THE DISPUTED LANDS

By Alexander B. Adams

THE DISPUTED LANDS

ALEXANDER B. ADAMS

G. P. PUTNAM'S SONS · NEW YORK

Library of Congress Cataloging in Publication Data

Adams, Alexander B
  The disputed lands.

  Bibliography: p.
  Includes index.
  1. The West—History. I. Title.
F591.A22   978   80-15405
ISBN 0-399-12530-2

PRINTED IN THE UNITED STATES OF AMERICA

To Frank and Virginia Gardner
with thoughts of all that we have shared and deep
appreciation for the years of friendship

CONTENTS

THE DISPUTED LANDS

An account of the long-contested country west of the Rocky Mountains—comprising the states of Arizona, California, Idaho, Nevada, Utah, Oregon, and Washington, and parts of Colorado, New Mexico, Montana, and Wyoming—from the appearance of the first Europeans to the closing of the frontier.

But this is not simply Western history. It is part of the history of the North and South, for those who came . . . were from those sections
—Alexander Majors, stagecoach operator, founder of the Pony Express, and frontiersman, 1893

A
CHRONOLOGY
OF HIGHLIGHTS IN THE HISTORY
OF THE WESTERN PORTION OF THE
UNITED STATES

*with some additional dates
in general American history
to serve as reference points*

By 1536 Spain was the principal power on the continents of North and South America. The Spanish held a firm base in the Caribbean; Cortés had conquered Mexico; Ponce de León had landed in Florida; Balboa had crossed the Isthmus of Panama; Spaniards had attempted to settle on the Texas coast; Magellan's expedition had sailed around the globe; and Pizarro had begun the conquest of Peru that was to bring him world renown.

Yet Spain's dominance in the New World was already being challenged. By the Treaty of Tordesillas, Brazil fell into the area allotted to Portugal; and Amerigo Vespucci, under the Portuguese flag, had sailed along its shore. John Cabot, a wealthy Italian, had explored the coast of North America on behalf of the British; Verrazano had sailed to the New World in the employ of the French; and Jacques Cartier had entered the St. Lawrence.

The lands west of the Rocky Mountains, however, were still unknown to Europeans. Perhaps they held an *el dorado* or a more direct route from the Atlantic to the Pacific and on to the wealth of the Indies. No one knew.

13

PART I
1536–1803

1536—Álvar Núñez Cabeza de Vaca and his companions reached Sonora. They were the first Europeans to cross the North American continent above the present boundary between the United States and Mexico.

1539—Francisco de Ulloa, a Spanish captain, explored the coast of Baja California.

Fray Marcos de Niza made an exploratory trip into what is now Arizona and New Mexico.

1540—Francisco Vasquéz de Coronado began the expedition that eventually carried him to Kansas.

Hernando de Alarcón explored the Colorado River.

1542—Juan Rodríguez Cabrillo sailed up the California coast. Coronado returned to Mexico.

1559—The Spanish attempted to settle in the Carolinas but shortly removed their colony to Pensacola, Florida.

1562—The French established a fort at the mouth of the St. John's River in Florida.

1565—A Spanish expedition under Miguel Lopez de Legaspi, accompanied by Andrés de Urdaneta, discovered a return route from the Philippines along the California coast.

The Spanish founded St. Augustine in Florida, thus reinforcing their hold on the East Coast of North America.

1576—Martin Frobisher made the first of his voyages to Canada, thus stimulating England's interest in the New World.

1579—After a successful privateering voyage in the Pacific, Francis Drake anchored in Drake's Bay north of San Francisco and in the name of England took possession of the land, calling it Albion.

1581—The Rodríguez-Chamuscado expedition attempted to reclaim the pueblos of the Río Grande.

15

1582—Antonio de Espejo led another expedition to the pueblos ostensibly to rescue Rodríguez.

1584—Francisco de Gali, returning from the Philippines, gave a brief account of the California coast as observed from the sea.

The British attempted to settle at Roanoke, North Carolina.

1587—Pedro de Unamuno, a Spanish explorer, landed on the California coast, probably near Morro Bay.

Thomas Cavendish captured a Spanish galleon off the coast of Baja California.

1588—The British defeated the Spanish Armada.

1590—Gaspar Castaño de Sosa made an unofficial attempt to settle in New Mexico and was arrested by a party sent to pursue him.

1593—Francisco Leyva de Bonilla and Antonio Gutiérrez de Humaña led another unofficial expedition to New Mexico. Both were killed during an effort to reach Kansas.

1595—Sebastián Rodríguez Cermeño explored the California coast north of Drake's Bay.

1598—Juan de Oñate, under contract to the Spanish crown, set forth to colonize New Mexico.

1602—Sebastián Vizcaíno sailed along the coast of California. His exaggerated reports of the harbor at Monterey later influenced Spanish exploration and settlement.

1609—Pedro de Peralta became governor of New Mexico, and the Spanish government assumed responsibility for supporting the colony. Peralta moved the capital to Santa Fé.

1620—The Pilgrims landed at Plymouth Rock.

1680—Popé led the Indians in a revolt against the Spaniards and drove them from New Mexico.

1682—La Salle discovered the mouth of the Mississippi and in the name of France claimed the river's entire watershed from the Apalachians to the Rockies.

1687—Eusebio Francisco Kino arrived in Pimería Alta and began his series of explorations.

1692—Diego de Vargas began the Spanish reconquest of New Mexico.

1697—The Treaty of Ryswick brought an end to King William's War.

1711—Kino's death ended his remarkable explorations.

1741—Vitus Jonassen Bering set sail on the second of his expeditions and discovered Alaska, thus giving the Russians a foothold in North America.

1751—The Upper Pimas in northern Sonora and southern Arizona revolted against the Spanish.

1754—The French and Indian War broke out between Great Britain and France.

1763—The Peace of Paris ended the French and Indian War. France, having ceded its land west of the Mississippi to Spain the previous year, surrendered most of its other possessions in North America to Great Britain.

1769—Gaspar de Portolá attempted to establish a settlement on Monterey Bay and discovered San Francisco Bay.

1770—The Spanish established a mission and presidio at Monterey, California.

1774—Juan Bautista de Anza made the first of his two journeys from Pimería Alta to Alta California. In the following year he escorted settlers to the San Francisco area.

1776—The American colonies declared their independence.

The Spanish founded a presidio and mission on San Francisco Bay.

1777—Juan Bautista de Anza was appointed governor of New Mexico in an effort to stabilize the frontier.

1778—James Cook visited the Pacific Coast of North America and learned about the high profits to be made in the fur trade with China.

1780—Anza helped open a route between New Mexico and Sonora.

1781—The Yuma Indians revolted, cutting the road from Sonora to California.

1792—Captain Robert Gray of Boston discovered the mouth of the Columbia River.

George Vancouver explored the West Coast on behalf of the British.

1793—Alexander Mackenzie led an expedition to the West Coast and became the first European to cross the continent from the Atlantic to the Pacific.

1803—The United States purchased Louisiana from France.

PART II
1804–46

1804—Lewis and Clark started on their expedition to find a route to the West Coast.

1805—Lewis and Clark reached the Pacific.

1806—Lewis and Clark returned to St. Louis from the West Coast. A Russian party under Count Rezanov visited San Francisco in an attempt to open trade with Alta California and perhaps expand their own empire down the coast.

Pike left on the expedition that eventually took him to Mexico.

1807—Pike returned from his expedition.

Aaron Burr was tried for treason.

The British forced the surrender of the American frigate *Chesapeake*.

Manuel Lisa began to expand the St. Louis fur trade up the Missouri River.

1810—Astor's ship, the *Tonquin*, sailed from New York for the mouth of the Columbia River.

1811—Hunt, leading the overland branch of Astor's expedition, left St. Louis for Oregon.

Astor's ship, the *Tonquin*, arrived at the mouth of the Columbia River.

The first contingent of the North-West Company appeared at Astoria.

1812—War was declared between the United States and Great Britain.

The Russians established a post, Fort Ross, in northern California.

Robert Stuart led an expedition from Astoria that discovered South Pass through the Rocky Mountains.

1813—The North-West Company took possession of Astoria.

1814—The Treaty of Ghent ended the War of 1812.

1816—Otto von Kotzebue, an officer in the Russian navy, visited San Francisco on an exploring expedition.

1817—The American sloop-of-war *Ontario* went on a mission of reasserting the claim of the United States to the Columbia River.

1818—Hypolite Bouchard, a Frenchman in the service of the revolting Spanish colonies in Latin America, attacked California.

Great Britain and the United States agreed on the joint occupancy of Oregon for ten years.

1819—In the Adams-Onís Treaty, Spain relinquished to the United States its claims in the West above the forty-second parallel.

1820—The Missouri Compromise settled the slavery issue for a time.

Stephen H. Long led a government-sponsored expedition into the edge of the Rocky Mountains.

1821—The Russians, who had been active on the West Coast, forbade any alien ships to approach the shore north of the fifty-second parallel.

Mexico became independent of Spain and began opening up its outposts to foreign visitors and trade.

1823—A presidential message to Congress contained the Monroe Doctrine.

1824—Henry Ashley took a pack train up the Platte River in the winter.

1825—On a limited scale the first rendezvous of fur trappers was held.

1826—Ashley sold his business to Smith, Jackson, and Sublette.

1827—Jedediah Smith returned from a trip to California and left again to continue his explorations of the West Coast, eventually reaching Fort Vancouver before turning east again.

Great Britain and the United States reached an agreement to continue their joint occupation of Oregon for another ten years.

James Ohio Pattie and a group of trappers started on a trip that brought them to California, where they were imprisoned by the Mexican authorities.

1829—Major Bennet Riley used oxen on the Great Plains.

1830—Hall J. Kelley, a schoolteacher turned propagandist, formed a society to encourage immigration to Oregon.

1832—South Carolina's legislature passed the Nullification Act, threatening to place the interests of a single state above those of the Union.

The Blackfeet attacked the annual rendezvous, resulting in the Battle of Pierre's Hole.

Nathaniel Wyeth made his first trip to the West Coast.

Captain Benjamin Bonneville entered the fur business.

Hall J. Kelley started for Oregon by way of Mexico.

1834—Wyeth started on his second trip to the West Coast. Jason and Daniel Lee accompanied him for the purpose of establishing a mission.

1835—Richard H. Dana, Jr., author of *Two Years Before the Mast,* arrived in California.

The secularization of the Spanish missions began.

Samuel Parker and Dr. Marcus Whitman went west to establish missions. Whitman returned east from the trappers' rendezvous to report their findings.

1836—Whitman and Henry H. Spalding went west as missionaries. They took their wives, who became the first women to cross the continent from ocean to ocean.

Texas declared its independence and defeated the Mexican army sent to subdue it.

California declared its independence of Mexico. Mexico made no immediate effort to reclaim it.

1837—The United States recognized the independence of Mexico.

William A. Slacum, a purser in the United States Navy, made a trip to Oregon and reported favorably on the country.

The Mexicans at Santa Rita del Cobre killed Juan José and thus reignited their war with the Apaches.

The Panic of 1837 affected many aspects of American life.

1838—Jason returned east to publicize Oregon and obtain new missionary recruits.

1839—John Sutter, whose workmen later on made the best-known gold strike, settled in California.

Jason Lee's new recruits left New York City for the West.

1840—Pierre-Jean de Smet, a Jesuit, visited the Flatheads and Pend d'Oreille Indians to determine whether to set up a mission among them.

1841—De Smet went west again. He assisted the Bidwell-Bartelson party, which is often considered the first party of immigrants.

The Texas Pioneers went to New Mexico, where they met a hostile reception.

Charles Wilkes visited the West Coast on an official American expedition.

1842—Lansford W. Hastings went to Oregon and then to California. His subsequent book led to greater interest in the West Coast.

Marcus Whitman returned east to plead the cause of the missions.

Commodore Thomas ap Catesby Jones "captured" Monterey in the mistaken belief that Mexico and the United States were at war.

1843—The American settlers in Oregon met to establish their own government.

John Charles Frémont led a survey expedition to Oregon.

1844—Frémont brought his expedition east again.

1845—Frémont started on another expedition to the West Coast, one that led him to flout the authorities in California.

1846—The United States gave notice that it intended to abrogate the joint occupancy of Oregon.

The United States declared war against Mexico.

PART III
1846–86

1846—Kearny marched from the Missouri, captured New Mexico, and by December he had entered California believing that the war in California was over.

June 14—a group of settlers captured the town of Sonoma, California, and in a few days declared themselves the Bear Flag Republic.

July 2—Commodore Sloat entered Monterey harbor and five days later raised the American flag over the city.

1847—January 8—the Americans defeated the Mexicans at the San Gabriel River, a battle that led to the recapture of Los Angeles and the suppression of the California uprising.

January 13—the remains of the Mexican army in California surrendered to the Americans.

February 2—Colonel Sterling Price began the attack on the Pueblo of Taos that ended the uprising in New Mexico.

February—the last survivors of the Donner party were evacuated.

July—the Mormons selected the site of their new city in Utah

November 29—the Cayuse Indians raided the mission at Waiilatpu and killed Marcus and Narcissa Whitman.

1848—February 2—the Treaty of Guadalupe Hidalgo was signed by Mexico and the United States. By its terms, the United States settled the question of Texas and obtained California and New Mexico.

James W. Marshall discovered gold on the American River in California.

August—Oregon received territorial status, and Joseph Lane was appointed its first governor.

December 5—in his annual message to Congress, Polk spoke about the extent of the gold found in California and submitted reports made by military and naval officers. This caught the attention of the people as no previous reports had.

1849—In the spring, the emigrants began moving in great numbers to California, most of them hoping to find gold.

California held a convention to write a state constitution, making it difficult for Congress to postpone the issue of whether the new lands should be slave or free.

1850—After reaching a series of compromises, Congress admitted California as a free state and organized New Mexico and Utah as territories without reference to slavery.

John Russell Bartlett began the survey of the new boundary between the United States and Mexico.

The Mormons organized the Perpetual Emigration Fund Company to provide assistance to Mormons moving to Utah.

1851—The first Committee of Vigilance of San Francisco was organized.

The first installments of Harriet Beecher Stowe's *Uncle Tom's Cabin* began to appear as a magazine serial and stimulated the abolitionist cause.

1853—Joseph Lane persuaded the Indians of southern Oregon to make peace.

Congress established Washington Territory.

The Gadsden Purchase from Mexico gave the United States some thirty thousand square miles of additional territory in Arizona and New Mexico and relieved the United States of the responsibility for preventing the Apaches from crossing the border to raid in Mexico.

1854—The Kansas-Nebraska Act passed Congress and split the country over the slavery issue.

1855—The Mormons suffered through a year of drought and grasshoppers.

1856—Frémont ran for president as the candidate of the Republican party.

The Mormons began their handcart emigration.

1857—Buchanan appointed a non-Mormon to be governor of Utah and provided him with an escort of troops in an effort to reestablish federal supremacy in the territory.

In the Mountain Meadows Massacre, a band of immigrants was wiped out by Indians with the help of some Mormons.

1858—The differences between the Mormons and the federal government were settled, and a military base was established near Salt Lake City.

Gold was discovered in Colorado, providing additional settlement between the Missouri River and the West Coast.

John Butterfield's stagecoach company instituted the first through mail and passenger service between the Missouri and the West Coast.

1859—Horace Greeley made a trip west to study the need for a transcontinental railroad.

The Comstock Lode in Nevada was discovered.

Oregon became a state.

1860—The Pony Express began service.

The Paiute Indian War in Nevada began.

Lincoln was elected president.

1861—The transcontinental telegraph line was completed.

The Pony Express discontinued service.

The Confederates fired on Fort Sumter.

The Confederacy invaded New Mexico and proclaimed the Confederate Territory of Arizona.

Cochise and the Apaches temporarily disrupted service on the Butterfield stagecoach line.

Congress organized Nevada and Colorado territories.

1862—The Confederacy extended its invasion of the Southwest but was driven back.

The California Column marched east and fought the Battle of Apache Pass.

Congress passed an act to subsidize two railroads, which would join and run from the Missouri to California.

Congress passed the Homestead Act.

1863—The ground was broken for the construction of the Central Pacific Railroad.

Arizona and Idaho were organized as territories.

Kit Carson defeated the Navajos and forced them to go on the reservation at Bosque Redondo.

1864—Nevada was admitted as a state.

Montana was organized as a territory.

Yosemite Valley was withdrawn from the public domain and deeded to California as a "reservation."

Congress gave the transcontinental railroad companies more liberal terms.

1865—Lee surrendered at Appomattox.

The Comstock Lode showed signs of giving out, and the prices of its mine stocks began to fall.

Samuel Bowles made a tour of the West and produced widely-read reports on his impressions.

1866—Congress passed a new Railroad Act. This authorized both railroads to continue until they met and started the race between the two.

1868—Congress created Wyoming Territory.

John Muir, later famous as a writer and a conservationist, moved to California.

Bret Harte published "The Luck of Roaring Camp," which began his career as a western writer.

1869—John Wesley Powell made his first trip down the Colorado River.

The Central Pacific joined the Union Pacific at Promontory Point, Utah, completing the transcontinental railroad.

1870—Congress passed the Hollman Resolution, recommending that no further land grants be made to railroads.

1871—Vincent Colyer attempted to make peace with the Indians of the Southwest.

General Crook was assigned to Arizona.

1872—General Oliver Otis Howard made his second peace mission to the Southwest and reached an agreement with Cochise and the Chiracahua Apaches.

The Modoc Indian War began.

1873—The Modoc Indians surrendered, and Captain Jack was hanged.

The Panic of 1873 brought the failure of Jay Cooke and affected business throughout the country.

The Mint Act of 1873 provided for the demonetization of silver.

The Timber Culture Act made another 160 acres available to settlers in return for planting 40 acres of trees.

The Big Bonanza was discovered at the Comstock Lode.

1875—The death of Cochise marked the beginning of renewed Apache raids in Arizona.

Fire destroyed much of Virginia City, Nevada.

1876—The Nez Percés that followed Joseph were ordered on the reservation.

Colorado was admitted as a state.

1877—The Nez Percés fled eastward. They surrendered early in January 1878.

Congress passed the Desert Land Act, which permitted the purchase of 640 acres at $1.25 an acre provided the purchaser irrigated them.

1878—The Timber and Stone Act made it possible to purchase 140 acres at $2.25 an acre.

The Paiutes and Bannocks broke from the reservation. The campaign against them lasted about three months.

The Bland-Allison Act provided for purchase by the Treasury of a limited amount of silver for coinage.

1880—Production at the Big Bonanza at Virginia City was declining radically.

The Apache leader Victorio was killed.

1881—Henry Villard organized his famous "blind pool" and raised enough capital to secure control of the Northern Pacific Railroad.

Helen Hunt Jackson's *A Century of Dishonor* appeared.

The Southern Pacific Railroad joined the Texas Pacific near El Paso.

1882—General Crook was reassigned to the Apache campaign.

1883—The last spike was driven to complete the Northern Pacific Railroad.

Crook fought his campaign in the Sierra Madre.

The Atchison, Topeka, and Santa Fé Railroad reached Needles and ran from there on the tracks of the Southern Pacific.

1885—The Nez Percé Indians were allowed to return to the Northwest.

Geronimo left the reservation for his final raids.

Congress appointed the Cullom committee to investigate the railroads' practices.

1886—Crook persuaded the Apaches to surrender, but under the influence of liquor some of them fled.

General Nelson A. Miles assumed command and led a campaign that resulted in the final surrender of Geronimo.

THE DISPUTED LANDS

As quietly and gently as a feather falling from a bird's wing, the fog began to creep in from the Pacific Ocean. It swirled along the edges of the Olympic Peninsula in present-day Washington, touched the rocky coast of Oregon, and floated around the cliffs that edge part of the shore of northern California. Farther south it slipped through the narrow passage that provides the entrance to the magnificent Bay of San Francisco, left the cypress trees of Monterey dripping wet, and circled the mountains that drop into the sea below the Big Sur, obscuring the points that pierce the surf and the rocks that stand like offshore sentinels.

As it moved inland, the air—wherever it touched the coastal ranges—rose, grew colder, and dropped some of its moisture in rain and heavy mist, forming the rain forest at the foot of Mount Olympus and the rivers that flow directly over the coastal plain into the sea. But it was then too dry to water the valleys beyond until it reached the Cascades and the Sierra Nevada. Their higher crests wrung out more water. Dark clouds released rain and snow on the mountains, creating waterfalls and rivers like the Merced, which pours out of the Yosemite Valley.

East of the Cascades, the skies over the Columbia Plateau, through which the Snake and Columbia rivers cut their ways, were blue. For the air, now parched, was translucent and blue. Further south, the Basin and Range area suffered, too, from lack of water, and much of the land was desert.

Still moving on its long journey from the Pacific to the Atlantic, the air mass from the ocean now reached the northern Rocky Mountains in today's Idaho and Utah. Partly replenished by the winds from Canada, it again formed clouds that fed the headwaters of the Snake and Columbia rivers. Farther south, the process took a little longer, the middle Rocky Mountains being offset to the east. Before reaching the southern Rockies at a lower latitude, the air cast its thin clouds over the dry Colorado Plateau, an enormous area containing such marvels as the Painted Desert, the Petrified Forest, and the unbelievable gorges of the Colorado River, including the greatest of them all, the Grand Canyon.

Having passed the Rockies and left what geologists call the Cordilleran Region of the United States, the air mass drifted on east across the Great Plains, the Central Lowlands, the Ozark Plateau, and the Appalachians to reach at last the coastal plain on the Atlantic seaboard.

In the year 1536—the year in which this account begins—the air mass, sometimes faint against the turquoise-colored skies, sometimes dark with moisture, made this lengthy trip from the West Coast to the East Coast of North America without casting a single cloud shadow on a European or wetting one with a single drop of rain or snow until it reached the northeast. Here Jacques Cartier had opened the St. Lawrence River to the French; and at the southern border of the present-day United States, three Spaniards and a Moorish slave were struggling from the Gulf of Mexico to what is now northern Sonora.

These four men, survivors of a shipwreck years earlier on the Texas coast, were the first to arrive from Europe and cross the continent so far north. Their descriptions of the land they saw induced white men to start penetrating the great area west of the Rocky Mountains.

That was not the last part of the continent to be explored nor the last to be settled, but title to it remained in dispute for three centuries; and even after the United States took possession of it, the resources of the nation were taxed to hold on to it. It is a tribute to the American people that they could unify a country that spanned the continent through the crises of the Mormon and Civil wars, especially during a period when transportation was slow and communications difficult.

It was not only the strength of the contending parties that made a transcontinental United States appear so remote; geography also stood in the way. By the middle of the Cenozoic era, what had been the Rocky Mountains was almost completely demolished by the forces of erosion, leaving only monadnocks standing above the surrounding plain while the streams drifted and wandered where they would. Then came a period of great uplifting. The surface of the earth trembled, and an arch began to emerge, rising faster and faster as the era progressed. The streams, once lazy and meandering, quickened their courses and thus heightened their erosive powers. They cut out the mountain basins that had been previously filled with deposits and wore away the softer material surrounding the remains of the former mountains, giving us the Rockies as we know them today.

The mountains formed a forbidding barrier in the path of the westward traveler, who had to find a route through their mysterious heights. They also had another adverse effect on the westward expansion of the American people. By creating a rain shadow, they turned the Great Plains to the east into a region that was long considered a desert and habitable only by Indians, trappers, and traders. This delayed the settlements that might otherwise have provided for a gradual assault on the Rockies.

Beyond the mountains the Colorado Plateau to the south offered no easy passage. Formed by another uplift that also quickened the streams, it was carved into an area of steep cliffs and deep canyons.

To the north, the Columbia Plateau was also inhospitable. During the Cenozoic era, molten lava flowed through rock fissures onto the surface and, being highly fluid, poured in every direction, filling old valleys and streambeds and creating a plateau. The immensity of the geologic disturbance is indicated by a single figure: An estimated 24,000 cubic miles of lava erupted from the earth and finally hardened on the surface.

The basin and range area came into being, not through an outburst of lava or an uplifting of the earth's surface. Instead rifts appeared in the older rocks, which slipped against each other; and some were raised to form new mountain ranges, creating a broken country, loved by many but uninviting to a traveler arriving from the east. And where the disturbances formed basins, the dry air provided no water, and the land became desert.

Two more obstacles still barred the way to the Pacific shore, two mountain ridges running parallel from north to south, the first divided into the Sierra Nevada and the Cascades. Although the central valleys of California, Oregon, and Washington might make an easterner feel at home, the coastal ranges remained between him and the ocean.

The movement of the people, therefore, could not be a simple sweep across the land, and they did not settle the interior of the country before they settled its outskirts. The farmlands of Oregon and the gold of California were goals long before the wheatfields and cattle ranges of Nebraska and Kansas; and this in itself testifies to the difficulties presented by geography to the unification of the nation.

The forces that carried the United States from sea to sea were varied. One of them was good fortune, for the luck of the Americans was sometimes incredible. How else to account for the discovery of the mouth of the Columbia River by a New England merchant seaman just after it had eluded a British exploring expedition? Or why else did James Marshall discover gold near Sutter's Fort just months after the Americans had annexed California and not before?

But the presence of luck did not alone account for the Americans' success. That came from a variety of factors, among them the contributions of other nations. The Spaniards opened the way to much of the western country, absorbed the initial stresses of exploration and conflict with the Indians, and also taught the Americans how to turn the arid ranges into cattle ranches. The British and the French helped mark the first trails into the unknown; and the French showed the Americans how to support their western advance with the fur trade, while the British provided the foundations of a social culture that could survive the strains that an undeveloped frontier placed upon it.

To these inheritances from others, the Americans added their own combination of qualities: a unique political structure that made the country a whole, not part fatherland and part colony; an outlook on life that was not always generous but never entirely selfish; a quality of mind that leavened the worst with humor; a national vision that could not be blocked by the next range of mountains or the next desert; and a group of individuals, some of them scoundrels, many of them heroes, who were equal to the challenge.

The Battle of Yorktown in 1781 established the western American boundary at the Mississippi; north of the Red River, the Louisiana Purchase soon placed it at the crest of the Rockies; beyond the mountains lay the disputed lands—a tangle of snow-covered peaks, arid basins such as Death Valley, deep canyons like those of the Snake and Colorado rivers, plateaus, fertile valleys, and an ocean-washed shore. The story of these lands is not merely the history of a section of the country; it is the story of the final testing of the American people before their nation emerged as a whole.

PART I
1536–1803

1. RUMORS OF TREASURE

*. . . these people [Indians north of Mexico] are
all very fond of romance, and are great liars,
particularly so where they have any interest.*

—Álvar Núñez Cabeza de Vaca, 1555

Every evening, when the shadows stretched their blackness across the plazas
and the sun started its flight over the rim of the earth, the pigeons of Mexico
City gathered in flocks to seek their roosts in the cathedral and churches that
the Spanish had built to displace the shrines of Montezuma. In the twilight,
the murmur of their cooing resembled human whispers like those of a
caballero to his loved one or of the men gossiping about the arrival of Álvar
Núñez Cabeza de Vaca.

Long abandoned for dead, he had appeared—dressed in tattered skins and
accompanied by three companions and numerous Indians—on the northwestern frontier of Mexico, hundreds of miles from his original destination.
He had been treasurer of an expedition headed by Pánfilo de Narváez, to
whom the crown had given a grant of land running from Florida to the Gulf
of Mexico, an empire if Narváez could settle and develop it. But Narváez
failed to meet the challenge. His expedition was finally wrecked on the coast

of Texas; and after several members had made unsuccessful attempts to reach Mexico by following the shoreline, Cabeza de Vaca and his companions started on an unmapped route toward the west.

Their journey was one of incredible hardship. They started in 1534 and finally reached Culiacán, Mexico, in 1536. With no equipment whatsoever—their scanty supply of European goods had already been exhausted—they trudged across the continent, each day seeing land that had never before been observed by European eyes. Sometimes they were abused by the Indians they met, but gradually they acquired fame as healers and medicine men, and this reputation gained them the assistance of many of the Indian bands they met.

When at last they found their way to the Mexican outposts, everyone was interested in their story; and at Mexico City, they commanded the ear of the viceroy, who was anxious to learn about that northern country through which no explorer had previously traveled.

In his written report describing all he had seen and heard, Cabeza de Vaca was circumspect, restraining his imagination and avoiding the rumors with which so many Spaniards filled the accounts of their discoveries. Yet interspersed throughout the final chapters of his tale were such comments as this: "The people gave us many deer and cotton shawls better than those of New Spain, many beads and certain corals . . . and fine turquoises that come from the north . . . To me they gave five emeralds made into arrow-heads . . . and they said the stones were brought from some lofty mountains that stand towards the north, where were populous towns and very large houses, and that they were purchased with plumes and the feathers of parrots." Or again: "Throughout this region, wheresoever the mountains extend, we saw clear traces of gold and lead, iron, copper, and other metals."

The "emeralds" were probably malachite, a carbonate of copper, and Cabeza de Vaca had neither the time nor the training to investigate the "traces" of metals he had observed. Nor was he able to bring back specimens of ore, since he had no means of carrying anything but the barest necessities. Therefore he had nothing to substantiate his remarks. Even so, they kindled the fancy of the Spaniards, who were ready to believe that the experiences of Cortés and Pizarro would be repeated in the north. The question in their minds was not whether the wealth existed but who would get it.

By virtue of his authority as Viceroy of Mexico, Antonio de Mendoza was able to control events in his own favor and was determined personally to sponsor the first expedition north and thus lay a claim to any riches that might be found. Therefore, he began assembling an army of men under his young protégé, Francisco Vásquez de Coronado, to explore the north. But before risking the enormous investment such an expedition entailed—under the Spanish system, Mendoza had to raise the funds himself by private subscription—he organized a scouting party to verify what Cabeza de Vaca had reported. Since it was cheaper to use a priest for this purpose than a contingent of armed men, he selected Fray Marcos de Niza, a veteran of Peru, and obtained as guide Estavanico, the Moorish slave who had belonged to one of Cabeza de Vaca's companions.

Fray Marcos began his trip in 1539. Almost immediately discord developed between Fray Marcos and Estavanico, who, according to one chronicler, "did not get on well with the friars, because he took the women that were given him and collected turquoises, and got together a stock of everything." Only a Moorish slave in the Spaniards' eyes, Estavanico's strong physique, unusual skin color, and simple disposition made him a hero to the Indians. As the chronicler noted, they brought him presents and women, which he accepted in what Fray Marcos considered an unchristian spirit. To rid himself of Estavanico's presence, Fray Marcos ordered him ahead as a scout, instructing him to report in person or by messenger any unusual discoveries. To prove their authenticity, the messengers were to carry crosses, the size of the cross indicating the importance of what the Moor had seen or learned.

A curious chase through the wilderness then developed. Estavanico, unwilling to surrender his freedom and enjoying his position among the Indians, did not reappear; but he sent back to Fray Marcos a number of crosses, some of them enormous, but he never made clear what he had found. So Fray Marcos kept following his elusive guide toward the north, while somewhere ahead the Moor marched proudly, his body adorned with hawks' bells and native gifts and surrounded by Indian followers, whom he treated more and more arrogantly.

The news of Mendoza's projected venture quickly reached Hernán Cortés, Mexico's original conqueror. Although out of favor with the king, who had made him subservient to the viceroy, his daring and avarice remained undampened. He equipped some small boats and placed them under the command of a sea captain, Francisco de Ulloa, with instructions to outflank Mendoza by going up the west coast of Mexico.

Geography, however, doomed the expedition. Coming to a dead end at the head of the Gulf of California, Ulloa was forced to turn back, round the point of Baja California, and then start north again, carrying the Spanish flag as far in that direction as it had ever gone before. But he found no gold-rich civilization, and Cortés soon after left Mexico for Spain on an equally unsuccessful attempt to regain the favor of the king.

Fray Marcos fared better—at least in his own imaginative account of his journey. Following Estavanico's trail, he went north through what is now Arizona, but no matter how fast he traveled, the Moor remained ahead, still sending back his vague messages of great discoveries.

Then suddenly everything changed. An Indian fleeing south brought Fray Marcos a story of disaster. Estavanico, growing more and more arrogant, had approached Cíbola, one of the Zuñi pueblos. Instead of the welcome he had come to expect as his due, he found himself forced to remain outside the pueblo while the Zuñis questioned him and debated their course of action. Finally they made their decision. Pouring out of their buildings one morning, they fell on Estavanico and massacred him and his followers except for the Indian with whom Fray Marcos first talked and two others whom he encountered later. (Some boys may have been taken prisoner and thus spared.)

According to the account Fray Marcos gave later, this startling news did not daunt him. In undertaking the expedition, he had offered his life to the service of God, so he proceeded to Cíbola; and although he did not attempt to enter the pueblo, he observed it carefully from afar before returning to Mexico.

Mendoza had no reason to doubt Fray Marcos's report. During his long service in the New World, the priest had gained an outstanding reputation for honesty; and yet his account of luxuriant valleys, prosperous towns, and a mighty city at Cíbola were so glowing the viceroy wondered whether his lonely journey in the wilderness might have overturned his imagination.

Consequently Mendoza sent a capable army officer, Melchior Díaz, on a second scouting expedition. The news Díaz brought back was extremely discouraging. Although he had not gone as far as Cíbola, wherever he had looked, he had seen only humble villages or small settlements in places where Fray Marcos had described prosperous communities, and what he heard about Cíbola indicated Fray Marcos was guilty of gross exaggeration.

In the face of this adverse information, the decision to march on was not easy, but Coronado made it. Caution, however, dictated a change in his plans. Instead of advancing with his entire strength, he selected a vanguard of approximately eighty horsemen, twenty-five infantry, and a few Indians, all of whom would serve under his direct command. They would be more mobile—and therefore more adaptable to the conditions they met—than the larger body, which would follow later.

The first weeks of his march confirmed Díaz's findings, not Fray Marcos's. The valley of the Sonora River was indeed well watered, and its fields appeared fertile; but the communities fell far short of Fray Marcos's glowing descriptions. A village Fray Marcos had particularly lauded lay off their proposed route, so Coronado dispatched Díaz to investigate it. What Díaz said on his return left little doubt the priest was a liar.

Gloom was overtaking the expedition, and the men looked at Fray Marcos with dark scowls. As they marched into Arizona and north to Cíbola, they could see ever more clearly that they were victims of a fervid imagination; and their disillusion was complete when they approached the Zuñi pueblo. Instead of the great city Fray Marcos had reported, it was, said a chronicler of the journey, "a little, unattractive village, looking as if it had been crumbled all up together."

Throughout, Coronado had tried to maintain friendly relations with the Indians he encountered and had given strict orders to his men not to molest them in any way. His pacific policy came to an end at Cíbola. For when he advanced with a small contingent to treat with the Zuñis gathered outside the pueblo, they replied by attacking him.

Instead of immediately ordering a general engagement, Coronado retreated to his main body and attempted again to speak to the Indians. This they mistook for a sign of cowardice and began shooting arrows. Failing in his efforts at peace, Coronado ordered the soldiers to charge. After their long march, both the Spaniards and their equipment were in poor condition. The strings of the crossbows, long exposed to the weather, snapped; and the musketeers were so weak they found it difficult to take steady aim, making it impossible to clear the Indians from the walls.

So Coronado led an assault on the adobe fortifications. Twice the Indians' rocks knocked him off his feet, and the second time one of his officers had to throw himself over his prostrate commander in order to save him. As it was, Coronado, whose handsome armor made him a conspicuous target, suffered several minor wounds, and an arrow stuck from one of his feet.

Although he himself was forced to withdraw from the fighting, other officers took his place, and the Indians soon gave way. In triumph, the Spanish entered the village and, for the first time in many weeks, had enough to eat. But an ample meal was not sufficient to suppress their disappointment. As they looked at the crude adobe buildings and the small unpretentious square, they realized the full extent of Fray Marcos's lies. Even his priestly garb and crucifix did not prevent their cursing him, and Coronado feared for the priest's life.

Once firmly established in the Zuñi village, Coronado questioned the Indians about other villages that might be near and sent Pedro de Tovar, one of his officers, to investigate the Hopi pueblos about which they told him. "When they reached the village," wrote the expedition's chronicler, "they entered the country so quietly that nobody observed them, because there were no settlements or farms between one village and another and the people do not leave the villages to go to their farms, especially at this time, when they had heard that Cíbola had been captured by very fierce people, who traveled on animals which ate people. This information," he added, "was generally believed by those who had never seen horses, although it was so strange as to cause much wonder."

After a brief fracas, started when one of the Indians struck a Spanish horse, the Spanish took possession of the pueblo. The victory was quickly and easily won, but it gained the Spanish little. Once again they were in a community of adobe buildings, small and crude by European standards and possessing little wealth except the Indians' agricultural products and a few turquoises.

This was more discouraging news for Coronado to report to Mendoza. After recounting his adventurous and difficult journey north, he wrote, "It now remains for me to tell about this city [Cíbola] and kingdom and province of which the Father Provincial [Fray Marcos] gave Your Lordship an account. In brief, I can assure you that in reality he has not told the truth in a single thing that he said, but everything is the reverse of what he said."

During his trip to the Hopis, Tovar had come across a mighty river—the Colorado—and the Indians had told him there were important villages downstream. Coronado therefore ordered another of his officers, García López de Cárdenas, to explore it further.

Accompanied by about twelve men, Cárdenas set out to pick up the river farther to the west. At last they came to a land that "was elevated and full of twisted pines, very cold, and lying open to the north." Suddenly there appeared before them a great gap in the earth—the Grand Canyon. Standing at the edge of this unbelievable natural miracle and with no means of gaining a perspective of its actual size, they at first thought the Colorado River at its bottom was only three feet wide.

For several days, they traveled along the rim, hunting for a possible downward trail; and when they found one, three of the lightest and most agile of the men volunteered to make the descent. Over the edge they went, clambering among the varicolored rocks that had been carved into strange shapes by the wind and water of past ages. To the astonishment of those remaining at the top, they soon disappeared from sight. About four o'clock in the afternoon, the volunteers reappeared, dirty and exhausted from their day's climb. For all their effort, they estimated they had gone only one-third of the way to the bottom. "Those who stayed above," wrote one of the men on Coronado's expedition, "had estimated that some huge rocks on the sides of the cliffs seemed to be about as tall as a man, but those who went down swore that when they reached these rocks they were bigger than the great tower of Seville."

This canyon was no minor obstacle, but a major gash in the earth across which even the Spaniards, who had fearlessly penetrated some of the most remote sites of the New World, were unable to find a way.

Cárdenas would have pursued his explorations further except for the shortage of water. The river flowed beneath them, but it was unreachable. Close to the rim water was nonexistent. In fact, each evening they had to travel a considerable distance away from the canyon in order to find enough to drink. Their guides told them this condition would grow worse if they followed the canyon's course downstream, so Cárdenas reluctantly turned back to the Zuñi village—the bearer of one more discouraging item of news: The route to the west was blocked by an impassable canyon.

The arrival of some Indians from the east, however, brought welcome hope. They told of other villages lying along a fine river, gave hints of riches, and reported that vast herds of wild "cattle" roamed the plains farther on. All this was good news in contrast to the gloomy information brought back by Tovar and Cárdenas, and Coronado ordered another of his officers, Hernando de Alvarado, to take a detachment of men east.

Their route carried them past the pueblo of Ácoma, perched high on a sheer-sided rock mesa and almost inaccessible except by a narrow, easily defended trail. The community contained no wealth, so they quickly left it, but they were greatly impressed by the impregnability of its fortifications.

Soon they reached the Río Grande (for that was the river the Indians had described) near present-day Isleta, New Mexico. From there they sent out messengers, each bearing a cross to signify peace, and were pleased that their overtures were met in a similar spirit. Delegations from about twelve villages arrived at their camp with presents of foods and hides. As Alvarado later reported to Coronado, these were an unwarlike people, more given to raising agricultural products than preying on their neighbors.

From the Río Grande, Alvarado led his men across the mountains to the Great Plains in search of the "cattle" the Indians had talked about. For once, the rumors they had heard proved true, and they discovered the enormous herds of buffalo that once grazed on the plains. Here at least was a source of meat for the army. They also heard tales of a fabulous civilization, centered in a city named Quivira, that lay somewhere farther east, but they could not locate it in the time Coronado had allotted them for their mission.

Before conducting a further search for this new city, Coronado decided to wait for more favorable weather. During the winter he spent on the Río Grande, a sea expedition under Hernando de Alarcón tried to bring him fresh supplies. Although Alarcón located the mouth of the Colorado River, thus adding to the Spaniards' geographical knowledge, he quickly realized it was not navigable. Mighty as the river was, it provided no entrance into the northern lands.

Some of the Río Grande pueblos had meanwhile revolted against the Spaniards' demands for food, but Coronado reestablished his control over them; and when spring came, he was prepared to set out again. Provisioning his entire army, he moved eastward toward the Great Plains, but once again the reports he heard from the Indians proved elusive. Quivira existed—many of them agreed on that point—but exactly where it was they were not sure.

When a growing shortage of supplies made it impractical to take so many men farther onto the plains, Coronado sent the majority back to the Río Grande and moved on with only a small group. The route on which their

39

principal guide took them led to the northeast and finally into present-day Kansas. But when, on the Arkansas River, they met the people of Quivira, their disappointment was complete. These were not an advanced group of people like the Aztecs and the Incas, but a humble race, living in straw buildings and dressed only in skins, for they did not know how to make cloth. And the only metal Coronado could find in their possession was a single copper disk, and that, he thought, had been brought there by one of his own men.

The discovery that Quivira was nothing more than a collection of huts, sweltering and poverty-stricken in the Kansas sun, completed the defeat of Coronado. He had gone to Cíbola; it had proved to be nothing but a community of mud buildings; neighboring villages were no more imposing; and much of the route west seemed blocked by the Grand Canyon. To the east, he had located the pueblos of the Río Grande Valley, and they contained no riches. The plains provided only untameable "cattle" and at their eastern edge were merely the humble villages of Quivira. In thousands of miles of travel, he had uncovered nothing to justify the expenses of the investors or to arouse the favor of the crown, nothing but mountains, deserts, endless plains, and relatively uncivilized peoples.

Infuriated by the series of fool's missions on which the Indians had lured him, he permitted his passion to overcome his restraint and committed one of the few ugly acts of his life. During the night, he seized the Indian guide who had told him of Quivira and, under the dark Kansas skies, garroted him. His revenge taken, he then ordered his men to make ready for the long trip back to the Río Grande, where he would decide what next to do.

In camp again by the timeless river, Coronado contemplated his future. Rarely had a nation sent so many men into so vast a territory and retrieved so little from the effort. His obviously was not to be the good fortune of another Cortés or Pizarro. And yet . . . ? As he pondered, fate took the decision out of his hands. Galloping on his horse, he slipped from the saddle and fell to the ground, where one of the hooves struck him in the head. Broken now in body as well as spirit, he could no longer wrestle against the hostile land and began the slow, inglorious march back to Mexico.

Although his expedition had failed to locate any treasure, optimism still prevailed in Mexico City; and Mendoza planned a second expedition, this one north by sea and under the command of Juan Rodríguez Cabrillo.

In June 1542 Cabrillo left the west coast of Mexico and after months of battling head winds reached one of the islands on the Santa Barbara Channel off the coast of present-day California. Here he fell and broke his arm. At the time the accident seemed so slight that the navigator, Bartolomé Ferrel, failed to note the incident in his log; but as they proceeded north, Cabrillo's condition grew worse, and they returned to the Santa Barbara Channel for the winter. Realizing that he was now about to die, Cabrillo pleaded with Ferrel to continue the expedition in the spring instead of returning to Mexico.

In obedience to his dead commander, Ferrel once again struggled against the head winds, driving past Point Reyes and reaching an area close to the present Oregon-California border. For badly equipped ships sailing through uncharted waters, the journey was a remarkable achievement. Yet as he walked the storm-tossed deck of his command, Ferrel wondered how much longer he could continue to struggle into the unknown seas of North America.

2. New Contestants

Ferrel deserved no discredit for turning back as he did. On his cruise he had seen few harbors in which he could take refuge, the shoreline presenting an almost unbroken stretch of beaches and rocks that afforded no protection. Heavy mists dripped water from his spars and, coming suddenly in dark gray swirls, obscured the course he was trying to set. Ahead lay only the unknown, menacing in its mystery, and holding no promise of anything but danger.

When he reached familiar waters again and made port in Mexico, he brought with him more knowledge of the geography of the West Coast than any man had ever possessed, but he had uncovered no coffers of gold nor any direct water route that Spanish ships could take to the Indies. The authorities, therefore, paid as little attention to his findings as they had to Ulloa's, and the fogs of ignorance, like the fogs of the Pacific, still enveloped the northern shoreline.

The failure of Ferrel or Coronado to find gold or a new passage between the oceans quenched Spain's interest in the lands to the north, and the caballeros who had once gossiped about Cabeza de Vaca's journey now turned their attention to the many other problems affecting the future of New Spain. Pressed on the east by the French and British (the French had built a base at the mouth of the St. Johns River in Florida and John Hawkins had forced his way to Hispañola and traded with the colonies there), the people of Mexico turned their eyes west toward the Philippines.

A practical obstacle, however, stood in the way of their exploitation. An agreement with Portugal prevented the Spanish from using the sea route around the Cape of Good Hope, and the Straits of Magellan were considered too hazardous for regular commerce. Therefore the west coast of Mexico was the logical base for the potential trade.

From there to the Philippines, the route presented no problem; the prevailing winds would carry Spanish ships directly to their destination, but they would have to find another course home with currents and winds that would bring them back to the North American shore.

On November 21, 1564, an expedition—under the command of Miguel Lopéz de Legaspi, who was accompanied by a friar, Andrés de Urdaneta—set out from Mexico to learn if such a return route existed. During the outward voyage, Alonso Arellano, captain of the smallest vessel, dashed ahead and, his ship being faster than the others, reached the Philippines before them. Anxious to secure as much credit as he could for himself, he hastily reprovisioned and, using information gained by earlier explorers, discovered the favorable conditions necessary to carry his ship back to the California coast. From there, the prevailing winds and currents carried him quickly to Mexico.

When Legaspi arrived in the Philippines, he found the natives hostile as the result of a previous Portuguese slave raid and possessed of little wealth except a few gold ornaments and a little cinnamon. Nevertheless, he decided to remain and cultivate their trade, while Urdaneta returned to Mexico on the largest of the ships. Following a course roughly similar to that taken by Arellano, he, too, arrived safely back in Mexico.

These two voyages gave a new, although indirect, importance to the area north of Mexico. For the coast of what is now California had gained strategic significance. Enemy ships sheltered in its harbors might be able to pounce on any galleons taking the best route back from the Philippines. So trade between the islands and Mexico depended on retention of the northern shoreline.

Their new interest in the Philippines, however, did not divert the Spanish from defending themselves against the inroads being made against their empire on the Atlantic Coast. During the year that Arellano and Urdaneta returned from the Philippines, the Spanish drove the French from their foothold in Florida and established a base of their own at St. Augustine, and they nearly captured John Hawkins at Vera Cruz.

Shaken by this experience, John Hawkins thereafter devoted himself to financing privateers and eventually became a high administrative officer in the navy. But his cousin, Francis Drake, who had fought with him at Vera Cruz, continued plundering the Spanish and even landed at the Isthmus of Panama, where he climbed a tree and caught a glimpse of the Pacific. The sight of those waters shimmering in the distance aroused his imagination, and he vowed that some day he would sail an English ship on the ocean that Spain and Portugal had reserved for themselves. In 1577, he left England to carry out his promise.

His cruise was successful. He plundered the Spanish until—his ambition sated and his men weary from long days of sailing and fighting—he decided to head for home.

"He thought it not good," wrote Francis Pretty, who accompanied him, "to return by way of the Straits [of Magellan], for two special causes—the one, lest the Spaniards should there wait and attend for him in great number and strength, whose hands, he, being left with but one ship, could not possibly escape. The other cause was the dangerous situation of the mouth of the Straits . . . where continual storms reigning and blustering . . . besides the shoals and sands."

So he turned north, resolved that if he could not find another passage back into the Atlantic (the nonexistent route for which Cabrillo and Ferrel had searched), he would continue across the Pacific and sail to England by way of the Cape of Good Hope. His course took him up the coast of California. Rocks and shoals often forced him away from the shore as he piloted the *Golden Hind* through the mysterious unknown waters, and sheets of fog blowing in from the ocean sometimes obscured the land. Thus he failed to notice the Golden Gate, that small entrance leading into the enormous harbor of San Francisco, and came to anchor farther north off Point Reyes in what is now known as Drake's Bay.

"In this bay we anchored," wrote Pretty, "and the people of the country having their houses close by the waterside, showed themselves unto us, and sent a present to our General [Drake]. When they came unto us, they greatly wondered at the things that we brought, but our General (according to his natural and accustomed humanity) courteously entreated them, and liberally bestowed on them necessary things to cover their nakedness, whereupon they supposed us to be gods, and would not be persuaded to the contrary. . . .

"Their houses are digged round about with earth, and have from the uttermost brims of the circle, clefts of wood set upon them, joined close together at the top like a spire steeple, which by reason of that closeness are very warm. Their bed is the ground with rushes strewed on it, and lying about the house, they have the fire in the midst. The men go naked, the women take bulrushes, and comb them after the manner of hemp, and therefore make their loose garments, which being knit about their middles, hang down about their hips, having also about their shoulders a skin of deer, with the hair upon it."

For the British sailors, far from their home port, the scene was a strange one—the long, rolling swell of the Pacific so unlike that of the Atlantic, the absence of any mark of European civilization, and the natives with their crude huts and belief in the Englishmen's divinity. Only the nearby cliffs, glistening white in the sunlight, were a reminder of the land they had left so long before, for in miniature they resembled those of Dover. Then "our General," continued Petty, "set up a monument of being there, as also of her majesty's right and title to the same, namely a plate, nailed upon a fair great post."

Having slipped into the ocean that Spain regarded as its own and having now claimed northern California, the security of which was essential to the growing Spanish commerce with the Philippines, Drake set sail for England. His arrival caused Queen Elizabeth considerable embarrassment. Fearful of trouble with Spain, she hesitated to honor him, but finally she made up her mind. On the deck of the *Golden Hind,* which had carried him around the world, she made him a knight. The meaning of her action was clear. England, which now had a valid claim to California under the law of that time, was the open enemy of Spain and a challenger of Spain's hegemony in North America.

Although the Spanish had increased their knowledge of the inland area north of Mexico through two more small expeditions, they still remained largely ignorant of California. In 1584, however, Francisco de Gali, captain of a galleon, wrote a brief account of the California coast as he observed it on his way back to Mexico from the Philippines. Reaching land somewhere in the vicinity of present-day Santa Cruz or Monterey, he continued along the shore on his way to Acapulco and reported that "there are many islands, which, though small, would seem to possess many good harbors." Although this misinformation—there are not many harbors—would scarcely assist future navigators seeking safety, it helped at least to strip some of the mystery from the unknown coast and make it seem less fearsome.

That same year the British tried to settle at Roanoke, Virginia, their first attempt to gain a permanent foothold in the New World. Even more important, Thomas Cavendish, another of England's great seamen and navigators, decided to emulate Drake, enter the Pacific, harass the Spanish in what they regarded as their own stronghold, and recoup the fortune he had squandered currying favor at the court. In 1856, he left England with three small ships acquired with the last of his credit, sailed through the Straits of Magellan, and began pillaging the western coast of South America.

As he pursued his northward course, a Spanish ship, under the command of Pedro de Unamuno, was heading east from the Philippines. On his own authority and without consulting the king in advance—a dangerous procedure for a Spanish official to follow—the viceroy had organized a small expedition to explore the California shore and search for safe harbors that might be used by passing ships or as centers for future settlement. Before safely reaching Acapulco, Unamuno met a government vessel carrying the startling news that a British corsair was loose in the Pacific. This was Cavendish, who was spreading terror along the whole length of the New World's western coast.

Not above torturing his prisoners to extract information from them and not above burning a church if it seemed to serve his purpose, Cavendish had sailed north, losing one of his ships but inflicting considerable damage on the Spanish and capturing booty for himself and his men. But he was still looking for the greatest prize of them all—the regular galleon from the Philippines. Those islands were not in themselves wealthy, as Legaspi had learned years before, but they were the key to the markets of China. Close enough to the mainland to be reached by Chinese junks, they had become a link in a long trade route—from China to the Philippines, to Mexico, overland to the Atlantic, and then on by sea to Spain, a route over which flowed silks of all kinds, velvets, brocades, preserves of fruits, spices, nails, saltpeter, and furniture—enough in a single shipment to provide a king's ransom. Much of the year's commerce was concentrated on board a single galleon. That ship probably represented the greatest prize sailing the oceans at the time, and because the Spanish felt relatively secure in the Pacific, it was not surrounded by a large guardian fleet.

Cavendish spotted his prey off Cape Lucas at the tip of Baja California. As soon as his lookout reported the galleon's sails, he began pursuing it and after three or four hours drew alongside. According to Pretty, who had also been with Drake, the Spaniards remained under cover, and made good use of their javelins, lances, and "an innumerable sort of great stones, which they threw overboard upon our heads and into our ship so fast, and being so many of them, that they put us off the ship again with the loss of two of our men, which were slain, and with the hurting of four or five." Forced away from the side of the galleon, the British "gave them a fresh encounter with our great ordnance and also with our small shot, raking them through and through, to the killing and maiming of many of their men."

As the Spanish captain still refused to surrender, Cavendish, "encouraging his men afresh with the whole noise of trumpets, gave them [the Spanish] the third encounter with our great ordnance and all our small shot . . . raking them through in divers places . . . They being thus discomforted and dispoiled, and their ship being in hazard of sinking by reason of the great shot which were made, whereof some were under water . . . set out a flag of truce and parleyed for mercy." This one capture more than justified the expense of the entire voyage; and Cavendish set sail for England, becoming the third man to circumnavigate the world. Spain no longer shared the waters of the globe only with Portugal, and even the seas off California were not sacred against the attacks of its enemies.

In an effort to destroy England's growing power, Spain had already assembled the greatest naval force ever seen and ordered it against the foe. As the Armada approached the British Isles, men like Hawkins, Drake, and Forbisher went out to meet it.

News of the outcome reached Cavendish and his men on their homebound voyage. "On the 3rd of September," wrote Francis Pretty, "we met with a Flemish hulk, which came from Lisbon, and declared unto us the overthrowing of the Spanish Fleet to," he added with understatement, "the singular rejoicing and comfort of us all."

Cavendish's raid shocked the Spanish authorities by demonstrating the vulnerability of the galleons. Although a few minor—and often unofficial— expeditions probed north by land, the main concern of the viceroy was protecting the important trade with the Philippines. To do this, Spanish seamen needed more knowledge of the California coast, so he appointed Sebastian Rodríguez Cermeño to explore it more carefully than Unamuno had done.

During the summer of 1595, Cermeño left the Philippines in a small ship named the *San Augustín*. Approaching the coast, the crew saw ahead of them a formidable sight: Dangerous reefs and heavy breakers presented an impenetrable barrier between them and the land. Nor could they find a welcoming harbor to the south. Instead a severe storm broke, and two-thirds of the crew had to bail the ship to keep it afloat. By this time, the men were so frightened and demoralized that three of the officers petitioned Cermeño to give up any further exploration and head straight for Acapulco.

Cermeño, however, would not let himself be dissuaded from his mission. Staying in sight of land, he continued to seek possible anchorages; and after several days, his lookout spied Drake's Bay, which the English navigator had claimed for Queen Elizabeth in 1579. Here the natives, as they had done with Drake, greeted him in a friendly fashion and received with pleasure the presents he had brought. But nature was less kind. A strong wind destroyed the *San Augustín* while it was at anchor and left the Spaniards—more than seventy men in all—to continue homeward in a small launch. Ahead of them lay more than two thousand miles of open water with a dangerous coast on one side and the great waves of the Pacific on the other. They had no charts; and as far as they knew, San Diego was the only mainland harbor that could offer them a safe refuge from the sea. But on its shores, they knew, dwelt Indians who were hostile.

3. Hope Will Not Die

It is difficult for those of our time . . . to picture to themselves the feelings of the men who lived in the sixteenth century. . . . A new and glorious world had been thrown open. But as to the precise spot where that world lay . . . they had very vague and confused conceptions.

—William H. Prescott, 1843

Cermeño's trip home—in a small launch crowded with seventy men—provided another instance of the heroism and daring of Spain's explorers. Always mindful of his assignment from the viceroy, Cermeño tried to make observations whenever he could, steering the launch as close to the coast as possible and largely disregarding the dangers of onshore currents and winds. But like Drake, he missed the narrow, obscure entrance into San Francisco Bay and did not touch land until he reached the general vicinity of the Bay of San Luis Obispo. The Indians they met there sold them some acorns, but that was all the food they could spare. Once again the crew pleaded with Cermeño to make haste for Acapulco; but once again he refused to be shaken in his purpose, talked them into a better humor, and let them kill and eat a dog they happened to have on board.

Anchoring later somewhere near the islands off Santa Barbara, the crew of the launch was delighted to see Indians approaching in small boats. Fortunately they brought with them twelve fish and a small seal they gave the Spaniards in exchange for some silk and cotton cloth. But these trade goods did not please them enough to produce more food. With handlines, however, the men caught some thirty more fish, thus providing themselves with the strength to continue their miserable journey. At another island where they anchored, they discovered some wild onions and prickly pears. These and a large dead fish they found on the shore were just enough to keep them from starving.

By this time, even Cermeño realized he could not conduct any further investigation of the coast in an overloaded small boat and with no provisions. So he agreed to sail directly to Mexico.

In the name of Spain, he had claimed the bay that Drake had taken in Queen Elizabeth's name, and he produced the most detailed report ever written about the California coast. Yet the information he brought back was not highly valued by the Spanish authorities. The defeat of the Armada and the rise of Britain as a seapower were all signs that the vast energies of Spain—the drive that had pushed men like Cortés and Pizarro into new worlds—was diminishing, and the *caballeros* were no longer so attracted by the unknown.

But the old spirit was not entirely dead. Juan de Oñate, the wealthy, ambitious scion of a leading Mexican family, retained the attitude of the earlier *conquistadores* and was certain he could wrest from the north the extensive riches he believed existed there.

Well connected and able to draw on extensive financial resources, Oñate seemed a highly desirable candidate to take over the exploration and settlement of that part of the continent. At least that was the opinion of the viceroy, who endorsed him for the post and helped him secure the necessary license from the king. Overjoyed at his good fortune and seeing in the future nothing but fame and wealth, Oñate appointed his nephews, Juan and Vicente de Zaldívar, as two of his most important assistants and began gathering the men and supplies required by his contract with the crown.

Although he assembled enough men and equipment to satisfy his contract—at vast expense to himself and his supporters—the arrival of a new viceroy, Gaspar de Zuñiga y Acevado, count of Monterrey, upset his hopes. For Monterrey was not as certain about Oñate's qualifications as his predecessor had been. By voicing his doubts he set in motion again the whole cumbersome bureaucracy of Spain, and Oñate spent the next three weary years defending his right to his contract. Finally in 1598 he secured permission to advance north at the head of his caravan.

Moving ahead of the main body, he found the Indians peaceful, and he safely explored the Río Grande Valley, selecting as his capital the pueblo of San Gabriel on the bank of the Chama River northwest of present-day Santa Fé. Although the pueblo contained four hundred Indian families, the town was not the metropolis they had pictured; and disgusted by the dusty streets, the absence of gold and silver, and by the poverty-stricken appearance of the Indians, some forty-five officers and men of Oñate's small force mutinied, declaring their intention to return immediately to Mexico. Oñate arrested the three ringleaders and threatened to garrote them; but heeding the pleas of the other soldiers and of the friars, he pardoned them. Their attitude, however, emphasized the need of his quickly finding a source of wealth or risking the disaffection of his tiny band. So he divided his men into three groups: one to guard the dusty Indian village that formed his capital; another, under Vicente de Zaldívar, to search for the "cattle"—the great buffalo herds that Coronado had reported; and another, headed by himself, to explore the lands west to the Pacific.

Zaldívar located the buffalo herds and discovered that the reports of their size had not been exaggerated, but the animals were completely intractable. His men could not drive or capture them, and the Spaniards gave up hope of making them the basis of an agricultural fortune.

Before Vicente returned, Oñate departed for the west, leaving Juan de Zaldívar to help guard the capital at San Gabriel until his brother came back. Oñate's route took him to the pueblos of Abó, Jumano, and Ácoma, the village perched on a mesa that Coronado's men had regarded as almost impregnable. Everywhere the Indians received him as a friend, supplying him with food and attending to his wants. From Ácoma he went on to the land of the Zuñis, still failing to find evidence of any great wealth but adding to Spain's knowledge of the country it claimed as its own. He then marched to the pueblos of the Hopis, ancient like Ácoma but less well protected by geography; and hearing rumors of some rich mines nearby, he sent one of his captains into north-central Arizona to seek them.

As soon as his brother, Vicente, returned from the Great Plains, Juan de Zaldívar, in compliance with his previous orders, selected about thirty men from the capital's garrison and began to march west to reinforce Oñate. The Indians' reception of Oñate had led the Spanish to believe their expeditions could purchase all the supplies they needed from the natives. So Juan de Zaldívar stopped to trade at Ácoma.

Making a temporary camp at the foot of the mesa, he asked the Indians for flour, wood, and water, for which he was willing to pay with hatchets and hawks' bells. The Indians were not anxious to do business with him, and the few soldiers permitted to climb the narrow trail to the top returned with little flour. Either the Europeans' trinkets had lost their appeal or the earlier demands of Oñate had exhausted the pueblo's patience and resources.

51

After several days, however, Zaldívar received permission to ascend to the top with eighteen soldiers and renew his efforts to obtain flour. The bright sun of the desert wind flared above the pueblo, lighting its adobe walls and the ladders leading to the upper apartments, as Zaldívar assembled his followers at the foot of the trail. Carefully he ordered them to behave themselves, to take nothing the Indians did not want to sell, and not to give vent to their growing impatience. But for all his precautions, he could not persuade the pueblo as a community to deal with him. Instead he had to bargain with individual Indians for flour, purchasing a little from one, a bit more from another.

As the tedious process went on, the sun slowly slipped through the turquoise-colored sky, the shadows fell longer across the alleyways between the buildings, and the reflections in the rock cistern that supplied the pueblo with some of its water grew darker. Yet Zaldívar had not obtained the quantity of flour he wanted. In an effort to close the bargaining before night forced him from the mesa, he sent one group of his soldiers off through the pueblo to trade on their own.

Suddenly he heard a shout. Then the latent hatred of the Indians erupted. Stones, sticks, and arrows fell on the Spaniards from every direction, and the Indians advanced on them waving war clubs. Taken by surprise, their small force divided, and with no place to flee, the Spaniards were quickly overwhelmed. A few escaped by making the dangerous leap from the top of the mesa to the protection of their friends waiting below with their horses. Looking back at the dreadful heights, they could see the Indians derisively waving the swords and harquebuses they had captured.

Oñate, having vainly waited for Juan de Zaldívar before proceeding to the Pacific, had turned back toward San Gabriel, deciding to postpone his journey to the ocean for another season. On the way he met the survivors of the massacre at Ácoma, and their news presented him with a serious dilemma. On the one hand, he could not afford to wage war against every pueblo; on the other, he could not let this assault against the Spanish pass unpunished. Otherwise the whole country might take up arms against him.

Wisely he postponed a decision until he had returned to San Gabriel. As the cold swept down from the mountains and entered the valley of the Río Grande, Oñate debated the question with his followers. After careful consideration his soldiers gave their consent to a punitive expedition against Ácoma, and the friars provided him with both moral and legal justification. So in January 1599, he sent Vicente de Zaldívar at the head of about seventy men to avenge his brother, Juan. It was a venture in the tradition of Cortés, for the command, small as it was, amounted to more than half of Oñate's entire force, and he was committing it to the capture of the best-fortified Indian stronghold in the known southwest.

Arriving at the foot of the mesa, Vicente de Zaldívar demanded the surrender of those responsible for the attack. The Indians, feeling secure in their fortress, failed either to apologize as Zaldívar requested or to offer up the guilty warriors as prisoners. Instead they hurled insults at the Spaniards and defiantly waved the mail and swords they had stripped from the bodies of Juan de Zaldívar's men. When they grew even bolder and attacked a detachment leading the Spaniards' horses to water, Zaldívar gave the order to counterattack.

The odds were heavily against the Spanish. Many hundreds of Indians stood on the rim of the mesa, all of them armed and anxious for battle. Supporting them were hundreds of women, also willing and able to take part in the fight. Zaldívar could not lay siege to the pueblo; he had neither the necessary men nor supplies. Nor could he make a direct assault, since two or three Indians with bows and arrows could have prevented an army from mounting the narrow trail to the top. Consequently he concentrated his men in a feint on one side of the mesa while some of his hardiest soldiers attempted to scale the cliffs on the other. Several succeeded in installing themselves on a high crag and were able to hold their position during the night.

The following day the battle started anew, but with the foothold they had won, the Spanish began to gain the advantage. Well disciplined and accustomed to fighting as a group, they pressed the Indians back, killing many of them while their own casualties numbered only six or seven wounded. At that point, Zaldívar offered the Indians a truce, but they had reached a frenzy in which victory or death seemed the only alternatives. An hour later they regretted their rashness and contritely brought Zaldívar more than eighty blankets in atonement. Cruel and determined as a fighter, Zaldívar nevertheless had a sense of propriety. He had come to punish malefactors, not to obtain tribute, so he rejected the blankets and demanded to know why in the first place the Indians had attacked the Spanish.

That night a relative calm hung over the pueblo. The Indians, huddled in their buildings, marveled at the fury that had struck them; the Spanish, on guard against a surprise attack, sprang to the alert at every shifting shadow.

The next morning Zaldívar began "arresting" some of the Indians, considering himself a law-enforcement officer rather than a soldier. The Indians resisted, and the battle on the blood-covered mesa broke out again. In the buildings of Ácoma were many kivas (the secret religious chambers) and other hidden rooms in which the Indians barricaded themselves in their desperate resolve never to surrender. The Spanish had now drawn artillery to the top, and with gunfire and flame Zaldívar forced the last of the Indians from their strongholds. When the fighting ended and Zaldívar tallied his prisoners, the effectiveness of his onslaught became apparent. Although he captured some five hundred women and children, only sixty or seventy fighting men were left alive. But the punishment of Ácoma was not yet complete.

He marched his prisoners back to Oñate, who assembled a court to try them. By Spanish standards the proceeding was scrupulously fair. The accused Indians were even defended by court-appointed counsel, but the outcome was never in doubt. The defendants were all found guilty, and Oñate handed down the sentences: The children under twelve years were to be placed in the custody of the friars; the women and men were each sentenced to twenty years of personal servitude; and each man over twenty-five was additionally punished by having one foot chopped off. Two Hopis had also been captured at the pueblo. Oñate ruled each was to lose his right hand and be sent back to his tribe as a warning never to assist the enemies of the Spanish.

Severe as the punishment was, it in part accomplished Oñate's purpose. Except for the Jumanos, whom he had to punish later, he had imposed peace of a sort on the land he had come to settle. But otherwise his plans met with frustration. Vicente de Zaldívar, sent to explore the west and perhaps discover a route to the Pacific, was turned back by geography and the Indians; Oñate's reports to the viceroy aroused little interest in Mexico, although a few more settlers came; and he fell into the trap that had nearly destroyed Coronado, for he listened to the rumors of Quivira—rich in gold and silver.

Oñate's journey in search of that mythical city started as Coronado's had with optimism and ended, too, in despair. On his return from the plains to the Río Grande Valley, he found many of his settlers had deserted and fled to Mexico, thus weakening his already small force and raising new questions with the government about the practicality of his settlement. But he did receive one compensation, however slight. In 1602 the court granted him the title of *adelantado*—or governor—of New Mexico. This had been promised him in his original contract, but among the snow-topped mountains and dusty deserts of the land of pueblos, promises—even those of a king—seemed too often like the mirages that made the sand at a distance look like water. And yet what did he govern? Hundreds of square miles of wilderness and a tiny Spanish settlement whose inhabitants were becoming desperate to find some means of making the country yield them a living.

So unsuccessful was Oñate's venture that the new viceroy, the count of Monterrey, lost interest in present-day New Mexico and turned his attention instead to the Pacific Coast. In 1602 he sent Sebastián Vizcaíno north to explore the shoreline in more detail. Utterly incompetent, Vizcaíno contributed nothing substantial to Spain's knowledge and, out of a desire to curry favor with the viceroy, reported one piece of gross misinformation. The bay he named Monterey (the misspelling has become traditional) was, he said, a magnificent harbor. Thus he lodged in the minds of the Spanish bureaucracy the idea that Monterey should be the center of any future development of California.

Oñate was more truthful in his reports, but his truthfulness emphasized one disappointing fact: He had found no sources of wealth. Yet he would not give up hope. Somewhere over the next ridge of mountains, beyond the next sunlit mesa, across the next desert valley, was the fortune he was seeking. So while the courtiers and clerks debated his future, in the fall of 1604 he set off on another expedition, this time to the Bay of California—or the Pacific; the Spanish cartographers were not certain whether they were one body of water or two, since they did not know if Baja California was an island or a peninsula.

Oñate stopped first at the now familiar Zuñi villages, where Fray Francisco de Escobar, who wrote an account of the trip, noted that the Indians received them hospitably, although he realistically pointed out that the community was poor and four of the six pueblos were in ruins. From there they marched to the Hopis, and Fray Francisco again accurately reported that by Spanish standards the villages contained no wealth.

But as the expedition continued farther west across Arizona, following first the Little Colorado and then the Big Williams Fork, his credulity increased, not out of naïveté but as a result of the Spaniards' expectation of the unexpected. After the discoveries in Mexico and Peru—gold-rich civilizations in the depths of the wilderness—the Spaniards were ready to believe almost anything they were told. This credulity, combined with the difficulties of interpreting the natives' language and the Indians' desire to please and impress their visitors, created miracles of the imagination.

One tribe, as Fray Francisco carefully reported, expressed familiarity with the silver in the plates the Spaniards, with their love of luxury, carried even on expeditions. The Indians claimed they found silver in such large chunks that to make bowls they merely had to carve them out. Even Fray Francisco doubted this, wondering if they had not confused the Spaniards' silver with tin; but as they had no bowls at hand to show him, he was not able to resolve his uncertainty.

At the Gulf of California, which they reached at the mouth of the Colorado, the tales they heard from the natives became even more wondrous—one tribe slept every night under water; another wore bracelets of golden metal; yet another had earlobes that dragged on the ground when they walked; and the males of still another had sexual organs so long that they wrapped them around their waists four times to keep from treading on them. Yet who would have believed the Incas capable of filling a storeroom with gold? But the stories of monstrous peoples and of bracelets and hunks of silver and of pearls drawn from the depths of the Gulf of California did not satisfy Oñate's need for a tangible economic return that would justify the expense of his administration.

Since Oñate's personal resources were exhausted and the Spanish authorities were unwilling to support him further, he had no choice but to resign his proud, but empty, office. In fact, the government would have been glad to abandon New Mexico entirely, but Fray Lázaro Ximínez, who had served as a courier from New Mexico to Mexico City, raised a disturbing issue: Seven thousand Indians had already been baptized.

Cynics might remark that the government used the church as an instrument of conquest, and often it did. Nevertheless it regarded the spread of Christianity as a serious mission and the protection of the converts from damnation as a major responsibility. It could not, therefore, desert the Pueblo Indians now that its friars had instructed them in Christianity. The only answer was to establish a subsidized government on a reduced scale. When the first choice of a new governor proved unacceptable to the settlers, Pedro de Peralta received the appointment. He immediately moved the capital to Santa Fé, while Oñate disappeared into the shadows.

Under Peralta, a relative calm possessed New Mexico. Gone was the spirit of the *conquistadores,* which, with its visions of gold and silver, had carried the Spanish into the far corners of the world. In its place had come the less adventurous attitude of salaried officials and the small settlers who hoped to earn a modest living from the crops they reaped in their meager fields. In the pueblos, the friars continued their endless work of converting the heathen, chanting their masses in the adobe churches and keeping a watchful eye against the recurrence of the outlandish practices of the kivas. The small garrison, its members scattered throughout the area, served as a police rather than a military force. And the great excitement for the entire populace was the arrival of the supply train from the south, the mules, horses, and wagons raising a cloud of desert dust as they brought the many goods the people could not produce for themselves and reminded them that, isolated as they were, they remained a part of one of the world's great empires.

Yet the calm in western North America was only illusory. For Henry Hudson, first under the Dutch and then under the British flag, sailed up the river and into the bay that both bear his name. The English, who had settled in what is now Virginia, fought with the French, who had settled in what is now Canada; and the Pilgrim Fathers landed at Plymouth Rock, bringing with them their austere theology. Perhaps most portentous of all, in 1670 the British founded the Hudson's Bay Company, thus providing an additional economic incentive for their nation's western exploration.

That same year the colony of New Mexico, surviving only with government subsidies, was swept by disaster. Famine struck both the Spanish and Indian villages, which held off starvation only by making stews of hides and old leather. Instead of relief, the following year brought further trouble—a pestilence that killed numerous people and destroyed many cattle.

As long as times were comparatively prosperous, the Indians had accepted the Spanish. The colorful ceremonies of the Catholic Church appealed to their sense of the dramatic, the demands of the authorities seemed few, and the change in their way of life remained for the most part inconsequential. But famine and disease raised doubts, and in the secret recesses of the kivas, the medicine men renewed the age-old ceremonies of the past and reminded the people of the gods they were beginning to forget. Away from the pueblos in hidden mountain valleys and by desert waterholes, the Apaches, too, were questioning the presence of white men in their land, and the warriors were discussing plans to drive them back south.

The Spanish governor was aware of the Indians' growing unrest but underestimated its extent and mistakenly blamed it entirely on the medicine men. In 1675, to repress their activities, he arrested forty-seven of them on charges of witchcraft and executed three. Instead of frightening the Indians into renouncing their practices, a band of warriors appeared and demanded the medicine men's release. Lacking the courage of Oñate when faced by the rebellion of Ácoma, the governor freed his remaining prisoners.

One of them was a particularly aggressive and intelligent Indian named Popé, who, instead of being subdued by his treatment, was angered and made more determined. Establishing his headquarters at Taos, he secretly maintained communications with the other pueblos and kept the spirit of unrest alive.

Although the Spanish regarded themselves as the masters of the country, they were exceedingly vulnerable. Despite New Mexico's poverty, it had attracted more and more settlers drawn from those who believed they could fare no worse—and perhaps might fare better—than they had in Mexico itself. They fanned out across the country, some settling near one pueblo, some near another. The priests, too, had established churches in many widely separated pueblos. If this population had been concentrated, it would have represented a formidable force. But scattered here and there over hundreds of square miles, it formed only small units that could be snuffed out one by one.

In a land where time was as endless as the desert sky, Popé could afford not to hurry. As the women with their *ollas* and their washing walked to the stream that divides the village of Taos and as the men tended their fields and occasional clouds gathered above the mountain that stands like a guardian near the pueblo, Popé continued weaving his plot to end Spanish rule in all New Mexico. Warriors, carefully chosen for their hatred of the Europeans, gathered to listen to him in the secret recesses of the pueblos; and couriers, chosen for their fidelity, went from village to village, quietly spreading Popé's message. Finally, in the heat of August 1680, all was ready.

The signal was prearranged. Popé took a piece of cord, tied knots in it, and handed it to trusted messengers. Each knot represented the number of days before the Indians were to strike, and as the cord was carried from pueblo to pueblo, one knot would be untied each night. Yet if the messengers were intercepted by the Spanish, what significance could an old cord possess? It would be overlooked, Popé was certain, or dismissed as another bit of Indian foolishness.

But Popé overestimated the loyalty of his own people. Three pueblo leaders who were not in sympathy with the revolt notified the Spanish governor, Antonio de Otermín, who ordered two messengers arrested and brought before him. From them he extorted the general nature of the plot but not its extent. Thinking the assault would be merely local, he prepared to defend Santa Fé and its immediate environs but failed to alert the other communities to their danger.

Aware that their plan was now known to the enemy, the Indians advanced the date of their uprising. In all but a few pueblos, the warriors suddenly attacked the clerics, civilians, and soldiers, and ransacked the churches, scattering their contents and breaking up the holy images.

Alonso García, commander of New Mexico's southern district, having received no warning from Otermín, was taken completely by surprise. Cut off from Santa Fé, he gathered the survivors of the first assaults at the friendly pueblo of Isleta and, from there, began to retreat south. With only about 150 soldiers to protect some 1,500 persons and facing the Pueblo Indians supported by the Apaches, he was fortunate to reach Socorro.

At Santa Fé, Otermín finally came to realize the magnitude of the revolt as those who had escaped from the Indians came straggling in from the surrounding pueblos; and the comparative lethargy that had marked his first response to the crisis was replaced by a more determined attitude. The change came just in time. For the Indians, who had concentrated their first efforts on the smaller Spanish bases, now congregated at Santa Fé, prepared to destroy the town and either force its inhabitants to leave or kill them. Offered this choice during a parley, the Spaniards expressed their desire to fight even though they were many times outnumbered.

Once again the discipline of the Europeans proved effective. In numerous skirmishes and two pitched battles, the Spaniards inflicted far more casualties than they received, but complete victory eluded them. With so few soldiers, they could not subdue an entire countryside, and they dared not remain where they were for fear of future attacks they would be unable to repulse. So after consultation with his officers and other leading citizens, Otermín gave the order to retreat to the south.

Marching down the Río Grande Valley with the remaining members of his settlement, he traveled through a desolate country, where no friends greeted him and enemies haunted his every campsite. Finally he effected a reunion with García. But instead of congratulating his junior officer for executing a relatively successful withdrawal, Otermín promptly arrested García for not coming to his aid.

4. OUTPOSTS ON THE COAST

So incessant was the desire of our Venerable Father Junípero [Serra] to found new missions that, dissatisfied with his efforts, he died with his thirst still unsated.

—Fray Francisco Palóu, 1787

Like an aging cougar that can do little more than growl, Spain's strength was failing, and it could not rush reinforcements to Otermín's aid. In 1681, when he finally assembled enough men to march back into New Mexico, he found the friendly pueblo of Iselta deserted. The church had been burned, and one of its bells—the clapper missing—had been dumped into the cemetery along with the Spaniards' 175-pound cannon. Pieces of a crucifix were strewn on the floor of the sacristy, and a cross lay on the ground in the main plaza. As he pushed farther north, he found that everything Spanish had been destroyed and the Indians were either openly hostile or afraid to befriend any white man. Reluctantly he gave up all thought of reconquering the province.

Spain's weakness also tempted its European enemies to whittle away at the New World. René-Robert Cavelier, sieur de La Salle, descended the

Mississippi and, by virtue of the international law of the time, claimed for France the river's entire watershed and later attempted to found a colony at the river's mouth. Yet in spite of its weakened state, Spain was not entirely void of men capable of carrying its banner into the remote frontiers. In 1682, Diego de Vargas successfully reconquered New Mexico, for Popé, like many revolutionaries, had proved better at plotting revolt than organizing his people to maintain what they had won. Once again emigrants from Mexico began to settle along the Río Grande.

While Vargas extended Spain's borders with the sword, a priest Eusebio Francisco Kino did so by peaceful means. Carrying his cross, he rode and walked throughout Pimería Alta—the land making up part of present-day Sonora and southern Arizona—founding missions, establishing herds of cattle to improve the lot of the inhabitants, and determining that Baja California was not an island but a part of the mainland. Patient when the Indians revolted, adroit at satisfying the demands of the secular authorities, and constantly spreading the Word of God, Father Kino carried civilization and, incidentally, the flag of Spain into the wilderness.

In 1711, at the age of sixty-nine and after twenty-four years of service in Pimería Alta, he arrived in the small Sonoran community of Magdalena to dedicate another of the many chapels that had been built under his supervision. After singing mass, he felt ill and lay down as usual on the two calfskins he now used as a mattress, covering himself with Indian blankets, and resting his head on the packsaddle that ordinarily served as his pillow. Although the father stationed at the mission tried to persuade him to move to a more comfortable bed, Father Kino refused, still adhering to the severe rules he had laid down for his own personal conduct. Concern for himself had not been part of his life, and neither was it part of his death. Stretched on the floor as always and making no concessions at the end, he died in Magdalena. The king of Spain had lost a great conqueror, albeit a conqueror of men's minds, and the God whom Father Kino adored had lost a great servant.

In the other parts of North America, Spain had not fared well. With the exception of present-day Mexico, Florida, and Texas, it had lost most of the eastern seaboard. In the interior, France had become familiar with the length of the Mississippi and was finally realizing La Salle's dream of establishing a colony at its mouth, while French explorers were also opening up the Missouri. Although the British settlements in the south were largely confined by the Appalachians, British fur traders from the Hudson Bay area were moving westward across what is now Canada; and British navigators were still entering the Pacific. In 1743, George Anson Anson, later a British admiral, captured a Manilla galleon, demonstrating again that no seas were closed to British ships.

From the north, the Spanish faced yet another threat. In 1741, Vitus

Jonassen Bering, a Dane who had joined the Russian navy, embarked on the second of his two trips to determine whether a land bridge connected Asia and North America. The discovery of Alaska during this voyage gave the Russians, too, a foothold in the New World, adding one more to the contending European powers.

Thus the Spaniards' possession of even the lands west of the Rockies was being challenged from many sides. Only in the south did the Spanish still control the approaches; and to make their hold firmer, they commenced a more intensive exploration and settlement of parts of Texas. Slightly to the west, however, their dominance was under attack by the Upper Pima Indians.

The eastern members of this tribe, which lived in northern Sonora and southern Arizona, were relatively advanced in their agricultural practices, in some instances irrigating their fields and, in others, planting their crops in the fresh silt brought down by the springtime floods. Being sedentary, they were—like the Pueblo Indians—more susceptible to the Spaniards' influence than the nomadic tribes like the Apaches and the Navajos.

Even in Kino's time, some of these Indians had rebelled against the Spanish, but they had been quickly put down. In 1751, however, their leader, Luís Oacpicagigua, who was a friend of the governor of Sonora and had fought other Indians on behalf of the Spanish, thought he could gain greater personal power by starting another rebellion. He had no difficulty finding reasons why the Indians should be dissatisfied with the white men's rule, for the Spanish system of colonization—successful as it was—had numerous faults.

Many of these arose from the conflicting interests of the three major participants—the soldiers, the clergy, and the settlers. The soldiers often accused the clergy of protecting Indians who were secretly hostile. The settlers, on the other hand, often urged that the mission lands, sometimes the prime holdings in a community, be secularized. They also looked on the priests as competitors for the Indians' labor, which they believed could be better used on their ranches or in their mines. On the other hand, the priests often placed their own interests above those of the soldiers and settlers. The resulting confusion and discord could lead to serious inconsistencies and, in some cases, severe injustices.

Playing on the wrongs of the past, some imagined and some real, Oacpicagigua was able to rally a substantial number of Indians to launch an attack on the Spanish outposts in Pimería Alta. Caught by surprise, the Spanish suffered heavy losses. The Pimas, however, like so many Indians, were unable to wage sustained warfare, and once their initial fury was exhausted, they began to disperse. Left with few supporters, Oacpicagigua fled to the Santa Catalina Mountains near modern Tucson. Since he could no longer take the offensive and the Spanish lacked the men to pursue him in the wilderness, both sides agreed to a peace in which the Spanish forgave the Indians in return for the Indians' renewed submission.

The Spanish, however, indirectly suffered long-lasting effects from the uprising. Each of the three elements in their frontier society blamed the other for the original outbreak; and the result of the quarreling was to diminish the influence of the Jesuits. Although a new presidio was established at the former Pima village of Bac, south of today's Tucson, the pioneering spirit instilled by Kino among the Jesuits on the northern frontier could not be revived. Like a wave dashing against the California shore to the west, the driving force had reached its highest mark and was now spent.

In the following years, Spain benefited from the French and Indian War that broke out between Great Britain and France. At first the fighting went heavily against the British, but then William Pitt, presumptuous and brilliant, came into office. "I know that I can save this country," he said, "and that no one else can," and set about proving he was right. The reverses that had been Britain's almost daily portion turned into a series of remarkable political and military triumphs, "It is necessary each morning," Horace Walpole remarked, "to inquire what victory there is, for fear of missing one." In 1763 the Peace of Paris ended the fighting and Great Britain received the lands that France had claimed in present-day Canada and the area reaching from the Appalachians to the Mississippi.

As for the other part of La Salle's claim—the land from the Mississippi to the Rockies—France had carefully placed it outside Britain's grasp. Anticipating their country's ultimate defeat, the nation's diplomats had transferred the territory the year before to Spain. Thus without firing a shot, Spain gained dominion over all access to the land west of the Rockies except from the north.

Discontented with the administration of Mexico—for the province was not producing the revenues he desired—Charles III of Spain followed the usual Spanish practice of appointing a *visitador-general* to make a thorough investigation and initiate any necessary reforms. To fill the position, he chose Joseph de Galvéz, a ruthless, ambitious lawyer who had worked his way upward from humble origins into the favor of the court.

While Galvéz was trying to reorganize the Mexican government, the Jesuits, of whom Father Kino had been a member, were coming into desperate times. Their enormous influence had created many enemies who, in one European court after another, intrigued for their downfall. In 1764 these enemies led Charles III to believe the Jesuits claimed his birth was illegitimate. Immediately he issued an edict expelling them; and Galvéz and the viceroy, with surprise raids and the use of soldiers, quickly carried out his order in Mexico. Regardless of his age, health, or service to Church and Crown, within days every Jesuit priest was shipped to the coast and thence out of the country. In this fashion, among many lamentations, those who had done so much to carry the Cross—and the insignia of Spain—to the frontiers of Mexico vanished from that land.

The expulsion of those able pioneers, however, did not mean that Galvéz intended to let Mexico's boundaries contract. On the contrary, he ambitiously dreamed of expanding them; and the settlement of Monterey—a location so temptingly and so misleadingly described by Vizcaíno—became his first objective. The colonizing expedition he organized was to leave in three sections, one by sea and two by land, from Baja California. One of the latter was under the direct command of an army captain, Gaspar de Portolá, who was also in overall charge.

With him, Portolá took Fray Junípero Serra, a Franciscan who was a worthy successor to Father Kino. Earlier when he had established a mission in the heart of the Mexican mountains, he had joined the Indians in carrying the beams for the new church, although he was so short he had to pad his shoulders to support his share of the load. In spite of a badly ulcerated leg, which made him painfully lame for life, he walked hundreds of miles to hold services; and he often flogged himself with chains or broken bits of wire to atone for his own sins and gain forgiveness for those of others.

Portolá's plan was to establish a base at San Diego before proceeding farther north, but even this limited objective proved almost beyond his capacity. One of the three ships assigned to the expedition was lost with all hands. (Ironically, it was named the *San José* after the saint selected as the expedition's patron.) Another took 110 days to beat up the coast from Baja California, arriving in San Diego with a crew so stricken with scurvy they could not lower their own boat to come ashore. Those marching by land, struggling over the mountains and across the deserts that hindered travel up the coast, found little more than a sick camp awaiting them after their long journey.

Portolá sent one ship with a skeleton crew back to Baja California for additional supplies. Then he designated those, including Fray Junípero, who were to remain at the base camp at San Diego while he marched north with the remainder to locate the Bay of Monterey. Following a circuitous route because of the obstacles in his way, he reached its shores farther to the north than he had planned. This error in his position and the failure of the bay to measure up to Vizcaíno's glowing description convinced him he had not yet gone far enough. Wearily pushing on, he found himself blocked by an enormous body of water that did not appear in any of the accounts he had read. This was San Francisco Bay, whose narrow, fog-enshrouded entrance had eluded Spain's sea captains. Portolá and his men, however, were in too great distress to appreciate their discovery. Believing they had either missed Monterey or that the bay had filled with sand and disappeared, they turned back to San Diego, arriving there shortly after New Year's, 1770.

In their absence, Fray Junípero had had great difficulty making any converts

63

among the Indians. Language was one barrier, for the Indians who had accompanied the expedition from Baja California did not speak the same tongue. Another was the Spaniards' illness, which made the Indians suspect their food and therefore refuse the sweets with which the priests had hoped to gain their friendship. Only one family brought a child to be baptized, and they snatched it away before the conclusion of the rite, much to the sorrow of Fray Junípero, who blamed his own sins for his inability to save even this one soul.

On the other hand, the Indians were fascinated by the Spaniards' clothing. They stole whatever they could and even tried to cut away the sails of the ship in order to get cloth to make their own. One Sunday, when most of the Spaniards were celebrating mass aboard the ship, they descended on the village, snatching up any loose clothing they found and stripping the sheets from the beds of the sick. The four soldiers still on shore quickly put on the several-layered leather jackets that served them as armor and started to counterattack. They were joined by the carpenter and the blacksmith, who, having just received Holy Communion, felt himself inspired. Without bothering to wear any of the protective clothing, he dashed through the village, shouting, "Long live the Faith of Jesus Christ, and may these dogs, enemies of that faith, die." Truer to the tenets of his belief, Fray Junípero remained in his hut praying that the lives of both sides be spared, the Spaniards' because they were his fellows, the Indians' because they had not been baptized and would therefore be damned.

At the end of the fighting, the Spaniards had suffered only one serious casualty—the death of Fray Junípero's servant. When the Indians returned a few days later, the Spaniards offered to care for the wounded. This sign of generosity—coupled with their effective defense of the village—gained them the Indians' respect; and so Portolá returned to a relatively calm community.

By the time the relief vessel reappeared, Portolá had come to the conclusion that the inadequate harbor he had seen was indeed the spot so inaccurately described by Vizcaíno; and although he thought the site a poor one, he was determined to carry out his orders. Leaving some of his men to maintain the settlement at San Diego, he once more marched north; and in June 1770 formally established the mission and presidio at Monterey. Then appointing one of his officers, Pedro Fages, to serve as commander at Alta California, he sailed back to Mexico.

In the north, the Russians were starting to exploit the area that Bering had opened up for them. The land, of course, was unsuitable for permanent settlers who wanted to farm, but it was rich in furs. Even though it was remote, Russian traders were becoming familiar with it, and Russian sea captains were learning the waters of the Pacific. So, too, were the British. For

James Cook, one of the most remarkable of the British navigators, had begun his series of voyages.

But Spain had at last two outposts along the shore—San Diego and Monterey. Neither one was strong enough to resist a concerted enemy attack; in fact Portolá wondered whether they could even be supplied except at unwarranted expense. Yet there they stood—evidence that Spain was not yet ready to surrender the empire its adventurers had won for it on the West Coast of North America.

Fray Junípero, in spite of his age—he had been well into his fifties when he left Baja California—and in spite of the continuing pain in his ulcerated leg, attended to the religious aspect of the colony by founding mission after mission along the length of California from San Diego north. Each of these required the conversion of an Indian congregation, the construction of a church and other buildings with unskilled labor, the cultivation of fields to make the mission partially self-supporting, the recruitment of priests from Mexico, and the maintenance of sufficiently good relations with the civil authorities to provide for its protection. The work was endless, and the indifference of the Indians discouraging; but Fray Junípero, devoted to his cause, persisted, and the string of missions gradually grew.

But the problem of communications between Alta California and Mexico still plagued the Spanish. Head winds made the sea voyage unreasonably long; and the land route from Baja California was unsatisfactory, since from Mexico the peninsula was as inaccessible as a distant island.

Juan Bautista de Anza, a handsome man, proud, ambitious, and somewhat disdainful of the opinions of others, had followed his father's career in the army and had often dreamed of finding an overland route between Pimería and Alta California. In 1771 he listened with interest to the reports brought back from the Colorado River by Fray Francisco Garcés, another of those priests who made interminable journeys into the wilderness. The Indians there had told him of seeing other white men, probably members of Portolá's expedition. Anza interpreted this as evidence that a land route existed between east and west, and he applied to the viceroy for permission to seek it out.

In 1774, he left Tubac, the presidio south of present-day Tucson, with slightly more than thirty men and two guides. One was Fray Francisco, who was willing to retrace his steps into the deserts and mountains of what is now western Arizona.

At the Colorado River, the leader of the Yuma Indians, Salvador Palma, greeted Fray Francisco as an old friend and received the expedition warmly. With a soldier's eye, Anza quickly noted that good relations with the Yumas was essential to anyone wishing to cross the river. So he liberally gave out presents and paid honor to Palma both in words and by hanging a medal around his neck.

Once on the other bank, the Spaniards were less than sixty miles from a point at which Fray Francisco had earlier seen gaps in the mountains—the only mountains, the Spaniards mistakenly believed, that stood in their way. But directly ahead lay a range of sand hills. Therefore Anza turned south along the right bank of the Colorado into a maze of dunes and the confusing lands of the lower Colorado. Finally in desperation he returned to the hospitable Yumas, who agreed to take care of half the livestock while the Spaniards made a fresh assault on the route to California.

This time Anza led his men to the southwest of his earlier course and then turned north through what is now known as the Anza-Borrego Desert of southern California. The land was grim and forbidding with strange geologic shapes silhouetted against the sky, and the whereabouts of drinking water was a constant question.

The men were encouraged by an Indian guide's growing recognition of the country through which they passed but discouraged by the local Indians' reports that other white men had been there before them. These, it proved, were a detachment of soldiers who had been pursuing some deserters from San Diego. This discovery meant that—for all their sufferings—Anza's expedition was not exploring entirely new territory. Their goal, however, was not San Diego, but Monterey; and the direct route there was still to be established. At least in this respect they continued to be pioneers. But being unfamiliar with the mountains, they did not know that a series of ridges fans out to the south. These deflected them seaward and brought them to San Gabriel Mission in the locality of the present city of Los Angeles and far short of their destination.

They continued on to Monterey by the more conventional route, as the way was now well known. In some respects they had failed in their original objective, but they had definitely established that the land between Pimería Alta and Alta California was passable to men on foot or horseback. The viceroy was so gratified by this discovery that he gave Anza a promotion in rank and instructed him to take a group of settlers to San Francisco Bay, which had been discovered by Portolá. In 1775 Anza left Tubac again, but this time with a much larger expedition—almost 150 settlers, their provisions, herds of cattle, some servants and muleteers, and an escort of soldiers.

While the viceroy was strengthening Spain's grip on California, he did not neglect the area farther north. A year earlier he had sent Juan Pérez, a Spanish navigator, to locate the Russian trading posts, which were causing Spain increasing concern. In the course of his voyage, Pérez discovered Nootka Sound in what is now Canada. Several more expeditions went out by sail the same year that Anza left Tubac. Bruno Hazeta discovered the area of the Columbia River; Juan de Bogeda traveled even farther north; and Juan Manuel de Ayala became the first man to take a ship through the Golden Gate into San Francisco Bay.

This spurt of activity, although enlarging Spain's geographical knowledge, did not provide what Spain most needed—a string of strong, defensible settlements along the coast. That was the purpose of Anza's second expedition. By bringing more settlers into the country, he might help establish the type of permanent colony that gave Great Britain such a firm grip on the eastern seaboard.

Near San Diego, his otherwise uneventful trip was briefly interrupted, for the surrounding Indians, having forgotten the lesson imposed on them earlier by the zealous blacksmith and his companions, had rebelled once more against the Spaniards living there. In a land where soldiers were few—the governor had about sixty at his call to protect the entire coast—Anza's escort provided invaluable reinforcements. As soon as the revolt was quelled, he went on to Monterey, where he found the officials less enthusiastic than the viceroy about San Francisco Bay. Nevertheless, he surveyed the area and helped determine possible locations for those two adjuncts of almost every Spanish settlement, a mission and a presidio—God and the sword standing together for the glory of Spain. Later in the year the sites were dedicated; but by that time Anza was back in Pimería Alta, his work well done and the Spanish empire slightly strengthened in the north.

On the evening of June 2, 1776, however, shortly after Anza had completed his mission, John Adams of Massachusetts, contemplating the events of that day at the Continental Congress, picked up his pen and wrote, "The greatest question was decided which was ever debated in America, and a greater, perhaps, never was nor will be decided among men. . . . Britain has been filled with folly, America with wisdom. It is the will of Heaven that the two countries shall be sundered for ever. . . .

"You will think me transported with enthusiasm," he continued, "but I am not. I am well aware of the toil and blood and treasure that it will cost us to maintain this declaration, and support and defend these states; yet, through all the gloom, I can see the rays of light and glory; that the end is worth all the means; that posterity will triumph in that day's transaction, even though we should rue it, which I trust in God we shall not."

In this spirit the delegates turned to Thomas Jefferson and asked him to draft a formal statement avowing the independence of the thirteen colonies from their mother country. Thus a new power—although young, weak, and uncertain in its steps toward the future—emerged upon the continent to join in the contest for its possession.

5. THE AMERICANS COME

*. . . and then we began to meet with the rock-
weed . . . which the Manilla ships generally fall in
with. Now and then a piece of wood also appeared.
But if we had not known that the continent of
North America was not far distant, we might, from
the few signs of the vicinity of land hitherto met
with, have concluded, that there was none within
some thousand leagues of us.*

—James Cook, 1778

Of all the obstacles—and there were many—that blocked the way between
Pimería Alta and Alta California, none was greater than the Colorado River
crossing. Here the men and animals, while they struggled with the current,
were almost defenseless; and so the friendship of the Yuma Indians was
indispensable. Consequently, Anza, to impress Palma with the power of
Spain, arranged to have the Indian leader pay a four-month visit to Mexico
City, where he was feted by the ecclesiastical and secular authorities, baptized

in the cathedral to the ringing of bells, and sent home to tell his fellow tribesmen about the wonders he had seen. The viceroy then appointed Anza governor of New Mexico, hoping he could bring peace to that troubled province, too.

While Anza prepared to undertake his new duties, Fray Junípero was busy expanding the California missions and, unfortunately, quarreling with the government authorities. Anyone who did not wholly support Fray Junípero's insatiable desire for new missions became his antagonist.

But Fray Junípero's influence stopped at San Francisco Bay. Beyond that point, the Spanish—their resources already drawn dangerously thin—made no effort to establish settlements, thus leaving the lands discovered by their navigators unprotected against other explorers. On these uninhabited shores, James Cook, the British seaman, landed in 1778; and he noted that, despite the absence of the Spanish, the white men were already affecting the Indians' lives. One of his crew members, John Ledyard, later wrote that "we found a few copper bracelets and three or four rough wrought knives with coarse wooden hafts among the natives at this place, but could not learn from the appearance of those articles or from any information they could give us how they became possessed of them, but it was generally thought they came from a great distance and not unlikely from Hudson's Bay." Then he added with considerable insight, "Commerce is diffusive and nothing will impede its progress among the uninformed part of mankind, but an intervention of too remote a communication by water, and as this cannot be the case with regard to the inhabitants of a continent, it seems entirely conclusive to suppose no part of America is without some sort of commercial intercourse, immediate or remote."

As Ledyard sensed, the influence of the Europeans had spread far beyond the last military fort and the most distant trading post. English and French traders were reaching into the west, and samples of their trade goods had preceded them. While the Spanish were still converting the Indians to Catholicism and looking hopefully for gold, silver, and gems, the British and French were finding their fortunes in furs.

As Cook's expedition continued along the coast, however, Ledyard noted in his journal that in spite of the speed with which traders from the east were penetrating the wilderness, other Europeans were even closer at hand— traders from the post established by the Russians in the country discovered by Bering. A new contestant had entered the struggle for possession of the western coast.

As the expedition drew near the settlement, Cook sent Ledyard ahead to inform them of the Englishmen's presence. "I found the whole village," he later wrote, "built partly underground, and covered with the turf at the bottom, and coarse grass at the tops. . . . They [the Russians] sleep on platforms built on each side of the hut, on which they have a number of Bear

69

and other skins, which renders them comfortable, & as they have been educated in a hardy manner, they need little or no other support than what they procure from the sea, and from hunting." Clearly the Russians were able to adjust to the rigors of life in the cold north in a way that the Spanish could not and had settled in permanently. They were even able to offer Ledyard the luxury of a hot bath, bringing him a copper cauldron filled with steaming water.

Earlier Cook's expedition had purchased some skins from the Indians, but it was not until later that the explorers learned the profit they might have earned. As Ledyard commented when he wrote an account of the voyage, "We purchased . . . about 1500 beaver, besides other skins . . . having no thought at the time of using them to other advantage than converting them to the purposes of clothing, but it afterwards happened that skins which did not cost the purchaser six-pence sterling sold in China for a 100 dollars." And he added, regretfully, "Neither did we purchase a quarter part of the beaver and other fur skins that we might have done, and most certainly should have done had we known of the opportunity of disposing of them to such an astonishing profit."

Here then was the secret that the Spanish had overlooked. Coming from their conquests of the Aztecs and Incas, they expected to find in the north duplicates of the civilizations they had already encountered, but the true riches were on the backs of animals trapped by apparently poverty-stricken Indians. Shortly after leaving the Russian post, Cook met his death in Hawaii—those islands he had named after his patron, Lord Sandwich—but his expedition continued without him and brought back the amazing news of the wealth that could be accumulated by those daring enough to follow the profitable example set by the Russians and enter the Chinese fur trade.

During the year in which Cook explored the coast of what is now Canada, the cause of American independence made a signal advance. The Battle of Saratoga ended England's hopes of splitting the colonies in half and brought prestige to the new nation. For the first time, many Europeans began to take seriously the Americans' aspirations; and France, which had been giving aid covertly, now became an open ally.

Unaware of this dramatic event, which would deeply affect the future of North America, Anza was absorbed in the immediate problems confronting the province of New Mexico. One of these was the raids of the Comanches, who swept in from the east. Scorning the practices of his predecessors, Anza took a new route across the mountains, caught the Indians by surprise, and defeated them in two battles, one of which took the life of their brilliant leader, Cuerno Verde.

This success left him free the following year to carry out a project long favored by both him and the viceroy: opening a trail between New Mexico and Sonora in northwestern Mexico that would bring the two provinces closer and reduce the cost of transporting supplies to New Mexico. In the late fall of 1780, he set out for Arispe with approximately a hundred and fifty men. This was a smaller force than he wanted, but many of the volunteers had dropped out when they realized that the journey would take them through the heartland of the Apaches. These Indians, among the most implacable of foes, had already won a fearsome reputation for their deadly raids, their ability to lie in ambush, and their ferocity in open battle.

Anza's journey took him a little to the east of present-day Deming, New Mexico, before he turned to the southwest. This added a considerable distance to his route, but he arrived safely in Arispe. Several other expeditions went out at the same time to support him, and they, too, met with success, even defeating some small bands of Apaches they encountered. At the same time, mindful of Anza's stress on the importance of the Colorado crossing, the authorities established two missions among the Yumas, placing them under the leadership of Fray Francisco Garcés, who had helped guide Anza to California.

After years of neglect, Spain was now taking energetic steps to strengthen its northern provinces, binding them together with a series of trails to make possible mutual trade and protection, reinforcing its friendships with its allies (Anza had already made one expedition to the Hopis in an attempt to secure their allegiance), and punishing its enemies. But the foundations of their northern empire were not strong. Men like Anza might march across the deserts, and mountains, but they left little behind them but their tracks, for few settlements extended into the north, and those that had been established, like the mission and presidios in California, were weak.

Even the strategic crossing at the Colorado River was left unguarded except for two missions and a tiny detachment of soldiers. In July, 1781, immediately after the departure of an emigrant train bound for Alta California, the Yumas decided to take vengeance for the insults and injuries they believed they had suffered from the Spanish. Quickly they attacked both missions and part of the military escort that had remained behind. Taken by surprise and with no presidio to which they could flee, the Spaniards suffered heavy losses, almost all their men being killed. A small military force—too small to punish the Indians—later marched to the crossing, buried the dead, and negotiated the release of the few survivors. But the road opened by Anza was closed, and Alta California was again separated from the rest of Mexico except for the long, impractical sea route up the coast.

The Spanish campaigns against the Comanches, Apaches, and Yumas were of minor importance, however, compared to the other events taking place in North America. In the year of the Yuma uprising, Cornwallis surrendered to the combined French and American forces at Yorktown; and two years later

John Ledyard, who had accompanied James Cook, published his account of the voyage. The slender volume was more significant than its unprepossessing size indicated, for it revealed to American readers the high prices obtainable in China for West Coast furs. Until now this had been the Russians' trade secret—the means by which they had been able to develop a firm foothold in North America without confronting the companies already in the business.

The largest and most prominent of these was the Hudson's Bay Company in Canada, which had long held a virtual monopoly in the north. It was now meeting competition, however, from the new North-West Company, formed by some of the Hudson's Bay Company's former employees. In the United States no one corporation dominated the field, but a young immigrant, John Jacob Astor, hoped to do so. (Even before disembarking from the ship that had brought him from Europe, he had decided that the prospects for making money were greater in buying and selling pelts than in opening a musical instrument store as he had originally intended.) Neither the two Canadian companies nor Astor was yet prepared to compete with the Russians, for none of them had the necessary establishments on the Pacific Coast. But Ledyard's book demonstrated that they had been overlooking a potentially rich business.

In California, Father Junípero, unaware of the business world and that trade was supplanting religion as a driving force in the creation of empires, continued to establish new missions in Alta California. Although in 1784 he was seventy years old, and although his leg hurt and his chest was now aching with pain, he still rode from one group of converts to another, believing that his God alone afford them the salvation they and all men deserved.

The previous year he had established another mission, making a total of nine, each created out of the wilderness. Yet he was not content. Then, too, he had another regret. Because he was not of sufficient rank within the Church, his authority to hold confirmation masses had been granted to him only temporarily, and this authority was about to expire. According to his itemized list, he had confirmed more than 5,300 persons; yet so many remained unconfirmed. It seemed to him that, for all his labors, his accomplishments had been so small.

On July 16, 1784, one of the ships from Baja California arrived at San Francisco, bringing with it the news that no additional missionaries were available to help him. This discouraging information, combined with the weariness he felt from having just finished tours of both the southern and northern missions, made him realize his usefulness was ending and his life coming to a close. When he asked for the Most Holy Viaticum—communion for those on the point of death—a priest offered to perform the service in the small room where he rested, but Fray Junípero insisted on going to the church. He was still able to walk, he said, and there was no reason for God to come to him when he could go to God.

A few days later he lay down on the roughhewn boards covered with a light blanket that served him as his bed. Across his breast lay the crucifix he had kept with him ever since his novitiate, carrying it on every journey and sleeping with it every night. Quietly he shut his eyes to rest and never reopened them. The priests for whom he had sent arrived too late to see him alive, but his example continued to inspire them. Fray Junípero was dead, but not his dream of lining Alta California with missions.

At the conclusion of the American Revolution, Spain successfully negotiated the return of Florida. This gave it control of the eastern coastline from approximately the middle of present-day Georgia around the entire shore of the Gulf of Mexico, which again became a Spanish sea, as it had been in the days before La Salle began searching for the mouth of the Mississippi. As for the United States itself, Spain was determined the new nation should not become a potent rival and, having failed to limit its territory to the Alleghenies, refused to cede it the right to navigate the Mississippi through Spanish lands. This further sealed off the Gulf of Mexico and so angered the western settlements they refused to back a treaty between the two countries. (To protect themselves in the future, they insisted on the constitutional provision that treaties must henceforth be approved by a two-thirds majority of the Senate.) At least on paper, Spain had maintained the security of the eastern approaches to its North American empire.

In New Mexico, Anza, struggling with more local problems, took further steps to protect the province from the Indians, especially the western Apaches, who had not been subdued by the campaigns waged against them during the opening of the road to Sonora. As they generally lived in small villages, the Spanish attacks had fallen only on isolated groups, and the vast majority of Apaches had remained untouched and still ready to fight the Spanish or raid their settlements.

The Navajos, another warlike tribe and related to the Apaches, often fought with them. One of Anza's first objects was to break up this alliance. In a series of meetings with leaders of the Navajos, he used a combination of threats and promises to achieve his purpose and even persuaded some of the Navajos to join his campaigns against their former allies.

Slowly he was relieving the pressure on the New Mexican settlements, but his success and Spain's diplomatic maneuvers in the east did not alleviate another danger that now menaced the nation's hold on the West Coast. For in Boston, a group of merchants who had read Ledyard's book outfitted two ships, the *Columbia,* under Captain John Kendrick, and a smaller vessel, the *Washington,* under Robert Gray, to enter the profitable fur trade Ledyard had

73

described. Although several British ships had made the voyage to the West Coast since the return of Cook's expedition, they had not yet published accounts of their journeys. Kendrick and Gray, therefore, could draw only on the rather scanty maps and descriptions prepared by Cook.

Off Cape Horn, the two ships became separated during a storm, but they reunited at their prearranged rendezvous in Nootka Sound on what is now Vancouver Island in the early fall of 1788. This harbor, discovered by Captain Cook, seemed an ideal center for conducting a fur trade, so the two ships lay there during the winter. In the early spring, Gray took the *Washington* and cruised the coast, north and south, stopping to trade with the Indians wherever they had furs to offer him. All that Ledyard and the other members of Cook's expedition had said seemed to be true, for at one spot they were able to buy sea otter pelts at the low cost of one simple iron chisel for each two hundred skins. In June, Gray returned to Nootka Sound, where he transferred his cargo to the *Columbia* for the voyage home.

Kendrick, having now acquired a taste for being his own master, sent Gray back to Boston in command of the *Columbia,* while he himself remained in the Pacific, using the *Washington* as though it belonged to him and trading on his own account. His death a few years later caused no grief among the Boston merchants, for his absconding with the ship had cost them much of their expected profits.

Gray, on the other hand, received a hero's welcome when he dropped anchor in Boston harbor. He had gone west from Nootka Sound (thus becoming the first captain to circumnavigate the globe under the American flag); and in a burst of patriotism, the citizens struck a medal bearing a picture of the two ships on one side and the names of the owners on the other. Several of the original partners, distressed by the expense of Kendrick's defection, dropped out of the partnership, but other investors, including Gray himself, took their place; and in approximately six weeks, they had re-outfitted the *Columbia* for another voyage, and Gray had again taken command.

While he had been away from the Pacific Northwest, the once quiet and remote harbor of Nootka Sound had suddenly become the center of a major international controversy. The Spanish, who now occasionally cruised up the coast to reaffirm their claims, discovered that a former British naval captain, John Meares, had established a trading center there. They seized some of the ships anchored offshore; and in retaliation Great Britain threatened to declare war and began assembling a fleet at Spithead. Spain's temper suddenly cooled, and it signed a conciliatory agreement with Great Britain, ceding commercial rights to its enemy and thus weakening its own claim to the area.

Before this, George Vancouver, another of Great Britain's famous explorers, had already been ordered to cruise the Pacific on a scientific expedition, so the government now gave him additional instructions to inspect Nootka Sound and the North American coast. Thus Vancouver and

Gray, although neither sea captain knew it, were engaged in a race of discovery, both heading at approximately the same time for the relatively unknown western shores of North America.

Gray arrived first, spent the remainder of 1791 buying furs, and then went into winter quarters on Vancouver Island. Vancouver, having already conducted surveys along the shores of Australia, New Zealand, Tahiti, and the Hawaiian Islands, sighted the coast in the spring of 1792. Inevitably the two ships met. Their missions were so different—Gray's purely commercial and Vancouver's scientific and diplomatic—that they saw no conflict between their purposes and sailed together for a while, exchanging information.

In July 1792, after he and Vancouver had gone their different ways, Gray's search for furs brought him to the mouth of what is now the Columbia River. Vancouver had passed that point, noticing the bay but not locating the river that formed it. Gray, however, desiring to purchase skins, was perhaps watching the shore more closely. Seeing a breach in the two sandbars that guarded the interior of the harbor, he sent his pinnace out ahead and, finding the way clear, sailed the *Columbia* nearer the land. He then observed that the water was becoming fresh and saw the river extending to the northeast.

Searching for a village whose inhabitants might have skins to trade, he decided to go up the river. Soon the shores were lined with Indians, twenty canoes came out to greet the Americans, and a brisk trade followed, the *Columbia* buying furs and salmon in return for nails, cloth, and sheets of copper. Then Gray decided to take his ship, a relatively small vessel, farther upstream. After some seven or eight miles, he ran aground on the shoals. By sending out a small boat, he learned he could continue on, but there seemed little point in doing so. Sea otters were the prized pelts, and the animals lived only in salt water. So he returned to the Indian village and then put out once more into the Pacific.

In this matter-of-fact fashion, his practical Yankee mind absorbed in trading, not in making history, Gray changed the course of his country's future. While the Columbia River had escaped the attention of both British and Spanish explorers, Gray had not only located it but entered it. Under the international law of the time, the nation discovering the mouth of a river could lay claim to its entire watershed. Almost without knowing it, Gray had, therefore, given the United States a legal basis for title to a vast area that included deserts, mountains, and fertile lands, running from the Pacific Ocean to the Rocky Mountains, a claim that the young nation could not yet enforce but which potentially cut deeply into those of Great Britain and Spain.

The log kept by one of Gray's officers describes their actions when they came to anchor several miles up the river. "I landed abreast the Ship," it reads, "with Capt. Gray to view the Country and take possession; leaving charge with the 2nd Officer." But the words "and take possession" were inserted in different ink and different handwriting, obviously at a later date when some one finally recognized the significance of the event.

After leaving the river, the *Columbia* struck a rock, and Gray was forced to put into Nootka Sound for repairs. The Spanish maintained a fort at the entrance, which, according to one of Gray's officers, "was no great thing, mounted with 6 Twenty-four and Thirty-six pounders. The platforms would not bear the weight of metal." But the Spanish could still impress the Americans. At a gala dinner, the governor served five courses to fifty-four men on silver plates. Furthermore, with each change of course, the dirty plates were removed—but left in the room where the Americans could see them accumulate until they made a total of more than two hundred and fifty. Shortly afterward, with the *Columbia* repaired and well laden with furs, Gray set his course to the east, traded his cargo in China, and returned to New England in 1793.

Almost exactly one week before Gray entered Boston harbor with the profits he had earned for his partners, a group of white men arrived on the West Coast under the leadership of a remarkable Scotsman, Alexander Mackenzie. One of the youngest men ever to be admitted to partnership in the North-West Company, which had been formed to compete with the Hudson's Bay Company, Mackenzie combined conflicting characteristics. Relatively uneducated, he had an extraordinary sense of the geopolitics of North America; a driver of men who could push them to their limits in the wilderness, he was shy in the presence of intellectuals and embarrassed by his own lack of formal training.

He had already explored to the mouth of the Canadian river that now bears his name and therefore knew, more certainly than anyone, that no Northwest Passage existed. If it had, his route to the Arctic would have intersected it. He then spent a year in England studying navigation; and when he returned to North America, his next objective was to reach the Pacific by land. Realizing he could not make the trip across the continent in one season, he established a base camp on Canada's Peace River; and in the spring of 1793, as soon as the ice had melted, he started up the river toward the west.

The whole party, including two Indian guides who were only vaguely familiar with part of the route, numbered less than ten men, and they carried with them merely the light provisions used by fur traders and a few articles to exchange for information and other assistance from the tribes they met. Speed was essential; each man knew they must reach the Pacific and return to their base before the snow and ice again blocked the rivers and mountain passes. Canyons and the swift water of rapids made the streams treacherous; deep forests and uncertain quagmires turned the land into a series of obstacles; but they crossed the Continental Divide and began the descent toward the coastline, completing a journey never before made by any man, red or white.

On July 20, 1793, Mackenzie noted in his journal that "at about eight [in the morning] we got out of the river, which discharges itself by various channels into the sea. The tide was out, and had left a large space covered with seaweed." In spite of the heavy fog that clung to the shore, those two signs—the tide and the seaweed—told them they had arrived at their destination.

Mackenzie did not stay long. He had to be back before winter, and the Indians, already accustomed to abuse from the traders who had come by water, were sometimes hostile and threatening. But he saw the sea otters—those most prized of all fur-bearing animals—and he had proved that the trade originated by the Russians and made known by Cook and Ledyard need not remain the private preserve of those with ships. The traders of eastern Canada could enter the business, too, and one more rival now stood on Spain's northern border.

Although John Jay's treaty with Great Britain ended the war and recognized the independence of the United States, it did little else. Many of the other issues between the two nations remained unresolved. The Senate finally approved the agreement, and Washington signed it reluctantly, but few Americans were pleased with it.

It did, however, improve the country's relations with Spain. Fearful of closer ties between the United States and Great Britain and a possible alliance between the two, Spain became more conciliatory, settled its major boundary differences with the new republic, agreed to restrain the Indians along its border, and granted the United States the right both to navigate the Mississippi and to transfer goods at New Orleans from one boat to another without paying duty.

Spain's efforts to placate its new eastern neighbor helped remove a threat on the eastern flank of its North American empire, but its government did not react prudently to the danger in the north. Renewed warfare with the British abrogated the Nootka Sound agreement and reopened the controversy in the Northwest. Yet Spain took few steps to protect itself from an attack coming from that direction.

A visitor to Monterey in 1796 reported that the "town shows ignorance of the arts and a stationary state of the country." The flour mill was so crude and inefficient it could barely fill a small order. "Industry," the visitor remarked, "is in general the feeble side of Spanish establishments and it is for this that they cost so dear to their government." Monterey was no exception. Lying in the California sun, the town had made little progress toward becoming self-sufficient or even toward being able to defend itself.

The days of Pizarro and Cortés were long over, and the treasure rooms of the Aztecs and Incas despoiled forever. The adventurer who extended the boundaries of the frontier no longer dressed in armor and ate off silver plates; he wore the simplest of clothing and dined on pemmican or hardtack. Russia,

France, England, and the United States had learned this. While Spain still dwelt in the past the Russians expanded their fur trade, the British drove overland to the ocean, the United States began sending ships to the far corners of the world and pioneers across the Appalachians, and the French, stirred by the contagious ambition of Napoleon, dreamed of regaining the territory once claimed on their behalf by La Salle.

Ready as a hawk to seize its prey, Napoleon began to negotiate with Spain to reacquire Louisiana. To Spain, the prospective sale was attractive. Its earlier efforts to restrict the United States had not been completely effective, and if Napoleon wished to drive a wedge into the heart of the North American continent, let him bear the expense of arming and patrolling it. The Spanish would be glad to remain behind his shield, for they were having enough trouble just maintaining their defenses on the West Coast.

An American sea captain who visited San Diego shortly after the start of the new century examined the settlement's fort and "found eight brass nine-pounders, mounted on carriages, which appeared to be in good order, and a plentiful supply of ball; but there was no appearance of their having been used for a long time."

The commandant, however, made up in show what his men lacked in training. When the Americans first arrived, they sent a boat to bring him on board. "This being done immediately," the captain later said, "he crowded the boat with his escort, and probably regretted the necessity of leaving on shore his horses . . . such a ridiculous display of 'little brief authority,' and pompous parade, I never before witnessed. Having saluted us on coming over the ship's side, he waited, before proceeding aft, until his escort were drawn up in two lines, with hats off in one hand, and drawn swords in the other, and then passed between them to the companionway."

His pretense was matched only by his rascality; he tried to confiscate the furs on visiting ships, apparently intending to sell them later for his own profit. But in his preoccupation with his own importance and his own welfare, he had failed to drill the troops under his command properly. When the American ship prepared to leave without paying the tribute the commandant demanded, he manned the fortress to block its exit. Since the vessel was armed only with three-pounders and had merely fifteen men on board, the odds were heavily against it. After approximately forty-five minutes, during which the fort bombarded the ship, the Americans fired only two broadsides. These sent the garrison running, and the ship proceeded safely out to sea.

Another sea captain visiting California at about the same time described the Spanish population as "of an indolent, harmless disposition, and fond of spirituous liquors. That they should not be industrious, is not surprising; their government does not encourage industry." The Spanish, he explained, understood the importance of California to the defense of Mexico, but "they have spread a number of defenceless inhabitants over the country, whom they could never enduce to act as enemies to those who should treat them well, by securing to them the enjoyments of liberty, property, and free trade." In conclusion he remarked that "the conquest of this country would be absolutely nothing; it would fall without effort to the most inconsiderable force."

Yet as far as the United States was concerned, Spain, at least temporarily, held one of the most strategic points in North America—the entrance to the Mississippi. Jefferson, who knew Spain was planning to transfer all of Louisiana to France, wrote to the American envoy at Paris, "There is on the globe one single spot, the possessor of which is our natural and habitual enemy. It is New Orleans, through which the produce of three-eighths of our territory must pass to market, and from its fertility it will ere long yield more than half of our whole produce, and contain more than half of our inhabitants . . . these circumstances render it impossible that France and the United States can long continue friends, when they meet in so irritable a position. They, as well as we, must be blind if they do not see this; and we must be very improvident if we do not begin to make arrangements on that hypothesis."

At first the French government seemed unresponsive to the American intermediaries' efforts to gain access to the sea, but Napoleon's plans for reestablishing France in the New World had gone awry. Santo Domingo, which he had intended to use as a staging area, broke out in irrepressible revolt, and the threat of renewed warfare in Europe again loomed large. In an abrupt change of strategy, he decided to abandon his proposed expansion in North America and divest himself entirely of Louisiana.

When his minister approached the United States envoy with the suggestion that he arrange the purchase—not merely of New Orleans area—but of all the western drainage basin of the Mississippi, he presented Jefferson with a problem of far-reaching consequences. Nothing in the Constitution, Jefferson believed, gave the executive branch the right to negotiate a purchase that would so alter the boundaries of the country and so upset the balance between east and west. Yet a dictator who had changed his mind as quickly as Napoleon might well change it again; the opportunity was one that must be seized at once or perhaps lost forever. Much against his own conscience, therefore, Jefferson concluded a treaty of purchase and presented it to the Senate.

The debate was acrimonious. Some questioned the validity of France's title; others objected to the expenditure; but behind their thinking lay the common fear that this enormous acquisition, coming while the government was still untried, might distort or destroy the compromises and ideals that had made possible its establishment.

Jefferson persisted against the opposition. For as one senator remarked, "To acquire an empire of perhaps half the extent of the one we possessed, from the most powerful and warlike nation on earth, without bloodshed, without the oppression of a single individual . . . is an achievement . . . [for] which the archives . . . cannot furnish a parallel." The necessary majority of the Senate agreed—and so did the nation. The treaty was ratified; and by virtue of a few words on paper, the United States took possession of more than nine hundred thousand square miles of territory and extended its boundaries to the crest of the Rockies. Between it and the Pacific lay only the lands still contested by Spain, France, and Russia—lands to which the United States could also lay partial claim; and Jefferson already had made plans to penetrate their mysteries.

PART II
1804–45

6. THE AMERICANS LOOK WEST

Should you reach the Pacific Ocean, inform yourself of the circumstances which may decide whether the furs of those parts may not be collected as advantageously at the head of the Missouri . . . as at Nootka Sound, or any other point of that coast; and that trade be consequently conducted through the Missouri and [the] United States more beneficially than by the circumnavigation now practiced.

—Thomas Jefferson
to Meriwether Lewis, 1803

The American Revolution and the Louisiana Purchase gave the United States title to the major portion of the middle area of North America; but except for the strip between the Atlantic Ocean and the Appalachian Mountains, the United States knew less about those lands than did most of the contending powers.

The Spaniards had explored Florida and the Southwest; they had been in Kansas four times before the British first tried to settle at Jamestown; their men had marched the length of California; and their ships had sailed far north of the present Canadian boundary. French fur trappers and explorers had been across the Great Plains and ranged the length of the Mississippi. British fur trappers had followed France's trails and had pressed beyond them, being the first white men to travel from the Atlantic to the Pacific.

All this time the Americans had mostly remained east of the Appalachians, were barely familiar with the watershed of the Ohio, and knew even less about the country beyond the Mississippi. Yet with the exuberance that was already part of their character, they felt themselves equal to the challenge of taking possession of the lands they now owned and of contending for those whose title still lay in doubt.

Although independent in spirit, they were willing to adopt the best of the techniques developed by the other cultures, learning from the fur traders of France and Great Britain and, later, from the cattlemen of Spain. But they also added some uniquely American ingredients to their westward expansion. After bitter debate at the Constitutional Convention, they had decided that most of the land west of the Appalachians would belong to the states in common and that its sale would provide some of the revenue the new nation sorely needed. The sales, however, would not be restricted to the wealthy; the minimum designated price for each acre and the size of the blocks of land available would make it possible for simple men to become landowners. This contrasted strongly with the previous European system of encouraging exploration and settlement with large land grants and trade monopolies.

American ingenuity did not stop with this encouragement to mass immigration. While the British, French, Spanish, and Russians who had come to North America were politically subordinate to those who remained at home, the United States had already devised a mechanism that would eventually make all its citizens politically equal. The Northwest Ordinance of 1787 set forth a procedure by which each area in the western lands would go through three stages: first, as an unorganized territory under the direct control of the federal government; then as an organized territory with certain rights and functions of its own; and finally as a full-fledged state with exactly the same rights and privileges as the older ones. For there would be no special concessions to seniority. Politically the pioneers would lose nothing by venturing west. Eventually they—or at least their descendants—would be on an equal footing with those who had remained at home. This concept, imaginative and daring, reversed the usual process of colonization, prevented the development of dependencies, and made the nation one whole. Rarely before had a people looked forward to their expansion with a greater sense of responsibility to those who would carry their flag.

★　　★　　★

Even before the Louisiana Purchase, Jefferson, partly stimulated by reading Alexander Mackenzie's journal, had conceived the idea of sending an American expedition overland to the West Coast. For this purpose he had chosen a young army officer and family friend, Meriwether Lewis, who had had frontier experience with the army and had acted as Jefferson's confidential secretary in Washington.

Lewis chose as his co-commander William Clark, a former officer under whom he had once served. Nothing could have been greater than the contrast between the two men. Lewis was introspective and given to self-doubts, frequently falling into dark moods. Clark, on the other hand, was completely an extrovert, self-confident, genial, and filled with physical vigor and a zest for living. Yet both men shared many characteristics: generosity, particularly toward each other; loyalty; a high regard for duty; and deep faith in their country. During their journey, neither man ever gave the other an order, a remarkable record in the strenuous circumstances under which they worked together.

While Lewis and Clark were preparing for their journey, the diplomats were still negotiating the actual transfer of Louisiana to the United States. Suspicious of Napoleon's intentions and angered by his resale of Louisiana, Spain had delayed turning the land over to France, and so France did not yet have title. Two transfer ceremonies were thus necessary: one from Spain to France, and the other from France to the United States. When they were eventually held at New Orleans and St. Louis, it took only hours to erase the ghosts of Coronado and La Salle from the country they had explored.

So many uncertainties had surrounded the transaction that Jefferson thought it wise to notify the Spanish government of the proposed expedition and to obtain for Lewis and Clark passports from both France and Great Britain. Particularly beyond the Rockies, no one was certain who owned what.

Jefferson's objectives for the expedition, which he set forth in a long letter of instructions to Lewis, were extensive. The men were to observe, and report on, almost every scientific aspect of the country through which they passed from its meteorology to its biology, from its topography to the anthropology of the Indian tribes they might meet, an assignment that would have taxed the energies of a much larger group. He also had a commercial motive in ordering the expedition. He hoped to find a link between the Missouri and one of the great West Coast rivers that would make it possible for the United States to participate directly in the prosperous fur trade along the Pacific shore. An overland route would obviate the need for the expensive sea voyage and give the United States a decided advantage.

Jefferson, like other national leaders, hoped to improve his nation's prosperity through exploration, but there the resemblance between the Lewis and Clark expedition and its predecessors ended. Coronado, Oñate, La Salle, and many other explorers of the past had received the official sanction of their governments, but they themselves had had to underwrite their expenses, hoping in return to make their fortunes. Some, like Alexander Mackenzie and La Vérendrye, the French fur trader who had searched the plains for a west-flowing river, had traveled unofficially but on behalf of their own business interests.

Neither Lewis nor Clark, however, expected any remuneration beyond their salaries and perhaps a bonus. They themselves would not obtain title to the lands over which they passed or receive trade monopolies. Theirs was to be a nationally sponsored expedition, not a speculative enterprise. Nor did the federal government expect to receive an immediate financial return.

The two men had responsibility for bringing back information, not bags of gold or bales of furs. Now a nation was making a national investment in itself and in the increment of its knowledge. Although almost unnoticed at the time, this was a dramatic revolution in the economics of exploring and developing the continent. The government was establishing the precedent that the initial costs should be borne by the people as a whole and not placed on the shoulders of commercial adventurers, and that the benefits should accrue to the people, not to a few individuals.

Having recruited the military and civilian personnel they would need, Lewis and Clark spent the winter of 1803–4 near St. Louis; and on May 14 of the following spring they began the ascent of the Missouri River on the first leg of their long trip. Their progress was slow, for they collected scientific data as they went and treated with the Indians, distributing presents and describing the might of the United States. Although the Indians had difficulty understanding what they were talking about, no nation ever had two more sincere propagandists working on its behalf.

By fall, they had reached the Mandan villages, which had first been discovered by La Vérendrye years before. These Indians, probably the most civilized of the Missouri River tribes, were a legend among the white men. Although the villages had suffered severely from smallpox and from attacks by the Sioux, they remained a focal point for the fur trade of the upper Missouri; and Lewis and Clark, while they were there, met Frenchmen and Englishmen who had come from Canada to do business with the Mandans and other nearby tribes.

After a bitterly cold winter the days began to warm, and the snow to melt. On April 7, 1805, Lewis and Clark watched the men who had agreed to accompany them only as far as the villages depart for St. Louis, carrying with them reports of the expedition's progress. Later that afternoon, the remainder boarded the two pirogues that had carried them upstream and six smaller boats they had built during the winter. To the echo of a swivel gun, which they fired in celebration of their departure, the men swung their boats into the river and headed for the West Coast.

During the next weeks, they followed the Missouri. If any river reached deep into the heart of the mountains that sea captains had seen from the Pacific, this must be the one. Under a sun that grew continually hotter as the days passed, they pushed their way upstream, sometimes rowing, sometimes poling, once in a while trying to sail, and sometimes dragging their boats behind them as they walked along the banks or waded in the water. They passed the mouth of the Yellowstone, which some men thought might reach the New Mexican settlements and thus provide a useful trade route; they encountered grizzly bears and learned firsthand that the reputation of these animals as dangerous was well deserved; they capsized a boat carrying most of their medical provisions and scientific instruments (they recovered most of its valuable cargo); and at last came to the mouth of Marias River.

Here they faced their most serious problem yet, for they were not sure which stream was the Missouri. To take the wrong course could delay them for weeks, thus preventing them from reaching the mountains before winter. By observing the rivers' currents carefully and by reconnoitering both of them, they made the right choice and came to the Falls of the Missouri, a series of impassable ledges over which the river poured with churning water and veils of spray. Here the topography forced them to make a long and arduous portage, dragging their boats over sixteen miles of the rough prairie land and fighting off a grizzly that attacked one of their men.

By June 15, 1805, weary but still in good spirits, they were ready to start moving upstream again. Lewis and Clark had proved an almost perfect complement to each other as leaders, pushing the men hard but conserving their strength, nursing them when they became ill, laughing at their jokes, and joining in their parties on those occasional evenings when Peter Cruzatte, one of the soldiers, played the violin he had brought with him.

On July 25 Clark, who had walked ahead of the boats, reached the Three Forks of the Missouri where the Jefferson, Gallatin, and Madison Rivers join to form the larger river. At this point, the expedition had reached truly unknown territory, and even the Indians whom they had questioned during their winter at the Mandan villages could tell them little about what lay beyond. Their principal hope was to meet the Shoshone Indians and obtain horses and guides.

For this reason, they had brought with them an Indian woman, Sacajawea, a native Shoshone who had been captured by raiding Indians and taken to the Mandan villages, where she had married a French trader. To secure her services, they had to hire her husband, too, a doubtful addition to their personnel as he was conceited, emotional, and slow-witted. They also had to

87

permit her to bring her son, Jean Baptiste, nicknamed "Pomp," who had been born only that winter.

"We are now very anxious to see the Snake [Shoshone] Indians," they wrote in their report, "After advancing for several hundred miles into this wild and mountainous country, we may soon expect that the game will abandon us. With no information of the route, we may be unable to find a passage across the mountains when we reach the head of the river—at least, such a pass as will lead us to the Columbia."

As they pushed up the Jefferson, they still saw no sign of the Indians whose horses and guides they needed so desperately. But during the second week of August, Sacajawea recognized the country through which they were traveling. At least they were certain that they had reached the lands of the Shoshones; and Lewis went ahead to see if he could find an Indian camp.

Walking along the trail with a soldier flanking him on either side, he observed an Indian about two miles away who was riding in his direction. Through his glass, he noticed that the horseman was different from any Indian he had seen before and rightly supposed he was a Shoshone.

When the men had come within a mile of each other, the Indian stopped. "Captain Lewis," according to the explorers' report, "immediately following his example, took his blanket from his knapsack, and holding it with both hands at the two corners, threw it above his head and unfolded it as he brought it to the ground, as if in the act of spreading it. This signal, which originates in the practice of spreading a robe or skin, as a seat for guests to whom they wish to show distinguished kindness, is the universal sign of friendship among the Indians on the Missouri River and the Rocky mountains."

The gesture did not overcome the Indian's suspicions, for he had noticed the two soldiers on Lewis's flanks, both of whom were still advancing. Lewis did not immediately signal them to stop for fear of alarming the Indian, so, according to the report, he first "took from his pack some beads, a looking-glass and a few trinkets, which he had brought for the purpose, and leaving his gun, advanced, unarmed, toward the Indian."

At the same time, he risked making a sign to the two soldiers. One of the men halted; the other did not see him. Lewis moved slowly ahead, holding out his offerings and rolling up his sleeve above his tanned hand and wrist to show that his skin was white. But when he was within a hundred and fifty paces, the Indian, aware of the one soldier who was still advancing, turned "his horse, and giving him the whip, leaped across the creek and disappeared in an instant among the willow-bushes. With him," continued Lewis, "vanished all the hopes, which the sight of him had inspired, of a friendly introduction to his countrymen."

Calling the two soldiers together, Lewis started to follow the Indian's tracks in the hope they would lead him to the man's village, but first they "fixed a small flag of the United States on a pole, which was carried by one of the men as a signal of their friendly intentions should the Indians observe them as they were advancing," as though that young flag, in which Lewis had such great faith, would have any significance for the Shoshones.

They did not overtake the Indian, but a trail they discovered the following day took them over Lemhi Pass near the present-day border of Montana and Idaho and brought them to the other side of the Continental Divide and into the drainage basin of the Columbia River. That night, as the explorers later reported, "having killed nothing in the course of the day, they supped on their last piece of pork, and trusted to fortune for some other food to mix with a little flour and parched meal, which was all that now remained of their provisions."

Still moving ahead of Clark, who was struggling with the boats as the river grew shallower, Lewis sighted several more Indians on August 13, but these, too, fled at his approach. But a little later he suddenly came on three more, an old woman, a young woman, and a child. The young woman raced away; but the other two, not having time to flee, sat on the ground with their heads bowed in submission. Lewis immediately brought out his presents and also painted their cheeks with vermillion as an indication of his friendliness. He so reassured them that they persuaded the fleeing woman to return, and the three of them agreed to lead Lewis to their camp.

They had gone only a few miles when they met a band of sixty warriors who, having heard that strangers were in the area, thought they must be a band of raiding Blackfeet. When the women told them of Lewis's peaceful behavior, "the whole body of warriors now came forward," Lewis later reported, "and our men received the caresses, with no small share of the grease and paint of their new friends. After this fraternal embrace, of which the motive was much more agreeable than the manner," Lewis invited the Indians to smoke a pipe with him, and secured permission to visit their camp.

Finally on August 30, Lewis and Clark were ready to push forward again. Their expedition had reached a critical and disappointing period. Although they had crossed the Continental Divide, they had failed to find a swift-flowing river that would carry them to the Columbia and on to the Pacific. Instead they had ahead of them weary miles of travel through unknown mountains. The Indians, from whom they had expected to purchase an ample herd of horses, would sell them only about thirty, a raiding party of Blackfeet having depleted their supply; and the only guide they could obtain, an Indian whom they nicknamed "Old Toby," had been on the trail just once, and that had been years before.

Since April, they had been traveling constantly over difficult terrain, walking, dragging their boats, making portages, puncturing their feet with cactus thorns, and suffering fevers and other illnesses. Yet they still were far from their goal. Worse yet, the year was growing late. The first touch of fall

89

would soon tinge the summer winds with cold, and an early snowstorm could block the passes for days. There was no question in their minds, however, of turning back.

In their report, the two captains related the hardships of the next days. ". . . the thickets of trees and brush through which we were obliged to cut our way required great labor; the road itself was over the steep and rocky sides of the hills, where the horses could not move without danger of slipping down, while their feet were bruised by the rocks and stumps of trees. Accustomed as these animals were to this kind of life, they suffered severely; several of them fell to some distance down the sides of the hills, some turned over with the baggage, one was crippled, and two gave out, exhausted with fatigue." It rained; the men had no time to hunt, and on September 3 "at dusk it commenced snowing, and continued till the ground was covered to the depth of two inches, when it changed into sleet."

The next day their fortune changed, for they encountered a band of Flathead Indians, who had never seen white men before. They were friendly and quickly proved willing to exchange some of their fresh horses for those that were worn out and also sell the explorers some additional ones in return for trade goods. For a few days the expedition traveled north along the eastern flank of the Bitterroot Mountains, seeking a way across them, and then turned west again. Game was once more scarce, and the terrain so rough that more horses slipped and fell or plunged down the mountainside.

On September 16, the snow started falling again, this time adding somewhere between six and eight inches to the old snow. The drifting white flakes cast a haze over the trail, so they could barely observe where they were going. By September 17, their situation was growing desperate. All they could see around them were the peaks of the Bitterroots. They seemed to have entered a trap from which there was no escaping.

Clark went on ahead and from a summit noticed off in the distance the magnificent and gentle Weippe Prairie of present-day Idaho, a gentle, rolling land covered with the camas plant whose roots provided one of the principal foods of the Nez Percé Indians. Pushing on as best he could with the six men accompanying him, he at last entered the prairie and located two villages of Nez Percés.

Communicating with strange Indians was not difficult. The sign language they used was almost universal; and many Indians, as well as many frontiersmen, could speak several languages, thus making it possible for those doing the interpreting to find a language in common.

Clark made his needs known and ever after considered the Nez Percés the most friendly Indians the explorers met on their journey. They offered Clark food immediately and sent supplies back to Lewis, who was struggling along behind trying to reach the prairie.

After learning from the Indians that they could travel the rest of the way by water, they asked for help in building canoes. But before starting work, the white men came down with an illness that produced violent diarrhea and vomiting. Digging into their medicine chest, the two captains produced patent pills and salts and began dosing their men.

Soon they were on their way down the Clearwater and Snake Rivers, leaving their horses in the care of the Nez Percés until their return. Their ordeal was not over, for they had to pass through swift water and over rapids where, in one instance, the rocks pierced a boat and sank it. But along the banks were camps of Nez Percés, who proved as friendly as the first bands they had met, offering them food and assistance when they needed it.

On October 16 they reached the Columbia, the goal for which they had strived so long. For a short time, they camped at the mouth of Snake, down which they had come, while they briefly explored up the Columbia. Then they were ready to go downstream again.

Since leaving St. Louis, they had met with many Indian tribes. All of them, except the Teton Sioux, had been friendly in varying degrees—although none so much so as the Nez Percés—and had accepted their presents and professions of amity. The Walla Wallas proved no exception, and their chief wanted them to remain a few days as his guest. But Lewis and Clark were anxious to press on, so they ordered the boats into the water once more, and continued their descent of the Columbia.

The river, however, did not run smoothly to the sea. In cutting its way through the Cascade Mountains that separated it from the Pacific, it had created a series of falls. The first of these was the Great Falls, where the water rushed between cliffs that were several thousand feet high and at one place dropped over a twenty-foot ledge. Shortly after came The Dalles, where the channel was only forty-five yards wide, and the water foamed and raced. Sometimes the men could guide their boats through these dangerous places, and when they could not do so and could not make a portage, they lowered them with ropes. Then came the Grand Rapids, several miles of angry water, which strained both their strength and their skill.

Nor were the Indians along the banks as friendly as those they had met before. A number of them were thieves and beggars, and many were infested with lice and fleas, which often deserted their Indian hosts for the white men. Two Walla Walla Indians, who had recently joined the expedition, became frightened and returned home; but the size of the party and the constant guard it kept prevented an Indian attack during the approximately fifty-five miles of dangerous navigation.

By November 2, the expedition had passed the Cascade Mountains; and on November 7, Clark thought they had arrived at the Pacific, making elated mention of the fact in his diary. But he was mistaken; they had merely reached the headwaters of the long estuary of the Columbia and still had miles to go before reaching the ocean.

7. BEYOND THE BOUNDARIES

The two great examples of English and Spanish America, are before our eyes. England gave us free liberty to pursue the dictates of our own judgment . . . by which means we increased in power, learning, and wealth . . . Spain pursued a different line of conduct towards her Mexican dominions, which . . . might be termed a conquered kingdom, rather than the settlement of a savage country.

—Zebulon Pike, 1810

Camping along the shore of the Columbia and beset by storms that whipped the river into waves and sent large logs beating against the sides of their fragile boats, the expedition continued down the estuary and at last, in the middle of November, saw the Pacific Ocean. The Corps of Discovery—as the two captains called their small group of men—had arrived at their destination, having traveled more than a year from St. Louis.

They were the second band of white men to cross the North American continent from ocean to ocean, but the first to carry with them the flag of the United States. They had brought that flag through unmapped wildernesses into which no white man had ventured before, arriving at the mouth of the river Robert Gray had discovered. By doing so, they had reinforced the claim of the United States to the rich Northwest.

When Thomas Jefferson had planned the Lewis and Clark expedition, he thought the explorers might well meet one of the seaborne fur traders on the West Coast. In such a case, he instructed them to send back word of their progress or, if they believed the return journey would be too difficult, to sail home.

But the broad mouth of the Columbia, storm-lashed and turbulent under November's skies, contained no American—or European—vessel of any kind. So the men were fated to remain for the winter without news from the outside world or a chance to replenish their supplies.

Although Lewis and Clark were stern disciplinarians, they realized the men would be happier during the long, lonely months to come if they were given a part in selecting their winter quarters. Although the men started searching immediately for a campground, the weather worked against them. Strong winds roiled the waters of the Columbia, and the waves were often too great for their small, unseaworthy canoes. Even when they finally were able to cross the river, the weather forced them to slink along in the safety of the shore or at times remain fixed in camp. Toward the end of November, the weather improved slightly, and Lewis went inland to find a site.

The life of those who remained behind was one of monotony and hardship. "Again we had a cloudy day, and the wind so high from the east that, having ventured in a boat with a view to hunt at some distance, we were obliged to return. We resumed our occupation of dressing leather and mending our old clothes, in which we passed the day." So Clark noted for December 1, 1805. The following day, he remarked that "this disagreeable food, pounded fish, has occasioned so much sickness among the men that it is now absolutely necessary to vary it." A successful hunting party put him in better temper, and the next day he remarked, "The wind was from the east and the morning fair; but, as if one whole day of fair weather was not permitted, toward night it began to rain."

When Lewis returned, he reported he had found a suitable site southwest of present-day Astoria, Oregon, on what is now the Lewis and Clark River—a "point of highland on its western bank . . . in a thick grove of lofty pines, about 200 yards from the water, and 30 feet above the level of the high tides." On December 7, the entire expedition moved there and began to prepare for winter.

Clark set out across the swampy ground to the west to find a spot where they could make salt, and Lewis supervised the construction of the "fort" in which they would live. Made of logs, two small low structures finally faced one another, each with four rooms. In one building lived the enlisted men; the other contained a room for the two captains, one for Sacajawea and her family, an orderly room, and a space for storing meat. Between the two structures was an open space about four yards long and three wide. This was flanked by two palisades, which ran from building to building, thus enclosing the entire area. Although it rained all day on December 24, the work continued, and that evening they moved into what the captains called "our huts," which they dignified with the name Fort Clatsop after a local Indian tribe.

For all their efforts to be gay, Christmas Day, 1805, presaged the gloomy weeks that lay ahead.

> We were awakened at daylight [the captains wrote] by a discharge of firearms, which was followed by a song from the men, as a compliment to us on the return of Christmas. . . . After breakfast we divided our remaining stock of tobacco . . . into two parts; one of which we distributed among such of the party as make use of it, making a present of a handkerchief to the others. The remainder of the day was passed in good spirits, though there was nothing in our situation to excite much gayety. The rain confined us to the house, and our only luxuries in honor of the season were some poor elk, so much spoiled that we ate it through sheer necessity, a few roots, and some spoiled pounded fish.
>
> The next day . . . brought a continuation of rain, accompanied with thunder, and a high wind from the southwest. We were therefore obliged to still remain in our huts, and endeavored to dry our wet articles before the fire. The fleas . . . have taken such possession of our clothes that we are obliged to have a regular search every day through our blankets as a necessary preliminary to sleeping at night. These animals, indeed, are so numerous that they are almost a calamity to the Indians of this country. When they have once obtained the mastery of any house it is impossible to expel them, and the Indians have frequently different houses, to which they resort occasionally when the fleas have rendered their permanent residence intolerable.

And so the winter continued with constant rain and dampness, a scarcity of fresh meat, and an overabundance of fleas. Then, too, there were the Indians. The Clatsops were generally friendly; if they had not been, the expedition would have been seriously endangered, for the fort was ill-equipped to resist a prolonged attack. But often they brought what purported to be presents and then demanded payment for them, and each visit introduced more fleas into the camp. Other tribes were less congenial, ill-humored and attempting to pilfer any unguarded supplies.

Although the two captains kept busy caring for those of the men who became sick, maintaining the morale of the others, and collecting more and more scientific information about the Indians and plantlife and wildlife of the area, they were glad as the weeks slipped away and spring drew nearer with its promise of reopening the mountain passes.

Originally they had planned to remain at Fort Clatsop until the first of April in the hope of meeting a fur-trading ship from which they could purchase new supplies.

About the middle of March, however, we had become seriously alarmed [the captains reported in their journal] for the want of food; the elk, our chief dependence, had at length deserted their usual haunts in our neighborhood and retreated to the mountains. We were too poor to purchase other food from the Indians, so that we were sometimes reduced, notwithstanding all the exertions of our hunters, to a single day's provision in advance. The men, too, whom the constant rains and confinement had rendered unhealthy, might, we hoped, be benefited by leaving the coast and resuming the exercise of traveling.

Therefore they hoped to delay their departure only long enough to permit the game to reappear on the Columbia Plateau over which they would have to travel before reaching the mountains. During the winter, the men had been dressing skins,

so that we now had a sufficient quantity of clothing, besides between 300 and 400 pairs of moccasins. [Moccasins wore out quickly on a trek as long as theirs.] But the whole stock of goods on which we are to depend, for the purchase of either horses or food . . . is so much diminished that it might all be tied in two handkerchiefs. We have in fact nothing but six blue robes, one scarlet, a coat and hat of the United States Artillery uniform, five robes made of our large flag, and a few old clothes trimmed with ribbon.

Before leaving, they wrote out several notices of their stay on the West Coast, posting one at Fort Clatsop and giving others to some of the Indians in the hope they might find their way into the hands of visiting sea captains. (One did and returned to the United States by way of Canton.) The weather continued unfavorable, and by March 22, "the rains and wind still confined us to the fort; but at last our provisions dwindled down to a single day's stock, and it became absolutely necessary to remove." So they sent a few hunters ahead, and the following afternoon left Fort Clatsop for the long journey home.

The route was now known to them; on the trip out they had established friendly relations with many of the Indians along the way; and they had learned about several shortcuts that would save them miles of travel; but they still had numerous difficulties to overcome. The strong current of the Columbia River, which had carried them safely to their goal, now opposed them. Pausing only long enough to explore briefly the Willamette River, they pushed on to The Dalles. There they found the rushing waters, fed by the early spring thaws, too much for them and traded some of their canoes for the few horses that the local Indians were willing to sell.

Farther up the river, they encountered Yellept, a friendly leader of the Walla Walla Indians, who had helped them on their journey west. Here the explorers obtained two more horses and, with the help of the Indians, ferried across the river and took a shortcut that led them near present-day Dayton, Washington, thus avoiding most of their previous route along the Snake River.

On May 4, they were back again in the country of the Nez Percés, who had proved so friendly to them before. The honesty of this tribe was exemplified by one of its members who gave Lewis and Clark two canisters of powder; his dog had dug them from one of the explorers' caches during the winter. He had carefully preserved them against their return. The horses, however, had not received the same care. Several of the Indians' leaders had quarreled over their custody, and the small herd had become scattered. But with the help of some of the Nez Percés, Lewis and Clark recovered all but a few.

Yet they were still unable to continue their trip east. Much to their discouragement, they learned from the Indians that the mountains would not be open for several more weeks, so they had to go into camp while the lengthening days slowly melted the snow and ice on the heights that separated them from home.

Many of their days were like those of the past winter. In their journal for May 17, 1806, the explorers noted that

> it rained during the greater part of the night, and our flimsy covering being insufficient for our protection, we lay in the water most of the time. What was more unlucky, our chronometer became wet, and in consequence somewhat rusty; but by care we hope to restore it. The rain continued nearly the whole day; on the high plains the snow is falling, and already two or three inches deep.

Food was again short, for game was scarce, and the salmon had not yet climbed that far up the river. Sometimes the men ate the native roots on which many of the Indians subsisted. Once in a while they had the luxury of horsemeat. Besides caring for the Americans, Clark in particular was often asked to cure sick Indians, who sometimes arrived in groups—one day four men, eight women and a child together. "The men were greatly afflicted with sore eyes," the explorers noted, "but the women had beside this a variety of other disorders. . . . After administering eye-water, rubbing the rheumatic patients with volatile liniment, and giving cathartics to others, they all thought themselves much relieved and returned highly satisfied to the village."

Anxious to leave behind them the wet spring, the sick Indians, and the scarcity of food, Lewis and Clark left in the middle of June on the next leg of their journey—the trip back over the Lolo Trail, which had led them through the Bitterroot Mountains the year before.

In the hollows and on the north sides of the hills [they noted] large quantities of snow still remain, in some places to the depth of two or three feet. Vegetation is proportionately retarded, the dog-tooth violet being just in bloom, and the honeysuckle, huckleberry, and a small species of white maple beginning to put forth their leaves. These appearances, in a part of the country comparatively low, are ill omens of the practicality of passing the mountains. But being determined to proceed, we . . . resumed our march.

That same day, as they reached higher altitudes, "we found much difficulty . . . in following the road, the greater part of it being covered with snow, which lies in great masses eight or ten feet deep, and would be impassable were it not so firm as to bear our horses." Soon they discovered a small glade with a little grass, not enough to feed their horses well, but more than they were likely to find farther on. So they made camp for the night.

The following morning, after climbing about three miles up into the mountains, "we found ourselves enveloped in snow from 12 to 15 feet in depth, even on the south side . . . with the fullest exposure to the sun." To move ahead was clearly impossible. The horses could neither dig for forage beneath the snow or live without it; and even if they could have survived, the heavy coating of white snow hid every sign of the trail. "To proceed, therefore, under such circumstances," the explorers wrote, "would be to hazard our being bewildered in the mountains, and to insure the loss of our horses; even should we be so fortunate as to escape with our lives, we might be obliged to abandon all our papers and our collections."

Occasionally one of their scouting parties, such as those that had reconnoitered the Three Forks of the Missouri, had retraced its steps, but never had the whole expedition retired before an obstacle. This time, however, Lewis and Clark decided a withdrawal was necessary—at least until they could obtain guides able to lead them over the snow-obscured route. After building scaffolds on which they placed the major portion of their supplies, instruments, and papers, they worked their way backward yielding the distance they had gained with so much trouble. "The mortification of being obliged to tread back our steps," the explorers noted, "rendered still more tedious a route always so obstructed by brush and fallen timber that it cannot be passed without difficulty."

By June 26, however, they had recruited the needed Indians and were again ascending the mountains. In slightly more than a week, some four feet of snow had melted; and, the two captains wrote "our guides traverse this trackless region with a kind of instinctive sagacity." By the end of the month, they reached the campsite on the eastern side of the Bitterroots where they had stopped on their journey west and which they had named Travelers Rest. They were now a short distance from present-day Missoula, Montana. Not having crossed the Continental Divide, they were still in the Pacific watershed; but the Bitterroot Mountains—the wilderness that had proved such a difficult part of their outward journey—were behind them. In a short while, they hoped, they would be on the Missouri, whose current would carry them in the direction of St. Louis and home.

During their journey, Lewis and Clark had been completely isolated from all but the Indians' world. Yet the comparative calm they had found at the mouth of the Columbia was deceptive, for the powers of Europe were still maneuvering for possession of the West Coast.

Nicholai Petrovich Rezanov, an official of the Russian-American Fur Company formed by the Russians to exploit their interests in North America, saw great possibilities in developing trade with California. Most immediately, it would provide food for the colony the Russians had established at Sitka, which was too far north to raise its own. Furthermore, he thought the trade itself would be extremely profitable, and he wanted some time in the future to extend Russia's settlements farther south.

In the spring of 1806, while Lewis and Clark were working their way back toward the Missouri, Rezanov entered San Francisco Bay on a ship named the *Juno*. The Spanish authorities were friendly, but suspicious and uncertain of their government's reaction to their trading with aliens.

Rezanov quickly learned, however, that the missions were as anxious to do business with him as the government was not. They had accumulated a surplus of grain but had no market. While the priests and the governor worked out a procedure that would satisfy the letter, if not the spirit, of the viceroy's instructions, Rezanov inspected the harbor and secretly visited one of the batteries, where he found only five brass cannon. Although Spain had increased the armament of its California port since Vancouver's cruise, its defenses were still pitifully weak. Spain, Rezanov noted, would have difficulty resisting a Russian advance down the coast.

With the *Juno* at last loaded with a cargo of grain, butter, and lard, Rezanov sailed back to Sitka to supply the Russian settlement there. At the same time, he dreamed of the great expansion of the Russian empire that might follow his advance into Alta California.

The Americans' ignorance of their own country was exemplified by their

98

uncertainty over its boundaries. The Atlantic Ocean formed a clear limit to the east. If La Salle's original claim held, it was bounded on the west by the Continental Divide, wherever that might be in the Rocky Mountains. Except for the Great Lakes area, numerous questions existed about the line between the United States and Canada. The exact limits of Spanish Florida were uncertain. And the southern boundary of the Louisiana Purchase probably ran along the Red River, although no one knew the exact course of that stream. But with their customary energy, the Americans were attempting to explore their possessions and settle their boundary disputes as quickly as possible.

Zebulon Pike, a young army officer, led a mission up the Mississippi, and when he returned, General James Wilkinson—that treacherous commander in the West—had a new mission for him: to treat with some of the Indians in the southern portion of the Louisiana Purchase, locate the source of the Red River, and perhaps secretly spy on the Spanish.

In the middle of July 1806, Pike left the vicinity of St. Louis in command of approximately twenty men. In addition, he had with him a number of Indian captives whom the Americans had ransomed from other tribes. As a gesture of goodwill, the government was returning them to their homes.

On his way to the Pawnee villages, he heard from an Indian the startling news that a force of six hundred Spaniards under the command of Lieutenant Don Falcundo Malgares was marching through the area. Reports of the Lewis and Clark expedition—reports that were grossly exaggerated—had already alarmed the Spanish government. Now that a military contingent under Pike was probing another of their borders, their reaction had been swift and impressive.

Fortunately Pike did not encounter Malgares; but when he visited the Pawnees, he found the tribe much more impressed by the Spanish display of arms than by the tiny group of Americans. Following instructions they had received from Malgares, they tried to block his way west; but when Pike, although greatly outnumbered, showed a willingness to fight them, they let him proceed.

Behind him was a tribe of vaguely hostile Indians; somewhere on his flank or ahead was an alien force approximately thirty times the size of his. He did not have the companionship that Lewis and Clark shared; he did not have the benefit of their careful preparations, for the Pike expedition was hastily conceived; but he did have the patriotism, determination, and courage of the two captains, who were then leading their men back toward St. Louis.

While Lewis and Clark remained a few days at Travelers Rest to give both the men and horses a chance to relax, the two leaders faced their greatest personal crisis of the entire trip. Devoted friends since they had first served together in the army, they had shared in every aspect of the expedition's long march; and even the weary months at Fort Clatsop, with the rain dripping

99

from the roof of their small cabin, had not eroded the relationship between them. Neither man had ever complained of the other, and they had taken equal responsibility for every decision and had worked equally hard to carry those decisions out. But at Travelers Rest, they planned to separate for the first time since they had left St. Louis almost two years before.

The reason was their desire to explore more closely two of the rivers they had passed during their ascent of the Missouri: the Yellowstone and the Marias. Since one river lay generally to the south and the other to the north, they could not now explore them together. So with grim forebodings, which they reflected in their journals, they separated at Travelers Rest, planning to meet later at the Missouri.

Clark made his way through the mountains to the Yellowstone's headwaters and then followed the stream to its confluence with the Missouri, where he camped and waited for Lewis. But the mosquitoes, descending in black clouds, made the campsite unlivable—the men could scarcely hold their guns steady to shoot game—and finally he was forced to descend the river, moving slowly and hoping everyday that his partner—and friend—would overtake him.

Lewis, traveling more directly east, reached the Missouri and then traveled up the Marias. To his disappointment, he learned that it did not take him into the area dominated by the Canadian trappers and traders; and on the way back, he was attacked by a band of Blackfeet, the first time that any members of the expedition had fought with Indians. Escaping from them, he raced back to the Missouri and finally rejoined Clark before reaching the Mandan villages.

Overjoyed at their reunion and thankful to find that neither of them had lost a man during their separation, they continued on their way, allowing the current of the Missouri to carry them through country that was now familiar.

On September 23, they arrived in St. Louis and learned that many of their friends had given them up as dead. They were, of course, the heroes of the moment. In the celebrations that followed, Mackenzie's dash across the continent was all but forgotten. He was British; Lewis and Clark were Americans. Not only had they brought back far more information—they were able to report on most of the long list of subjects that Jefferson had given them—they had carried the nation's flag overland to the Pacific and for several months had flown it above the palisades of Fort Clatsop. It was a deed of which a young nation could—and did—feel proud.

About two months later in the middle of November 1806, Pike was traveling up the Arkansas River and saw ahead the peaks of the Rocky Mountains rising above the level of the plains. "Their appearance," he wrote, "can easily be imagined by those who have crossed the Alleghany; but their sides were whiter as if covered by snow, or a white stone." In the heart of those mountains was the source of the Red River, which he had been assigned to locate.

Making a semi-permanent camp near present-day Pueblo, Colorado, he set out with a small detachment to observe—and perhaps climb—the mountain he called Grand Peak and which is known today as Pikes Peak. As they reached higher and higher altitudes, the inadequacy of the expedition's preparations became more and more evident. For the men finally stood waist deep in snow with only cotton clothing to protect them and no warmer equipment waiting for them at their base camp. Just as he had barely missed finding the headwaters of the Mississippi, Pike never climbed the peak that carried his name. The distance was too great, the weather too cold, and any further attempt would have been suicidal.

After returning to camp, Pike continued up the Arkansas. Choosing between the several tributaries that flowed into the river, he selected the wrong one, advanced to its source, and mistakenly believed he had found the origin of the Arkansas. Then with the great mountains rising around him, he began a search for the Red River. Once more his unlucky fortune intervened. He rightly surmised that the Spanish officer, Malgares, had followed a trail through the Rockies from Santa Fé and that his route was probably the best way into the mountains. But he wrongly guessed that a trail he had found was the one made by Malgares. Instead it was an Indian trail. When it finally brought him to a large river, the water was flowing in the wrong direction. Realizing that it must be the south fork of the Platte, Pike wearily turned back.

The expedition's rations were short; their guns in disrepair (they needed guns both for protection and to obtain food); their clothing was in tatters; many of their blankets had been torn up to make inadequate substitutes for their worn-out footgear; and winter had arrived. Only a man of Pike's perseverance would have continued, but he was soon rewarded by finding a river he thought surely must be the Red. Following it eastward, he and his men believed they had completed their mission and were at last on their way home. But when they came to the edge of the mountains and the plains stretched out before them, they saw they had once more been mistaken. The river was again the Arkansas.

Pike would not admit defeat. Near the site of present-day Cañon, Colorado, he established a camp where he could leave his exhausted and now practically useless horses in the care of some of the men who were also disabled. With the remainder, he set out across the mountains on foot, ill-equipped and in the middle of winter. The venture was foolhardy, but so, too, would have been the journey home. Between him and St. Louis lay the wind-lashed, snow-covered Great Plains and the uncertain Pawnee Indians. And at the end of that trail was failure. Better, he thought, to risk the dangers of the Rockies in winter and seek shelter on their western slopes.

The heavy snow and bitter weather drove away the game. Several of the men became so weak and tortured by the cold they could go no farther, and Pike had to leave them and hope he could rescue them later. He himself tried

101

to do more work than any of the others, sparing himself no task, but his example failed to keep one of the men from thinking of mutiny. Only by extreme care did Pike avert an uprising against his authority. So depressed did he become during those weeks in the mountains that at one time he contemplated walking off into the white world that lay around him and letting the cold and hunger bring him final peace. But he resisted the temptation and finally led his men to the banks of the Río Grande in the San Luís Valley of Colorado.

The boundaries of the United States were ill-defined, but Pike was now definitely in Spanish territory and, what is more, he was leading a military force. Whether, as he later contended, he thought he had found the Red River and intended to follow it east, or whether he actually knew where he was is a matter of conjecture.

Inevitably the Spanish learned of his presence. With the Russians probing their frontier in California, Lewis and Clark circling around the north, and now Pike penetrating their boundary just above Santa Fé, they were justly nervous. In no time, a Spanish soldier and an Indian arrived at Pike's camp, which he was busy fortifying. Obviously they were spying on his position and determining the size of his party. Then came a detachment of fifty dragoons and fifty militia with a polite request that Pike proceed to Santa Fé to be questioned by the governor of New Mexico.

"I was induced," Pike wrote, "to consent to the measure, by conviction, that the officer had positive orders to bring me in, and as I had no orders to commit hostilities, and indeed had committed myself, although innocently, by violating their territory, I conceived it would appear better to show a will to come to an explanation . . . yet my situation was so eligible [he was referring to the manner in which he had fortified his camp], and I could so easily have put them at defiance, that it was with great reluctance I suffered all our labor to be lost."

Despite the words he entered in his journal, Pike had no chance to fight back. Isolated in a foreign land with no easy escape route, he could not have resisted any prolonged siege of his little encampment. Without being able even to secure permission from the Spanish to await the arrival of the men and horses he had left behind on the Arkansas, he and his expedition were marched to Santa Fé, ostensibly as guests of the governor, but actually as his prisoners. The Spanish commander was delighted with Pike's peaceful acquiescence; but his men, who wished to fight, "were likewise fearful of treachery."

8. OUTPOST ON THE PACIFIC

Your petitioners . . . beg leave to suggest for consideration, whether they have not some claim to national attention and encouragement, from the nature and importance of their undertaking: which though hazardous and uncertain as to their private emolument, must, at any rate, redound to the public security and advantage.

—John Jacob Astor, to Congress, 1812

When Pike arrived in Santa Fé, the governor of New Mexico was polite but skeptical. Obviously he did not believe what Pike said; and his examination of the explorer's papers, all of which the authorities had seized, merely reinforced his doubts that Pike had become lost and that his entry into Mexican territory had been an error.

If Pike wondered whether his predicament was serious, he had only to look at the American who served as the governor's interpreter. He and nine others had attempted to trade illegally with the Spanish. One had been killed in an ambush. The survivors were forced to roll dice to determine which one of them would be hanged, and the remaining eight—among them the interpreter—were sentenced to servitude for the rest of their lives.

Yet the Spanish knew little about the Americans. Pike and his men were dressed in the roughest of clothes, having left many of their belongings at the camp on the Arkansas. "A greater proof," he later reported, "cannot be given of the ignorance of the common people, than their asking if we lived in houses or camps like the Indians, or if we wore hats in our country."

Underlying this ignorance was a sense of fear. A Spanish officer asked Pike to give him a written statement that he had been friendly to the Americans. "This paper," Pike noted, "he seemed to estimate as a very valuable acquisition, as he was decidedly of the opinion we would invade the country the ensuing spring."

Perplexed by Pike and uncertain what to do with him, the governor sent him to Chihuahua for further interrogation. The Chihuahuan governor also treated him kindly but once again made it clear he was a prisoner.

"You have given us and yourself a great deal of trouble," he said to Pike, to which Pike responded, "On my part unsought and on that of the Spanish voluntary."

Sharp retorts did not divert the governor of Chihuahua, who, like his counterpart in New Mexico, became convinced Pike was a spy. But he feared exacerbating relations between Spain and the United States. Although Pike's original command was now widely separated, so each man's case would have to be considered later on an individual basis, he sent Pike himself under a military escort to the American boundary near Natchitoches, Louisiana, and there released him.

Pike's first reaction on reaching the United States was simply one of relief that his adventure was finally over. "Language," he wrote, "cannot express the gaiety of my heart, when I once more beheld the standard of my country waved aloft."

In spite of the explorations of Lewis and Clark and of Pike—Pike never received the credit he deserved for his travels—the edge of the frontier still lay close to St. Louis. When the city's businessmen were not speculating on the possibility of trade with Santa Fé, they were talking about furs, for furs were the life blood of the community's economy.

The one disruptive element in their lives was an upstart named Manuel Lisa. Not connected with any of the leading families, he had been doing his best to overturn their monopolies and acquire a large portion of the business for himself. Tempestuous and rough, he was an unpleasant adversary; but he had a vision that some of the older traders lacked and the courage and tenacity to carry it out. In 1807 he formed a company for the purpose of ascending the Missouri River and trading at the limits of the Louisiana Purchase. After passing the Mandan villages, he went up the Yellowstone, which Clark had explored on the way home; and at the mouth of the Bighorn, he built a fort to serve as a base for him and his men. For Lisa was adopting the practice of the Hudson's Bay and North-West Companies, establishing posts deep in Indian territory and supplementing his trade with the natives by sending out white trappers who worked directly for him on a contract basis.

The only other American trader who compared to Lisa in imagination, daring, and enterprise was John Jacob Astor. Ever since his decision to enter the fur business, he had been accumulating a fortune. So far, he had confined his activities to the east of the Mississippi, but now he began considering the profits made by those who had entered the trade on the West Coast.

"The comprehensive mind of Mr. Astor," wrote Alexander Ross, one of his partners, "could not but see these things in their true light, and to perceive that if such a limited and desultory traffic [carried on by individual ship captains] produced such immense profits, what might not be expected from a well-regulated trade, supported by capital and prosecuted with system: at all events, the Russian trade would then be confined within its own limits, and the coasting vessels must soon disappear altogether."

After first contemplating a cooperative effort with the North-West Company, Astor decided to form his own company—with himself as the majority stockholder—and establish a major trading post on the Columbia River. "By this means," Ross continued, "he contemplated carrying off the furs of all the countries west of the Rocky Mountains; at the same time forming a chain of trading posts across the Continent, from the Atlantic to the Pacific, along the waters of the great Missouri." In time, therefore, he would link his western operation with those he already owned in the East, making him dominant in the fur business from coast to coast.

If successful, he would greatly enhance his own fortune, but the enterprise was of such scope and national significance that it stirred the imagination of many other Americans. "This grand commercial scheme," Ross said, ". . . gave much satisfaction to the American public . . . for all the rich cargoes of furs and peltries . . . were to be shipped in American vessels for the great China mart, there to be sold, and the proceeds invested in a return cargo of . . . articles of high demand in the United States; which would not only prevent to some extent the American specie going out of the Union for such articles, but also turn the barren wilds of the North and Far West into a source of national wealth."

Two problems, however, gave Astor concern. One was the inexperience of Americans at running a large-scale fur business. This he solved by raiding the personnel of the North-West Company. The other problem was the reaction of Great Britain, for Astor's plan might "arouse them to assert more speedily their claims of prior discovery to the Oregon quarter." This possibility Astor brushed aside. He thought his employment of so many British citizens would work in his favor, and he believed that territorial claims should be argued by governments, not by private citizens. Whichever flag finally flew over Oregon, Astor hoped to govern its commerce.

In September 1810, his ship, the *Tonquin,* sailed from New York under the command of Jonathan Thorn, an experienced seaman and a veteran of the Tripoli wars. On board were a number of Astor's employees and several former North-West men to whom he had given partnerships.

Another group was to proceed overland to the Columbia under the leadership of William Price Hunt, who was Astor's principal partner and personal representative. Originally from New Jersey, Hunt had had no previous experience in the fur business. This may have been the reason Astor selected him, for he was less likely than some of the others to question Astor's judgment. His first assignment was to recruit additional personnel and assemble them at St. Louis in preparation for the trip, while the *Tonquin* went ahead and prepared the base.

The only American competitor who thought in Astor's broad terms was Manuel Lisa. He, too, planned a chain of forts down the Missouri; but desperately short of capital from the beginning, he was beleaguered by many difficulties. The Blackfeet, with whom Lewis had fought, were taking a heavy toll; the Non-Intercourse Act, which prohibited trade with Great Britain, made it difficult to buy the English goods the Indians preferred and that were offered by the Canadian fur companies; and he was having trouble obtaining credit. Except for the disloyalty of some of his employees (they had given his plans to the North-West Company), events were favoring Astor.

After a voyage during which Astor's partners and Captain Thorn quarreled bitterly over their authority and after stopping at the Hawaiian Islands—a customary practice for sailing ships bound for the Northwest—the *Tonquin* arrived off the coast of Oregon in March 1811. As they approached the Columbia River, they could see why its discovery had eluded so many navigators. It is, wrote Ross, "remarkable for its sand-bars and high surf at all seasons. . . . The bar, or rather the chain of sand-banks, over which the huge waves and foaming breakers roll so awfully, is a league broad, and extends in a white foaming sheet for many miles, both south and north of the mouth of the river."

Thorn was nevertheless determined to get his ship past the barrier. First he sent out a small boat to look for a channel between the bars; that boat was lost. The next day he ordered several similar searches made for a passage, but without success until the ship's pinnace located a channel. "We followed . . . [the pinnace] and advanced between the breakers with a favorable wind," wrote Gabriel Franchère, a former Canadian clerk who had joined the expedition, "so that we passed the boat on our starboard, within pistol-shot. We made signs to her to return on board, but she could not accomplish it; the ebb tide carried her with such rapidity that in a few minutes we had lost sight of her amidst the tremendous breakers that surrounded us. It was near nightfall, the wind began to give way, and the water was so low with the ebb that we struck six or seven times with violence: the breakers broke over the ship and threatened to submerge her. At last we passed from two and three-quarters fathoms of water to seven, where we were obliged to drop anchor, the wind having entirely failed us. We were far, however, from being out of danger, and the darkness came to add to the horror of our situation: our vessel, though at anchor, threatened to be carried away every moment by the tide; the best bower [anchor] was let go and it kept two men at the wheel to hold her head in the right direction. However, Providence came to our succor: the flood succeeded to the ebb, and the wind rising out of the offing, we weighed both anchors in spite of the obscurity of the night and succeeded . . . in gaining a little bay or cove . . . where we found a good anchorage."

Thorn had fulfilled his mission of bringing the *Tonquin* into the mouth of the Columbia River, but the cost had been high. For eight lives had been lost crossing the bars. It was an ominous beginning for Astor's great venture.

After picking out a suitable site, the men started building the trading post to be named Astoria and which would be their principal base. For Captain Thorn, this was a time of trial. He continued to quarrel with the partners over their respective responsibilities, and he grew annoyed with the Indians that came onboard the *Tonquin*. What he considered their sloppy manners offended his sense of seamanship, and he could not abide their petty pilfering. Finally in the first week of June, he had unloaded his ship and was free to sail north and trade with the Indians along the coast.

Alexander McKay, who had traveled with the Canadian explorer, Mackenzie, was charged with the actual dealings with the Indians; but at Vancouver Island he went ashore to visit one of their villages and ended up spending the night with them. During his absence, Thorn undertook to conduct the trade on his own.

All went well until the Indians, who were as skillful at bargaining as the white men, began to raise the price of otter skins. When their leader derisively refused Thorn's highest price, the captain lost his temper. He grabbed a skin the Indian was offering, pushed it in his face, kicked the other pelts aside, and ordered the Indians from the ship.

When McKay returned, the interpreter told him what had happened. Both of them were alarmed, for they knew the Indians' pride. But Thorn, pointing out the superiority of his cannon and firearms, expressed no concern; and his confidence seemed justified by the peace that hung over the *Tonquin* that night.

In the morning, while McKay was still asleep, a canoe with some twenty Indians arrived at the side of the ship. Smiling and waving skins, they obviously wished to continue trading, and the watch permitted them to come on board. Another canoe arrived, and its passengers were also allowed on deck. Then another, and another.

Soon the ship was crowded with Indians, and the officer of the watch, becoming alarmed, called McKay. One glance at the crowd that had accumulated made him suggest to Thorn that he should get the ship under way as soon as possible. At the same time, the interpreter noticed the Indians were wearing short skin capes that probably concealed weapons.

As even more Indians crowded on board, Thorn gave the order to set the sails. The Indians, apparently alarmed by the imminent departure of the ship, immediately offered to trade on Thorn's terms; and a brisk business followed, the most popular item being knives.

While the crew was busy readying the ship and the other men were occupied trading, the Indians attacked. The ship's clerk was the first to fall, struck in the back as he was leaning on a bale of skins. McKay, who had been sitting on the taffrail, was knocked overboard by a blow from a war club. When he dropped into the water, the women, who had remained in the canoes, fell on him and quickly dispatched him. Thorn drew a knife and began to slash his way to the cabin where the firearms were stored, but his effort failed; and his body, too, slid into the water. Everywhere on board, the seamen and traders were fighting futilely for their lives. Those who were aloft at the time looked on with horror at the bloodshed taking place below them, swung down from the rigging, and dashed for the cabin. Four of them made it to that uncertain refuge, where they were joined by the clerk who, although wounded, had not been killed.

The five men grabbed the guns that were available and kept up a steady fire that finally drove the Indians back in confusion. But the sails were flapping loose, and an onshore wind threatened to carry them toward land if they cut the anchor free. Four of the men decided to make their escape during the night in one of the boats, but the ship's clerk refused to go with them. Already severely wounded, he was determined to avenge his friends and himself.

The next day he appeared on deck; and when the Indians came out to visit the scene of their victory, he smiled at them as though nothing had happened and invited them on board again. Overcome with curiosity, they clambered up the sides, but the clerk had disappeared. Busy below decks, he had opened up the ship's store of powder. Now he threw a burning light onto it.

The explosion rocked the shore. Pieces of planking, bits of masts and other gear, and the bodies of approximately a hundred Indians flew into the air. When the enormous sound and flare of light had passed, quiet came back to the bay, and the Indians remaining on land stood in amazement. Never had they seen such destruction.

The four survivors who had left the ship the previous night tried to make their way toward the open sea, but the wind was too strong. Finally they landed in a small cove, planning to remain hidden there until the weather changed; but the Indians found them before the wind veered, took them as prisoners back to their village, and there killed them. The interpreter was the only survivor of the almost thirty men who had sailed from Astoria on the *Tonquin*. Because he was an Indian, although of a different tribe, his life was spared, but he was kept a prisoner. He made his escape, however, and returned to the base with the awful news.

The loss of the *Tonquin* was a costly blow to Astor and one that disrupted his plans, but there were other disturbing developments to come. Those who had remained at Astoria after the departure of the ship were visited by two strange Indians dressed in long deerskin robes, more like the clothing worn by Indians nearer the Rockies than by those on the Pacific Coast. They reported there were other white men coming down the Columbia River; and since it was too early for the overland expedition under Wilson Price Hunt, the traders at Astoria could only believe they must be employees of the North-West Company.

On July 15, 1811, their suspicion was confirmed. "Toward midday we saw a large canoe with a flag displayed at her stern," wrote Franchère. "We knew not who it could be. . . . We were soon relieved of our uncertainty by the arrival of the canoe. . . . The flag she bore was British, and her crew was composed of eight Canadian boatsmen or voyageurs. A well-dressed man, who appeared to be the commander, was the first to leap ashore, and addressing us without ceremony, said that his name was David Thompson and that he was one of the partners of the North-West Company."

He was also one of the company's great geographers, whose maps served Canadian travelers for many years. "He was provided with a sextant, chronometer, and barometer," Franchère noted, "and during a week's sojourn which he made at our place had an opportunity to make several astronomical observations."

The purpose of his trip had been to forestall Astor on the Columbia River, but he had arrived a few weeks too late. Nevertheless he and Duncan McDougal, Astor's senior representative at Astor, started playing a cat-and-mouse game with each other. "McDougal received him [Thompson] like a brother," Ross later wrote. "Nothing was too good for Mr. Thompson; he had access everywhere; saw and examined everything; and whatever he asked for he got, as if he had been one of ourselves. . . . His . . . visit had evidently no other object but to discourage us—a maneuvre of the North-West policy to extend their own trade at the expense of ours; but he failed. The dangers and the difficulties, which he took great pains to paint in their worst colours, did not deter us. He forgot that in speaking to us, he was speaking to north-westerns—men as experienced and as cunning as himself. . . .

"Everyone knew this, and knowing it, how could we account for the more than warm and unreserved welcome Mr. Thompson met with from Astor's representative. Unless, as some thought at the time," Ross wisely surmised, "McDougal was trying to pay back Mr. Thompson with his own coin, by putting on a fair face, so as to dupe him into an avowal of his real object. This is more than probable, for in point of acuteness, duplicity, and diplomatic craft, they were perhaps well matched."

So well matched, in fact, that neither could gain the advantage over the other. Thompson left to report his failure to his partners, but McDougal knew that at the first show of weakness, the North-West Company would be glad to seize Astoria.

Wilson Price Hunt, whom Astor had chosen as his principal representative and partner in his Northwest venture, had recruited the additional men he needed and was ready to leave for the Pacific Coast in the spring of 1811. By then he had made the acquaintance of most of the leading merchants of St. Louis and had been joined by two other businessmen, Ramsay Crooks and Robert McClellan.

Manuel Lisa, still beleaguered by his shortage of capital and the attacks of the Blackfeet, was also planning to ascend the Missouri. Hunt left first, but because he had the larger of the two parties, Lisa was anxious to catch up with him and enjoy his protection while they passed the Sioux and other unfriendly tribes on the river. Thus began a race that finally ended at the Arikaras' village. Despite Lisa's overtures, however, Hunt remained suspicious of him, not realizing that when they were among Indians all white men had to cooperate.

The news coming down the river was not good. The Indians were in an unpleasant mood, and the Blackfeet were still harassing Lisa's outposts. Hunt, therefore, began to question his original plan to follow Lewis and Clark's route, because it would take him right through the heart of the Blackfeet's country. Instead he decided to buy horses from the Indians, leave the Missouri before reaching the Mandans' villages, and head in a westerly direction by land.

The purchase of the necessary livestock took considerable time, as he had to bargain for each horse individually; but on July 18, 1811, he set out, using as guides several men who had worked for Lisa. At this point his inexperience as a frontiersman became apparent. Lewis and Clark had left the Mandan villages early in the spring and had pressed forward vigorously in order to cross the mountains before the first snows fell. Hunt was not leaving the Missouri until the middle of the summer, and yet he still saw no need to hurry.

Crooks became ill and had to be carried on a litter, and Hunt had not been able to obtain enough horses to mount all his men. Yet even these handicaps did not account for his slow pace. He allowed his men to camp leisurely, and he stopped often to hunt for buffalo when he should have been racing to get

110

across the Rockies as quickly as possible. But by September 9, he had only reached the Bighorn River at a point southeast of today's Yellowstone National Park in Wyoming. Ahead of him were the Rocky Mountains and beyond those ridges the long and virtually unknown trail to the coastal mountains, which he had to cross before reaching his final goal. Already the days were shortening, the first touch of fall was about to chill the air, followed by the winter snows, snows unlike anything Hunt had known.

9. Casualty of War

The situation of our country, fellow-citizens, is not without its difficulties. . . . With more than one nation we have serious and unsettled controversies, and with one, powerful in the means and habits of war, we are at war.

—James Madison, 1812

Although Astor's men had arrived first on the Columbia, thus establishing a claim prior to that of the North-West Company, the *Tonquin* was gone and with it his immediate hope of trading to the north and contesting the British and the Russians. Now Hunt, with more than eighty men—the largest part of the expedition—was still on the eastern slopes of the Rockies with winter just in the offing. Meanwhile relations between the United States and Great Britain were rapidly deteriorating. War between the two countries would leave the post at Astoria exposed to British naval vessels with little hope of assistance. Astor's careful plans were going badly awry.

Unlike Lisa, however, Astor was a man of large capital and broad business interests. Astoria was, therefore, only one of his many concerns. As Ross commented, "Had he . . . acquired such insight into the practice of the Indian as he so eminently attained in all other branches of trade; had his mind been so liberal as it was acute, or as ready to award merit as to find fault; or were he as conversant with human nature as he was expert in a bargain; and had he also begun his undertaking, not at the commencement of a war, but at its close . . . success might have crowned his ambition." As it was, his Astoria venture had moved beyond the range of his personal supervision and was hurtling toward disaster, first in the person of Captain Thorn, who against Astor's specific instructions had allowed Indians aboard the *Tonquin,* now in the person of Hunt, who failed to comprehend the rigors of a winter in the mountainous country of the West.

With the help of a band of Crow Indians, Hunt found his way past the Bighorn Mountains and, continuing westward, caught a glimpse of the Grand Tetons—an inspiring sight even to those fighting their way through the wilderness. By the middle of September he had reached the valley of the Green River. Although food was important, he was not justified in stopping for approximately ten days to shoot buffalo and cure the meat. Continuing on his leisurely way, he reached the Snake River. Here his men wanted to build canoes and make the rest of the journey by boat, but from what the Indians told them and from what they saw during a brief scouting expedition, they realized the river was unnavigable. Shortly afterward Hunt released four men to remain in that area for the winter as a trapping party.

On October 8, 1811, he reached an abandoned post that had been used by some of Lisa's men, who had spent the winter in the mountains to escape the Blackfeet. Once more the flowing waters of the Snake River lured the men who, tired of traveling without enough horses, dreamed of floating downstream in boats. Hunt gave in to them, and they spent another week building canoes before they took off again, leaving behind their horses and another small party of trappers.

For a short time, they could only congratulate themselves on their decision. The river swiftly and easily carried them toward their destination, but soon it became a twisting, dangerous monster with swift rapids and deep canyons. For a single day it improved with only two rapids giving the men cause for worry; then it again became worse. The canoe bearing Ramsay Crooks capsized; one of the men was drowned; and the river engulfed many of the expedition's supplies.

Hunt ordered a halt while he followed the river's course for about thirty-five miles on foot. Below him he saw the water pouring over falls that were ten to forty feet high and racing through rapid after rapid. In only two places could he even reach the water's edge because of the steep canyon walls.

As they had food for only a few days more, Hunt told the men to split up before they died of hunger. Two scouting parties were to search for friendly

Indians who might sell them something to eat, and Crooks was to return to the fort formerly occupied by Lisa's men. Perhaps the employees whom Hunt had left there could give them some help. In a few days, Crooks was back, but he brought no assistance. He had gone only a short distance before he realized he could never reach his goal before winter and turned back to rejoin Hunt.

In his far-distant office in New York, Astor had no way of knowing that his plans were falling apart. Hunt's expedition, designed to bring personnel and supplies to the small fort on the Columbia River, was floundering in what is now Idaho, uncertain how to proceed and with winter baying at its heels. Giving each man an allotment of food, Hunt divided those still in camp into two groups. One under the leadership of Crooks was to go down the right-hand bank of the Snake; the other, with himself at their head, would advance along the opposite side. At least some of them might make it to the base at Astoria, which, small and insecure as it was, offered them their best chance for survival.

Two scouting parties were already out. They encountered each other and joined forces, choosing as their leader Alexander McKenzie, a former employee of the North-West Company. Although not related to the man who had crossed the continent, he was an experienced frontiersman. This group were the first to reach Astoria, straggling up to the fort in the middle of January 1812. Commenting later on their arrival, Alexander Ross said, "They suffered much, and were at one time five days without a mouthful to eat, when, fortunately, they caught a beaver; and on this small animal and its skin, scarcely a mouthful to each, the whole party had to subsist for three days. At this time some of them were so reduced that McKenzie himself had to carry on his own back two of his men's blankets, being a strong and robust man, and long accustomed to the hardships and hard fare of the north. He alone, of all the party, stood the trial well; and, by still cheering and encouraging his men on, he brought them at length to the main waters of the Columbia . . . from whence they descended with the current to the long-looked-for Astoria."

Crooks, becoming ill and unable to move as fast as Hunt, lagged behind. Hunt, seeking a passable route through the unknown, fighting the cold weather, and struggling through the snowstorms that finally overtook him, reached Astoria a month after McKenzie. "The emaciated, downcast looks and tattered garments of our friends," Alexander Ross later wrote, "all bespoke their extreme sufferings during a long and severe winter." He then added, "To that Being alone who preserveth all those who put their trust in Him, were in this instance due, and at all times, our thanksgiving and gratitude."

Astor in his New York office was uninformed about the fate of his various expeditions but still confident that his plan would work. He had entered into a contract with the Russians to supply them, too—he knew he would need all the allies he could obtain—and so he sent out another ship, the *Beaver,* with goods for both Astoria and the Russian posts. On May 6, 1812, it arrived off the mouth of the Columbia River and faced the same turbulent waters that had proved so dangerous to the men on the *Tonquin.* Although it fired signal guns, no answer came from shore; and the captain was fearful the Indians had overrun the post and destroyed it. But after repeated attempts to make those on land aware of his arrival, two boats came out to greet him and pilot him over the bar. That day there was great rejoicing at Astoria.

A few days later a small group of the company returned from an expedition they had made to an outpost they had established on one of the Columbia's tributaries. They, too, brought good news. As they were descending the river, they heard a voice calling to them in English. At first they suspected some trick on the part of the Indians—they had already engaged in one fight with them—and were hesitant about approaching close to land. But finally they realized that Crooks and one companion were standing there, so worn and changed from their experiences that they were barely recognizable. But at last, approximately a year after leaving St. Louis, the remnants of Hunt's expedition were reunited just as a new crisis was developing.

By sending representatives to meet with the American peace commissioners after the Revolution, Great Britain had tacitly admitted defeat. But neither its government nor its people could believe that the greatest sea power in the world, the one nation capable of contesting Napoleon, had really suffered such a reverse at the hands of a former colony. Its attitude, therefore, had remained arrogant, its regard for the terms of the treaty casual, and its military actions, particularly on the oceans, those of a dominant nation toward its vassal. The conciliatory measures adopted by successive American administrations succeeded only in irritating the people of the United States without materially placating those of Great Britain. So the two rushed forward toward an inevitable conflict, and on June 18, 1812, the United States declared war on Great Britain.

Rarely, if ever, has a country determined to fight a major adversary more poorly equipped. It had little in the way of armaments, its leading officers were for the most part incompetent or, in the case of Wilkinson, corrupt; its army was too small; and its finances barely able to withstand the demands of peace, much less those of combat. Except for a few initial victories at sea— none of them decisive—the opening campaigns of the War of 1812 drove home these points to the American public. Instead of easily marching into Canada, the United States was badly beaten and found itself hard put to defend its own frontiers. In the few years since Yorktown, it had expanded its boundaries to the edges of Louisiana and, by Astor's establishment at Astoria, reinforced its claim to the edge of the Pacific. But by engaging in the war, it had converted these acquisitions into possible prizes for the enemy to capture

115

without, at the same time, providing the means to defend them. That burden fell on the fur traders.

Even Astor, the best capitalized of them all and therefore the best able to survive in adverse times, was hard pressed to sustain Astoria. The sea routes to the mouth of the Columbia instantly became more dangerous and risky than before; and the land routes had not proven themselves an adequate substitute. Lewis and Clark had required two seasons to reach the ocean, and their trail ran through the country of the ferocious and hostile Blackfeet. On the other hand, Hunt's journey farther south had been slow and hazardous. If his experience was indicative, valuable cargoes could not be shipped back and forth by the route he had followed.

Other problems were also threatening Astor's enterprise. Some of the partners to whom he had offered shares in the company in return for their services were becoming disillusioned; and the Russians, whose support he had hoped to gain, were proving no more honorable than himself in living up to the spirit of an agreement. He had seen himself as their chief supplier, thus checking their advance, but they had flanked him and established a base in Alta California. Located on Bodega Bay only a relatively few miles north of San Francisco, its construction alarmed the Spanish, who regarded the post as a major encroachment on their territory. But the Russians were tough, determined, and unyielding, and the Spanish reluctantly accepted their assurances that the fort would be used only to supply their northern posts with beef.

Yet Astor's men, although their position was increasingly precarious, were making a contribution toward the expansion of the United States. In addition to establishing and maintaining a post at the mouth of the Columbia and thus reinforcing the nation's hold on the area, they were exploring upstream and extending their activities even further afield into such areas as the present-day state of Utah.

One of their most significant achievements came toward the end of 1812. Realizing that it was imperative that Astor have news of the expedition and its needs, they decided to undertake another journey across the continent. As the leader, they chose Robert Stuart, a young and relatively untried man, but one whose abilities had impressed them. To go with him, they selected four of their hardiest members. Ramsay Crooks and Robert McClellan, the two businessmen who had joined Hunt in St. Louis, were now disillusioned with the prospects at Astoria and decided to return, too.

With a smaller number of men, a better knowledge of the country, and an earlier start in the year, this new overland expedition fared better than Hunt's, but still met with many hardships—days when the men were desperately short of food, stormy weather, encounters with Indians, some of whom drove off their horses and forced them to proceed on foot, illness that caused

116

them to spend time in camp while Ramsay Crooks recovered, and the near madness of McClellan, who, against all common sense, left the party rather than climb another mountain ridge. (He was encountered again days later, almost dead from starvation and exhaustion.) These events were to be expected by those making the transcontinental crossing; the unexpected was the discovery of South Pass.

This breach in the barrier of the Rockies is located in the southwestern quarter of present-day Wyoming, and it afforded the best route through the mountains that had been found. Avoiding the northern country of the Blackfeet and the maze through which Lewis and Clark had pushed their way and improving greatly on the devious route taken by Hunt, South Pass had only a gradual grade both ways and was well watered its entire length. For the first time, the Americans had a practical route through the mountains that split the continent.

The opening months of 1813 brought little encouraging diplomatic or military news, and Astor was perplexed. He had commissioned yet another ship to visit Astoria but, with the uncertain international situation, debated whether he should order it to sea. He still had had no word that Hunt had arrived at Astoria. In fact, rumors were current that the entire expedition had been wiped out. Reports also reached him that the North-West Company was sending an armed ship of twenty guns to found a competing establishment at the mouth of the Columbia. His appeal to the government for forty or fifty men to help defend Astoria was denied by an administration deeply engrossed in defending areas nearer home. And the Indians, unrestrained by either combatant, were blocking many of the routes east of the Rockies.

Astor, however, was not yet ready to abandon his dream. Raising his stake in Astoria even higher, he reconfirmed his agreement with the Russians to act in concert and ordered his ship to weigh anchor and head for the West Coast. On board was the man he had designated to take over Hunt's functions if Hunt had not arrived; and to him, Astor expressed his thoughts. "If I were on the spot, I would defy them all [the North-West Company and the British]; but as it is, everything depends on you and your friends about you. Our enterprise is grand, and deserves success; and I hope in God it will meet it." Always desperately fond of the dollars he could make, Astor nevertheless often used pious terms to express his wishes, and so he added, "If my object was merely gain of money, I should say, think whether it is best to save what we can, and abandon the place; but the very idea is like dagger to my heart."

Astor's determination was great, but it was not equal to the events of 1813. While he remained in ignorance of conditions at Astoria, news of the war between the United States and Great Britain had been brought to the Astorians by John G. McTavish of the North-West Company. Smiling at the predicament in which his information placed them, he had approached one of their outposts with a copy of Madison's proclamation and had advised them that an armed ship was sailing for the mouth of the Columbia.

Hunt had temporarily left with the *Beaver* to take supplies to the Russians, so Duncan McDougal was again in charge at the fort. Taking stock of his situation, he saw little grounds to hope they could hold out. No word had come from the *Beaver*. Therefore it might have met a disaster like the *Tonquin*'s. Astor's new ship, the *Lark,* had not arrived. The departure of Hunt and the need to send men out into the country to trap and trade had depleted the fort's manpower, and meanwhile some of the neighboring tribes had become hostile, so much so that he had had to increase the fortifications at the post and even then feared a surprise attack. The imminent arrival of the North-West Company's men and a British armed ship seemed to make his position hopeless. After conferring with the partners who were then at the post, he decided Astoria must be abandoned and began making preparations to leave.

Hunt had meanwhile reached the Russian settlements and found their trade was much more extensive than he had realized. Not only were they collecting skins in the north, they were also outfitting ships—including some belonging to the Americans—to trap and trade along the coast of Alta California, intruding on territory that Astor would have liked to exploit.

Originally Hunt had intended to return directly to Astoria, but the *Beaver*'s captain produced instructions from Astor indicating he was to give preference to the Russians' cargoes rather than his own. Therefore Hunt next found himself in the Hawaiian Islands and headed for Canton. To get back to Astoria, where he thought his presence might be needed, he had to charter a boat.

His arrival did not change the decision to abandon the post. At first he objected, but when McDougal outlined the situation, he reluctantly agreed they would be unable to resist the combined onslaught of the British navy and the North-West Company. Therefore he departed from the Columbia on his chartered vessel, taking with him some of the post's supplies and personnel.

Soon McTavish arrived at the head of about seventy-five men from the North-West Company. He confirmed the news that a British privateer escorted by a frigate was soon to arrive, for the North-West Company had persuaded the British government that Astoria was an important American settlement, one well worth capturing.

The waiting game began. McDougal had not planned to give up the post until later in the year; McTavish could not force his hand until the arrival of the British ships; and neither side wished to fight, for hostilities between them would inevitably arouse the Indians. Besides, McDougal, being a former employee in the North-West Company, knew McTavish well, and the two men regarded each other as friends. In fact, when McTavish began to run short of supplies, McDougal sold him what he needed. "As the season advanced," Franchère wrote, "and their ship did not arrive our new neighbors found themselves in a very disagreeable situation, without food, or merchandise wherewith to procure it from the natives; viewed by the latter with a distrustful and hostile eye, as being our enemies, and therefore exposed to attack and plunder on their part with impunity; supplied with good hunters, indeed, but wanting ammunition to render their skill available. Weary, at length, of applying to us incessantly for food (which we furnished them with a sparing hand), unable either to retrace their steps through the wilderness or to remain in their present position, they came to the conclusion of proposing to buy of us the whole establishment."

Indeed, this seemed like a practical solution to the problem. The North-West Company would gain the post along with its business, and Astor would obtain some recompense for his loss.

The negotiations were protracted, McDougal sparring for the highest price he could get, McTavish realizing that the appearance of the ships would tip the balance entirely in his favor. But when the ships did not appear, he finally consented to pay a relatively small price for the supplies of the fort and for the skins that were already on hand; and on October 23, 1813, the American flag was hauled down and supplanted by the British.

On November 30, the first of the expected British vessels arrived at the mouth of the Columbia. "The officers visited the fort," Franchère later wrote, ". . . and seemed to me in general very much dissatisfied with their fool's errand, as they called it; they had expected to find a number of American vessels loaded with rich furs, and had calculated in advance their share of the booty of Astoria. They had not met a vessel, and their astonishment was at its height when they saw that our establishment had been transferred to the North-West Company and was under the British flag. . . . The Captain landed after dark; when we showed him the next morning the palisades and log bastions of the factory [as trading posts were often called], he inquired if there was not another; on being assured there was no other he cried out, with an air of the greatest astonishment: 'What! is this the fort which was represented to me as so formidable! Good God! I could batter it down in two hours with a four-pounder!'"

The British officers might have been disillusioned by Astoria, but both the fort and the land on which it stood now belonged to Great Britain, and the only American settlement west of the Rockies no longer existed.

10. A Time of Change

. . . it is manifest that all those Provinces [Spain's continental possessions in the New World] are not only in the full enjoyment of their independence, but . . . that there is not the remotest prospect of their being deprived of it.

—James Monroe, 1822

Many Americans had entered the War of 1812 with light hearts and high hopes, picturing themselves as conquerors of large portions of Canada and triumphant negotiators of their outstanding differences with Great Britain. But the vision and the reality had little in common.

The opening months brought defeat and humiliation almost everywhere except at sea; and even on the oceans, the American navy ultimately proved unequal to the British. In 1813, however, a victory broke the dismaying list of defeats. In a well-executed attack—but one that cost its commander his life—the Americans captured the Canadian city of Toronto (then called York). Finally in death Zebulon Pike achieved the glory that had eluded him in life.

Elsewhere the gloomy news persisted, and the Americans' hold on the continent shriveled like a flower exposed to the desert sun. Gone was their foothold in the Northwest and their control of the Great Plains. Even Lisa, tenacious and tough, could no longer conduct his far-flung Indian trade and retreated like every other merchant toward St. Louis.

Fortunately for the Americans, the British, too, were disillusioned. Although they slashed here and there, they could not destroy the Americans' resistance. So in 1814 both sides agreed to go to the negotiating table but made little progress until the failure of the final British offensive. Then the delegates began bargaining in earnest, and, on Christmas Eve, 1814, concluded the Treaty of Ghent.

In many respects, the treaty was a futile document. It settled none of the great issues between the two nations, avoiding some, postponing others, and merely suggesting the machinery by which the remainder might be resolved in the future. To Astor, still smarting from the loss of Astoria, its terms were bitter. Pending the later discussion of boundary issues, each nation was to relinquish any territory it had seized during the hostilities. Thus the British navy's "capture" of Astoria became void, and the land on which it stood reverted to the United States. But before the arrival of the warships, Astor's partners had legally sold the post itself to the North-West Company. Therefore its transfer was a private transaction between willing parties and, consequently, valid.

Astor was beside himself. In a letter, he said, "Had our place and our property been fairly captured, I should have preferred it. I should not feel as if I were disgraced." Hoping to enlist the government's support, he importuned every official he knew and wielded his considerable influence to its full extent. But to no avail.

His loss was heavy. Even the *Lark,* the last of the vessels he sent to Astoria, had been shipwrecked off Hawaii. From his enormous investment, he had only salvaged the payment he received from the North-West Company. Luckily his fortune was sufficiently great to absorb the cost, but his venture indicated that the government's assistance was necessary for the rapid expansion of the new republic. Private capital alone did not have the necessary resources, and the wisdom of Jefferson's decision to finance the Lewis and Clark expedition as a national service was affirmed.

Peace did not bring tranquillity to North America. A mood of restlessness was sweeping across the continent especially in those parts of it that still retained close ties to the Old World. In Canada the North-West Company, grown powerful through the efforts of its explorers and traders, challenged the settlements authorized by the British government along the Red River of the north. Even though the company's partners eventually lost this test of strength, their attempt reflected the colony's growing discontent with regulations set down in London.

In Mexico, the spirit of revolt that was shaking most of Spain's overseas empire began to spread. Armed revolutionaries roamed the countryside, throwing fear into the hearts of Spanish officials and sympathizers. Finally the authorities captured the rebels' leader, Father José Morelos. His ecclesiastical superiors defrocked him and symbolically removed the holy oils from his hands by physically scraping them, a ceremony so painful that the onlookers wept at his suffering. Then the Church turned him over to the secular authorities, who shot him. The fall of his bullet-riddled body, however, did not end the people's thoughts of revolt. They only awaited another leader, one more capable of uniting large segments of the population.

The United States had already won its freedom from Europe; but its boundaries with Canada had yet to be settled through commissions provided by the Treaty of Ghent. East Florida remained a Spanish possession and a refuge for escaped slaves and Seminole Indians, and Amelia Island, located a short distance offshore near the Florida–Georgia border, served as a center for freebooters and outlaws. West of the Mississippi, the trappers and traders had to battle anew to regain the control they had lost while the nation fought an even greater foe than geography and Indians. Astor, however, had had all he wanted of adventures so far from his New York office. Frustrated in his attempt to repossess Astoria, he was content, at least for the time being, to restrict his operations to the land east of the Missouri, leaving the West Coast to the Russians, the Spanish, the British, and a few American shipowners.

Alta California remained relatively untouched by the ferment elsewhere, continuing in its placid ways as though the world would never change. In the fall of 1816, Otto von Kotzebue, a Russian naval officer, arrived at San Francisco on a government exploring expedition. As he entered the harbor, he saw the Spanish ensign was not flying at the presidio. On landing, he learned the reason: The halyard was broken, and no one in the garrison had either the skill or the energy to replace it.

As individuals, the Spanish did not lack courage. To von Kotzebue's amazement, they went out on horseback and roped a wild bear, bringing it back alive to stage a bull and bear fight for his entertainment. But of industry, or faith in the future, he saw little.

Summing up conditions in California, he commented, "California costs the Spanish government a great sum, without any other advantage than the annual conversion of some hundreds of Indians. . . . It is truly lamentable to see this beautiful country thus neglected."

Yet all this time, as von Kotzebue remarked, "Sea-otters are very frequently met with upon the shores of California; and, as they have not been seen here at all in former times, it is to be supposed, that they have withdrawn thither from the Alioutskan [Aleutian] Islands, and from the northern parts of America, to escape the persecutions they were exposed to there." The wealth the Spanish so much desired was spilling over into Alta California through the activities of the Russians. Yet the Spanish were too indolent to grasp it.

The weakness of their California defenses was clearly revealed by the cruise of a Frenchman, Hypolite Bouchard, who had joined the revolutionists in Argentina and been given command of two ships. In the late fall of 1818 he appeared at Monterey. After a brisk exchange with the Spanish battery, he landed about three miles away. Before the Spanish could bring up their fieldpieces, he and his men marched toward the fort and soon overran it. "We then turned the guns on the town," wrote an Englishman, Peter Corney, who commanded one of the two ships, ". . . and after firing a few rounds, the Commodore [Bouchard] sent me with a party to assault the place, while he kept possession of the fort. As we approached the town, the Spaniards again fled, after discharging their field-pieces, and we entered without opposition."

Farther down the coast, Bouchard sacked another town and lost three men, whom a quick-riding group of Spaniards lassoed. (They appeared more adept with their *riatas* than their guns.) By agreeing to spare Santa Barbara, he recovered the three men and went on to attack another community farther south and found it "well stocked with everything but money," Peter Corney wrote, ". . . and about two o'clock we marched back, though not in the order we went, many of the men being intoxicated, and some were so much so, that we had to lash them on the field-pieces and drag them to the beach."

Bouchard's raids underscored the weakness of California's defenses; but the same remoteness that made it difficult for Spain to protect its province also prevented an invader from occupying it permanently. So the Spanish authorities, embroiled in bitter struggles elsewhere, merely shrugged their shoulders and let California drift along in semi-isolation.

Spain could not, however, treat its differences with the United States in the same manner and, by ignoring them, dispel them. The United States had already forced the sale of East Florida and was now asking Spain to relinquish its claims to West Florida and also to the land west of the Rockies and north of the forty-second parallel, which is the present boundary between California and Oregon. Spain was in no position to resist the demands of its aggressive neighbor, who had demonstrated its willingness to use arms to get what it wanted in East Florida. So in 1819, it agreed to the Adams-Onís Treaty. This gave the United States what it asked for in return for abandoning its own slight claim to Texas. Thus Spain surrendered more of its empire and the legacy of its great explorers.

For the diplomats of the United States, those were busy times. While some of them were prying Florida loose from the Spaniards and picking up Spain's claims in the Pacific Northwest, others were occupied with the question of Astoria. Even though Astor himself had finally given up hope of regaining his former trading post, the government had not lost sight of the importance of effecting its claim to the lower stretches of the Columbia River. James Monroe was president and John Quincy Adams secretary of state, both men who wanted to see the United States expand. In the early fall of 1817, the government therefore ordered the sloop-of-war *Ontario* to the West Coast with orders to reassert America's claims. When the British learned about the ship's mission, they lodged a strong protest; but the Americans replied that they were merely exercising a right permitted by the Treaty of Ghent.

The manner in which they did so became a comedy of bureaucratic squabbling and diplomatic maneuvering. The ship's captain and the State Department's representative soon quarreled, and the ship's captain left the representative in Chile and sailed north without him. On the banks of the Columbia River, he placed lead plates reasserting the claims of the United States; but apparently fearing trouble from the representatives of the North-West Company, he did not notify them. Later the diplomatic representative secured passage on another ship to the Columbia. He, too, claimed the land in the name of the United States but this time in the presence of a British naval captain and a member of the North-West Company, neither of whom raised any objections. This was a diplomatic error on their part, for they permitted the claim to include a larger area than Great Britain had previously acknowledged.

The point arose when the Americans began negotiating a northern boundary with Great Britain. Both sides agreed on the forty-ninth parallel from the Lake o' the Woods to the Rocky Mountains, but the Americans wanted the line to continue straight on to the Pacific; the British insisted that it drop south and give them Oregon. Their case, however, had been weakened by the acquiescence of their representatives at the ceremony held a little earlier. Finally both sides agreed to occupy the territory jointly for ten years. Perhaps in a decade the question would resolve itself.

Meanwhile, the Russians were pushing their own frontiers outward. The Spanish, by surrendering to the United States their claim to the coast above the forty-second parallel, had created a buffer zone between themselves and the Russians. Nevertheless, the Russians still had their base, Fort Ross, north of San Francisco near Bodega Bay, and their ships frequently went as far south as Santa Barbara. On the West Coast, conditions were changing rapidly. The British were still an important influence through their fur companies, the Russians were expanding, the Spanish empire was shrinking. But in those times of flux, the American role, except for the cruises made by its independent ship captains, was limited to arguing with Great Britain about the Oregon Territory.

The forces at work, although strong, were not stable, and therefore the end was not predictable. In the United States, the Panic of 1819 had blunted the nation's optimism; and the issue of slavery—with its horrifying implications—had again arisen. But in 1820 the Missouri Compromise temporarily calmed the fears of the North over slavery, and as the nation recovered from the financial panic as well, its self-confidence became restored.

The timing was fortunate, for events were accelerating. The following year the Hudson's Bay Company and the North-West Company merged. Until then these two giant organizations had been fierce competitors for the fur trade, and the struggles between them had been partisan and sometimes vicious. Now they presented a common front with the single purpose of controlling the fur-rich country of the West. At the same time, the Russians took a more aggressive stand. The tsar issued a ukase that forbade any foreign ships to approach the North American coast above the fifty-first parallel (a line that lies near the northern tip of Vancouver Island), thus adding much of the present-day Canadian shore to the claim he had already established in Alaska. At the same time, he made no sign that Russians would withdraw from the post they had established south of that line or that they would curtail the movement of their ships along the coast of California.

The event with the greatest potential for change occurred in Mexico, where the death of Morelos had not quieted the spirit of unrest. In 1820 Augustín de Iturbide, a military commander, was sent to put down one of the rebellious armies that still roamed the Mexican countryside. Even before undertaking this assignment, Iturbide had considered heading a revolutionary movement of his own and had formulated a program for the Mexican people. During the military campaign, he joined forces with his opponents, seized a shipment of silver pesos to finance his effort, and early in 1821 published his plan for converting Mexico into an independent constitutional monarchy. Whereas other revolutionists had appealed to specific groups within Mexico's rather complicated society, Iturbide's program was more universal. Soon he had almost the entire nation on his side, and the newly arrived viceroy could do little except recognize the country's independence.

The effect of the political upheaval was almost immediately apparent in the outposts of Mexico. Relieved at last of the restrictions placed upon them by the suspicious, self-centered government in Spain, the inhabitants were eager to open their marketplaces to foreign trade and immigration, whose benefits had been so long denied them.

Moses Austin, with the permission of the new government, began to bring American immigrants into Texas. Another adventurer, named Hugh Glenn, thought the New Mexicans might now welcome foreigners and organized an expedition to trade with them. To avoid risking the loss of his goods, Glenn left his party on the outskirts of the province and went ahead to test the reaction of the New Mexicans to his arrival. Jacob Fowler, one of his companions, noted in his journal in January 1822 that "we now under stand that the mackeson [Mexican] provence Has de Clared Indepndance of the mother Country and is desirous of a traid With the people of the united States

Conl Glann [Colonel Glenn] also advises me that He Had obtained premition to Hunt to trap and traid In the Spanish provences."

The results, however, were not as advantageous as Glenn had expected, for the New Mexicans were not rich. In February, Fowler reached Taos and commented, "We Heare found the people extremely poor, and Bread Stuff could not be Head among them as the [they] Said the grass hoppers Head Eat up all their grain for the last two years and the [they] had to Pack all their grain about one Hunderd miles—for their own use—We found them Eaqually Scarce of Meet and Ware [were] offered one quarter of a dollar a pound for the meet We Braght in With Us. . . . We must Soon leave this Reeched place— and now in the dead of Winter and the Waters frosen tite Exsept the River Delnort [Rio Grande del Norte] Which is Said to be oppen to Which We Intend to go as soon as possible to Catch Beaver to live on as there is no other game In this part of the Country."

Although New Mexico did not contain the lode of riches that many had imagined, it continued to prove an irresistible lure to the adventurous just as it always had since the time of Coronado. Thomas James, a merchant who had lost his business during the Panic of 1819, joined another American, John McKnight, in a similar trading expedition. McKnight's principal interest was in finding his brother, who had trespassed on Spanish territory years before and been held a prisoner ever since. James, however, was only concerned with making money, and Santa Fé proved a disappointment.

As he told the story later, "The spring was nearly gone and most of my goods remained unsold. Money was very scarce, and I had little prospect of selling them at any price. I offered them at cost, and at last found a purchaser . . . who paid me one thousand dollars in cash and an equal sum in horses and mules." This left James with "a large quantity of brown and grey cloths which were unsaleable in the Spanish market, blue and other colors being preferred," and a debt owed him by the governor, who explained that since he himself had not been paid for ten years he could not settle his account.

William Becknell, another Missouri businessman, had gone to trade with the Indians. Learning from some Spanish soldiers he met that Mexico had gained its independence and might welcome foreign traders, he, too, had traveled to Santa Fé. He enjoyed better commercial success than James; and when he returned home, his reports to his neighbors stimulated further interest in this new outlet for business. He also made a mechanical improvement in the trade. On a return trip the following year, he took with him three wagons. Contrary to the common belief, these were able to navigate the rough terrain and opened up the possibility of carrying larger and more diverse cargoes.

Like the New Mexicans, the governor of California also prepared to welcome foreign visitors. The British—with their post on the Columbia River—were in a good position to take advantage of this change in policy; but the directors of the Hudson's Bay Company (the name of the North-West Company had disappeared in the merger) had other problems on their minds. For all their effort to seize the Columbia River, their business there was not proving profitable. In 1822 they instructed George Simpson, their chief operating officer in North America, to reduce the losses at Fort George, the name now given to Astoria.

If these could be brought to "a small sum," it might be worthwhile to maintain the post to help protect "the more valuable districts to the North of it." The fate of the British in the Pacific Northwest depended, therefore, almost entirely on the ledger books of the Hudson's Bay Company. If the directors could turn the entries for Fort George from red to black, the British would remain. If not, their flag would retreat to "the more valuable districts to the north," driven back, not by a conquering army, but by the absence of sufficient fur-bearing animals.

11. Growing Ambitions

. . . until Europe shall find it a settled geograph-
ical element that the United States and North
America are identical, any effort on our part to
reason the world out of a belief that we are
ambitious will have no other effect than to convince
them that we add to our ambition hypocrisy.

—John Quincy Adams, 1819

As yet no nation controlled the lands west of the Rockies. Mexico had the largest number of settlements and the largest number of inhabitants, but its people had long been subjected to the debilitating effects of Spanish colonial rule; and their new government, unstable and untested, was more occupied with survival than expansion.

Great Britain had entrusted its westward expansion to a commercial company. Although the government could—and did—assist the Hudson's Bay Company diplomatically, no Francis Drake was ready to risk his life on the western shores of North America for the glory of his country.

Russia was moving aggressively to expand its territory, but it was handicapped by geography. Its posts on the edges of the icy northern seas were difficult to supply and could not be made self-supporting. Therefore their status as Russian possessions was tenuous in spite of the tsar's ukase.

The United States had been pushed back during the War of 1812; and although some of its citizens dreamed of a nation that would extend from ocean to ocean, it was having difficulty reestablishing its dominion over the lands it had already acquired through conquest or purchase. On the West Coast, it had no permanent posts at all, merely claims based on the discovery of Captain Gray, the acquisition of the Spanish rights above the forty-second parallel, and the attempt of Astor to establish a fur-trading base. So as the fogs swept eastward from the Pacific, turned into clouds, and began their long journey toward the Atlantic, they no longer passed over lands that were unknown to Europeans. But the struggle to gain control of those lands might go in any direction.

Great Britain and the United States had been antagonists in international affairs for almost fifty years; but they found a common cause in opposing the tsar's ukase.

Nevertheless, John Quincy Adams, secretary of state, did not solely rely on Britain's cooperation. Regardless of what the British did, his position was clear, and he expressed it in forceful terms to the American ambassador to Russia. "The United States," he wrote, "can admit no part of these claims. Their right of navigation and fishing is perfect, and has been in constant exercise from the earliest times . . . throughout the whole extent of the Southern Ocean, subject only to the ordinary exceptions and exclusions of the territorial jurisdictions, which, so far as Russian rights are concerned, are confined to certain *islands* north of the fifty-fifth degree of latitude, and have no existence on the continent of America." Since the Russians were having trouble supplying their posts and were thinking of relinquishing them anyway, the subsequent negotiations were, as Monroe said, a "friendly proceeding"; and the tsar withdrew his ukase.

Having forced the Russians to retreat for the first time since they had started expanding on the West Coast, Monroe became even more aggressive. In his message to Congress in December 1823, he said, "It is impossible that the Allied Powers [the Quadruple Alliance of Austria, Russia, Prussia, and France] should extend their political system to any portion of either continent [North or South America] without endangering our peace and happiness; nor can anyone believe that our southern brethren [the Latin American nations], if not left to themselves, would adopt it of their own accord. It would be equally impossible, therefore, that we should behold such interposition in any form with indifference."

This was a strong challenge for a minor power to make to some of the greatest nations in the world. Yet the growing self-confidence of the United

States was largely justified. During the War of 1812, it had brought Great Britain to the conference table. Since then it had successfully negotiated several territorial disputes. Between 1810 and 1820, its population had jumped by almost two and a half million persons; its government had proved firm and stable during a variety of crises; and even along the frontier in the West, it was rapidly regaining the position it had held earlier, largely because of an aggressive fur trader, Joshua Pilcher, who had taken over the business once headed by Manuel Lisa and was pressing back up the Missouri into the land of the Blackfeet.

In 1822 he faced two new competitors in the field: William Henry Ashley, a gunpowder manufacturer and Missouri politician, and Andrew Henry, formerly one of the most successful and adventurous of Manuel Lisa's men. During the first year of their partnership, Ashley and Henry endured many trials, including the upset of one of their keelboats with the loss of all its cargo. The second year, 1823, they suffered an even greater disaster. While moving his supplies up the Missouri, Ashley was attacked by the Arikaras, who drove him back downstream with heavy losses.

The season was now late, but like most men in business, Ashley and Henry could not afford the cost of a year's inactivity. So they divided into three groups. Ashley returned to St. Louis to handle the partnership's business there. Henry went to the Yellowstone and prepared to push on into the dangerous country of the Blackfeet. And the third, under the leadership of Jedediah Smith, set off almost directly west to spend the winter on the other side of the mountains.

Even among America's many remarkable frontiersmen, Jedediah Smith was outstanding for his imagination, leadership, literacy, and his religious faith. (He was a devout Methodist all his life.) Among the men with him on this journey was Edward Fitzpatrick, whose left hand was later injured in a firearms accident and who consequently came to be known by the Indians as "Broken Hand." Cool in moments of crisis and effective as an organizer, he was also skilled at understanding the Indians. Another member of Smith's group was William Sublette, one of several brothers who later distinguished themselves in the fur trade.

Their journey was filled with hardship. Before they had crossed the plains, two men nearly died of thirst; Smith himself was badly mauled by a grizzly bear; and in the mountains, they struggled against deep snows and savage cold as they made their way to the western slopes of the Rockies.

After they had divided into two successful trapping parties and had reunited in June, Smith made a far-reaching decision. Instead of returning to St. Louis with his entire party, he sent Fitzpatrick back alone with the furs while he and the other men remained in the mountains to continue trapping. With that, he started to revolutionize the American fur trade. For he had dispensed with the cost of building supporting forts to serve as bases, and he had kept his men in the field for the entire twelve months. No one in Washington—not even John Quincy Adams, who had expressed such a strong interest in his nation's westward expansion—knew of this decision. Neither did the statesmen in Europe who were trying to influence the future of the New World. While they debated, planned, and exchanged diplomatic correspondence, Jedediah Smith and his small contingent of trappers were shaping the course of events. For they had adopted a strategy that made it possible for Americans to reach deeper and deeper into the land beyond the Rockies.

During the next few months, these few men crossed mountain ranges, followed unknown streams, trekked through hidden basins, and located passes over divides—turning the unknown into the known and learning the trails that other Americans could later follow. One group, of which William Sublette was the senior member (such free adventurers recognized leaders only in an informal sense), followed the Green and Bear rivers.

Smith and the other men struck more directly west and with great success trapped along some of the tributaries of the Snake River. In the early fall, they came across a party of the Hudson's Bay Company's men who had been attacked by a band of Snake Indians. Just as quick to take advantage of their plight as the North-West Company had been to seize Astoria, Smith demanded their remaining furs in return for escorting them to the Hudson's Bay Company's headquarters at Flathead House near present-day Thompson Falls, Montana.

There Smith met Peter Skene Ogden, who, in addition to being an important figure in the company's management, was a scholar of Indian ways. From Ogden, Smith learned the surprising extent of the company's activities in the country around the Snake River. About sixty men worked in the territory, and during the last four years they had taken somewhere between eighty thousand and eighty-five thousand beaver skins. It was the British, not the Americans, who were exploiting the resources of the land they both claimed.

After spending several weeks at Flathead House, Smith returned with Ogden to the Snake River and then rejoined the rest of his trappers near the Great Salt Lake. Toward the end of May, he encountered another band of Hudson's Bay Company men and once again was able to take advantage of his competitors. By offering higher prices than Ogden was prepared to pay, he persuaded the men to desert their employer and bring with them all the skins they had obtained.

Smith's operation was so successful that when Henry withdrew from the partnership, Ashley decided he would continue alone. Abandoning the Upper Missouri, he planned to concentrate on the areas west of the Rockies and carry Smith's ideas even further. Instead of sending a man back to St. Louis at the end of the season with the furs, he would meet the trappers in the mountains, pick up their furs, and resupply them. This would give Smith and the others even more mobility.

In the early winter of 1824, he left St. Louis with a pack train of provisions. The route he chose to the mountains was the Platte. This had been traveled several times, but no one had ever followed it in the dead of winter with so many animals to feed.

The cold was intense, the snow lay two feet deep, and the wind blew swirling white clouds into the air and around the heads of men and horses. But game was plentiful, and Ashley's hunters kept the men well supplied with food, while the horses browsed on the grass of the many islands in the river. But the Pawnee Indians whom he met warned him that conditions would change once he reached the forks where the north branch met the south. From there on, they told him, he would find the game scarce and browse almost nonexistent. The only safe route in winter was along the South Platte. But this ran for a considerable distance along the eastern foothills of the Rockies and thus would carry him many miles out of his way. Yet Ashley realized the Indians had no reason to lie to him and took their advice.

The cold became more and more bitter. Forage was difficult to find, and his horses grew thinner and thinner. Yet always to the west stood the barrier of the Rockies, forbidding and seemingly impenetrable. Although not an experienced frontiersman like Henry, Ashley realized the futility—and danger—of attacking the mountains without an adequate plan, so he made a base camp and scouted for a pass through the crags. Finally he located what he thought was one; and when he set out again, he followed the boulder-covered streambed of Cache la Poudre Canyon near present-day Fort Collins, Colorado. With a relatively slight climb, this route through weird rock formations brought him well into the mountains. To his surprise, once he had reached the top of the front range, the mountains appeared less stern and steep; and instead of the glaring, unbroken white of winter, parts of the land were bare of snow; and occasionally a touch of spring promised that a new season was coming. Passing to the south of the Medicine Bow Mountains, he reached the Laramie River on March 10 and was pleased to find a plentiful supply of dead wood to use for fires.

He then crossed the Continental Divide into the drainage system of the Green River. Here he released some of his men to go trapping, while with the others he selected a general meeting place.

Approximately a hundred and fifty men gathered at the spot he chose. After calculating the value of each trapper's pelts, Ashley deducted the amount he had advanced him the year before, sold him the goods he wanted for the coming season, and credited him with any balance that might remain. This was the point in the year when Ashley's own capital requirements were at their highest. He had outstanding—either in direct outlay or in debt—the goods for both the previous and the future season, plus their cost of transportation. Not until he returned to St. Louis and sold the furs would he have any funds coming in. Yet he was not concerned. As he counted the packs of skins—each pack contained about a hundred pounds—and added to them forty-five packs he had collected earlier and cached, he knew the year had been a profitable one, provided he could get the skins safely to civilization.

During the outward journey, hostile Indians had stolen some of his pack animals, and the remainder were exhausted from the long trip. Since the Platte was unnavigable, he went farther north to pick up the Bighorn and Yellowstone rivers, which carried him to the Missouri. There he almost immediately met Henry Atkinson, who—with a large military escort—had been sent up the river to make peace agreements with the Indians who lived along its banks. Surrounded by soldiers, Ashley and his furs were now safe for the remainder of his journey.

In St. Louis at last, he counted his profits. He had returned with approximately half a ton of beaver skins, a good-sized fortune and proof that his new approach to the fur business was practical. Becknell had changed the Santa Fé trade by using wagons. Ashley had an even more revolutionary effect on the fur business. By eliminating a string of supporting forts, he had greatly reduced the amount of capital needed to enter the trade; and by meeting his trappers in the field, he had greatly increased the range of their travels. The United States had laid a claim on the Northwest when Captain Gray discovered the Columbia. Now the presence of American trappers— made possible by Ashley's innovation—was giving that claim substance.

Americans were also penetrating beyond the Rockies in the Southwest. Trade with Santa Fé was now open to them; and even merchants with relatively small means could participate by underwriting a single shipment. Meeting at predesignated sites in Missouri, those going to Santa Fé formed a single caravan for their mutual protection during the long journey. When they reached New Mexico, often after fighting the Indians along the way, they found themselves welcomed by the majority of citizens for the variety of goods they brought and for the diversion they created in the otherwise isolated life of the province. The officials, however, were not always so pleasant. Sometimes gracious and helpful, often they were pompous and glad to extort an extra peso or two to eke out their uncertain salaries.

Some of the Americans who went to New Mexico were trappers; and they, too, had problems with the officials. James Ohio Pattie, who came with his father to seek their fortunes, commented on the reaction of the governor when they asked for a trapping license. "His reply," Pattie wrote, "was that, he did not know if he was allowed by the law to do so; but if upon examination it lay in his power, he would inform us on the morrow. . . . According to this request, we went to the place appointed, the succeeding day. . . . We were told by the governor, that he had found nothing, that would justify him, in giving us the legal permission we desired. We then proposed to him to give us liberty to trap upon the condition, that we paid him five per cent on the beaver we might catch. He said, he would consider this proposition, and give us an answer the next day at the same hour. The thoughts of our hearts were not at all favorable to this person, as we left him."

Despite the obvious uncertainty of their relationship with the governor, Pattie's group went on to Taos, which had become the center in which the New Mexican trappers gathered. Because these men were not associated with a large organization like Ashley's, they formed their own informal combinations to provide themselves with protection in the mountains. Yet these arrangements were not always happy ones. As Pattie explained, "Men bound only by their own will and sense of right, to the duties of such a sort of partnership are certain to grow restless, and to form smaller clans, disposed to dislike and separate from each other, to parties of one by one to three by three. They thus expose themselves to be cut up in detail by the savages, who comprehend all their movements."

Although the Taos trappers, as they came to be called, ranged north and west, the major activity in the fur business continued to be concentrated on the Missouri River and in Ashley's Rocky Mountain Fur Company. Ashley, however, realized the best opportunities lay in financing the operation, not actually running it. After the rendezvous of 1826, he sold the company to three of his ablest men, Jedediah Smith, David E. Jackson, and William L. Sublette. In this way, he could trim his investment each year to the outlook for the marketplace and rid himself of the responsibility of supervising so many men.

The new partners, unlike Ashley, were field men, not financiers; and their futures lay in the development of larger sources of beaver skins. The partners, therefore, came to the conclusion that while Sublette and Jackson remained close to their present trapping grounds, Smith would explore farther west and perhaps go as far as California.

Moving south and slightly west in what is now Utah, he went into present-day Nevada, passed through the Mojave Desert, and crossed the Colorado River near the site of Needles, California. This route took him over country utterly unlike the territory he had previously explored, much of it desert. His horses and mules gave out, and sometimes he and his followers went days without eating. But at last he reached San Gabriel Mission near the present-day city of Los Angeles.

Founded in 1791—one of the earliest of the California missions—it employed about a thousand Indians to tend its fields and its livestock and perform other duties. Each year it slaughtered two thousand to three thousand head of livestock, selling the hides to the increasing number of foreign ships—many of them American—that now stopped at California ports. Yet the Americans noticed that the Mexicans did not make full use of the rich land that surrounded them.

Nor had they overcome the Spaniards' old suspicion of aliens. Although boats were now allowed to stop at California's ports, the people of San Gabriel wondered whether some nefarious purpose lay behind Smith's visit. They treated him well, but he had to make a trip to San Diego and explain his motives to the governor. Even then several days passed while the governor debated with himself the course of action he should follow. Only after several sea captains joined to attest to Smith's character and the truth of his statements would the governor permit him to return to San Gabriel and start on his way home. Mexico might welcome foreign trade, but there were limits to the government's trust.

Smith went north about three hundred miles and then attempted to cross the Sierra Nevada. The snow had fallen, the mountains were covered with ice, and men and horses were numb with the cold. To make the passage with his entire group seemed out of the question, so Smith left some of them in California. With two men, seven horses, and two mules to carry a supply of hay and food, he started back to Utah.

The snow on the mountains lay four to eight feet deep. It had melted in the sun and packed, so his horses and mules sank into it only a foot or so, and he was able to reach the other side of the range. There he entered country as barren as any he had ever seen. The Indians he met made their meals of seeds and grasshoppers, and for the white men there was little either to eat or drink. Working his way across Nevada, he arrived at Utah's Bear Lake in time for the rendezvous of 1827. The rigors of the journey showed in the state of his livestock. Of the seven horses and two mules with which he had started, only one horse and one mule were left; and these were so weak they could barely carry the scanty supply of equipment still remaining.

The partners were not in the least discouraged by the hardships Smith had undergone and were determined to continue extending their activities in the territory so long dominated by the Hudson's Bay Company. As they discussed their plans, Albert Gallatin, the American ambassador to London, was negotiating the future of the Oregon Territory with the British government. Wisely he realized that to ask for too much was to risk losing everything, for Britain, alarmed by the stand the United States had taken over European interference in the New World, was in no mood to compromise on any issue involving its own position in the Western Hemisphere.

Gallatin, therefore, concentrated on reducing the tensions between the two nations and obtaining an extension of the agreement providing for the joint occupation of the contested area. This was not the compromise most Americans wanted, but Gallatin unknowingly gained for the fur trappers what they needed, time: time to follow the trails taken by the employees of the Hudson's Bay Company, time to pioneer new ones, time to enforce America's claim to the Northwest by the presence of American citizens. Aware only that they were trying to expand their business, Jedediah Smith and his partners had become foremost figures in settling the future of a large part of the continent.

12. Past the Mountain Barrier

The more we became acquainted with the beautiful country around San Francisco, the more . . . it was impossible to resist joining in the remark of Vancouver, "why such an extent of territory should have been subjugated, and . . . turned to no account whatever, is a mystery in the science of state policy not easily explained."

—Frederick W. Beechey, 1827

Jedediah Smith set out again from Utah to California in the middle of July 1827, taking with him eighteen men and two Indian women and safely reached the present site of Needles, California. Lulled into a sense of security by the apparent friendliness of the Indians, he began to cross the Colorado—that barrier to east-west travel that had so concerned Anza. While his party was almost evenly divided by the great river—some on one side and some on the other—the Indians attacked, and more than half the white men fell. The survivors, who were on the west bank, had little time to lose. Scattering their

137

supplies on the ground in the hope the Indians would pause to collect the loot, they started fleeing in the general direction of California. But their ruse did not work. The Indians quickly abandoned the tempting prizes and raced after them.

Since they were still close to the river, Smith and his men dashed to the inadequate cover of a grove of cottonwoods. There they discovered they had salvaged only five guns—five shots to save themselves from the Indians' onslaught before they could reload. For hand-to-hand fighting, they cut cottonwood poles, lashing their knives to the ends and thus improvising crude lances. But their marksmanship alone won them safety. With their five shots, they brought down three Indians—two dead and one wounded. This swift retaliation so discouraged the others they broke off their attack.

Left without horses and almost no supplies, the small band pushed westward toward present-day Los Angeles and then turned north toward the Stanislaus River, which flows out of the Sierra Nevada north of Yosemite Valley. Here the men Smith had left behind the previous season were still encamped and waiting, but the meeting of the two groups was a disillusionment for each: Neither had the supplies for which both were desperate. So Smith immediately went for help to the nearest mission, San José, and once again found himself entangled in the mesh of suspicion and bureaucracy that was the legacy of Spain.

The father who headed the mission accused him of entering the country illegally and took away his horses. Finally Smith secured permission to go to Monterey—under the guard of four soldiers—where he appealed to the governor personally. That official was not pleased to see him, for the Bible-reading trapper presented a problem he did not know how to solve. Sometimes he considered sending him to the higher authorities in Mexico; sometimes he thought of forcing him to leave California by ship to prevent his further exploration of the West Coast. During his vacillations, a number of American captains, whose vessels were anchored in Monterey harbor, entered the negotiations. When one of them agreed to post bond for Smith's good behavior, the governor gave him permission to leave California by land—but as soon as possible.

Rather than make the dreadful trip back across the Sierra Nevadas, Smith decided to go north and explore more of the western country. He therefore instructed his men to meet him at San Francisco. This community was no longer the isolated outpost it had formerly been, but a port of call for many foreign vessels. At one dinner Smith attended, he met six captains whose home ports were in Massachusetts. Also present was Captain Frederick W. Beechey, a famous explorer and a captain in the British navy. Yet the Mexican residents had not changed greatly and were still failing to make effective use of San Francisco's resources. As Beechey reported on his return to England, such neglect of an opportunity was incomprehensible.

Although Smith's party was desperately short of supplies, they were not poverty-stricken, for they had collected approximately fifteen hundred pounds of beaver skins. These he sold for about four thousand dollars, obtaining the money he needed to re-equip his men.

But his wrangles with the Mexican authorities and the purchase of supplies consumed much time. So he did not start his trip home until the middle of December 1827. Struggling through land rarely, if ever, traveled by white men, he moved up the valley of the Sacramento River, past the general location of modern California's capital, toward the mountains that block the way into Oregon. Almost every day presented new obstacles—swamps, cliffs, a bear that mauled one of his men, a mule that kicked Smith himself, canyons and steep ascents. Yet the small party persevered on their route, trapping for beaver as they went and observing the coastal redwoods, the tallest of all trees.

By July 12, 1828, Smith and his party had reached the present-day state of Oregon and, having veered toward the west, were near the Pacific Ocean. A large number of Umpqua Indians had joined them and were proving helpful by selling berries, fish, and beaver skins for trade goods. One of them, however, stole an ax. Smith, determined to stop such thievery before it became rampant, ordered him seized and tied up until he returned the tool.

They were then close to the Willamette Valley and only a short distance from Fort Vancouver, the Hudson's Bay Company's post. But first they had to cross an expanse of marshy land, made even more soggy by a recent thunderstorm. Smith, leaving most of his men in camp, went ahead to explore for the best possible route. When he returned from this brief—and routine—reconnoiter, he found that disaster had struck. The Umpqua Indians, angry over the treatment of the thief or disturbed because a trapper had tried to molest an Indian woman, had attacked the camp during his absence. The bodies of his friends lay on the ground, and his supplies and packs of beaver skins were gone.

Revenge was impossible. So Smith, accompanied by the man who had been with him on his scouting expedition, made his way as quickly as possible to Fort Vancouver. There they found one other survivor, named Arthur Black. He had just finished cleaning and reloading his gun when the Indians rushed the camp. Firing it at them, he ran in the opposite direction and somehow eluded them.

For John McLoughlin, who was in charge of the company's Columbia River operation, the arrival of these refugees presented a problem. By birth a Canadian and by profession a physician, McLoughlin was an enormous man. Unwilling to discard the fashionable clothes he had brought from civilization, he continued to wear them, although they were soon heavily patched. These and his heavy beard, which, one observer said, would have done justice to a grizzly bear, and the many weapons he carried when he was away from the fort gave him an unusual appearance; but he was a man of outstanding intelligence, skillful at dealing with both the Indians and the company's trappers, ruthless as a business competitor, but fully conscious of the responsibilities that devolved on him under the joint occupation agreement and therefore hospitable to Americans.

Smith was naturally anxious for revenge, but McLoughlin's chief trader, Alexander McLeod, was more cautious. He recognized that an attack on one white man was an attack on them all. On the other hand, he doubted that the Hudson's Bay Company had the resources for a prolonged fight with the Umpquas, nor did he think it wise to antagonize Indians with whom the company wanted to continue trading.

But he agreed to let Smith accompany him on a friendly tour of the country south of Fort Vancouver. Moving from band to band—and stopping also to bury the dead at Smith's former camp—McLeod recovered almost forty of Smith's horses, some of his traps, and many of his beaver skins. The effort, according to a Hudson's Bay Company official, cost the company about a thousand pounds, but it demonstrated its adherence to the conditions of the joint occupancy.

Smith, with the driving energy that had carried him so deep into strange territory, was now ready to return to Great Salt Lake. But the Hudson's Bay Company, familiar with the dangers of the western winters, refused to let him depart so late in the year. Instead they offered to buy his skins and to supply him with horses if he would wait until spring. So Christmas, 1828, found Smith still at Fort Vancouver, a captive of the cold and snow and anxiously waiting for the first signs of spring's thaw.

The trappers working out of Taos and Santa Fé were also roaming farther and farther west of the Rockies, following the line of mountains north and pushing toward the Pacific into present-day Arizona, where they trapped along the Gila and even as far as the Colorado. They, too, found themselves in a running battle with the Mexican authorities. The combination of venal officials, the remains of the Spanish bureaucracy, and the vagueness of the laws provided ample opportunities for misunderstandings, if not downright corruption. Ill will grew on both sides, and occasionally the Mexicans called out their troops and the Americans ostentatiously oiled their guns. Two cultures were in conflict: the Americans, brash, independent, and aggressive; the Mexicans, steeped in respect for protocol and rank and uninterested in the laborious and dangerous task of trapping.

In 1827, the year that Jedediah Smith had returned from his first trip to California, James Ohio Pattie joined his father, Sylvester, on a trapping expedition out of New Mexico. Sylvester hoped to find a West Coast port where he could sell his skins, perhaps to an American or British sea captain. This would enable him to make a longer trip, entering country that had not been so heavily trapped, and would also allow him to dispose of his catch without being under the eye of the rapacious New Mexican governor.

During the years since Fray Marcos and Coronado had ventured into the Southwest and Mackenzie had made his daring trip across Canada, the overland routes had become more and more familiar. In fact, only the year before some trappers from New Mexico had made a quick visit to California. But the territory between the Rockies and the ocean was still clouded with mystery.

Pattie followed the Gila River to the Colorado, where the party disagreed and split into two groups. The dissension did not deter Pattie from pursuing his original purpose—to find a western trade outlet. With considerable logic—but little knowledge of geography—he assumed the Mexicans must have had a settlement at the mouth of the Colorado, for he believed such a large river must end in a great harbor. He did not know that the sediment carried by the river had created an enormous delta and a shallow upstream channel, making the site impractical for foreign trade.

When he and his men at last saw the reality that was so far from their imaginings, they felt like animals caught in a net. As James commented later, "The fierce billows [of the Gulf of California] shut us in from below, the river current from above, and murderous savages on either hand on the shore. We had a rich cargo of furs, a little independence for each one of us, could we have disposed of them, as we had hoped, among the Spanish people, whom we had expected to have found here. There were no such settlements. — Every side on which we looked offered an array of danger, famine and death. In this predicament, what were furs to us?"

They had gone too far to return now to New Mexico, so they decided to go back up the river, cache their beaver skins, and, with their loads thus lightened, strike out for the Pacific Coast. Shortly after leaving the Colorado, Pattie wrote, "We began to suffer severely from thirst. The earth, also, was so loose and sandy, that at every step we sank up to our ankles."

Making friends with a band of Indians they met, they obtained two guides. But even then their sufferings did not end. "We . . . hurried on through the drifted sand," Pattie later wrote, "in which we sank up to our ankles at every step." When they tried to rest for a few minutes in the shade of a small tree that somehow had defied the dry land, their Indian guides urged them onward. There was no time to rest if they hoped to get to the next far-distant source of water.

The mountains they finally reached contained water, but their sufferings were not ended. Weakened from their journey, they had difficulty ascending each ridge, and the sharp stones underfoot cut through their thin deerskin moccasins and into their flesh. Yet they finally arrived at Mission Catalina in Baja California, an exhausted band of men.

The Mexican authorities took no pity on them and immediately placed them in jail, feeding them only corn mush. After holding them about a week, the authorities, being unable to decide what to do, sent the entire group under guard to San Diego.

There the governor, José María Echeandía, assumed a hostile view of what he regarded as their trespass. He took away their arms, placed them each in solitary confinement and, although he interrogated them in detail, would not believe their story. Separated from each other and fed only the poorest of food, the men wondered at the fate that had spared them in the desert only to deliver them into a Mexican jail. The cruelest blow came when Sylvester Pattie smuggled word to his son that he was dying. Even in this emergency, the governor would not permit James to see his father.

Yet some Mexicans tried to be kindly to the desperate men. The sergeant who had them in his custody interceded several times on their behalf and did what little he could to ameliorate their treatment; and his sister, whom James described as both beautiful and gracious, came to visit them regularly. She even found a dark suit James could wear to his father's burial.

"A lieutenant conducted the ceremonies," James later recalled, "and when I arrived at the grave he ordered the crowd to give way, that I might see the coffin let down, and the grave filled. . . . I had scarce time to draw a second breath, before the grave was half filled with earth. I was led back to my prison, the young lady walking by my side in tears. I would gladly have found relief for my own oppressed heart in tears, if they would have flowed. But the sources were dried, and tears would not come to my relief."

Meanwhile he was worried about the beaver skins, for the cache in which he had left them would not protect them if the river flooded. He was in the tantalizing position of being a prisoner while he had a small fortune only a relatively short distance away. At last he secured permission from the governor for his men to retrieve them provided he himself remained as a hostage against their return. This was a dangerous commitment to make, for the others, once free, might refuse to return to captivity. Or they might be killed by Indians, since they were almost defenseless. "Their only arms," Pattie commented, "were old Spanish muskets, which, when fired, I would almost as soon have stood before as behind."

Nevertheless they successfully completed the trip; and although two of them did desert and return to New Mexico, the governor overlooked this defection. He remanded the others to jail, however, and once more the Americans resumed their old routine with little hope they could persuade the governor to set them free.

Their salvation came in the form of a smallpox epidemic. This dread disease appeared in Alta California, and the governor was terrified that it would spread to San Diego. In his father's medicine kit, Pattie had some smallpox vaccine, and he used his scanty supply to start bargaining with the governor. Each side had its desires. The governor wanted as many people as possible protected, particularly those who were physically near him. Pattie wanted freedom, not only for himself but also for his entire party.

At this demand, the governor "said he might as well let loose so many wolves to ravage his county," Pattie wrote. Finally they agreed that Pattie would vaccinate the people in San Diego and then go north along the coast, vaccinating both Mexicans and Indians as he went. In return, the governor would give him and his men passports good for one year in California and would pay Pattie for his services.

Then began a remarkable journey through California. Pattie moved from one settlement and mission to another and vaccinated, according to his account, about twenty thousand people, replenishing his stock with pus from those he had already treated.

But when he tried to collect their promised payment from the Mexicans, they offered him, instead of cash, a thousand head of livestock and the land on which to graze them, adding the provision that he must become both a Catholic and a Mexican citizen. These terms were unacceptable to him.

While he was in Monterey trying to negotiate his claim, he saw at firsthand the instability of the government. Joaquín Solís, a former convict who had been sent to California as a settler, led a revolt, which quickly gained the support of the local militia and of the foreign colony, which had grown to almost forty persons, Scotch, Irish, English, Dutch, and Americans. For Solís had spread the word he favored greater privileges for aliens. When he marched against Governor Echeandía, who was then at Santa Barbara, Pattie was ready to join him and have a chance to shoot at his old enemy. But the attitude of the foreigners changed when they learned that Solís was really more interested in suppressing the aliens than in encouraging their activities and they decided to support the existing government.

The bloodless battle that took place at Santa Barbara between Solís and the government forces drew nothing but contempt from Pattie. "A continual firing had been kept up on both sides," he said, "during . . . three days, at the expiration of which Gen. Solís, having expended his ammunition, and consumed his provisions, was compelled to withdraw, having sustained no loss, except that of one horse from a sustained action of three days!"

With Solís's rout, the foreign colony took steps to secure Monterey for the governor, locking up the garrison, seizing their ammunition and arms, helping to capture Solís himself, and hoisting the American flag over Monterey. When Echeandía arrived, they turned the community over to him; and he, in his gratitude, ordered the American flag saluted.

The feelings of amity that now existed between the legitimate government and the aliens did not make Pattie more cordial to Encheandía. The two met, and Pattie was not satisfied with the governor's offer. There were only two things he wanted: payment for his beaver skins and his medical services, and the right to return to the United States.

But payment in cash was out of the question. The governor had no money, nor could he draw on the central government, which was itself in deep trouble. In 1829 the president of Mexico, who had been elected by a single vote, was replaced by a candidate selected by Congress; the Spanish had landed an invasion force of 2,700 men to try to regain their former province; the treasury was empty; and foreign claims against the country had mounted up. In this time of crisis, the central government had little interest in California.

To Pattie, almost nothing was more important than getting away from it. Speaking of the United States, he told the governor, "If I could once more place my foot upon its free soil, and enjoy the priceless blessings of its liberty . . . I should be satisfied." At last he procured his release from the governor and a passport that permitted him to visit Mexico City on his way home. There he claimed reimbursement for his furs, his time spent in what he considered illegal imprisonment, and his medical services, but he received no compensation from the virtually bankrupt government. After he returned to the United States, he wrote, with the assistance of a local minister, an account of his adventures. The resulting book was popular; and although his tale of the hardships he had suffered was not the sort to encourage others to go west, its portrayal of the capricious injustice of Mexican rule and the inefficiency of the Mexican government made an impression on many readers.

Interest in the Far West was not limited to a few adventurers like Pattie and Jedediah Smith or to the diplomats in Washington who were working on the Oregon question. The general public was becoming more and more concerned about those far-distant lands.

One reason was the single-minded obsession of a man in Massachusetts named Hall J. Kelley. A schoolteacher, author of several popular textbooks, and an engineer, Kelley had been fascinated by Lewis and Clark's accounts of the Oregon Territory. Convinced it was rich in resources, he saw it as a place that would support many of the unemployed of the East, and he also believed the Indians would benefit from the introduction of Christianity. What was important was to settle it quickly, for the presence of Americans would resolve the issue of ownership.

In 1828 he wrote a memorial to Congress requesting the government to assist with the founding of a colony on the northwest coast. Although several similar petitions were submitted at the same time, Congress took no action. In 1829 Kelley established a "society for the encouragement of the settlement of Oregon by Americans"; and in the winter of 1830, the year Pattie returned to the United States, he made one of several trips to Washington to arouse concern over the issue he had espoused. In 1830 he also published at Boston *A Geographical Sketch of that Part of North America called Oregon.*

"The local position of that country [the Oregon Territory]; its physical

144

appearance and productions; its qualities of soil and climate, suggest, not only the practicability of founding a colony in it; but the consequent beneficial results to our Republic." So wrote Hall Kelley in his booklet.

He was only one of the growing numbers who foresaw a virtually unlimited future for the United States. They believed without question their country was destined to greatness, both physically and morally, and that the benefits of American government should be extended to other peoples and other areas. Yet in the midst of their optimism, the forces of destruction were eating away at the core of the nation.

The centrifugal forces that threatened to send the sections of the country flying apart had been accelerated by the tariff which the older Southern states found so harmful to their economies. Unable to secure the tariff's repeal in Congress, South Carolina had taken the stand that the acts of the federal government could, if the occasion warranted, be nullified by a single state—a doctrine that effectually proposed the dissolution of the Union when the strains became too great. This view was held not just by a small minority of radicals; it received the support—or at least the serious consideration—of some of the nation's most prominent citizens.

Opposed to them were those who remained the Union's ardent defenders. Ostensibly the Hayne-Webster debate in the Senate turned on the disposition of the public lands, but the underlying question was the stability of the Union. In his response to Hayne, Daniel Webster spoke words that became famous to generations of Americans, for he expressed the thoughts of many of them when he said, "While the Union lasts, we have high, exciting, gratifying prospects spread out before us, for us and for our children. Beyond that I seek not to penetrate the veil."

Upon the supremacy of this view depended the future of the United States, not only in the East, but also west of the Rockies. Smith, Pattie, and other frontiersmen might press into California and the country so long dominated by the Hudson's Bay Company, and men like Hall Kelley might try to encourage the settlement of the lands west of the great mountain ridges, but none of them could conquer the Far West by themselves. Behind them must stand a united nation.

The men who roamed the country west of the Rockies were composed of every type of character and were drawn from many different ranks of society. Some were little more than brutes, who trapped beavers for most of the year, survived in an elemental way, and once a year drank and brawled at the rendezvous. Some, like Jedediah Smith, were God-fearing and never forgot the traditions of their upbringing. Some were braggarts like James Beckworth. Some, like Kit Carson, were taciturn and withdrawing. When, in his old age, Carson wrote his autobiography, it made a smaller volume than most of those written by others describing encounters with him. Some, like Pattie, returned soon to home. Others thirsted after adventure as a drunkard thirsts after liquor, never quite getting their fill until old age tempered their spirits.

It was not merely curiosity that drove them, although they could be curious about the Indians, the condition of Mexico, and sometimes just about what lay beyond the next ridge or the next river. Nor was it money alone that impelled them to travel hundreds of miles over deserts and through mountain ranges. Some of them wanted to become rich, but there were other ways of making a fortune in the young America of the 1830s. What they all had in common was an inability to stay still. They preferred a campfire to a blaze within a cast-iron stove, liked drinking from a spring rather than from a well, and were glad not to sleep in the same bed every night but, with sundown, to cast their blankets into a new niche in the earth.

Individually they did little to change the course of history. Even Smith's dramatic ventures into unknown lands would have been made by someone else if Smith had not been there, and William Wolfskill and George Yount, who explored the Great Basin country and entered California in 1831, were not so much the leaders of destiny but the servants of it. If they had not made their journeys, other men would have done so. Yet taken together, they represented a powerful force for exploration and expansion. Few nations have ever had so many independent spirits carrying its frontier forward in so many directions at once, piercing every nook and corner of a vast strange land, without the benefit of a central organization and making so little demands on the capital resources of the country. In America, this was important. Its financiers or its government would have been hard pressed to raise the funds to do on a formal basis what these men did out of the restlessness of their souls.

But Jedediah Smith was at last growing weary of his incessant travels. Although the fur business continued to be profitable, he decided to leave it in favor of the Santa Fé trade. In 1829 this commerce had received important recognition from the federal government. The presence of the richly laden caravans was a constant temptation to the Indians, who swept down on them in increasing numbers and with ever greater frequency. In response to the traders' pleas for help, the government assigned them an armed escort, under the command of Major Bennet Riley, to convoy them as far as the Mexican border. Of lasting consequence was his use of oxen instead of mules and horses, the traditional draft animals employed until then on the Great Plains.

The choice of oxen had not been Riley's; they had been assigned to him by the War Department to save money. But to the surprise of everyone, they proved adaptable to the rigorous conditions prevailing on the plains. Much cheaper than either mules or horses, they offered other advantages, too. Less temperamental than mules and less skittery than horses, they were far easier to drive. Furthermore, if the supplies they carried were used up on a long journey, the animals could be butchered and eaten. For persons of modest means, they offered a practical form of transportation across the Great Plains.

When Smith entered the Santa Fé trade, the business was flourishing. In 1832, a congressional report said in part, "With all the disadvantages, which have been encountered, this trade has continued to increase steadily for a period of nine years, and the circulating medium of Missouri now consists principally of Mexican dollars."

He did not live long enough, however, to enjoy the profits, for he was shortly afterward killed by Indians. But if he had lived, he might also have taken some satisfaction in knowing that California, which had treated him so poorly, and its governor, Echeandía, had entered a period of chaos and discord.

In 1829 a liberal Mexican party had taken over the central government and had appointed a liberal governor, who was instructed to enforce a new policy in California: the secularization of the missions.

Throughout the years the missions had played an essential role in California's life. They were centers of culture; they kept the Indians in subservience and converted them, not only to Christianity but also into an important pool of labor. They were the chief suppliers of provisions for the presidios and were also the strongholds of California's traditionalism. If they were secularized, their lands would be distributed to laymen—with an obvious struggle to see who would get them—and the structure of California's economy and society disrupted.

The governor whom the new administration chose was fiercely opposed to the missions, but before he could take office, another change occurred in the central government. This time a conservative group gained control, and immediately, a new governor, Manuel Victoria, was appointed.

He arrived just in time to revoke the decree that had already been issued secularizing the missions. At the same time he took steps to repress what he considered the subversive elements in California. This brought about a rebellion, one of its leaders being Echeandía. Forces representing the two sides met near Los Angeles toward the end of 1831. Instead of resulting in a bloodless stalemate, several casualties occurred.

The central government, facing even greater crises near Mexico City—an armed revolt, the defeat of the troops sent to quell it, and soon the resignation of the president—had neither the energy to participate in a California civil war nor the desire to lose its great seacoast province. So it wisely recalled Victoria. This created political problems, for the province became, in effect, divided in two with two separate, temporary governors. But it prevented internal warfare from breaking out or the secession of the province.

Americans had already become contemptuous of Mexico's government, both federal and local. But the United States, brash and cocky in so many ways, was in no position to deride the instability of its neighbor. For its own foundations traversed a fault line whose ominous workings presaged a catastrophe greater than any earthquake.

In 1832, the year after Victoria's battle with the California rebels, the legislature of South Carolina, following the principle it had stated earlier, declared the tariff acts passed by Congress null and void and prohibited the collection of federal duties at South Carolina's ports. If the federal government used force to override the will of the legislature, violence would be met by violence and South Carolina would secede. In his moving defense of the Union, Webster had said, "When my eyes shall be turned to behold for the last time the sun in heaven, may I not see him shining on the broken and dishonored fragments of a once glorious Union; on States dissevered, discordant, belligerent; on a land rent with civil feuds, or drenched, it may be, in fraternal blood!" But the horrible day that Webster dreaded was threatening to come with a burst of gunfire and make the revolutions of Mexico seem trivial.

13. THE TRAILS BECOME BROADER

So far from deriding the disposition to explore unknown regions, we should consider judicious travellers as so many benefactors to mankind.

—John B. Wyeth, 1833

The Union's future was as uncertain as an obscure mountain trail followed by a trapper in a snowstorm, and the abyss was only one misstep away. Many believed the United States might someday bridge the continent and touch both oceans, but the dream was separated from the present by a gap as wide as any canyon to be found in the Rockies.

Even if the Union itself survived the forces that were threatening to blow it apart, its hold on the West Coast was slight. American seamen regularly visited that distant shore, but they were mostly transients whose presence added little to the American claims. Government-sponsored exploration of the West had continued after Lewis and Clark; but the government, bound by diplomatic considerations, could not enforce claims where the title remained with another nation or was in dispute. The trappers, too, had made their contribution. Without expense to the central government, they had unraveled many of the mysteries of the land beyond the Rockies, but their passage left little more impress on the land itself than the wind's.

If the United States hoped to take hold of the transmountain West, it needed to enter yet another stage—when more permanent settlers went west, groups whose stakes went deeper into the land surrounding them and who, once having linked their fortunes to the country, would remain and become a part of it.

This stage of development was just starting when South Carolina thundered its denunciations of the central government. Hall Kelley had failed to secure the support of the government in establishing a settlement in Oregon; but his intense enthusiasm had attracted the attention of a successful Massachusetts merchant, Nathaniel Wyeth. During the winter of 1831–32, Wyeth began enlisting a group of young New Englanders to go west. "The real and avowed object of this hardy-looking enterprise," according to Nathaniel's nephew, John B. Wyeth, "was to go to the river Columbia . . . and there and thereabouts commence a fur trade by trafficking with the Indians, as well as beaver and other hunting by ourselves. We went upon shares . . . and our association was to last during five years."

This arrangement was quite different from those that had prevailed before and was more in the nature of a joint stock company, each member owning an interest in the overall enterprise. It attracted, as Wyeth had hoped, a wide variety of investors, including a physician, a gunsmith, a blacksmith, carpenters, fishermen, farmers, and laborers—not a one of them with any previous experience in the West. This, too, was a marked change. Although tenderfeet had been welcomed on previous trapping expeditions, they had usually been accompanied by experienced men.

Another change was also taking place in the type of person planning to go beyond the Rockies. Many French and Spanish explorers had been missionaries, but religion had not played the same role in the expansion of the United States. About the time South Carolina was assuming its defiant stand, however, the Flathead Indians sent several members of their tribe to St. Louis to interest one of the Protestant sects in establishing a mission in their part of the country. To be successful, both of these trends—one to attract ordinary investors and the other to create missions—required a peaceful, stable nation, not one split by internal warfare. Certainly this consideration did not enter Andrew Jackson's mind when South Carolina presented him with the constitutional crisis, but he moved quickly to preserve the institution he so revered—the Union. His firm action and a conciliatory attitude on the part of both the North and South soon brought about a compromise. Temporary peace having been restored, the nation's westward movement could continue undistracted.

Despite their common interest in Oregon, Hall J. Kelley and Nathaniel Wyeth were not compatible. Kelley was a visionary propagandist; Wyeth, a businessman. In 1832, when Wyeth was ready to lead his company west, Kelley was no longer a member.

At St. Louis, Wyeth began to realize that many of his ideas had been based on fantasies as impractical as Kelley's. In preparation for the journey, he had drilled his men by camping on an island in Boston Harbor. Such an experience had little to do with the world they were now entering. He had dressed them in a semi-uniform of striped cotton shirts, rawhide boots, pantaloons, and woolen jackets. The similarity of their clothing had impressed some observers in the East; in the West, it seemed ridiculous. Three vehicles he had designed to double as boats and wagons proved worthless. Even more important, he had not counted on the high state of development of the fur business. Not a chance existed of picking up an extra dollar or two by trapping during the journey. The existing firms had established near monopolies for many miles around. And he quickly learned that an inexperienced group such as his would have difficulty just crossing the Great Plains.

Adaptable and not afraid to admit his mistakes, Wyeth sold his wagons for much less than they had cost him to build and made arrangements to travel with the Rocky Mountain Fur Company—Ashley's former concern—as far as the annual rendezvous.

The meeting that year was held at Pierre's Hole in the Teton Mountains in eastern Idaho. "This valley," wrote one contemporary, "is . . . from 70 to 80 miles in length, with a high mountain on the east and west. . . . The river runs immediately through the center, with a beautiful grove of timber along the bank; from this timber to the mountain, a distance of four or five miles, there is nothing but a smooth plain."

In this hidden valley—far distant from civilization—the trappers gathered to conduct their annual business. Here they sold the furs they had collected during the past season, purchased the supplies they would need for the next, and settled their accounts with the company. The rendezvous was also their annual vacation. Protected by the sheer number of men who gathered, they could relax and indulge in the violent sports they liked—heavy drinking, fighting, and chasing after the Indian women who were present—while those of more sober taste, like Jedediah Smith, watched from the sidelines.

This year was particularly notable, for as the rendezvous was breaking up, the Blackfeet, the most feared of all the tribes who harassed the trappers, attacked them. "We thought we could rush right on them [the Blackfeet] and drive them out of the brush into the plain and have a decisive battle at once," wrote one of the trappers. "We advanced with all possible speed, and a full determination of success, until we discovered their fort [it was unusual for the Indians to have constructed any sort of defensive position] by receiving a most destructive fire from the enclosure. This throwed our ranks into complete confusion, & we all retreated into the plain."

Fitzpatrick, one of the partners in the Rocky Mountain Fur Company and an old-timer in the mountains, took charge and directed the men to surround the Indians' fort. "A continual fire was kept up," the writer went on, "doing more or less execution until late in the afternoon, when we advanced to close quarters, having nothing but the thickness of their breast work between us, and having them completely surrounded on all sides to prevent any escaping."

Victory was at hand for the trappers when the Indians "commenced the most tremendous yells and shouts of triumph, which seemed to move heaven and earth. Quick as thought a report spread through all quarters, that the plain was covered with Blackfeet Indians coming to reinforce the besieged. So complete was the consternation in our ranks, created by this stratagem, that . . . every man thought only of his own security, and ran for life without ever looking round, which would at once have convinced him of his folly. In a short time it was ascertained that it was only a stratagem, and our men began to collect together. . . . The rage of some was unbounded, and approached to madness." But it was too late to start the advance again, and the Blackfeet slipped away.

The fight, the only major attack on the rendezvous, came to be known as the Battle of Pierre's Hole, and the casualties of the Americans were heavy— some thirty-two dead. To several in Wyeth's company, it proved a final discouragement, and they joined the party taking the furs back from the rendezvous to St. Louis. When he finally reached home, Wyeth's nephew wrote an account of his journey that he hoped would prevent others from trying to make it. "Reader," he said, "the book you have in your hands is . . . written . . . particularly to warn young farmers and mechanics not to leave a certainty for an uncertainty, and straggle away over a sixth part of the globe in search of what they leave behind them at home."

His words made sense, but they did not dispel the vision held by many that Oregon was a land of fertile valleys and of forests rich in furs, where a man, free from the constraints of an older society, could make a fortune. To the ambitious, the adventurous, and the repressed, it continued to hold an appeal that was becoming as strong as that of *el dorado* for the Spanish.

Nor did the Battle of Pierre's Hole deter Nathaniel Wyeth, although approximately half his original party had deserted him. He reached the Hudson's Bay Company's post at Walla Walla in time to prevent starvation from depleting his ranks still further and from there he went in a boat loaned him by the company to Fort Vancouver, where Dr. McLoughlin welcomed the group with his usual friendliness.

Wyeth was much impressed by McLoughlin's extensive operations. In addition to carrying on the fur business, he was raising large quantities of wheat, barley, potatoes, and other staples, feeding sheep, hogs, cows, and horses, and also growing apples, peaches, and grapes. At the same time, some of his men were busy building a seventy-ton schooner.

Wyeth, of course, could not remain indefinitely as McLoughlin's guest. At the same time, he began to recognize the futility of his original plan. The men still with him were far too few to conduct a business in that far-off land, and most of them were already asking him to be released from their contracts. "In a word," wrote Washington Irving, the contemporary chronicler of the American fur trade, "his expedition proved a failure. He lost everything invested in it, but his hopes. These were as strong as ever. He took note of everything, therefore, that could be of service to him in the further prosecution of his project; collected all the information within his reach, and then set off, accompanied by merely two men, on his return journey across the continent. . . . in full confidence of being able to form a company for the salmon fishery and fur trade of the Columbia."

Wyeth's optimism contrasted strongly with the disillusion of his nephew, but it was shared by others. Captain Benjamin Bonneville, an officer in the army, was so impressed by the possibilities in the fur trade that he secured a leave of absence to engage in it. A man of considerable charm and good connections, he was able to raise enough capital to form a sizeable expedition. Like Wyeth, he quickly discovered that the trans-Rocky Mountain West only surrendered its treasures to patience and experience and that a young army officer could not necessarily succeed in the business. But he took wagons across South Pass—thus opening up the possibility of improved transportation across the continent—and his men, like those of Jedediah Smith, wandered into many isolated places, making the natural routes of the Far West better and better known.

Kelley's spirits, too, remained undashed. Abandoned, as he felt, by Wyeth, he left New York in 1832 to go to the West Coast by way of Mexico. After a short stay in Washington, where he again vainly tried to interest the federal government in his enterprise, he continued to be haunted by trouble. Before he left the United States, his own followers stole some of his supplies; he lost more on the ship to Mexico; the customs officials there levied heavy duties against him; and he did not reach Mexico City until the middle of the following year. From there, he went to the coast, crossed over to Baja California, and on to San Diego, enduring many hardships and not arriving in Alta California until April 1834.

When at last he reached Monterey, he brashly asked the governor for permission to explore the country and, of course, was refused. Frustrated in every desire, Kelley joined Ewing Young, an experienced frontiersman, who was going to Fort Vancouver to sell some horses.

His entry into Oregon was not as grand as he had hoped it would be. He caught malaria (a Hudson's Bay Company official, whom he encountered, treated him and arranged to have him taken part of the way by canoe), but his quota of misfortunes seemed inexhaustible. Dr. McLoughlin, usually so friendly, regarded him with deep suspicion, for the governor of California had sent word ahead that some of the horses the Americans were bringing had been stolen. Thus Kelley found himself a pariah and assigned to live in a small building at a distance from the center of activities.

It was now October 1834. While Kelley had been following his long and roundabout route to his promised land, he had not been alone in his interest in the West Coast. Joseph Walker, one of Bonneville's trappers, made the overland journey to California, and some of his men remained behind when he left; Thomas Oliver Larkin, like Wyeth, a native of Massachusetts, moved to California and established a flourishing retail business, and a widow whom he met on the voyage to California and subsequently married became the first American woman to reside in California; and Nathaniel Wyeth's hope to finance another expedition to Oregon had been realized. For an agreement he had secured from the Rocky Mountain Fur Company to supply some of the goods needed at the next rendezvous assured the investors of at least a partial return on their outlay.

Nor had the Flathead Indians' plea for a mission passed unnoticed. The Methodists asked Jason Lee, a man with previous missionary expeience, to answer the call and assigned his nephew, Daniel Lee, to help him. Since missions require capital, too, Lee went on a fund-raising tour, during the course of which he made Wyeth's acquaintance and accepted the fur trader's offer of assistance. The combination of commerce and religion brought the apparent potentials of Oregon to an even wider audience, probably a larger one than Kelley could have ever reached.

In April 1834, or about the time that Kelley had arrived at San Diego, Wyeth was in Independence, Missouri, and had made arrangements to travel with the Rocky Mountain Fur Company's supply train to the rendezvous. He had also extended the protection of his own group to both the Lees and to Thomas Nutall, a distinguished young botanist who had already studied the flora of the Missouri, and John K. Townsend, an ornithologist. The presence of these professional scientists reflected another aspect of the nation's broadening interest in the Far West.

As they moved across the Great Plains, their days were much like those of other travelers, sometimes pleasant, sometimes filled with hardship and discomfort, and often mundane and unchallenging. But when they arrived at the rendezvous, Wyeth received a shock. The Rocky Mountain Fur Company refused to honor its contract to purchase from him the goods it had ordered the year before.

No court existed to which he could make an appeal, and he could not dispose of the goods himself in competition with the powerful company. Helpless to right the wrong done to him, he accepted the injury with grace, merely noting the episode in one sentence in his journal.

Continuing toward Oregon, he stopped on the Snake River and erected a trading post, stocking it with the goods that were now surplus. The fort, which he named Hall after his oldest investor, took two weeks to build, and he left twelve men in charge. Although this was not in his original plan, he saw it as a means of selling the supplies the Rocky Mountain Fur Company had refused to buy.

In spite of the hardships of the journey to Fort Vancouver, the young and physicially fit quickly adjusted to them. "We have passed for months," Townsend remarked in his journal, "through a country swarming with Indians who thirsted for our blood, and whose greatest pride and glory consisted in securing the scalp of a white man. . . . To those who have always enjoyed the comforts and security of civilized life, it may seem strange that persons who know themselves to be constantly exposed to such dangers . . . should yet sleep soundly and refreshingly, and feel themselves at ease; such however is the fact. . . . I never in my life enjoyed rest more than when travelling through the country of which I speak."

Wyeth, for all his ability and determination, had placed himself in a position that offered him only the slightest chance for success. Two companies dominated the field—companies strong in personnel, experience, and financial resources—and both were determined to make every penny they could, ruthlessly and quickly. For the Hudson's Bay people realized that the settlement of the Oregon question would force them to withdraw from much of the country in which they now trapped, and therefore they might as well take quickly every pelt they could. Understanding this, the Americans knew that every skin they missed would go to the British. This intense competition was taking place when new manufactured products were depressing the market for furs, thus making it even more difficult for a newcomer like Wyeth.

Nevertheless he attempted to establish a rival post about eight miles from Fort Vancouver, importing livestock from California and the Hawaiian Islands and planting crops of wheat, corn, potatoes, beans, and other staples. Emulating McLoughlin, he hoped to make it self-sufficient. But he could not overcome the difficulties that beset him. In 1835 he moved back to Fort Hall and spent part of the following year there. By then he had to admit to himself he was not succeeding. He made one more journey back to the Columbia and then returned to Fort Hall and from there to the East by way of Taos.

Before the end of the year, the failure of several European banks was among the omens that ushered in the Panic of 1837. In later years, Wyeth commented, "The commercial distress of that time precluded the further prosecution of our enterprise, that had so far yielded little but misfortunes. It remained only to close out the active business." By selling his two posts and liquidating his other assets, Wyeth was able to pay off his debts and turn to other forms of business.

Kelley arrived back in the East in September 1836, or about the same time as Wyeth. He had helped publicize Oregon, but the members of Congress, whom he repeatedly petitioned, did not think his role in the eventual

155

acquisition of the territory sufficiently great to merit a reward. Increasingly unwelcome as a supplicant, he spent the remainder of his life trying to persuade them otherwise.

Three men, each representing an entirely different point of view, had gone west; and two of them had failed completely. Kelley, the promoter, had shattered himself in his search for notoriety and financial success. He had been too early, for the nation was not ready for the mass movement he had been ready to stimulate. Wyeth, the man of commercial enterprise, had been too late. The year after he made his first trip west, John Jacob Astor, shrewdest of all American fur dealers, realized the best days of the business were coming to a close, sold out, and began concentrating his investments in New York real estate.

Of the three men, Jason Lee alone went at the right time. For if the day of the trapper was drawing to a close and that of the settler not yet come, the missionary's moment had arrived. In a land in which an isolated settler could not survive, a mission—with its outside support—could. Thus Lee, like the Spanish missionaries, served as a precursor of those to follow.

When he reached Fort Vancouver, he was glad to find the ship bringing him additional supplies arriving at almost the same time, thus he was well equipped for the adventure he was undertaking. Originally he had planned to work among the Flatheads and Nez Percés, but he followed McLoughlin's advice and decided to establish his mission about sixty miles up the rich Willamette Valley and by the end of October was ready to move into the log structure he had erected.

Catholicism had been the predominant Christian sect on the West Coast, brought along passively by the French-Canadians, who did not build missions, and actively by the Spanish, who did. But like the fur business, it was on the wane and losing influence. Richard H. Dana, Jr., who later became a prominent Boston lawyer, arrived in California on the journey he was to make famous in *Two Years Before the Mast*. Describing the situation, he said,

Ever since the independence of Mexico, the missions had been going down; until, at last a law was passed, stripping them of all their possessions, and confining the priests to their spiritual duties, at the same time declaring all the Indians free and independent *Rancheros*. The change in the condition of the Indians was, as may be supposed, only nominal; they are virtually serfs, as much as they ever were. But in the missions the change was complete. The priests now have no power, except in their religious character, and the great possessions of the missions are given over to be preyed upon by the harpies of the civil power . . . who usually end, in a few years, by making themselves fortunes, and leaving their stewardships worse than they found

156

them. . . . Trade was much diminished, credit impaired, and the venerable missions were going rapidly to decay.

One immediate economic effect was an increase in the number of hides available for export. The priests, knowing they would lose their missions, attempted to salvage as much of their wealth as possible for the Church. This could best be done by immediately slaughtering the herds of cattle and collecting cash for their skins. Around some missions the bodies of dead cattle stank unpleasantly in the California sun, the missionaries having too little time to bury the skinned corpses or drag them away.

Yet the secularization of the missions did not effect any fundamental improvements. Dana noted the continuing venality of the government officials, the instability of the administration, and the uncertainty of justice and joined the many others who had commented on the inability of the Mexicans to take advantage of the blessings the land offered them. "Such are the people," he concluded, "who inhabit a country embracing four or five hundred miles of seacoast, with several good harbors; with fine forests in the north; the waters filled with fish, and the plains covered with thousands of herds of cattle; blessed with a climate than which there can be no better in the world; free from all manner of diseases, whether epidemic or endemic; and with a soil in which corn yields seventy to eighty fold. In the hands of an enterprising people, what a country this might be!"

Contrasted to the Mexicans' attitude toward California was the Americans' vigorous interest in Oregon. Samuel Parker, minister of the Congregational Church at Middlefield, Massachusetts, had also been attracted by the Indians' plea for Protestant missions. The American Board of Commissioners for the Foreign Missions, representing both the Congregationalists and the Presbyterians, did not welcome his offer to serve as a missionary. His age—fifty-four—was against him, and they hesitated to move into a field in which the Methodists were already pioneering. But they finally yielded to his importunings, gave him the appointment, and permitted him to employ a physician, Dr. Marcus Whitman, as his second in command.

Outwardly the two men were extreme opposites, Whitman, robust, an extrovert, and quickly assuming the dress of a frontiersman; Parker, aloof, wearing a white stock and tall hat, and almost a prude in his conversation. Yet the two men had many qualities in common. Both were enthusiastic about their new assignment and excited about the country. They also shared the animosity of the trappers toward them, an animosity based on their strict observance of the Sabbath and their intolerance of drinking. They earned respect as frontiersmen, however, when they stopped at a post that was stricken by cholera. Whitman's ceaseless efforts were relatively successful in controlling the disease.

Although the two missionaries marveled at the land through which they

157

passed, the trip to the rendezvous—once so adventurous—had now become almost routine. The party stopped for a short rest at Fort Laramie, the new post constructed by fur trappers on the Laramie River in Wyoming, and then continued on to the rendezvous, which was held near Hams Fork in southwestern Wyoming.

Many of the trappers had not seen a doctor for years, and Whitman found himself busy. James Bridger, one of Ashley's first employees, had been carrying an Indian arrowhead in his back for three years. The operation was complicated by the distorted shape of the arrowhead, but Whitman successfully removed it. This encouraged another trapper to ask him to cut out an arrowhead embedded in his shoulder. Soon numerous others were requesting similar medical assistance.

Parker was appalled at the brutality of the trappers. Kit Carson, for example, accepted a duel-to-the-death challenge from a drunken bully. (He quickly secured the advantage and spared the bully's life.) On the other hand, Parker had a chance to talk to the Nez Percés and Flatheads who were gathered there. "The oldest chief arose," Parker noted, "and said he was old and did not expect to know much more . . . but his heart was made glad, very glad, to see what he had never seen before . . . a minister of the Gospel." The Indians' friendly reception made the two missionaries confident their assignment was practical, so Whitman returned home to recruit more help while Parker continued west.

As he retraced his steps, Whitman's thoughts were not wholly occupied with mission business, for he was engaged to Narcissa Prentiss, a young woman whose fervor suited her for a missionary's wife although her sheltered upbringing did not. Whitman's trip beyond South Pass had convinced him that a woman could make the journey to the West Coast. Her family did not object to the hazardous life he offered her, but they questioned the propriety of her traveling with Whitman's new recruit, the Reverend Henry H. Spalding, for he had once been her suitor. Spalding, however, was bringing his wife, Eliza, and since Narcissa would also be under the protection of her husband, they at last set aside their misgivings.

The two women, Narcissa and Eliza, were the first to cross the continent above the Gulf of Mexico; and the trip, as would be expected, was difficult for them. The sun poured down with blazing light; the dust swirled around them, seeping into their clothes and bedding and hair; the wind blew constantly and steadily, setting their nerves on edge with its monotonous moaning. At Fort Laramie they paused for rest, and the fort seemed to them miraculously civilized after their days crossing the plains. At Fort Hall, the post that Wyeth had built on the Snake River, Narcissa could not help observing that the small vegetable garden looked scrawny and unkempt, quite unlike the prosperous gardens she had known at home.

Yet she tried not to despair or complain, although in the journal she kept for her family she advised her sisters to appreciate the simple luxuries surrounding them—luxuries like freshly baked bread. Even the driest crust, she said, was worth savoring. Whitman himself had made the common mistake of trying to carry too much luggage. On leaving Missouri, each irreplaceable object brought from home seemed invaluable, but as the long weeks passed, the weight became insufferable. Oxen and men were weary, and every article that had to be loaded, unloaded, ferried across a river, or pulled up a steep grade became like the stone of Sisyphus. As other travelers did, Whitman soon wondered at the miscellany of belongings he was laboring to take to Oregon and began to discard the less necessary. Even his wagon seemed more than he could take across the continent, and he resolved to abandon it, salvaging only the wheels, which would be difficult to replace. Narcissa had with her a small trunk filled with personal items from home; and the condemnation of the wagon meant the trunk must go, too. The thought of being separated from these reminders of her life at home was almost more than the young bride could bear. A Hudson's Bay Company man with whom they were traveling noticed her distress and offered to carry it for her, and her gratitude was great.

John Townsend, the ornithologist who had accompanied Wyeth, was at Walla Walla when Whitman and his party reached the fort. "Doctor Whitman," he noted in his journal, "presented me with a large pacquet of letters from my beloved friends at home. I need not speak of the emotions excited by their reception, nor of the trembling anxiety with which I tore open the first envelope and devoured the contents. This is the first intelligence which I have received from them."

Once he had read his correspondence, Townsend took time to observe the new emigrants. "They appear admirably qualified," he noted, "their minds being fully alive to the mortifications and trials incident to a residence among wild Indians; but they do not shrink from the task, believing it to be their religious duty to engage in this work. The ladies," he added, "have borne the journey astonishingly; they look robust and healthy."

But the trip left Narcissa weary, although her spirits remained high. At Fort Vancouver, she immediately began to think of ways she could make her life in the wilderness more civilized. The bunks at the trading post were covered with Indian blankets, but a few had mattresses stuffed with the feathers of game fowl. Those were the kind she intended to have in her new home. The floors, she remarked, were rather dirty, because they were swept only with hemlock boughs. So in her first letter home she asked her family to send her some broom corn seed. (Letters between East and West were generally carried by visiting ships.) She also wanted them to send her some fruit tree seeds. Narcissa was a woman who was determined never to leave her past ways behind her.

The Northwest had changed greatly between the time that Lewis and Clark had come down the Columbia to spend the winter on the edge of the continent and the arrival of the Whitmans and Spaldings. The mists still floated in from the ocean, bringing the dampness that added to the land's fertility; the waves stormed against the shore, striking the rocks and breaking into foam as they crossed the shoals at the entrance to the Columbia; the sea otters, although in smaller numbers, swam among the kelp beds; and deer and beaver still fed along the inland streams. But the mystery was gone. Many valleys and mountain crests remained untouched by the feet of white men, but the unexplored areas were becoming fewer and smaller. The trappers, both American and British, had spread into the remote corners of the wilderness in their frantic search for furs. Except at their forts, where they attempted to make themselves semi-independent of the outside world, they left the soil untilled, the grass ungrazed. For they were nomads whose travels were dictated by the presence of the fur-bearing animals they sought.

Now, however, there were missions directed by men who were intent on remaining. Jason Lee was well established near the present-day city of Salem, Oregon. Whitman started his mission at Waiilatpu, a few miles from Walla Walla, and administered to the Cayuse Indians. And Henry Spalding moved up the Clearwater among the Nez Percés, choosing a place the Indians called Lapwai. White men—and white women—had arrived to become part of the land, not merely to trap and leave, but to plant and stay. And to the south, where the Mexicans had inherited the lands the Spaniards had conquered, new forces were also gathering, forces as potentially violent and dangerous as the San Andreas fault or the volcano that formed Crater Lake. In 1836 those forces were growing in intensity.

14. THE MISSIONARIES COME

Between the laughing and the crying,
The living and the dying,
The singing and the sighing,
The wheels roll west.

— Trail Song, *c.* 1844

As the Americans moved westward, strengthening their slight claim to part of the land west of the Rockies, the Mexicans were facing many problems in their northern provinces. Texas (then a part of Coahuila) simmered with unrest. By 1836, the Americans, whose immigration Mexico had encouraged, greatly outnumbered the native population, but they had never been assimilated. Instead of taking conciliatory steps, Santa Ana, the corrupt politician and general who was then Mexico's president, personally led a punitive expedition against them. After the bloody battle at the Alamo, the Texans defeated him at San Jacinto and forced him to recognize their independence.

California, too, was restive under Santa Ana. Although its people were predominantly Mexican, they were weary of receiving dictates and officials

161

from Mexico City. When Santa Ana's administration sent them a governor who insisted on enforcing the regulations of the central government, they expelled him. A young Californian, Juan Bautista Alvarado, became the leader of the rebellious portion of the population, seized control of Monterey, and sent most of the officials home. On November 7, 1836, only a few months after Texas had done so, California declared its independence: and Alvarado became its head.

A year earlier the Mexican Congress had proclaimed Los Angeles the capital of the state, but Alvarado preferred Monterey. As a concession to southern California, however, he made Los Angeles a second, subsidiary capital with a local governor to whom he gave considerable power.

California was still so inaccessible that sending troops would raise major logistical problems; it had no aggressive neighbors, and the population, unlike the Texans, was largely Mexican and generally sympathetic to Mexico. So the government ignored the revolt, confirmed Alvarado as governor, and thus without bloodshed or expending a single bullet brought California back under the Mexican flag.

The area's position, however, remained precarious. Alexander Forbes, an Englishman who made a study of both Baja and Alta California, remarked of the latter, "The want of frequent communications with Mexico renders it quite uncertain what may be at present [June 1838] the state of the country; but it is, at least evident, evident now, if there was any doubt formerly, that it is at this moment in a state which cannot prevent its being taken possession of by any foreign force which may present itself."

After discussing the fears of the British government that Russia might move down the coast, Forbes pointed out that "the danger does not lie there. There is another restless and enterprising neighbor from whom they will soon most probably have to defend themselves. . . . The northern American tide of population [the United States] must roll on southward, and overwhelm . . . California."

He saw, however, one other possibility. Mexico had been plunging deeper and deeper into debt, relying on British loans to balance its budget. "There have been some thoughts," Forbes continued, "of proposing to the Mexican government that it should endeavor to cancel the English debt—which now exceeds fifty millions of dollars—by a transfer of California to the creditors." In Forbes's opinion, California was a ripe plum, ready for the picking.

Although New Mexico remained loyal to the central government, its economy received a severe blow. Among its few profitable enterprises were the copper mines at Santa Rita del Cobre, located southwest of Santa Fé. Although isolated from the few troops stationed at more populous centers, the community had reached an informal agreement with the Apaches that roamed the area, whose local leader, Juan José, left the small settlement untouched in return for presents of horses, bolts of cloth, and other articles

162

that his people liked. The Mexicans also tacitly agreed not to expand their activities beyond mining the copper. Therefore they had no farms, ranches, or small industries that would have made them self-supporting and were entirely dependent on the *conducta,* or wagon train, that came regularly from Chihuahua.

The first move that upset the delicate balance between the Apaches and Santa Rita del Cobre came from the government of Sonora. In 1835 it placed a bounty on the scalp of any Apache, hostile or friendly, warrior, woman, or child. The measure was taken in response to the Apaches' continual attacks throughout the area, but the events it touched off soon embroiled Santa Rita del Cobre far to the northeast. For the government of Chihuahua followed suit, and Juan José and his followers were immediately worth a hundred pesos each—if they were dead. (Women and children commanded a lesser price.) The temptation to collect the bounty was great.

A trapper and trader, James Johnson, knew Juan José—he had encountered the Apache while trapping on the Gila River—and thought he could easily lure the Indians into a trap and translate their deaths into Mexican currency. Some of the people of Santa Rita del Cobre, blind to the potential consequences of their evil act, were willing to help him; and together they invited Juan José to a party at which they promised to serve plenty to eat and drink and to give out presents.

Near the meeting place, Johnson hid a howitzer; and as soon as the unsuspecting Apaches became relaxed and careless, he ordered it fired into their midst. At the same time the white men grabbed their guns and began shooting. Juan José was wounded, but not mortally, and fell to the ground, grappling with his nearest adversary. Even then he did not comprehend the treachery that surrounded him and trustingly called to Johnson for help. Johnson put another bullet into him.

When the fight was over, Johnson and his fellow conspirators enjoyed their moment of triumph. Gleefully they removed the grizzly bits of human skin and hair. All they now had to do was present the scalps to the authorities and collect their money—a sizable sum for such a brief day's work.

Mangas Colorados, a brilliant Apache leader, had been one of the few to escape; and to him fell the leadership of the bands. In the past he had opposed the policy of Juan José. Now in view of Johnson's treachery, his opinions prevailed, and the Apaches were ready to break the fragile truce they had made.

Their method of warfare precluded a mass assault on Santa Rita del Cobre, and they relied instead on grinding up their enemies piece by piece. The first to suffer their vengeance was a party of fifteen trappers on the Gila River. The Apaches left them dead and then attacked another band of three white men.

These swift and deadly raids did not divert them from their principal goal: revenge on Santa Rita del Cobre. To all outward appearances, nothing had changed at the mining community except that occasional Apache visitors no longer walked its streets. But when the date arrived for the *conducta* to roll across the plains below the settlement, leaving a trail of desert dust hanging in the air, nothing appeared. The great space extending to the south remained empty without a trace of human activity in its vast solitude. Day after day drifted by; the community's supplies dwindled; the faces of its inhabitants showed their growing concern; and the eyes of the lookouts were weary and strained. Slowly Santa Rita del Cobre realized that the *conducta* was not coming; the Apaches had destroyed it; and the community was cut off from the goods it needed for survival.

Some argued that a small force should be sent to Chihuahua to spread the alarm and secure reinforcements. Others feared that by dividing their forces, they would invite destruction. At last they all agreed to abandon their town and seek safety together farther south. After loading every available wagon with their belongings, the men oiled their guns, and the procession started on its way.

The Apaches knew little of siege warfare, but they were experts at attacking a moving body. Again and again they struck the caravan, cutting off stragglers, capturing or killing horses and mules, and shooting the men who rode as guards. For the Mexicans the journey became a voyage into death. The greedy men who had condoned Johnson's slaughter of Juan José were being repaid, not with Mexican pesos but Apache bullets and arrows. Of the hundreds of men, women, and children who had left Santa Rita del Cobre, only a few survived. But Mexico had lost even more than a community and a profitable enterprise; it had also lost the peace it had made with some of the Apache bands.

As if all this was not a sufficient burden for the struggling republic to bear, it had not gained international respect; and Europe thought it could bully it. When Mexico refused to pay excessive reparations to France for damage resulting from some riots years earlier, the French navy blockaded Veracruz in 1838 and bombarded it. Santa Ana, who had been thrown out of the government after San Jacinto, rushed to the city's defense, but fled in his underwear when a French landing party moved toward the building in which he was staying. Subsequently a cannonball shattered his right leg below the knee. Although his participation in the engagement had accomplished little— the fleet sailed away only after the government agreed to make the demanded payments—the reputation of Santa Ana was restored. In fact, he later ordered his amputated leg disinterred and reburied—with military honors—at Mexico City. But the episode clearly demonstrated that Mexico could not resist the strong-arm tactics of a foreign power.

Canada, the other neighbor of the United States, was also having problems. Earlier the British had divided it into two provinces, Upper and Lower Canada, the one predominantly British, the other largely French. In 1837 rebellion broke out in both. The French-Canadians unsuccessfully took up arms against British domination; and the Canadians of English descent rebelled against the controls that prevented them from playing a greater part in their own government. For the moment at least, Canada was too preoccupied with its internal affairs to concentrate on external expansion.

The United States was not immune to the gray malaise that seemed to be sweeping North America. "The depression which prevailed from 1837 to 1843," wrote Hugh McCullogh, earlier a banker and later secretary of the treasury, "cannot be understood by any who did not witness it. It was widespread and all-pervading. It affected all classes."

On the frontier, one of the victims was the fur business. Changing techniques in the manufacture of hats—beaver had once been the prime material—coupled with a belief that cholera might be spread by furs had already depressed the market for pelts. The lean years following the Panic of 1837 finally ended the trade as a major part of the nation's economy.

The government, having first undertaken the expense of exploring the West, had long let the major burden fall on the shoulders of the fur trappers, and they had carried it nobly. But by 1837 their days of aggressive exploration were over. With a weakened Mexico to the south and a divided Canada to the north, the United States had an unusual opportunity to penetrate the lands west of the Rockies, but it must find a new means of doing so.

Four forces were replacing the fur trade in keeping alive the Americans' interest in the Far West: patriotism, agriculture, general commerce, and religion. Patriotism made them unwilling to relinquish the claims they had already established; and to find out what was at stake, Congress authorized a naval purser, William A. Slacum, to visit the Oregon Territory and report his findings.

"I consider the Willhamett [Willamette] as the finest grazing country in the world," he said. "Here there are no droughts, as on the Pampas of Buenos Ayres, or the plains of California, while the lands abound with richer grasses, both in winter and summer. . . . The river called 'Rougues' [the Rogue River in southern Oregon] abounds with the finest timber west of the Rocky mountains; and it may be fairly estimated that the valleys of the rivers certainly within the limits of the United States [that is, south of the Columbia] contain at least 14,000,000 of acres of land of first quality, equal to the best lands of Missouri or Illinois."

To a New England farmer, looking at his rock-filled hills, or one from the South whose land had been worn out by raising tobacco, those words told of an Eden. ". . . the finest grazing country in the world . . . no droughts . . . the finest timber . . . acres of land of first quality." The United States was still an agricultural nation and Slacum's report, bearing the official endorsement of the government, stirred the hearts of patriots and husbandmen alike.

Commerce, too, was looking west. John Marsh had had an eccentric career even for a Harvard graduate. He had married an Indian woman, sold guns to her friends and relatives, and had been forced to flee a federal warrant for his arrest. His wanderings took him to California, where he presented his Harvard bachelor's diploma as evidence he was a physician. Soon he had built up a lucrative practice—he accepted his fees in cowhides—established a ranch, and became a successful businessman. To enhance his own prosperity, he encouraged emigration from the United States.

While Marsh was tight-fisted, John Sutter, another new arrival, was open-handed and expansive. A Swiss who had been forced to leave his native land because of unpaid debts, Sutter in 1839 brought to California the type of energy so lacking among the Mexicans. With hard work, a willingness to take chances, and an astute sense of opportunity, Sutter soon developed an enormous and prosperous ranch in the Sacramento Valley on California's frontier. Although temperamentally so different, both he and Marsh shared a common interest in encouraging American emigration as a means of stimulating their own businesses.

To the forces of business, patriotism, and agriculture was added religion. Although Americans had never been a particularly evangelical people, they had not lost sight of the missionaries whom they had sent to the frontier.

When Jason Lee returned to the East in 1838, he found considerable interest in his work and toured more than eighty cities, raising money and enlisting recruits. Approximately fifty persons, including ministers, a physician, and several craftsmen, met at New York in October 1839 to board the ship Lee had chartered to carry them to the West.

Until now the Roman Catholic Church, although it had led the French and Spanish banners into many faraway places, had played little part in extending the frontier of western America: but there now came on the scene a remarkable Jesuit, Pierre-Jean de Smet. A Belgian by birth, he had been educated at a seminary near St. Louis and had served as a missionary among some of the more eastern Indians. Possessed of a strong physique, a love of adventure, and endless enthusiasm, he welcomed any assignment that would carry him into the wilderness. Gladly he undertook to visit the northwestern Indians and determine the feasibility of establishing Catholic missions among them.

In 1840 he joined the caravan of the American Fur Company to the annual rendezvous, the last that was to be held. There he met a deputation from the Flathead and Pend d'Oreille Indians, who guided him to Pierre's Hole, where their tribes had concentrated.

Catholicism's mystic ritualism and de Smet's enthusiasm, combined with his shrewd understanding of primitive minds, made his visit immediately successful. When he rang his small hand bell to call the Indians together, they came running, and those who were sick asked their friends to carry them.

166

"This zeal for prayer and instruction (and I preached to them regularly four times a day)," de Smet wrote, "instead of declining, increased up to the time of my departure. . . . The day after my arrival among them, I had nothing more urgent to do than to translate the prayers into their language, with the aid of a good interpreter. Fifteen days later, at instructions, I promised a medal to the first who should be able to recite without a mistake the *Pater*, the *Ave*, the *Credo*, the ten commandments of God and the four acts. A chief rose: 'Father,' he said, 'your medal belongs to me.' And to my great surprise, he recited all these prayers without missing a word . . ."

During his relatively brief stay with the Flatheads and the Pend d'Oreilles, de Smet baptized nearly six hundred persons. Many of the others, he wrote, "ardently desired to obtain the same favors . . . but since the absence of missionaries could only be momentary I thought it prudent to put them off until the following year, to give them a high idea of the dignity of the sacrament."

As the year 1840 opened and these new forces gathered strength in the United States, the Mexicans retained title to an area of extraordinary contrasts: expanses of desert almost barren of trees except for cottonwoods and mesquite; snow-covered mountains with primeval forests; the arid basin that reached from the southern deserts to more northern and colder climates; and the rich, well-soaked country of parts of coastal California. Yet over this entire region, the Mexicans exerted only the control of a weak and worn-out system of government, enmeshed in the privileges and traditions of the past and unable to look to the future.

Neither had the British adapted to the changing times. Dr. McLoughlin still presided over their interests at Fort Vancouver with nominal sway over the rain forests of the seacoast, the deep canyons of the Columbia River and its tributaries, and the strange lava region of the Columbia Plateau. But for all his vigor and energy, the doctor was letting time slip by him. Although he encouraged retired employees of the Hudson's Bay Company to start farms in the region he controlled, his principal reliance was still on the vanishing fur trade.

The Russians had decided to give up. Preoccupied by events elsewhere and constantly foiled by the problem of supplying their North American posts, they sold their California fort to John Sutter and quietly retreated to the north. Whatever dreams they had had of expanding down the coast were now surrendered to the demands of reality.

On the other hand, wanting to encourage more American settlers, both John Marsh and a former trapper, Antoine Ribidoux, had sent east glowing accounts of life in California. And Slacum's report on Oregon was still widely read. By the time de Smet was ready to go west again, he found approximately sixty men, women, and children gathered at Sapling Grove,

Missouri—"some for health," as de Smet later reported, "others for science or pleasure; but the greater number to seek their fortune in the too highly boasted land of California."

His appearance was a godsend. As one of the emigrants, John Bidwell, commented later, "In five days after our arrival we were ready to start, but no one knew where to go, not even the captain. Finally a man came up, one of the last to arrive, and announced that a company of Catholic missionaries were on their way from St. Louis to the Flathead nation of Indians with an old Rocky Mountaineer for a guide, and that if we would wait another day they would be up with us. At first we were independent, and thought we could not afford to wait for a slow missionary party. But when we found that no one knew which way to go, we sobered down and waited for them to come up; and it was well that we did, for probably not one of us would have ever reached California, because of our inexperience."

Instead of outpacing de Smet's party, some of the emigrants had difficulty keeping up with the fast-moving priest. As a guide, he had employed Thomas Fitzpatrick, the former fur trapper, and both men knew the need for speed in order to beat the winter. Fortunately for their own safety, the emigrants began to realize how dependent they were on the more experienced men. In fact, when they reached Soda Springs, Idaho (in the southeastern corner of the present state), about half of the emigrants abandoned their intention of going to California and stayed with Fitzpatrick and de Smet. As for the others, "We were now thrown entirely upon our own resources," Bitwell later commented. "All the country beyond was to us a veritable *terra incognita,* and we only knew that California lay to the west."

With the few facts Fitzpatrick could tell them and some information they picked up at Fort Hall, they set out on the southern route across Utah toward the formidable barrier of the Sierra Nevada. In afteryears, Bidwell could still vividly recall the journey—the bitter, nauseating water they drank from the Humboldt Sink, the narrow distance by which they missed the rich meadows that would have revived their livestock, the dwindling number of oxen on whom they were dependent for food, the short tempers, and the growing dissension.

Before they reached the Sierras, John Bartleson, who had insisted upon being elected captain, decided to take a few chosen companions and desert the others. In a few days, however, he was back. "Bartleson, who when we started from Missouri was a portly man, was reduced to half his former girth," Bidwell later wrote. "He said: 'Boys, if I ever get back to Missouri I will never leave that country. I would gladly eat out of the troughs with my hogs.' He seemed to be heartily sick of his late experience, but," Bidwell added, "that did not prevent him from leaving us twice after that."

By the time the men had crossed the mountains and started the descent into the San Joaquin Valley, they were completely demoralized. "When night came," Bidwell said, "our company was strung along for three or four miles, and every man slept where darkness overtook him."

John Marsh's ranch, when they finally straggled into it, was not the utopia they had pictured. Marsh complained about their inability to pay his prices for food and charged them five dollars for Mexican passports, which, they later learned, they could obtain free. John Sutter, however, was a different personality. He "received us with open arms," Bidwell wrote, "and in a princely fashion, for he was a man of the most polite address and the most courteous manners, a man who could shine in any society."

De Smet, staying farther north, went from Soda Springs to Fort Hall, where his warm personality favorably impressed the employees of the Hudson's Bay Company. From there he searched for a location for the mission he wished to establish, finally choosing one on the Bitterroot River south of present-day Missoula, Montana. This site, which was far from the new east-west routes across the continent, was in the country Lewis and Clark had explored so many years before. The palisades of St. Mary's—as de Smet called the new mission—surrounded a small oasis of civilization in the wilderness.

Where once only fur trappers had traveled and built their forts, missionaries had now spread a chain of establishments reaching from the Continental Divide to the West Coast. Granted that the chain lacked many links and that hundreds of miles often separated one mission from another, their existence brought a new element to life in the Far West, one that supplemented the small—but growing—number of settlements near the ocean.

Although the Bidwell-Bartleson party became the best known of those who tried to move west that year, they were not alone. Mexico might feel hemmed in and threatened by the Texans, but the Texans themselves were having difficulties. Burdened by debt and plagued by a stagnant economy, their republic offered little to its citizens, so a group of them launched an expedition to open up trade with Santa Fé; and if the rumors that New Mexico was discontented with Mexican rule proved true, they planned to offer it an opportunity to be annexed by Texas.

About three hundred men assembled at Austin to make this trip, among them, George Kendall, founder of the New Orleans *Picayune,* who thought it might make a good story. The others included soldiers and merchants and three commissioners empowered to deal with New Mexico if the province wanted to join Texas.

Unfamiliar with the route to their goal, they struggled through the Cross Timbers, which lie partly in Texas and partly in Oklahoma, and reached the rim of caprock that guards the eastern approaches to the Llano Estacado, the Staked Plains, of west Texas. Their supplies were now almost depleted, the men exhausted, and Indians were harassing them. When a small scouting party, sent ahead to get help from New Mexico, failed to return, Hugh McLeod, the leader, ordered approximately a hundred men to leave their wagons behind and make a dash for assistance.

Crossing the Llano Estacado—an enormous plain cut by deep, sharp-sided canyons that constantly blocked their way—they reached New Mexico only to find that the citizens, instead of feeling friendly toward the Texans, regarded them with the deepest enmity, an emotion stirred up by the governor Manuel Armijo.

The earlier scouting group were already prisoners, and a band of local militia soon surrounded the second. By guile the Mexicans persuaded them to surrender their arms and then prepared to execute them. Only the pleas of a local landowner spared their lives, but by Armijo's orders, they were imprisoned in a small building and told to look out the window.

As they watched, another of the Texans was marched across the plaza under a small guard. He had been caught trying to escape and was now to suffer death. "A horrible death it was, too!" Kendall wrote. "His cowardly executioners led him to a house near the same corner of the square we were in, not twenty yards from us, and after heartlessly pushing him upon his knees, with his head against the wall, six of the guards stepped back about six paces, and at the order of the corporal *shot the poor fellow in the back!* Even at that distance the executioners but half did their barbarous work; for the man was only wounded, and lay writhing upon the ground in great agony. The corporal stepped up, and with a pistol ended his sufferings. . . . So close was the pistol that the man's shirt was set on fire, and continued to burn until it was extinguished by his blood!"

Armijo then appeared, lectured the Texans on the futility of trying to escape, and ordered them to watch the execution of another of their comrades. This man's "hands were tied closely behind him," Kendall wrote, "and as he approached us we could plainly see that his left ear and cheek had been cut entirely off, and that his left arm was also much hacked, apparently by a sword." Without permitting their prisoner to talk to his former comrades, the Mexican soldiers shot this Texan, too.

Later the Mexicans captured the remainder of the Texas Pioneers—as the original expedition was called. Some of the men experienced long periods of suffering in the worst of Mexican jails, some—through the intervention of American and British diplomats—were finally allowed to return home. From this experience, none of the Texans gained any respect for the Mexicans. They noted with scorn their corrupt system of justice, their inefficient local government, their unwillingness to engage in productive labor, and the poor training and bad discipline of their soldiers.

George Simpson, the Hudson's Bay Company official, made a visit to California later the same year and, although he was British—and not Texan—

came to many of the same conclusions. After a stay in San Francisco, he remarked,

> On the score of industry, these good folks [the people at San Francisco], as also their brethren of the other ports, are perhaps the least promising colonists of a new country in the world, being, in this respect, decidedly inferior to what the savages themselves had become under the training of the priests. . . .
>
> In the missions the wool used to be manufactured into coarse cloth; and it is, in fact, because the Californians are too lazy to weave or spin—too lazy, I suspect, even to clip and wash the raw material—that the sheep have been literally destroyed to make more room for the horned cattle. In the missions soap and leather used to be made; but in such vulgar processes the Californians advance no farther than nature herself had advanced before them, excepting to put each animal's tallow in one place and its hide in another.

He, too, had no respect for either their soldiers or the military prowess of their *rancheros* in controlling the Indians who were constantly raiding their herds. "For such a state of things, however, the public authorities," he said, "are far more to blame than private individuals. Contented with extorting the amount of their own salaries from the missions and the foreign trade, they care little for the general welfare and security, though a band of fifty resolute horsemen, provided they chastised only the actual marauders, could hold at bay all the savages, with their wretched bows and arrows, between Somona and San Diego."

He also foresaw the effect that energetic people might have on the future of California. Although he did not personally meet Sutter, he said that "if Sutter really has the talent and the courage to make the most of his position, he is not unlikely to render California a second Texas. Even now, the Americans only want a rallying point for carrying into effect their theory, that the English race is destined by 'divine right' to expel the Spaniards from their ancient seats . . ."

Yet the American government's intentions were completely peaceful when it instructed Charles Wilkes, a naval officer, to examine the western edge of the continent as well as some of the Pacific islands. Reporting on Jason Lee's mission he said that "it has not been as successful as the lovers of the cause wished. One cause of its failure is that the Indians hereabouts are few; they are remnants of scattered tribes, who are nomadic in their habits, and little inclined to undergo the restraints of any kind of discipline or confinement." On the other hand, Whitman's mission was "flourishing under the care of himself and wife."

Wilkes was critical of some aspects of Oregon and California. He regretted, for example, the treacherous entrance to the Columbia River and pointed out that some of the land would be difficult to farm. But comments such as these did not detract from his overall enthusiasm, which equalled Slacum's. Here was another publication that set many Americans thinking about the better lot they might enjoy if they moved West.

15. LEARNING THE LAND

It yet remains for others to explore, discover, and make known, many of the hidden resources of interest, with which these remote, new, and peculiar regions, most probably abound.

—Overton Johnson, 1846

Although the title to Oregon had not yet been settled, the trickle that had started to the West Coast continued to run, and farmers who were discontented with their eastern lands began to gather in Missouri to start the journey over the plains and mountains to the richer, more fertile country that lay near the Pacific Ocean. One young man, Lansford Hastings, had gone to Independence, Missouri, to join a party heading west and found others there "waiting very patiently until their number should be so increased as to afford protection and insure the safety of all, when they contemplated setting out together, for their favorite place of destination, Oregon territory. The number of emigrants continued to increase with such rapidity that on the 15th day of May, our company consisted of one hundred and sixty persons, giving

173

us a force of eighty armed men, which was thought ample for our purpose."[7]

To provide for order during their trip, the emigrants set up their own form of government, which quickly broke down, the minority on every issue resenting the decision of majority. So great was their dissension, they separated into two groups. Even this did not satisfy them, so shortly they joined together again.

After leaving Fort Laramie, they met Fitzpatrick, the former trapper, who proved willing to serve as their guide. For the first time, the band of neophytes found themselves led by a man who knew the wilderness, but even Fitzpatrick could not hold them together. Before they reached Fort Hall, they again divided into two groups, one remaining behind to dispose of their wagons and reload their belongings, the other proceeding ahead with another trapper as their guide.

Just before arriving at Fort Walla Walla, they came to Dr. Whitman's mission. "He received us," Hastings later wrote, "with the utmost kindness and attention, and insisted upon our remaining a few days with him. . . . Our stay with the doctor included the Sabbath, during which day we attended divine service, at his residence. In the forenoon, he delivered a discourse to the Indians, in their own language, to which they appeared to be very attentive, evidently comprehending the truths and doctrines inculcated. Having had a few hours intermission, we again convened, when the doctor delivered a very able discourse to our company, the other members of the mission, and his family." Amid his many other duties—supervising the school, tending the sick, and guiding the mission's secular activities—Whitman still found time to prepare several sermons a week. "The doctor," Hastings concluded, "is not only a very kind and honorable gentlemen, but he is no doubt, a very good man, and a devoted christian."

In spite of the long trip he had made to get there, Hastings was not satisfied with Oregon and decided to see what California had to offer. "But," he discovered, "traveling from Oregon to California, like traveling from the States to Oregon, is attended with imminent dangers, from innumerable hostile Indians; it became necessary to obtain a party of armed men, sufficient in numbers, to insure our entire safety."

On the way to California with fifty emigrants he had recruited, Hastings met a party coming in the opposite direction. Some of them were drovers who were taking cattle to Oregon for sale; others, however, were emigrants who did not like California. "We, of course," Hastings commented, "had nothing very favorable to say of Oregon, for we were then in search of a desirable place of abode, which in our view, could not be found in Oregon; nor had they much to say in favor of California. They all concurred in the opinion, that California was, beyond any doubt, one of the most delightful countries in the known world, both in point of mildness of climate, and

174

fertility of soil; but they remarked, that they had been seriously oppressed there, and that they would seek refuge, *for the time being,* in Oregon." Thus neither group liked what it had labored so hard to reach. Hastings was discontented with the land; the California emigrants were unhappy with the Mexican government.

Sutter, however, was well entrenched and glad to see the new arrivals. "It really appeared," Hastings remarked, "to afford him the greatest delight, to be thus enabled, to render important aid, to citizens of his former, adopted country."

Hastings liked California, and so did the other members of the expedition. They were "determined to remain there," said Hastings, "and make California the future home, not only of themselves, but also, of their friends and relatives."

California had received a new set of propagandists. Once American opinion had been centered principally on Oregon, to which the nation had some claim. Now some of the nation's enthusiasm was turning toward California, which, however ill-protected and mismanaged it might be, still belonged to Mexico—although its grip was so tenuous that the area had almost fallen into American hands. Thomas ap Catesby Jones (the "ap" stands for "son" attached to a name) was commodore of the fleet that the United States maintained in the Pacific. Receiving information that mistakenly led him to believe his country was at war with Mexico, he set sail for Monterey, entered the bay, and demanded the surrender of the Mexican authorities. Since they had no means of resisting him, they permitted him to hoist the American flag over the capital while they persuaded him of his error. Greatly embarrassed, Jones then lowered the flag, raised his sails, and took off for the Pacific in an exit that was as ignominious as his arrival had been triumphant.

Although the Protestant missions in Oregon were expanding and attracting more workers, the Indians were often volatile, helpful at one time, obstreperous at another. Communications with the missions' headquarters in the East were so slow the missionaries could not receive the guidance they desired. And some of the men and women who had decided to dedicate their lives to the enlightenment of the Indians were not temperamentally equipped for the work. Internal strife also disrupted the missions' operations. Relatively isolated and yet mutually dependent, they often irritated each other and fell to quarreling.

Even Whitman, for all his physical energy and spiritual devotion, sometimes found himself unequal to the task he had undertaken. On occasion the Indians became insulting and threatening, and although he was able to hold his temper, the incidents bothered him and made him feel uncertain in his relations with the people he had come to help.

The Catholic priests—some of them encouraged by the Hudson's Bay

Company—were making inroads among his converts. And then he faced the problem of dealing with Spalding. The two men had had difficulty agreeing ever since their trip across the continent, and for that reason had set up separate missions. But they had to meet regularly to determine overall policy, and few of those meetings were peaceful. The strain between the two finally became so great the controlling board in the East ordered them to abandon both missions and return home. By the time Whitman received these instructions, he and Spalding had patched up their differences. In the fall of 1842, he therefore decided to return east to plead for permission to continue their work.

Meanwhile he had become aware of the importance of the increasing number of emigrants and visualized the time when Oregon would be a land of farmers, not of trappers. Leaving Narcissa to supervise the activities at Waiilatpu, as he called his mission, he began his hasty preparations for his trip. Traveling with as little equipment as possible and with only one man for a companion, he raced against the winter storms, avoiding the better-traveled route in favor of Taos in the hope of evading hostile Indians. In spite of his haste, cold weather overtook him, and much of his journey was accomplished in snow so deep the pack mules would sink out of sight except for their ears. On some days the two men covered such a short distance they could still see the smoke from their old campfire as they made a new one for the coming night.

Nevertheless, Whitman finally reached Washington, D.C., where he had little difficulty in obtaining audiences with several influential officials. Later he drafted some proposed legislation for them and suggested a line of military posts that could supply travelers and help keep the Indians from attacking them. Later his supporters claimed he had discussed the future boundaries of Oregon, but apparently he assumed in his Washington discussions that the line would run along the Columbia River.

From Washington he went to New York City. His frontier dress, which he had not yet abandoned, made him a colorful figure on the city's streets, and he was interviewed by Horace Greeley. But in Boston the members of the mission board disapproved of his clothing and were distressed over the dissension that seemed to rend the two missions. But Whitman was persuasive. The board finally voted to rescind its previous order and, his objective attained, he returned to Oregon, where he and Spalding continued their work of trying to help the Indians.

Somewhere over the great forests of the West, forests that had never known the bite of an ax and whose trees reached to the skies, a faint rain cloud gathered, grew, and turned darker. Streaks of lightning flashed from its interior, and one of them struck a tree, which exploded with a blast as its sap suddenly became heated. A touch of the lightning licked at a dead branch, setting it aglow, but in the rain that accompanied the storm, the fire merely smoldered. By the time the rain had passed, the fire was hidden beneath the soft litter that covered the forest floor, and there it remained almost invisible. Suddenly the winds dried the leaves and the tree trunks and fanned the flame. It rose from the earth and licked at the trunk of a tree. Then it broke through the covering of the forest floor a hundred feet away and blazed at another trunk. Soon it attacked another and another. The trees looked like pyres, smoke and flames reaching the length of them, and the whole forest was ablaze.

In much the same fashion, the American western emigration took place. First a few sea captains had approached the shores, then a trickle of fur trappers had crossed the continent, lonely, roaming men with no intention of remaining. Then arrived a few missionaries, a few settlers, a few more men and women to help the original missionaries. The total numbers hardly counted against the vast space they were occupying. But they were like the flame hidden under the forest floor. Suddenly the great outburst came. In 1843, after listening to the reports of the missionaries and men like Hall Kelley, large groups of men and women decided to go west, and 1843 became known as the "Year of the Great Migration."

In later times, when the dust from the wagons had settled again into the soil and the sound of the last oxen's hooves striking stone had disappeared in the vast blackness of the past, scholars began to examine the western movement and ascribed it to many causes. Some spoke of "manifest destiny"—a contemporary phrase—as though the fate of a nation had dropped from the hands of its people into the laps of the gods, which may be true, but only partially so. Others talked of the economic disturbances in the East, the decline of the land's fertility, the pressures of European immigration, and other measurable reasons. But they do not suffice to explain what happened, for similar factors in other countries have produced dissimilar results.

What was different about the Americans was the buoyancy and self-confidence of their natures—their ability to laugh at themselves (Fray Marcos or Coronado could hardly be imaged making jokes at their own expense), and their faith in themselves as a people. To this was added the role of the government—never all-encompassing, as it had been in Spain's territories, never relying solely on commercial enterprise as the British had done with the Hudson's Bay Company and their own western venture. The Americans, probably more by luck than by philosophy, had produced limited government help at the right times to relieve the crises and had withdrawn it when it might have proved stultifying.

Perhaps most important of all was the absence of any spirit of colonialism—an absence that was almost unique among expanding nations. Ever since the opening of the Old Northwest Territory in the days immediately following the Revolution, the United States had determined that its western territories would become part of the whole, that the inhabitants of one part would not be inferior to the inhabitants of another. As long as he remained in the New World, George Simpson, the Hudson's Bay Company official, might be one of the most powerful and influential men in Canada, but he could not vote for a member of the British Parliament and, at home, was considered a "colonial"—a citizen, yes, but of a lower sort than those who resided in England.

The Reverend Parker or Marcus Whitman, on the other hand, knew that in time—and by a precise process—the land they stood on would be part of a state and that they themselves would enjoy equal rights and standing with the people they had left behind. Those moving westward suffered no civil or social loss as did those who advanced the boundaries of Spain, France, or Great Britain. They carried the American flag—and its government—with them.

This idea was so intoxicating that the Americans in Oregon decided to hasten the procedure. No matter that the diplomats had not yet settled the boundary dispute, no matter that by international agreement no government officials were permitted to function in Oregon. On May 15, 1843, a delegation of Americans met to discuss the formation of their own government.

The Hudson's Bay Company, naturally enough, did everything it could to discourage the idea. Earlier it had met with the settlers and told them that if they included the area north of the Columbia, the company would exercise its influence among its employees and other dependents, thus threatening to outvote the Americans. "The district committee," wrote William H. Gray, who had gone west with Whitman and Spalding as their business agent, "contended that the influence and vote would defeat us, and make us an English or Hudson's Bay Company settlement. We could, without the interference of the company, manage our own affairs with such of the French [Canadian] settlers as chose to remain and vote with us . . . Besides, we were confident we should receive a large immigration in the fall, and in that case we could extend our settlements . . . and laws . . .

"Another prominent, and perhaps the most prominent reason of all was, we were afraid to attempt to enforce any laws we might wish to adopt, or think necessary among ourselves, upon the servants of the company . . . and we . . . wisely concluded if they would not openly interfere with us, we would not openly interfere with them, till we were strong enough to outnumber and control them."

To assert their independence, the Americans in Oregon built a crude statehouse "with poles set upright, one end in the ground, grooved on two sides, and filled with poles and split timber," as Gray described it. But they were ahead of their time and, without an international agreement and the backing of the federal government, were unlikely to make much progress against the powerful Hudson's Bay Company.

By fall gloom was overtaking the settlers. But the largest emigrant party yet was on its way—some nine hundred people carrying their belongings in about a hundred and twenty wagons and bringing with them five thousand head of livestock. When it reached Oregon, one of its members, Overton Johnson, later said, "Our arrival had a great effect on the country. The people were beginning to feel lonesome, and to fear it would be long before these far-distant wilds of Western America would be settled. Property was of doubtful value, and their once high anticipations were fading away. . . . Instantly everything revived; improvements went rapidly on, and the expectations of the people were again excited."

He noted the functioning of the local government, pointing out that it "is intended only to be temporary, and subject to the disposition of the Government of the United States, whenever she extends her jurisdiction over the Territory." At the same time, it "regulated the making of land claims, determining who might hold the claims, and deciding what steps should be necessary, in order that persons might be secure in the possession of lands."

Although a settler restricted himself to the prescribed 640 acres, and although he marked the corners and carefully entered his claim in the territorial register, his title remained doubtful. The United States did not own this land, and each citizen of Oregon, no matter how carefully he followed the local law, ran the risk of losing everything for which he had traveled so far and worked so hard.

Yet Washington had not completely forgotten the settlers in Oregon, and while they were filing their land claims, John Charles Frémont was leading an expedition down the Oregon Trail to the West Coast, ostensibly to survey the land on behalf of the Topographical Corps but in actuality to demonstrate that the flag could go where it wished and to warn the Indians that the inexperienced emigrants, with their overloaded wagons and herds of slow-moving cattle, were not the easy targets they might seem.

Frémont was the traditional schoolgirl's romantic vision of all that a young army officer should be, debonair, handsome, gay, and adventurous. The illegitimate son of a French father and Virginian mother, he had started life with no money or influence. Much to the wrath of Thomas Hart Benton, senator from Missouri, he had secretly married the senator's daughter, Jessie. Rather than never see his daughter again—the alternative Jessie offered him— the senator accepted his new son-in-law and did everything he could to forward his career. But it was not political influence alone that had won Frémont his assignment. Previously he had worked for Joseph Nicolas Nicollet, one of the most brilliant members of the Topographical Corps, and only the year before had led an expedition up the Oregon Trail as far as Fort

179

Laramie. So even without his father-in-law's influence behind him, he was well equipped to conduct a survey of the whole trail.

The expedition started off uneventfully except for a brief controversy over a cannon. Exceeding his orders, Frémont requisitioned a howitzer. Since this was to be a peaceful, scientific expedition, not a warlike, invading party, orders went out immediately for Frémont to return to the capital and explain himself. Jessie, rather than see command of the expedition fall to someone else, intercepted the orders and sent word to Frémont by private messenger to hurry off. Frémont thus escaped being relieved of his command, and Senator Benton was able to quiet official action against either his beloved daughter or his son-in-law.

Because he had already explored the route along the Platte River, Frémont went farther south, hoping to find a new pass through the Rocky Mountains. On the way he was joined by Kit Carson, the mountain man, who was now using his skills to make a living out of the growing settlement of the country. The previous year Carson had served with Frémont, and both men had benefited. Frémont obtained the help of an experienced frontiersman; Carson, uneducated but extremely intelligent, discovered a whole new world and, through Frémont's subsequent reports, gained the notoriety that later made him a prominent figure in American lore.

At the base of the Rockies, Frémont divided his men into two groups: One would follow the Oregon Train with the former mountain man, Fitzpatrick, as their guide and scout; the other, under his own command and accompanied by Carson, would take a more devious route, exploring as they went and eventually rejoining the first party at Fort Hall.

As Ashley had done so many years earlier, Frémont went up Cache la Poudre Canyon in Colorado and picked up the usual route to Oregon, now so heavily traveled that it needed no further marking to enable a novice to find it. As Frémont commented, "The broad smooth highway, where the numerous heavy wagons of the migrants had entirely beaten and crushed the artemisia [sagebrush], was a happy exchange to our poor animals for the sharp rocks and tough shrubs among which they had been toiling so long."

From the usual route west, Frémont turned south to observe Great Salt Lake. He was not, of course, the first man to visit it, but he was the first with scientific training. Consequently he studied it for several days, taking observations and venturing out on it with an inflatable boat that he had brought along. This was not easy work, for, as he had earlier observed, "We discovered that two of the [three] cylinders leaked so much as to require one man constantly at the bellows, to keep them sufficiently full of air to support the boat."

Nevertheless, he was determined to explore the lake in his strange craft. "So long as we could touch the bottom with our paddles," he later said, "we were very gay; but gradually as the water deepened, we became more still in our frail bateau of gum cloth distended with air, and with pasted seams. Although the day was very calm, there was a considerable swell on the lake; and there were white patches of foam on the surface . . . recalling the recollection of the whirlpool stories. [The lake had been the subject of campfire tales since its first discovery.] The water continued to deepen as we advanced; the lake becoming almost transparently clear, of an extremely beautiful bright green color; and the spray, which was thrown into the boat and over our clothes, was directly converted into a crust of common salt, which covered also our hands and arms."

In spite of the frailty of his boat, Frémont landed on a distant shore, spent the night, and returned to his camp the following day, both he and his men happy to feel solid land again underfoot. But he reluctantly realized it was impractical to make any more studies. "As we looked over the vast expanse of water . . . and strained our eyes along the silent shores over which hung so much doubt and uncertainty . . . I could hardly repress the almost irresistible desire to continue our exploration; but the lengthening snow on the mountains was a plain indication of the advancing season, and our frail linen boat appeared so insecure that I was unwilling to trust our lives to the uncertainties of the lake. I therefore unwillingly resolved to terminate our survey here, and remain satisfied for the present with what we had been able to add to the unknown geography of the region."

At Fort Hall, Frémont rejoined the party which Fitzpatrick had been guiding. Fall was spreading its cold winds through the valleys and over the mountain crests, whispering of the bitter days and hard traveling that lay ahead. Frémont therefore gave his men the choice of continuing on with him or returning east, and a number chose to make their way back to the Missouri. After purchasing a few horses and oxen from the man in charge at Fort Hall, Frémont took the trail again, but he did so with regrets that the post was in British hands.

During the emigrants' "recent passage," he remarked, "they had been able to obtain, at very high prices and in insufficient quantity, only such assistance as could be afforded by a small and remote trading post—and at that a foreign one—which, in the supply of its own wants, had necessarily drawn around it some of the resources of civilization, but which obtained nearly all its supplies from the distant depot of Vancouver [Dr. McLoughlin's base on the Columbia]." In the expansionist spirit of his father-in-law, Frémont noted that "an American military post sufficiently strong to give their road a perfect security against the Indian tribes, who are unsettled in locality and very *uncertain* in their disposition, and which, with the necessary facilities for the repair of their equipage, would be able to afford them relief in stock and grain from the produce of the post, would be of extraordinary value to the emigration." Frémont saw the government assuming an even greater role in the movement west by constructing and maintaining a whole string of such

181

forts, thus guarding the entire trail and acting as supply agent for the emigrants.

After a short stop at Fort Boisé—another of the Hudson's Bay Company's outposts—and seeing "the snowy mass of Mount Hood, standing high out above the surrounding country, at a distance of 180 miles," Frémont reached Dr. Whitman's mission, which at the time consisted of a single adobe building, the mill having burned down. Yet Frémont found ample confirmation of his previous remarks that the emigrants needed centers to which they could turn for supplies and help. For at Whitman's he observed a large number of new arrivals, "men, women, and children, in robust health, all indemnifying themselves for previous scanty fare, in a hasty consumption of potatoes, which are produced here of a remarkably good quality."

At The Dalles, Frémont made camp and, leaving the majority of his men behind, went ahead with a few selected companions to Fort Vancouver, thus connecting his survey with Wilkes's. In spite of the opposition of some of the Americans to the Hudson's Bay Company, Dr. McLoughlin was continuing to play his helpful role. On his way downstream, Frémont had noticed several camps of emigrants, and at Fort Vancouver he found many more gathered. "Others have already crossed the river into their land of promise—the Willamette Valley," he wrote. "Others were daily arriving; and all of them had been furnished with shelter, so far as it could be afforded by the buildings connected with the establishment. Necessary clothing and provisions (the latter to be afterwards returned in kind from the produce of their labor) were also furnished. This friendly assistance was of great value to the emigrants, whose families were otherwise exposed to much suffering in the winter rains."

Returning to The Dalles with a good supply of peas, flour, and tallow and having obtained more than a hundred horses and mules, as well as some cattle, Frémont was ready to start back even though the season was late. But his ambitious, adventurous spirit revolted at routinely retracing his steps. Instead he decided to exceed his orders and go south to explore the Great Basin between the Rockies and the Sierra Nevada.

"It was," he noted, "a serious enterprise, at the commencement of winter, to undertake the traverse of such a region, and with a party consisting only of twenty-five persons . . . most of them young, several being under twenty-one years of age. All knew that a strange country was to be explored, and dangers and hardships to be encountered; but no one blenched at the prospect."

PART III
1845–86

16. A Time of Expansion

Nor was there room for complaint that our propositions for settlement were unreasonable; permission was not given our envoy to make any proposition whatever. Nor can it be objected that we, on our part, would not listen to any reasonable terms of their suggestion; the Mexican government refused all negotiation.

—James Polk, 1846

If the American settlers in Oregon felt deserted and remote, they had reason to. Separated from the rest of the country by months of travel, functioning under a form of government that was not recognized even by their own people, and constantly dependent on the goodwill of the Hudson's Bay Company, they appeared to be the orphans of the western movement. Even Frémont's expedition, which represented the best that Senators Benton and Linn could persuade Congress to do for them, remained in Oregon only a short time before its restless, ambitious leader plunged off into new territories. Yet they were not forgotten, either by the United States or by Great Britain, the other power that controlled their destinies.

185

In February 1844, while the winter rains were falling on the Oregon coast and the cold damp was rising from the Potomac and blowing across Washington, the British ambassador wrote the American secretary of state that the British government was anxious to settle the boundaries of the Oregon or Columbia Territory. He said he had been "instructed to lose no time into entering into communication" on this subject. The secretary of state was ready to start negotiations, but fate had decided the Americans in Oregon would have to wait awhile longer for the resolution of their problem. During a brief cruise on board a naval vessel on the Potomac, a gun exploded, and the secretary of state was killed. Thus settlement of the boundary question was again postponed, but it had at last risen high on the agenda of issues to be discussed by the two countries.

Far from the warm rooms in which the diplomats wrote their correspondence and did their negotiating, Frémont had been marching toward the south along the eastern slopes of the Cascade Mountains, reaching one of the marshes of southern Oregon in bitterly cold weather. Dry in summer and covered with a lush growth of green grass, their winter wetness had turned to ice, white and shimmering and offering nothing to hold him. By Christmas Day, which the men celebrated by firing the howitzer—its most useful function so far—they had almost reached the present-day boundary between Oregon and Nevada and shortly afterward crossed it.

By the time Frémont arrived at Pyramid Lake in Nevada, his men were weary, his pack train growing smaller as the result of dying animals and Indian raids and his small herd of beef cattle exhausted. Yet he persisted in his southward course, pushing his weary men forward until they came within a few miles of the modern city of Reno, Nevada.

Here he paused to take stock of his position, for it was apparent he could not continue the present line of his march and that his homeward "detour" should be brought to a stop. In the distance he could see columns of smoke rising in the air, a sure sign he was being observed by Indians, although they had made no effort to attack him. After briefly following a stream he mistakenly thought might flow to the Pacific he returned to camp. "Examining into the condition of the animals . . . ," he explained, "I found their feet so much cut up by the rocks, and so many of them lame, that it was evidently impossible that they could cross the country to the Rocky mountains. Every piece of iron that could be used for the purpose had been converted into nails, and we could make no further use of the shoes we had remaining." Having decided he could not go east, as his orders instructed him to, and that he could not spend the winter in what is now Nevada, he continued, "I therefore . . . determined to cross the Sierra Nevada into the valley of the Sacramento, wherever a practicable pass could be found. My decision was heard with joy by the people, and diffused new life throughout the camp."

Whether or not his course of action "was heard with joy," it was injudicious. Crossing the Sierra Nevada in wintertime was no light task even for the most experienced frontiersmen, and Frémont did not even know where the passes lay. Furthermore, California's government, as he most certainly realized, was hostile to unauthorized intrusions. In addition, his orders said nothing about going to California; he was merely told to explore the route to Oregon. No young army officer who was not related to a powerful senator would have dared to set up such a plan.

On January 31, the expedition made camp in sight of a mountain crest, which, they thought, finally represented the main ridge of the Sierra Nevada. They had hardly lighted their fires when they were visited by a large number of Indians. One of them, an older man who particularly inspired Frémont's trust, said that "before the snows fell, it was six sleeps to the place where the whites lived, but that now it was impossible to cross the mountains on account of the deep snow; and showing us . . . that it was over our heads," he urged Frémont not to advance further. Frémont, however, was not to be discouraged.

The days that followed were grim. As the snow became deeper, he organized a group of ten men, mounted on the best horses, who took turns going ahead, trampling a pathway through the white wasteland. On February 4, 1844, less than three weeks before the British ambassador wrote his letter to the American secretary of state, the horses that had been breaking the path went only a few hundred yards and then, exhausted, refused to push further into the great banks that lay ahead.

That evening their Indian guide, "who," Frémont said, "comprehended [the problem] even more readily than ourselves, and believed our situation hopeless, covered his head with his blanket and began to weep and lament."

After a night during which it was too cold to sleep, Frémont instructed his men to make sledges and snowshoes in order to continue their journey. He himself went ahead and reached a peak from which he could survey the surrounding country. "Far below us," he wrote, "dimmed by the distance, was a large snowless valley, bounded on the western side, at the distance of about a hundred miles, by a low range of mountains, which Carson recognized with delight as the mountains bordering the coast. . . . Between us, then, and this low coast range, was the valley of the Sacramento; and no one who had not accompanied us through the incidents of our life for the last few months could realize the delight with which at last we looked down upon it."

Fighting for every yard, they began moving forward again. They were short of food, the men and animals were worn out, and many of the men became snow-blind, suffering not only the loss of sight that accompanies that affliction but also the great pain.

On the evening of February 11, Frémont said he "received a message from

Mr. Fitzpatrick [who was behind], acquainting me with the utter failure of his attempts to get our mules and horses over the snow—the half-hidden trail had proved entirely too slight to support them, and they had broken through, and were plunging about or lying half buried in the snow." Frémont sent back word to return the animals to the nearest partially clear ground, "and, after having made mauls and shovels, turn in all the strength of his party to open and beat a road through the snow, strengthening it with branches and boughs of the pines." As a result of their hard work, the following day the two parties came in sight of each other, separated by a distance of only three miles.

Continuing ahead, Frémont "travelled along the crests of narrow ridges, extending down from the mountain in the direction of the valley, from which the snow was fast melting away. . . . Toward sundown . . . we encamped on the head water of a little creek, where at last the water found its way to the Pacific."

They had finally made their way over what is now known as Carson Pass at an elevation of more than eighty-five hundred feet; but, Frémont said, "we had hard and doubtful labor yet before us, as the snow appeared to be heavier where the timber began further down, with few open spots."

Two of the men became deranged. One who had gone in search of a horse lost his way and, when he finally regained the camp, told of a trip lasting several days. The other, believing it was summer, stripped off his clothes and tried to swim in a roaring mountain torrent. "The times were severe," Frémont said, "when stout men lost their minds from extremity of suffering—when horses died—and when mules and horses, ready to die of starvation, were killed for food. Yet," he added in a tribute to his men, "there was no murmuring or hesitation."

Their courage and perseverance finally brought them to an Indian village, where one of the natives spoke excellent Spanish. Explaining that he was an employee of John Sutter, he told them they "were upon the *Río de los Americanos* [the American River], and that it joined the Sacramento river about 10 miles below. Never did a name sound more sweetly!" Frémont said, "we felt ourselves among our countrymen; for the name of *American,* in these distant parts, is applied to the citizens of the United States."

In a short time, they met Sutter himself and, as usual, he placed himself and his facilities completely at their service. In Oregon, John McLoughlin was the man to whom Americans turned when they needed help, however ungrateful they might be once they had established themselves; in California, it was John Sutter, commander of his own fort and prince of his own domain. Under his protection, Frémont need not worry about the Spanish authorities—Sutter could settle any problems they might raise—nor fret about supplies—he was well stocked.

Life at John Sutter's was a sharp contrast with crossing the Sierra Nevada in winter. Instead of cold, there was warmth; instead of starvation, there was a plenteous supply of food; instead of loneliness, there was the companionship of friendly humans, all anxious to make the members of the expedition as comfortable as possible. Yet Frémont—for all his faults—was not one to be seduced by the lotus-eaters, and in two weeks was rested, fully re-equipped with a new herd of livestock, and ready to start for the East.

Unwilling to retrace his steps, he planned to march south some five hundred miles, cross the Sierra Nevada at a lower point, and take a more southerly route. His decision reflected the versatility of the explorers of his time who were willing to trade a canoe for a horse, woods for a desert, or snowshoes for a hot sandy trail. Within a few weeks, he was traveling by night instead of day, trying to avoid the pitiless glare of a sun whose heat he would have welcomed during those bleak days crossing the Sierra Nevada. Early in May, he approached the present site of Las Vegas, Nevada, and the most difficult part of the return trip lay ahead—a stretch of land with so little water the men were forced to eat the pulp of cacti to satisfy their thirst. But they finally reached Mountain Meadows in Utah, where water and grass were again available, and the horrors of the desert lay behind them.

As these men, with their suffering and hardship, were doing what they could to expand the nation they loved so well, others in different circumstances were also working toward the same end. John C. Calhoun, former vice-president and now secretary of state, was trying to resolve the question of Texas. Independence had not proved the answer to the Texans' problems, but the United States was reluctant to annex the republic, partly out of respect for its treaty obligations to Mexico and partly from fear of again raising the issue of slavery. A diplomatic flirtation between Texas and Great Britain whetted America's appetite, but the annexation treaty negotiated by Calhoun was defeated in the Senate. Although the United States had grown much stronger, it was divided politically, not only over slavery but also over the question of its own expansion.

This fact was evident during the national conventions held that May in Baltimore, while Frémont was leading his small band back toward the Missouri. The Whigs, who then held office, were in disarray. Tyler, the first vice-president to succeed on the death of a president, was so heartily disliked by his own party that most of his cabinet had resigned and no true Whig would consider him a candidate. By acclamation, they selected Henry Clay, who had left the Senate two years before in disgust over the failure of his various programs.

Martin Van Buren of New York, who had already served as president, was the logical choice of the Democrats; but in April he had written a letter taking a firm stand against the annexation of Texas, thus committing himself beforehand on an issue over which public opinion was both strong and divided. In each ballot, he dropped further behind while no other candidate gained the votes to take his place. Threatened with a deadlock, the delegates turned with relief to James Polk, a politician with little national reputation. In two ballots he won, to become the first "dark horse" nominee of a national convention.

Of the two candidates, Polk was the quicker to sense the nation's mood—and dilemma. On three of its borders, it was touched by regions of political instability—California, Texas, and Oregon. Proving that the Whig politicians had been wrong, Polk came out for the annexation of Texas and thus ensured his election.

Calhoun, too, sensed that the majority of people wanted to expand their boundaries. He, therefore, responded favorably when the British ambassador again raised the question of Oregon. "The government of the United States," he wrote in reply to the ambassador's note, "participates in the anxious desire of that of Great Britain that the subject may be early and satisfactorily arranged."

But eager as he was to settle the question, Calhoun was not so eager that he was willing to bargain away the position of the United States. On the contrary, he sternly informed the British ambassador that "the undersigned cannot assent to the conclusion . . . that Great Britain possesses and exercises, in common with the United States, a right of joint occupancy in the Oregon territory. . . . He claims, and he thinks he has shown, a clear title on the part of the United States, to the whole region drained by the Columbia." This unconciliatory attitude made an immediate settlement impossible and served notice that the American government would not be easily satisfied.

Texas was ready for annexation; Oregon was the legitimate object of diplomatic negotiations; California, however, belonged under international law to Mexico, which had no intention of relinquishing it. Yet it was California that was attracting the attention of an increasing number of Americans, even among those who had originally set Oregon as their goal.

For all his efforts to reach the territory, Overton Johnson, who had emigrated in 1843, was already having doubts about Oregon. Although he found much to praise, he also thought some aspects of the country were unequal to the much closer Mississippi Valley. "After balancing the advantages and disadvantages, we cannot determine which is, in reality, superior."

Johnson left Oregon in June 1844, less than a year after his arrival, and went to California. Nor was he alone in seeking a better place to settle permanently, for his expedition was made up of almost forty men, women and children.

Like most other American emigrants, the party first stopped at John Sutter's, and then Johnson set out to explore northern California. Both it and Oregon, he decided, held merits not to be found farther east. "As the farmer's stock can live well all winter," he wrote, "not only throughout California,

190

but through nearly the whole of Oregon, he will here possess one advantage . . . he will not be compelled, as he is in most parts of the great and fertile Valley of the Mississippi, to labor six months to produce grain and provender, to feed out, at the expense of another six months' labor to his stock. And there is not only in the territory of Oregon, but also in the province of California, another great advantage, that is, indeed, paramount to all others: which is, health." In 1845, having completed his informal survey of Oregon and the northern part of California, Johnson began the trip back to the East. That even California could not satisfy every emigrant was evidenced by the size of his party, which included approximately fifteen persons.

Johnson was returning to a United States that was considerably larger than the nation he had left a relatively short time before. Tyler, rejected so completely by his own political party, still understood the country better than some of the men who had ended his political life, and therefore he was determined—notwithstanding the reluctance of the Senate—to complete the annexation before the end of his term. His unwitting allies were the Mexicans themselves. When they protested the annexation negotiations, they used terms many Americans found offensive, thus rallying public opinion against their own cause.

On December 18, 1844, he proposed to Congress that it approve a resolution calling for annexation. To pass, this required only a majority in each house, not a two-thirds majority of the Senate. Although the subterfuge evoked considerable criticism, Tyler had correctly calculated the will of the nation. After its passage, Tyler sent a copy of the resolution to the Texas government. At a convention called on July 4, 1845, Texas approved its provisions. Although the final formalities were not completed until December, for all practical purposes, Texas had become the twenty-eighth state by the time Johnson reached the Missouri.

This added thousands of square miles to the territory of the United States and placed its western boundary along the entire length of the Rocky Mountains from what is now the Big Bend National Park in the south to the forty-ninth parallel in the north, thus completing the acquisition of the watershed draining east from the great range. It also brought the United States to the border of New Mexico, thus eliminating the quasi no-man's-land that once separated it from the Mexican province.

If "manifest destiny" was at work, it had taken a long time to make itself evident. Texas had remained a rejected suitor for almost a decade, and for an even greater period, the settlement of the Oregon question had held a low priority among the issues to be settled with Great Britain. But once the American people had decided, in effect, to override their own Senate and take Texas out of the international limbo in which it had been uncomfortably resting, the forces of expansion were finally released and would not be satisfied without further acquisitions.

191

This spirit was reflected in the increasing number of emigrants that year. When Joel Palmer, a former member of the Indiana legislature, decided to go west and seek a better fortune, he joined a group of emigrants at Independence, Missouri. Soon they overtook a company of thirty-eight wagons with about a thousand head of loose cattle. Three days later they encountered another band of twenty-eight wagons and by nightfall had caught up with yet another, consisting of approximately a hundred wagons with some two thousand head of loose stock. This was a far cry from a few years before when the bands of men and herds of animals had been isolated and tiny.

Frémont's return and the reports he prepared also incited further interest in the Far West, although his preoccupation with his work almost destroyed his personal reputation. Looking for a horizon with which to check the accuracy of a sextant, he chose the top of a large granite carriage step outside a Washington church. For several successive nights, while waiting for the stars to rotate into the positions he wanted, he rested against the stone. Jumping to conclusions, the deacon reported to Senator Benton that his son-in-law had become a drunkard incapable of finding his own way home. The report fell on unbelieving ears, however, and as there was no consequent blotch on Frémont's record, he received the command of yet another western expedition.

Because he had access to many of the most important members of the government, Frémont was well informed concerning the administration's long-term objectives. "The President and Mr. Bancroft," he later wrote (Bancroft was secretary of the navy and close to Polk), "held it impossible for Mexico, situated as things then were, to retain possession of California, and therefore it was right to negotiate with Mexico for the acquisition of that which to her could be of no use. This it was hoped to accomplish by peaceful negotiation; but if Mexico, in resenting the acceptance of the offer of Texas to join us, should begin a war with us, by taking possession of the province."

War was in the air. In December 1845, a senator introduced a resolution calling for an examination into the country's military defenses. Such a measure could only be interpreted as a preparation for hostilities; and while much of the country was enthusiastic, others, like Daniel Webster, expressed grave reservations. "Every member of the Senate knows," he said, "and every man of intelligence knows, that unnecessary alarm and apprehension about the preservation of the public peace is a great evil. It disturbs the affairs of the country." Yet even Webster, cautious as he was on this issue, was realistic about the direction the nation was taking and the impossibility of running against the tide. ". . . at the same time," he concluded, "as far as I am concerned, if gentlemen think the time has come for enlarging the defences of the country . . . I am ready to cooperate with them." Even those who did not support expansion would, in the event of war, support their nation.

Yet the United States was still at peace with Mexico and therefore the purposes of Frémont's expedition were estraordinary. He was to explore the Southern Rocky Mountains, the northern Río Grande, the Colorado River, the Great Salt Lake area, and the passes through the Cascades and the Sierra Nevada. The reason was to establish better lines of communication between East and West; but, as Frémont himself noted, "The geographical examinations proposed to be made were in greater part in Mexican territory." The only excuse for such an expedition was the likelihood of hostilities, or, as Frémont later remarked, "In arranging this expedition, the eventualities of war were taken into consideration."

In the summer of 1845, Frémont set off with approximately sixty men, slightly too many for a purely exploratory expedition and yet too few to have much military consequence. With the help of experienced frontiersmen like Kit Carson, Frémont made a relatively uneventful trip through the Great Basin and, crossing the Sierra Nevada, reached John Sutter's establishment on December 10, 1845. There he was greeted by John Bidwell, the former captain of an emigrant group who had become one of Sutter's trusted employees. Bidwell, in Frémont's opinion, was something less than cordial, leading Frémont to believe that Sutter's sympathies lay with the Mexicans. In this, he was mistaken. Bidwell had been taking a realistic look at the Swiss emigrant's accounts and realized that his open-handed generosity to all newcomers and other expenditures had placed him heavily in debt. Only a miracle or the most rigorous economies would save him. But common sense and the threat of bankruptcy were not enough to quench Sutter's spirit. When he returned to his headquarters, he complied with all Frémont's requests as though money were of no concern.

For an assignment in California, Frémont was clearly the wrong man for the job. Even the political situation was unclear, for in February 1844 the Californians had once again disposed of the governor appointed by the central government. In his place, two men held power: José Castro, the military commander, who operated out of Monterey; and Pio Pico, who held the title of governor and made his headquarters in Los Angeles. Of the two, Castro had the greater influence, for although Pico controlled the legislature, Castro dominated the Monterey customshouse, which produced most of the province's income. To add to the complications, much of the population was in favor of—or indifferent to—an American annexation, thus giving rise to the possibility of a bloodless conquest.

In such a delicate situation—and with the United States and Mexico on the verge of war over issues elsewhere that could not be reconciled—a more moderate and seasoned officer would have adhered closely to his original assignment. He would have realized that the limited force at his disposal could not truly affect the course of events but that his presence as a military commander might create embarrassment for his government. Instead of moving north toward Oregon, however, Frémont, anxious to be in the center of activity and to share in any glory, stayed in California. Worse yet, he did not quietly remain in the friendly seclusion of Sutter's establishment. Instead he marched south down the San Joaquin Valley in the center of California, disciplining the Indians and searching for the main body of his men whom he had left behind when he had dashed ahead to Sutter's.

Failing to locate the soldiers, he returned to Sutter's Fort, visited San Francisco, and from there went on to Monterey. Walking the streets of the old town—the original Monterey almost forgotten and his name now misspelled—Frémont visited Thomas O. Larkin, the redwood exporter and businessman who served as the American consul. He also called on Castro, the military commander, and protested that he was merely a man of science, entitled to purchase the supplies he needed. Although his excuses were weak and he was clearly in violation of international law, Castro decided to ignore his unusual behavior.

In the weeks that followed, Frémont showed little judgment and a great desire for fame. He finally located the remainder of his party—they had misunderstood the rendezvous—but instead of retiring to the north or continuing the exploration assigned to him, went into camp fairly near the present-day city of San José, California. After a brief rest, he moved again, this time toward the southwest and the most heavily populated part of that area of California, stopping near the present city of Salinas, not far from Monterey.

For this action, he could give no reasonable excuse. Even years later he tried to explain it away by saying that he was merely looking for a place where he might eventually obtain property and settle. But there he remained, an army officer at the head of sixty armed men, not far from one of the province's two capitals. It was a position designed to create the maximum trouble for the American government if peace prevailed and, with so small a force, of almost no value if hostilities commenced.

With good reason, the Californian authorities were annoyed. No nation could tolerate the presence of unauthorized military personnel of another country in its midst, particularly when the commander's stated purpose was at such variance with his actions. Quite properly Castro sent a messenger with a protest, to which Frémont replied in unjustifiably haughty terms.

"Surprised both at the message and the terms in which it was worded," Frémont later said, "I expressed to the envoy my astonishment at General Castro's breach of good faith, and the rudeness with which he committed it. . . . I peremptorily refused compliance to an order insulting to my Government and myself."

Having delivered this incredible reply, Frémont moved his men to the top of a small neighboring mountain, now known as Frémont Peak, and began to build a fort over which he raised the American flag.

Castro, of course, could no longer ignore the impetuous young officer and sent troops to dislodge him. When a detachment of Mexican horsemen began to advance, Frémont moved forward with forty of his men. Since he held the superior position, the Mexicans wisely withdrew, but greater and greater numbers of them began to assemble at the foot of the mountain. The outcome of any battle became more and more certain regardless of what Frémont did, and he began looking for a way to extricate himself.

"Later in the afternoon of the third day," he wrote, "the pole bearing our flag fell to the ground. Thinking I had remained as long as the occasion required, I took advantage of the accident to say to the men that this was an indication for us to move camp, and accordingly I gave the order to prepare to move."

He then tried to justify his conduct. "The protecting favor which the usage of all civilized governments and people accords to scientific expeditions imposed on me, even here, a corresponding obligation; and I now felt myself bound to go on my way, having given General Castro sufficient time to execute his threat."

Frémont's forces were too small and California too remote for his vainglorious maneuvers to affect the policy the American government was pursuing. Polk and his cabinet had three objectives: to defend Texas against the Mexicans' threatened attack and resolve the dispute over the republic's southern boundary; to acquire California before some other nation seized it; and to acquire also the land, much of it unsettled, that lay between Texas and California.

For the land outside Texas, Polk was willing to pay and pay well. In November 1845, he had appointed John Slidell, a Louisiana lawyer and politician, minister plenipotentiary to negotiate the purchase with Mexico. He also ordered General Zachary Taylor to take up a position near Corpus Christi, Texas, on the edge of the area that was contested by Texas and Mexico.

Polk hoped for peace. It seemed to him that everything could be worked out to the advantage of both nations, particularly since Mexico, chronically in debt ever since it had gained its independence, already owed the United States a considerable sum of money. Under Polk's plan, this debt would be cancelled, and the United States would pay a large premium on top of it. But he did not count on the national pride of the Mexicans. José Joaquin Herrerra, president of Mexico, might have been interested in negotiating, but the army, traditionally a source of patronage, was filled with commissioned officers, proud of their positions and contemptuous of the Americans. Any negotiations would be an affront to their honor, and their feelings were shared by the populace. Herrerra's government was quickly overthrown, and a warlike but over-imbibing general took his place as president. Slidell received instructions to leave the country immediately, and the stage was set for battle.

When his peaceful approach failed, Polk ordered Taylor to take up a new position on the Rió Grande, thus occupying the territory that Mexico and Texas had been disputing. Taylor moved forward in March 1846. The opposing Mexican general ordered him to withdraw. Taylor retaliated by blockading the Rió Grande. On April 25, 1846, a Mexican detachment crossed the Rió Grande and attacked some of the American general's dragoons, inflicting several casualties and taking a few prisoners.

In Washington Polk was considering his next step. The expulsion of Slidell convinced him little was to be gained by further attempts at negotiation, and in late April he started preparing a declaration of war on Mexico. A meeting with Slidell, who had returned to Washington, heightened his belief that war was inevitable, but several of his cabinet members were reluctant to take so drastic a step.

At the same time, Polk was trying to draw the Oregon question to a conclusion. The secretary of state told the British ambassador, "Our own American title to the extent of the valley of the Columbia . . . extends our exclusive rights over the whole territory in dispute, as against Great Britain."

He then reminded the British that Polk had expressed a willingness to compromise on the issue although this represented a reversal of his previous stand. "Such being the opinion of the President in regard to the title of the United States," the secretary of state continued, "he would not have consented to yield any portion of the Oregon territory, had he not found himself embarrassed, if not committed, by the acts of his predecessors." Polk was warning the British that the threat of war with Mexico was not going to weaken his stand on Oregon but that he was willing to compromise to honor the position taken by previous administrations.

Mexico, however, continued to occupy his greater attention. On Saturday, May 9, 1846, he convened the cabinet. Several members were still uncertain that the circumstances warranted war. During the day, Polk learned about the attack on Taylor's forces and reconvened the cabinet. The news startled those that were hesitant and removed their lingering doubts. All day Sunday—although it was against his scruples—Polk worked on his message to Congress, which was delivered on May 11. "In further vindication of our rights and defense of our territory," he said, "I invoke the prompt action of Congress to recognize the existence of the war, and to place at the disposition of the executive the means of prosecuting the war with vigor."

17. Marching to War

. . . I have seen with great pleasure the alacrity with which volunteers have rushed to the public service. A spirit of patriotism and devotion to the country's interest has been manifested of which we can be justly proud.

—Daniel Webster, 1846

Few nations have embarked on a warlike policy as ill prepared as the United States in 1846. To oppose the approximately six thousand Mexican troops gathered at the Rió Grande, General Taylor had only about twenty-two hundred men and officers. Yet collecting this relatively small number had been a challenge to the War Department, which had had to strip the defenses of the northern border and the Atlantic Coast.

Confusion over the mobilization of the nation's manpower created additional problems. Without waiting for proper authorization, General Edmund P. Gaines in New Orleans began calling for volunteers on his own. A veteran of the War of 1812 and the fighting against the Seminoles, Gaines's enthusiasm was greater than his common sense. What Taylor needed were trained soldiers; what Gaines produced were large numbers of raw recruits whom Taylor now had to care for and supply.

Furthermore the nation was not united behind Polk's aggressive policy. In February 1846, shortly before actual hostilities broke out, Representative Truman Smith of Connecticut charged that "the policy of this administration is adapted to bring on us three wars at one and the same time. 1. A war with Great Britain. 2. A war with Mexico. And 3. A war with all the Indian tribes on our western and northwestern frontier." After recounting the possible costs in human lives and damage to the nation's economy, he said, "In conclusion, I wish to notice for a moment what has been said on the *destiny* of this great republic." Smith did not concur that a manifest fate was leading the United States toward the expansion of its territory. He thought its energies might be better devoted to other ends, such as education, and the improvement of the public morals. "And especially," he hoped, "let us keep clear of that greatest of all curses to republics, unnecessary war."

John C. Calhoun, who had now returned to the Senate after serving in Tyler's cabinet, was also alarmed by Polk's bellicose strategy; and in March 1846, when Polk announced the sudden abrogation by the United States of the agreement for the joint occupancy of Oregon, he told the Senate, "I see nothing to hope from war, be its result what it may. On the contrary, I believe that the most successful and triumphant war that could be waged . . . would be disastrous to us."

Yet Polk's timing turned out to be right, and he launched the United States on its dangerous adventure when the current of history carried it over obstacles that ordinarily would have proved insurmountable. Fighting against numerically superior forces, Taylor immediately won a series of victories that placed his army inside his opponents' territory in contrast to the opening days of the War of 1812.

Then came the astounding news that the British—in spite of their irritation over Polk's unilateral action in abrogating the joint occupancy of Oregon— were willing to relax their demands. The influences bearing on their decision were many and varied, including a change of government and several domestic crises. Even the Hudson's Bay Company, which had the primary British stake in the area, seemed to have lost interest in it. Having almost exhausted the furs to the south, it was willing to withdraw from the Columbia River north to Vancouver Island.

The British, therefore, would agree to a boundary line at the forty-ninth parallel with a loop going south to encompass Vancouver Island; and they were willing to surrender their rights to navigation on the Columbia River with the provision, however, that the Hudson's Bay Company could still travel on that great river unimpeded.

Their sudden conciliatory mood caught Polk off guard and placed him in an embarrassing position. Many Americans, particularly among the members of his own party, had wanted the boundary at 54°41', a line that would have carried the United States far north into what is now Canada. As an expansionist, Polk had favored their views and was afraid that the acceptance of anything less would alienate his supporters. Yet although he was a gambler, he tempered his risk-taking with realism, and he knew the British would probably never offer better terms.

Wisely he submitted the offer to his cabinet. If they unanimously approved its acceptance, he would then send it on to the Senate. But the cabinet's opinion was not unanimous.

With a divided cabinet and his own past extremist statements against him, Polk decided on a course that would, in effect, place the decision in other hands. On June 8, 1846, he sent a message to the Senate saying, "In the early periods of the Government the opinion and the advice of the Senate were often taken in advance upon important questions of our foreign policy. General Washington repeatedly consulted the Senate and asked their previous advice. . . . For these reasons I invite the consideration of the Senate to the proposal of the British Government for the settlement of the Oregon question, and ask their advice on the subject." He then stated that if two-thirds of the Senate—the majority required to ratify a treaty—approved the offer, he would accept. Or he would make any changes such a majority suggested. If they failed to approve the offer, he would reject it.

A clever politician, Polk avoided personal responsibility for a decision; but acting also like a wise statesman, he involved more persons in the settlement of an issue that could be divisive. The Senate took up the question in executive session; and since the expansionists had been somewhat tempered by the acquisition of Texas and the war with Mexico, the terms were approved by thirty-eight to twelve. So the question of Oregon, which had roiled relations between the British and the Americans for several decades, was suddenly quieted; and the settlers who had advanced beyond the recognized boundary of the United States were now living on American soil.

Although Polk had a busy schedule, negotiating with the British and dealing with the Mexican War, he did not forget that his objectives also included the acquisition of New Mexico, California, and the land that lay between. American ships were in the Pacific with orders to take California if war broke out, a naval ensign had already reached the province as a secret agent, and what became known as the Army of the West was ready to march from the Mississippi to reinforce the navy.

Stephen Watts Kearny was in command and started west about the time Polk was considering the British offer. The regular troops assigned to him were the First Dragoons, or mounted infantrymen, some of whom had been withdrawn from the Upper Missouri. He was also authorized to enlist volunteers from Missouri, many of them men from sedentary occupations and with no military experience. In addition, he was instructed to form a batallion of Mormons and, by offering them a trip west at the government's expense, remove them from the areas where they were likely to come into conflict with the local residents.

Polk intended to supply additional troops later, a company of the Third Artillery to sail from New York City and a regiment of New York Infantry Volunteers. In the meanwhile, Kearny was to be dependent on the small force assigned to him.

The task given him was staggering. He was to conquer New Mexico and then continue on to California and engage in whatever hostilities might still be continuing on the West Coast.

Although Texas was disputed land, it might be regarded as generally friendly, but from the New Mexican line to California was a march several hundred miles longer than the march Napoleon made from the Neiman River to Moscow. Although Mexico's army was far smaller than the tsar's, Kearny counted his men by the hundreds, while Napoleon counted his by the thousands. Napoleon took with him large quantities of supplies; Kearny knew he would have to live off the country—a country that for many square miles included nothing but desert. He did not have to face the Cossacks, but he had no idea whether the Indians, especially the Apaches, would prove friendly or whether they would launch their harassing raids. Furthermore the countryside over which Napoleon led his soldiers was well known; Mexicans had traveled from Santa Fé to California with some frequency, but no roads marked the route and few towns would provide opportunities to replenish the army's supplies or rest its men. The winters in what is now New Mexico and Arizona were not cold and bitter like those of Russia, but Russia could not duplicate the heat and lack of water that Kearny was likely to encounter.

These considerations did not disturb Kearny, who faced the campaign with a soldier's optimism. Some of his officers, however, were disappointed by the assignment, not because it was so overawing, but because they thought it would prove too easy and that the glory would be won by those fighting farther to the south against the main concentration of Mexican troops. Philip St. George Cooke, a captain of dragoons, was especially upset by this assignment. But he soon found that his commanding officer had carefully selected him to perform an unusual mission: Under a flag of truce, he was to go in advance of the troops and treat with Governor Armijo in Santa Fé.

With a few men and two merchants who wished to trade at Santa Fé—one of them was an American, James W. Magoffin—Cooke set off. Whereas Armijo had prepared and executed a brutal welcome for the ill-equipped unmilitary expedition of the Texas Pioneers, he acted differently when threatened by a relatively large force of regular soldiers. At the outlying towns, where the Texas Pioneers had been manhandled and bullied, the officials received Cooke courteously; and he made his way without difficulty into Santa Fé.

"For the first time," Cooke later said, "I thought it would not be amiss to air my flag of truce; so I placed a white handkerchief on the point of my sabre, and the officer of the guard advancing to meet me, I announced my mission in a sentence of very formal book–Spanish: he gave me a direction to the right I thought, and looking up a narrow street, I saw a friendly signal, pushed on, and emerging found myself and party on the plaza, crowded by . . . soldiers and countrymen."

These, however, were not like the hostile crowds the Texas Pioneers encountered; and instead of being taken prisoner, Cooke was permitted to go into the governor's palace. "I entered from the hall, a large and lofty apartment, with a carpeted earth floor," Cooke wrote, "and discovered the governor seated at a table, with six or eight military and civil officials standing. There was no mistaking the governor . . . he wore a blue frock coat, with a rolling collar and a general's shoulder straps, blue stripped trousers with gold lace, and a red sash."

Armijo rose and took the letter Kearny had sent him. "He said," Cooke continued, "he had ordered quarters for me, and . . . he hoped I would remain as long as it pleased me."

During the succeeding days, Magoffin, who had many acquaintances in the town, went about his business, met with the governor, and introduced Cooke to Santa Fé's social life. The governor asked Cooke a number of questions about the strength of the American forces. "General Armijo," Cooke said, "with little or no military experience, distrustful of the loyalty of the population he had habitually fleeced, and of their feeble ignorance which has been much impressed by our long commercial intercourse, is said to be in painful doubt and irresolution."

In later years, when the war was long over, the battle flags furled, and the ink on the treaties dry and fading, Cooke would describe his mission to Santa Fé, but not its purpose or its outcome. On those topics he remained discreetly silent, not mentioning whether he had been successful or not, or the role that Magoffin, with his outgoing, jovial manner and deep knowledge of Mexican customs, might have played.

But after Cooke had reported back to Kearny and the Army of the West moved forward, it encountered no resistance. The local authorities in each town surrendered quickly and listened respectfully while Kearny assured them they would be continued in office under the new sovereignty and that the rights of their people would be respected. At one easily defended pass outside of Santa Fé, the Americans discovered the remains of a breastwork but only two Mexicans. One of them was New Mexico's acting secretary of state, who brought Kearny a letter from the lieutenant governor. This informed the American commander that Armijo had fled to the south and that the Americans could enter the capital without opposition. By that evening Kearny was riding down the streets of Santa Fé, where nothing remained of

201

the city's defenders except nine pieces of artillery, one of them bearing the pathetic stamping—"Barcelona, 1778."

After the war Magoffin filed a large expense account with the American government, and the amount was paid without question. And Cooke, having met the approval of his superior officers, continued to rise in rank. The purpose—and the success of his mission—was now apparent. As every trader knew, Armijo was a man with a price. And the Americans had purchased from him the conquest of hundreds of square miles of his nation's countryside.

In New Mexico, Kearny's principal problem was not facing a hostile army or an angry population but finding enough supplies for his troops. Never strong, the province's economy had declined even further in recent years, for the Indians—especially the Navajos—had depleted the herds of sheep that had provided the basis for what little wealth it did have. Even feeding the horses was a problem, for there was no grain or hay to be purchased.

Their easy conquest, moreover, had not helped the morale of his soldiers. The thoughts of many were expressed by Cooke, when he said, "Our position here has been unfortunate, irksome, disheartening—so far from the 'sabre clash' of the sunny South! . . . That a soldier should pass through a war without distinction I used to think—and does not the world?—is to be set down to his fault or want of merit."

A brief foray to the south convinced Kearny that Armijo did not intend to return, so before the end of September 1846, he divided his force into three columns. When the Mormon Battalion arrived, it would come under Cooke's command and build a road between New Mexico and California. The Missouri Volunteers, when they were relieved by reinforcements expected from the east, would march to Chihuahua and join the troops already there. The third column, numbering approximately three hundred men, would meanwhile advance toward California under Kearny's personal command.

The trail from New Mexico to California was not clearly marked; and Cooke summed up Kearny's problem by saying, "To-morrow, three hundred wilderness-worn dragoons, in shabby and patched clothing, who have long been on short allowances of food, set forth to conquer or 'annex' a Pacific empire; to take a leap in the dark of a thousand miles of wild plains and mountains, only known in vague reports as unwatered, and with several deserts of two or three marches where a camel might starve if not perish of thirst."

When Kendall, the editor of the New Orleans *Picayune,* returned from his adventure with the Texas Pioneers, he had remarked that the conquest of Mexico would not be easy, for what the nation lacked in fortifications and trained soldiers was made up for by its geography. Kearny was not launching his soldiers against an army; he was launching them against a land.

Before he left the Rió Grande, he met Kit Carson, who had gone with

Frémont on his expedition to California. On his way to Washington with dispatches from Frémont and Stockton he brought news that the navy had been victorious and the war in California was over. Kearny, therefore, decided to leave two hundred more men in New Mexico, as they would not be needed on the West Coast, and proceed with a column of only a hundred. He also persuaded Carson that his skills were wasted taking messages to the capital and that he would render his country a greater service by guiding the Army of the West.

On his way down the Rió Grande Valley, Kearny saw firsthand evidence of the continued ferocity of the Apaches. One of the towns he entered had suffered from an Apache attack only the day before, the Indians having killed numerous inhabitants and run off with many of the community's horses and mules. Near Santa Rita del Cobre, however, he learned that the Apaches' hatred was directed at the Mexicans, not all white men.

A group of Apaches appeared with their leader, Mangas Colorados, and watched with interest as the soldiers responded to the bugle call "Boots and Saddles." "The order, quickness and quietude of our movements seemed to impress them," William H. Emory, Kearny's topographical engineer, later reported. "One of the chiefs, after eyeing the general [Kearny] with apparent great admiration, broke out in a vehement manner: 'You have taken New Mexico, and will soon take California; go, then, and take Chihuahua, Durango, and Sonora. We will help you. . . . The Mexicans are rascals, we hate and will kill them all." There burst out the smothered fire of three hundred years!

Before the soldiers moved on, the Apaches, according to Emory, "swore eternal friendship to the whites, and everlasting hatred to the Mexicans. . . . The road was open to the Americans now and forever." But, Emory added, "Carson, with a twinkle of his keen hazel eye, observed to me, 'I would not trust one of them.'"

A contrast to the nomadic Apaches were the Pima Indians, whom the expedition encountered later. "To us," Emory later said, "it was rare sight to be thrown in the midst of what is termed wild Indians, surpassing many of the Christian nations in agriculture, little behind them in the useful arts, and immeasurably before them in honesty and virtue." Each of their adobe houses, he noted, "consists of a dome-shaped, wicker-work, about six feet high, and from twenty to fifty feet in diameter, thatched with straw or corn stalks. In front is usually a large arbor, on which is piled the cotton in the pod, for drying.

"In the houses were stored water melons, pumpkins, beans, corn, and wheat, the last three articles generally in large baskets. . . . A few chickens and dogs were seen, but no other domestic animals, except horses, mules, and oxen. Their implements of husbandry were the axe (of steel), wooden hoes, shovels, and harrows."

Seeing these two tribes, so widely different in their way of life, and observing some of the ancient Indian ruins gave Emory and other members of the expedition a sense of the wide variety of Indian culture. It was as impossible to find a common denominator as it was to place a single classification on all the peoples of Europe.

The following day, Emory and two companions went on a short exploring trip near the camp. "On our return," Emory recounted, "we met a Mexican, well mounted and muffled in his blanket. I asked him where he was going; he said to hunt horses. As he passed, I observed in each of his holsters the neck of a bottle, and on his croup a fresh made sack, with other evidences of preparation for a journey. Much against his taste, I invited him to follow me to camp; several times he begged me to let him go for a moment, that he would soon return. His anxiety to be released increased my determination not to comply with his request. I took him to General Kearny and explained to him the suspicious circumstances under which I had taken him, and that his capture would prove of some importance. He was immediately searched, and in his wallet was found the mail from California, which was of course opened."

The news it contained belied the tidings Carson had brought. Instead of being at peace, California was at war. In a counterrevolt, the Mexicans had driven the Americans from Santa Barbara, Los Angeles, and several other communities, and the Mexican flag was again flying over much of California. On hearing Kit Carson's news, Kearny had left two-thirds of his force in New Mexico. Now he stood on the edge of hostile territory with only a small column of travel-weary soldiers, short of supplies and more ready for a rest than a battle, yet with the prospect of stiff fighting ahead.

18. The Fruits of War

Some of the Californians are quietly awaiting the result, some are indifferent on the subject, and others against it.

—Thomas O. Larkin, 1846

In planning to acquire California, the American government had to take into account several possibilities: Mexico might be willing to sell it; the Californians might revolt and ask the United States to take possession; they might fight, but not hard; or—although this seemed remote—they might wage vigorous warfare. Each possibility required its own strategy, often in conflict with the others. And this complex problem had to be administered from a command post thousands of miles away in distance and months away in time. Nevertheless the government's planning was realistic.

The commander of the Pacific squadron, John D. Sloat, was ordered, in the event of war, to move up the coast and take possession, peacefully or otherwise, of the California ports, particularly Monterey, one of its two capitals and the headquarters of its military commander. Kearny, of course, had been ordered to proceed by land and, after capturing New Mexico, continue to California and join in any fighting that might be taking place there. Thus, if the plan to purchase California fell through, a pincer attack could be launched on the province, one arm by sea and one approaching from the east.

To make sure its strategy was understood, the government also sent a secret emissary, Archibald H. Gillespie, a lieutenant of marines, to inform the American consul at Monterey, Thomas O. Larkin, of the government's plans. Although Larkin was a merchant—not a soldier—he understood the Californians well and could be counted on to conduct any negotiations and to advise the army and navy. Polk intended to add California to the United States with as little bloodshed as possible.

There were, however, several factors that neither he nor his administration took into account. One was Frémont. Although he had been assigned to lead a purely scientific expedition, it soon became apparent he had military ambitions and was prepared to take every opportunity to satisfy them. Anther factor was the romantic nature of Gillespie. Letting him near Frémont was like trying to put out a prairie fire by smothering it with dried grass.

Another complication was the presence of comparatively large numbers of aliens, many of them either Americans or men who considered themselves allied with the Americans. Living mostly in the north, they had never been assimilated into the Mexican population. In fact, the majority had come to California in the expectation that it would shortly be part of the United States. They were not ill-intentioned or evil people; but they knew that the country would be run more efficiently under the American flag and that a change in sovereignty was inevitable. As far as they were concerned, every day that passed was one in which the benefits of American acquisition were lost; and they were growing impatient.

The combination of these factors quickly upset the government's original plans and turned the conquest of California into a drama that ranged from tragedy to comedy, from order to confusion, and destroyed the goodwill of many of the Mexicans that men like Larkin had been courting for years.

Gillespie quickly joined Frémont, not the quiet, clear-thinking Larkin; and the news he brought fired Frémont's already overstimulated ardor. At a time like this, Frémont could not think of withdrawing his men from the scene of action. But while he dreamed of defeating the Mexicans and emerging a hero, Frémont forgot to post sentinels around his camp that night. The Klamath Indians attacked in the darkness and killed three men. The following day, Frémont, in turn, attacked the nearest Klamath camp, killed most of its warriors, and set fire to its supplies. He was literally a firebrand let loose in a delicate situation.

On hearing of Frémont's return to the Sacramento Valley, Castro justifiably became alarmed. He began mobilizing his troops at Santa Clara, south of San Francisco, and sent out scouting expeditions to obtain horses and supplies. One of these collected a herd of about two hundred horses near Sonoma, California, north of San Francisco. A group of American settlers were not willing to see such a prize escape and seized the horses. Having committed this overt act of war, they decided to go a step further and captured, with little effort, the town of Sonoma, a completely senseless achievement, for the community had absolutely no military value for either side.

Furthermore its most prominent citizen was Mariano Guadalupe Vallejo, a rich Californian who had long been active in the province's public life and was also known to be friendly toward the Americans. In accord with the usual Mexican custom of bestowing titles, he was also the *commandante* of Sonoma, a commander without a command, but nevertheless in the eyes of the American attackers a military figure. They, therefore, declared him a prisoner of war and sent him off to be locked up at Sutter's Fort. This was highly embarrassing to Sutter, who was both a friend of Vallejo and who also hoped to be a helpful intermediary between the Mexicans and the Americans.

Once started, the uprising at Sonoma soon swelled to comic-opera proportions. Frémont quickly joined it; and the settlers selected their civilian leader, William F. Ide—a newly arrived Mormon—designed a flag that contained a large bear, declared themselves the "Bear Flag Republic," and called on other residents of California to support them.

Castro responded by sending fifty men north to recapture Sonoma. They met the Bear Flag soldiers at Olompali, near Sonoma, engaged in a skirmish, and withdrew, their mission uncompleted. Frémont then marched on to San Francisco, where he spiked the Mexicans' cannons. This was another useless act, since the guns were so old and decrepit they could not have been fired without causing more danger to the gunners than to the target.

Meanwhile the significant action was taking place toward the south, where the power of the Mexicans was concentrated. Commodore Sloat, pursuant to his orders, had sailed into the bay at Monterey and dropped anchor, prepared to salute the Mexican flag. But there was no flag—somehow it had gotten lost—and the Mexicans' powder magazine was empty, so they could not have returned the honor.

Once ashore he wisely consulted Larkin. Both men were anxious to acquire California as peacefully as possible, but events had outdistanced their desires. The Bear Flag uprising had been too arrogant for the Mexicans to ignore, so on July 7—even after five days of negotiation—they refused to surrender. Without waiting any longer, Sloat raised the American flag over Monterey and ordered the commander of an American ship at San Francisco to hoist it over that community, too. He then issued a proclamation announcing that California had become part of the United States. Castro and Pico, the commander and the governor, were realistic about the odds facing them and announced that resistance was useless and quietly withdrew. Momentarily it looked as though Polk's policy would succeed in spite of another difficulty that arose.

Sloat was both sick and feeling old, so he welcomed the arrival in Monterey of Commodore Robert D. Stockton. Turning his command over to the younger man, he sailed for home. Stockton had had wide experience in the navy and had spent ten years in private business before returning to the service, where he devoted much of his time to encouraging the use of steam power instead of sail. (Later he became a senator and worked for the abolition of flogging in the navy.)

Such a man might have been expected to continue the moderation practiced by Sloat. Instead, he issued a second proclamation, using far harsher terms, and placed Frémont in command of the newly constituted California Battalion of Mounted Riflemen with Gillespie as his second in command.

By August, Stockton had gained control of southern California, including Los Angeles, and sent Kit Carson to Washington with word that the war was over, the mission Carson was fulfilling when he met Kearny in New Mexico. But Stockton then committed a serious blunder. He made Gillespie, who had little understanding of the Mexican temperament, commander of Los Angeles, and also permitted him to declare martial law. Nothing could have been better designed to irritate the people, who had shown themselves willing to accept American rule but had demonstrated no willingness to put up with bombast, regulations, and red tape. In a short time they were in revolt under the leadership of José María Flores and several other former Mexican officers.

Until then Gillespie had had a contemptuous attitude toward the Mexicans, but he quickly learned the difference between a Mexican who had joined the army because he could not otherwise make a living and a Mexican who was fighting to overthrow an oppressor. By September 24, Gillespie was pinned down near the center of Los Angeles; and Stockton began organizing a rescue column that included Frémont and the California Battalion. Before they could arrive, Gillespie was forced to surrender.

The success of the uprising at Los Angeles inspired other Californians to revolt. A group of Mexicans attacked a ranch about twenty-five miles from Los Angeles and captured a number of Americans; and the outbreak, although never well planned and coordinated, spread into the northern part of California.

One of its saddest victims was Thomas O. Larkin, the consul who had worked so hard for understanding between the Americans and the Mexicans. His wife had moved to San Francisco, where conditions were less unsettled, only to have their daughter fall seriously ill. Hearing that his daughter might die, Larkin rushed to join his wife at the child's bedside; and on the way, the insurgent Mexicans captured him. He was then forced to watch—with bitterly torn emotions—a fight between some Mexicans and Americans.

After defeating the Americans, his captors took him first to Santa Barbara and then to Los Angeles. His position was ambivalent. As the leading American diplomat in California and a prominent citizen, he was an important hostage, one to be guarded closely and perhaps executed. Yet he also had many acquaintances among his jailors, who treated him with respect and did him favors. For a man of his standing, accustomed to commanding—not obeying—it was a trying experience, compounded by his knowledge that the fighting was probably unnecessary. As he pointed out to his wife he had known that the Sonoma uprising would only make the conquest of California more difficult and that the aggressive attitudes of Stockton and Gillespie were creating additional problems.

The Americans, in spite of the turn of events against them, were not ready to concede defeat. When Gillespie reached San Diego—he had been paroled on his promise to embark at that port—he found that reinforcements had already arrived with control of the sea, the Americans could quickly move up and down the coast and forgetting his surrender, he was prepared to march back to Los Angeles.

The Mexicans were ready. About fifteen miles away, they had prepared their defenses, which included a cannon that had once been used in Los Angeles for the state ceremonies in which the Mexicans so delighted. When the Americans had taken over the town, it had been buried. Now the Mexicans had dug it up again, cleaned it off, and mounted it on wagon wheels. Able to move it quickly from one point to another, and using powder they had made themselves, they stopped the American advance. If the United States was to retake the town it had lost, it needed more troops and better leadership.

And so by December 1846, when Kearny entered southern California, Los Angeles was again in Mexican hands, and no American—not even one of Larkin's standing—could consider himself safe.

As they reached the last mountains that separated them from the coast, Kearny's men were in a somber mood. What they eagerly anticipated were good meals and a chance to rest, not a battle. But at the first ranch at which they stopped, they received their first intimation of the bad news awaiting them, but the man in charge of the ranch did not know any details. So Kearny sent for an Englishman who lived about fifteen miles away.

"His dress," Emory said, "was a black velvet English hunting coat, a pair of black velvet trousers, cut off at the knee and open on the outside to the hip, beneath which were drawers of spotless white; his leggins were of black buckskin, and his heels armed with spurs six inches long." In better times, his weird dress might have caused the men to laugh, but the information he brought was too serious. Stockton still held San Diego, but all the neighboring country had reverted to the Mexicans. While stressing his neutrality, the Englishman said he would carry a message to Stockton, since he was going to San Diego anyway. At least the two branches of the American invading force could establish some sort of communication.

With a party of about thirty-five Americans, Gillespie marched from San Diego to meet them. He warned Kearny that the road to the coast was not clear and that the Mexicans were gathered in force at a point called San Pascual, which was only a few miles ahead.

Before daybreak, the Americans started their advance on the enemy, whose campfires glowed in the darkness. The fighting was fierce and sharp, mostly hand to hand; and although they drove the Mexicans from the field, they had learned that the people of California, when aroused, were courageous combatants. The Americans suffered more than thirty casualties—a high percentage of the small number engaged—and both Kearny and Gillespie were wounded, Kearny so badly that he temporarily turned over the command to one of his junior officers.

"When night closed in," Emory said, "the bodies of the dead were buried under a willow to the east of our camp, with no other accompaniment than the howling of myriads of wolves, attracted by the smell. Thus were put to rest together, and forever, a band of brave and heroic men. The long march of 2,000 miles had brought our little command, both officers and men, to know each other well. Community of hardships, dangers and privations, had produced relations of mutual regard which caused their loss to sink deeply in our memories."

Kearny's battered column—the Army of the West—needed help. He dispatched messengers to Stockton, hoping they could get past the enemy; meanwhile he made camp where he was. "Our provisions were exhausted," Emory wrote, "our horses dead, our mules on their last legs, and our men, now reduced to one third their number, were ragged, worn down by fatigue, and emaciated. . . . Our position was defensible, but the ground, covered with rocks and cacti, made it difficult to get a smooth place to rest, even for the wounded. The night was cold and damp, and notwithstanding our excessive fatigues of the day and night previous, sleep was impossible."

The following morning the men started their dreary, somber march to the coast, carrying their wounded with them, as best they could. Descending on a nearby ranchería, they found it had no browse for their remaining mules but were able to round up some cattle, which gave them the promise of a good meal in the evening. Shortly the Mexicans fell upon them again. The Americans drove the enemy back, but in the process lost the herd of cattle they had seized and faced the prospect of another day without enough food.

Hope came to them, however, when the Mexican commander offered to exchange prisoners, for one was a courier whom Kearny had sent to San Diego. He had gotten through, being captured only on his return. Although the dispatches he brought back were never recovered by the Americans, at least they knew that Stockton was aware of their predicament.

On the night of December 10, while the tired soldiers tried to get some rest before fighting off another enemy attack in the morning, one of the sentinels heard a man speaking English. A few minutes later the sound of a marching column broke the quiet. A hundred sailors and eighty marines had arrived from San Diego.

This gave the Americans a numerical superiority that ensured their safety, and the rest of their march was uneventful. Crossing over a hill they saw the Pacific for the first time, "the sight producing strange but agreeable notions," Emory wrote. "One of the mountain men, who had never seen the ocean before, opened his arms and exclaimed: 'Lord! there is a great prairie without a tree.'"

Kearny's safe arrival at San Diego prevented the Mexicans from using the one strategy most likely to bring them success—attacking and defeating the Americans in small groups. But it still left the United States faced with the problem of subduing a large area in which revolt, although sporadic and not well coordinated, was widespread.

One key to victory was the recapture of Los Angeles. So the Americans organized a fresh attack under the leadership of Kearny. The forces he commanded were a miscellany—fifty dragoons, fifty volunteers, forty sailors acting as artillerymen, and nearly a hundred and fifty sailors and marines serving as infantry.

His men's morale was high when, on January 8, 1847, they met the Mexicans at the San Gabriel River just outside Los Angeles. The site lent itself to the Mexicans' defense. The river, although only about knee deep, was close to a hundred yards wide and filled with quicksand. On the opposite side, a hill gave the Mexicans a superior position from which they could shoot down on the advancing Americans.

Stockton, who had a reputation as a fine artilleryman, proved himself as capable on land as he was at sea and, refusing to remain on the far side of the San Gabriel, maneuvered his guns across the treacherous terrain and placed them where they would be most effective. Kearny meanwhile had led his dragoons and converted seamen across the river, at the same time fighting off an attack on his rear.

Although the land generally favored the Mexicans, one feature of it proved enormously helpful to the Americans. On the Mexicans' side of the river, according to Emory, "there was a natural banquette, breast high. Under this the [Americans] line was deployed. To this accident of the ground is to be attributed the little loss we sustained from the enemy's artillery, which showered grape and round shot over our heads. In an hour and twenty minutes our baggage train had all crossed, the artillery of the enemy was silenced, and a charge made on the hill."

To Kit Carson, this was merely another of the many fights in which he had

211

been engaged. Having stripped himself to a red shirt and trousers and having bound a handkerchief around his head, he tied his horse to his arm, so the animal could not run off. He then lighted his pipe and was ready to do battle. He never took his pipe out of his mouth except to fire. After every shot, he replaced it in his mouth, reloaded, and was ready to fire again; and each time he pulled the trigger, he brought down a Mexican.

After the Americans had consolidated themselves on the Mexican bank of the river, "the enemy pitched his camp on the hills in view," Emory said, "but when morning came he was gone. We had no means of pursuit, and scarcely the power of locomotion, such was the wretched condition of our wagon train."

The next day the Mexicans regrouped in a horseshoe formation with their artillery placed on the Americans' right flank and two smaller guns in front. This, they hoped, would hold the Americans in check while they charged against the left. The Americans waited until they were about a hundred yards away before shooting and knocking many of them from their saddles. "A round of grape was then fired upon them," Emory said, "and they scattered. A charge was made simultaneously with this on our rear with about the same success. We considered this the beginning of the fight but it was the end of it. The Californians, the most expert horsemen in the world, stripped the dead horses on the field, without dismounting, and carried off most of their saddles, bridles, and all their dead and wounded on horseback to the hills on the right.

A day later three emissaries entered the American camp under a flag of truce and offered to surrender Los Angeles if the Americans agreed to respect the residents' persons and property. These terms were acceptable; but suspicious of the Mexicans, the Americans "moved into the town," Emory said, "in the same order we should have done if expecting an attack. It was a wise precaution, for the streets were full of desperate and drunken fellows, who brandished their arms and saluted us with every term of reproach."

This victory was almost counterbalanced by the troubles that were now stirring in New Mexico. When Kearny left Santa Fé, he had every reason to believe the province was securely in American hands. Armijo was gone, his route south paved with American money; the population seemed content; and Kearny had installed what appeared to be an acceptable new government. But as in the days of the Pueblo revolt, when the Indians under Popé drove out the Spanish, the surface calm belied the powerful currents running underneath. Once again in the kivas the older men—with the encouragement of the Mexicans—were planning to rise up against their new conquerors.

19. VICTORY WITHOUT GLORY

Now, fellow-citizens, let us look calmly at our true situation. We are two thousand five hundred miles from any point from which we can receive the least assistance by land; and seventeen thousand miles by water.

—William H. Gray, addressing the provisional legislature of Oregon, 1843

The capture of New Mexico had been easy, too easy as the Mexicans now began to think. Without firing a shot, they had permitted Kearny to take the province. But if they were to revolt, they needed allies.

The greatest fighters in that part of the continent were the Apaches and the Navajos, but they had fought so long and hard against the Mexicans they could hardly be trusted in an alliance against the Americans.

The relations between the Pueblo Indians and the Mexicans were different. Their warfare against Coronado and their uprising under Popé had proved the Pueblo Indians were courageous fighters; but since the priests still lived among them and the Mexicans had often established communities near their villages, the two groups frequently communicated with each other. Skillfully the Mexicans played on the Pueblo Indians' emotions and, with the promise of supporting them, roused them into preparing to fight the Americans. The center of the plotting was the Taos Pueblo, close to the town of the same name.

The outbreak started prematurely on January 19, 1847, shortly after the fall of Los Angeles. A Taos Indian had been arrested by the sheriff for theft, and a large crowd gathered at the jail to demand his release. When the sheriff refused to free his prisoner, the mob resorted to force; and the slaying of the sheriff unleashed the crowd's desire for blood. In no time at all, the Indians were calling for the lives of all Americans and seeking them out in their homes and offices. Charles Bent, a member of the famous fur-trading family and the man appointed by Kearny as governor, was one of the victims. The Indians cut off his head and carried it back to the pueblo as a trophy.

As soon as he heard of the uprising, Colonel Sterling Price, whom Kearny had appointed military commander of New Mexico, rushed north. The Mexicans, who had been urging the Indians on, melted into the landscape; and the Indians, as they had done since ancient times, fled to what they considered the security of their pueblo. Price, with a force of several hundred men, arrived at the pueblo on February 2, 1847. The Indians clustered around their church, almost as though they thought the white man's God could keep the white men away, and hurled insults at the American soldiers just as they had hurled insults at Coronado's men years before. Price made a half-hearted attempt to reduce the pueblo, then withdrew, and went into camp.

The following day he took up the battle again, this time in earnest. The adobe walls of the church and the other pueblo buildings could not withstand the pounding of his artillery. Pieces of dried adobe flew in the air or exploded into dust; and although the Indians fought hard, they could neither retreat from their pueblo nor defend it. When the walls were shattered, the Americans charged; and one of Bent's former partners had the satisfaction of killing the Indian who was wearing the slaughtered governor's coat.

In trying to defend their community, the Indians suffered about a hundred and fifty casualties. To finish his task, Price rounded up the Indian ringleaders of the anti-American plot and held a public hanging a few days later.

The capture of Taos and the drastic punishment of its principal warriors quickly dispirited the other pueblos. They fell back into the spirit of sullen acquiescence that had marked their relationships with their conquerors for several hundred years, while the Mexicans, realizing their cause was lost, hoped merely that the Americans would not learn the names of those who had been inciting the Indians.

In California and New Mexico, the war did not end in a vast battle with large armies opposing each other. Nor did triumphant soldiers march with glistening sabers and well-oiled guns into a great city to be followed by frock-coated statesmen. It came to a conclusion in the dusty remains of the church of Taos and the equally dusty streets of Los Angeles, where drunken, frustrated men called insults at the victors. A little sporadic fighting still continued in California, but it was meaningless.

As Emory commented, the battle outside Los Angeles "had forever broken the Mexican authority in California, and they were daily coming in, in large parties, to sue for peace . . . yet small parties of the more desperate and revengeful hung about the mountains and roads; refusing or hesitating to yield obedience to their leaders." These small bands, while they constituted an occasional danger to individual travelers, were incapable of retaking the country.

The fighting was over, and the land conquered, but the maps had not yet been officially redrawn. That would have to await the outcome of the fighting thousands of miles away and closer to the heart of Mexico. Meanwhile neither the actual victors nor the nation as a whole were universally triumphant over the capture of a small empire at so low a cost in money or lives. Enthusiasm for migrating westward waned, partly because many had been disappointed and partly because the nightmarish news about the Donner party was widespread.

When the party had gathered in Missouri during the late spring of 1846, no one—particularly its members—would have expected it to become nationally famous. It was merely a group of men, women, and children, discontented with their lives at home, unfamiliar with the wilderness, and hopeful that somewhere on the West Coast they could find a better future. As their leader, they chose George Donner, who with his brother, Jacob, headed the largest family group within the party. Their days on the trail were like those of most emigrant parties: Sometimes they bickered and fought; sometimes they joined in sorrow, as they did when an elderly member of the company died, or in gaiety, as during their celebration of Independence Day near Fort Laramie. They were united, too, in their common ignorance of the trail and the ways of frontier living. Consequently they accepted as true the claims of Lansford Hastings—now a self-designated expert on the trail to California—that he had discovered a new and easier way to reach the coast; and they did not understand the urgent need to make haste in order to cross the mountains before the snows began. Even Frémont, with a disciplined band of hardy explorers, had almost failed to pass the crest of the Sierra Nevada in wintertime; and the Donner party was neither disciplined nor hardy.

It took them until October to reach the Humboldt Sink, where the Humboldt River, flowing across Nevada with the promise of reaching the Pacific, suddenly turns into alkaline pools and disappears beneath the earth. The Donner party was already in trouble, for with a long distance yet to go, their food was running short. Two men had gone ahead to secure help from John Sutter (whenever emigrants were having difficulties, they counted on the Swiss to help them), but they had not reappeared. Morale was low. One member of the party, James F. Reed, had knived another, probably in self-defense. Some of them thought he should be hanged; others were for letting him go free. Finally they decided to banish him and then commuted the sentence to sending him to Sutter's, too, in case the first two men did not get there.

At the Humboldt Sink, the Indians slipped up during the night and ran off with almost thirty head of cattle. This seriously depleted their herd, forcing them to abandon more wagons and to carry some of their goods on their backs. Only small children and those who were sick could now ride. The others had to walk—often without shoes—over the sharp rocks.

The situation dramatically improved on October 19, 1846. Thomas Stanton, one of the first two men who had gone ahead to Sutter's, returned. He had reached the Sacramento River, and Sutter had sent him back with mules and provisions. For the Donner party, this was a reprieve from death; but instead of pressing on, they paused to rest near the present-day city of Reno. They had heard the snows did not ordinarily start in the Sierra Nevada until around Thanksgiving Day. But this year the storms came early. On October 23, they could see dark clouds gathering ahead of them and began to hurry. But they were too late. The snow began falling, and soon six inches covered the ground.

The flakes floated gently in the dark air, but they brought terror, and the Donner party, never well organized to begin with, started to disintegrate. Some made a wild dash forward; others traveled more slowly behind. At Donner Lake they came together again, those in the lead unable to find a way over the mountains. When Frémont had crossed the mountains in the winter, every man had his specific duty to perform, and all worked in unison. In the Donner party, each family or group of friends worked for itself, one trying one route or one system of moving through the snow, while another did something contrary. At last, as the result of repeated failures, even the most independent of them realized they must make a plan for concerted action. So they returned to their camp at Donner Lake, prepared to start anew on the following day.

But that night snow started falling, not a mere six inches this time, but great swirls of it, deadly and stifling. Under its cover, the land seemed to change form. Logs and rocks disappeared; ravines took on the appearance of level land; slopes lost their steepness; and cliffs and banks rose where none existed. With this change into a world of fantasy—the rocky trails covered by a quagmire of white—the Donner party entered into weeks of horror in which death stalked them mercilessly and their deepest traditions of behavior crumbled.

Approximately eighty people were huddled on the eastern side of the Sierra Nevada with almost no food and only a slight chance of survival. They built a few cabins to give shelter against the snow and wind, but there was little to cook over their campfires. In November, a small party started ahead, not only in the hope of obtaining relief for the others, but to lighten the drain on the remaining supplies. At the end of the first day, they returned exhausted, some of them so beaten in spirit they could barely make any effort to help either themselves or others.

Fifteen of them, however, decided to try once more, among them Thomas Stanton, who had brought back the supplies from Sutter's Fort. But this time the strength had gone out of him. He fell behind, caught up, fell behind, caught up, and at last failed to leave the camp when the others set out the next morning. He assured them he would be with them soon, but he remained where he was, and it was not until the following spring that his body was found, partially devoured by animals that did not distinguish between one form of carrion or another.

The suffering of those who went ahead was intense, and so, too, was that of those who remained behind. "The families shared with one another," wrote one of the survivors, "as long as they had anything to share. Each one's portion was very small. The hides [of the last cattle] were boiled, and the bones were burned brown and eaten. We tried to eat a decayed buffalo robe, but it was too tough, and there was no nourishment in it. Some of the few mice that came into camp were caught and eaten."

Even keeping a fire going proved to be a task of enormous proportions. If they felled a tree, it often disappeared beneath the snow, and when they lighted a fire, it sank deeper and deeper into the snow, until it was at the bottom of a watery pit, making it difficult to get close to it or put on fresh logs.

The fifteen persons going ahead suffered equal torture. One man became so cold in spite of the four shirts he was wearing that he felt nothing when he sat with his back to the fire. Only the smell of his scorching flesh told him the shirts had burned through. Two Indian guides whom Sutter had sent to help them lay dying beside the trail. Since their end was near anyway, the party hastened the death of one of them in the hope that his body would help save some of the living. For they were reduced now to cannibalism, and so, too, were those who had remained behind.

The next weeks were a ghastly blend of snowstorms, frustrations, suffering, horror, and incidents of self-sacrifice and devotion. Even though some of the advance party reached Sutter's and word of the disaster quickly spread, the war with Mexico hindered the recruitment of relief parties, because many of the more vigorous and able young men had gone off to fight. (The demands of the Mexican War in California were not great, but neither were the resources on which the military were able to draw.) Often those attempting to help had almost as much difficulty crossing the mountains as the emigrants themselves. Reed, who had been banished for knifing one of the travelers, tried once, turned back, and then tried again before he finally succeeded in reaching his fellow emigrants. Each relief party could bring with it only a small amount of food and other supplies and could escort out only a limited number of survivors. It was an agonizing operation that demanded many life-or-death decisions from its participants. Who should be helped, and who abandoned? Should families break up, or should the stronger remain with the weaker? By February 1847, the horrible experience was over. Those who could be saved had crossed the mountains, but behind them lay a trail of the dead and memories that would haunt them for the rest of their lives.

In June 1847, General Kearny visited the campsite on the far side of the Sierra Nevada to inspect what was left and bury the corpses. "Near the principal cabins," wrote one of the men accompanying him, "I saw bodies entire, with the exception that the abdomens had been cut open and the entrails extracted. Their flesh had either been wasted by famine or evaporated by exposure to the dry atmosphere, and they presented the appearance of mummies. Strewn around the cabins were dislocated and broken skulls (in some instances sawed asunder with care, for the purpose of extracting the brains), human skeletons, in short, in every variety of mutilation." In a few words, he summed up his reaction by saying simply, "A more revolting and appalling spectacle I never witnessed."

Kearny ordered the human remains buried in a common pit and set fire to the cabins and other signs of the party's existence. But the flames could not eradicate the impression made on the nation. At such a cost, perhaps the trip to California was not worth it.

Even the men most directly responsible for the conquest of this vast area were not as triumphant as might have been expected, but ended their successful military campaign in bickering and intrigue. When Stockton was ready to leave California, Frémont asked him to be appointed governor. Stockton had absolutely no authority as a member of the navy to promote an army officer over his commanding general's head. Nevertheless that is what he did, and Frémont used his new position to defy Kearny. His patience exhausted, Kearny arrested the junior officer and sent him back to Washington to appear before a court-martial, which found him guilty of disobeying orders and sentenced him to dismissal. Polk approved the findings but remanded the sentence. But Frémont resigned anyway and devoted the rest of his life to business and politics.

In spite of its inglorious ending, the successful conclusion of the war in California should have brought rejoicing to the people of Oregon. With the boundary dispute settled and the United States replacing a jealous and suspicious neighbor to the south, the people of Oregon should have enjoyed a new sense of security. But instead the year 1847 made them feel in some ways more abandoned and remote than before.

Almost every settler in Oregon had hoped that as soon as the United States secured possession of Oregon, the government would affirm their titles to the land they had taken up. But Congress was in a hesitant mood, and all the settlers obtained was a weak, provisional government, not much better than what they had enjoyed before. Meanwhile they were faced with a crisis as great as any they had experienced.

At Waiilatpu, the mission he had founded, Marcus Whitman continued his work of converting the Cayuse Indians to Christianity and tending to their physical ailments. At the same time, he had taken on an additional burden. His establishment was directly on the trail to Oregon and had become a regular stopping place for the emigrant trains. Hardly a one of them did not need assistance of some sort—a sick child required care, a wagon wheel needed a new rim, an axle had to be replaced—the list was endless.

Not only was the mission a center of religious and medical services for all who wanted them, Marcus and Narcissa Whitman operated a school and a mill, grazed cattle, and planted crops. Out of the wilderness, they had created a complete, and almost independent, community, one that could serve as a model for other settlers. Yet an element of unrest ran through the area like an underground stream, invisible but erosive.

At Waiilatpu, two cultures met without an opportunity for either to adjust to the other. The emigrants, travel-weary and anxious to reach their goal farther west, were likely to treat any Indians brusquely. The Indians, seeing the white men stop briefly and pass on, marveled at their numbers but had no opportunity to know them. Marcus and Narcissa could not bridge the gap. Devoted as they both were to their cause and to the people they served, they never fully understood the Indians as some of the mountain men did. There were reasons for this. They obviously could not lead the Indians' life; they were there to set a white man's example for the natives—to alter, not participate in, many of the Indians' customs. Also, for all their earnestness, they seemed to lack the particular ability of a few white men, especially the trappers, to understand the Indians' mind. They had friends among the Indians but little intimacy.

The personal position of Marcus was also a dangerous one. Wilkes, when he had been exploring the Northwest several years before, had reported: "The practice of medicine [among the Indians], although profitable, is one of great danger, for if the patient should die it becomes the duty of the next of kin to revenge his death on the person by whose means he died. Such was the case of Mr. Black, an officer of the Hudson's Bay Company, in charge of one of the northern posts; he administered some medicine to a chief who requested it of him; after taking it he died. His nearest of kin sought Mr. Black's quarters, under the guise of friendship, and shot him in his own apartment."

Whitman knew this custom and occasionally refused to do anything for a patient whom he was sure he could not save. Otherwise he assumed the risk of death along with the other dangers of being a missionary.

In the fall of 1847, as California was adjusting itself to its new rulers, Whitman's medical and political skills were tested to the utmost: his knowledge of medicine in checking the epidemic of virulent measles that swept through parts of Oregon, his diplomacy in trying to explain to the Indians why fewer of their people recovered from the disease than white men. The reasons were twofold: They had less immunity, and they often failed to follow Whitman's directions. In fact, once he had treated them, they were likely to pursue their own cure by giving the patient sweat baths and then immersing him in cold water.

As fatalities among the Indians began to soar during the early weeks of November 1847, some of the Indians started to mutter against Whitman and the other white men. Whitman, however, was their particular target. After all, he was the medicine man who seemed to cure white children and adults more often than Indians; and they knew he understood how to brew poisons, for they had seen him kill wolves with strychnine. Some of them spoke of killing him. Whitman heard the rumors but, busy as he was with more mission children coming down with the disease, paid little attention to them.

John Settle, an emigrant who had gone to work at Waiilatpu, took the reports more seriously. He advised Whitman to leave the mission and, when the doctor refused, loaded his own belongings on his wagon, rounded up his cattle, and departed with his family.

The next day Spalding, who with his wife, Eliza, still headed the mission at Lapwai, arrived at Waiilatpu. He also had heard of a plot to kill Whitman and warned the doctor. While he was there, a messenger arrived to ask Whitman to treat some of the Indians on the Umatilla River. (While many of the Indians feared him, many of them still wanted his services.) Whitman agreed to go, thinking he could accomplish a second objective at the same time: discussing his problem with the Catholics who were establishing a mission on the river. Whitman had even been considering the possibility of turning Waiilatpu over to the Catholics if that is what the Cayuses desired.

One of the Indians at the village was a friend and again warned him that his life was in danger. By this time Whitman was beginning to take the rumors more seriously, for they were coming from too many different sources to be ignored. After treating the sick and briefly visiting the Catholics, he departed hastily for Waiilatpu, arriving at about ten in the evening of Sunday, November 28, 1847. Some of the mission staff were already asleep while others sat up caring for the children who were ill with measles. Whitman spoke briefly to Narcissa, sent her to bed, and then, in spite of his long ride, took over the duty of watching the sick.

The next morning, Monday, November 29, was cold, and the buildings of Waiilatpu stood gray in an autumn fog. Narcissa was upset, for Whitman had just discussed with her his growing concern for their safety. Otherwise life at the mission continued its routine—Whitman conducted burial services for three more Indian children who had died during the night, one man was grinding wheat at the mill, another, a tailor, was making clothes, and others were catching one of the cattle for butchering.

After lunch everyone went back to his task, and Whitman, weary from his long ride the evening before and the press of his morning's work, sat down in the living room to read for a little while. Narcissa, who was taking her turn nursing the mission's sick children, left to go out to the kitchen and get some milk. A large number of Indians had entered the mission, and one of them insolently insisted that she get him milk, too. Narcissa retreated to the sitting room and, when the Indian tried to force his way in after her, bolted the door.

The Indian banged on the door and demanded that Marcus bring him some medicine. Getting an appropriate drug from the medicine closet, Marcus, telling Narcissa to lock the door behind him, left the sitting room for the kitchen. Sitting down at a table, he began talking to an Indian named Tiloukaikt. Meanwhile the Indian who had demanded the medicine, a warrior named Tomahas, moved up behind him. Whitman did not notice him. Tomahas pulled out a tomahawk hidden under his blanket and struck Whitman on the head. A second blow knocked him out of his chair onto the floor. Tiloukaikt, who had been sitting in front of him, began slashing his face, and another Indian fired a shot into his neck. Although this sudden assault had not killed the doctor, he was mortally wounded with only a few more hours to live.

The only other white man in the room fired twice with his pistol at the Indians, wounding two before he himself was killed. Also in the kitchen was Mary Ann Bridger, the half-breed daughter of Jim Bridger, the mountain man, who had entrusted her to the Whitmans to raise. She fled from the kitchen outdoors, ran around the building, and entered it by another entrance to bring Narcissa the terrible news.

From that day for the next several weeks, horror and terror were the lot of the people at Waiilatpu. As was often the case with Indians, they had not worked out a coordinated plan of attack. It would almost have been better for the survivors if they had, killing those whom they hated, sparing the others, and leaving quickly. As it was, they worked either individually or in small groups; and they passed separate judgments on the white men, women, and children whom they happened to encounter.

The white man who had been butchering the beef was at least armed with

221

an ax when the Indians first attacked. Swinging it over his shoulder, he laid about him with surprising effectiveness until the Indians brought him down and then, to show their hatred, disemboweled him. The tailor had no weapon. He was killed as he sat cross-legged on the table, his needle and thread in his hand. The schoolteacher also had no means of resistance. When he heard the sound of shots and went out to investigate, the Indians killed him easily. The children he left behind in the schoolroom took temporary refuge in the loft above. One family, who had been sleeping in the room usually reserved for passing emigrants, remembered that some of the floorboards were loose. Lifing them up, they found room to hide underneath; and one of the children could later recall the terrifying sound of Indians walking on the floor above their heads.

Narcissa seized the first opportunity to drag Whitman from the kitchen to the sitting room and placed him on the settee. Soon he lost all consciousness and passed beyond any help she could give him. With a number of other survivors, she then took refuge in the attic. Being unarmed, the small group had no means of resisting and therefore were willing to talk to an Indian who came to them in the self-designated role of an emissary. He reported the others were about to burn down the building and, in effect, guaranteed them safe conduct if they left immediately.

Some of the refugees preferred to risk being burned alive than to leave the slight shelter the attic offered them. Narcissa, however, took the Indian at his word. By the time she reached the living room, where she had been when the day's horrors started, she collapsed. A white man who had accompanied her from the attic laid her on the settee; and he and a half-breed, following the shouted instructions of the Indians, used it as a litter to carry her outdoors toward the building usually reserved for emigrants.

The sight of the woman who had tried so hard to help them seemed to infuriate the Indians. Shots rang out. One bullet struck Narcissa in the cheek. The white man accompanying her dropped his end of the settee and fell to the ground. More shots followed. One Indian stepped forward and began slashing at Narcissa's face with his quirt. But she was past pain and horror, and the dream she had shared with Whitman ended for both of them that afternoon in the blood-splattered surroundings of Waiilatpu.

As darkness dropped its shadows over the mission, the American dead totaled six men, one woman, and two boys. The casualties they had inflicted on the Indians were slight. Few of them had been armed. Several, however, had escaped. One man seized a gun from his Indian attackers and used it to hold them off while he retreated toward the river. Leaping into the water, he swam to the other side and made his way to Fort Walla Walla, the Hudson's Bay Company's post.

Another man, although wounded, was able to get free and make the journey to Lapwai to warn the Spaldings. Since the Nez Percés, among whom they lived, were still friendly, they had no reason to fear an immediate assault, but they stayed away from the country of the Cayuses. The family that had hidden beneath the floorboards of the emigrants' house also escaped to Fort Walla Walla, taking with them several children. An artist who had planned a visit to Waiilatpu met an Indian and learned what had happened, so he turned back with the news. In this way, the outside world learned of the terror that had taken place.

On Wednesday, one of the Catholic priests visited Waiilatpu to offer any relief he could. Because the Cayuses did not associate him with the mission, they did not molest him, but what he found was appalling. Aside from those who had escaped, the only surviving men were wounded and could do nothing to help the women and children who remained. The Indians were in an uncertain mood. Some had continued killing; some were stricken by what had already happened; and others were fearful of the revenge the Americans might take against their tribe. They had almost fifty captives, the majority of them children, and most of the remainder women. These helpless people were the Indians' hostages against the settlers of Oregon taking revenge, and the priest could do nothing to secure their release.

If they were to be freed, help must come from the outside, but from where? Spalding was impotent; he had barely escaped with his own life. William McBean, the trader in charge at Fort Walla Walla, was not one of the daring adventurers who were so common in the Hudson's Bay Company and had barely enough men to defend his own post if the Indians attacked it. The weak, provisional government of Oregon possessed almost no authority and no manpower. It governed largely by consent and had little capacity to wage war against a remote tribe. Yet these were the principal sources of succor to which the captives at Waiillatpu could look.

20. Retreat and Advance

Did we have any suffering, affliction, hunger, thirst, and fatigue? I can bear testimony that the pioneers . . . can look back to that period of their lives as to a time when they experienced the fulfillment of David's words: "Hungry and thirsty their souls fainteth in them. Then they cried unto the Lord in their trouble, and he delivered them out of their distresses."

—Orson Pratt, 1867, describing the first days
of the Mormons' Utah settlement

The weakness of Oregon's government and its consequent inability to defend its people from an attack like that on Waiilatpu stemmed from Congress's reluctance to organize the area as a territory. In turn, this reluctance arose from the unpopularity of the Mexican War among large segments of the population and the fear that the geographical expansion of the country would lead to the spread of slavery. This sentiment was expressed in fiery terms in a resolution written by Charles Sumner and passed by the Massachusetts legislature.

"The object of the bold policy of annexation [admitting Texas to the Union]," the resolution said, "was not only to strengthen the 'Slave Power.' The same object is now proposed by the Mexican War. This is another link in the gigantic chain by which our country and the Constitution are to be bound to the 'Slave Power.'" This bitter feeling muted discussion of establishing governments for the newly acquired lands. No one wanted to light the powder keg.

Thus Oregon found itself, for all its hopes, almost like an orphan when it was confronted with the Indian attack on Waiilatpu. Nevertheless, its provisional legislature adopted a resolution bravely declaring that "the governor [also provisional] be, and is hereby, authorized and required to raise, arm, and equip a company of riflemen, not to exceed fifty men . . . and disptach them forthwith to occupy the mission station at the Dalles." What the legislature intended was a holding action to prevent the Indian uprising from spreading down the river while it arranged for stronger measures.

At the same time the people of Oregon prepared a memorial to Congress. "We feel sensibly our weakness and inability to enter into a war with powerful tribes of Indians," it said in part. ". . . We are deficient in many of the grand essentials of war,—such as men, arms, and treasures; for them our sole reliance is on the government of the United States."

Having discussed the issue that most immediately concerned them, they took up several other points relating to the formation of a government and ended with this plea: "If it be at all the intention of our honored parent to spread her guardian wing over her sons and daughters in Oregon, she will surely not refuse to do so now." The legislature entrusted the memorial to Joe Meek, an old mountain man, and appointed him their messenger to carry it overland to Washington and see that it was presented to Congress.

Nothing that happened so far helped the prisoners held by the Cayuses. Fifty untrained riflemen could not effect their release. In fact, the appearance of armed men in the Cayuses' country was likely to frighten the Indians and encourage them to take desperate steps.

Earlier the citizens might have turned to John McLoughlin for help, but he had retired from the Hudson's Bay Company. Taking his place was Peter Skene Ogden, another of the company's famous traders. He decided to act on his own accord. Taking enough boats to bring the Americans back if he was successful but without making any display of force, he went to Fort Walla Walla and sent out word he wanted to see the Cayuses.

Since they had no quarrel with the English and were dependent on the Hudson's Bay Company for supplies, they responded. Probably few other white men in Oregon could have conducted the negotiations that followed. Carefully Ogden avoided promising the Indians any immunity from an

American attack, but skillfully he kept referring to the captives, not as hostages, but as subjects for barter. For the Indians often took prisoners merely to ransom them.

The bargaining followed a slow and tortuous path, since the Indians regarded trading as both an art and a social occasion. Ogden's temper, after years of experience, was equal to such drawn-out proceedings. At the end of the life-or-death negotiations, carried on among the bleak surroundings of Fort Walla Walla, he purchased the captives' freedom and, with a supplemental payment to the Nez Percés, secured a safe conduct for the members of the Lapwai mission to join them.

About a week after his arrival, this extraordinary man had the group assembled on the bank of the Columbia River ready to embark on the boats he had brought with him. (Generously he later told the Hudson's Bay Company that if they did not approve the expense, they could charge it to his account.) For approximately a month, the men, women, and children had lived in terror. Now, thanks to a single fur trader, they were safe.

The year 1847 was a curious time for the people of the United States. They had had many triumphs, and yet little seemed to have been settled finally. The one group ready to take full advantage of the changing conditions was the Mormons, and they did so out of desperation. Wherever they tried to settle, their numbers and cohesiveness brought them a degree of political power, but never popularity. Invariably their neighbors thought of them as practitioners of dark arts and regarded them with a suspicion that soon turned to hatred. If they were ever to be free of prejudice and persecution, they must establish a colony remote from others.

For a while they had considered moving to California and even sent a delegation to inspect the possibilities of establishing a settlement there. The young men who joined the Mormon Battalion under Cooke did so largely to obtain free transportation. But even before they reached California, Brigham Young, the Mormons' leader, changed his mind. In the basin of Utah's Great Salt Lake, he thought, the Mormons would have more of the isolation they desired.

Early in April 1847, the first Mormon party, composed of just under a hundred and fifty persons, set out from Winter Quarters, their encampment near the site of present-day Omaha, Nebraska. The others were to wait eight or ten weeks until the grass was richer and then follow to the site the advance party would have picked out.

Along the trail the advance party met several old-time fur traders. (One of them was Jim Bridger.) From them they learned as much as they could about the country toward which they were headed; and they were also joined by

Samuel Brannan, the Mormon who had led the contingent of several hundred Mormons to California by boat. He had returned for the specific purpose of meeting them and brought with him some copies of the newspaper he had already established. But his appearance did not divert Brigham Young from his new choice. The future center of Mormonism was to be at the Great Salt Lake, and Young had already sent word to the members of the Mormon Battalion to join him there.

On July 22, 1847, a small group of the advance party was near the lake, and all that remained was to pick the precise location for their future town. This they did on July 23, 1847; and without waiting for Brigham Young to come up with the main body they gave thanks to God and set to work. "We called camp together," Orson Pratt, one of the Mormon leaders, noted in his journal, "and it fell to my lot to offer up prayer and thanksgiving in behalf of our company, all of whom had been preserved from the Missouri River to this point; and, after dedicating ourselves and the land unto the Lord, and imploring his blessings upon our labours, we appointed various committees to attend to different branches of business, preparatory to putting in crops, and in about two hours after our arrival we began to plough, and the same afternoon built a dam to irrigate the soil, which at the spot where we were ploughing was exceedingly dry."

The following day Brigham Young arrived. He confirmed the choice of the site, and the Mormons began laying out the community they called Great Salt Lake City. This was to be no ramshackle frontier settlement but a well laid-out, dignified city. The streets were eight rods wide and formed blocks of eight acres each, divided into eight building lots. These were so placed that no house would face another on the opposite side of the street, an esthetic arrangement made possible by the plentiful supply of land. But the Mormons were not unmindful of the debt they owed God. One of the blocks was reserved for the construction of a temple. Later the remainder of the Mormon migration of that year arrived; and although the land still belonged to Mexico—General Winfield Scott had not yet reached Mexico City and forced the Mexicans to surrender—the Mormons had few doubts about their ability to hold what they had taken.

Missionary work and the recruitment of new converts had always been an essential part of the church; and now, in their enthusiasm over their New Zion, they intensified their efforts to gain additional members. Yet the community at Salt Lake City was ill equipped to support those who were already there. Not being wealthy, they had been unable to purchase all the supplies they needed, especially wheat, and many of them were without such fundamental necessities as teams to do their plowing. Starvation was not an empty word to those who ventured into the wilderness. The Donner party's fate the year before was common knowledge; and Samuel Brannan, returning east, had passed the remains of their horrible encampment. The Mormons knew that a similar destiny might await them.

On January 8, 1848, as the Mormons were struggling through their first Utah winter, the captives taken by the Indians at Waiilatpu arrived at Portland, Oregon, delivered by the kind and wise intervention of Peter Skene Ogden. The same day the volunteer troops sent by Oregon to secure their release fought a skirmish near The Dalles with some Indians who had stolen a herd of cattle. The next month they had several more small fights with the Indians, inflicting a few casualties but failing to win a decisive victory.

Early in March they reached Waiilatpu and looked at the ruins of Marcus Whitman's dream. Although the adobe walls were still standing, the buildings were charred hulks; and the once happy mission presented an ugly sight. Vigorously the temporary soldiers set about converting it into a fort, but soon their short-term enlistments were about to run out, and none of them wished to make a career of soldiering. So they alerted the few remaining white men on the upper Columbia and withdrew. By their show of force, they had somewhat intimidated the Indians, but they had not identified—much less arrested—the ringleaders in the attack on Waiilatpu, and they had stirred up ill will by stealing some of the Indians' horses and cattle.

The American troops at Mexico City did considerably better. The Mexican government finally bowed to the inevitable and negotiated the Treaty of Guadalupe Hidalgo, which was signed on February 2, 1848. By its provisions, the Americans obtained official title to the lands they wanted. In return they agreed to assume responsibility for some financial claims against the Mexican government and to pay a premium as well. Ironically the whole sum amounted to approximately three-fifths of what Polk had originally been prepared to offer. The Mexicans, therefore, lost not only the war but also an opportunity to settle on much more favorable terms.

Gradually the disjointed pieces left over from 1847 were coming together, and the United States was beginning to consolidate its gains. The Waiilatpu captives had been released, and Mexico had acknowledged the transfer of their former provinces to the Americans. The Mormons, too, after their uncertain start of the year before, were establishing a base in the center of the newly acquired lands. One Mormon, who was a small boy at the time, later recalled that he had been hungry every day during the winter of 1847–48 and that for months his appetite was not satisfied. But the season was mild with little snow, and the discipline of the Mormons told. They carefully rationed their food and shared their equipment; and when spring came, the entire community went to work planting the crops that would see them through the coming year. They had plenty of corn seed, for it was light and easy to

228

transport, and also some beans, peas, and a few other vegetables. But they had no potatoes so a small party went to southern California with pack animals and purchased some.

The crops did well. Under the Utah sun, the plants flourished, pushing their heads through the soil and appearing in neat green rows that promised well for the coming winter—a winter that would be different from the one just passed. But before the produce was ready to harvest, swarms of grasshoppers appeared. The Mormons flooded their irrigation ditches, hoping to drown the insects, but the grasshoppers seemed impervious to the effects of the water. Even when they were caught in the ditches' current and washed downstream, they would climb to the bank, quickly dry themselves, and return to eat again. So voracious were they that they would munch on the dead and disabled of their own kind, and some that had been crushed but were still alive would eat the injured portions of their own bodies.

Every man, woman, and child was enlisted in this strange battle on the outcome of which depended the colony's future, for no bands of skulking Indians could have presented a greater threat than those black clouds of insects with their steady and deadly nibbling. First the Mormons squashed those that were still outside the cultivated plots, hoping their dead bodies would divert the others from the fresh plants. Then they tackled those within the plots, but the odds were against them. Every time they reworked a row, they found that new grasshoppers had replaced those they had killed, and the numbers of grasshoppers seemed endless. Only when night came did they stop their incredible chewing. Then they clustered in the nearby bushes and under loose pieces of sod and at daybreak began their dreadful invasion again.

No matter how hard the Mormons battled, no matter how many insects they killed, the ceaseless chewing on those precious leaves continued, and the Mormons' New Zion seemed doomed. Just as disaster had come from the skies, however, so did salvation. A flock of sea gulls appeared, and then another and another. The birds were as hungry for the grasshoppers as the grasshoppers were for the fresh crops. Up and down the rows they went, their strong beaks snapping up the insects right and left. At night when the grasshoppers withdrew, the gulls went to a large field about half a mile away to rest; and when morning came, they returned with the grasshoppers and renewed their feast. What men could not do, the sea gulls accomplished, and the settlement was saved. Today the gull is the state bird of Utah.

While the sprouts of the Mormons' crops had been pushing their way through the soil and reaching for the sun, Joe Meek, the emissary whom the people of Oregon had sent to Washington, was making his way across the continent. By May 18, 1848, he had reached St. Louis, and the editor of the *Republican* seized this chance to get a firsthand story of events in the West.

229

Other papers quickly picked up the *Republican*'s account, and the attack on Waiilatpu had just the right mixture of blood and tragedy to capture the nation's sympathy.

When Meek arrived in Washington toward the end of May, the capital knew all about the deaths of Marcus and Narcissa Whitman. Because of the slavery issue, most politicians still wanted to postpone establishing governments in the newly conquered territories, but the tale carried by Meek could not be ignored. Who could deny protection to the residents of Oregon in their pathetic plight?

Meek had no difficulty seeing Polk and presenting the case of the people of the Northwest. Polk promptly gave their petition to Congress along with a strongly worded message of his own. "The memorialists," he said, "are citizens of the United States. They express ardent attachment to their native land, and in their present perilous and distressed situation they earnestly invoke the aid and protection of their Government. . . . I therefore . . . recommend that laws be promptly passed establishing a Territorial government and granting authority to raise an adequate volunteer force for the defense and protection of its inhabitants."

The House responded by quickly passing the necessary measure; the Senate followed suit in less than two weeks; and Polk signed the bill the next day. As the territory's first governor, he appointed Joseph Lane of Indiana, who had won fame in the Mexican War, and as United States Marshall, Joe Meek, the former mountain man who had carried Oregon's plea to the capital. Both men met in Indiana and, because the season was growing late, took the southern route through New Mexico and California to Oregon, arriving in Oregon City on March 2, 1849. Marcus Whitman's death had not been completely futile. The emotion it aroused had certainly hastened the process by which Oregon attained territorial status.

The most important changes, however, took place in California. Just as many persons had foreseen, the area's economy began to quicken once it came under the American flag. Monterey, with its insufficient harbor, began to lose importance, and the commercial activity of California shifted north to San Francisco, which, until 1847, had been known as Yerba Buena. Thomas Larkin recognized the change and began liquidating his holdings in Monterey and buying building lots in San Francisco. Also, in cooperation with some partners, he laid out another community across the bay.

The market for real estate was good. The conquest of California gave Americans a greater sense of security in making investments; and many of the troops, particularly those from New York, decided to remain. Their presence, coupled with the regular emigration, caused a rise in population and a consequent demand for building lots.

Sutter, in addition to his many other enterprises, had necessarily been a producer of lumber. His men usually went up into the Sierra Nevada with a whipsaw and cut about a hundred to a hundred and twenty-five feet a day. This was slow and expensive, and for some time, he had been looking for a suitable location for a sawmill. Bidwell, who had gone back to work for him, later said, "The year after the war [with Mexico] Sutter's needs for lumber were even greater than ever, although his embarrassments had increased and his ability to undertake new enterprises became less. Yet, never discouraged, nothing daunted, another hunt must be made for a mill-site."

The man John Sutter chose as his partner was James W. Marshall, an emigrant who had come to California by way of Oregon. Originally a wheelwright by trade, he had a bent for working with wood that enabled him to make spinning wheels, looms, shuttles, and other equipment Sutter needed. Bidwell drew up the contract between the two men. As he recalled, "Sutter was to furnish the means; Marshall was to build and run the mill, and have a share of the lumber for his compensation. His idea was to haul the lumber part way and raft it down the American River to the Sacramento and thence, his part of it . . . to San Francisco for a market."

Bidwell did not think much of the arrangement. The site chosen by Marshall on the South Fork of the American River was near a plentiful supply of trees, but, said Bidwell, "it is hard to conceive how any sane man could have been so wide of the mark. . . . Surely no other man than Marshall ever entertained so wild a scheme as that of rafting sawed lumber down the cañons of the American River, and no other man than Sutter would have been so confiding and credulous as to patronize him."

Marshall, who prided himself on being able to handle every sort of mechanical problem, designed a mill that included several improvements Bidwell had never seen, but he placed the wheel so low it would not run. "The remedy," Bidwell remarked later, "was to dig a channel or tail-race to conduct away the water."

The digging was difficult work and required several weeks. At the end of each day, Marshall stopped the mill wheel and raised the gate. All night long the water poured through its course, carrying with it the sediment the diggers had left, and by morning had flushed the channel. While the Indians he employed were having breakfast, Marshall studied the flow of water and decided where the Indians should dig next. He then closed the gate, thereby shutting off the water, and as soon as the Indians had finished eating, he was ready to put them to work.

One morning in August 1847, as the California sun was rising in the sky and water was streaming through the tailrace, Marshall was making his usual inspection. As he was watching the running water, he saw the sun's light reflected from the bottom of the channel. Stooping over, he picked the glittering material out of the tailrace and held it in his hand.

Always in the hearts of men who wandered through the wilderness was the hope they might find gold. It had brought the Spaniards to California many years before, and even in recent years, travelers through the lonely mountains had occasionally searched a stream bed, thinking that perhaps they might be the ones to find a fortune. The majority discovered nothing at all; the few who did were usually disappointed to learn that what they had located was not gold, but "fool's gold," which often looked more like gold than the real metal but which was worthless.

Marshall had no knowledge of metallurgy and therefore no means of evaluating what he held in his hand. He might have made a great discovery; he might be just one more in that legion whose hopes had been dashed by reality. Like so many others in California, when in doubt he turned for advice to John Sutter. As soon as he could, he saddled his horse and rode for Sutter's Fort, taking his sample with him.

21. Stampede for Wealth

*We passed through the Golden Gate . . . and,
landing, I saw with astonishment the great change
that had come over San Francisco. The little idle
place I had left . . . was now, by the potent power
of gold, metamorphized into a canvas city of several
thousand people.*

—Joseph W. Revere, February 1849

Sutter, although not an assayer, knew a little more about metallurgy than Marshall. He subjected Marshall's sample to a few simple tests and looked up the subject in his encyclopedia. After finishing his brief and rather amateurish analysis, he concluded that Marshall had indeed found gold in the tailrace. But in what quantities did it exist? A few widely scattered particles of dust, or even nuggets, would hardly make a man rich.

Marshall was excited by his discovery; Sutter much less so. He did lease some land surrounding the mill site from the Indians and confirmed the lease with the American military authorities, but his greatest concern was a possible interruption in the construction of his sawmill. Sutter, who had proved himself more far-sighted than most persons, was blind to California's greatest immediate opportunity. Reluctantly, he permitted his workmen to pan for gold on Sundays if they would continue building the mill the other days of the week.

For the time being, everyone was satisfied. The workmen collected small bags of gold dust that added a bonus to their regular pay, and yet construction on the mill continued apace.

News of the discovery, of course, leaked out, but it created no great stir. The hopes of gold-hunters had been so often disappointed that even the most eager among them were disillusioned, and mere rumors or even factual reports of small discoveries were not enough to rouse them. As Bidwell later said, "There was no excitement at first, not for three or four months— because the mine was not known to be rich, or to exist anywhere except at the sawmill, or to be available to anyone except Sutter, to whom everyone conceded that it belonged."

Samuel Brannan, who had headed the Mormon delegation to California, operated a store at Sutter's Fort. Shrewdly he concocted a plan to make some money, not out of the gold itself but out of the subsidiary market that a gold rush would create. Quietly he accumulated gold offered as payment at his store until he had an impressive amount, while at the same time he bought up all the supplies that would be used by prospectors, such as tents, shovels, and pickaxes. After he had cornered the market, he was ready to set off a gold rush. On May 12, 1848, he was in San Francisco. With a container of gold in one hand for all to see, he loudly announced that gold had been discovered in the American River. The samples he showed were, of course, the result of many Sundays of work, but no one knew this.

Seeing Brannan's gold and hearing his inflamatory words, man after man left San Francisco to go prospecting, buying his equipment from Brannan at inflated prices. Brannan made a small fortune from his scheme, but he had also seriously miscalculated. As one prospector after another went out, loaded down with equipment purchased from Brannan, and actually found gold, what had started as a limited speculation fired by one merchant's avarice, quickly turned into a real gold rush.

William R. Grimshaw, a young man who had left a mercantile career in New York to go to sea, arrived in San Francisco the October following Brannan's dramatic announcement and saw the effect it had had on the small community. A barque lying in the harbor was completely deserted, everyone from the captain to the cook having abandoned it to go seeking gold. The frame of a new hotel was standing unfinished, there being no workmen to complete the job. A partially built wharf jutted into the bay. It would have received heavy use in those hectic days, but the owner could find no one willing to do such trivial labor, regardless of wages, when gold might be found along the American and Sacramento rivers. A whaling ship from New

234

Bedford entered the port to pick up water and fresh provisions. The ship's agent told the captain to leave immediately or he would lose his entire crew.

Grimshaw himself resisted—at least for a while—the gold craze and went to work for Brannan and his partners. Their store at Sutter's Fort (often called New Helvetia at the time) was a large adobe building about a hundred feet long and thirty wide, one of only two buildings outside the fort. Up in the loft were stocks of old hides and other remnants of the days before the gold rush had started. The downstairs was devoted to filling the needs of the gold prospectors at outrageous prices. Glass beads to use in buying food or labor from the Indians were available at twenty dollars a pound, marked up from their original cost of something like five cents. Boston crackers went for sixteen dollars a tin, sardines, five dollars. Twenty pounds of baking soda cost four hundred dollars, and quinine, at Brannan's prices, was worth sixteen to twenty dollars an ounce—approximately the same as its weight in gold—and was always in demand.

At least once while Grimshaw was there, Brannan was caught at his own game. He needed some turpentine to treat a harness sore on one of his mules. As this was a commodity he did not have in stock, he turned to the small drugstore that operated within the fort. The price: five dollars for two-thirds of a cup. When Grimshaw recalled the incident years later, he remembered that he heard Brannan "murmur audibly."

Even at the exorbitant prices charged, trade flourished. One enterprising man set himself up in the business of making pans, essential equipment of every prospector. Filling the bottom with two or three inches of river sand or loose dirt, he held it just under the surface of the water and began rotating it. Gradually the lighter material was swept over the side; and after he had removed the stones and pebbles by hand, what remained at the bottom might be gold. Such a method was dependent on an easily extractable supply of gold, but it required little capital investment. For sixteen dollars, a miner could obtain a pan from the industrious manufacturer, who worked night and day making them and yet never seemed to have enough on hand to meet the demand.

No one asked the price of anything. Each man simply placed his order at the store and, when it was filled, poured out enough gold dust to pay for it. Anyone entering the gold fields could obtain credit, no matter how uncertain his past record may have been. If, in those early days, he survived, he would be more than able to pay back what he owed, and business was both so brisk and so profitable that losses could easily be absorbed. By the spring of 1849, Brannan was ready to send money back to San Francisco; and when Grimshaw helped him fill his buckskin bags with dust ready for shipment, he had about fifty thousand dollars' worth.

The easy money of the gold miners had a serious impact on the social structure of northern California. Those that suffered were the Indians. Most of them belonged to primitive tribes, who had little clothing and ate the simplest food. Before Marshall picked the samples from the tailrace, they had reached an informal arrangement with the landholders in the area. In the late summer, when the need for labor was at its greatest, the Indians would appear to help with the harvest. For this, they were usually paid in beef and cloth, which substantially raised their standard of living. The rest of the year they were content to exist much as they had always done.

The sudden influx of miners upset this arrangement. The new arrivals would sell the Indians liquor, which the older landholders rarely did; and the Indians quickly learned the value of the gold the white men were seeking. Often they "panned" for gold themselves, using baskets woven by their women; and when they located a particularly productive area, they tried to hold it for their own use. This brought them into direct conflict with the white men, and the Indians almost always lost their claim—if not their lives.

Among the white men themselves, the weak often went unprotected. Congress had been no more disposed to establish a government for California than it had been to set one up in Oregon. Consequently the military commanders had taken over the Mexican system and filled the positions with their own appointees. These often received no remuneration and understood that their titles were largely honorary.

So informality and expediency marked the governmental process. When a murder occurred at Sutter's Fort, the American *alcalde* promptly resigned rather than have anything to do with the case. The responsibility, therefore, fell on the second *alcalde*. He considered the problem only briefly before he, too, resigned. The accused would have gone untried if Brannan had not insisted on a trial and agreed to serve both as judge and prosecutor, two offices no one else would fill.

Brandy and water were available in the courtroom to those who wished refreshment, but smoking presented a problem in decorum. "Judge" Brannan ruled, however, that since the Mexican women in California used tobacco, smoking could be permitted. Anyone attending, whether a member of the prosecution or the defense or merely a curious spectator, could cross-examine the witnesses; and when the trial ended, the jury wandered off without rendering a verdict. When they were reassembled by the "sheriff," they announced they could not agree, so "Judge" Brannan held the defendant for retrial. Since Sutter's Fort contained no jail and the "sheriff" had no restraining irons, the spectators voted to free him on bail. His second trial resulted in his acquittal; and the amusement over, everyone went back to work.

In those days of poor communications, when the east-west news traveled slowly, the East did not immediately understand the immensity of the gold discovery. The news spread first through California, causing an exodus of workers from other jobs and mass desertions by the soldiers and sailors stationed in the new American territory. In fact, holding their units together was the major concern of American military commanders.

Men and women in Oregon also heard the news, and the agricultural riches of that new territory lost their appeal. Some of the Mormons, too, were willing to desert their New Zion—for all its promise of a life free from persecution—in exchange for a chance at great wealth. Because Hawaii was a natural stopping point for ships doing business on the West Coast, the people of those islands began to join the mad rush. The news also traveled down the coastline, reaching Mexico, Peru, and Chile. Instead of the Spanish language becoming less common after the American conquest, probably more people in California spoke it in late 1848 than at the time of Kearny's victory at Los Angeles. The hopes that had lured the Spaniards north hundreds of years before had finally been realized by the Americans, and the descendents of the *conquistadores* came to try for their share of what their ancestors had missed.

Those with a great stake in the discovery were not only the miners who left their jobs and their homes, but the members of the current federal administration. Polk had pursued his policy of expansionism against the wishes of important segments of the population, but in the tailrace of James Marshall's mill, he had found his justification. Almost no one could quarrel with his acquiring for his country the largest source of gold yet discovered in North America.

The interests of the administration, therefore, were being served by the activity on the West Coast. When the army commander in California sent Lieutenant Edward F. Beale to Washington in the early fall of 1848 to report what was happening, he gave Beale some samples of the actual gold to take with him. Beale failed, however, to have a galvanizing effect on public opinion.

The administration handled its next publicity with more flamboyance. In December, a second officer brought with him a full tea caddy of gold, which was placed on display at the Department of War. Crowds went to see it, and samples were sent to the mint at Philadelphia, which reported that some of it was of the same standard as that used for making American coins. What ignited this new interest was not so much the gold itself as the time of its appearance in Washington. Only two days before, Polk made his fourth and final annual report to the two houses of Congress. At his own request, he was not a candidate for renomination to a second term; and his remarks, therefore, were as much a summary of the eventful four years of his administration as a recommendation for future legislation.

The discovery of gold in California featured largely in his message. "The accounts of the abundance of gold in that territory are of such an extraordinary character as would scarcely command belief if they were not corroborated by the authentic reports of officers in the public service." Polk was not relying on rumors. Naval and military officers in California had been enlisted by the administration in obtaining a realistic estimate of the extent of the gold discoveries, and Polk attached their reports to his annual message. "The explorations already made," he said, summing up the officers' findings, "warrant the belief that the supply is very large and that gold is found at various places in an extensive district."

The crowds who went to see the tea caddy were familiar with what Polk had said and were confident that this was no schemer's plot to entrap the unwary. Those who lived too far away to visit the War Department's building also read Polk's words with astonishment and—hope. The farmer's young son who knew the family homestead could not support him as well as his older brothers, the lawyer whose practice was failing, the doctor whose patients never seemed to come in sufficient numbers, the merchant whose store would not pass the break-even point, the laborer whose horizon was limited by a low hourly wage, all these and many more whose expectations exceeded their circumstances read the president's message and the official accounts he had submitted and began to dream.

The adventurous, too, read the accounts with quickening heartbeats, and those who always yearned for the rainbow and who liked to match themselves against the dangers offered by nature and their fellow men. Here was the challenge that would take them from the humdrum and the everyday, that would place them in strange surroundings with an opportunity to test their wits and their physical strength. These were the honorable. But the dishonorable also read the reports—the gamblers, the thieves, the men with a derringer in the tails of their coats or, less fashionably, a pair of brass knuckles in their trouser pockets, the men whose livelihoods depended on marked cards or fake stock certificates and the toughs who lurked in the darkest and gloomiest portions of the cities, the wharf rats, the pickpockets, the thieves, and the murderers. Wherever money was flowing in such quantities, some might drift into their hands whether they found a mine of their own, cheated a neighbor, or robbed a traveler in the lonely mountains.

In every rank of society, men and women dreamed of California's gold; and by spring a large number of them were ready to join the search for the Americans' Quivira, a Quivira more tangible than Coronado's and yet, for many of them, no less elusive.

There were three principal routes by which these emigrants could get to the gold fields. The most comfortable and luxurious was to take a ship around Cape Horn. Although the weather might be bad at the tip of South America and the voyage somewhat hazardous, the passenger had a bunk to sleep in, meals each day, and could generally count on the captain to get him there safely. This form of transportation, however, was expensive—often about four hundred dollars a passenger—so the ships, although busy, carried only a small portion of the emigrants.

Another route, used particularly by those who lived on the Gulf Coast, took them by water either to Mexico or Panama. After crossing to the Pacific, they reembarked and went up the coast to California by water. The price, although not as high as for the longer journey around the Horn, was still beyond the reach of many families, and the traveler faced the problem of dealing with foreign authorities, who might not be friendly, and the chance of contracting one of the diseases prevalent in both Panama and Mexico.

The most popular way to get to California was to travel across the United States, using either the southern route followed by Kearny and later marked by Cooke or the northern route first opened by the fur trappers. The southern route was the less popular of the two. Although it had now been traveled by numerous persons and no longer presented many of the dangers that had beset Anza on his journey from Arizona to California, both the country and the Indians remained inhospitable. The long stretches of desert were forbidding, and some of the fiercest Indian tribes, like the Navajos and the Apaches, lived along the trail. Most emigrants, therefore, took the better known route across South Pass and, having learned from the fate of the Donner party, respected the awesome winters of the mountains and made sure they had completed their journey before the snow fell.

Most of them had little idea of what to expect on the way or what they would find in California. Almost all of them were inexperienced at frontier living, but they had plenty of companionship during the entire trip. The trail across the continent was beset by many dangers, tragedies, and discomforts, but loneliness was not one of them. Starting in the year 1849, as soon as the grass turned green and the snows melted in the mountains, the trail to California—and also Oregon, for there were men and women to whom a productive farm seemed better than finding gold—became an almost continuous line of humans, wagons, and livestock. Some started out in companies and stayed together for the entire journey; others quarreled and broke with their original companions, but they soon attached themselves to new parties whom they met on the road. One group would pass another and forge ahead, only perhaps to be overtaken themselves a few days or weeks later. Sometimes, if the forage around a campsite was sufficient, several groups would spend the night together, their spirits high, their wagon covers embellished with outlandish slogans that proclaimed the places from which they had come. News passed quickly along this vast line. Those behind learned of the presence of old friends ahead. Conditions on the trail, the state of the rivers, and other items that affected their passage were reported back and forth in a steady stream of gossip, rumors, and factual information.

Interest in the West caused the Bureau of Topographical Engineers to send

Captain Howard Stansbury on a survey expedition to the valley of the Great Salt Lake. Although he left late in the year, when many of the emigrants had already started, he made a typical entry in his journal on June 12, 1849. "We have been in company with multitudes of emigrants the whole day," he wrote. "The road has been lined to a long extent with their wagons, whose white covers, glittering in the sunlight, resembled at a distance, ships upon the ocean."

He then noted one specific party as an example of the general unpreparedness with which the emigrants entered this new life. "We passed a company from Boston," he said, "consisting of seventy persons, one hundred and forty pack and riding mules, a number of riding horses, and a drove of cattle for beef. The expedition, as might be expected, and is too generally the case, was badly conducted: the mules were overloaded, and the manner of securing and arranging the packs elicited many a sarcastic criticism from our company." The load itself, of course, suffered from such mishandling. Worse yet was the fate of the animal carrying it. Even if it could walk with relative balance and ease, the pack saddle was likely to wear bad sores into its back which, after a day's march, could make the animal virtually useless.

Alonzo Delano, a businessman from Illinois, who had left earlier in the year when the trail was less crowded, remarked, "Although I speak particularly of our own train . . . the reader should bear in mind that there were probably twenty thousand people on the road west of the Missouri, and that our train did not travel for an hour without seeing many others, and hundreds of men. For days we would travel in company with other trains, which would stop to rest, when we would pass them; and then perhaps we would lay up, and they pass us. Sometimes we would meet again after many days, and others, perhaps, never. As near as we could ascertain, there were about a thousand wagons before us, and probably four or five thousand behind us."

The Indians presented a relatively minor problem. Although they often raided the emigrants' herds, running off with livestock during the night, they did not make a concerted attack on the long line of wagons. Such unified action was alien to their tradition, and the numbers of white men too great to make victory at all certain. Finding forage, however, was often troublesome. The first emigrants of the season grazed their herds near the trail, but as the year progressed, those areas became barren; and subsequent travelers had to wander farther and farther away each night in order to be able to feed their animals. The result was a wide swath cut across the face of the land.

Supplies also posed a difficulty. Most of the emigrants, like Narcissa Whitman so many years before, quickly learned they had brought too many of the wrong things, too few of the right. They were overburdened with bulky articles like anvils, stoves, beds, and other paraphernalia of houses and barns, most of which was useless during the trek and only added to the heavy loads pulled by the animals. As a consequence, they tried, unsuccessfully, to sell much of it to their fellow travelers, gave it away, or merely dumped it along the trail, which became lined with heaps of discarded belongings, each heap a graveyard memorializing the past. On the other hand, the supplies they did need, like a new wagon wheel rim, were often difficult, if not impossible, to obtain. The forts and trading posts along the way tried to keep stocks of goods the emigrants might want, but they were not equipped to enter the general merchandise business. Such items, therefore, commanded large premiums.

The economic effect of this migration was enormous. California, after years of somnolence, suddenly came to life. Real estate values soared. Ranch lands and even building lots that could have been obtained for next to nothing now commanded tremendous prices; and land that previously was not worth the cost of a survey became the subject of title battles. Every sort of business that supplied the new population, whether tent and trouser-makers like Levi Straus or the importers or producers of foodstuffs, found a quick market for what they had to sell.

Even the older industries of California revived. Cattle raising had once been an important occupation of the missions, but as the herds prospered and outgrew the missionaries' ability to dispose of their meat, they had been slaughtered only for their hides. But this had changed. An American who stayed with a Mexican family told of gathering a herd of three hundred beef cattle to be taken to the mining areas. In addition, he said that "anyone finding an animal of two years or older without a brand had the right to keep it. . . . It was these that Hernando [the son of the Mexican family] and his herdsmen were in search of, and as fast as captured they were branded, driven to his father's ranch, and ultimately to the mines and sold for beef." So great was the sudden demand for meat that California ranchers could not fill it easily, and speculators began bringing cattle and sheep from places as far away as Arizona and Texas.

The Mormons benefited greatly from the heavy passage of people. Originally they had sought seclusion, but soon they were doing a brisk business with the emigrants, purchasing belongings they could no longer carry and selling them the supplies they so desperately needed. "Pack mules and horses," commented one Mormon newspaper, "that were worth twenty-five or thirty dollars in ordinary times, would readily bring two hundred dollars in the most valuable property at the lowest price. Goods and other property were daily offered at auction in all parts of the city. For a light Yankee wagon, sometimes three or four great heavy ones would be offered in exchange, and a yoke of oxen thrown in at that." On the other hand, "common domestic sheeting sold from five to ten cents per yard by the bolt. The best of spades and shovels for fifty cents each. Vests that cost in St. Louis one dollar and fifty cents each, were sold at Salt Lake for three bits or 37½ cents. Full chests of joiners' tools that would cost 150 dollars in the east, were sold in that place for 25 dollars. Indeed, almost every article, except sugar and coffee, is selling, on an average, fifty percent below wholesale prices in the eastern cities." Heavy wagons for a light one, sheets and joiners' tools for draft animals—at any price these were bargains for the overloaded, under-equipped emigrants who still had hundreds of miles to go. Nowhere else on the trail could they readily dispose of what they did not want and obtain what they needed.

The generally unfavorable reputation of the Mormons among many Americans and their monopoly of the emigrants' market caused many complaints, but Stansbury strongly defended them. "In their dealings with the crowds of emigrants that passed through their city," he wrote, "the Mormons were even fair and upright, taking no advantage of the necessitous condition of many, if not most of them [the emigrants]. They sold them such provisions as they could spare, at moderate prices, and such as they themselves paid in their dealings with each other."

For the Mormons, this unexpected economic activity in their New Zion was a blessing. When Brigham Young changed their projected center from California to Utah, he could not have foreseen they were obtaining the best of two worlds: On the one hand, they were free from interfering and critical neighbors and could manage their new community as they wished; on the other, the passage of the emigrants provided them with a market that was approximately equal to their capacities.

No similar benefits, however, accrued to the nation as a whole. The United States had long produced a small amount of gold; but in 1849, the first year of the gold rush, the amount exceeded that of all the previous years combined since 1791. Polk believed that coins minted from California's gold would replace the foreign coins that were in general circulation. In fact, almost the opposite happened. By 1852, dollar amounts were usually paid in bank notes, and fractional amounts in silver. Gold coins continued to be rare.

Nor did the new farmlands in California and the other acquired areas suddenly make America's foreign trade burgeon and convert the nation into an exporting country, as Polk had hoped. The United States had had a favorable balance of international payments in 1842, but in spite of the discovery of gold, it did not have one again until 1858.

On the other hand, the expansion of the United States created economic problems of the very sort Polk had long sought to avoid. About a year before, in December 1847, he had addressed Congress sternly on the question of the federal government's financing what were usually called "internal improvements"—canals, highways, and other public enterprises. "In some of the States," he said, "systems of internal improvements have been projected . . . many of which, if taken separately, were not of sufficient importance to justify a tax on the entire State . . . and yet by a combination of local interests, operating on a majority of the legislature, the whole have been authorized and the States plunged into heavy debts. . . . If the abuse of power has been so fatal in the States, where the systems of taxation are direct and the representatives responsible at short periods to small masses of constituents, how much greater danger of abuse is to be apprehended in the General Government. . . ."

Polk did not take into account that whenever the United States expanded beyond the ability of private capital to support the growth, the people would call on the federal government for help. Thus the settlers of Oregon, unable to raise the funds to protect themselves, asked the federal government for troops. Their voices were not the only ones raised in pleas for help. The routes across the continent were not considered satisfactory, and the government soon found itself involved in surveys and road building. The cry for public assistance was never stilled. Although revenues eventually increased and often exceeded expenditures, the gross debt of the federal government never again became as small as it had been in 1846 before the Americans embarked on their great adventure of enlargement.

Such considerations were of little interest to the men in the mining camps. The national debt and the economic fate of the Mormons were no concern of theirs; they had come to the gold fields to make money. The gold they were seeking was not the gold embedded in veins of quartz. Although those were the richest concentrations, mining and grinding the quartz required heavy machinery and more capital than most of the miners possessed. They were looking for placer gold, which erosion had already freed from the surrounding quartz. Now it lay loose in the bottoms of streams or rivers or in gravel and dirt where the water had swept it. Once a prospector had located a place where such gold had collected, he "panned" the waste material away.

In addition to being difficult work, panning was also slow. One man could handle about fifty pans a day, far less than another man could dig. So the pan soon gave way to the "rocker," a somewhat more complicated device. The motion was provided by a handle, which even an inexperienced man could soon learn to move in the proper manner, and its capacity was much greater.

With experience, the men developed other means of separating the gold from the base material that enveloped it, machines like the "long tom," for example. In almost every instance, the various methods had one point in common—they required water. In the earliest days, this was not much of a problem. Most of the placers were on a stream or river, but as those claims became worked out and new ones were discovered farther away, the problem of water became increasingly critical. For miners built sluices to carry it to their mines, diverting it from the stream where it had originated and making it unavailable for others' use.

The riparian law of the East could not answer the resulting questions.

243

Consequently the miners had to develop their own law. The basic principle, stated briefly, was this: The first person to use water acquired a right to it that no one else could take away. From then on, he could continue to use the same amount no matter how many other demands might be laid on that particular stream. A second user had a second priority, and so on, until the capacity of the stream was exhausted. And, importantly, it did not make any difference whether he used the water at its original site or carried it away.

Long after the gold rush was over and the miners had dispersed, the code they had established for the use of water continued in effect. Even in parts of the country where mining was not practiced but where water was scarce for ranching, farming, or urban development, water was treated under the miners' law.

Rich or poor, honest or dishonest, the miners all lived in the mining camps that sprang up wherever gold was found. Temporary settlements, they had many similarities—poor housing, a largely male population, high prices because of the difficulty of bringing in enough supplies, a relatively free-and-easy attitude toward life, and, eventually, crime.

Sutter's Fort, as the center of the original gold discoveries, soon all but disappeared under the influx of miners. In his wildest dreams, Sutter had never imagined anything like this. "When we reached Sacramento City," wrote J. W. Gibson, a newcomer from Missouri, ". . . it was not necessary to ask where the city was. The whole valley was covered with tents and lunch stands. There must have been several thousand people there. They had come in from everywhere, off the plains by caravan, up the river from San Francisco by boat, and from every other place in the world, it seemed to me. There were as yet no houses. People, men mostly, lived in tents and the lunch counters consisted of the sideboards of the wagons laid upon poles supported by forks driven into the ground. Meals were a uniform price, $1.00, but lodging was free. Just spread your blanket down on the grass anywhere and make yourself at home."

The community made a similar impression on Alonzo Delano when he arrived. "It was first laid out in the spring of 1849, on the east bank of the Sacramento River, here less than one-eighth of a mile wide, and is about a mile and a half west of Sutter's Fort. Lots were originally sold for $200 each, but within a year sales were made as high as $30,000. There were not a dozen wood or frame buildings in the whole city, but they were chiefly made of canvas, stretched over light supporters; or were simply tents, arranged along the streets. The stores, like the dwellings were of cloth, and property and merchandise of all kinds lay exposed."

What struck both Gibson and Delano, as well as other new arrivals, was the honesty of the people. The merchants had no fear that thieves would carry off their merchandise. Such general honesty, however, could not last. With so much gold dust and cash in circulation and few safe places in which to store it,

244

the temptation to steal grew greater and greater, and more people succumbed to it.

For many men, their hard work in the gold fields brought them only a small return. When Gibson arrived in Sacramento, he and his friends promptly set out for the gold fields and "twenty miles up the American River we each took up a claim and went to work." Since the time was August 1849, the gold rush still was young, and many of the best locations had not yet been discovered. "Each man," Gibson later said, "had his own pan and with it and the water of the river, he washed the gravel away from the loose gold. We worked there several weeks and so far as we could see, exhausted the gold that was in our claims. We found on estimating the result of our work that each man had averaged about sixteen dollars a day for every day he had worked." Earnings such as those were not enough to make a man wealthy, particularly in view of the high cost of food and other supplies.

On their second claim, Gibson and his party did not fare as well. During the winter months, his brother and another man came down with scurvy, and Gibson himself developed a lighter case of the same ailment. "I was very much afraid it would become serious," he later recalled. "I could walk flat footed on my left foot, but had to tip-toe on my right, and all the balance of that winter I did the cooking, provided the wood, and ran the errands, hobbling along the best I could."

Their dreams of riches were not being realized. In fact, Gibson added, "We were somewhat troubled by finances. Everything was going out and nothing coming in." Fortunately they had a good stock of provisions, for in their camp, he noted, the price for a sack of flour had risen to two hundred dollars.

Yet miners like Gibson presented a target for the gamblers, thieves, robbers, and murderers who had begun to cluster around the gold centers. Delano, who spent some time on a tributary of the Feather River in northern California, later described the gradual deterioration of morale in the camp where he was living. When he first arrived, everyone went to work immediately after breakfast; and when evening came, they sat around several large fires and talked of their homes and passed on rumors of new discoveries.

Then a monte dealer appeared. "A change had been gradually coming over many of our people," Delano said later, "and for three or four days several industrious men had commenced drinking, and after the monte bank was set up, it seemed as if the long smothered fire burst forth into a flame. Labor, with few exceptions, seemed suspended, and a great many miners spent their time in riot and debauchery. Some scarcely ate their meals, some would not go to their cabins, but building large fires, would lay down, exposed to the frost; and one night, in the rain. Even after the monte dealer had cleaned out nearly all who would play, the game was kept up by the miners themselves in a small way, till the fragments of their purses were exhausted. There were two companies at work near me, who, when I first went there, were taking

245

out daily in each company, from one hundred to one hundred and fifty dollars. This they continued to do for more than two weeks, when it seemed that the gold blistered their fingers, and they began a career of drinking and gambling, until it was gone."

Then, instead of returning to work on their claims, they began a futile search for richer placer deposits in the nearby valleys. "Among the miners," Delano continued, "was one who lost nine hundred dollars, another eight—their whole summer's work—and went off poor and penniless."

Gamblers were among the least of the criminals who haunted the mining camps. Only a short distance from Delano's camp, three miners from Vermont settled down in the shelter of their tent one evening. Above them the peaks of the mountains rose like dark shadows, and the stream that flowed by their tent whispered in its familiar tone. About ten o'clock, one of them, a miner named Ward, suddenly awoke to find a man standing over him with a hatchet poised to strike. Ward leaped to his feet, avoided another man, ran out of the tent and over a pile of rocks, and reached a cabin about two hundred yards away.

His screams of "murder, murder" waked the men inside, and they dashed with him back to his tent. The killers had split the heads of his companions with their hatchet, tossed their bodies into the stream, and fled with the four hundred dollars they found. Although the miners heard somebody moving along the hillside above them, the night was so dark and the country so steep they were unable to pursue the fugitive sound. When daylight came, they could only bury the dead, for there were no authorities to whom they could report the crime.

What little government existed was informal and ineffective unless a man like Brannan exercised leadership. In southern Oregon, where small amounts of gold had also been discovered, two miners named Sprenger and Sim worked a claim together. While Sim went to the nearest large settlement to purchase supplies, Sprenger had an accident that crippled him. When Sim returned and found his partner helpless, he threw him out of the cabin they had shared and refused him his rightful portion of the proceeds from their claim. The miners had already chosen one of their own members to serve as their leader, giving him the Spanish title of *alcalde*. Sprenger appealed to him, but Sim had presented his case first, using false witnesses and, as became apparent, bribe money to win a favorable opinion.

Unable to perform any hard work, Sprenger lived as best he could on the charity of his fellow miners without, however, giving up hope that he could obtain a just decision against Sim. Among the miners he located an able lawyer, who agreed to handle his case, although every day he spent representing Sprenger meant a day lost working his claim.

The logical course was to file an appeal with the territorial courts, but on second thought he realized this was impractical. Months would pass, and in the meanwhile Sim would be working the joint claim, and by the time the courts acted, it might be worthless.

At the lawyer's instigation, about a thousand miners took the day off from their work—at considerable cost to themselves—and met to consider the next step. By vote, they appointed a committee to call on the *alcalde* and ask him to rehear Sprenger's case before a jury. The *alcalde* barricaded himself in his cabin, thus bringing justice to a standstill.

When the committee reported back to the assembled miners, the crowd was faced with difficult choices. They could seize the *alcalde,* drive him from the camp, and declare his office open. But a resort to violence did not appeal to the majority. Proud of their nation's democratic tradition—then less than a hundred years old—they wished to right Sprenger's wrong but preserve the legal process. Assembled in the open air, their claims lying idle, the miners wanted justice—or at least a fair hearing—for Sprenger, but the means of getting it, short of using force, seemed even more elusive than a rich find of placer gold. But after discussing the problem, several of the miners came up with the answer.

22. GOVERNMENT AND JUSTICE

There are too many hung juries and too few hung
men.

—San Francisco crowd, 1856

During the gold rush, the need for government was proportionate to the concentration of people and the potential wealth to be made in an area. In Oregon, the territorial government was adequate to the relatively small demands made upon it. It had, for example, launched a small second war against the Cayuse Indians as soon as the necessary federal troops arrived—a war that brought peace and safety for the few persons interested in settling on the upper Columbia River. But as Sprenger's lawyer had learned, it was inadequate to preserve order in the gold fields.

In that case, the miners acted on their own but with consideration for the rights of those involved and respect for democratic procedures. Disregarding the *alcalde,* they appointed a judge, gave him authority to appoint the necessary court officials, and ordered an entirely fresh trial. At the conclusion, the jury was split. Some wanted to hang the man who had cheated his crippled partner; others favored hanging the *alcalde.*

The "judge," however, reminded them that responsibility for determining

248

the sentence was his, not theirs. He ordered Sprenger's former partner to pay the costs of Sprenger's illness and give him half of everything he had taken from the mine. The crowd was not entirely satisfied with either the verdict or the sentence, for neither touched the *alcalde*. So they marched to the *alcalde*'s cabin and demanded his resignation. Faced by the angry crowd, he quickly surrendered his office, and the mining camp returned to normal.

In California, cases that demanded justice were far more frequent and the form of government even weaker. For although Oregon was a territory, California in 1849 remained under a military governor. Since American military tradition had left its officers unprepared for the role of proconsul, the commander of California was anxious to free himself of the responsibility for the area's civilian government. Without waiting for Congress to establish a territory—the usual first step toward statehood—he divided the former Mexican province into districts, decided on the number of delegates to represent each one, and called a constitutional convention to meet at Monterey on September 1, 1849.

At the convention, a few men like Thomas Larkin represented the old California, but for the most part the delegates were both young and newly arrived. The constitution they adopted was not particularly unusual, being founded in large part on other state constitutions. On one important point, however, the delegates made a significant social advance: They adopted from the Mexican law separate property rights for women.

On three issues, they took the initiative away from Congress. One of these concerned the form of government under which California would operate. As a territory, its taxes would be lower, since the federal government would assume many of the costs. But with a cavalier disregard for their pocketbooks, the delegates wanted to eliminate this stage and have Congress create a state of California immediately. They also recommended what the boundaries should be.

The most important national issue—and therefore the most important problem for the convention to consider—was slavery. A group of Texans unwittingly helped decide this question. They had arrived at one of the gold-bearing rivers with some fifteen slaves. Each of the Texans took up a claim in his own name and then took up claims in the names of their slaves, thus securing control of approximately a third of a mile of stream bed. Although the Texans were driven away by other miners, they had raised a horrible possibility, and the story of their attempted scheme quickly passed from delegate to delegate. Nothing could have been better calculated to make California a free state.

In November 1849, the constitution was presented to the people, who voted its adoption by an overwhelming majority and, at the same time, elected their officials. The two men chosen provisionally as senators were Frémont, who had returned to California and enjoyed wide popularity in spite

249

of his court-martial, and a disappointed former Tennessee politician, William McK. Gwin. Yet the offices of these two ambitious men, as well as the government of California, were merely empty shadows until Congress voted its approval. For Congress had the final determination on the admission of states. And that was one question—with the decision whether a state should be slave or free—that Congress wished to avoid.

The debate over slavery in the newly acquired lands had little practical basis. In one of his many famous speeches, Webster set forth the opinion of others as well as himself when he said, "I have no more apprehension . . . of the introduction or establishment of African slavery in these territories, than I have of its introduction into and establishment in Massachusetts." Whatever Congress willed, geography had made the conquered areas unsuitable for slavery.

This cold fact did not temper the hot feelings that the question still aroused, particularly in the Congress that assembled in December 1849. So divided were its members that more than sixty ballots were necessary merely to choose a speaker. Yet the people of California, by the vote at their convention, had stripped this indecisive Congress of the politicians' last refuge—postponement. The constitution written by the delegates assembled at Monterey demanded an answer—either positive or negative.

The thin threads that held the Union together were stretched mightily in the months that followed, as the extremists of both South and North pressed their cases, and the admission of California might have split the nation apart except for the intervention of two old antagonists. Henry Clay and Daniel Webster had often opposed each other, but at this moment of crisis they rose to new heights of statesmanship and made common cause of the preservation of the Union.

Clay, long a defender of Southern interests, said in the Senate, "If Kentucky tomorrow unfurls the banner of resistance unjustly, I will never fight under that banner. I owe a paramount allegiance to the whole Union—a subordinate one to my own state." And Webster, old and reaching the end of his career, echoed Clay's thoughts in even stronger words. "For myself," he told the Senate, "I propose . . . to abide by the principles and the purposes which I have avowed. I shall stand by the Union, and by all who stand by it."

In early September 1850, the legislators finally adopted various measures that were designed to resolve the differences between North and South. California became a free state, Utah and Nevada were organized as territories but without any mention of slavery. In addition, Congress strengthened the law governing fugitive slaves and abolished slavery in the District of Columbia,

This collection of bills was designed to hold the Union together for a few more years, but it left unresolved a number of other problems. California had the form of a government but not yet the substance, leaving the lawless elements of its society almost as uncontrolled as they had been before. And the new boundary between Mexico and the United States had been fixed only on paper, not on the ground. Although the United States had conquered thousands of square miles, it was not sure what it really had gained.

The Treaty of Guadalupe Hidalgo, which ended the Mexican War, provided for a joint commission to lay out the actual boundary between the United States and Mexico. Frémont had obtained the appointment to head the commission but preferred to serve as senator from California. The position, therefore, went to John Russell Bartlett, a New York bookseller and historian, who began his three-year assignment in 1850.

The commissioners from the two countries met at El Paso, and while one group went east, Bartlett and his Mexican counterpart headed west. One of the first questions they had to settle was the precise location of several points specifically mentioned in the treaty, for the maps available to the negotiators had proved inaccurate. Bartlett was also to recommend a proposed route for an east-west road to help bind the sections of the country together and, most important, he was to give the American people—and their government—a detailed description of what they had won by their recourse to arms.

At Santa Rita del Cobre, where the bounty-hungry Mexicans and the American trader had ambushed Juan José, he received a visit from Mangas Colorados, the leader who had succeeded to Juan José's place. The Apache told Bartlett he had followed him part of the way and that "he thought we ran a great risk in going so far with so small a party; as there were many bad Indians prone to theft and murder in the country through which he passed, and whom he could not control." The idea of having been closely watched by this famous Apache was not reassuring, but Mangas Colorados recalled his meetings with Kearny and Cooke, when they had traveled through his country, and said that "he was a friend of the Americans, and that his people desired to be at peace with us."

Bartlett thought it his duty to describe to the Indians the new border between Mexico and the United States—an idea that was incomprehensible to the Apaches, who roamed where they wished—and said the United States would always protect the Indians just "as long as they conducted themselves properly and committed no thefts or murders." Otherwise, he explained, the Americans would punish them "and by our treaty with Mexico, we were bound to extend to her people the same protection."

This provision of the agreement between the United States and Mexico had been made by diplomats who had never fought the Apaches; and Mangas Colorados could not understand it. "Our protection of the Mexicans," Bartlett said, "he did not seem to relish; and could not comprehend why we should aid them in any way after we had conquered them, or what business it was to the Americans if the Apaches chose to steal their mules, as they had always done, or to make wives of their Mexican women, or prisoners of their children."

To show his good feelings toward the Apaches, Bartlett gave them cloth, shirts, beads, and other articles but refused them whiskey. Not believing that an American expedition would be without that "indispensable article," as Bartlett called it in his report, they looked questioningly at every bottle. Losing his patience, Bartlett said, "I one day handed them a bottle of catsup and another of vinegar, and told them to ascertain for themselves. A taste put a stop to their investigations, and they were afterwards less inquisitive."

When Bartlett finished the survey, he returned to Rhode Island, where he had been born, and helped assemble one of the outstanding libraries of Americana. His published account of the boundary survey acquainted many people with the parts of the Southwest through which he had traveled and thus contributed to the nation's knowledge of itself. But the results also showed that the Treaty of Guadalupe Hidalgo had not given the United States what the country desired—a good southern route between east and west. That lay even farther south and still within the territory of Mexico.

California's admission as a state did nothing immediately to relieve its problems. More thousands of people from every walk of life and every background were rushing to the gold fields, bringing with them their own respect—or disrespect—for the law. Murder, theft, and claim-jumping became common crimes, but the demoralizing effect of speculation and quick money was not limited to the mining areas. The value of food, clothing, tools, and other necessities of a miner's life were soaring, providing tempting opportunities for the dishonest.

Land was one of the most volatile subjects of trade. A gambling tent in San Francisco, where land could have been obtained for next to nothing only a year or so previous, rented for forty thousand dollars a year, although it covered only three hundred square feet. Land outside the cities also rose in price if it produced any of the commodities wanted by the growing hordes of emigrants; and if it contained a suspicion of gold, there was no end to the price that might be asked or the lengths to which men would go to secure control of it. Before going east, Frémont had given Larkin three thousand dollars with which to obtain some land for him. Larkin chose a Mexican grant at Mariposa, California, which, although enormous in size, was apparently useful for little but raising cattle. But when Frémont returned to California in 1849, he learned that gold had been discovered on it. In the space of a few months his original three-thousand-dollar investment was worth millions. How many millions no one could be sure. But . . . and the buts were many. Was the original Mexican grant valid? Drawn up casually since the land was worth so little at the time, what exactly did it cover? Had the original grantee lived up to the terms imposed on him, thereby validating his title? Did a Mexican grant also include the mineral rights? And even if these questions could all be answered satisfactorily, how could a landowner keep off the crowds of miners who recognized no law—neither Mexican nor American—except the law they themselves had established?

Frémont put his own workers on the land to pan gold for him and, by so doing, gained a small fortune, but he could not prevent individual miners from taking a large part of the placer gold. Soon he installed a mill for crushing the gold-bearing quartz, becoming one of the first, if not the first, in California to engage in this more advanced—and more expensive—method of extracting gold. In order to finance the large undertaking he envisioned, he enlisted European capital in the exploitation of his property, becoming involved in a spider's web of leases and other legal obligations. Meanwhile he engaged in a constant battle, sometimes legal, sometimes physical, to retain the largest area that might be covered by the original deed. On at least one occasion, he had to call on the governor for troops in order to dislodge interloping miners who seized one of his shafts. A pack of wolves surrounding a carcass were no less aggressive than the people of California when they knew where gold was located.

Yet Frémont fared better than John Sutter. When the gold rush started, Sutter had just finished transplanting two thousand fruit trees from various parts of California and was establishing himself in the flour business. Already overextended financially, his difficulty in getting workers caused him to lose more than two-thirds of his wheat crop, which lay in the fields unharvested, and so slowed the construction of his flour mill that he lost another twenty-five thousand dollars. The gold on his own property did not compensate him. Like Frémont, he was unable to fend off the tide of miners who began to stake out claims on land that he had thought belonged to him, and he found his Mexican land titles challenged. So great were the stakes that every device, legal or illegal, was used to take possession of the property of others. No man could feel safe.

Contributing to the lawlessness were two factors resulting from the gold rush itself. One was the influx of criminals. Among them were men who came from the British penal colony in Australia. These swarmed into California by the thousands and, forming a society of their own, brought with them their traditional disrespect for law and order. Another factor was the unwillingness of the better class of citizens to forego the chance of becoming wealthy in order to serve in government, leaving the public offices open to those who hoped to use them to augment their personal fortunes. "There is scarce an officer intrusted with the execution of our state government," complained one San Francisco newspaper, "scarce a legislator chosen to frame the laws . . . scarce a judicial officer from the bench of the supreme court down to the clerk of a village justice of the peace, scarce a functionary belonging to the municipal administration of our cities and incorporated towns, who has not entered upon his duties and responsibilities as the means of making money. . . . His devotion to the well-being and advancement of the community . . . is measured by the dollars and cents to be acquired . . . rather than by any prospective regard to the influence which his official career may have upon the destinies of the community of which he has no intention to become permanently concerned."

When John Sutter discovered a group of five men stealing large numbers of his cattle, he called on the sheriff to pursue them and furnished him with a posse of his own employees. The sheriff followed the thieves to Sacramento, where they were loading the cattle onto boats to take them down the river to San Francisco. He called on them to stop and threatened to fire on them. But the men laughed at him, pushed out into the stream, and left the sheriff standing helpless on the shore. If a man of Sutter's standing and connections could not secure justice on his own behalf, there was little chance for anyone else.

Basic to the problem was the evil of bribery. If the jailer would not set the accused free for a price, either the judge or prosecutor might be susceptible to an offer of money. If these men proved to be honest—or the price they demanded exorbitant—the votes of one or two jurors were usually available for a modest sum. More often, rather than let the case even come to trial, the friends of the accused arranged for the disappearance of some of the key witnesses, who for a slight payment would fade away into the crowds descending on the cities and mining camps. As the state had no means of organizing their pursuit and returning them to the court having jurisdiction, the proceedings would be dismissed.

The miners, having a community of interest, maintained a semblance of order. Should anarchy break loose in the camps, almost everyone would be the loser. In the cities, no common bond existed, and sea captains, merchants, honest gambling proprietors, and hotel owners had few mutual ties except their morality and growing impatience with the dominance of the criminal element.

In February 1851 their impatience could no longer be restrained when a violent attack occurred on a noted San Francisco merchant, J. C. Jansen, who was assaulted in his store and robbed of two thousand dollars. For once the police responded quickly and within a short time had arrested two suspects.

The case was eventually complicated by an extraordinary instance of mistaken identity; but unaware of this confusion, the respectable citizens of San Francisco assembled in a crowd numbering several thousand and demanded the immediate trial and punishment of the two men in custody. An informal court promptly tried the accused *in absentia,* but, stumbling over the question of identity, failed to reach a verdict of guilty. Before dispersing, the

254

infuriated crowd threatened the "jury," who had to draw their revolvers to defend themselves.

An official jury, deliberating after this outburst of violence, later found both men guilty. One of them escaped, and the other—he who was innocent—was held over to stand trial for another offense committed by his look-alike and finally obtained his freedom. Meanwhile the people of San Francisco, grown weary of their government, had developed a taste for handling their problems in their own way.

In addition to murder, robbery, burglary, and mayhem, San Francisco suffered from fires that its volunteer departments could not control. In May 1851, exactly one year after the last great fire, an even larger one swept across the city, taking several lives and destroying almost three-quarters of the city. The damage, at San Francisco's inflated prices, ran into the millions. As the people labored among the ashes, the suspicion grew in their minds that arsonists had started the blaze to provide an opportunity for plundering. The discovery of ten thousand dollars of loot hidden in the houses of some of the Australian immigrants enhanced this suspicion.

Growing increasingly uneasy, the citizens organized their own night patrol system. About a hundred men volunteered to take turns augmenting the seventy-five man regular police force. Since the mayor swore the volunteers into service and the city marshal supervised them, they operated legally within the existing government.

On June 2, 1851, another fire broke out. It had originated near the waterfront in the room of a man named Benjamin Lewis; and when investigators discovered he had some oil-soaked cloth in his possession, the authorities jailed him on a charge of arson. During his arraignment, a fire engine responded to another call. Word immediately flashed through the crowd that Lewis's friends were attempting to distract the authorities' attention so they could rescue him. With that, the mood of the people became sullen. The owner of the building where the fire had started called on the crowd to forget about the courts and exercise their own justice. Only when the court officials convinced the crowd that Lewis would receive an honest trial did the people begin to leave. They had had a taste, however, of the power they could exert by mass action.

The majority of the city, weary of ineffective law enforcement, supported the people's new attitude. The following morning, one of the newspapers commented editorially, "Although strongly opposed, as must be every lover of fair play, to the summary execution of even such a character as Lewis, without a patient and impartial trial—we yet must declare that we regard the demonstration of yesterday with the highest satisfaction." Since government could not protect the people, let the people protect themselves.

This sentiment, of course, was not confined to San Francisco. The miners had been pioneers, not only in finding gold, but in safeguarding their own property and lives; and the citizens of Sacramento had already become aroused over the extent of criminal activity in their community. But San Francisco, as the leading city in California, was getting ready to set the others an example.

On June 8, an anonymous reader of the *Alta* openly proposed that a committee of citizens should be formed to prevent the landing of more emigrants from Australia and that each of the city's wards should form a "committee of vigilance" to drive out criminals. On the same day, another San Franciscan discussed the problem with a friend, and they both decided to talk to Samuel Brannan, the Mormon businessman who had started the gold rush and who had also presided over the "trial" at Sutter's Fort. Brannan was receptive and suggested calling a larger meeting at the California Engine House, which, like most volunteer fire companies, served as a focus for the discussion of community affairs. The meeting there was later adjourned to a building owned by Brannan, where debate on the subject could be carried on with greater privacy.

These were men of action. For months they had watched conditions deteriorate in northern California. At first they had thought that statehood would be a remedy, but more criminals walked the street than ever before and more rascals filled the official posts. The answer was a secret society dedicated to the preservation of law and order. The formal constitution they adopted unequivocally asserted their devotion to the law, but it also clearly stated they would not permit any arsonist, thief, burglar, or murderer to escape unpunished through "quibbles of the law" or through the corruption or laxity of the police or other law enforcement officials.

The leaders were largely men of prominence, they were armed, they had numerous resources on which they could draw, and they were determined. The penalties they could invoke, however, were limited. They had no jails and no means of imposing fines. Therefore the culprits they seized would face one of two punishments: banishment or death.

A quick means of bringing the committee together was agreed upon, a signal that did not openly avow their existence but would notify the members they were needed. Two rings on the bell of the California Engine Company could be heard at a distance and, followed by a silence before being repeated, was unlike any fire call. The sound above the noise of San Francisco's streets henceforth brought men running to Samuel Brannan's building. A whispered password at the door, and the chosen few were admitted, grim-faced and ready to do what they saw as their duty. Those San Franciscan criminals for whom no church bell would ever reverently toll would find a substitute in the double clang coming from the California Engine Company. No priest, minister, or sexton pulled on the rope, but the meaning was just as certain.

23. FAILURES OF GOVERNMENT

*No hour of no day but we listened for the yell of
the Apache. At no time was any man's rifle out of
his reach.*

—William H. C. Whiting, 1849

In 1851, the United States seemed to have every reason to be content with
itself. Its domain now extended from ocean to ocean, spanning the temperate
middle of North America and surpassing the wildest dreams of those men
who had gathered at the Continental Congress less than a hundred years
before.

On the high seas it was gaining a supremacy that would have astonished the
ship captains who fought in the War of 1812. The gold rush had placed a
premium on speed because of the willingness of passengers to pay high fares
and shippers to pay high rates. In 1850 orders began to arrive at American
shipyards for the fastest possible vessels, regardless of how expensive they
were to build and man, or whether cargo space was sacrificed for speed. A
new era opened—the time of the famous clippers, which set and broke speed

records again and again and which evoked admiration wherever they appeared.

As for the slavery issue, the Compromise of 1850, that package of legislative bills arrived at with so much debate and after so much hesitation, seemed, in the minds of many, to have solved the question. The South, its economy burgeoning, felt secure and self-confident; the North, beginning to become industrialized, still contained many abolitionists, but the majority of the people considered themselves less threatened by the South and within a year would even see one of their own, Franklin Pierce of New Hampshire, elected president.

Yet under the surface, events were not moving as smoothly as they seemed to be, and small thunderheads of future trouble were rising in the otherwise blue sky of the nation's prosperity. The new territories acquired during the hectic days of the late 1840s were proving expensive, as each one demanded service from the federal government. During his term as a senator, Frémont, for example, introduced a number of bills calling for benefits for his state: the donation of public lands for educational purposes, the establishment of asylums, a grant for a university, and the construction by the federal government of a transcontinental wagon road. Utah, which had been denied statehood, nevertheless needed twenty thousand dollars for the erection of public buildings, five thousand for a library, and twenty-four thousand to pay its legislature. New Mexico and Oregon required similar federal assistance. In 1851 the federal budget amounted to almost forty-eight million dollars, a tiny sum compared to later years but almost double what it had been in 1846 when the great expansion first started.

Yet these expenditures did not satisfy people. The Mormons had wished for statehood and the name Deseret. Instead they had received a territory called Utah along with an influx of unwanted, Washington-appointed officials. Brigham Young had sought isolation and independence in the desert; instead his area was filled with emigrants bound for California, who complained bitterly about the prices the Mormons charged them for the supplies and services they needed.

In Oregon, the men and women had been anxious to obtain territorial status; now that they had it, they found it unsatisfactory. As one of their own historians noted, "Oregon passed through the most irksome stage of her existence. The territorial form of government, although in theory superior to the provincial, turned out to be practically at least as annoying, with this additional disadvantage—that whereas, under the provincial *régime,* the people were drawn into close union by the threat of external perils, under the territorial they were divided against one another by local and political antagonisms. The average character of the population was lowered as its numbers increased; the tedium and difficulty of communicating with Washington were savagely felt, as well as the futility of attempting to negotiate business there through the medium of a single delegate, who had no vote."

In New Mexico, problems were also arising. While the Apaches expressed friendship toward the Americans, their attitude was largely based on the assumption that they had a common enemy in Mexico. They had no respect for the American government and did not propose to let it interfere with their ancient ways.

Bartlett's survey was beginning to reveal that the American negotiators had not secured a practical southern route between the East and West. Kearny's march and the struggle to seize the area had failed in one of its most important objectives.

In California, the long debate over its admission as a state had not produced the stable government the people had envisioned. The experience of one man, who lived on San Francisco Bay, revealed the conditions under which many Californians lived. "I was alone on the extreme tip of the peninsula," he later said. "All passing boats, to or from the Bay, were obliged to round this point; on which occasions it often happened that people came on shore, especially at night, and atacked my house. To shoot me in bed would have been easy, as board walls could not resist rifle balls. So I made an inner wall of planks, a foot from the bed, and filled the space with sand; I also laid a powder mine under my threshold, as a last resort. A loose plank in the floor was my greatest safeguard, as, when beset by large numbers I could lift it, slip into the cellar and creep into the long, high grass behind the house, whence I could make a circuit behind the foe, and, sheltered by stones and holes and sure of an easy retreat, I could open fire from my double barrelled rifle."

This settler, like many others outside the cities, joined his neighbors in a mutual defense program. The result, he said, was that "the California rascals retired from the country to the larger towns, where they were safer. Popular justice was not so easily administered there, for the simple reason that five men will agree more readily than five hundred; and though five men were enough to hang a thief on a creek . . . five hundred could not have erected a gibbet in Sacramento or San Francisco."

The San Francisco Committee of Vigilance was about to prove him wrong.

John Jenkins was typical of the riffraff attracted to California. Taking advantage of the nighttime, he slipped into a business office on the waterfront, dragged the safe outside, and prepared to load it into a small boat that he had waiting. Before he could do so, the owner appeared. Jenkins dropped the safe into the water, leapt into his boat, and fled. But the cries of the owner alerted a boatman who was returning from a visit to an offshore vessel. He caught Jenkins and brought him back to land.

The commotion attracted a number of people, who assisted the boatman in getting Jenkins onto the shore and helped hold him. Several of them were for marching him directly to the city jail and turning him over to the police. Several others were not. As members of the Committee of Vigilance, they thought the new organization could handle the case with swifter and surer justice.

The ringing of the bell soon brought the committee together, and the "trial" commenced that night. Jenkins did not help himself by serving as his own "attorney." He was an Australian, it turned out, and there could have been no poorer reference than that in San Francisco in 1851. He had been involved with the roughest elements in town, had kept a notorious rooming house, and was suspected of murdering the man to whom he had finally sold it. He ranted at the committee, insulted them, and called them names, until even the most moderate members turned against him. The verdict was death by hanging.

With consideration for the victim's soul, some of the members went in search of a minister. But his prayers and exhortation did nothing to soften Jenkins's attitude; he remained as tough and as abusive as before.

Meanwhile a crowd had gathered outside. Although the committee was willing to flout the law, it was sensitive to public opinion. So Samuel Brannan addressed the gathering, explaining Jenkins's crime, and, like a Roman emperor consulting the mob over the fate of a gladiator, asked whether or not the sentence should be carried out. Some shouted no, but the majority favored a quick hanging.

Just before two o'clock in the morning, when San Francisco would normally be asleep, the committee emerged from their meeting place. Jenkins was in the center, his hands fastened and a guard standing at each side. Around the three men was a cordon of rope held by other members to keep the crowd back and to prevent Jenkins's friends from rescuing him. The rest marched as additional guards, all armed and ready to shoot down any person who tried to interfere.

While the fire companies tolled their bells, the procession walked toward the square where the hanging was to take place. Once Jenkins's friends tried to extricate him from the hands of the committee; once the police tried to stop the death march; in neither instance did they succeed. When the procession arrived at the square and several committee members were placing one end of the hangman's rope over a building beam, some of Jenkins's friends rushed forward and seized him by the legs. In the struggle that followed, Jenkins was the victim. While his friends pulled in one direction, members of the committee pulled in the other, dragging on the rope that was already around his neck. At least one eye-witness said he had been strangled to death before the committee got the rope over the beam and officially hanged him.

The next morning, when most of the committee had gone home after their busy night's work, the coroner appeared, cut down the dead man, and ordered an inquest, thus placing the committee under the scrutiny of the city's officials.

The inquest lasted for several days. At first the committee was not sufficiently sure of its standing with the public to testify openly about its organization and activities. But as the inquest continued, it became more and more apparent that the people of San Francisco favored the committee over the government. When a leading politician tried to harangue a crowd with arguments against the committee, the people threatened to manhandle him; and by the time the inquest was finished, the committee no longer saw a need to be so secretive or defensive.

This exhibition of self-reliance brought temporary relief to San Francisco by squashing some of the more virulent criminal groups and making others realize that even if they foiled the law, they might not escape punishment. Other communities followed San Francisco's example, taking the law into their own hands when their officials failed to protect them. But total crime in California did not decrease, for the emigrants were coming in an ever larger flood.

Starting near the Missouri, a great track lay across the face of the continent, a track of wagon ruts bordered by the goods the emigrants had unloaded along the way and by a broad expanse of closely cropped land, where their livestock had grazed. Indians who saw this "trail" sometimes believed the exodus from the East was about to end. Surely, they thought, no more white men existed toward the rising sun, for they must have all passed by already.

The wagons formed an almost continuous line, the leading members of one party merging with the group ahead, while those in the rear found themselves overtaken by the party behind. So relentless was the pounding of the wheels on the rock and soil that a century and a half later the marks still remained in that dry country, memorials to the thousands of men and women who left their homes in order to found new ones in the West.

The influx by sea was also tremendous. San Francisco Bay was constantly filled with ships, some just entering the Golden Gate, some tied to the wharves and unloading the cargoes that would command such high prices in the California market, and some hoisting their sails and preparing to depart, often with little more than a skeleton crew, many sailors having deserted to try their luck in the gold mines.

As time passed, the ardor of the prospectors did not dim, but their expectations became lower. No longer did they think they would find nuggets of gold among the river sands waiting to be picked up with only casual effort. Even the new arrivals quickly learned that panning was not easy and the returns, if any, were often meager. "In an early day," wrote an emigrant who watched the changing attitude, "men were not content with doing well, and were not satisfied with a fair remuneration. Ten dollars per day was looked upon as not sufficient to pay. Now the mines are better understood, and generally, if a miner finds diggings which pay from three to five dollars, he continues to work."

In spite of the disappointments suffered by many miners, California continued to be the goal of the majority of emigrants. But Oregon was not forgotten. In 1852, Hall J. Kelley, still the promoter, brought out a book featuring the territory's many advantages and, incidentally, stressing his supposed role in developing it and his claim to some sort of reimbursement for his time and expense. Whem the emigrant trains came to the point where the Oregon and California trails divided, many of them still took the northern fork, preferring a fertile farm to the chances of finding a placer mine. And the discovery of gold in southern Oregon also brought additional men from California.

The impact of crowds of strangers in both California and Oregon upset the Indians' way of life. In California they had long become accustomed to the rule of the Spaniards and had accepted their own role as second-class citizens. The Spaniards, however, had concentrated their settlements and missions along the coast, and their influence had little effect on the Indians in the foothills of the Sierra Nevada.

An imaginative entrepreneur, named James D. Savage, took advantage of their comparative ignorance. Soon he had the Indians—some reports said hundreds of them—hunting the stream beds for gold, which he purchased from them at ridiculously low prices. Only the Yosemite Indians, who lived farther east, caused him trouble. Their attacks on his posts as well as on other white miners moving into the area produced a short conflict. Savage led a punitive expedition against them, during which he entered the Yosemite Valley and saw its marvelous beauty.

In Oregon the Indian problem was more difficult. Not having been subjugated by the Spaniards, they had remained more independent and therefore a greater threat to the white settlements in such fertile areas as the Willamette Valley. In 1850 the government embarked on a policy of persuading the Indians along the coast to move east of the Cascades and thus out of the way of the men and women who wanted to farm the land. Such a policy was unrealistic, for the Indians on the coast had no desire to move, and the Indians who already lived on the other side of the mountains had no desire to receive them. So the three commissioners appointed to conduct the negotiations quickly adopted a policy of "buying" the Indians' lands but allowing them to retain a reservation.

These agreements were made without either of the two parties understanding what they were doing. The concept of land ownership was as alien to the Indians of western Oregon as it was to most of the Indians in North America. They wandered where they could, concentrating largely on those areas from which another tribe was unable to expel them. The thought that ownership could be complete and irrevocable and transferred through a piece of paper was incomprehensible. The American commissioners were also at a disadvantage. Ahead of the country was a future they had absolutely no way of foreseeing, a future that would make many of their concessions difficult to maintain. Yet they worked in good faith, avoiding the solutions Spain had used that had usually resulted either in the assimilation of the Indians into the peon classes or their extermination.

Each of the nineteen agreements arranged by the commissioners was in the form of a treaty. This practice had started in the nation's colonial days when the white men and the Indian tribes were more nearly equals and dealt with each other as separate nations, but the practice continued because of the jealousy of the Senate. Treaties required the consent only of the Senate, the concurrence of the House not being dictated by the Constitution. Thus the Senate could maintain sole control over the negotiations and the transfers of land that usually accompanied them.

The Senate rejected all the Oregon Indian treaties on the ground that the appropriations were excessive and the terms of the agreements too loose. The failure of the treaties to win approval came at a critical moment. Although the northwestern Indians—with the exception of those that had attacked Marcus Whitman—had been generally friendly, they were becoming increasingly resentful of the intrusion of the Americans. In the late summer of 1853, the Klamath, Shasta, and Rogue River Indians decided to make a unified attack on the white men and drive them out of southern Oregon. Without any previous warning, they began their raids.

Joseph Lane, who had been the first governor of Oregon, took command of the counteroffensive and, leading a group of volunteers and a few regular soldiers, pursued the Indians until they made camp in a well-protected ravine. After completely surrounding them, Lane ordered an assault that proved costly to both sides. Several Americans were killed, and Lane himself received a serious wound in his right shoulder. The Indians' casualties were even greater; and when they learned that Lane was the commander of their opponents, they offered to make a truce because they trusted him. In a week's additional time, they said, they would get their people together, meet Lane at an appointed place, and surrender. When one of the Indian leaders offered his son as a pledge of their good faith, Lane accepted their terms. At that point, his trouble with the white settlers began.

Many settlers favored immediate extermination; and when the Indians failed to appear on September 1—the date set for the meeting—they were ready to start. With the greatest difficulty, Lane restrained them.

A few days later the Indians arrived—the slight difference in time meant little to them—and the talks between the two parties began. While they were progressing, a group of volunteers showed up, bringing with them a howitzer and a company of dragoons. Since the military strength was now overwhelmingly on the side of the Americans, the extremists were for beginning an offensive immediately. Once again Lane had to draw on all his political and diplomatic skills to hold them back.

The road followed by the peacemaker—whether he was white or red—was often rough, largely because the leaders of both races had difficulty controlling their own people. That happened during Lane's negotiations with the Indians of southern Oregon.

With only about ten white men accompanying him, he stood in the middle of a large group of warriors, pleading with them to give up their war effort. While he was talking, an Indian messenger arrived with the news that a band of Americans had captured a warrior, tortured him, and killed him. His own people had effectively condemned Lane to death.

Whether Lane could win a reprieve depended on his own wits. Surrounded by angry warriors and still suffering from the wound he had received earlier, he calmly emphasized two points. The men who had killed the Indian were criminals, and he himself would try to capture their leader and punish him. At the same time, he freely admitted that the Indians could kill him. But what purpose would that serve? It would neither prove they were brave, since he was outnumbered, nor would it provide any settlement between the white men and the tribes fighting them. A remarkably persuasive man, as well as a courageous one, Lane was able to make the Indians understand the truth of what he was saying. The negotiations continued and brought temporary peace to the people of Oregon.

Politically, however, they were still in turmoil. Territorial status had brought them some benefits, such as greater federal protection, but it made them victims of politics. For territorial offices were regarded as legitimate spoils by the party victorious at the national polls. Furthermore, Oregon Territory was far too large to be governed efficiently. In 1853, the same year that Lane quieted the uprising of the Indians in southern Oregon, Congress voted to establish Washington Territory. Since the question of slavery was not involved, the measure passed without the acrimonious debate that had marked the year 1850.

In Utah, the Mormons were also struggling with the problem of size. Congress, in its desperation to end the bitter debates of 1850, had included in Utah Territory most of what is now Nevada as well as parts of Colorado and Wyoming. With their characteristic energy, the Mormons were sending parties of colonizers into the areas surrounding Great Salt Lake to establish here and there small dots of Mormon influence. Hardworking as they were, however, the task of consolidating the government of the entire area was beyond their capacity, and they concentrated on problems close to the center of the territory, where they were building a prosperous and strong community in spite of the disadvantages of the desert they had chosen for their New Zion.

Yet they continued to exercise their usual talent for making themselves disliked. Many of the emigrants, who purchased their supplies and relied on them for succor, complained that they charged too much; and Benjamin G. Ferris, who served as territorial secretary during this period, would not even give them credit for their accomplishments. Writing of the emigrants who were forced to stop over in Utah to earn the means of continuing their journey, he said, "Hundreds remain all winter, and work for a bare living; and a large number of the indications of industry and enterprise, in the form of buildings, fences, water-ditches, and other improvements for which the Mormons have received credit, owe their existence to the toil of these temporary sojourners."

In his dislike for the people, Ferris accused Brigham Young of using unseemly language in his public utterances and said of the Mormon boys that "it is a common thing for them to retail at school the disgusting intimacies which they have witnessed at home. Young men who have graduated in these primary institutions of vice [the Mormon schools] are licentious to a degree that will not bear description." Reports such as these helped to drive a breach between the Mormons and the rest of America. Politically Utah was part of the United States; culturally, in the view of many, it was a separate land.

In New Mexico Territory life was continuing much as it had before. The American conquest of what now constitutes New Mexico and Arizona had not appreciably quickened the pace of life, and the people's casual attitude toward their territorial government was evident in the experience of David Meriwether, who was appointed governor in 1853. When he first heard he was being considered for the office, Meriwether declined. He had once been held a prisoner by the New Mexicans before the province became part of the United States, and he had no desire to see Santa Fé again. Furthermore, he did not believe there was much future in the position. Only the personal arguments of President Pierce persuaded him to accept.

After his arrival in Santa Fé, he learned that the post imposed numerous responsibilities on the incumbent but gave him little means with which to carry them out. Any number of persons wanted federal positions, but the governor had little patronage at his disposal, and many of the applicants were clearly unqualified. Several of those who wished to be attorney general had never read law. In fact, one of them was a blacksmith.

To control the fifty or sixty thousand Indians that were in his charge Meriwether had three Indian agents, two of whom, he believed, had never seen an Indian before. To make the problem worse, his predecessor as governor had already spent most of the Indian appropriation, so he did not have sufficient funds to pay the agents' travel costs or to hire interpreters for them.

Beyond New Mexico lay a vast desert country, little changed since the days of the Spaniards and still largely controlled by Indians. A few New Mexicans, however, ventured through it to go to the California gold mines or to drive livestock to the burgeoning California markets. A number of men made good profits in this business, one of them being a French-Canadian named François Xavier Aubry, who had come to the United States to make his fortune. Several characteristics distinguished him from others who made the trip to California, or as Aubry also did, engaged in the Santa Fé trade.

One was his obsession with speed. A skillful long-distance rider, he again and again set new records for the trip between Missouri and Santa Fé, sometimes riding his mules to death in the process, sometimes traveling part of the way on foot when he could not obtain a mount. Even the hardiest westerners marveled at the pace he kept.

Another distinguishing characteristic was his interest in routes. Many of the merchants who went to Santa Fé or those who drove livestock to California took the best way they knew but paid relatively little attention to the alternatives. Not Aubry. In spite of the speed with which he traveled, he kept records of his journeys and made comparisons of one route with another, all in the interest of improving communications between the various parts of the Southwest.

On a trip from California in 1853, he made a discovery that presaged the opening of some of the relatively unknown areas of what is now Arizona. Often he traveled alone, but this time he had a small company of men with him. After crossing the Colorado River, he wrote in his journal, "On one occasion whilst at rest for a few minutes in a deep gully about a mile from the crossing . . . a Mexican mule boy discovered something glistening upon the ground, which on examination proved to be gold. We at once commenced washing sand in our tin cups, and in every one discovered particles of gold."

This was the lure that should bring settlers into the land except for one major deterrent: The Indians were no more peaceful than they had been under the Mexicans. Even as Aubry and his companions tried to pan a little of the gold, a band watched them from a nearby height, and their attitude toward the white men was uncertain. Aubry was daring but not foolish; and the lives of his company were worth more to him than a few bags of gold dust.

How wise he had been not to tarry in an unprotected spot was demonstrated a few days later when Indians did attack his party. After the fight, Aubry noted in his journal, "Our condition at present is bad enough. I have eight wounds upon me, five of which cause me much suffering; and at the same time, my mule having given out, I have to walk the whole distance. Thirteen of us are now wounded, and one is sick, so that we have only four

266

men in good health." Adding to their suffering was the loss of their canteens during their fight, making it impossible for them to carry water from one spot to another, and they were also reduced to eating half rations of horse meat. The inhospitality of the Southwest's Indians and terrain formed a barrier against its quick settlement that even the presence of gold could not remove.

. The United States government also was learning the clause in the Treaty of Guadalupe Hidalgo requiring the Americans to protect the Mexicans from Apache raids was impossible to enforce. That and the failure of the treaty to include some of the land that seemed necessary for a southern transcontinental route put the diplomats to work again. Santa Ana, who came and went in Mexican politics, was once more in control of the government and once more thirsty for money. In 1853, through the Gadsen Purchase, the United States was able to obtain what is now its southern border and also secure relief from the treaty obligation to keep the Apaches in check.

Other tribes west of the Rockies were also opposing the Americans' advance. In 1852, the Modocs of California staged a raid on a wagon train carrying sixty-five men and women west. Only one survivor remained to tell what had happened. When Meriwether arrived in New Mexico, he found the territory in an uproar over the raid of a band of Navajos. Sporadic Indian attacks, the breakdown of government in California, and the growing gap between the people of Utah and the rest of the country demonstrated that it had been easier to gain title to the lands beyond the Rockies than to obtain control of them. Yet the greatest threat to the unity of the nation came not from the strain of absorbing the newly acquired territory but from the old issue of slavery.

The year 1851 had marked the serial publication of an inflammatory book that seized the imaginations of thousands of people. *Uncle Tom's Cabin* enjoyed such success as a magazine story that it immediately appeared as a book. Three hundred thousand people (or the equivalent today of approximately 2.5 million) purchased the volume, thrilled to Eliza's flight across the frozen Ohio River, wept over Uncle Tom's fatal beating, and passed the book on to their family and friends. The controversy quieted by the politicians was raised anew by the novelist.

On one national issue, however, almost everyone agreed: the need for better communications. The federal government was already engaged in building roads, but better than wagon roads were railroads. These had proved themselves efficient east of the Mississippi, and there was no reason why they should not eventually link the East and the West.

The cost of surveying possible routes fell on the federal government, for the potential return from a transcontinental railroad did not at that time warrant the investment of private capital. As various sections of the country hoped that such a railroad would eventually pass through lands in which they were interested, the pressure on Congress was heavy to survey numerous possibilities.

Four routes were clearly the most practical. The southern ran across Texas and on to Yuma and San Diego. One just north of that went along the thirty-fifth parallel. (This was the route favored by Aubry after his own explorations of the Southwest.) The central route went from St. Louis across the mountains to Great Salt Lake and roughly followed the emigrants' trail to California. The fourth and last went to the north of that and was more or less based on the trail opened by Lewis and Clark.

But to survey a railroad route was different than selecting one. An advantage would accrue to the section of the country through which a railroad passed. And which should it be? North or South? Congress preferred to avoid that question and continue the uneasy peace that existed between the two factions. Then early in 1854, Stephen A. Douglas, senator from Illinois, threw a firebrand into the powder keg.

24. VIOLENCE AND JUSTICE

. . . the Vigilance Committee acted wisely . . .
in not dissolving. The whole organization re-
mained unaltered and imparted to the officeholders
as well as to the criminals the persuasion of the
undeniable truth, that at any moment, when neces-
sary, the Committee could again repress crime.

—Gustav Bergenroth, 1851

The problem raised by Douglas came from his effort to organize part of the Great Plains as Nebraska Territory. This, in turn, was occasioned by his interest in a transcontinental railroad. In spite of their disagreement on many points, most congressmen concurred that a railroad should not run through an ungoverned—and perhaps ungovernable—wilderness. Some sort of social structure, capable of developing towns and enforcing at least a minimum of law, should exist along its right of way. If the central route, which Douglas favored, was to have any chance of selection, the country immediately beyond the Missouri must be given a government.

Douglas was wise in the ways of Congress. He knew that some concession must be made to the South in order to secure its votes, so he adopted one of the features of the Compromise of 1850. In that delicate and successful arrangement, the territories had been given the option of later deciding themselves whether they wanted to be admitted as slave or as free states. Nothing, at least on the surface, could appear to be more logical or democratic, and Douglas proposed applying the same principle to Nebraska Territory. This was, however, in direct contravention to the earlier Missouri Compromise.

The South grabbed the opportunity to demand the outright repeal of the Missouri Compromise. Time had silenced the great voices of Clay and Webster, and no one with their prestige and gifts of oratory spoke out to place the Union above all other considerations.

The original bill, which had been introduced in December 1853, was considerably changed during the bitter debates that followed, and instead of one territory, it soon proposed the establishment of two: Nebraska and Kansas.

For the extremists of the South, its passage represented a major victory; for those of the North, a defeat that was unacceptable. Since the bill still gave the local residents the option of deciding whether they would apply for admission as a free or a slave state, both sides mustered their strength to populate the new territories—particularly Kansas—with emigrants that favored their cause. When these efforts left the future still in doubt, both sides turned to force; and a nation that could not quiet the violence taking place in its geographical center obviously could do little to bring peace and responsible government to its farthest frontier.

Although a semblance of order had been restored to San Francisco by the Committee of Vigilance of 1851, conditions had again deteriorated. Political corruption was rife, and when the machine could not command a majority in any other way, it could count on its unique ballot boxes to give them one. These were designed with false bottoms. By means of a skillfully hidden slide, which pulled out to permit access to the interior, a worker could insert extra ballots even after the lock had been closed and sealed with wax. And if this feature failed in the face of an avalanche of ballots for the adversaries, the ballot box could be lost or smashed and its contents sent flying to the winds. The better citizens, however, did not intervene in the governmental process until in 1856 two rapidly succeeding events stirred them to action.

Charles Cora was a well-known San Francisco gambler. His trade was not by itself sufficient to condemn him in the free-wheeling life of the city, but he also had a notorious affair with Arabella Ryan, the madam and apparent owner of a highly profitable house of prostitution. This relationship might not have attracted undue attention until one evening the pair obtained seats at the theater close to William H. Richardson, then the United States marshal.

270

The occasion was gala, and Richardson left the theater that night convinced that he and his wife had been ridiculed by the proximity and behavior of Cora and his mistress. The next evening he met Cora on the street—and here the details of the story as presented in court varied. Cora later insisted that Richardson had drawn a derringer and threatened to kill him. As a consequence he had drawn his own derringer and killed Richardson in self-defense. The prosecution argued otherwise, charging Cora with outright murder.

The trial caused such a commotion in San Francisco that the judge ordered the jury sequestered, and for more than a week its members were separated from their family and friends. At the conclusion, they all agreed on a verdict of guilty except for one man who persisted in supporting Cora in his contention that he had fired the fatal shot only to save his own life. In the opinion of the other jurors, their dissenting member had been bribed, and this opinion soon became common throughout the city.

One of the vocal proponents of this view was James King of William, editor of the San Francisco *Bulletin*. (He had adopted the "of William" as part of his name to distinguish himself from others also called James King, William being his father's name.) He had come to California a few years earlier, made a considerable fortune in the banking business, lost it, and turned to journalism, a field in which he quickly earned a reputation as one of the muckrakers of his day.

One of his particular targets was James P. Casey, a machine politician who had been elected a county supervisor and who was supposed to be the mastermind behind the trick ballot boxes. By some journalistic detective work, King had learned that Casey was a former inmate of New York State's penitentiary and acquainted his readers with that fact while they were still in an uproar over the hung jury in the Cora trial. Casey immediately called on King, who refused to print a retraction.

That same day, on his way home, King met Casey, who drew a pistol and shot him in the chest. Some of King's friends immediately started chasing Casey, who fled to the city jail, where his own friends in the city administration could protect him. When a crowd gathered, Casey's friends carried him to the county prison. Since news of the shooting had spread rapidly, the crowd grew even larger. The usual role of the jailers and the mob was reversed. The purpose of the jailers was to set Casey free, the purpose of the mob, to prevent his escape.

On the night of May 14, 1856, San Francisco was in turmoil. The mistrial of Cora and the shooting of King—all on the same day—made many persons believe the Committee of Vigilance should be resurrected. The former members agreed and placed an advertisement in the newspapers announcing a meeting for the following day. Without much debate, they chose as their leader William T. Coleman, a prominent merchant.

One of their earliest steps was to use their financial strength. The only newspaper in San Francisco that had condemned the reformation of the committee was the *Herald,* which that morning had said editorially, "We see that a number of highly respectable merchants, some of them our warm friends, have called a meeting of the old Vigilance Committee. . . . We wish to be understood as most unqualifiedly condemning the movement." Much of the *Herald*'s revenue came from San Francisco's auctioneers, who handled most of the ships' cargoes brought into the city. A notice signed by many important merchants almost immediately appeared in the other papers advising the auctioneers to stop advertising in the *Herald* as the signers no longer read it. Anyone questioning the power of the vigilantes had only to look at the *Herald*'s fate. From one of the largest newspapers in town it quickly became one of the smallest.

Compared to the committee formed in 1851, the new group was larger and more formal and soon numbered several thousand men. Because the opposition they faced might be stronger, they organized themselves into military companies of a hundred men each and armed themselves from a shipment of rifles that had just been landed in the city. Next they secured a building to serve as headquarters, fortifying it with sandbags and placing military guards around it. Anyone who doubted the seriousness of their intentions had only to visit Fort Gunnybags, as they called it, to realize that these men were willing and prepared to challenge the constituted authorities. Later in July the committee opened its doors to the public, and it was reported at the time that six thousand men were enrolled and divided into companies of dragoons, cavalry, infantry, and—most surprising of all—artillery. They had secured cannons from visiting ships, cannon then being frequently used for the defense of trading vessels.

Despite its general popularity, the committee was not allowed to take over San Francisco unopposed. Many who supported it financially—probably for business reasons, if nothing else—would not play an active role in its affairs. Others joined what became known as the Law and Order party. This was composed of the officeholders, of course, but aligned with them were many private citizens who had no use for the city's criminals or for political dishonesty, but who believed such evils should be remedied through the courts, not by private individuals.

The Law and Order party quickly secured the support of the state's governor, who came from Sacramento two days after the committee's initial meeting. First he called on William Tecumseh Sherman, later a Civil War general, but than a San Francisco banker who had recently been appointed commander of the militia. Sherman joined him when he spoke to Coleman, the committee's leader. Young and inexperienced in politics, the governor agreed to permit the committee to station its own men within the county jail to ensure that neither Cora nor Casey was rescued by their friends. In return, he thought he had secured Coleman's assurance that the committee would not attempt to remove the prisoners. But the two men had misunderstood each other. Coleman believed he had only promised to notify the authorities in advance if the committee decided to take possession of the prisoners and try them.

Events in San Francisco were moving rapidly. King had been shot on May 14, 1856, and the committee had organized that evening. Two days later the governor had met with Coleman. On May 18, Coleman decided to take the two prisoners from the jail and bring them to trial before the committee. That Sunday morning broke clear over San Francisco, and the bay glimmered under a cloudless sky. At nine thirty, Coleman ordered the committee's observers at the prison to withdraw. At eleven the governor received a notice from the committee stating that the prisoners were going to be seized. Shortly after twelve the committee's forces surrounded the jail. This was no shouting mob, but a serious-minded mass of thousands of determined men, all armed and all obeying their elected officers. Around the jail they placed a cordon, permitting no one to enter or leave. A six-pound cannon, originally the property of the militia, stood aimed at the front of the building, and the committee loaded it conspicuously and lighted the match that could be used to fire it.

A messenger rode up to the prison door and tapped on it with the handle of his whip. To the person opening it, he handed a message directed to the sheriff. "You are hereby required," it said, "to surrender forthwith the possession of the county jail now under your charge to the citizens who present this demand, and prevent the effusion of blood by instant compliance." The note bore no name, being signed merely "Committee of Vigilance." Against such an overwhelming force, the sheriff had little chance and surrendered his two prisoners.

The "trial" of Cora took place first. Although the committee went through the traditional motions, it had from the first decided that legal technicalities were not to stand in the way of "justice." The outcome, therefore, was almost certain before the first evidence was taken. While the case against Cora was being heard, King, the editor of the *Bulletin,* died of the pistol wound he had received from Casey. Everyone in San Francisco, including all the members of the committee, quickly heard the news; and the practical effect was a death sentence for both Cora and Casey.

The day of King's funeral services was set as the time for the prisoners' execution. Several thousand members of the committee stood guard outside Fort Gunnybags, while inside a priest spent several hours with the condemned men. Then they were brought to the main committee room on the second floor, where the committee had already made its preparations. Two planks lay on the floor and extended out two windows, the ends being hinged so they would drop when a weight was placed on them. Projecting out the tops of the

273

windows were two beams to which the hangman's ropes were attached. Casey and Cora entered the room wearing white robes and white caps. Briefly they stood in the windows, looking at the sky above them and the hostile, expectant crowd below, which included not a single friend. Then the executioners pulled the caps down over their faces, adjusted the nooses around their necks, and led them forward. The hinges turned downward, and their bodies dangled in the air.

Having hanged two men, defied the state's governor, put the sheriff to rout, and destroyed the one newspaper that had dared criticize its members, the committee had so firmly established itself in San Francisco that it could now use lesser measures to accomplish its purposes. The means it adopted was banishment. One by one it made up a list of the least desirable people in San Francisco and asked them to leave, either of their own free will or with the committee's forcible assistance. Since a departure by land meant the exiles might return after only a brief absence, the committee usually booked passage for them on a boat leaving for distant ports. As a matter of conscience, it usually gave the deportees their choice of destination and, if they had no money, paid their passage. Few, if any, of those ordered to leave refused to obey. The white-robed bodies of Cora and Casey had shown them the fate that otherwise awaited them.

Whatever anyone may have thought of the Committee of Vigilance—whether they were destroying angels purging their city or a group of hoodlums undermining the judicial system—one point was clear: Their leadership was superb. Coleman and his associates never allowed the organization to degenerate into an uncontrolled mob. By using banishment as a punishment instead of death, they forestalled the reaction that would have come against extremism. And by carefully selecting as their targets the most notorious residents of San Francisco, they kept the people on their side. As a result, the position of the committee was practically impregnable. Neither force nor public opinion could prevail against it.

The governor of California, frustrated by his previous experience in dealing with the committee, decided on another attempt to regain control. The point on which he seized was the release of a deputy sheriff whom the committee held as a prisoner. When the committee refused to recognize a writ of habeas corpus issued by Judge David S. Terry of the state supreme court, the governor declared martial law and ordered Sherman to call out the militia.

Sherman had agreed to do this provided the federal government would supply arms. But the army commander in California said he would have to obtain authorization from the president. Since the militia was not anxious to confront their fellow citizens anyway and certainly could not do so without an adequate supply of weapons, Sherman saw the effort as hopeless and resigned. The governor had accomplished nothing except to lose the support of the public, even outside San Francisco.

"No revolution other than a moral one can be produced in this state," said the Sacramento *Union,* "unless the commander in chief gives his order to fire upon the citizens of San Francisco. Should this fatal order be given such a storm of revolution would sweep over the state as had never been witnessed in these United States." Coleman and his associates had the support not only of the citizens of San Francisco but of many other Californians as well. More than seven years had elapsed since Kearny had captured Los Angeles and six years since Congress had admitted California as a state. But government did not yet exercise real sovereignty over the area.

San Francisco was not a single city in revolt against its government; it was the prominent representative of a whole order of thinking. Throughout many parts of the West, as the ordinary machinery of government failed to meet the demands of frontier society, the citizens resorted to the tactics used by the Commiteee of Vigilance of San Francisco. The people of Los Angeles and Sacramento, for example, also knew how to take the law into their own hands when the occasion required it. But San Francisco remained the outstanding example, the model that others could follow. For that reason, the governor believed it of the utmost importance to reassert his authority.

Judge Terry, who had already shown an active interest in the governor's cause, discovered a provision in the federal statutes that required the army, in spite of the commanding general's attitude, to supply the militia with a limited number of arms. Through this clause and by other means, a few shipments of guns, destined for the Law and Order party, began to reach northern California, and it became an objective of the Vigilance Committee to intercept them.

On June 20, 1856, the committee, which had its friends and spies in many circles, learned that the schooner *Julia* was on its way to San Francisco from Sacramento and on board were some of the guns held in the name of the governor. At dusk about twelve committee members boarded a small sloop and began cruising the bay in search of the schooner. As they pushed in a northerly direction, the wind and the tide both turned against them, and they came to anchor at San Pablo Bay on the eastern shore of San Francisco Bay and waited for either the tide or the wind to change direction. When they again set sail, they inspected several vessels but found no schooners named *Julia.* In the blackness it was difficult to see the ships, but about midnight they noticed a vessel anchored off a point and carrying no lights, in itself a suspicious circumstance.

Approaching quietly, the committee members made out the name *Julia.* No sign came from the boat as the twelve men climbed over its side. The entire crew, as well as three Law and Order party members, were sound asleep, unaware that word of their cargo had reached San Francisco before them. Quickly the vigilantes seized them and then found what they were looking

275

for—150 guns. Taking the guns and the three party members with them, the vigilantes returned to San Francisco, pleased with their night's work.

Back in San Francisco, the committee considered the cases of the prisoners. At least two of them were notorious characters, but the committee had no specific charges against them and decided to let them go free. Their leader was James R. ("Rube") Maloney; and although he had surrendered peacefully, being captured while he was asleep, he deeply resented the treatment he had received and went from saloon to saloon, drinking and building up his resentment and finally meeting Judge Terry.

At that point a horrible thought occurred to the Committee of Vigilance. Maloney's evidence in the hands of a prosecutor might be turned into a case of piracy. Ever since the committee had been organized, both its leadership and the leaders of its opponents had taken a curious and ambivalent attitude toward the law. On the one hand, the governor had considered the vigilantes as insurrectionists and cause for declaring martial law; on the other, he had tried to serve them with a writ of habeas corpus, a writ usually served only on legally designated jailers, not on kidnappers. The committee had felt free to hang two men as the result of an extralegal "court" proceeding, which under the law was equal to murder. Yet they were worried that the charge of piracy might be leveled at them. So they sent one of their members, Sterling A. Hopkins, to "arrest" Maloney and place him beyond the reach of the authorities.

Hopkins found Maloney in conference with Terry but did not make the "arrest," for Maloney, Terry, and several other men in the room all drew their pistols. Quickly retreating, Hopkins went in search of reinforcements but, returning with four more men to support him, found that Maloney, Terry, and their companions had disappeared. Rushing back to the street, he saw them all heading for the armory, one of the strongest defensive posts still under the control of the government.

Both parties were armed, and since Hopkins and his men could not get ahead of Terry and Maloney to cut them off, Hopkins rushed past the men separating him from Maloney. As he tried to do so, one of those guarding Maloney covered Hopkins with his gun while the others seized him and forced him to the ground.

The situation had changed abruptly from Hopkins's original assignment—to "arrest" Maloney single-handedly. Guns were now pointing in every direction, the men holding them were nervous, and inevitably one went off. The bullet did no damage, but Terry believed it had been aimed at him. Whipping out a bowie knife, he lunged at Hopkins and stabbed him in the neck.

The other committee members thought Hopkins was fatally wounded. They charged; Terry, Maloney, and the rest rushed toward the armory, entered, and had time to slam the door shut as their pursuers dashed up behind them. Two members of the committee remained outside the door to prevent the fugitives from escaping, while the others removed the bleeding Hopkins and reported the event to Coleman.

The leader of the vigilantes followed his first instinct—to capture and punish anyone guilty of wounding a committee member in the course of his "official" duties. If assailants could escape with impunity, no vigilante could count on being safe. The ruffian element might pick them off one by one.

Soon the fire company bell was ringing the alarm, and vigilantes poured into the streets. Carters unharnessed their horses and, leaving their wagons standing, became cavalrymen. Storekeepers abandoned their customers, and one vigilante, whose sprained ankle prevented him from walking, comandeered the cart of a tradesman delivering kerosene. As empty cans clattered onto the pavement and full ones slopped over, he raced to the scene of action. In a few minutes the armory in which Terry and Maloney had taken refuge was surrounded by armed and angry vigilantes, a group too large and powerful for the sheriff to disperse.

The negotiations between the besieged and the besiegers moved quickly. The vigilantes demanded the surrender of the men who had dared defy them; those inside the armory demanded their safety. The committee, of course, would not guarantee that they would go unpunished, but they did agree to protect them from attacks by any other group. On these obviously poor terms, the fugitives surrendered.

This was a victory that destroyed the victors. Hanging without due process a known gambler and a cheating politician was one thing; holding prisoner an associate justice of the state's supreme court was another. With the curious distinctions that marked the Californians' attitude toward the law, the second action raised serious questions of ethics, and even the committee members were not unanimously agreed on what to do next but finally decided to hold a "trial."

The proceedings concluded on July 22, 1856, with speeches by the "prosecutor" and by Terry, who acted as his own attorney. The person who saved both sides, however, was neither of the two lawyers, but Hopkins. To the relief of everyone concerned, Hopkins did not die.

With his survival, the committee could afford to be magnanimous; and although they found Terry guilty of a number of the counts in their original indictment, they ordered his release with a recommendation that he resign from the state supreme court. The decision was rendered by the vigilantes' executive committee, but it did not meet the approval of many of the members, who failed to see any distinction between a judge and the hoodlums they had been summarily banishing. Only by using the greatest diplomatic skill were Coleman and the other leaders able to secure a vote from the delegates of the general membership that confirmed their ruling.

Terry was free, and the days of the Committee of Vigilance of San

Francisco were ended. From the beginning, the committee's leadership had shown an unusual sense of timing, and they were aware that they had gone too far. Instead of waiting for the public to turn against them, they declared their job done and prepared to disband. To slink off quietly would be an admission of defeat and would have removed the threat that the committee could be reestablished at some future time. Coleman and the other leaders realized this and understood the psychological importance of bringing the affairs of the committee to a close with a fanfare. Consequently they arranged one of the most spectacular ceremonies San Francisco had ever seen.

On August 18, 1856, at ten o'clock in the morning, the military companies into which the vigilantes were divided began assembling and shortly afterward passed in review before the executive committee, whose members were mounted. Then came an enormous parade with the entire Committee of Vigilance of San Francisco marching—under arms—through the city's principal streets, while the spectators cheered and shouted and the women among them tossed flowers. The sun was low in the sky when the great parade neared its conclusion. Still marching in the companies to which they were assigned, the men came to Fort Gunnybags, now to be restored to civilian status, and stacked their arms. The show was over and the marchers went home, "proud," in the words of one of them, "of the new peace they had brought to the community we all loved."

During the elections of the following November, the vigilantes campaigned vigorously, and the men they supported swept into office. The costs of government were drastically reduced, and for a time the city was relieved of some of the more obnoxious members of its population. But the reform movement lacked the structure and continuing purpose that might have made its effects enduring. After a while the expense of San Francisco's government again began to rise, political office once more became a way of life for certain men rather than a form of service, and the memory of the Committee of Vigilance began to fade except among those who treasured recollections of the city's pioneer days. The numbered medallions given each member became items that collectors of California historical items began to seek, and some of the certificates of membership, official documents, and reminiscences of members were filed in libraries. For a while an aura of romance hung around the committee, for the masked man coming to the aid of society has always held appeal. Then attitudes began to change. The extralegality of the vigilantes' actions brought criticism from historians and social commentators; but the committee, regardless of what later generations might think of it, had become the prototype of the vigilante movement in the western United States. When the ordinary citizens believed the judicial process no longer served their fundamental interests, they established their own system of

278

justice. Yet in most instances, just as the San Franciscans had done, they preserved the semblance of the Anglo-Saxon code if not its substance. Even at the most lawless of times, the shadow of the law remained.

In the turmoil of life in California, fortunes were made quickly and lost with as much dispatch. Today's pauper was yesterday's millionaire, and the man without a penny in his pocket might soon be a person of influence and wealth. In fate's whirligig, the old-timers seemed to enjoy no advantage. Larkin, the once powerful American consul, soon found himself surpassed in influence by men who only a few years previous had barely known the whereabouts of Monterey and San Francisco Bay. Sutter, who had gambled so heavily on California's future, saw his land covered with squatters and himself besieged with lawsuits. In time, he was glad to settle for a modest pension voted him by the California legislature and died in comparative obscurity.

Frémont fared better. His lands at Mariposa never made him a rich man, but he found an outlet for his energy and ambition in the search for a railroad route and in politics. In 1856, the year the Committee of Vigilance in San Francisco was resuscitated, Frémont secured the presidential nomination of the Republican party. Newly formed to express the point of view of the antislavery men, neither the party's machinery nor its cause was sufficient to bring it victory at the polls. Given these circumstances, Frémont secured a highly creditable number of votes. This represented his greatest achievement; and although he acquired notoriety of a sort during the Civil War, he never again commanded the support of so many people nor came closer to gratifying his large ambition.

In Utah the problems faced by Brigham Young were less immediately spectacular but of greater lasting importance. The remote wilderness of Utah permitted the Mormons to escape persecution, but Young realized they could never be prosperous or politically powerful unless their community grew. So he kept pressing the Mormon missionaries, particularly in Europe, not only to make converts, but to encourage the newly initiated to move to Utah.

The program was enormously successful. Among the poor were many who caught the Mormons' vision, and deserted what little they had to make the long journey to the strange world of Utah. Because they were poor, the expense of the trip proved a major deterrent for some, so in 1849, the Mormons raised five thousand dollars to assist them and in 1850 formally organized their effort as the Perpetual Emigration Fund Company. In 1852, the church decided to use some of the money it had raised not merely to bring people who had already reached the Missouri, but to help them all the way from Europe. In a statement in their foreign publication, the Mormons announced to their readers, "Let all who can procure a loaf of bread and one garment on their backs, be assured there is water plenty and pure by the way, and doubt no longer, but come next year to the place of gathering, even in flocks, as doves fly to their windows before the storm."

That year slightly more than two hundred and fifty individuals received financial assistance, and when they arrived the Mormons greeted them with a band, an artillery salute, and presents of cakes and melons. In 1855, the number of emigrants to Utah amounted to more than four thousand persons, of which nearly a quarter had received money from the Perpetual Emigration Fund Company for a total of about $150,000.

But the year 1855 brought the Mormon colonies in Utah to the verge of disaster. The grasshoppers returned in vast, swirling hordes and descended again into the fields. This time no sea gulls came to the rescue, and the insects fed liberally on the Mormons' crops. This invasion, coupled with a drought during the summer, cut seriously into the Mormons' food supply, forcing them to adopt rationing and greatly reducing contributions to the emigrant fund.

Many Mormons counseled against encouraging further emigration for a time, particularly among those who could not afford to pay their own way. But Brigham Young was not to be defeated by adversity. If the Mormons could no longer provide wagons and oxen, they could supply handcarts in which the emigrants could carry their belongings as they walked across the Great Plains and the Rocky Mountains. With an optimist's exuberance, Young even saw advantages in this method of travel. Because they would not need forage for their livestock, the emigrants could start earlier in the year, thus avoiding the less healthy summer days.

Surely many potential recruits questioned Young's reassuring words, but in June 1856 several hundred were ready to start out from Iowa City, where they had gathered at the end of the railroad. With twenty persons assigned to each tent, overcrowding made adequate sanitary conditions impossible, and many died during the several weeks they camped there.

With the discipline that characterized the Mormons and helped make them successful, a limit was placed on the amount they were allowed to carry. To circumvent the rule, some members of this first group put on extra clothing under the garments they ordinarily wore. Others persisted throughout the entire journey in "wearing" some of their belongings. One older woman carried a teapot and a collander attached to her apron string from Iowa City to Salt Lake City.

The first part of the journey was the easiest, taking the emigrants to Florence, Nebraska, near present-day Omaha. As they were passing through land that had already been settled, they could purchase what they needed as they went along. But from there on, they faced the hazards of the wilderness without some of the equipment that made existence easier for other travelers.

Buffalo, for example, were a usual source of food on the Great Plains, but the handcart emigrants had no horses and therefore could not pursue them.

The carts themselves, to save money, were made entirely of wood with no metal parts, and this presented its own difficulties. For the axles tended to wear out or to bind; and grease, which might have relieved the problem, was practically nonexistent. Dragging a handcart whose wheels would not turn was back-breaking. Yet they persevered. One newspaper editor who watched them admitted he could not share their religious faith, but he certainly admired their courage and fortitude.

This courage carried them over every obstacle and hardship. Sometimes they were short of food. One woman was bitten by a rattlesnake, and another was run over by a handcart. Rain so drenched them that even in their tents they stood up to their knees in water. And when a relief train came from Salt Lake City with wagons of flour, they found they were expected to pay for it at the rate of eighteen cents a pound.

But at Salt Lake City, Brigham Young received them with honors. "The procession," according to the *Deseret News,* "reached the Public Square about sunset, where the Lancers, Bands and carriages were formed in a line facing the line of handcarts; and after a few remarks by President Young, accompanied by his blessing, the spectators and escort retired and the companies pitched their tents, at the end of a walk, and pull upwards of 1,300 miles. This journey," the article continued with a touch of Brigham Young's own optimism, "has been performed with less than the average amount of mortality usually attending ox trains; and all, though somewhat fatigued, stepped out with alacrity to the last, and appeared buoyant and cheerful."

The statement reflected the Mormons' propaganda, and the article's concluding remarks underlined the substance of the Mormons' appeal. "And thus has been successfully accomplished a plan, devised by the wisdom and foresight of our President [Brigham Young], for rapidly gathering the poor, almost entirely independent of the wealth so closely hoarded beyond their reach."

The third company that year was composed of emigrants from Wales, some of them pathetically unequipped for the march over the plains and mountains. One man had a wooden leg, and the pad that protected his stump was not sufficient for so long a walk. Becoming painfully lame, he tried riding in the handcart pulled by his wife, but she was pregnant and could not draw so heavy a load. One of the leaders finally allowed him the special privilege of riding in a commissary wagon. In the same tent with the lame man were two who were blind, one who was missing an arm, and a widow who had five small children. Another couple had three children, one of them a cripple who had to ride in their cart. The mother became so exhausted pulling him she died on the road, and her husband died shortly after reaching Utah. A

281

grandfather, too, had to be carried in a cart, all the long distance from Iowa.

Although Young had cited an early start as one of the advantages of travel by handcart, the fourth and fifth companies in 1856 did not begin the trip until late in the season. Like every other company, the fourth had to travel light, and when they were caught in the early fall snows of the mountains, they had neither adequate food nor sufficient clothing.

On October 4, 1856, Brigham Young learned of their predicament. Taken by surprise, for he had not realized so many converts had been recruited, he called on the entire community of Utah for aid. Fortunately the semiannual conference of the Mormons was being held at the time, so large numbers of Mormons were gathered at Salt Lake City, making it unnecessary to send word to the outlying communities. Within a short time a relief expedition was under way.

In spite of the haste with which it was organized, it started none too soon. When it arrived at the encampment of the fourth company, it found people already dying of cold, exposure, and hunger. Of approximately four hundred who had left Iowa, almost sixty-five died before they reached Salt Lake City.

The fifth and last company was in even worse condition. The first man to reach them found many had already lost one or more of their limbs as a result of the cold. When the frozen parts were still attached to their bodies, he washed them with soap and water until they fell off and then with a pair of scissors cut off the remaining shreds of flesh.

At last the wagons with food and other supplies arrived, and the remnants of the original company were able to continue their sorry, plodding way. When they arrived in Salt Lake City, some 135 to 150 people who had started out for Utah were dead beside the trail, and many of those who had survived were maimed for life. In total numbers of dead and injured, the Mormons had suffered one of the greatest catastrophes that had occurred on the westward trail.

Although many voices were raised against the use of handcarts in the future, Brigham Young was resolute, insisting it was not the method of transportation but rather the lack of supplies and the poor timing that had created the disaster. So winning the argument with his own people, he pressed on with his plans for bringing more converts to Utah.

His struggle with his own people over the issue of handcarts was easily won, but his other antagonist at the time was more powerful. Having moved to Utah to gain freedom, Young resented the interference of the appointed territorial officials and did everything he could to circumvent them and render them powerless. To win his battle with them, he was willing to take on anyone—including the United States government and its armed forces.

25. The Stages Roll

I know what hell is like. I've had twenty-four days of it.

—A passenger disembarking from
the overland stage, 1859

Conflict between the Mormons and the rest of the United States was almost inevitable with the right and wrong apportioned on either side. The Mormons had a long history of persecution. Wherever they had lived, they had found their neighbors' hands raised against them, and they remembered clearly that their original leader, Joseph Smith, had been killed while being held in a jail by Gentiles, the name they gave to non-Mormons. By their own light, they had tried again and again to live in peace, but others would not let them.

On the other hand, they had given cause for some of the reaction against them. Polygamy alone was an issue that bred distrust and gave rise to tales of their licentiousness. Then there were the Danites, those secret enforcers who reported directly to Brigham Young and made it dangerous to oppose his will. About them, the Mormons were ambivalent, sometimes denying their existence, sometimes boasting of the vengeance they would take on those—Mormon or Gentile—who obstructed their leader's wishes.

The Gentiles who dealt with the Mormons also had other causes for complaint. Anyone who lived in Utah abided by the Mormons' will or he did not prosper, and the Mormons' will was Brigham Young. He had a stranglehold on the church, and influence in local government. Thus he exercised both temporal and ecclesiastic power.

Often he used his position for the benefit of the entire community. On the other hand, he was not above using some of his authority to enhance his own position and increase his own wealth. For example, he secured control of the best site for cutting wood within a reasonable distance of Salt Lake City. Although he permitted others to cut there, too, he demanded as payment one wagonload out of three. This one coup would have made him a relatively wealthy man, but he and his closest followers controlled other sources of Utah's riches: good grazing grounds, rich farmlands, and irrigation rights. This self-interest, combined with his great power and his jealousy of the federal government, were sufficient cause for the appointed officials to dislike him. Some were adventurers of the worst sort, only anxious to make money from their office. (One left his wife at home and brought a prostitute with him in her place.) Others were able and competent, but they often interfered with Young's plans. In either case, he disliked them, and they returned his animosity by writing disparaging reports that led many Americans to believe Young was trying to set up a separate country.

Then there was the question of the Indians. The Mormons were generally successful at reaching friendly agreements with the neighboring tribes, but when they negotiated, they always made a clear distinction between Mormons and "Americans." This distinction, which was reported by the federal Indian agent in the area, aroused suspicion. Did it mean the Mormons were attempting to make allies of the tribes against other white men?

Stephen Douglas, the successful proponent of the Kansas-Nebraska Bill, had once been a Mormon supporter but now took a different position. In a violent statement, he denounced them as "bound by horrid oaths and penalties to recognize and maintain the authority of Brigham Young, and the government of which he is the head, as paramount to that of the United States." He proposed that Congress repeal the law establishing Utah Territory on the ground that "they [the Mormons] are alien enemies." If the territorial government was rescinded, Douglas argued, Mormon criminals, from Brigham Young on down, could be arrested and tried before the courts of nearby states such as Missouri, where the judges, prosecutors, and juries would be free of Mormon influence.

In this atmosphere of mutual distrust, James Buchanan, who had defeated Frémont in the presidential election of 1856, had to name a governor for Utah. Reappointing Brigham Young would have been the easiest course, but several of Buchanan's advisers argued that the federal government should reassert its authority over the territory. Therefore Buchanan chose a Gentile— or non-Mormon—Alfred Cumming, and selected Gentiles for all the other posts. To reinforce the authority of his new appointees and to impress the Indians along the emigrants' trail, he decided to give them an escort of approximately twenty-five hundred soldiers.

Unfortunately he did not announce his plan publicly, so some Mormon men were surprised to encounter the advancing army on the trail and overhear the soldiers talking. The enlisted men of that day were often ruffians and toughs, and the thought of the Mormons' polygamy led them to make many lewd remarks. They could easily dispose of any truculent Mormon men, they told each other, while the sex-hungry, loose women of Utah rushed into their arms. Upset by this talk and the sight of the army, the Mormons dashed back to Salt Lake City, where Young was celebrating the tenth anniversary of the sect's arrival in Utah.

On hearing the news, Brigham Young told the crowd that had gathered he would fight the army and, if unsuccessful, burn down every farm and town and move south. Judging by Young's attitude, Buchanan faced a possible civil war between Utah Territory and the rest of the United States.

The hold of the United States on the western portion of the country was weak. Not only were the Mormons in apparent revolt, but communications between East and West were slow, uncertain, and expensive. A transcontinental railroad seemed the answer, but such a large, costly undertaking required unanimity on the choice of a route, and that unanimity seemed as far off as ever. In the absence of a through railroad, the next most important service was transcontinental mail. As a consequence, several mail routes had been developed with federal assistance, some going by way of central America, and some partly across the continent to terminal points where the mail was picked up by another carrier.

In 1856, Congress authorized service between San Diego and San Antonio via El Paso, and the postmaster general awarded the contract to James E. Birch, a stagecoach operator. Many tales were told about the Jackass Mail, as the line was nicknamed. Sometimes the passengers were left behind while the mail went ahead in saddlebags. Whenever another team, or whatever else had been missing was available, the passengers wearily took their cramped positions again and recommenced the bouncing, joggling trip. The discomforts, hazards, and hardships of the journey were no cause for surprise. What was astonishing was that the Jackass Mail operated as well as it did. Birch had performed a minor miracle in opening his line and keeping it running. But it obviously did not meet the nation's needs, for neither San Antonio nor San Diego was a sufficiently important terminus.

In 1857, after numerous previous attempts had failed, Congress finally

285

passed a bill providing for service between the Missouri River and San Francisco. The time allowed the contractor for the trip was twenty-five days, and he was to supply four-horse coaches or spring wagons that were suitable for carrying passengers as well as mail.

Everyone understood that where the mail went, the first railroad was likely to follow. So the choice of the route would affect the future balance between North and South.

Congress wished to avoid making the decision. Consequently the bill provided that those bidding for the contract were to name their own starting point on the Missouri and how they would proceed from there. The law also gave the postmaster general the right to select the contractor. This meant, in effect, that he could select the route, for he could choose the bidder whose proposed line most appealed to him.

In fact, he made his wishes widely known. One eastern terminal was to be in the vicinity of St. Louis, thus satisfying Congress's requirement that the line should start at the Missouri. But there was to be another also. That was Memphis, Tennessee, for the postmaster general wanted his native state to benefit. These two feeder lines were to converge at Little Rock, Arkansas, and the main line was to run from there to a point near El Paso and along the southern route to Yuma. The contractor was free to decide how he was to get the rest of the way to San Francisco.

The criticism was immediate and loud. Clearly the postmaster general was favoring the South. But he had worked out a careful set of arguments to defend his decision, and the contract went to a syndicate headed by an experienced operator, John Butterfield. Within the space of a year, he was to build the necessary stagecoach stations, buy the coaches themselves, collect enough livestock, and hire the personnel—an enormous task, but one Butterfield was ready to undertake.

With the first transcontinental mail about to start and troops marching toward Utah, Buchanan's administration was attempting to gain control of the vast area beyond the Rockies, but the two steps it had undertaken were easier to plan than to carry out.

Stewart Van Vliet, a captain in the Quartermaster Corps, went ahead of the main body of troops sent by Buchanan to Salt Lake City to make arrangements for the billeting and supply of the soldiers. He immediately became aware that the army was marching straight into a hornets' nest. Although the Mormons did not abuse him personally, they made it clear they were ready to resist what they considered an invasion. Young himself told Van Vliet that "when these troops arrive, they will find Utah a desert. Every house will be burned to the ground, every tree cut down, and every field laid waste. We have three years' provisions on hand, which we will cache, and then take to the mountains and bid defiance to all the powers of the government."

Yet neither side was truly prepared for war. The Mormons had proved themselves superb colonizers, but they had little military experience, relatively few weapons, no artillery except some guns salvaged from the Mexican War, and no means of replenishing their supply of gunpowder. The army, although it had been building up its strength since the demobilization after the Mexican War, was about one-third of its size in 1848. Yet it was now called on to defend and police a much larger area than ever before.

Although the Mormons were ready to fight the army, they remained friendly to other Americans and, during that tense summer, allowed the emigrant trains to pass freely through Utah. But in September 1857, just as the season was coming to an end, a particularly obnoxious group of 135 emigrants appeared. Among them were some ruffians from states in which the Mormons had been persecuted. They disdained anything to do with Mormonism, boasted of having killed Joseph Smith, and made a display of prodding two oxen they had named after Mormon leaders.

The party encountered no problems either from the Mormons or the Indians until they made camp at a spot called Mountain Meadows near Cedar City in southwest Utah. There they were attacked by Indians, and drawing their wagons together to form a temporary fort, prepared to fight.

Under ordinary circumstances, the Mormons would have come to their aid. In this instance, however, a group of them, enflamed by the threat of the advancing troops and the unpleasant remarks made by some of the emigrants, decided to help the Indians destroy them.

According to John D. Lee, a highly respected Mormon who later confessed to the crime and was hanged at the spot, "The emigrants were to be decoyed from their stronghold under a promise of protection." Then at a signal, Lee explained, the Mormons "were to shoot down the men; the Indians were to kill all of the women and the larger children, and the drivers of the wagons and I were to kill the wounded and sick men that were in the wagons. Two men were to be placed on horses near by, to overtake and kill any of the emigrants that might escape from the first assault."

The plan contained almost every element of the horrible: deception of the worst sort, white men allied with Indians against white men—a concept that amounted to treason in the Far West—and the annihilation of men, women, and children.

"As I entered the fortifications," Lee continued in his confession made later under the shadow of the hangman's noose, "men, women, and children gathered around me in wild consternation. Some felt that the time of their happy deliverance had come, while others, though in deep distress, and all in tears, looked upon me with doubt, distrust and terror." But they had little choice except to do what they were told and trust the Mormons.

The plan worked out as the Mormons intended. After the shooting was over, Lee said, "I walked along the line where the emigrants had been killed, and saw many bodies lying dead and naked on the field, near by where the women lay. I saw ten children; they had been killed close to each other; they were from ten to sixteen years of age. The bodies of the women and children were scattered along the ground for quite a distance before I came to where the men were killed."

Despite the stern oath of secrecy taken by each Mormon participant, word of the massacre reached the outer world. Brigham Young repeatedly asserted his own innocence but he also made it clear that he would stop at nothing to keep the advancing army out of Utah.

Lot Smith, a major in the Mormon militia, was given command of less than fifty men and ordered to halt some of the army's wagon trains and either force them to turn back or burn them. The first one he intercepted agreed to return to Missouri, but on its backward trail it met a column of soldiers, so it turned around and proceeded again toward Utah. Smith resolved never to be so lenient in the future.

Shortly afterward his scouts reported that another train of twenty-six wagons was nearby. Including the drivers, Lot quickly figured about forty men would be accompanying it, in other words a force no greater than his own. But when he approached the train, he discovered he had misunderstood his scouts' reports. There were not one but two trains of twenty-six wagons each.

"It was expected by my men," he later wrote, "that on finding out the real number of wagons and men, I would not go further than to make some general inquiries and passing our sortie upon the train as a joke would go on until some more favorable time. But it seemed to me that it was no time for joking. I arranged my men, and we advanced until our horses' heads came into the light of the fire. Then I discovered we had the advantage, for looking back into the darkness, I could not see where my line of troops ended, and could imagine my . . . followers stringing out to a hundred or more as well as not."

Bewildered by Smith's show of confidence and not knowing how many Mormons were behind him, the two wagon trains surrendered. Smith searched them for goods his men could use; and this time, instead of ordering them to turn back, he set them afire. "While riding from wagon to wagon," he later recalled, "with torch in hand and the wind blowing, the covers seemed to me to catch very slowly." He mentioned this to one of his followers. "He replied, swinging his long torch over his head: 'By Saint Patrick, ain't it beautiful! I never saw anything better in all my life.'"

The loss of the two trains was a serious blow to the federal government. Furthermore, the Mormons, who had earlier purchased Bridger's Fort, burned it to the ground, so the troops could not use it for shelter during the winter. Young was carrying out his threat; and as reports of these offensive activities reached Washington, President Buchanan began to realize that gaining control of Utah Territory was not going to be easy.

In Congress sentiment was as fiery as Young's. One of the senators from New York referred to the Mormons as "the internal enemy which is lodged within a Territory across the path which leads from our Atlantic to our Pacific settlements." Another senator stated, "I am one of those who believe that this rebellion, or insurrection, or whatever else you may term it, in Utah, should be crushed; and crushed effectually, if it shall be necessary to sacrifice every individual in that country."

At this critical point, when war seemed inevitable, a Philadelphia lawyer, Thomas L. Kane, offered his services as a mediator, services that Buchanan accepted. Because the mountain passes were now blocked with snow, Kane went to California and approached Utah from the west. With infinite tact, he persuaded Brigham Young to accept Cumming as the new territorial governor. Then he rode to the army's headquarters at the burned-out ruins of Fort Bridger and persuaded Cumming—against the advice of the army commander—to ride with him back to Salt Lake City and talk with Young himself.

Kane was a public servant in the true sense of the often misused words. Self-effacing and willing to endure the hardships of long travel—hardships that were severe for a city-bred lawyer—he effected an understanding between Cumming and Young, as a result of which the Mormons agreed to accept Cumming as their governor, although they remained fearful of the army.

He then returned to the army's headquarters in the mountains to consult with the commander. With the military, he had more difficulty than with the Mormons; but the commanding general finally reassured the Mormons that they need not fear for their lives or property if they did not resist his entry into Salt Lake City. Kane, exhausted by his long journeys, returned to Washington to report to Buchanan.

Meanwhile Buchanan, unaware of Kane's success, appointed a Commission of Reconciliation and gave the two commissioners a presidential pardon to extend to the Mormons if they submitted to the laws of the United States. In April 1858, the commissioners traveled west and early in June they reached Salt Lake City, accompanied by Cumming, who had joined them.

Kane had done his work well. Although many differences still existed between the Mormons and the federal government, the bitter hostility of the previous fall was gone; and in an atmosphere of better understanding, the two sides negotiated an agreement whereby the Mormons once more recognized their responsibilities as American citizens.

On June 27 the army reached Salt Lake City. No cheering crowds awaited them, only a handful of men who had been left there to set fire to the buildings if the army failed to abide by its promise to respect Mormon property. But the Mormon War, as it was called, had ended, and the army set about constructing a permanent base in Utah at Cedar Valley about thirty-five miles from Salt Lake City. The establishment of this post greatly strengthened the Americans' hold on the trail across the center of their country at the same time that they were also opening up the southern route to greater use.

Butterfield's contract gave him only a year to prepare for regular service, and he used it well. The difficulties he faced, however, did not result from penny-pinching on the part of the postmaster general. In 1848 the Post Office Department's revenues had exceeded its expenditures by more than $200,000, but that fortunate condition had been changing rapidly. By 1853, expenditures exceeded revenues by almost $2 million, and the annual deficit rapidly continued its upward rise. In 1858, the year Butterfield was to start his line in operation, it passed $5.25 milion. These high costs were not entirely the result of too many contracts for service or to excessive prices paid by the postmaster general but arose from a basic economic problem confronting the nation. Its period of great expansion had carried its boundaries from coast to coast, but the land was not evenly settled. From the Atlantic Coast to the Mississippi and beyond to the Missouri, the emigrants had moved steadily westward, leaving behind them no large, relatively unpopulated areas. But west of the Missouri River existed an enormous blank, which most of the settlers had leap-frogged. No mail or stagecoach service and no regular freight line could expect to make much money out of intermediate stops in that part of the country, for there was little to stop for. As a consequence, most of the profitable western freight lines were those with contracts to supply government posts, and neither transcontinental stage lines nor postal service could exist without heavy subsidies.

The lack of towns was one of the problems that plagued Butterfield just in laying out the route. For hundreds of miles he could buy nothing locally, neither goods, services, nor labor. Almost everything had to be imported from afar—the coaches that would carry the mail and passengers, the horses and mules that would draw them, the men who drive and feed the teams, the ammunition and guns that would protect them, replacement parts, food, and even the utensils in which his personnel would cook their meals.

Each station had to be designed to house a keeper and from two to six additional men to perform the tasks of defending the post and servicing the stagecoaches as they came through. If the livestock could not graze nearby— and they could not at many of the stations—Butterfield had to cart in hay and oats. Where the stations were liable to Indian attack, he could not be content with building the usual corrals of wood. Instead they had to have walls that were seven or more feet high and were constructed out of adobe, sod, or, if possible, rock. Those stations were like small fortresses. Even when this work was well under way, Butterfield still had the task of buying the livestock. Hundreds of mules and horses had to be selected and bargained over. If Butterfield needed excellent men to run his stage line, he also needed the best animals he could afford. They had to be powerful, steady, and enduring.

There were other difficulties, too. When Colonel James B. Leach, who was in charge of constructing the military road between Yuma and El Paso, approached the partly built Dragoon stagecoach station east of Tucson, he was struck by the silence that seemed to hang over the spot like a warning. The stage was scheduled to run within the same month, but instead of workers hastily finishing the buildings and wranglers guarding the herd, not a person could be seen.

Approaching cautiously, for who knew what danger those quiet walls might contain, Leach found only two survivors out of an original complement of seven men—four Americans and three Mexicans. Two of the Americans were dead, one with his head still lying on the saddle he had been using as a pillow, his skull cracked open by a hatchet. Of the two men who were still alive, one was unconscious and dying, the other suffered from a slash that had nearly severed his arm and from a thirst that left his mouth swollen. Although water was near, he had been too weak to get it. From him, Leach heard a horrible story.

A few nights previously, the four Americans had gone to sleep, leaving the three Mexicans on guard. The one survivor had awakened to find the Mexicans hacking at his three companions, and he himself received the blow on his arm. In spite of his wound, he was able to grab a rifle. Although in his condition he could not shoot the gun, the sight of one of their intended victims with a rifle frightened the Mexicans, who ran off.

They were not, of course, apprehended. In the desert they could have gone in any direction. Nor was the reason for their crime ever discovered. Probably they had planned to run off with the herd of livestock. At the lonely posts that Butterfield was establishing almost anything could happen, and he had to be ready for every contingency, no mean feat along a route that extended for many hundreds of miles through unsettled lands.

Although the postmaster general could be pleased with the progress Butterfield was making, no impartial observer could fail to note that he had made his decision on the basis of sectionalism, not logic and efficiency. But fate was intervening, and in spite of the postmaster general's machinations, the balance was already being swung in favor of the central route, which, in turn, would favor the North.

Ever since the early days of the California gold rush, rumors had drifted through the frontier that there was gold in Colorado on the eastern slopes of the Rocky Mountains. Occasionally a westward-moving band of emigrants had paused to pan the streams that rushed down from the crests, but no one had made any discoveries that warranted further prospecting. Green Russell was a Georgian who had made enough money in the California gold fields to live comfortably in his native state. But the Panic of 1857 upset his plans for retirement, and he decided to move to Kansas. Once there he recalled the stories of Colorado gold and organized a party to search for the precious metal in the lonely, remote valleys that had seen few white men since the beaver trappers had passed.

He and his companions quickly found a little gold but not enough to merit their having abandoned their homes for the long, dangerous journey. Although discouraged, they kept moving from spot to spot like all earnest prospectors, constantly hunting for a richer placer. Their efforts were unrewarded, and the party broke up, some leaving the mountains for a surer living closer to civilization, some remaining to continue the gamble for greater riches. A trickle of miners started to follow Russell, and by winter several communities had grown up along the eastern slopes of the Rockies. Shortly the finds came richer, and by the spring of the following year, a new gold rush was in progress.

This movement of people was just what was needed to increase the utility of the route through the center of the country. Although the Colorado gold miners were not on the main trail, their population could help provide the sort of intermediate business that had been so lacking on any of the routes. In just a few years, the central path had gained the settlement of the Mormons at Salt Lake City, the establishment of a large military base near that community, and now the new mining communities of Colorado. But as long as the postmaster general insisted on the southern route, it made no difference. For still no transcontinental service could survive without the government subsidy.

By September 1858, right on schedule, Butterfield's first coaches were ready to roll, one from the East, the other from San Francisco. At the crack of the driver's whip, the teams leapt forward, and the band that was to bind the two parts of the country together had been welded.

Strangely the departure from San Francisco failed to stir that usually enthusiastic community. The hour was midnight, but darkness meant little to a city where the gaming houses and bars operated at all hours. Even the papers paid little attention to the occasion except to list the names of the first eight passengers with the exception of the one who was most important of all—the postal inspector whose report would confirm that Butterfield had lived up to the terms of his contract.

The stage from the East, which took to the road the following day, carried only one through passenger, a young man named Waterman Orsmby, a correspondent for the *New York Herald*. Its editor, Horace Greeley, was a proponent of western development; and even if San Francisco was nonchalant about this new enterprise, Greeley's New York readership would receive a detailed account of the long journey.

The coach left with as little celebration as the coach from San Francisco.

John Butterfield's son held the reins, being relieved from time to time by his father, who was traveling the first leg. At Springfield, Missouri, which they reached sixteen and a half hours ahead of schedule, "we drove off to the post office," Ormsby reported, "and took on a small through mail for San Francisco, and also the postmaster and another citizen, who wished to have it to say that they had ridden in the first coach from Springfield containing the overland mail. It was gratifying to me, as one of the few evidences of interest in the enterprise that we met."

At Fort Smith, Arkansas, they picked up the mail from Memphis, the mail the pro-South postmaster general had insisted be included in the contract, and had the satisfaction of noting that they were more than twenty-five hours ahead of schedule.

When they reached the Red River, they were so far ahead of time that the stationmaster did not expect them, and the team they were to use next was still out at pasture. This cost them a two-hour delay, and there were more to come. At one station in Texas, the mules had not been broken in thoroughly, and it took the men about a half hour to harness each one. At another station, the relay teams had not arrived, and the driver had to continue at a much slower pace with the weary animals he had hoped to replace. By the time they reached El Paso, they were forty-two hours behind and had met the eastbound stage, which was eight hours behind. (It had left San Francisco more than a day ahead of time; hence the meeting east of the halfway point.)

The run across southern New Mexico and Arizona was one of the most difficult and dangerous of the entire route. The heat could be death-dealing, water was scarce, and the Apaches, still unfriendly and untamed, wandered throughout the area. Only a few days before they had demanded presents from one of the stations. But on raced the team with Ormsby making note of the horrible murders that had taken place at Dragoon Station. At Tucson, they were still behind schedule, but they had recovered almost eleven hours of lost time.

Directly ahead lay a sandy, hot stretch of almost four hundred miles. Coming east, the first stage had lost some forty hours on this one part of the route. The man in charge of the section had considered himself disgraced. So he had driven another eastbound stage himself, covering the mileage in quick time; and he was ready to drive the westbound team. Furthermore, he had ordered fresh teams placed at every station where the sand was deep. The combination of his foresight and his skilled hands on the reins enabled him to cut time from the schedule. At Los Angeles, the mail was only twenty-two hours and forty minutes behind.

In drawing up his original plan, Butterfield had built in an allowance of almost twenty-four hours. A small part of this allowance was left, and it was almost certain, barring an accident, that the mail would reach San Francisco in the twenty-five days demanded by the contract.

Up into the mountains and down into the California town of Visalia raced the coach, the teams sweating, the drivers taking advantage of every slope in the road, the men at the stations switching the teams as swiftly as possible. The people of Visalia were among the few so far who appreciated the historic significance of the occasion. Almost the entire population, consisting of about five hundred persons, were up at midnight to greet the driver and his passengers. To celebrate, they exploded some powder, making it sound as though an eight-pounder had gone off.

With this salute echoing in their ears, the driver and his passengers continued the long race against time. As they dashed down one hill, Ormsby expected to see the driver "put down the brakes with all his might but he merely rested his foot on them, saying 'it's best to keep the wheels rolling, or they'll slide.'" Ormsby estimated that they must be moving at between fifteen and twenty miles an hour.

With such driving and with the support they received at the stations along the way, the stage rolled into San Francisco just twenty-three days and twenty-three hours after John Butterfield had picked up the mailbags in St. Louis.

Everyone was jubilant. Butterfield notified Buchanan that he had met the contract, and the president replied in glowing terms about this new bond that would hold the two parts of the nation together.

Travel on one of Butterfield's coaches was fast, but not comfortable. For a period of approximately three weeks, the passenger was shut into a small world, sometimes hot, sometimes freezing cold, through pouring rains, miles of desert, dragging slowly up mountains, dashing down steep slopes, fearful of Indian attacks, wary of bandits if the cargo was valuable, and dependent always on the elements, the drivers, and the station attendants. The drivers made little effort to avoid the bumps in the road. As they explained to complaining passengers, they tried to guide their teams as little as possible. If the weather turned bad or the night was black and visibility just a few feet, the teams could follow the road if they knew it. But they could not learn their way if the drivers constantly steered them.

Inside the coach, the passengers were jammed one against another. Privacy was nonexistent, and the through passengers had to abide each other's closeness. For more than twenty days, the coach became almost a world in itself, a microcosm in which entire human dramas were played out.

Dr. J. C. Tucker made the trip from Missouri to California and later recounted his experiences. Among his fellow passengers was a young man whom everyone called "Texas," a German who—at two hundred pounds— occupied more than his share of seating space, and two French gamblers accompanied by two French women, one of them young, pretty, and vivacious.

Much to Texas's annoyance, "Dutchy"—as they called the German—

always insisted on being next to the window, thereby getting more than his share of fresh air just as he was getting more than his rightful portion of the seat. When it began to rain, they closed the windows, making it even more stuffy inside; and at this point, Dutchy reached in his pocket, drew out an ill-smelling pipe, and lighted it.

Dr. Turner and Texas had also wanted to smoke but had refrained from doing so out of courtesy to the two women. At Dutchy's breach of courtesy, they both complained, and the two women also showed signs of displeasure. Dutchy thereupon opened the window and let the rain, as well as the fresh air, pour into the coach. At this, the restraints that had held Texas's temper in check snapped. He leaned over, grabbed Dutchy's pipe from his hands, and threw it out the window.

Lack of room prevented a fight, so Dutchy took a long pull at his flask—flasks were standard traveling equipment—and fell asleep. But his snores were almost as bad as the smoke from his sour pipe.

As the stage rocked over the next bump, Texas reached over, opened the door, and gave Dutchy a slight shove. With Texas's assistance, the bump was enough to throw him out of the coach and onto the ground. Texas jumped out after him and with mock sympathy picked him up and brushed him off, but Dutchy was not in the least misled by his solicitude and wanted to fight him then and there.

But the mail could not stop while two passengers settled their differences. Dutchy was so furious and unpleasant, the men would not let him sit with them again and made him ride outside. At the next station he started off, according to the driver, to swear out warrants for the arrest of Texas and Dr. Tucker. Taking advantage of his absence and using the excuse that he could not wait, the driver signaled his team, and off they went with Dutchy left behind.

The expulsion of the German did not settle all the personal problems between the passengers. In between tormenting Dutchy, Texas—a handsome young man in a buckskin suit—had been flirting with the younger of the two French women, feeling no restraint since her two escorts were professional gamblers and therefore outside the usual social code.

Often passengers riding the stage amused themselves by practicing their marksmanship on objects they passed. A hawk was sitting on a tree; and as the team raced by, it rose slowly. Texas lifted his pistol and with part skill and part luck shot off the bird's head. No one could fail to admire what he had done, the young woman included, and so Texas offered her his gun and invited her to try hitting the next suitable target.

This was too much for the younger of her companions. Speaking English for the first time, he swore at Texas and told him not to speak to the woman again. As his treatment of the German had indicated, Texas's rein on his temper was as light as the driver's foot on the brake when they were racing downhill. He immediately flared up and told the Frenchman since he could speak English after all, he could apologize at the next station.

As soon as the stage stopped, Texas leapt out and walked back of the station house. The older of the Frenchmen followed, and soon the two men returned. Texas explained to Dr. Tucker that the younger Frenchman wished to fight a duel, and he asked Tucker to be his second. What Texas proposed was this: A large corral stood in back of the station house. It contained two gates. Texas would enter by the north gate, the Frenchman by the south. They would begin firing at the sight of each other.

The older Frenchman protested vigorously at these terms. What he had in mind for his principal was a more civilized duel. In fact, he even had with him a pair of dueling pistols. But Dr. Tucker reminded him that Texas, as the person who had been challenged, could set his conditions and choose the weapons.

So while the men at the station changed the teams—even a duel could not slow down the mail—and while the women remained in the station house, Texas and the younger Frenchman took up their positions at the two entrances of the corral. Dr. Tucker threw his handkerchief in the air as a signal, and the men entered the enclosure, each holding in his hand a cocked revolver.

26. Across the Continent

. . . notwithstanding our demerits, we have much reason to believe . . . that we have enjoyed the special protection of Divine Providence ever since our origin as a nation.

—James Buchanan, 1859

Of the two duelists entering the corral, the Frenchman was obviously the more experienced, advancing sideways to present as small a target as possible. Texas, brasher and more scornful of danger, walked forward in normal fashion, his chest and shoulders fully exposed. The Frenchman fired first, two shots rapidly following each other. One went wild, but the other shattered Texas's left arm near the wrist. With the blood pouring from his wound, Texas moved forward and fired almost simultaneously with the Frenchman's third shot. He missed, and the Frenchman's bullet merely knocked off Texas's hat.

Realizing he could afford to waste no more shots, Texas took a different course, and without advancing farther, he calmly dropped to one knee, rested the barrel of his gun across his wounded arm to steady his aim, and fired again just as the Frenchman was once more preparing to pull his own trigger. But he had not time to finish. Texas's shot caught him in the heart, and he fell dead.

The drama was over. The station hands had come running at the sound of shots, but they now returned to work. Even a duel to the death could not be allowed to interfere with the schedule. The men quickly finished harnessing the fresh team, the driver jumped aboard, whip in hand. The two French women and their remaining companion stayed behind to bury the dead. Texas got into the stage, followed by Dr. Tucker, who had grabbed the roller towel to make bandages and some shingles from which he could fashion splints. Medical treatment could be given while they still raced toward California.

Fights of this sort were not ordinary occurrences on the Overland Mail. Usually if tempers erupted, the passengers themselves maintained order, separating the contestants and imposing peace on them for the remainder of the journey. But there were other adventures—accidents, teams that had not been properly broken, and once in a while a visitation from Indians. Often they were merely curious and, after examining the coach, would let it go on its way. Sometimes they attacked either the stage or one of the stations, the latter being the better prize of the two because of the livestock. Then the stage would descend on a bitter scene. The wounded or dead bodies, the missing livestock, and sometimes the charred ruins of the buildings stood witness that the land and its people were still wild and untamed.

More often the journey contained little adventure, but a large stock of boredom and discomfort. Even the toughest frontiersman grew restless at spending week after week in the jostling coach, able to stretch his legs only during the brief stops at the stations, where they ate their hasty meals. Women were not frequent passengers, but when they did travel they were almost invariably safe. If they were ladies, almost every man was their protector; if they were not, they were still precious beings in a society that was largely male. For them, the windows were raised or lowered at their wish, and the best seats reserved; but such courtesies did not spare even them the boredom and the general hardship.

Although Butterfield was meeting the terms of his contract, in Washington pressure continued for improving the service along the central route. Instead of dividing the route between two contractors, its proponents wanted a single contractor and a larger subsidy that would pay for better equipment, more livestock, and additional personnel. To obtain this change, they had to refute the postmaster general by proving the central route was faster even in the winter. And so they arranged an unusual contest.

Congress, in those days, went into session at the end of the year, and the president delivered his annual message in December. Three advance copies would be sent to St. Louis. As soon as the telegraph reported that the president had begun speaking, the copies would be handed to representatives of the central and southern routes and also to the steamship company that used the route across Central America. The first to deliver the speech to California would obviously be the fastest.

The December date placed the central route at a disadvantage because of the weather, but its opponents decided to make the odds even greater. When the copies arrived, there were only two. The one for the representative of the central route was missing.

On December 14, 1858, the representative of the central route was finally able to procure a copy from a St. Louis newspaper, six precious days behind the others, six days during which the others not only got a headstart but during which the winter's storms began on the Great Plains and in the mountains.

The operators of the central route had lost time waiting to obtain the third copy of the message and more time making the trip by steamboat up the ice-filled Missouri from St. Louis to St. Joseph, the actual start of their line. From there they had carried the message to California—in spite of heavy snows—in seventeen days and twelve hours, substantially faster than either of their competitors. But this computation required consideration of two "ifs": if the copy had been delivered on time, and if the race had started at St. Joseph on the Missouri River instead of at St. Louis. Some people understood this, but the majority overlooked it.

To the company that held the contract from St. Joseph to Salt Lake City, the race was fatal. Its owner, John Hockaday, one of the great figures in American staging, had overextended himself putting extra stock on the line and making other special preparations. Reaping no reward from the contest, he had little means of paying his creditors.

With the Colorado gold rush beginning to boom, a market for transportation service had developed between the Missouri and the eastern slopes of the Rockies, the very element most needed to make any line self-sufficient. If Hockaday had concentrated his investment on making a southern loop toward the new town of Denver instead of attempting to race Butterfield, he might have become a wealthy man. Instead two freighters, William H. Russell and John S. Jones, had formed a company to provide that service.

A further blow awaited Hockaday. One of those rare economy drives had started in Congress with some members questioning the skyrocketing costs of providing postal service to the West. They were helped by the death in early 1859 of the postmaster general, who had been most generous in subsidizing new routes. His replacement was more parsimonious and immediately began to look for ways of reducing the post office budget.

Within a short time, he cut out some of the smaller routes and reduced the subsidies awarded to the others by requiring less service of them. Butterfield

299

alone escaped the blow. His original contract still had time to run and was so worded that it could not be amended. Hockaday, the unfortunate contractor for the route between St. Joseph and Salt Lake City, found himself driven out of business.

But hands were waiting to pick up what remained. Russell and Jones, who had started the freight line to the Colorado mines, had enlarged their operation by providing stagecoach service just before the gold rush started in earnest. By being slightly premature, they had overanticipated their revenue and were unable to meet the bills for their new investment. Russell was also a partner in another firm, Russell, Majors and Waddell, and apparently had used their credit. To try and recover the losses, Russell, Majors and Waddell took over the line and also bought out Hockaday, thinking that by combining the two they might make them profitable.

Just before this purchase took place, a traveler boarded the stage for Colorado with the intention of transferring later to the Salt Lake City stage and continuing across the country. To a casual observer, he appeared like a strange, ineffectual person with mild, pale eyes peering through his spectacles, thin, light hair, and a high, shrill voice. He was dressed in expensive clothes but wore them carelessly, his string tie slipping toward one side of his neck or the other, his trousers snagged awkwardly on the top of his boots. Usually he carried a large umbrella whose whalebone ribs made it extraordinarily bulky and on his head he generally wore a large white hat. To the rough frontiersmen who often hung around the larger stagecoach stations, he might have appeared a figure of fun, a gullible easterner who could serve as the butt of jokes. But those who recognized him—and many did—knew him as one of the outstanding journalists of his day, Horace Greeley, editor of the *New York Tribune*.

A man of energy and liberal thinking, Greeley had created an outspoken but unsensational paper, one that was quoted widely by other journals throughout the country. He also lectured frequently and was the author of several books, all of which brought him further recognition and widened the audience that listened to his every word. A believer in the greatness of the United States, he was a strong advocate of a transcontinental railroad, and one of the purposes of his trip was to observe at firsthand the central route.

In Colorado he carefully inspected the gold mines and wrote a report that was cautiously enthusiastic. From there, he headed north to Fort Laramie, where he had to wait five days before catching the westbound stage. "I alone," he told his readers, "perched on the summit of its seventeen mail bags as passenger—he who had thus far filled that exalted post kindly giving way for me, and agreeing to take instead the slower wagon that was to follow the next morning." Both the five-day wait and the overcrowded stage were the result of the postmaster general's economy drive, and so, too, was a further delay as they came near the Platte. Instead of a station house and a fresh team waiting for them, they made camp and let the mules loose to graze. When they were ready to start again, it took two hours to locate the livestock. This was the type of operation to which Hockaday had been forced to resort.

At this point, Greeley was on the old overland trail to California and Oregon, the trail over which so many emigrants had passed. In his reports to his readers, he pointed out that they were already familiar with much of it, since accounts of the westward journey had been printed and reprinted throughout the East.

But he did have something to say about the expenditure of the public's money by the government. "Of the seventeen bags [of mail] on which I have ridden for the last four days and better, at least sixteen are filled with large bound books, mainly Patent Office reports, I judge, but all of them undoubtedly works ordered printed at the public cost—*your* cost, reader!—by Congress, and now on their way to certain favored Mormons, franked (by proxy) 'Pub. Doc. Free, J. M. Bernhisel, M. C.' I do not blame Mr. B. for clutching his share of this public plunder, and distributing it so as to increase his own popularity and importance; but I do protest against this business of printing books by wholesale at the cost of the whole people for free distribution to a part only."

After commenting on the custom of senators' and representatives' using public funds for their own campaign purposes—a custom that was to continue virtually unchecked—Greeley gave his readers a quick analysis of the economics of the overland mail. "Of the one hundred and ninety thousand dollars per annum paid for carrying the Salt Lake mail," he wrote, "nine-tenths is absorbed in the cost of carrying these franked documents to people who contribute little or nothing to the support of the government in any way. Is this fair? Each Patent Office report will have cost the treasury four or five dollars by the time it reaches its destination, and will not be valued by the receiver at twenty-five cents."

Senators had argued that the high cost of mail service to the West was entirely justified as a means of holding families and friends together, but in actuality most of the money did not go for such high purposes. Politics or sectionalism was at the bottom of most of the excessive expenditures.

When they arrived in Salt Lake City, Greeley interviewed Brigham Young. "He was very plainly dressed in thin summer clothing, and with no air of sanctimony or fanaticism," Greeley wrote. "In appearance, he is a portly, frank, good-natured, rather thickset man of fifty-five, seeming to enjoy life, and to be in no particular hurry to get to heaven. His associates are plain men, evidently born and reared to a life of labor, and looking as little like crafty hypocrites or swindlers as any body of men I ever met. The absence of cant or snuffle from their manner was marked and general; yet I think," Greeley added, "I may fairly say that their Mormonism has not impoverished them— that they were generally poor men when they embraced it, and are now in very comfortable circumstances."

In fact, Brigham Young was frank enough to tell Greeley that he himself was worth about a quarter of a million dollars, a sizable fortune in those days. But Young emphasized that none of it came from the church, for no official was allowed to receive payment for his work.

On two points, Greeley was particularly curious. One was Brigham Young's attitude toward slavery, for Greeley was a leader among the antislavery forces in the East. Young said that those who arrived in Utah with slaves were permitted to keep them but that Utah would never become a slave state. Its geography and climate made slavery uneconomical.

The other issue on which Greeley questioned Young was polygamy. The Mormon leader readily admitted that some of the Mormons had more than one wife, although some did not. He himself had fifteen, but some of these, he said, were old women whom he had merely taken under his protection. Young was perfectly straightforward on the subject, and Greeley reported—but could not accept—his views.

In summing up his impressions, he asked the rhetorical question, "Do I regard the great body of these Mormons as knaves and hypocrites?" And he answered, "Assuredly not. I do not believe there was ever a religion whereof the great mass of the adherents were not sincere and honest. Hypocrites and knaves there are in all sects; it is quite possible that some of the magnates of the Mormon Church regard this so-called religion (with all others) as a contrivance for the enslavement and fleecing of the many, and the aggrandizement of the few; but I cannot believe that a sect, so considerable and so vigorous as the Mormon, was ever founded in conscious imposture."

Yet the remedy Greeley proposed for settling the difference between the United States and the Mormons was extreme. The church was the all-powerful authority in the territory, rich because of the ten percent tithe it imposed on all its members and influential because of its tight grip on the juries, the courts, and its hold on the minds of the people. "In short," Greeley said, "the federal judiciary, the federal executive, and the federal army, as now existing in Utah, are three transparent shams." The church, on the other hand, "spends little or nothing, yet rules everything; while the federal government, though spending two or three million per annum here, and keeping up a fussy parade of authority, is powerless and despised." Therefore, he concluded, "Let Brigham be reappointed governor; withdraw the present federal officeholders and army; open short and better roads to California . . . and notify the emigrants that, if they choose to pass through Utah, they will do so at their own risk. Let the Mormons have the territory to themselves—it is worth very little to others."

Greeley also commented directly on the role the government was playing in the economy. At Camp Floyd, the newly established army base near Salt Lake City, the buildings were constructed of adobe bricks, which were made by Mexicans working at the site. But wood was needed for the roofs and for window framing, doors, and other details. As Brigham Young had already secured control of the best source of timber near Salt Lake City, his three saw-mills were busy cutting the boards the army required. Delivering lumber at seventy dollars a thousand feet, his profit on this one contract alone must have amounted to more than fifty thousand dollars by Greeley's calculation.

The army base also needed supplies from Leavenworth, Kansas, and allowed its contractors twenty-two cents a pound for transporting them. These supplies included flour. Flour was also produced in Utah, and the War Department was willing to pay the same price for it as for flour brought from the East. Thus the army's price for local flour was the prime Missouri price plus an additional twenty-two cents. The contractors, therefore, easily sold their contracts to local producers at a profit of seven cents a pound without doing anything to earn the money. Greeley estimated they had cleared $170,000 on this one transaction.

Even when the government occasionally tried to save money, Greeley noted, it failed to get the most for what it did spend. The reduction in mail service over the central route from a weekly to a semimonthly service decreased the subsidy the government was paying, but it increased the cost to the operators of the lines. The large bulk of mail, much of it worthless, as Greeley had pointed out, made it impossible for the operators to carry two weeks' accumulation in one wagon or stage. So they had to run two at the same time and therefore needed twice the number of wagons and teams. Therefore they asked to be allowed to carry the mail on a weekly basis for the same price. At least, they figured, they would not lose quite so much money. But the postal authorities refused to permit this. So instead of weekly service at no additional cost to the government, those who lived along the route, including the soldiers stationed at Camp Floyd, received their mail only semimonthly.

There were several obvious conclusions to be drawn from Greeley's observations, but perhaps the most significant was the desirability of having connections in Washington. Those who did reaped large amounts from the government's expenditures in the West; those who did not could expect only illogical, bureaucratic treatment.

Between Salt Lake City and California, Greeley, although he was one of America's greatest editors and reporters, missed an important story. For without his being aware of it, western Nevada was on the verge of a great change. Near Carson City in what is now Nevada, a miner named William Prouse had found a small amount of gold in 1850, enough to attract a few other miners, most of them working only during the spring and summer months when the run-off from the Sierra Nevada provided ample water.

A small community named Johntown, which no longer appears on most Nevada maps, sprang up nearby and soon boasted a saloon. The Mormons, less interested in prospecting than in commerce, probably made more money catering to the miners' needs and wants than most of the miners made. For the discoveries were not rich. By 1857, the citizens of Johntown were spending most of their time hunting and pursuing other carefree activities. Most serious prospectors believed the area was dead.

A few members of the community kept working, however. One of them, James ("Old Virginia") Finney, finally found an outcrop that led him to suspect the presence of gold, and soon he and some men with him were panning about twenty-five dollars worth a day, not a substantial amount but enough to keep them working. News of their discovery had a resuscitating effect on the area. If Finney and his friends could find a little gold again, why could not the others?

Patrick McLaughlin and Peter O'Riley thought so and chose a spot called Six Mile Canyon. Like most Nevada miners, they were troubled by the lack of water and set about enlarging a spring toward the head of the canyon. While digging it out, they came across some yellowish sand containing quartz and a black mineral they were unable to identify. As far as they were concerned, the black material was a nuisance, but the gold in the sand was sufficiently rich to make them continue working.

In a community as small as Johntown, secrecy was next to impossible; and Henry P. ("Pancake") Comstock soon learned what was going on. Even among the unsavory characters that often flocked to mining camps, Comstock seems to stand out as a man for whom the others had little use, considering him somewhat crazy as well as dishonest. Glad to profit by someone else's work, Comstock remembered that he may have once laid claim to the spring in which McLaughlin and O'Riley had found gold. Accompanied by an acquaintance named Emmanuel Penrod, Comstock went to see the two miners. Perhaps his claim was legitimate or perhaps he was merely a glib talker, but in any case he persuaded them to admit Penrod and himself to full partnership.

Inspecting the spring, Penrod determined that the source of gold the original prospectors had found was a quartz vein. Under the mining laws of the time, this permitted them to stake out a larger area than would have been possible for a placer. But because the men were dealing with rock, not loose placer gold, they needed some sort of crusher. The kind most commonly employed by those too impecunious to construct a mill was an arrastra, a machine known to the Spaniards for centuries and originally designed for wheat. It consisted of a circular container into which the ore could be poured. A spindle stood in the middle, and from its arms hung rocks that were dragged over the ore as the spindle turned. Not only was the machine simple and inexpensive to build, the only power required was a horse or mule. Harnessed to a long arm on the spindle, it walked round and round, revolving the spindle and dragging the crushing rocks over the ore. The construction of an arrastra, however, was beyond the ability of the four partners, and they took in one more man in return for building a machine for them.

304

There were now two new mines relatively close to each other, both of them making reasonable returns for their owners, but nothing spectacular; and the miners continued to be bothered by the strange bluish material. As it was heavy, they could not dispose of it by blowing it away with the wind or by swirling water over their crushed ore, the two methods commonly used for getting rid of extraneous matter. Finally some of the miners sent samples to an assayer to find out what it was that was so plaguing them.

Horace Greeley was only partly aware of what was taking place as he rode through western Nevada with the mail. Although he had heard that some of the miners were becoming rich, the shortage of water limited the number of claims that could be worked. Johntown did not impress him particularly; Carson City, he reported, "though it has few houses as yet, aspires to be the emporium of the new gold region, and perhaps of the embryo state of Nevada." But he noted that Genoa, "though a village of but forty or fifty houses," seemed to be the leading community.

Nevada was on the verge of an enormous change. To an extent he sensed this, but as he traveled into the mountains and down into the valleys of California, he thought the future of Nevada's Carson Valley, once irrigation ditches were dug from the Carson River, lay in agriculture. Rarely had Horace Greeley made so great an error.

27. Blessings and a Curse

The presidential election was . . . in progress, and I wished to see . . . the working of a system which has been facetiously called "universal suffering and vote by bullet."

—Richard Burton, 1860

Greeley was fascinated by California, not only by its size and many material advantages but also by its physical beauty. He visited Yosemite Valley, and as he stood on the valley floor in the darkness, its full effect came over him. "That first, full deliberate gaze up the opposite height!" he wrote for his readers. "Can I ever forget it? The valley is here scarcely half a mile wide, while its northern wall of mainly naked, perpendicular granite is at least four thousand feet high—probably more. But the modicum of moonlight that fell into this awful gorge gave to that precipice a vagueness of outline, an indefinite vastness, a ghostly and weird spirituality. Had the mountain spoken to me in audible voice . . . I should hardly have been surprised."

He also visited the redwood trees and was astounded at their age and size.

He quickly noted their extraordinarily shallow roots and recognized this as one of their weaknesses, although he considered them vulnerable to winds rather than to the undercutting of flooding water, which has proved to be—next to man—the most destructive force working against them. But he was absolutely accurate when he looked into the future. "I am sure they will be more prized and treasured," he said, "a thousand years hence than now, should they, by extreme care and caution, be preserved so long, and that thousands will then visit them, over smooth and spacious roads, for every one who now toils over the rugged bridlepath by which I reached them."

Greeley's pale but keen eyes took in the esthetics of the California landscape, but they were not blind to the new state's material advantages and disadvantages. He visited Frémont, whom he had supported as a presidential candidate, and observed the difficulties encountered by California business-men because of the murkiness of many land titles. He also realized that mining in California was in a transition period, passing from the days in which a single man with a pan might make a fortune into an era when mining was becoming the business of corporations. For the early prospectors had taken most of the easily mined gold, which had collected in the sands and gravels over thousands of years and could not be replaced. What remained were the quartz veins, which required expensive equipment and large numbers of employees. "It takes a mine to run a mine," he said, quoting a popular saying of the time.

The large agricultural areas of California impressed Greeley. The amount of land, he calculated, equaled all that in New England, highly fertile and well watered by the moisture coming in from the Pacific. In addition to mining, other industries were making rapid progress: construction, fencing, and wine-making, to name only a few.

Excited as he was by all that he had seen during his trip across the United States, Greeley had never forgotten the fundamental purpose of his journey: to examine the prospects for a railroad. Everything he had seen convinced him a railroad was a necessity for both the military protection of the western portion of the United States and to ensure the development of its resources.

As for the specific route, although Greeley's sympathies lay with the North both as a resident of New York and a member of the antislavery forces, he did not propose one over the other, being willing to compromise on this point in order to secure the railway itself. Let private organizations, he suggested, come forth with plans for building a railroad with government support. Congress could then select the plan that seemed the most practical.

Greeley was optimistic in thinking that such a simple solution would settle a problem that had bothered Congress for so long and which involved a question so emotional and enduring as slavery. But in western Nevada, through which he had ridden with the mail, events were making the

307

construction of a railroad more practical by creating another intermediate market that a railroad could serve. For the assayer's report on the ore taken from the new discovery contained some remarkable information.

The miners of western Nevada were much like those in California and Colorado, but a few of them were luckier than almost any other prospectors in the United States. That bluish-gray material that had made their work so difficult, clogging up their machinery and refusing to wash or blow away, contained silver, large quantities of it. And the ore contained gold, too. From the samples he had examined, one assayer believed the ore ran to about three thousand dollars a ton in silver and—almost like a bonus—more than $850 a ton in gold. This was a fortune indeed.

In the informal society that composed Johntown, record-keeping was not precise, therefore the early history of one of America's greatest mineral finds is somewhat vague. But certain facts clearly emerge from those early days. Pancake Comstock attached his name to the Lode he had not discovered, and Old Virginia Finney had the honor of giving his name to Virginia City, the town that almost immediately began to spring up.

Another fact also emerges. Despite all the secrecy that the original miners enjoined on their fellows and on the assayers, word quickly spread that the Washoe Range of western Nevada contained riches beyond the dreams of the most avaricious miner. As a consequence, prospectors, lawyers, gamblers, bankers, doctors, adventurers, and ruffians began to pour into the area, the majority of them from California.

Pancake Comstock, never noted for his good sense except in the way he had worked himself into the original partnership, became wild and erratic. At one instant he would dismiss his claim as a mere nothing and is reported to have sold it for a dollar in a fit of disillusion. (A committee of miners quickly abrogated the sale and got it back for him.) At other times, he thought himself a millionaire—which, indeed, he would have been if he managed things right—and showed his generosity by giving away gold and staking out claims for those persons who had attracted his attention and favor.

But now that he had acquired the fabulous wealth about which he had dreamed so long, he quickly lost it. Thinking he was outwitting the new arrivals who were flocking to Nevada, he sold out for a few thousand dollars. And so did the other original miners, forty thousand dollars being the highest price any of them received. Less than two decades later, an effort was made to discover what had become of them. About half of them were dead, and most of them had little or no money. The men who eventually developed the Comstock Lode were not the prospectors and frontiersmen, but the mining promoters and bankers, many of them with their roots in California. As Greeley had foreseen, the day of the simple prospector was ending, and it was this new group who knew how to meet the demands of commercial mining.

* * *

An investment in the Comstock mining area, with the uncertain legality of some of the titles and the difficulty of processing the ore—originally much of it carried on pack animals to California—was a gamble, one that required a steady nerve and access to the capital needed for quartz mining. George Hearst, for example, had to give up his interest in another profitable mine to raise the funds to try his luck in the Comstock. But these investors were not the only businessmen taking risks in the Far West. The stagecoach and freighting firm of Russell, Majors and Waddell was also making an extraordinary and dangerous gamble on the future.

Of the three partners, John Russell was the promoter, the one who pushed the others into taking chances. His premature investment in the line to Colorado had already forced his partners to come to his rescue and had also led to their buying out Hockaday. In itself, this was a poor purchase. Alexander Majors, one of the partners, later recalled that Hockaday "had a few stages, light, cheap vehicles, and but a few mules, and no stations along the route. They traveled the same team for several hundred miles before changing, stopping every few hours and turning them loose to graze, and then hitching them up again and going along."

The first step of Russell, Majors and Waddell was to strengthen the operation. "As soon as we bought them out," Majors later said, "we built good stations and stables . . . all the way from Missouri to Salt Lake, and supplied them with hay and grain for the horses and provisions for the men, so they would only have to drive a team from one station to the next, changing at every station." This investment made it possible for the new owners to shorten the scheduled time to Salt Lake City and increase the frequency of the service they offered. With the gold fields in Colorado and the new mines in what is now western Nevada, the partners had considerable hope they would recapture what they had spent.

Russell, however, was a man whose dreams followed each other in rapid succession, and no sooner was one realized than he had another. Having inveigled his partners into buying up two additional lines, he now came up with a new idea. The central route across the country was, in his opinion, the best. Once Congress and the nation were convinced of this, the southern route would be discarded for the through mail, and Russell, Majors and Waddell would receive the principal contract. In this belief, Russell was encouraged by William McK. Gwin, the senator from California, who promised to promote the necessary legislation.

Thus was conceived the idea of the Pony Express—one of the most glamorous and least practical enterprises ever undertaken by American business. The partners' goal was to carry the mail from St. Joseph, Missouri—the terminus of the railroad and the telegraph—to California on a regular ten-day schedule. This was a distance of almost two thousand miles through wild country—the dry, long flat stretches of the Great Plains, several mountain ranges whose peaks were covered with snow much of the year, and the desert regions of what are now Utah and Nevada. Over this terrain, the riders would average two hundred miles every twenty-four hours, including the time taken out to change horses and men.

Later Alexander Majors recalled the preparations he and his partners made. "Five hundred of the fleetest horses to be procured were immediately purchased," he wrote, "and the services of over two hundred competent men engaged. Eighty of these men were selected for express riders. Lightweights were deemed the most eligible for the purpose; the lighter the man the better for the horse, as some portions of the route had to be traversed at a speed of twenty miles an hour."

The general plan was for each man to ride between three stations, changing horses at the second, and giving the mail to a fresh rider at the third. The stopover at each station was to be no more than two minutes, which meant everything had to be in readiness when the station personnel first heard the pounding of hooves in the distance.

As soon as the rider had dismounted, the station workers grabbed the *mochila* from his saddle. This was like a leather apron that fitted over the saddle and formed the rider's seat. From each side hung two pockets. Three of these carried the through mail. The fourth contained mail to be dropped off along the way and a time sheet on which the stationmaster marked the hour of arrival, thus creating a record of the actual progress made for the entire route.

Service such as this could not be cheap. The price was five dollars for half an ounce, which meant that copies of newspapers carried by the Pony Express were specially printed on tissue paper and the letters written on the lightest of stock. Yet the demand for news and information between East and West was so great the firm anticipated it would fill the pouches of its *mochilas.*

On April 3, a special train pulled into St. Joseph with the first Pony Express mail from New York. The mayor made a speech, and so did Alexander Majors on behalf of the firm. Then the *mochila,* filled with mail, was placed over the saddle, the rider mounted, and dashed toward the bank of the Missouri, where a ferry was waiting. The captain pushed off quickly and as soon as he touched the opposite side of the river, the rider galloped down the trail to the West.

The Pony Express was the woof out of which legends are woven. Stagecoaches might be stopped by Indians and highwaymen and their stations attacked, but the odds against them were less unfavorable. In addition to the driver, they often carried a guard, and the passengers were generally armed.

The Pony Express rider did not enjoy this advantage. He rode alone. All the protection he had was his own wits and the speed of his horse. After riding several hundred miles through the worst of weather—and a single rider often did—the body became numb with weariness and the brain less acute.

The mount, too, was not always fresh in spite of the most careful of plans. During its run, it might have plowed through deep snow, swum across rivers, raced up mountains, and sometimes had not been replaced at the last station. For more than once, when the rider pulled to a stop, he found the stationmaster dead, the herd raided, or some other catastrophe that prevented him from swinging onto a fresh mount to continue his journey.

Decades later, long after the last Pony Express rider had thrown his *mochila* over the saddle and galloped into the distance, the apparent list of riders continued to grow and grow. No man who had actually carried the mail was ever likely to forget the experience; and with the passing years and the growing faintness of memory, men who had worked briefly at a station—perhaps merely wrangling the remounts—would find his friends and grandchildren more interested if he put down the pitchfork he had actually used and at least in his imagination slipped into the saddle himself. Some even claimed to have been Pony Express couriers who could not have been much more than four or five years old at the time.

One reason for the numerous stories was the outbreak that spring of the Paiute War in Nevada. With the mining boom and the rapid growth of Virginia City, friction between the Indians and the white men quickly developed. In 1860, while Russell, Majors and Waddell were getting the Pony Express into operation, the Paiutes and the Bannocks met at Pyramid Lake near the California border to determine what they could do to drive the white men out.

As was often the case with Indian outbreaks, a small band of warriors, more impatient than the others and operating independently, launched the first attack. Why they chose the Pony Express station operated by a man named James O. Williams later became a matter of conjecture. Some said the men there had abused an Indian woman; others did not believe so. In any case, the Indians killed everyone except Williams, who was away, and set fire to the buildings. They then prepared to attack a nearby ranch; but dawn was breaking, their courage failed them, and they retreated.

News of the attack swept quickly over the Carson Valley as neighbor told neighbor what had happened, and the immediate response of the majority was to send out a punitive expedition. More than a hundred volunteers took up their arms and marched in the direction of Pyramid Lake to exterminate the Paiutes. With the typical self-confidence of inexperienced frontiersmen, they believed the task would be simple, particularly because the Paiutes were one of the poorer and more backward tribes.

But a surprise awaited them. The Indians laid an ambush, caught the volunteers off guard, killed more than seventy, and wounded many of the remainder. It was one of the worst defeats ever suffered by white men in a battle with Indians, and word of the disaster spread horror through the Carson Valley. Each ranch, each little settlement began looking to its

311

defenses. The commanding general in California ordered a hundred and fifty soldiers to march to Nevada as quickly as possible, while a call went out for more volunteers. Soon somewhere between eight hundred and a thousand men assembled and retraced the steps of the previous volunteers toward Pyramid Lake. Near the site of present-day Wadsworth, Nevada, the Indians and the white men met.

This time the white men were not overconfident. With superior arms and better organization, they inflicted heavy casualties on the Indians, winning a victory but not ending the war. For the Indians fled into the wilderness where they could not be pursued and took up the type of fighting they knew best—guerrilla warfare. And the targets that were among the most vulnerable were the small stations operated by the Pony Express.

From this circumstance came some of the best-known tales of the courageous riders who kept up the mail service through Nevada. One was Robert H. Haslam, better known to his friends as "Pony Bob." He rode into the station on the Carson River and found no remount waiting for him, as all the station personnel were off fighting the Paiutes. Continuing with his tired pony, he traveled the fifteen miles to the next station, which was to have been the end of his lap.

The next rider refused to carry the mail because of the Indians. So Pony Bob agreed to go on. When he reached the end of the second man's route, he had covered 185 miles, stopping only long enough to eat and change horses. After nine hours of rest, he rode off again with the return mail.

"When I arrived at Cold Springs [one of the stations he had visited only a few hours before]," he recalled, "I found to my horror that the station had been attacked by Indians, and the keeper killed and all the horses taken away. What course to pursue I decided in a moment—I would go on. I watered my horse—having ridden him thirty miles on time, he was pretty tired—and started for Sand Springs, thirty-seven miles away.

"It was growing dark," he continued, "and my road lay through heavy sagebrush, high enough in some places to conceal a horse. I kept a bright lookout, and closely watched every motion of my poor horse's ears, which is a signal for danger in an Indian country. I was prepared for a fight, but the stillness of the night, and the howling of the wolves and coyotes made cold chills run through me at times, but I reached Sand Springs in safety."

There Pony Bob persuaded the stationkeeper to leave his post and come with him on his next lap. "He took my advice," Pony Bob commented, "and so probably saved his life," for the following morning another nearby station was attacked. At his next stop, Pony Bob found the men on the alert, because they had seen a party of fifty Indians maneuvering around their station, but they had not been attacked, so Pony Bob remounted to continue his ride, only three and a half hours behind schedule in spite of the problems and dangers he had encountered.

312

But his work was not yet done. At the next station, the Pony Express agent asked him to keep on riding. So after resting for two and a half hours, he carried the mail up into the Sierra Nevada, having traveled a total distance of 380 miles and almost keeping up with the tight schedule set by the owners of the lines.

During those troubled times, a rider on one occasion rounded a bend in the trail and found himself in a Paiute camp. Fortunately at that moment the Indians only wanted tobacco. The rider gave them half of what he had, and when they demanded more, leveled his rifle at them. As they were not in a warlike mood, they let him go.

Indian attacks, blizzards, dust storms, floods, these were all among the hazards regularly encountered by the Pony Express, and yet the riders kept the mails on schedule, day after day, month after month, the hoofbeats of their ponies writing a unique chapter in their country's history. But like so many romantics, they were riding toward oblivion almost as fast as they carried the mails. For even as they began their remarkable service, the end was already in sight. Racing ponies could not keep up with the technological developments of the time.

As the lands west of the Rockies became better known and more heavily settled, interest in them expanded far beyond the borders of the United States. European investors were studying the opportunities for making money—the Rothschilds, for example, were represented in California—and European readers thrilled to the accounts of Indians, stagecoaches, and even to lurid rumors of the Danites. Richard Burton, one of the most noted of England's travel writers and explorers, thought a book about that part of the world would be as widely read as his previous reports on the Nile and other far-off places.

In the fall of 1860, as the Pony Express riders were pounding along the trail between St. Joseph and California, he came to this country to study the Mormons. Like Greeley before him, he was an experienced observer, but he was even more unbiased, since the sectional differences in the United States were no concern of his.

Of Brigham Young, whom he interviewed at Salt Lake City, he reported, "His manner is at once affable and impressive, simple and courteous; his want of pretension contrasts favourably with certain pseudoprophets that I have seen."

This description, from the pen of a world traveler who had known many men of different qualities, belied the picture of a self-serving demon cloaked in darkness, of a man ruling a hell on earth in which all must do his bidding and virtuous maidens were enslaved to satisfy the lecherous. In summation, Burton said of Mormonism that "its genius was essentially Anglo-American" and could not have flourished except in a new hemisphere. It was "rationalistic" and "Simplificative: its fondness for facilitation has led it through literalism into complete . . . materialism." In conclusion, he added, "It is essentially Practical." This was the reason it could build a prosperous society in the middle of the desert and why Brigham Young could amass a small fortune in a few years.

Yet Burton recognized the enormous gap that separated the Mormons from the Gentiles. "The excessive positivism with which each side maintains its facts, and the palpable sacrifice of truth to party feeling, would make it impossible for any but an eye-witness, who . . . had preserved his impartiality, to separate the wheat from the chaff" in Mormon history.

As he intended to leave by ship from California, Burton continued on the westbound stage, visiting Carson City. "A mining discovery," Burton said, "never fails to attract from afar a flock of legal vultures—attorneys, lawyers, and judges. As the most valuable claims are mostly parted with by the ignorant fortunate for a song, it is usual to seek some flaw in the deed of sale, and a large proportion of the property finds its way into the pockets of the acute professional, who works on half profits. Consequently in these parts there is generally a large amount of unscrupulous talent." Among those he especially noted was Judge Terry, who had opposed the vigilantes in San Francisco. Since then the judge had shot and killed one of California's senators in a duel.

In a mining camp, where violence was common, the shooting of a senator would not handicap a man's career. "In a peculiar fit of liveliness," Burton said, "an intoxicated gentleman will discharge his revolver in a ballroom, and when a 'shyooting' begins in the thin walled frame houses, those not concerned avoid bullets and splinters by jumping into their beds."

When Burton sailed from California, he left behind him a country that was trying to pull its far-flung sections together with stagecoaches and the Pony Express, and yet was tearing itself apart. Fourteen years before it had embarked on a policy of expansion that had carried its borders from the Atlantic to the Pacific. Yet now it was preparing to divide itself, and this time there were no great voices to speak in behalf of the Union. In Congress only smaller men forged the future, and they were not equal to the crisis that was overtaking the country.

In the lands west of the Rocky Mountains, the bitterness of the dispute touched many people, some favoring the South, some the North, but only in California and Oregon could they make their opinions effective. For those were the only two areas that had been admitted to statehood and thus played a direct role in the determination of national affairs.

Oregon's statehood had come rather quietly. By the end of 1858, it had fulfilled all the technical requirements for statehood, having attained the necessary population and prepared its constitution. The bill admitting Oregon passed the Senate but remained locked up in the House committee. On

January 7, 1859, the year the Comstock Lode was discovered, the committee chairman announced plans to release it. The Republicans in the House decided to vote against it as a means of influencing the administration's policies in Kansas, but enough of them defected to permit its passage by a slim majority.

In the presidential election that year the voters had their choice of four major candidates, reflecting the divided state of the nation's emotions. Lincoln won, receiving the support of both California and Oregon, by a narrow margin in the first state and a larger one in the second. The defection of both, however, would not have changed the outcome.

The election signaled the course the nation would ultimately take and made it impossible to postpone the issue by further compromise. On December 12, 1860, the South Carolina legislature unanimously agreed that "the Union now subsisting between South Carolina and other states under the name of 'The United States of America' is hereby dissolved."

That, which so many had struggled to prevent, had come about. The nation, which had only recently seemed to fulfill its destiny by spreading from ocean to ocean, was in risk of falling apart and becoming two opposing states, no longer linked by a common government and a faith in its own greatness.

28. The War and the West

*The struggle of today is not altogether for today;
it is for a vast future also.*

—Abraham Lincoln, 1861

If pride in the nation or affection for the Union did not call for the support of the moderates, common sense should have. The United States needed its entire energy for its own development, as it was still far less of a nation in fact that it was in the atlases.

The vastness of the undeveloped areas was not what made the United States weak and less than a whole nation. Many countries have had large wild hinterlands until late in their histories. But in the case of the United States this was not hinterland; geographically, much of it was heartland. The developed areas did not gradually fan out into inaccessible wilderness, as would have been more normal. Instead the farthest reaches were more heavily populated than many of those closer to the eastern seaboard.

As an added complication, the part of the country most distant from the capital and from the financial and industrial centers was not isolated. A traveler from Europe, for example, could reach California with not much more inconvenience than it took to go from New York, Washington, or Charleston. America's outposts were not protected by a barrier of wilderness except from its own people.

The physical bonds that held this empire together were slight. The Pony Express raced along the central route, beset by the Paiute Indians and its increasing deficit. The stagecoach that followed in its dusty wake provided relatively poor service in spite of the investments made by Russell, Majors and Waddell. The line ran only to Salt Lake City, where the weary passenger was still forced to transfer to another line before going on to California. Those who rode the route sometimes spoke enthusiastically of their adventures but never of their comfort.

The only through transportation across the country remained Butterfield's "ox bow," sweeping far south to satisfy the requirements of the former postmaster general, and even it was uncertain. This became evident when the theft of some cattle and the kidnapping of a Mexican boy interrupted the passage of the stages for several days and almost stopped them for an indefinite period.

On Butterfield's route, one of the most dangerous parts was the long, dusty road that led across southern New Mexico and Arizona, for here water was scarce and the Apaches were largely in control. The critical point was Apache Pass in the Chiracahua Mountains, where the road left the surrounding plains to wind through a narrow gap at the foot of the Dos Cabezas, a smaller group of mountains that were almost a spur of the Chiracahuas. The road could have turned to the north and avoided the mountains altogether, but Apache Pass contained the vital asset: water.

This was the homeland of the Chiracahua Apaches and their capable leader, Cochise. The safety of both the station and the stagecoaches was almost entirely dependent on their friendship, and Butterfield had immediately gone about securing it with presents. In fact, relations between the Indians and the company became so good that the some of the Chiracahua Apaches were frequent visitors at the station and occasionally cut firewood for it.

In February 1861, when Second Lieutenant George N. Bascom received orders to recover some stolen livestock and a Mexican boy who had been kidnapped by Indians, he focused his suspicions on the Chiracahuas without considering the possibility that some other tribe might have been involved. Leading approximately sixty soldiers, Bascom arrived at Apache Pass and found Cochise paying one of his visits to the stagecoach station. Without consulting Butterfield's employees, he invited Cochise to his tent and then treacherously tried to seize him as a hostage. Cochise quickly drew his knife, slashed the canvas wall of the tent, and escaped through the opening he had made; but several other Indians who had accompanied him were either killed or kept as prisoners by the soldiers.

As Cochise was completely innocent of either the theft or the kidnapping

317

(this was later confirmed by the boy), Bascom's treachery rankled him all the more. He rallied his warriors, seized the station house, captured a nearby wagon train, and took several Americans as hostages. He was then ready to bargain with Bascom for the release of the Indians Bascom had captured in the tent. But Bascom, with more martial ardor than diplomatic common sense, refused to deal with him, forcing Cochise to take steps to increase his bargaining power. This he intended to do by capturing both the eastbound and westbound stages, which were due to arrive soon.

Through the carelessness of the Apache lookouts, the westbound stage slipped into the station unobserved. The eastbound coach was not so fortunate. Apache gunfire wounded the driver and killed one of the mules. The passengers leaped out, and while some of them held back the Indians with their guns, others cut the dead mule loose, pulled the wounded driver inside, and started off again. With a new driver at the reins, the stage raced along the road to the station. Ahead of them lay a small arroyo. The Indians had removed the planks from the bridge, but the mules, according to later accounts, leaped across while the stage skidded on its axles over the wooden spans. By a miracle it reached the station and the protection of Bascom's soldiers.

That night two American messengers slipped past the Apaches in the darkness, one carrying the news to Tucson and the other to an army post. Detachments of troops rushed to the rescue, and against these odds Cochise knew his chances of victory were slight. So he killed his prisoners, mutilated their bodies, as the Apaches often did with those they hated, and retired into the mountains where no white men dared follow him.

In the rush of events taking place in the East, this battle was not of much concern, but it revealed the fragility of the communications link between the Atlantic and the Pacific. The unfortunate combination of a single Indian raid and an uncompromising lieutenant could cut it. During this period, the United States needed to devote its full energy to holding East and West together. Instead many of its finest leaders were determined to rip the country apart even further. For about two months after the fighting at Apache Pass, the Confederates fired on Fort Sumter, and the Civil War began.

Texas was far removed from the major battlefields; and although its heart was behind the Southern cause, distance lessened its ability to put troops on the major fronts. Traditionally, Texans had turned west when they thought of expanding. It was logical, therefore, for them to think of making a drive in the direction of California.

In the summer of 1861, about the time the North and South were testing themselves at Bull Run, Colonel John R. Baylor marched to El Paso and easily captured the nearby federal fort. Isolated from the rest of the Union and impossible to supply, no one could have expected it to resist. He then crossed over to the New Mexican town of Mesilla, captured it with equal ease, and afterward met and quickly defeated the troops at the next federal post.

318

After this string of victories, Baylor proclaimed the existence of the Confederate Territory of Arizona, which included most of the southern parts of today's New Mexico and Arizona, thus—in theory—bringing the boundary of the Confederacy almost to California. In actuality, of course, hundreds of miles of rough country, many Apache warriors, and several remaining forts stood between him and the outermost limits of the domain he had created. But he had opened the road to Albuquerque and Santa Fé.

Although his action did not influence the main theater of war, it had a regional effect. The people of Tucson, Arizona, held a meeting and elected a delegate to the Confederate Congress; the Congress itself confirmed the establishment of the territory; and Jefferson Davis appointed Baylor governor. By the beginning of 1862, part of the transmountain Southwest was under the Confederate government.

The chief beneficiaries were not the Confederacy or its sympathizers, but the Apaches. Without understanding the white man's affairs or the cause for which the North and South were fighting, the Apaches did recognize that the white men appeared distracted and that the number of federal soldiers stationed through their land was growing smaller. Sensing their opportunity, they—and a number of other tribes—began to run rampant. Both the North and South had lost what the Confederay called Arizona. It had reverted to the Indians.

While the Far West often boasted about its independent spirit and self-reliance, since the decline of the fur business it had become increasingly dependent on Washington and looked to the federal government for roads, troops, subsidized mail and other services, as well as grants of land to help pay some of the costs of local development. But Congress had been handicapped in providing assistance by its own deep divisions, whether the immediate question was the admittance of a state or the choice of a principal route across the country.

The bombardment of Fort Sumter changed this. For the first time in decades, Congress was rid of the slavery issue. This was immediately reflected in the aggressive manner in which it tackled issues that had long been postponed. One of these was the selection of a transcontinental route. As its proponents had long urged, the central route seemed the most practical.

Russell, Majors and Waddell should have been the beneficiaries of this decision. They had gambled large sums on improving stagecoach and mail service along the route and, at enormous expense, had established the Pony Express. And meanwhile they had suffered a serious blow. For the year before, in 1860, Congress had passed an act to encourage the construction of a transcontinental telegraph line. The subsidy was not to be more than $400,000 a year for ten years; and the work had to be completed by the end of July 1862, and the contractors were meeting the deadline.

Hiram Sibley, president of the Western Union Telegraph Company, had promoted the legislation and was the one who received the contract. He immediately formed two companies, one to build from the east, the other from the west, until they met at Salt Lake City. Just as Butterfield knew the stagecoach business thoroughly, Sibley was an expert at constructing and managing telegraph lines, and the work went ahead with precision. Ten men in a row each dug holes, the first to finish walked to the head of the row and started digging another. Then came wagons with the wire, insulators, and other equipment. They were accompanied by teams that raised the poles and attached the wire. Nothing was left to happenstance, for the subsidy voted by Congress was more than sufficient to permit Sibley to use the best materials, hire the best men, and still make a substantial profit.

By the spring of 1861, the line coming from the west had only four hundred miles to go before it reached Salt Lake City. The line from the east was behind schedule, but the company then began to build from Salt Lake City to meet the teams crossing Nebraska. On October 24, 1861, the lines from east and west joined, and Americans were able to send messages across their nation in a matter of hours. This was the end of the Pony Express.

It had arrived in glory; it went out in shame. Russell, the promoter, had overplayed his hand in arranging the company's finances. Using his best salesmanship, he had persuaded the War Department to issue acceptances against which he could borrow funds with the understanding that the acceptances would not be presented for payment. This expedient failed when the banks became ready to call their loans, and Russell borrowed some bonds to serve as additional collateral. The person who held the bonds was an employee of the commissioner of Indian affairs in Washington, and the bonds, it turned out, belonged in an Indian trust fund. The result was a major scandal. All that could save the firm was the contract to carry the through mail. But they did not receive it.

In 1861, with the slavery issue no longer crippling its debates, Congress could at last establish the necessary governments west of the Rockies. Clearly Utah had been far too large, to say nothing of the problem created by having Mormons control areas where the population was predominantly non-Mormon. So in 1861, Congress established Nevada and Colorado Territories.

One of the extraordinary and unexpected effects of this action was to create a new era in American literature. The man appointed secretary of Nevada Territory was named Clemens, and his brother Samuel, not yet well known as Mark Twain, decided to go with him. The Mississippi steamboats had been driven from the river by the war, and his brief experience as a soldier made him certain he had neither the taste nor the talent for a military career. While he was in Nevada, he worked as a reporter for one of the Virginia City newspapers and later described his western experiences in his book *Roughing It*. At last he had found his place in American society, and from that time on his work exemplified a type of writing that was distinctly American—humorous, extravagent, and yet perceptive.

Of his first impression of Carson City, which had been named the capital, he later wrote,

It was a "wooden" town; its population two thousand souls. The main street consisted of four or five blocks of little white frame stores which were too high to sit down on, but not too high for various other purposes; in fact, hardly high enough. They were packed close together, side by side, as if room was scarce in that mighty plain . . . it was two o'clock now, and according to custom the daily "Washoe Zephyr" set in; a soaring dust-drift about the size of the United States set up edgewise came with it, and the capital of Nevada Territory disappeared from view. Still, there were sights to be seen which were not wholly uninteresting to newcomers; for the vast dust-cloud was thickly freckled with things strange to the upper air—things living and dead . . . —hats, chickens, and parasols sailing in the remote heavens; blankets, tin signs, sagebrush, and shingles a shade lower; door-mats and buffalo-robes lower still; shovels and coal-scuttles on the next grade; glass doors, cats, and little children on the next; disrupted lumber yards, light buggies, and wheel barrows on the next; and down only thirty or forty feet above ground was a scurrying storm of emigrating roofs and vacant lots. . . .

But seriously, a Washoe wind is by no means a trifling matter. It blows flimsy houses down, lifts shingle roofs occasionally, rolls up tin ones like sheet music, now and then blows a stage-coach over and spills the passengers.

Continuing with his first impressions of Carson City, Mark Twain said,

We found the state palace of the Governor of Nevada Territory to consist of a white frame one-story house with two small rooms in it and a stanchion-supported shed in front—for grandeur—it compelled the respect of the citizen and inspired the Indians with awe. . . .

The Secretary and I took quarters in the "ranch" of a worthy French lady by the name of Bridget O'Flannigan, a camp-follower of His Excellency the Governor. She had known him in his prosperity as commander-in-chief of the Metropolitan Police of New York, and she would not desert him in his adversity as Governor of Nevada.

Thus wrote Twain, one of the best-loved of American authors, often expanding the facts to capture the fancy of a nation in an expansive mood, irreverent of authority and dignity, and yet sensitive to human needs and wants.

Farther to the west a group of men were entertaining dreams that even Mark Twain might have thought extravagant, both in their scope and the riches that might result. Their principal leader was a brilliant young engineer named Theodore D. Judah, well known for his fanatic obsession with railroads. He had constructed bridges, done surveying, and had built the Niagara Gorge Railroad as well as part of the road that later became the Erie. He had come to California at the request of some businessmen to build a railroad between Sacramento and Folsom, the first railroad in the state. Working with inexperienced labor, he completed the project and saved a day's travel for those going to the mines. But the placer deposits that formed the reason for constructing the railroad in the first place began to give out, traffic diminished, and the owners' original intention of extending their operations to other parts of the state gave way to apathetic indifference. Judah was a railroad engineer without a railroad either to run or to construct.

His enthusiasm was not diminished by the lack of interest he encountered whenever he brought up his favorite topic: a railroad running from California across the continent. Hard times had not made him lower his sights. On the contrary, he had raised them; and while he could still become absorbed in plans for short, less consequential lines, the subject to which he always returned was the concept of a line that would carry passengers and freight from the Pacific to the Atlantic. So engrossed was he with this one idea that he sooned earned a reputation as a fanatic, and people grew weary of hearing him talk.

With the outbreak of the Civil War he became certain that at last the time had arrived. Like everyone else he followed all the debates and speculation on the subject and read the government surveys, but he went further than the others, for he incorporated the Central Pacific Railroad. His first efforts to sell stock in San Francisco met with failure—someone was always promoting a railroad and none of them had materialized—but he met a more receptive audience in Sacramento. Less sophisticated than the financiers and bankers of the larger city, they listened as Judah spoke to them in practical, down-to-earth terms instead of expounding his usual visions. What he stressed was the importance of a railroad leading from Sacramento to Nevada if they wished to make money out of the market developing around the new mines.

Four of those showing early interest in his plans were an unimpressive group of local merchants: Leland Stanford, a wholesale grocer; Charles Crocker, who was in the dry-goods business; and two others, Collis P. Huntington and Mark Hopkins, who were partners in a hardware store. They were not the kind of men who would ordinarily launch a business requiring millions in capital, but the Far West was not an ordinary place. In a land where gold might lie at the bottom of a silted stream, dreams were not limited by the usual considerations. With the help of these men, Judah raised enough money to survey a possible route over the Sierra Nevada, the most immediate geographic obstacle facing anyone trying to build a wagon road or a railroad east from California. Then Judah left for Washington to interest Congress in his plans.

He was right about his timing. Although Congress, distracted by the war and busy filling the positions left vacant by the Southern members, was not yet ready to promote a railroad, it was in a mood to listen to Judah. Its members were impressed by his knowledge of the business and his familiarity with the terrain of California; and when at last they were prepared to take up the subject formally, he was the established expert.

Everyone agreed that building a railroad was fraught with enormous problems, not merely those of engineering. No one thought that private capital could carry the burden, for the same geographic and economic factors that had made it difficult to develop transcontinental stagecoach service applied on a much greater scale. Government support was needed—in large amounts—but what form should it take?

James Buchanan, who was strongly in favor of a transcontinental railroad, had earlier raised doubts concerning the government supporting such a vast project. Addressing Congress, he had said, "I repeat . . . that it would be inexpedient for the Government to undertake this great work. . . . This would increase the patronage of the Executive to a dangerous extent and would foster a system of jobbing and corruption which no vigilance on the part of Federal officials could prevent."

Yet the nation wanted a railroad. Since the people were so determined, Congress set about drawing up a plan, keeping in mind that the work should be done by private contractors and the railroad should be owned by private organizations, but that a large part of the financial support would have to come from the government.

In 1862 Congress passed a bill that provided for the establishment of two companies, one to build and operate the railroad from the Missouri west, and the other from California east. Each road would receive its right of way as a gift from the public lands. In addition, it would receive a grant of ten alternate sections of land for each mile of construction, which it would sell in order to raise some of the cash it would need. Theoretically the land retained by the government would rise sufficiently in value to more than compensate the taxpayers for the acreage given away. Since the railroads could not sell their holdings at premium prices until after the road had been built, they would have to have an immediate source of cash. This the government agreed to supply by permitting the railroads to sell thirty-year government bonds at the rate of $16,000 to $48,000 a mile, depending on the terrain.

From the government's point of view, the arrangement seemed clever. It would put up no money at all, and what it lost on the land grants would be recovered by the rising value of the remaining public property. Judah, who was an engineer, not a financier, was delighted with the outcome and glad to receive the western contract for the Central Pacific. He rushed back to California to tell his partners and to start work. In the East, the act resulted in the formation of the Union Pacific Railroad, which would build west from the Missouri. In 1862 it looked at last as though the United States would have its transcontinental railroad about which so many people had talked for so long a time. Few were aware that the arrangement devised by Congress could not possibly work.

Although the North was taking an active step to tighten its ties with the Far West, in the Southwest it was losing the struggle. Baylor seemed firmly in control of the Confederate Territory of Arizona except for the Apaches. In March 1862, he ordered his subordinates to persuade them, or any other tribes, to come together for the ostensible purpose of making peace and then to slaughter the adults. It is to Jefferson Davis's credit that, when he learned of these orders, he put an effective end to Baylor's further advancement in the army.

The Union commander in the Southwest was Colonel Edward R. S. Canby. Handicapped by the loss of several important officers to the Confederate cause, Canby nevertheless had a force of several thousand men, enough to pose a serious threat to Baylor if Baylor should attempt to enlarge his newly formed territory by pushing north toward Santa Fé. So the two armies remained at a distance of more than a hundred miles, while the Apaches, at least for the moment, were the real victors.

One of the former members of the Union command in New Mexico was Henry H. Sibley, who had joined the Confederacy. An experienced officer with a thorough knowledge of the country, he believed that all of New Mexico Territory, not merely the southern portion, could be brought into the Confederacy; and he proposed to Jefferson Davis an advance that would carry the Confederate line far beyond Mesilla. Receiving permission to proceed with his plan, Sibley marched into New Mexico toward the end of 1861 with a force of almost two thousand men, many of them veterans of previous fighting.

The principal barrier between him and northern New Mexico was Fort Craig, located on the Río Grande and protecting Santa Fé. Here Canby had concentrated his men.

Sibley was outnumbered by Canby, but many of Canby's men were local volunteers with little or no military experience and, because of their Mexican heritage, often unable to understand English. Sibley, therefore, decided to march against Fort Craig and crossed the Rió Grande at the town of Valverde. Anticipating this move, Canby left the fort and took up a position on the right bank. The battle that followed was bloody and pointless. Numerous men fell on both sides, including Lieutenant Bascom, whose mishandling of Cochise had put the Chiracahua Apaches on the warpath.

324

At first the fighting went in favor of the Union. Then a charge by Sibley broke up the untrained federal forces, and the Confederates were enabled to cross the river. Canby retreated to Fort Craig. Without pursuing him or laying siege to the fort itself, Sibley moved north and occupied Santa Fé without difficulty, but he had left his supply lines blocked.

Earlier Sibley sent about two hundred soldiers to Tucson, where they met no opposition. A few scouts from this detachment went on to Yuma, thus reaching the edge of California. Baylor's original proclamation setting up the Confederate Territory had been largely bombast, but it was now something of a reality.

Sibley's next objective was Fort Union to the east of Santa Fé. Originally planned to guard the Santa Fé trail, it had become the center of the remaining Union activity in the area and, according to the report Canby received, was well stocked with the supplies he needed. The governor of Colorado Territory organized a nondescript military force that called themselves the "Pike's Peakers" and who rushed south to cut Sibley off from Fort Union. Although both sides later claimed a victory, Sibley lost his supply train and had to retreat. From that moment the Confederate cause west of the Rockies was ended.

One of the reasons for Sibley's return to Texas was the advance of the "California Column," a group of volunteers under Colonel James H. Carleton, who were marching east from the Pacific. At their approach. Sibley's small force in Yuma fled; and when they reached Tucson, they were joined in their flight by the Confederate soldiers who had remained there. Fortunately for them, the Apaches attacked them only at Dragoon Springs, killing three of their members but permitting the remainder to go through Apache Pass unopposed.

As Carleton moved quickly behind them, he feared the Indians more than the white men. Before leaving Tucson, he put Captain Thomas Roberts in command of an advance guard with John C. Cremony, a student of Indian ways, in charge of the wagon train.

Following the former route of the Butterfield stagecoach line, Roberts marched to Dragoon Springs, which had a good supply of water for his men and livestock. The next water was at Apache Pass, where Bascom and Cochise had fought. Roberts marched ahead to secure the pass before the wagons came up.

Cremony later described what happened. "Roberts," he wrote, ". . . entered the pass with the ordinary precautions. He had penetrated two-thirds of the way, when from both sides of that battlemented gorge a fearful rain of fire and lead was poured upon his troops, within a range from thirty to eighty yards. On either hand the rocks afforded natural and almost unassailable defenses. Every tree concealed a warrior, and each warrior boasted his rifle, six-shooter and knife. A better armed host could scarcely be imagined. From behind every species of shelter came the angry hissing missiles, and not a soul to be seen. Quickly, vigorously, and bravely did his men respond, but to what effect? They were expending ammunition to no purpose, their foes were invisible: there was no way to escalade those impregnable natural fortresses; the howitzers were useless, and the men doubtful how to attack the foe."

The arms of the Apaches were probably not so plentiful as Cremony said, for Indians always had difficulty getting guns and ammunition; but he did not exaggerate the ability of the Apaches to hide during a battle. They confused more than one commander who would have been glad to fight his foe if only he could have found them.

Roberts wisely drew back and reorganized his force, sending out flankers and preparing his howitzers to fire against the upper slopes of the pass. Most Indians, including the Apaches, were not accustomed to any kind of artillery fire. This time his advance brought him to the stagecoach station and, most important in the Southwest, to water.

Behind him was the wagon train, far more awkward to maneuver and far more difficult to defend. If it approached the pass and was taken by surprise, the chances of its survival would be slight. The Apaches, extraordinary fighters but never particularly good at strategy, failed to guard against the escape of messengers, so Roberts was able to warn Cremony of the danger and also lead back enough men—with the howitzers—to protect the wagon train.

After Cremony had joined him west of the mountains, he once again used his howitzers to advantage. As one of the Indians later remarked, the artillery turned the day. The Indians were frightened by the effect of those guns, which, compared to the rifle fire with which they were familiar, was terrifying. Roberts brought the wagon train to the spring; and the Indians, completely disheartened by his advance, withdrew. Apache Pass now belonged to the California Column.

When Carleton arrived, the Indians were gone, but he sensed at once the importance of the pass to any military force trying to hold Arizona and maintain communications between the East and the West. So when he marched on, he left a small detachment behind with instructions to establish a permanent post named Fort Bowie.

By the time Carleton reached New Mexico, Sibley had already retreated to Texas. Although the Union had reconquered the Southwest, what Carleton governed was, like Baylor's former territory, only a shell. In a few centers of population, the white men still controlled the land; but in most of it, the Indians, and particularly the Apaches, had regained their former dominance.

Mangas Colorados, the leader who had succeeded Juan José after the massacre at Santa Rita del Cobre, had been wounded at the battle with Captain Roberts. Recovering, he resumed his fight with the white men, but not for long. The following year, a group of prospectors under the leadership of an old-time frontiersman, Joseph Reddeford Walker, were attempting to get to the mines along the Gila River, but whichever route they tried, the Apaches barred their way. In an encounter with Mangas Colorados, they persuaded him to treat with them under a flag of truce. As soon as he came forward to speak with them, they drew their guns and made him a prisoner.

All they wanted was a prominent hostage to protect them while they traveled through the Apaches' country; but a general, at whose encampment they stopped, insisted on taking possession of so distinguished a prisoner. Furthermore, he ordered his sentinels to shoot Mangas Colorados if he tried to escape. During the night, while the Apache leader was attempting to sleep by the campfire, the sentries took turns prodding him with their bayonets, which they first heated in the flames. When he finally leapt to his feet under this torture, they claimed he was trying to get away and killed him.

This did nothing to quiet the Apaches. Rather it increased their growing belief that Americans were no more to be trusted than the Spaniards or the Mexicans. Since the Union could not spare any appreciable numbers of troops, the situation became worse and worse.

One traveler who visited Tucson about this time described the condition of that community, which was supporting the occupying Union soldiers and was beleaguered by the Apaches, all at the same time. "The citizens who are permitted to live here at all," he wrote, "still live very much in the Greaser style—the tenantable houses having been taken away from them for the use of the officers and soldiers who are protecting their property from the Apaches. But then, they have claims for rent, which they can probably sell for something when any body comes along disposed to deal in that sort of paper. Formerly they were troubled a good deal about the care of their cattle and sheep; now they have no trouble at all; the sheep and cattle have fallen into the hands of the Apaches, who have become unusually bold in their depredations." The Civil War had turned the Southwest into a battlefield, but the struggle was between Indians and white men, and, in those parts that espoused the South's side, civilians and an occupying army of undisciplined volunteers.

Most of the West beyond the Rockies, however, was relatively unaffected by the Civil War. Containing little of strategic importance for either side, neither the North nor the South made any further forays into it. In some areas, sympathizers of one cause or the other became involved in local disputes that had no national consequence. Senator Gwin of California, who had once pledged his support to Russell, Majors and Waddell in securing the mail contract, was imprisoned because of his pronounced Southern views. Released from jail, he tried to encourage the settlement of parts of Mexico by Southerners, a program that produced nothing except his renewed imprisonment. Dramatic as it was, his quick fall from senator to convict affected little except his personal life. Such was the limited scope of most outbursts of partisan feeling in the Far West.

In western Nevada, the principal preoccupation was making money. The Comstock Lode was pouring out its riches to ever larger syndicates and companies. Nevertheless there was wealth to spare for individuals, and Mark Twain pictured what was happening. Speaking of the *Territorial Enterprise,* the newspaper for which he worked, he said the two men who owned it had found it "a poverty-stricken weekly journal, gasping for breath and likely to die. They bought it, type, fixtures, good will, and all for a thousand dollars on long time. The editorial sanctum, news-room, press-room, publication office, bed-chamber, parlor, and kitchen were all compressed into one apartment, and it was a small one, too. The editors and printers slept on the floor, a Chinaman did their cooking, and the 'imposing-stone' was the general dinner-table.

"But now things were changed," he continued. "The paper was a great daily, printed by steam; there were five editors and . . . the columns crowded. The paper was clearing from six to ten thousand dollars a month." Even given Mark Twain's tendency to exaggerate, western Nevada was enjoying unbelievable prosperity.

The main distributors of the wealth were, of course, the mining companies. "The 'Gould & Curry' company [which was operating one of the original finds] were erecting a monster hundred-stamp mill at a cost that ultimately fell little short of a million dollars," Mark Twain said. "The superintendent . . . drove a fine pair of horses which were a present from the company, and his salary was twelve thousand dollars a year. . . . Money was wonderfully plenty. The trouble was, not how to get it—but how to spend it, how to lavish it, get rid of it, squander it."

During the Civil War, the Far West was a curious composite of contrasts— Oregon quietly making use of its fertile valleys, California putting its senator in jail, the Southwest terrorized by Indians, Utah still controlled by the hardworking Mormons, and Nevada enjoying some of the greatest local prosperity the nation had ever seen. Remote as it was from the principal scenes of action, however, the Far West was not forgotten by the federal government. That same year, Congress passed legislation that affected it more deeply than any legislation except those acts necessary to acquire the territory in the first place. For many it represented the culmination of a dream held for years.

29. Civilization Advances

The absence of good female society . . . is likewise an evil of great magnitude; for men become rough, stern and cruel.

—Thomas Dimsdale, 1866

One of the great blessings enjoyed by the United States was the public domain, those millions of acres that belonged to the people as a whole and were held in trust for them by the federal government. They had also been the cause of more debate since the Constitutional Convention than almost any other issue, including slavery. For nearly everyone had an opinion on their disposal.

In the early days of the republic, these lands had represented almost the only capital the new nation possessed. With the debt from the Revolution still to be paid and with insignificant sources of revenue, the legislators—and the people—believed the sale of land would pay a large part of the cost of government. Then, when the country began to make internal improvements, the public lands provided much of the capital. Grants of acreage were made for many purposes, including the construction of dikes, roads, canals, and railroads. Grants of land had also been made to some of the states to help them start school systems and provide other public services.

All this time there had been a concurrent demand for free land for individual settlers, a demand that was particularly strong along the frontier. Why should the man who had gone beyond the last of the older settlements and faced the hazards of nature and the Indians have to pay the federal government for land that he himself had made habitable?

Over the years several concessions had been made to the individual pioneer, but these laws did not satisfy the wishes of the frontiersmen. What they wanted was land that was absolutely free.

Many liberal groups in the eastern cities agreed with them. Free land, they argued, would absorb the unemployed, the immigrants pouring in from Europe, the children of farmers in the poorer agricultural areas, and all the others who formed a pool of labor that kept wages down and made the lot of the worker difficult. And for those already in the West and who had capital, free homesites promised faster settlement and thus a quickly growing market for the goods and services they had to offer.

But their ideas did not prevail. Even when land sales began to account for an inappreciable percent of the federal revenue—less than one per cent of the total in some of the years after 1850—many were opposed to the thought of giving acres away.

Most important was the influence of the South. Free farms for small individual farmers was antipodal to the plantation system. Furthermore, a flood of small farmers sweeping westward might disrupt the balance in Congress by giving the antislavery areas a greater representation in the House of Representatives. Time and again the liberals had pushed legislation that would make farmland available free; again and again the legislation had been either rejected or emasculated.

With the coming of the Civil War, the debate was ended, just as the debate had been ended on the selection of a principal route for the mail and eventually for a railroad. In 1862 Congress passed the Homestead Act, which, despite its many faults, was an extraordinary piece of legislation. Anyone who was twenty-one years or the head of a family could take possession of 160 acres of land in the public domain, and the only payment required of him was a few modest fees. But he had to swear that the land was for his own use and agree to make certain improvements during the next five years, such as building fences, barns, and a dwelling place. In other words, he had to live on the land and convert it into his home.

The law contained many imperfections. No sure way existed to determine whether the applicant really wanted the acreage for his own use. He might, for example, be a cowhand staking out a waterhole that he would later turn over to his employer. No corps of inspectors could personally examine all the "improvements" and make certain they actually existed. More than one settler placed a small model of a log cabin on his land and swore he had put a "house" on it. Nor was the gift of land to the settler quite so munificent as Congress had intended. In the fertile regions of the country, 160 acres made a good farm, but in many parts of the West, where rain was scarce, 160 acres was insufficient, and a family tied to a farm that size would find only poverty. Consequently Congress eventually had to change the law, making it possible to acquire additional land under certain circumstances.

Nevertheless, the enthusiasm that attended the passage of the original Homestead Act was not misplaced. It was unique and generous; and its ultimate effect on Americans extended far beyond those who eventually took up holdings. For thousands of others who never did the thought that they could become farm owners sustained them in times of adversity and took the grayness out of their daily lives. This point, overlooked by most historians, may have been the act's most important impact. More than the torch in the hand of the Statue of Liberty, this one law presented a beacon of hope to the multitudes.

At the same time, Congress passed the Morrill Act, another piece of democratic legislation drawing on the resources of the public lands. This provided grants of acreage to the states for the purpose of establishing colleges. (Those states that had no public lands within their boundaries were given scrip.) These "land grant colleges," as they came to be known, concentrated on agriculture and mechanics. Their purpose was to give every man's son the technical skills necessary to hold a good job or operate a profitable farm. Advanced education was no longer to be the privilege of a few.

The third great democratic act that same year was Lincoln's proclamation freeing the slaves. Placing the Union above the slavery issue, he at first had hesitated to take the final step to eliminate the evil that had destroyed the bonds between the states. But in the fall of 1862, he thought the time was right. On the first of January, all slaves in states still in rebellion would be free. As a practical matter, the federal troops had to secure the surrender of those states before the proclamation became effective, but the government had at last avowed there was no place in the Union for slavery.

In 1862, the United States had acted like a wealthy nation. It had authorized the largest construction project in its history, one to daunt the best of engineers and the most skillful of financiers. It had offered a farm free to anyone with the courage and persistence to carve one out of the land and an inexpensive education to anyone who wished to go to college. It had also destroyed millions of dollars of "property rights," so the "property" could become human beings.

Yet it was not wealthy. Europe had no confidence in an eventual Union victory, so American credit was weak abroad. Federal bonds sold at a discount—no one really wanted them—and American currency was falling in value. Even with new issues of greenbacks, the government could not always meet its bills, and the soldiers in the field often had to wait to collect their pay.

On the other hand, new riches had just been discovered within its boundaries, not long-term riches like fields that might someday be cleared and cultivated, but riches in the form of metals that were immediately saleable. For gold was found in Idaho, which was organized now as a territory, and in Montana, not yet one. Once more, men abandoned what they already possessed in the hopes of obtaining more, the news of fresh discoveries acting on them as Cabeza da Vaca's reports had once acted on the Spaniards. Most of them failed to find the riches they sought, but the discoveries sent them racing into areas that otherwise might have remained unexplored and unsettled for decades to come.

The sudden wealth again brought the lawless from the shady places in which they usually resided to plunder what others had dug from the earth; and the miners once more had to make their own laws and enforce them. In Montana, the problem was particularly complex, for the leader of the band of highwaymen who terrorized the countryside proved to be none other than Sheriff Henry Plummer himself, who used his office to shield those whom the public mistakenly thought he was trying to catch.

During the period, one of the most remarkable characteristics of the nation was its seemingly bottomless reserve of energy. Here it was, engaged in a bitter Civil War that was disrupting the nation and splitting families. (Sibley and Canby who had fought each other in New Mexico were brothers-in-law.) Yet men kept moving into the Far West, wrestling with its mountains, its deserts, its rivers, and its Indians. And they were still able to make progress, however slow and faltering, with their great construction project.

In January 1863, a reporter from the Sacramento *Union* watched Leland Stanford, the local dry goods dealer, pick up a shovel and dig a spadeful of dirt to start work on the Central Pacific's first railbed. "We may now look forward with confidence," the paper said, "to the day, not far distant, when the Pacific will be bound to the Atlantic by iron bonds."

The optimism of the writer exceeded the reality. Judah's enthusiasm and Huntington's ability to raise money were both being sorely tested. At that point, Judah did not even have his first shipment of rails from the East (there were no steel-making facilities in the West), and Huntington was meeting the resistance to the sale of stock that was to plague him for a number of years to come. An act of Congress and the chartering of a corporation were only first steps in a long endeavor.

Labor was another problem that plagued the rapid construction of the railroad. In those days before the invention of large earth-moving equipment, human and animal muscles did much of the work now accomplished by power. Earth was moved by the shovelful, and hills leveled with pickaxes.

Almost every visitor to California commented on the high cost of labor, for the influx of newcomers had never relieved the shortage. In 1854, however, a large number of Chinese came to the United States, and they did for the Californians of that time what the Indians had done for the Spanish under the mission system—all the menial jobs.

The trade—for that is what the importation of "coolies" became—was not limited to the United States. Many other nations also drew on this labor supply, usually on terms that resembled those of an indentured servant's. But the imported Chinese had few defenses against abuse, for he could not speak the language well and his race set him apart.

As one contemporary journalist remarked, "Almost every one has imbibed the indefinite idea of it [the trade] as a gigantic wrong, in some way involving outrages against human liberty that have called down the opprobrium and legislative denunciation of civilized governments. . . . Gigantic outrages have been enacted; but more than this, an old form of slavery has been instituted under a new name, and many a deluded Coolie is today under a more hopeless and terrible bondage than the African from the Gaboon." Whatever the world might think of Chinese labor, it was on these workmen that the partners in the Central Pacific Railroad largely depended. Four small-town businessmen, an engineer whom many regarded as practically unbalanced, and a corps of imported Chinese laborers—these were the ingredients for the construction of an American transcontinental railroad.

The Southwest did not share in the prosperity and general growth of the rest of the Far West during the Civil War. Even the death of Mangas Colorados, killed by the soldiers in 1863, had not brought any respite from the Indian warfare. But Congress had not forgotten the people living there. Recognizing the futility of trying to govern from Santa Fé what is now Arizona, it created Arizona Territory, and it encouraged Carleton in his war on the Indians.

Carleton was a realist and realized the defeat of small bands of Indians had little effect, because the remaining bands continued to be just as active as before. He therefore determined to kill all the males—as Baylor had wanted to do earlier—or place them on a reservation. He had already selected a place, the Bosque Redondo in eastern New Mexico. Far from any settlement and away from the mountains, the area could be guarded; and although the water was poor and the climate unlike that to which many of the Southwest Indians were accustomed, he thought it suitable for converting them from war to a more peaceful way of life.

His first successful campaign was against the Mescalero Apaches. These Indians were closely related to the Chiricahua Apaches like Cochise and to those of whom Mangas Colorados had been the leader; but living farther east, they were better adjusted to life on the plains. Their surrender and removal to the reservation at Bosque Redondo did not affect the general Apache warfare around Apache Pass and the Gila River, but it did end one source of raids against the white men's settlements and herds.

Carleton next turned his attention to the Navajos. Related to the Apaches, this tribe had been one of the scourges of the Southwest since the appearance of the Spaniards. Hard-fighting warriors and good horsemen, they had come and gone as they pleased without regard for any soldiers, whether they were Spanish, Mexican, or American.

Many army campaigns against the Indians had been based on European concepts of warfare, with large forces attempting to maneuver the enemy into a pitched and set battle on a limited field. Even the Americans, who had done guerrilla fighting during the eastern Indian wars and during the Revolution, seemed to forget the lessons they had learned. Carleton was aware of this, and his orders to his subordinates might well have been copied by other commanders assigned to the same sort of duty.

"The troops must be kept after the Indians," he told his subordinates, "not in big bodies, with military noises and smokes, and the gleam of arms by day, and fires, and talk, and comfortable sleep by night; but in small parties moving stealthily to their haunts and lying patiently in wait for them. . . .

"An Indian is a more watchful and a more wary animal than a deer. He must be hunted with skill; he cannot be blundered upon."

The person in New Mexico who knew more about this type of fighting than anyone was Kit Carson, now a respected and prosperous citizen of the territory. Carson was more than willing to help wage war against the Navajos and was successful in enlisting the help of some of their old-time enemies, the Utes.

The campaign that followed was one designed to eliminate the Navajos once and for all as an impediment to white settlement. Wherever the soldiers found Indian dwellings or herds, they destroyed them. It was the same scorched-earth policy that Sherman used in his march across Georgia, an effort to cut off the enemy from his supplies. As a result of Carson's tactics, several bands came to parley with the troops. The answer was always the same: They must either surrender and go to Bosque Redondo or face the burning of their villages and fields and—death. There was no other choice.

Already hungry and bewildered by this offensive, which did not stop with the surrender of a band or two, some of them capitulated. But Carleton was not satisfied with the results. After several months of fighting and marching, the soldiers had captured only a small part of the total tribe. The rest remained free and ready to continue their raids as soon as the troops withdrew. So Carson kept on pressing them.

One of the mysterious and beautiful places in the Navajo country was the Canyon de Chelly, a deep gorge cut into the surrounding plain with cliffs along the sides, cliffs too steep either to climb or descend. Through the bottom of the canyon ran a stream, supplying it with water; and clinging to the surrounding canyon walls were the ruins of cliff dwellings. Erroneously, the Navajos believed they were descendants of those ancient occupants, and the thought that their ancestors were looking down on them when they were in the canyon added to their sense of security. This was both their church and their fortress. Few white men were familiar with it, and if the white men entered it, the ghosts of the men who had once lived in the ruins would come to the Navajos' aid.

Carson knew the Navajos' attitude toward the Canyon de Chelly and their belief that it represented their ultimate refuge. So he did not slacken his pursuit as they drew nearer and nearer to it.

This was the act of a skilled Indian fighter and a courageous man, for the farther he advanced, the farther he was from his own source of supplies and from reinforcements. Soon his soldiers were marching along the canyon floor, burning dwellings and destroying any food they uncovered, while others held firm possession of the heights. It was January, cold winds swept through the canyon, and the Navajos had less to keep them warm and less to eat than usual at that time of year. They were already hungry and cold, and the ghosts who lurked in the shadowy places among the cliff dwellings did nothing to help them. This factor, almost as much as the actual military invasion, broke their will to resist.

Large numbers agreed to go to Bosque Redondo. The remainder fled farther away or drifted south to join the Apaches. The winter snows, drifting into the canyon, not only covered the canyon floor; they also buried the proud past of the Navajos.

Kit Carson had already dictated the short manuscript that was to become his official *Autobiography,* but he did not take the papers out and add some remarks about his campaign. Such was the modesty of the man. But he also did not underestimate what had been accomplished, remarking in his official report, "We have shown the Indians that in no place, however formidable or inaccessible in their opinion, are they safe from the pursuit of the troops."

By 1864, the year the Navajos began surrendering in large numbers, the war in the East was turning in the favor of the North. The Battle of Gettysburg had marked the greatest advance the South would make into the land of its enemy, and from that point on, its actions were largely defensive, trying to avoid the heavy blows that Grant relentlessly gave its army.

Congress, nevertheless, still had time for the land beyond the Rockies. Montana was rapidly gaining in population because of its gold, so Congress organized it as a territory, the first step toward statehood. In Nevada, already a territory, many of the people were active in preparing it for statehood by writing a constitution. They were tired of federal officials, including the appointed judges. The bench was called upon to settle some of the conflicting claims arising out of the Comstock Lode, which was generating almost as much legal strife as it was silver. No matter which way the judges decided, they made enemies, and criticism of them was heard in every direction.

A few people in Nevada who were more pragmatic understood that statehood was not the cure for every evil and would only increase their local taxes. For as long as Nevada remained a territory, the federal government absorbed most of the cost of government services. The Humboldt *Register* thundered out that it was "dead-set against engaging to help support any more lunk-heads till times get better. . . . If we have a State Government we'll have more fat-headed officers to support; and if we undertake to support them without taxing the mines, we'll run hopelessly into debt. If we do tax them, we'll stop the development of them." ·

This commonsense approach did not appeal to the majority. There was something glorious about being a state, and the additional expense made little difference. No one with pride would choose to live in Nevada Territory when he might be a citizen of the state of Nevada. So great was their enthusiasm that they did not use the mail to send their new constitution to Washington for approval; they telegraphed it. This display of local pride cost them almost $3,500, a large sum in those days and a nice bit of business for the telegraph company. Lincoln proclaimed Nevada a state on October 31, 1864, which allowed the people time to prepare to vote in the presidential election. Every post went to a Republican, the party that Lincoln headed.

Since Nevada had already settled its boundary dispute with California, the colorful days were gone when Aurora was the seat for a county in California and one in Nevada, and its residents voted in both elections. Such undignified times were over.

One of Congress's actions that year had a particularly far-reaching effect. Many a traveler to California had been taken out to see the Yosemite Valley and, as Greeley had done, found the site magnificent. The concept of national parks had not been developed, but with unusual foresight Congress withdrew the valley from the public domain and gave it to California as a "reservation" to be maintained unspoiled for the enjoyment of everyone. It was a move that showed a sensitive awareness of esthetic values and respect for the nation's natural resources that was surprising in a country rich in undeveloped land and occupied with the horror of war.

The railroads that would ultimately bring thousands of eastern visitors to California to see the Yosemite and the state's other sights were not, however, faring well. Judah had died almost immediately after construction on the Central Pacific had started, and the loss of his driving personality and engineering skill was serious. Nevertheless he had planned sufficiently well so that his company had made far more progress than the Union Pacific, which was still largely a corporation on paper only.

The principal problem of the Central Pacific was money. Building a railroad of any size was a major undertaking for a country with as little capital as the United States. Under the best of circumstances, stock in such a questionable enterprise would have been difficult to sell, and the company could not issue bonds itself because of the government's first lien to secure its own securities. Furthermore, Congress had decreed that none of the stock could be sold below par.

The purpose of this provision was clear. Congress was trying to make it impossible for the principal stockholders to favor themselves and their friends by selling stock at a discount and thus using the potential resources of the railroads for their personal profit rather than for raising the money needed to pay the construction bills. What Congress overlooked and what any experienced underwriter could have told them was the virtual impossibility of maintaining a market for the stock without ever letting the price dip below par. Thus a thousand dollars of treasury stock might not mean the company could purchase a thousand dollars worth of construction. Under the rules set down by Congress, it might not be able to sell the stock at all.

To overcome this difficulty, both companies adopted a procedure that had been used by other railroads. They formed special companies to do the construction work under contract. In the case of the Union Pacific, the principal shareholders bought a Pennsylvania concern called the Credit Mobilier; the Central Pacific established one called Crocker and Company, a name that was later changed to the Contract and Finance Company. If the stock was selling, for example, at 50 percent of its par value, the railroad could overestimate the cost of the work to be done, pay the construction company at the par value of the stock for the inflated estimate. The construction company could then sell the stock in the marketplace at its going price—for no restrictions applied to the stock's resale—and recoup its money. Thus a job that might cost a thousand dollars could be paid for with stock worth two thousand dollars at par and which the construction company could sell on the market at half price to regain the thousand actually due it.

Up to a point, this was a logical way of circumventing the congressional restriction, but it did not work well in actual practice. For it lent itself to enormous abuses. In the first place, the owners of the two construction companies were the principals of the two railroads, so they controlled both the letting of the contracts and the performance of them. And if they could inflate the estimated cost of the work to compensate for the stock's depressed value, they could easily inflate it further to ensure an additional profit for themselves. That is precisely what they did.

As the two railroads inched their way across the continent, one pushing toward the east, the other headed west, they were being drained of their assets, and the principals in each case were becoming wealthy men. The Credit Mobilier was eventually the target of an extensive congressional

337

investigation—but too late to recoup the money lost. The company formed by Crocker and his associates never received the same scrutiny. Each partner had kept his own records, making a thorough analysis impossible, and the problem was further complicated by a fire in 1873 that burned what books the company had kept. In the end, the nation got the railroad it so much wanted but at a cost that was much higher than it should have been.

The year 1865 brought two of the most important events in American history. By April 9, Lee's army had suffered heavily from Grant's hammering, and as there was no escape route remaining open, the Confederates surrendered at Appomattox. When Lee offered his sword to Grant, the end had come.

In the midst of its joy over this conclusion to years of costly, bloody fighting, the nation was shocked by the news of Lincoln's assassination. At the best, reconstruction would have been a difficult time, as generosity and forgiveness conflicted with avarice and vengeance. With Lincoln gone, the times were even worse. Yet with the resiliency it had consistently shown, the nation pulled itself from the shadows of war to the sunshine of peace.

The Far West had not suffered much during the Civil War. It had stayed within the Union, and Congress had returned its loyalty with the Homestead Act, the acts for the construction of the railroads, the maintenance of through service for mail and passengers, and by setting up territories or states in almost all the area, thus bringing it formal government. Enough men were left over from the draft calls to provide an increase in population. Practically everywhere, except in those mining camps whose gold and silver was exhausted, the population had grown. Even Montana, once dominated by the fearsome Blackfeet, was becoming settled with miners, and soon the new territory's economy was expanding to include cattle and other forms of ranching. Idaho, too, had benefited from the discovery of precious minerals, and regions that had once been known only to the mountain men were now occupied by miners and the people who supplied their wants.

Along the central route, finally selected for the telegraph and the railroad, the Far West had changed greatly since those days in 1846 when soldiers had marched forth to fight Mexico and diplomats had matched wits with British statesmen. Samuel Bowles, editor of the Springfield, Massachusetts, *Republican,* one of the nation's outstanding newspapers, made a tour of inspection in the company of Schuyler Colfax, speaker of the House of Representatives. Once again the country had the benefit of the remarks of an experienced observer.

About three years had gone by since Congress had passed the original Railroad Act, which it had amended in 1864 to make the terms more liberal. Yet Atchison, Kansas, just across the Missouri River, was as far as Bowles could go by rail. From there, he had to use the stagecoach, just as Greeley had done, to Placerville, California, before meeting the railroad coming from the west. The great dreams of a transcontinental line was still in the offing.

At Virginia City, Bowles reported on the Comstock Lode and remarked that "no silver mines worth working here have yet been found off from it . . . although thousands of dollars and years of labor have been spent in the search. Nor had the working of this ledge [the Comstock] been attended with uniform success. At least as many companies have failed . . . as have succeeded."

Even the companies still working were not enjoying the glorious days of a short time earlier. The Gould and Curry Company had paid its stockholders $4 million in dividends on an investment of $180,000; but, he pointed out the value of its holdings had dropped considerably. "At one time," he reported, "the mine sold at the rate of six thousand dollars a foot, but now it is down to about eighteen hundred; for, though it is producing bullion at the rate of two millions a year, and pays handsome monthly dividends uninterruptedly, it has about exhausted all the valuable ore in its mine at the present depth, and is working up mainly the poorer ore at lower depth. . . ."

Virginia City was already showing signs of maturity, compared to some of the newer mining camps. When Mark Twain had arrived, he had commented on the community's crude appearance, rowdyism, and disrespect for human life. Bowles noted that it now "puts its gambling behind an extra door; it is beginning to recognize the Sabbath, has many churches open, and closes part of its stores on that day; is exceedingly well built, in large proportion with solid brick stores and warehouses." The "fast and fascinating times of 1862–63 are over," he said.

The community was becoming civilized, and the days of the frontier were almost ended. Instead of lonely prospectors like Old Virginia, he noted that "eastern capital and eastern men are now coming hither in force, and promise soon to start up anew the rather dormant life of the State, and give rapid and profitable development to its great mining wealth." But he warned the easterners not to consider the westerners naïve. The investors of Montgomery Street in San Francisco, he pointed out, were just as smart as those from Wall Street in New York.

Bowles also reported on the new mines in Idaho. They were, he said, "perhaps exciting the most interest at present among the people of the Coast; and they are also beginning to divide enticements with those of Nevada and Colorado, for eastern speculators and capitalists." Yet he concluded that he "did not see that Idaho really offers any better inducements for emigration and capital than Nevada and Colorado."

Although Bowles, like most Americans, was excited over the development of the nation's resources, he noted that in many instances the biggest profits were made by the speculators, not those doing the actual work, and he was keenly aware of the destruction of much of the California countryside as a result of hydraulic mining. In this process, the earth was removed from gold-bearing slopes by forcing streams of water over it. "All these operations," Bowles said, "create a wide waste. . . . Tornado, flood, earthquake and volcano combined could hardly make greater havoc, spread wider ruin and wreck." Streams that should have been clear ran with mud and sand and gravel, covering fertile fields and making them worthless for growing crops.

He also remarked on the wide gap between the Californians and the Chinese, who had not become assimilated. "They look down even with contempt upon our newer, rougher civilization, regarding us as barbaric in fact, and calling us in their hearts, if not in speech, 'the foreign devils.' And our conduct towards them has inevitably intensified these feelings—it has driven them back upon their naturally self-contained natures and habits." The abyss between the two cultures could not be bridged. The Chinese seemed remote and inscrutable. Given to strange customs and often addicted to opium, their alien ways were occasionally a cause for suspicion and fear. California had become dependent on them but did not understand them.

Ever since the gold rush in California, Oregon had faded from the limelight, but in many ways its people had benefited. "They lack many of the advantages of their neighbors . . . ," Bowles said, "their agriculture is less varied, but it is more sure; mining has not poured such irregular and intoxicating wealth into their laps . . . but they have builded what they have got more slowly and more wisely than the Californians; they have less severe reaction from hot and unhealthy growth to encounter—less to unlearn; and they seem sure, not of organizing the first State on the Pacific Coast . . . but of a steadily prosperous, healthy and moral one."

The Far West was a strange mixture of extremes. Many of its cities like San Francisco were well developed communities, ranking with those of the older sections of the nation and offering similar amenities. Some like Virginia City were maturing. Others were still wild, like some of those in Montana where the citizens had to rely on themselves even for the enforcement of a minimum of law. In parts of the Far West, men and women visited their friends in the evenings and engaged in normal social pursuits. In others, like parts of the Southwest, they hardly dared leave their houses when darkness came. In fact, they lived in terror much of the time, for the land around them was a great unexplored void filled with their Indian enemies.

The measure of an area's civilization was often the presence of women. When the trappers had first crossed the mountains, no women accompanied them except for the Indians who, at the best, became wives, and, at the worst, camp followers. The appearance of Narcissa Whitman and Eliza Spaulding in the Northwest opened a new era there. Narcissa's wish for better brooms to sweep her floors may not have seemed significant in itself, but it was an indication of a new and more cultivated way of life. Men might be content with the wild and rough; women were not. Under their insistent pressure, they brought civilization to the wilderness.

Not all the first-comers had the standards of Narcissa nor her gentle ways. Thomas Dimsdale, who lived in Montana and was a member of the vigilance committee that ended the criminal career of Sheriff Plummer, left a picture of the women in the early days of a mining camp. Many of them were, in the phrase of the times, "of easy virtue," and "receiving fabulous sums for their purchased favors."

The more common form of female entertainment was found at the "Hurdy-Gurdy" house. A large room was dominated by a long bar at one end. The men crowded around it, buying drinks at high prices and in large quantities. At the end of the bar ran a railing, which cut off one section of the room. "Beyond the barrier," said Dimsdale, "sit the dancing women, called 'hurdy-gurdies,' sometimes dressed in uniform, but, more generally, habited according to the dictates of individual caprice, in the finest clothes that money can buy, and which are fashioned in the most attractive styles that fancy can suggest. On one side is a raised orchestra. The music suddenly strikes up, and the summons, 'Take your partners for the next dance,' is promptly answered by some of the male spectators, who paying a dollar in gold for a ticket, approach the ladies' bench, and—in style polite, or otherwise, according to antecedents—invite one of the ladies to dance."

Describing a single dancer out of many, Dimsdale went on to say, "How sedate she looks during the first figure, never smiling till the termination of 'promenade, eight,' when she shows her little white hands in fixing her handsome brooch in its place, and settling her glistening ear-rings. . . . No wonder that a wild mountaineer would be willing to pay—not one dollar, but all that he has in his purse, for a dance and an approving smile from so beautiful a woman."

At the conclusion of the set of dances, the caller shouted out "gents to the right" and "promenade to the bar." As soon as the women had rested and the men had ordered enough drinks to keep the bartender busy and the receipts rolling in, the process was repeated. A good-looking girl who was also a good dancer might collect more than fifty tickets in an evening, splitting the miner's dollar fifty-fifty with the proprietor—"A great deal of money," Dimsdale commented, "to earn in such a fashion; but fifty sets of quadrilles of four waltzes . . . is very hard work." Many of the girls did not limit their business to the "Hurdy-Gurdy" house but played the men for more money in their off-hours; and those who were most successful often made in a week more "than a well-educated girl would make in two years in an Eastern city."

The dances were frequented by everyone. "You can see Judges, the Legislative corps, and everyone," Dimsdale said, "but the Minister. He never ventures further than to engage in conversation with a friend at the door, and

341

while intently watching the performance, lectures on the evil of such places with considerable force; but his attention is evidently more fixed upon the dancers than on his lecture."

Washington, which had achieved territorial status in 1853, approached the problem of women in a different fashion. Asa Mercer, president of the territorial university, decided to go on a recruiting trip in the East. The territorial treasury was low, so the governor could not finance the venture, but Mercer raised some money from his friends. In May 1864, he reappeared at Seattle with eleven young women. Just before the next election, the *Seattle Gazette* called attention to what he had achieved. "It is to the efforts of Mr. Mercer—joined with the wishes of the darlings themselves—that the eleven accomplished and beautiful young ladies, whose arrival was lately announced, have been added to our population." The paper urged the community—and especially the bachelors—to vote for Mercer as councilman in return "for his efforts in encouraging this much needed kind of immigration." The electorate responded, and Mercer won office.

So successful was this venture that he went East again, hoping to enlist the help of Lincoln, whom he had known in school. But Lincoln had just been assassinated, so he appealed to General Grant for a steamship to carry his recruits back to Washington Territory. This appeal failed, but he obtained the help of Ben Holladay, the stagecoach operator, who purchased a steamship to carry the women west.

Mercer then toured New England, preaching the benefits of living in Washington. According to his own account, he had signed up a large number of women when the *New York Herald,* always given to sensationalism, ran an article erroneously giving his motives the worst interpretation. Many recruits promptly dropped out, but he succeeded in bringing fifty women, far fewer than he had hoped but nonetheless a considerable addition to Washington's predominantly male population.

In one way or another the women were coming, taking their places not only in the older communities like Santa Fé and San Francisco, but in the more remote areas. And their arrival in increasing numbers signaled that the end of the frontier was coming, too.

30. The Last Spike

The secret of the harmonious control of so vast and varied a population, extending over so great an area as the United States, is found in railroad transportation.

—G.L. Lansing,
controller of the Southern Pacific
in defense of the Central Pacific, 1889

The settlement of the East had been spurred by a number of incentives: greater financial opportunity, religious freedom, escape from constricting social conditions, and political tolerance. This had produced a dissimilarity among the original colonies that made their eventual union surprising. In the development of the Far West, many of these incentives played a part, but the one that predominated was the chance to make money.

At first, it had been the fur trade in which even a man of no means and little education could become wealthy. Then it was agriculture, the lure of rich, prosperous farms in Oregon. The Mormons had moved west to find religious freedom, one of the few groups of settlers to do so. With the advent of the gold rush in California, the major influence became mining. The prospect of finding gold had brought thousands of people to the West Coast and then sent them scurrying into Nevada, Arizona, Idaho, and Montana. The ancestors of many of those who became leading families had arrived with picks over their shoulders and pans under their arms.

In Montana the original motive of Granville Stuart had been to find gold. Now he was a leading citizen of the territory and branching into other activities, such as ranching. For once news reached the outside that Montana's earth and rocks contained gold, the crowd had come rushing, bringing with them a demand for food, hardware, a newspaper, clothing, and all the other goods and services they needed. The number of western emigrants to Montana had become so great that the government, just recovered from one war, was fighting the Indians to keep open the Bozeman Trail, which provided a shortcut from the plains to the gold fields of Montana.

Although the mining business was booming in Montana, Idaho, Arizona, and parts of Nevada, it seemed to be dying at the Comstock Lode. As Bowles had reported, the finest ores had been exhausted, and the enormous cost of supplies and labor had eaten heavily into the profits of the owners. The investors had poured more than $5 million into the largest companies, $5 million into the smaller ones, and perhaps $1 million to $2 million into individual mines. The total dividends paid out had amounted to slightly more than $11 million, making a deficit for the entire operation. By the summer of 1865, the market value of the Comstock mines had fallen from $40 million two years before to $12 million, but the worst had not yet happened. Before the end of the year, they had dropped even lower, to about $4 million. This occurred in spite of several optimistic studies of the geology of the Comstock, the first of which appeared that same fall.

The decline in the Comstock's stock did not dampen Congress's enthusiasm for the West. Aside from the physical protection of the settlers, the greatest contribution it could make was to see that the railroad was finished. Construction of the Central Pacific was moving along, and the railroad was showing an operating profit on the stretch that was already in service. With a labor force of about eight thousand men, the larger number of them Chinese, the road had pushed almost to the summit of the Sierra Nevada, an accomplishment that had required building trestles, some a hundred feet high, and long tunnels through the rock.

Pleased with the results achieved so far, Congress passed the Railroad Act of 1866 in order to encourage both companies to work harder. The most important provision was the elimination of a specific terminal point for either railroad. Both were to continue construction until they met. Thus the one that worked the faster would end up with the greater government subsidy and the longest mileage of track. This began what became a famous and dramatic

344

race. Another provision allowed the companies to draw two-thirds of the government bonds for each mile finished when they had completed the grading, even though they had not laid the track. This got them quicker access to the cash they needed to pay their bills.

Not content with just one transcontinental railroad, Congress also chartered another—the Atlantic and Pacific Railroad. This was to run from Springfield, Missouri, to Albuquerque, Needles, and on to California, following the thirty-fifth parallel, the route recommended so many years previously by the explorer and trader, François Aubry. Almost a decade before, Horace Greeley had foreseen the need to protect whatever railroad was finally built by giving it a monopoly. In view of the slight market for railroad services for most of the long run, he was right. But Congress was now encouraging the construction of competing lines before even the first one had been finished. It was a victory for enthusiasm over its traditional enemy, economic logic.

James F. Rusling, a lawyer who also wrote for some of the leading periodicals of the day, made a trip west in 1866. In Idaho, he found that Boise, the center of the mining activity, seemed to have as its chief business "drinking whiskey and gambling. The saloons," he reported, "were the handsomest buildings in town." Yet even there a more refined attitude was beginning to make its inroads against the more boisterous element. "The Episcopalians and Presbyterians already had their churches up," he said, "and the Methodists were soon expecting to build theirs."

He noticed that the Chinese were treated in Idaho as they were treated elsewhere in the Far West—as inferior persons. Three or four miners had robbed and killed a Chinese; but when they were arrested, the judge freed them, because the only witnesses were other Chinese and therefore incompetent to testify. Nevertheless, throughout the West a strong sense of justice prevailed. When the judge let the criminals go free, another group of miners promptly caught and hanged them.

Portland, Oregon, was booming. Originally dependent on agriculture, it had now become an important trading center. "The great Oregon Steam Navigation Company had their headquarters here," Rusling said, "and pour into her lap all the rich trade of the Columbia and its far-reaching tributaries, that tap Idaho, Montana, and even British America [Canada] itself. So, also, the coastwise steamers, from San Francisco up, all made Portland their terminus, and added largely to her commerce. . . . Nearer to the Sandwich Islands [Hawaii] and China, by several hundred miles, than California, she had already opened a brisk trade with both. . . "

Farther south, he found Los Angeles to be "a brisk and thriving town" of about five thousand. "The Americans seemed to own most of the houses and lands," he said, "the Europeans—chiefly Jews—to do the business, the native Californians to do the loafing, and the Indians to perform the labor."

San Diego, however, had fallen into decay. Its population had dropped to two or three hundred, its courthouse was "a tumble-down adobe," and its jail, "literally a cage, made of boiler-iron, six or seven feet square at the farthest."

Tucson, although larger, was not much more prosperous. "It boasted several saloons, one rather imposing, and some good stores; but no bank, newspaper, school-house, or church, except a rude adobe structure, where a Mexican padre officiated on Sunday to a small audience." One reason for its stagnation was the Apaches, who seemed to "claim original, and pretty much undisputed, jurisdiction over most of the country there. Merchants complained that the Apaches raided their teams and trains *en route,* and ranchmen that the wily rascals levied contributions regularly on their live stock, as soon as it was worth anything, and did not hesitate to scalp and kill, as well as steal. Farming or grazing under such circumstances . . . could hardly be called very lucrative or enticing. . . ."

More than one year after Appomattox, the Far West was going through several stages at once. Many of its communities were long past the frontier stage, some were leaving it, but in the Southwest, the Americans had barely dented the wilderness and were living under conditions reminiscent of many years previous.

Like most other observers, Rusling agreed that of all the activities in the West, the railroad held the most promise for the area; and after a slow start, the Central Pacific was at last making good progress. But ahead of it lay the greatest of the challenges, the summit of the Sierra Nevada, and one of its greatest enemies—winter.

When the Union Pacific and Central Pacific railroads were chartered, each faced its own separate physical problems. The grade from the Missouri River to the Rockies was steadily upward; but the land, except for its tilt toward the mountains, was relatively flat, making construction comparatively easy. On the other hand, the Union Pacific faced more trouble with war-like tribes.

The Central Pacific had the advantage of passing through land that had been largely wrested from the Indians. In California, the long occupancy by white men had greatly reduced their threat, and in Nevada the Paiutes had been slowly driven into submission since their outbreak in the days of the Pony Express. But the Sierra Nevada presented an obstacle unlike any of those faced by the Union Pacific. No easy pass existed over their summits; and as Frémont or Jedediah Smith could have testified, their winters were like the Arctic. As the fall winds of 1866 nipped the leaves of the hardwoods and sent the hibernating animals into their holes, the Central Pacific still had to cross the highest part of the mountains. This meant digging eleven tunnels over a twenty-mile stretch of track.

The snow that year was heavy. Storm followed storm; one lasted for thirteen days and brought with it ten feet of snow; others were lighter, but their accumulation kept adding to the total depth. Overhanging masses of snow created avalanches. Some of these were brought down by blasting, but in at least one instance the snow broke loose and in its mad rush down the mountainside carried away a bunkhouse with all its occupants. To get to and from the tunnels, the men had to dig secondary tunnels through the snow that blocked the approaches. Sometimes the wind blew with such force that great drifts formed where the men had already cleared a way, the snow tunnels had to be reinforced, and men could get lost walking only short distances because of the blinding white that surrounded them.

The foremen and other skilled workers exercised considerable ingenuity in keeping the operation going. When powder seemed too slow a method of blasting the rock, they made their own nitróglycerin on the mountaintops, doubling the pace of their advance through the rock with the use of this highly volatile and treacherous explosive. Only two accidents occurred, about the same number, they remarked afterwards, that would have taken place if they had continued using powder.

When they needed a steam engine, they brought it to the summits by dragging it with oxen, sometimes making only fourteen inches at a time through the snow. They learned to walk on snowshoes, experimenting with different types until they found one that suited the prevailing conditions. But they flatly balked at using steam drills. No arguments advanced by the "Big Four," as the original partners came to be known, would make them try that new tool. They were as obstinate about this as they were obstinate about keeping going in spite of the snow and cold.

Everyone spoke highly of the ability of the Chinese to get the job done, although they were paid less than white labor. (They received the same cash wages but had to supply their own food.) Every so often, to the surprise of their white supervisors, they would stop work, frightened by some "devil" lurking in the mountains or by some other danger the foremen did not always understand. But soon they were back at their jobs, moving tons of earth and shattered rock with their shovels. Night and day the sound of their digging could be heard in the tunnels, for they worked three eight-hour shifts and thus kept going around the clock. The foremen, who had more responsibility but less physical labor to perform, were divided into only two twelve-hour shifts.

The Big Four were roundly criticized by many for the profits they made and for their tactics in getting what they wanted, but they deserved credit for the magnitude of the operation they had undertaken. Sometimes they had as many as ten thousand men at once dispersed along the line, all of whom had to be fed and housed and supplied with tools, rails, and other equipment. The logistics alone were staggering, and they still had to make sure that cash was available to meet their bills. Even with the subsidies paid by the government this was not easy, for many financiers doubted their ability to finish the road.

347

For men whose previous business experience had been limited to running local enterprises, their performance was astounding. And when the winter of 1866–67 was finished, and the snows began to melt, the Central Pacific was still moving forward.

The crowd of men working throughout the winter at the summit of the Sierra Nevada was indicative of the times. The day of the lonely mountain man or small exploring party was almost gone, and the population living at the summit of the Sierra Nevada that winter was greater than that of many western towns.

Going, too, were the miners who owned their own claims. Now many of them worked for wages just like the Chinese on the railroad. In 1867 the once-independent men at the Comstock Lode organized the Miners' Union and demanded better working conditions. In the old days, when they did not like what they were earning, they picked up their shovels and picks and moved to another, richer location. Now they marched against their bosses. For the most part, they were peaceful, although, according to reports, they did tie one foreman to the hoisting cable and send him up and down, and another foreman took refuge with a Catholic priest for fear of his life. Finally the men settled for four dollars for an eight-hour day, still a long time to work in the hot, wet, badly ventilated mines. None of those who had come to California in 1849 would have been content with such pay and conditions of work even though these wages were higher than those offered by the railroad.

At the same time a new business was developing that would soon become typically western—cattle ranching. Cattle had long played an important part in the life of the Spanish, both for meat and hides. But Americans had never taken up ranching on a large scale. During the gold rush in California, when food was short and prices high on the West Coast, a few men had driven livestock to that growing market, but no one had thought of taking them to the Northeast.

Around 1867, two circumstances combined to make beef a more important industry. During the Civil War, the herds in Texas had been neglected; and since the range was well suited to them, they had grown enormously and were running wild. Anyone who could catch them was welcome to them, their number surpassing anything the local market could absorb. But with the advance of several railroads from the East, even though the railheads were hundreds of miles away, it became possible to ship them to eastern slaughterhouses. Soon the famous drives started from Texas. Because the market proved profitable, ranches sprang up farther north, as the ranchers of the Far West began to see that rail service would make possible a new use for the thousands of acres that were too dry for farming.

Even more of those acres were passing out of the public domain and entering private ownership, for the federal government had finally adopted a formal code regulating mining rights—a code that required many subsequent revisions—and the Homestead Act was attracting increasing numbers. In 1863 slightly more than eight thousand persons took out homesteads, a large number of new farms to start within one year. At the end of 1867—the year the Central Pacific weathered the storms at the summit of the Sierra Nevada— that rate had doubled to almost seventeen thousand and was still rising, and it approximately doubled again in the next four years. Although many of the homesteads were east of the Rockies, the movement filled up many of the once-empty places farther west. The ghosts of the mountain men, carrying their rifles and beaver traps, were being pushed off the trails by men with ploughs and domestic livestock, not to say perhaps a wife and children as well.

As the land west of the Rockies increased in population, the need for formal government became greater. In 1868, Congress created Wyoming Territory. This filled the last void. The entire area was now composed of states or territories.

Another change was the type of man who held power in the West. Formerly John Sutter had wrestled with the land and built a "fort." Many of his men went armed against bandits, Indians, and others who might break the public peace. His was almost a feudal fief with himself as overlord and in direct control of the activities in which his fortune was based. Sutter was gone now; the influx of people for which he had always hoped had literally pushed him off his land.

His place had been taken, in large part, by the bankers and financiers. Asbury Harpending did not open new trails through the mountains or trade with Indians. He speculated in land in San Francisco, happy when he could buy a piece of property for $150,000 instead of the $300,000 he was prepared to pay and proud of his part in developing the area around Market Street.

One of his friends and associates was William C. Ralston, who founded the Bank of California and used it as the center of his many activities, which included gaining control of the Comstock by foreclosing on mortgages his bank had made. Personable and quick-witted, he was always willing to finance a new venture if he thought he could make a profit from it. His enterprises ran from a watch factory to the most sumptuous hotel in San Francisco, from real estate to manufacturing furniture and helping the Big Four of the Central Pacific. (In dealing with them, however, he found they knew more tricks than he did.) In all his activities, he was the promoter, the planner, the financier, not the actual manager. Twenty years previously his counterpart could only have been found east of the Missouri. In the end, Ralston's many ventures collapsed, and he died shortly afterward, perhaps a suicide. But although he was one of the more flamboyant of his type, there were now many others like him in the West that was leaving its youth behind.

Books and articles had been written about the West. Most of them had been personal records such as diaries and journals, reports similar to those prepared by Frémont and Wilkes, or promotional tracts like those of Kelley and Hastings; but, with the exception of Washington Irving years before, few had regarded the area as a topic for literature. That, too, was changing. Whereas at first the reading public's desire had been for information, some of the inhabitants of the Far West now began to realize that their lives were different, set apart from those of people in other parts of the United States and a fit subject for more imaginative treatment.

Mark Twain, former steamboat pilot, had not yet published *Roughing It,* the story of his days in Virginia City, but had already gained considerable fame with *The Celebrated Jumping Frog of Calaveras County*, which appeared in book form while the Central Pacific was rushing down from the mountains to meet the Union Pacific. Just a year later, Cincinnatus H. ("Joaquin") Miller brought out his first poems, followed in 1869 with a volume that gave him his pen name Joaquin. So romantic that his accounts could not be trusted, he made a success of his eventual appearance in England. People there thought of him as a true frontier poet, forgiving him his most obvious mistakes on the ground that he had had no opportunity to learn better. It made little difference to them whether, according to his own version, he had lived with an Indian princess on the slopes of Mount Shasta, or whether, as seemed more likely, he had shared quarters with an ordinary Indian woman who had rescued him from the jail where he was being held on charges of horse theft. When he returned to the United States, his popularity began to wane, but he had shown that the West could be an inspiration for poetry, even if his own was not of the best.

At the same time, San Francisco's interest in literature was sufficiently great to bring about the establishment of the *Overland Monthly,* a new publication edited by Bret Harte. His experience publishing "The Luck of Roaring Camp" indicated that San Francisco was no longer a frontier city of uncontrolled tastes but a center of conservative prudery. As editor, Harte sent his rather sentimental story directly to the printer and was surprised when he was later called into his publisher's office.

"The Luck" was a baby born in a mining camp, a baby of obviously illegitimate birth but winning ways who turned the community of hardened miners into a collection of bewhiskered nursemaids. That "The Luck" died in sad circumstances and his illegitimacy was only incidental to the tale made no difference to the publisher's feelings. The printer, as Harte said later, was so shocked that he sent the proofs directly to the publisher "with the emphatic declaration that the matter thereof was so indecent, irreligious, and improper that his proof-reader—a young lady—had with difficulty been induced to continue its perusal, and that he, as a friend of the publisher and a well-wisher of the magazine, was impelled to present to him personally this shameless evidence of the manner in which the editor was imperilling the future of the enterprise."

Harte naturally objected to the deletion of the story from the magazine, and the fair-minded publisher submitted the proofs to others to read. The majority also condemned it; but a final jury composed of three men whose judgment the publisher particularly trusted could not reach an agreement. So he yielded to Harte as editor and permitted him to let the story appear.

"The secular press, with one or two exceptions, received it coolly," Harte later recalled, "and referred to its 'singularity'; the religious press frantically excommunicated it, and anathematized it as the off-spring of evil; the high promise of the 'Overland Monthly' was said to have been ruined at its birth; Christians were cautioned against pollution by its contact; practical business men were gravely urged to condemn and frown down upon this picture of California society that was not conducive to Eastern immigration; its hapless author was held up to obloquy as a man who had abused a sacred trust."

Outside California the reaction was different. The publishers of the *Atlantic Monthly* wrote and asked if "the author of 'The Luck of Roaring Camp'"—they did not know his name—would send them a similar story for publication. And other letters arrived expressing the readers' enthusiasm for the tale. These so encouraged Harte that he wrote more stories, "swelling," to use his own words, "these records of a picturesque passing civilization." One of the keystones of his success was his consciousness that the West he had known was a "picturesque passing civilization." It now needed not a reporter but a memorialist of its ancient glory.

The year that Bret Harte was struggling with San Francisco's censorious readers, another writer arrived in California. John Muir had proved himself a practical businessman and a competent inventor, but an industrial accident blinded him permanently in one eye and temporarily in the other. During his period of total blindness, he reconsidered his career and vowed to himself that if he regained partial sight, he would use it to look at the wonders of nature. In California, he almost at once made a trip by foot through the San Joaquin Valley and up the Merced River to Yosemite. Thus began a relationship between the man and the valley that lasted for approximately half a century.

Muir did not immediately start writing. Instead—between the jobs that supported him, for he was a practical man—he began to make the careful observations he later turned into forceful arguments for the preservation of the Yosemite and other wild and beautiful parts of the West. When the state of California proved an indifferent trustee of the valley Congress had given it as a "reservation," Muir became the leading influence in the establishment of the Yosemite National Park and voiced opinions on the preservation of the wilderness that have remained influential for decades after his death. But his coming, too, was a signal that the Old West, brash and arrogant, was yielding to new influences.

Muir was not alone. John Wesley Powell, on the staff of the Illinois State Normal University, had taken an interest in the scientific exploration of his country. Physically he was ill-equipped to carry out his ideas, for he had lost one arm in the Civil War, and the places he wanted to go required rugged traveling. But Powell did not let his handicap deter him.

In 1869 he journeyed down the Colorado River, seeing sights that had never been observed by a white man and gaining a sense of the land that few others possessed. In 1871, he repeated the river voyage and in his first popular reports combined the two journeys in order to make them more dramatic. For Powell wanted to stir the public's interest in its own land.

When Congress created the United States Geological Survey, largely at Powell's urging, he logically became its first head.

Others, starting with Lewis and Clark, had been financed by the government to explore the land and, in effect, catalogue its contents. Powell's mission was to assess it. One of his many contributions was an evaluation of the aridity of large sections of the West and its relation to the 160-acre limit on homesteads. What Powell collected was the knowledge essential to the nation's wise use of its resources; and if it has not succeeded as well as many would desire, Powell prevented it from doing worse. The work done by men like him and Muir was, however, unspectacular. The eyes of the majority were hypnotized by one of the most flamboyant races in the history of the country.

When Congress amended its previous railroad acts and provided that the Central Pacific and the Union Pacific would end wherever they met, it sent both companies into a spasm of activity. The prize for speed was high. Each additional mile of track represented more government subsidies and longer runs when the track was completed. To the Central Pacific, the prospect was especially alluring. It had finished building the most difficult and expensive part of its line, the section crossing the Sierra Nevada, and ahead of it now lay easier terrain. The Big Four had done well financially in the towering mountains; they could do even better for themselves over the flatter desert country. Their surveying crews were soon working far beyond their railhead and were talking to Brigham Young about hiring men to continue the survey east beyond Salt Lake City.

The Union Pacific had its surveyors out, too. They were busy in Nevada, while the grades that had been prepared were hundreds of miles behind them and the end of the tracks even farther back. This was obviously a wasteful operation, for sometimes the crews were working parallel to each other, duplicating each other's efforts.

Behind the surveyors and the men who did the grading came those who laid the rails, also working with remarkable speed. A reporter from the San Francisco *Alta California* wrote a report describing the scene on a day the men were trying to set a record. "See that car loaded with iron coming up the track," he wrote. "It is wheeled along by a pair of horses. . . . They are met by another car of similar pattern coming down, after leaving its load at the front. The latter is bowled along (for the grade descends) by the men on each side, using their feet like oars. Surely this must be *contretemps* for vehicles which cannot pass on a single track—but stop—the down platform car is stopped in an instant, it is lifted up, standing on the edge, and the loaded car passes on to the front. . . ."

There the horses were released to dash back for the next load—no time was to be lost—while four men grabbed the rails and laid them over the ties that had already been put in place. Another crew placed the spikes in position and bolted each rail to the one behind it. A gang of Chinese followed close behind. They drove the spikes home and added others; and as they moved on, their places were taken by another squad of Chinese, half of whom had picks and the other half shovels. Those with picks loosened a small amount of earth; those with shovels used the dirt to bury the ends of the ties. While he watched, the reporter for the *Alta California* timed the men. They laid 240 feet of rail in a minute and twenty seconds or, as he commented, at about the same pace as the earlier ox teams had crossed the continent.

The magnitude of the task could be measured in terms of the mass of material that had to be handled. A mile of completed track required two hundred tons of rails and ten tons of spikes. Once a locomotive had deposited this at the railhead for transfer to the horse-drawn cars, all this material was moved entirely by men and horses. Where the roadbed curved, the process slowed, because the men had to lay the rails on blocks and beat them with hammers into the necessary bend.

To keep going, the support services had to be on a similar scale. On a dirt road to the right of the track was a parade of wagons carrying the ties. A similar road on the left was filled with the all-important water carts and wagons carrying tools. In addition, the twelve to fourteen hundred working-men had to be fed and housed. A train of cars with wooden bunkhouses and kitchens came up at the close of the day and formed what amounted to a movable village for the night. The following morning the process began again.

The race for mileage got completely out of control, as neither railroad showed any sign of being willing to give in to the other. Although the government would obviously pay only one subsidy if the tracks ran alongside each other, the managements of both companies kept rushing forward in an incredible waste of money that endangered the future of the loser. Ulysses S. Grant, who had just become president, saw he must intervene. Huntington had become skillful in dealing with the government; but the Union Pacific had the advantage, its chief engineer being a former general and a friend of Grant. The companies could either settle the issue themselves, Grant told him, or he himself would settle it for them. In April 1869, Congress confirmed their agreement to meet at Promontory Point in Utah. Immediately the race slackened, extra men were laid off, and the two companies began to resume construction at their more normal speed.

Early in May, several special trains, operated for the occasion by the Central Pacific, arrived at the railhead to take part in the scheduled ceremonies marking the joining of the rails. But the passengers found only a miserable, temporary village, sodden in a late spring rain, with no signs of the expected dignitaries from the Union Pacific who had left Omaha. By telegraph they sent word they had been delayed by a storm to the east, which had created floods and washouts. Furthermore, the Union Pacific was having difficulty keeping some of its men at work, for it was running out of cash. While they waited, Leland Stanford had his Central Pacific train pulled back, and his guests looked around for ways to amuse themselves.

The Central Pacific train had arrived on May 7, 1869. Now the final ceremonies were postponed until May 10, a day that broke with the weather so cold the water froze in the pails. Still there was no sign of the dignitaries from the Union Pacific. Noon passed, and the rails on the eastern side of the gap in the tracks remained empty. Finally in the middle of the afternoon, the waiting crowd of workmen and Central Pacific officials heard a locomotive in the distance. It pushed a Pullman car into place, and the leading officer of the Union Pacific Railroad descended the steps. The ceremony was ready to begin.

A specially selected crew brought the last rail forward and laid it on the ties, the final tie being made of California laurel with silver plates bearing the names of the management of both companies. The telegraph company had an operator on hand to report the final proceedings, and while he waited with the line cleared all the way through to both coasts, a minister delivered the benediction. Then came the presentation of special spikes donated by Arizona, Idaho, and other Western areas, all of them symbolizing the mineral resources of their donors, mostly gold and silver. The presentation of each one required a speech.

When these were done, the final spike—made from California gold—was placed into the predrilled guide hole, and Leland Stanford picked up the silver mallet with which he was to drive it into place. He swung—and missed. Then came the turn of the leading representative of the Union Pacific. He was no more skilled than Stanford, for he, too, swung, and missed. Several engineers stepped forward and gently tapped the spike into place, while the telegraph operator sent the news across the nation. The transcontinental railroad, over which so many people had dreamed and fought and argued for years, was a reality. Passengers could now travel by rail from the Atlantic to the Pacific by train, and the day of the oxen was over. Their sturdy shoulders had moved a nation thousands of miles westward, but their place was taken by locomotives. Instead of dust rising above the trail, a line of smoke marked the

354

westward passage of the travelers; and what once took weeks to accomplish now required only a few days.

The news not only engrossed the nation's attention; Europe, too, was deeply interested, and the London *Daily News* sent a reporter, William F. Rae, to make the trip across the continent. Although much was said of through transportation to California, such service did not exist. The soft soil near the Missouri River had made it impossible for the engineers to find adequate footings for a bridge, so travelers were forced to cross the river by boat.

On boarding the train at Omaha, Rae began talking to his fellow passengers. "To nearly every one the journey is a new one," he said, "partaking of the character of a daring enterprise. Some who profess to be well informed mis-spend their time in endeavors to excite the fears of the timid and the apprehensions of the excitable. They enlarge on the dangers incident to a line constructed too hurriedly. They draw ghastly pictures to be faced in the event of wild Indians putting obstructions in the way of the train, and attacking the passengers."

At Promontory Point, he noticed the results of the two companies' competitive race and how they had carried their lines beyond their present terminal points. "These unfinished roadways," he said, "are still to be seen side by side with the completed line. As one result of the disagreement, there are few through trains [even from Omaha]. In general the passengers have to change carriages, secure fresh sleeping berths, and get their luggage moved from one train to the other."

The switch to the Central Pacific was not an improvement. Instead of Pullman cars, the Central Pacific had "what it calls 'silver palace cars,' of which the name is the best part." The service on these was poor, and the attendants rude. Through at least part of Utah, the alkali dust from the surrounding desert filled the cars, burning the throats of the passengers; and at one point, they were stopped for eight hours when the train ran into a herd of cattle and the locomotive was thrown from the rails. But Rae marveled at what the builders had accomplished, laying their rails through a wilderness of arid areas and high mountains, covering part of the track with snow sheds that blocked the view but made the trains able to move during the heavy winter storms. And even though the railhead still stopped short of San Francisco and most of the passengers traveled the last few miles across the bay by boat, and even though the schedule was somewhat erratic, he considered the transcontinental railroad one of the three great achievements of the time, the other two being the Suez Canal and the Atlantic cable.

Yet the outward appearance of both railroads was misleading. The tracks would support the trains, but not for long. Many of the grades were poor, the ballast badly laid, and the trestles so weak they soon had to be replaced. The construction companies, in each case dominated by the railroads' insiders, had made a maximum of profit and done a minimum of work, just enough to make it possible for the trains to run and to satisfy the government's minimum requirements.

Financially both companies were little more than hollow shells. Congress had intended to set them up so they could finish the construction and be healthy concerns able to maintain a good service. But the subsidies it had provided were in the pockets of the promoters, not in the railroads' treasuries. In fact, many of the original investors in the Union Pacific had already taken steps to get rid of their stock, knowing it was almost worthless.

The Big Four were not as astute and held on to their Central Pacific certificates too long. All of them were wealthy, but their wealth was composed of what they had made building the railroad, not their ownership of its track and rolling stock. The American people at last had their transcontinental railroad, but they should have had a better railroad more cheaply.

31. After the Railroad

Said the Union: "Don't reflect, or
I'll run over some Director."
Said the Central: "I'm Pacific;
But when riled, I'm quite terrific."

—Bret Harte,
"What the Engines Said," 1882

The West was already changing before the completion of the first transcontinental railroad, and the trains puffing from the Missouri River across the
deserts and plains to the West hastened the process. Even the management of
the railroads themselves had changed. No longer primarily concerned with
the construction of the tracks, they had become "big business" in the crudest
sense of nineteenth-century America. While romance might ride with the
engineer or sweat with the tough crews at the railheads, the power—and the

money—was to be found in the board rooms and among the security dealers.

The profits were made not by building and running a good railroad but by buying and selling shares, securing transportation monopolies, picking up key routes that another company might want, and promoting stocks and bonds. Jim Bridger and Kit Carson could deal with the wiliest Indians, but they would have been as helpless doing business with a railroad tycoon as the tycoon would have been trapping beavers under the eyes of hostile Blackfeet.

Through their construction contracts, the Big Four had done well by themselves; but now for the first time, their limited experience as small-town businessmen told against them. If they had been more familiar with the men who occupied the offices on Boston's State Street or in New York's financial district, they would have realized that their secrets were not well hidden. Almost every serious investor knew the four men had drained the company. And those handsomely engraved stock certificates were almost worthless on the security markets. To make a profit on their holdings the Big Four should have sold out much sooner. But not being men to lament over lost opportunities, they set about restoring value to their shares by acquiring additional properties.

California was the place they knew best. There they were friendly with the bankers, had great influence in politics, and understood the people and the markets. Unlike the easterners who ventured far from home to invest in western railroads, the Big Four wisely stuck to the land with which they were familiar. In a series of well-coordinated steps, they ran the Central Pacific's tracks from Sacramento to San Francisco, so no one could undercut them in that major metropolis; they gained control of the principal terminals and wharves, linking their railroad directly to the maritime commerce of the port; and by buying up the Southern Pacific of California, a state-charted railroad, they began to gain control of central California's business. They expanded their original empire out of adversity.

Wells, Fargo and Company, which had been purchasing one stagecoach line after another, including the central route, realized its monopoly of passenger transportation was ending and began concentrating on its express business. Even before the last spike was in place, it started selling off its lines. Usually the buyer was a former employee, and the prices were reasonable. Wells, Fargo and Company, however, generally inserted a standard condition into the terms of sale: For at least a year, the new owner could not make express deliveries or carry gold or silver for anyone but the company. Stagecoaches might be disappearing, but the company's directors realized there would still be a demand for express service and for the equivalent of today's armored car trade.

In California, the merchants found the immediate results of the railroad's completion disappointing. Instead of opening up the markets of the East to them and thus increasing their incomes, it cut transportation costs and reduced the price of many articles sold in California. Their profits dropped, although in time the increased number of emigrants brought some of them prosperity.

In 1869, the year the railroad was completed, California's frontier days were gone, its days of cultured sophistication still to come. Those who had arrived in 1849, only twenty years before, called themselves the "pioneers" and were regarded as a separate and distinguished group. But the British journalist, Rae, noted that few, if any, of California's new millionaires had learned the obligations of having money. They might be generous in their hospitality to their friends, particularly in buying drinks, but they had no sense of philanthropy. As a specific example, Rae cited the difficulty of finding financial support for a public library. Huntington could have served him as another example. Although his fortune was in the millions, his total gifts during his lifetime amounted to only a few thousands; and on his death, his will provided only for his family.

Rae believed the railroad in time would break down the Westerners' insularity. "Their comparative isolation," he said, "has led to the growth of a local pride hardly justified by facts and not deserving of admiration. The young men who left their homes in the Eastern States twenty years ago, and are now wealthy citizens of California, have remained practically ignorant of the changes which, during that long interval, have been wrought in the cities of their birth. They have not known that progress has moved with gigantic strides in New York, St. Louis, and Chicago as well as San Francisco and Sacramento. They compare what they see around them with what they imagine to exist elsewhere and they glory in their achievements."

Even without the railroad, the Westerners were being carried into the mainstream of American life. The legal case of a Chinese illustrated the point. Involved in a criminal proceeding, the federal judge before whom he appeared ruled that under the Sixteenth Amendment to the Constitution, which had been adopted to provide equal rights for blacks, he could testify in his own behalf. Until then, Chinese had not been permitted to serve as witnesses. In winning freedom for the blacks of the South, the Union had also won it for the Chinese of the West, for the West was not exempt from the social progress taking place elsewhere in the country.

Even without the influences of the courts and the railroad, the West could no longer remain outside the orbit of national affairs. During the days of the fur trade, fluctuations in the market obviously affected the prices of skins and the amount of credit the companies could secure. But the influences had been rather remote. Even the Civil War had left much of the West untouched. But in 1869 when the New York speculator Jay Gould tried to corner the gold market, he also nearly destroyed the banking system on the far side of the Rockies.

As Gould drove up its price, gold began to leave the West in large amounts, and the banks grew short of the specie needed to pay their depositors' withdrawals. Ralston, who ran the Bank of California, had just lent a large sum to the Central Pacific and his reserves were depleted. In his vaults was a quantity of gold bars, but government policy prohibited his exchanging these for gold currency at the subtreasury in San Francisco.

Rumors began to float through San Francisco that the bank—and others— were insolvent. When the rumors were at their height, Ralston called two friends into his office, explained the situation to them, and asked them to come to the bank at one o'clock in the morning. He advised them to dress in old clothes because they would have plenty of hard physical work to do.

As the streets of San Francisco lay deserted and dark except in those sections of the city where the saloons and gambling halls remained open and prostitutes still plied their business, the two men met Ralston along with another trusted bank employee. Ralston and his two friends walked to the subtreasury on Montgomery Street. The building was dark except for one faint light still burning inside. While his two friends waited, Ralston opened the unlocked door and disappeared, only to reappear shortly with several sacks of coins. These he asked his helpers to carry back to the Bank of California where they would receive "something" in exchange. The "something" proved to be bar of gold, which the trusted employee had removed from the bank's vaults and had waiting.

Down the black streets went the two men, carrying their burden to the subtreasury. Ralston was waiting at the door with more sacks of coins. Back went the faithful two with their new loads. Once more the bank employee counted out the value and gave them gold bars of equal worth in return. As the night wore on, the two men traipsed back and forth, growing exhausted under the weights they were carrying but unobserved by passing strangers.

When the depositors began to appear the next morning in anticipation of a run on the bank, Ralston brought out the bags he had collected the night before and in a loud voice instructed his tellers to pay everyone who wished to withdraw their money. At this assurance that their funds were safe, the crowd melted away, but another crowd had been forming at a neighboring bank.

Ralston entered its lobby, climbed on a box so he could be seen and heard, and announced that the Bank of California had plenty of cash on hand and if they would just step over to its office, it would honor any withdrawals they wished to make. The crowd, convinced that Ralston meant what he said, dispersed. A few days later Gould's corner collapsed, the price of gold sank, and conditions returned more nearly to normal. Ralston's helpers that dark night never learned what arrangements he had made with his friends in the subtreasury, whether he had bribed them or whether they had merely shared his concern for the California banking system. In any case, he had acted with ingenuity and audacity. But above all the incident demonstrated clearly how

360

dependent the western banking system, whose center was at San Francisco, had become on events taking place on the other side of the continent.

Even the owners of the railroads found themselves somewhat surprised by the form their business took after the track was completed. Originally they had expected the enormous trade between Europe and the Far East to come to the Atlantic Coast, be transshipped by rail to the West, and then go by ship across the Pacific. Every figure showed this would be the most economical way of sending goods back and forth. But six months after the last tie was laid, the Suez Canal opened. By obviating the long journey around Africa, it made the use of the railroad impractical. On the other hand, the rise in emigration and permanent population was greater than the promoters had expected.

In 1871 the number of those taking up land under the Homestead Act rose to a new high of almost forty thousand. Out of a total population of forty million people, this appears small, but compared with the population of parts of the West, it was enormous. If each homestead supported a man, his wife, and three children, the resulting total was greater than the populations of Montana, Idaho, Wyoming, Arizona, and Washington combined, although, of course, not all of the homesteads were west of the Rocky Mountains. The federal government was also continuing to sell land as well as giving it away. In 1870 it offered for sale more than a million and a half acres in New Mexico alone. A further stimulation to settlement was the sale of the scrip that had been issued under the Morrill Act for the encouragement of education. This gave settlers an additional way to acquire acreage.

With experience, Congress was taking a somewhat sterner view of the manner in which the public lands were being distributed. In 1870 it passed the Hollman Resolution, which urged that the lands be held for actual home-steaders and that grants to railroads should be discontinued. It also became slowly aware of the many abuses taking place under the existing laws and the way in which they were being administered. One of the biggest loopholes for the unscrupulous was the preemption provision, which provided that settlers who had moved onto land before it was surveyed retained first rights to its ownership. This was intended to prevent pioneer families from being ejected from acres they had taken up on the fringe of the frontier, acres that had required all their strength and ingenuity to defend from the Indians and from nature.

When members of a government commission later visited the redwood forests of California, they "saw little huts or kennels built of 'shakes' that were totally unfit for human habitations . . . which were the sole improvements made under the homestead and pre-emption laws, and by means of which large areas of red-wood forests . . . had been taken under pretenses of settlement and cultivation." Wasteful as they were, however, the public land laws were encouraging further emigration to the West and pushing the frontier back from the fertile, watered valleys into the mountains and deserts, where living was more difficult.

With the increased population came more civilization and a greater interest in the West both as a place and as an aspect of American life. Women, too, were becoming more numerous and more influential. They did not hold the public offices or head the vigilante committees, but their opinions carried weight and, again and again, they were the ones entrusted with the education of the next generation, a task for which most of the men considered themselves unsuited. So important were women that in 1871 the citizens of Idaho seriously debated giving them the vote. The measure failed to pass only by a tie. Wyoming, Montana, and Utah were other places in the West that early began the process of enfranchising women, and California had already given them property rights. This was taking place a half century before the Constitution was amended to give them the vote and reflected the progressive spirit that was evident in a part of the country that was closer to its frontier days.

Violence, however, had not disappeared. Wherever wealth lay unprotected, whether in herds of cattle roaming the mountains or in gold bars carried on a stagecoach, crime was likely to be present. Even in the best of circumstances, law enforcement was handicapped by the lack of equipment and training that was characteristic of the most advanced police departments of the time. In addition, the western officer often suffered from poor communications, vast distances, and, in sparsely populated areas, lack of assistance. The crime rate in many communities was not high when compared with other places with a predominantly young male population. But the nature of the country often made the struggle between an officer and a criminal a man-to-man struggle. Thus sprang up many tales that provided material for historians and novelists alike and that have become a vital part of the West's tradition.

In at least one instance, violence broke out in its ugliest form within what had become a major city, a scene far removed from the lonely trails down which legendary sheriffs pursued their suspects. In 1871, the year in which Idaho considered the progressive move of establishing woman suffrage, two Chinese factions started fighting in Los Angeles. A policeman, assisted by a prominent citizen who had been standing nearby, tried to intervene. A shot from a building wounded the citizen, who died shortly after.

News of his death spread through the city, and soon an angry mob had gathered. The magnificent work of the Chinese in building the Central Pacific Railroad had not improved their general reputation as mysterious aliens given to opium smoking and underhanded dealings. The crowd, angry and determined, broke into the building from which the shot had been fired and captured eight Chinese.

Most vigilante actions in the West were marked with some respect for justice; this was not. Only one shot had been involved, but the crowd held eight prisoners. Obviously only one of the eight could have committed the killing, but the crowd made no effort to determine his identity. They set about beating and kicking all their prisoners, tied ropes around their necks, and marched them to a corral. The wooden stringer holding the posts of the gate together seemed like an appropriate gallows. Within a few minutes, the eight Chinese were dead.

The night's horrors were not over. Looters began breaking into the Chinese houses, for many Chinese were reputed to be rich. The crowd seized any person who interfered with their orgy of pillaging, killing some nineteen additional Chinese before dawn broke and the city's more respectable and law-abiding elements had restored order. The incident received wide publicity across the nation, and many expressed horror at the behavior of the people of Los Angeles. The event, however, was not typical of the West or inherent in the frontier. It might have occurred in any race-conscious city, however "civilized."

But violence more directly associated with the frontier had not yet disappeared. Even with more settlers, a transcontinental railroad, and army posts established over much of the area, the United States had not yet gained undisputed control of the land west of the Rockies. For many of the Indians had not finally surrendered.

In some places they were quiescent, abiding by the white men's rules unless they were pushed too far. In others they were still the masters of their old lands, able to ride where they wanted and still terrorizing the countryside. This was especially true in Arizona, where the Apaches had not been conquered. To handle the problem, one of the toughest military tasks of the day, the army assigned an unassuming general, a man who eschewed military display and dress uniforms, but was one of its most relentless fighters.

The arrival in Tucson of General George Crook was attended by no ceremony. He had quietly slipped out of San Francisco, where he had been stationed, and even the driver of the stagecoach on which he traveled did not know he was taking over a new command. Once in the city, he wasted no time on formalities but began talking to the better-informed citizens in an effort to assess the situation. It was not good.

As the Spanish had learned hundreds of years before, the Apaches were unusual enemies. Their physical endurance was almost unbelievable. They could outwalk and outride almost any white man, including the toughest of pioneers. They lived off the country even in the desert, traveling light and fast, and they had no stocks of supplies that could be attacked and destroyed. Since they rarely congregated in large numbers, each battle involved only a few of their warriors. Except when they were cornered, they would not fight unless they had the advantage, simply melting away, and the most astute commanders had trouble finding their trails and, if they did, could not keep pace with them. In a battle, they were deadly. They wore no headdresses or other ornaments that made them easy to see; they could find hiding places where no other person—white or red—would have believed one existed; and they were extremely courageous and determined, fearing little and bowing to no one.

To complicate Crook's problem, the whole nation was in an uproar over the Apache question at that moment. A large number of Aravaipa Apaches had informally surrendered to Lieutenant Royal Whitman at Camp Grant in Arizona and refused to move anywhere else, preferring to remain under Whitman's protection. In the absence of specific orders from the army, Whitman did the best he could, finding areas in which they could live and occasionally soliciting jobs for them among the neighboring white men. Except for the burdensome responsibility on Whitman, the arrangement worked out well until a group of Tucson residents, angry over the repeated raids of other Apaches, decided to avenge themselves. The Apaches they could locate the most easily were those living near Camp Grant; and so, drawing guns from the territorial arsenal, they headed in that direction.

The Aravaipa Apaches, although they had no formal agreement with the government, thought they had made peace, and therefore they had posted no lookouts. The men from Tucson were able to approach their *rancherías* undetected in the night; and when they opened fire, the slaughter was ghastly. Women and children were killed indiscriminately with the warriors, and those few Apaches fortunate enough to escape vowed never to trust the Americans again.

Many persons, particularly among those living west of the Rockies, thought the citizens of Tucson had done the right thing. Like Carleton earlier, they believed there would be no peace until the Indians were exterminated. East of the Rockies the prevailing reaction was one of horror. All those who sympathized with the Indians generally—and there were many who did—regarded this as another example of American perfidy and a good reason for overhauling American policy. Crook's arrival in Arizona came when this domestic controversy was at its height.

Outwardly at least, he did not let it bother him. He had a job to do and set about performing it. Realizing that Mexicans understood the Apaches better than the Americans, he employed a group of fifty of them as scouts and marched through the Apaches' country in the hope that some of them would resist him. But, as they usually did at the sight of a large force, the Apaches avoided a battle. At the end of the march, however, Crook came to the conclusion that while the Mexicans made good scouts, Apaches themselves would be even more effective and began enlisting them from among those who had already gone on the reservation.

They were to be the keystone of Crook's strategy. No commander had succeeded in defeating the Apaches with West Point tactics, so he planned to fight them the way they themselves fought. Many people questioned how he was able to enroll Indians to wage war against their fellows. But many reservation Apaches were convinced some sort of peace had to be made with the white men and the sooner the better. They were not only willing to help, they were glad to return to the life they knew so well—days spent under the desert sun, nights by their campfires or traveling through the mountains, the constant danger, the surprise attack. This was an improvement over sitting on a reservation with little to do, particularly as Crook chose the white commanders of the scouts with the greatest of care, selecting men who sympathized with their ways and at least partially matched them in endurance.

Before he could continue his campaign, however, he noticed in the newspapers a report that Washington was sending out another representative to treat with the Apaches and other Indians, a Quaker artist named Vincent Colyer. Ulysses S. Grant, being a man of war, knew its horrors as well as anyone. He was also a man of personal integrity and was appalled at the corruption that marked many of the government's dealings with the Indians. More than one Indian agent made a small fortune out of the contracts he was supposed to supervise, and so Grant decided to place the various tribes under the patronage of different churches. This would eliminate the graft, he thought. At the same time he hoped that men of goodwill might persuade the Indians to make peace even if others had failed.

Crook was disgusted with the news of Colyer's arrival. He, too, was a man of great integrity. Corrupt Indian agents angered him just as they angered Grant, and, like Grant, he wished to avoid warfare whenever possible. But he also believed Indians like the Apaches would never live peacefully on a reservation until they had been pursued and defeated in the field. But with Colyer active in the Southwest, he thought he should suspend his operations and see what the Quaker could accomplish.

Colyer was a man of justice, but he had no experience with Indians and little time to complete his assignment. At Santa Fé, he learned some citizens intended to emulate the people of Tucson and launch an attack on the Warm Springs Apaches who were already on a reservation. He therefore ordered a new reservation prepared for them, although he did not understand that the Warm Springs Apaches could not adapt to the geography and climate of the place he had chosen.

He set up another reservation at Camp Apache in Arizona for other Apaches who had surrendered. He then went to Camp Grant, where he met with some of the Aravaipa Apaches who had finally returned. His idealism was evident, and their leader said he was such a good man he could not have been born of mortal parents. When Crook heard this statement, he decided Colyer was not only foolish but gullible; and when he finally met Colyer personally, the Quaker failed to make the general change his mind. Then

Colyer was gone, his assignment being merely temporary, and Crook again had the field to himself.

Given the amount of time in which he had to work and his lack of permanent authority, Colyer had done about as well as anybody could have, but shortly after his departure, Indians attacked a stage near Wickenburg, Arizona, and killed six Americans. Once again the West was in an uproar, demanding firmer punishment for all Indians; and the government gave Crook greater powers to deal with them as he wished. In December 1871, he issued an order that all Indians must be on a reservation by February 15 of the coming year or face severe punishment.

Before he could start his campaign to round up those who had not obeyed, the government in Washington once more changed its mind. Instead of supporting Crook's aggressive policy, it sent out another peace commissioner, General Oliver Otis Howard, a one-armed veteran of the Civil War. In recent years, he had concerned himself with the well-being of the freed blacks and was now glad to help resolve the Indian question. Quite pompous and somewhat conceited, he was nevertheless a man of great personal courage and, like Colyer, motivated by goodwill and a Christian sense of his responsibility to all humans.

One of his first official acts was to visit the Aravaipa Apaches at Camp Grant, where he opened his council with the Indians by dropping on his knees and starting to pray. This so startled the Apaches, who thought he might be casting a curse on them, that they fled. It took time and tact to persuade them to reassemble. After talking to them, Howard established the San Carlos reservation on the Gila River in Arizona and sent them to live there. After making a few other arrangements, he returned to Washington, taking with him several Apache leaders, it being the belief of the government that the sight of the East's great cities would so impress the Indians they would no longer dare to fight.

In August 1872, Howard was back in Arizona. First he settled the unrest that had arisen among the Warm Springs Apaches by moving them back to the reservation from which Colyer had taken them. His next mission was to make peace with Cochise and the Chiracahuas. No bureaucrat in Washington could have devised a more difficult task. Fort Bowie, the post established by Carleton, still stood at Apache Pass, keeping the route open and maintaining a semblance of order in the immediate vicinity. But Cochise himself was as free—and as elusive—as he had been when he was fighting Bascom and no more inclined to trust any American. No one knew where he was, much less how to reach him to hold a council. The only signs of his presence were the bodies and burning wagons that remained after one of his raids.

Howard talked to the few reservation Indians and the one or two white men who had known him. They agreed to help find the Apache leader, but they insisted Howard must take no soldiers with him. Cochise had a deep hatred for troops, and if any appeared, he would either attack or, if he thought the odds were against him, flee. Thus it was that Howard finally entered Cochise's stronghold in the Dragoon Mountains of Arizona, accompanied only by his aide, a white man named Thomas Jeffords, whom Cochise trusted, and two friendly Apaches. It was an act that called for the highest personal courage.

When Howard reached the Apaches' camp, only women and children remained. The warriors had all left—a bad sign, for it could only mean the men were prepared for war. Nevertheless he spent the night there, outwardly calm enough to play with some of the children, inwardly wondering whether he would be alive when the sun broke over the horizon.

The following morning, he was not only alive; Cochise appeared to talk with him. The two Apaches who had come with Howard vouched for the general's honesty, as did Jeffords. Cochise agreed to gather the Chiracahua warriors for a council, provided Howard assured him no soldiers would attack them when they were assembling. Howard himself rode to Fort Bowie and told the commander he was to permit the Apaches to move freely. For those who did not trust Indians, this was a difficult order to follow, but Howard had Grant's authority behind him.

During their council with Howard, the Chiracahuas agreed to go on a reservation, but they insisted on several conditions: The site for the reservation must include the Dragoon Mountains and the broad valley that extended in the direction of Apache Pass; Jeffords must be the Indian agent in charge; and no troops should be stationed within the reservation or interfere in any way in its affairs. Such an arrangement was far too favorable to the Indians, many argued. Under its terms, the Indians would receive government rations and a refuge. Yet they would be free to come and go as they pleased, for there was no way to check on their movements. To some this was worse than having no agreement with them at all.

These people underestimated Cochise's good faith and the willingness of the Chiracahuas to follow his leadership. The raids did not completely stop. Cochise could not discipline every Apache remaining in the Southwest, particularly those who had not been parties to the agreement. Nor could he exercise complete authority over those who had, any more than a white official could guarantee the good behavior of every American. But the system set up by Howard worked, the raids became substantially fewer, and Crook's role was reduced from policy-maker to policeman.

The country of the Apaches was not the only part of the land west of the Rockies to remain outside the control of the United States government. For some time the Modoc Indians of northern California had presented another unsolved problem. As more settlers moved west, the Modocs were placed on the Klamaths' reservation in southern Oregon, a step designed to avoid the expense of an additional agency but one that was utterly impractical. The reservation was too small for two tribes, and furthermore the Klamaths and the Modocs were traditional enemies.

In 1870, an Indian leader named Captain Jack left the reservation and, with approximately four hundred Modocs, returned to the lands that had once belonged to his tribe. Inevitably conflicts between his people and the settlers began to occur, and the government started negotiations for his return to the reservation.

When these failed, troops were sent in 1872 to force Captain Jack's surrender. The commander entered the Modocs' village, shots broke the quiet, and the small detachment of soldiers retreated before the superior number of Indians. Realizing that more soldiers would come to avenge their fellows, the Modocs also retreated, choosing as their stronghold a place known as the Lava Beds; and on their way, they killed a number of settlers.

Although additional troops were rushed to the area, Grant continued to follow his policy of trying to hold peace councils before declaring war. General Canby, who had fought the Confederates in New Mexico, was then commander of the army's Department of the Pacific. He was chosen to head a commission on which a Methodist minister and an Indian agent and subagent also served.

The Lava Beds were not a place where white men liked to go. Composed of the outpourings of a geological eruption, the rocks were twisted and deformed into strange structures. In places deep ravines ran through them, making it possible for men to move about unseen; and air bubbles in the original lava had created caves in which Indians could hide. For those who knew them, the Lava Beds offered an almost impenetrable stronghold; for those who did not, they could be a deathtrap of ambushes. Nevertheless Canby finally located Captain Jack in the bleak wilderness and, with friendly Indians serving as emissaries, arranged a meeting with him.

On April 11, 1873, the four white men who formed the peace commission met with Captain Jack to discuss possible terms of peace. General Canby brought out some cigars, which he passed around to both the Indians and the Americans. Then the negotiations were ready to start. Suddenly Captain Jack drew a pistol and fired at Canby. The gun failed to go off, but at the sound of the shot other Indians drew their guns and started firing, too. Canby and one other commissioner were killed, one was seriously wounded, but the fourth was able to flee, since he had a small pistol with which he was able to hold off his pursuers.

Many Americans had accused both the Westerners and the soldiers of treachery toward the Indians. Here the case was reversed. Treachery, broken promises, and violence were not restricted to one side. Both Indians and white men shared ignoble, as well as noble, qualities. The reaction of the War Department was immediate. General Sherman, who was then the army's commander, issued orders from Washington to inflict "the most severe punishment" on the Modocs.

Canby's successor in the field was Colonel Alvan C. Gillem. Although he greatly outnumbered the Modocs and was equipped with mortars, he could not locate the Indians among the rocks they knew so well. When he finally discovered their camp, his attack failed. The Indians slipped away, while the Americans suffered several casualties.

In an effort to find the Indians again, Colonel Gillem sent some seventy soldiers and almost twenty friendly Indians on a reconnaissance through the Lava Beds on April 26, 1873. Badly commanded, they advanced without putting out flankers; and when lunchtime came and they had seen no Indians, they rested together in a cluster without first placing sentinels.

Slinking among the rocks, the Modocs drew closer and closer around the target the soldiers presented until they were within easy rifle range. Then they began firing. The echoes of their shots bounced off the rugged rocks as the startled soldiers tried to find their enemy in order to fire back. But the Indians, taking advantage of the natural cover, seemed almost invisible. As many settlers had said, the Lava Beds were no place for a white man.

32. THE DYING FRONTIER

*The work that remains is one of time. A miracle
cannot be performed in the Indian's case.*

—General Nelson A. Miles, 1896

The battle with the Modocs was an unmitigated disaster. When Gillem wrote
his official account, he had to report that three commissioned officers had
been killed, one was missing, and another wounded, as was the assistant
surgeon. They had borne the main burden of the fighting, most of the other
members of the force having fled. Of the enlisted men, thirteen were killed
and sixteen wounded. The majority of these casualties occurred while the
Indians were chasing them through the strange contorted rocks.

General Jefferson C. Davis, Canby's replacement, disliked his name. A
staunch Union supporter during the Civil War and no relation to the
Confederate president, he carefully used his middle initial to differentiate
himself from the South's leader. But when he arrived in California to succeed
Canby as commander of the Department of the Pacific, he found something
to dislike more—the conduct of the enlisted men during the battle with the
Modocs. "The result was conspicuous cowardice on the part of the men who

ran away," he reported. "My recommendation is, however, that they be kept here, trained, and made to fight. I shall take such steps while here as to insure this training."

While the nation expressed amazement that such a large number of soldiers had been unable to capture a relatively small band of Indians, Davis took personal charge of the campaign. Constantly harassed by Davis and running short of ammunition, some of the Modocs advised Captain Jack to surrender; and when he refused to do so, they deserted him. In June 1873, Captain Jack himself realized the end had come. When the soldiers approached him, he made no effort to resist.

Sherman regarded the Modocs as military enemies, not civil insurrectionists, and therefore ordered the court-martial of those Indians who had plotted the murder of Canby. The proceedings were quick. Two Indians were released on the ground they were not principal figures in the shooting of the commissioners. Four others, including Captain Jack, were sentenced to death and hanged in the presence of their tribe.

Although the treatment of Captain Jack seemed brutal, the government was not anti-Indian but was trying to solve the difficult problem of satisfying the settlers, finding places for the Indians to live, and maintaining peace between two cultures that were often incompatible. No man—or group of men—could have succeeded. No wonder the results often seemed contradictory.

While Captain Jack and the Modocs were in revolt against the Americans, Joseph, leader of the Nez Percés was negotiating with them. The area originally occupied by the tribe had included the Wallowa Valley in Oregon, but the valley had been ceded to the Americans several years earlier. Joseph protested he had not been a party to the negotiations and that neither he nor his followers had signed the agreement. A government commission concluded the law was on Joseph's side, so Grant made the valley a reservation and ordered the white settlers to leave. It was a victory, however short-lived, for the Indian cause.

In line with the government's policy of assigning responsibility for the Indian tribes to various religious sects, the Presbyterians were placed in charge of the Nez Percés; and Henry Spalding was sent back to them in his old age. To help him, he had as an assistant one of those extraordinary women who, in their quiet way, did so much to bring civilization to the Far West.

Sue McBeth, a native of Scotland, had previously taught Indians, nursed soldiers during the Civil War, been a missionary in the tough sections of St. Louis, and had joined the staff of a college in Iowa. Now she was willing to give up that relatively secure life to work with the Nez Percés in what were still the remote parts of Idaho. She was disliked by some of the chiefs, because she realized, as they did not, that the old days were disappearing and the

371

Indians would have to learn new skills. But whatever they thought of her, she was a symbol of those members of the white race who made heavy personal sacrifices to benefit the Indians.

The world of the mission, despite the strain of guiding the Indians toward a different mode of life, seemed calm compared to the turmoil into which the rest of the country was thrown that year. Congress investigated the Credit Mobilier, the construction company that had built the Union Pacific, and the revelations undermined the natural optimism of the Americans. They had taken such pride in the completion of the railroad and were shattered to learn they had been defrauded and that even their government could be bribed. The records of the similar construction company set up by the Big Four of the Central Pacific disappeared in a questionable fire, but the flames kindled the suspicion it had not served the public to any better purpose.

To add to the problems of 1873, a financial depression struck Europe. The United States, constantly expanding at a rate faster than its own resources could support, had drawn heavily on capital from across the Atlantic. When Europe could no longer supply it, the uncertain structure of the American economy began to collapse. One of its principal weaknesses had been overspeculation in unprofitable railroads, which required ever larger investments without producing returns. The failure of Jay Cooke's banking house was the signal for the panic to begin. His fall also brought to a halt the construction of the Northern Pacific Railroad, in which he had invested heavily and which had reached Bismarck, North Dakota.

At the same time Congress passed legislation that would later provide the basis for bitter political dispute, although it went almost unnoticed at the time. Ever since the nation's recovery from the Civil War, the legislature had been considering the revision of the Mint Act; and the monetary experts, after long consideration, had finally agreed to a bill, which, among many other provisions, discontinued the minting of silver. Since silver had been selling at a substantial premium above gold, the silver producers paid little heed to the measure, for as a practical matter, they sold their bullion on the open market, not the Treasury. But 1873 was the beginning of two long trends: increased silver production and lower prices. Later the silver producers claimed they had been tricked into approving the bill's passage. It was a political time bomb, beyond the comprehension of most frontiersmen, but one that would become a rallying point for the silver states of the maturing West.

Despite the speculation in railroad stocks, several companies were pushing forward aggressively to seize territories that were still open. The Atchison, Topeka and Santa Fé had reached the Rockies; and in California the Big Four, through their control of the Southern Pacific of California, were taking steps to secure for themselves the southern route into California. The two most practical crossings over the Colorado River were at Needles and Yuma. If the

Big Four could take possession of them, they could protect themselves from being outflanked by another railroad.

Although big business in the form of investment bankers and railroad companies dominated the nation's attention, Congress had not forgotten the small individual settler. On his shoulders, in the long run, depended the success of the others. Unless he moved west, the railroads would have no traffic to carry, the industries no consumers to buy their products, and the bankers no securities to underwrite. Much of the area between the Rockies and the mountains on the West Coast would remain in reality what it had been so often called—the Great American Desert.

Clearly the 160-acre homestead, which Congress had once thought so generous, was an insufficient inducement. Therefore Congress passed the Timber Culture Act, which permitted a settler to secure an additional 160 acres provided he planted 40 acres of it with trees. Not only would the act enable the settler to secure a more realistic allotment of land, many believed the trees themselves would improve the climate by increasing the rainfall. Whatever the railroads actually thought, they subscribed to the theory in public. For they had become the great promoters of the West, outdoing even Hall Kelley.

While some men were trying to induce more rainfall on the land, others were trying to wrest from it the riches that were already there, riches others had overlooked. Since the output of the Comstock Lode had started declining, stocks in the mining companies had fallen. Yet a few geologists believed its ore was not exhausted, and a man named Adolph Sutro had invested heavily in a horizontal tunnel he thought would make possible much deeper mining. The large companies, however, would not do business with him.

John W. Mackay, who had come from Ireland as a boy, moved to California in 1851 and acquired considerable mining experience. Unlike many miners, who were often boisterous, frolicking men, Mackay was a serious student of mining methods. One of his contemporaries wrote of him, "Mr. Mackay is one of the most modest and unassuming of men, yet he is a shrewd observer of character and of all that is going on in the world about him. Generally he has but little to say, but that little is to the point—goes directly to the bull's eye. He is not often misunderstood. He most thoroughly understands mining in all its branches, as there is nothing required to be done in a mine that he has not done with his own hands. No man is more ready to adopt improvements than Mr. Mackay. He is ever ready to spend money for labor-saving machinery."

This description of Mackay underlines some of his distinctive qualities. He would never have had to hire someone to build an arrastre for him, as the early owners of the Comstock did; and unlike San Francisco bankers, he was less interested in financial maneuvers than he was in extracting ore and refining it. He thought the lower grade ores of the Comstock could be profitably mined by using better equipment and advanced methods. So as others began to desert the Comstock, he began buying up a company there.

As his principal partner, he chose James G. Fair, another man with practical mining experience behind him. The same contemporary who described Mackay said, "Mr. Fair is a man who never talks when he is acting, and no one knows exactly what 'Uncle Jimmy,' as the 'boys' call him, is up to. You see the hole by which he goes into the ground, but when once he is down out of sight you never know in what direction he is going."

Even after he became many times a millionaire he spent many of his hours "in miner's garb down in the seething lower levels, and 'poking about' in all manner of old abandoned drifts and tunnels, as though he were working for four dollars per day and had a very hard and exacting boss. He is a shrewd and enterprising businessman, and thoroughly understands mines and mining." Like Mackay, he, too, was interested in machinery, always willing to give a new idea a trial. Although the two men took in several other partners, they were the leading spirits in the effort to make a profit from what remained of the Comstock.

The prices of stocks in the Comstock mining companies rose and fell erratically. Sometimes a rumor—often set off by a speculator—would send them soaring. Then they would plummet until some miner found a previously undiscovered deposit of gold and silver that produced a profit. This would send the optimists running to the San Francisco Stock Exchange with orders to "buy." Meanwhile Fair and Mackay now controlled the Consolidated Virginia and hoped to find a new source of ore by digging deeper. Their original plan was to take the shaft down to the thousand-foot level and then move westward six hundred feet toward the lode. This would have cost them about $200,000 and, as it later turned out, would have been a complete loss, for nothing lay in that direction.

Instead at the last minute they decided to work from the shaft of the Gould and Curry Company north and west back to the Consolidated Virginia mine. The owner of the Gould and Curry, a man who had already made a fortune from the Comstock, gave them permission with the contemptuous remark that he would be glad to help "those Irishmen" lose some of their money.

While digging their tunnel, they came across a vein of low-grade ore and, in accordance with the mining practice of the time, decided to follow it. In March 1873, the low-grade ore gave way to ore of high quality almost directly under Virginia City itself. For years the community of miners had been walking back and forth from their homes to their saloons and churches—according to their taste—and passing over one of the richest deposits ever found in the United States.

The "Big Bonanza," as the new find of silver and gold came to be called, set Virginia City booming again and mining stocks soaring, this time, however, with reason. Mackay and Fair became extremely wealthy, although they never lost their simple ways with the men who worked for them. It was typical of the West that its greatest riches often came from the least expected places and those who found them were the singularly lucky, the unusually perceptive, or the uncommonly persistent.

The people of Arizona were not as fortunate as those of western Nevada. As Virginia City burst into life again, Arizona Territory was still threatened by the Apaches. The reservations set up by Colyer and Howard and the campaigning of Crook had brought relief from the devastating raids of a few years previous, but bands of these fierce Indians still roved the southern part of the area, drifting back and forth across the international border and occasionally striking some lonely traveler or a rancher.

In 1875, the year after the Big Bonanza, Cochise died. Among most Indian tribes, the authority of the "chiefs," as the white men designated the leaders, was uncertain and depended largely on their momentary standing among their own people. Today they might be able to speak with authority; tomorrow theirs was just one voice among many. Cochise had been a notable exception, occupying a place among the Chiracahua Apaches that was unique.

A white man who was staying at the reservation later wrote, "I shall never forget their lamenting over Cochise's death. Quite a number of Indians were camped near the agency, mostly women and children, and they had evidently gathered to await the news of their chief's death. When it came, the howl that went up from these people was fearful to listen to. They were scattered around in the nooks and ravines in parties, and as the howling from one *ranchería* would lag, it would be renewed with vigor in another. This was kept up through the night and until daylight the next morning. Everything then became quiet, and throughout the next day almost the stillness of death reigned."

The Indians carried Cochise's body to the Dragoon Mountains and left it there, exactly where, no white man knew, and now, no Indian. Even more individualistic than most tribes, the Apaches had no successor for Cochise; and without their great leader, they divided into small bands that often struggled against each other, and the work of Jeffords and Howard came undone. Moreover, during this critical period, Crook had been transferred to the Great Plains to take part in the Indian fighting there.

At Virginia City, the boom continued in spite of the declining price for silver. The passage of the Resumption Act of 1875 called for the minting of a limited number of silver dollars. Although this had little effect on the world market, the silver producers had won a minor victory. And meanwhile the ore—millions of dollars' worth each month—came to the surface and was taken to the stamp mills for processing.

In the early morning of October 26, 1875, some of the lodgers in the rooming house kept by Kate Shea, better known to her acquaintances as "Crazy Kate," got into a drunken brawl. At least that is what the occupants of the nearby houses later reported. In the course of the struggle, they knocked over a coal-oil lamp. The pool of oil broke into flames, and soon Crazy Kate's establishment was on fire and then another building and another.

Some of the buildings in Virginia City were of the best kind, but not those surrounding Crazy Kate's. "In addition to their being constructed of wood," wrote William Wright of the *Enterprise,* "nearly the whole of the buildings in the neighborhood were lined with cotton cloth, on which was pasted paper as on a plastered wall. The partitions dividing the rooms, and the ceilings of all the rooms, were also constructed of muslin and wallpaper. . . . Almost instantly the column of fire that was at first seen to arise began to assume the form of a pyramid. The base of this pyramid rapidly extended into the sides of the houses in all directions—the glass falling in showers from the windows to give ingress to the flames—and structure after structure burst out in sheets of fire more rapidly than could be counted or noted down."

With such a start, there was no containing the flames. "While the whole face of the mountain seemed a sea of fire with great billows tossing to and fro," Wright said, "the sounds that reached the ear were as fearful as the scene spread before the eye. From the armories of the various military companies, from the gunsmith shops, and from many of the variety-stores there came a constant roar of exploding cartridges, guns, pistols, firecrackers, bombs, rockets, and all manner of fireworks, sounding like the discharge of small arms in a great battle. Amid and above all this din were heard the frequent and startling discharges of giant-powder, gunpowder, and Hercules powder, as building after building was blown up in various parts of the town. As the fire began to approach the great mining works these heavy reports became more frequent and terrific. The miners carried into the buildings not a few cartridges only of the powerful explosives they were using, but whole boxes of them" to destroy the structures and perhaps check the fire's advance.

"At times great whirlwinds came down the side of the mountain and waltzed about in the midst of the burning buildings, carrying spirals of flame and fiery missiles thousands of feet into the air," Wright added, but "by the blowing up of buildings, and by almost superhuman exertions at carrying water and wetting the roofs and sides of the houses, the progress of the fire was stayed at a few important points."

Virginia City was in ruins. Many of its residents had lost their homes, much of the surface property of the mining companies had been destroyed, and their shares dropped on the San Francisco Exchange, as investors tried to get rid of their holdings. But calm returned. The people of Virginia City set about rebuilding their community, and those who had put money into the Comstock Lode remembered that the great deposits of ore were still safe under the ground. Within days the work of rebuilding commenced, and the price of mining shares climbed up again. Soon Virginia City was back about its normal business, and the Big Bonanza was once more pouring wealth into the West.

Nevada's problem was more immediate, dramatic, and more quickly solved than Arizona's. Conditions on the Chiracahua reservation had deteriorated after Cochise's death, and many of the bands had resumed the practice of raiding both the Americans and the Mexicans. On the San Carlos reservation, however, they had improved since the agency had been placed under the supervision of an extraordinary member of the Dutch Reformed Church, John Clum. He had had no previous experience with Indians, but he showed an immediate aptitude for the job. One of his underlying philosophies was to permit the Apaches, insofar as possible, to manage their own affairs; and to forward this purpose, he established Apache courts and an Apache police force. The latter were extraordinarily able and effective and were the civilian counterpart of Crook's Apache scouts, now largely disbanded.

To reduce expense, open up more land for settlement, and gain better control of their movements, the government decided to move the Chiracahuas from the reservation chosen for them by Cochise and place them with the other Apaches already at San Carlos. The decision had more ramifications than Washington supposed, for the San Carlos reservation was crowded, and the climate and terrain were different from those to which the Chiracahuas were accustomed.

John Clum received the unenviable assignment of supervising the removal. Knowing from experience that the sight of soldiers always frightened the Apaches, he asked the commanding general in Arizona to have troops on hand but out of sight while he tried to effect the transfer using only his Apache police. His tactics proved remarkably successful. A few Indians, including the warrior Geronimo, fled to the mountains and kept their freedom, but the majority of the tribe did what Clum and his police told them to.

He was far more successful than General Howard, who had again been called on to negotiate with Indians. Although Grant had created a reservation for the Nez Percés in the Wallowa Valley, the pressure of the settlers for additional land became more than the government could resist. Howard, as military commander of the territory, was a member of the commission appointed to talk with the Indians. The results of the "negotiation"—if it could be called that—were not surprising. The commission told the Nez Percés they must join the others of their tribe on the other reservation assigned to them.

377

The deadline was first set for April 1, 1877. This was not realistic. The Indians could not move their children, old people, and livestock while the ground was frozen and snow blocked some of the trails. In another meeting with Howard, they obtained a postponement until the middle of June.

Some of the Indians, like Joseph, favored the move. Although they did not want to leave the valley, they realized, as many of the others did not, that the white men were too strong to resist and that it was better for the tribe to submit peacefully than to fight a losing battle. Reluctantly the others agreed, and they started the journey with only a few days to spare.

During one of their stops, a warrior taunted another Nez Percé, Wahlitis, for not having avenged his father's death at the hands of a white man about two years earlier. Such remarks to a proud young Indian were almost unbearable; and to redeem his honor, Wahlitis with several friends left the camp and killed four white men along the Salmon River. When the warriors returned and said what they had done, the blood lust of the others was aroused. In the next few days, more than twelve other whites were killed by parties of Nez Percés, and that part of Idaho was thrown into a state of terror, as settlers feared to leave their houses and thought every movement in the grass might be a marauding Indian. Joseph, who had been away from the camp when the raids started, was torn between obeying the Americans' instructions and standing by his people. Finally he rode off to join the rebellious warriors at White Bird Canyon, where they had made a new camp.

Howard had demonstrated personal courage and common sense in his dealings with the Apaches, but hope for any compromise with the Nez Percés had passed. A commander who gave in to them now would have been dismissed from his post if the settlers had not shot him first. Howard ordered ninety soldiers, accompanied by some volunteers and friendly Indians and commanded by Captain David Perry, to compel the Nez Percés to go on the reservation.

The Indians were uncertain what to do. Some were for fighting, some for fleeing, some for talking with the advancing soldiers. When Perry neared their camp, they sent out a party of six warriors under a flag of truce, while others prepared to move the camp or, picking up their guns, lurked on the flanks of the route by which the soldiers were approaching.

While he watched the Indians with the flag of truce, one of the volunteers noticed the other Indians with their guns. Losing his nerve, he fired and missed. An Indian promptly returned the fire, killing one of Perry's trumpeters, and a general battle started.

The soldiers, badly trained and poorly led, were unprepared for the viciousness of the attack. Indians seemed to appear from everywhere, driving wedges between the white men and separating them into small groups. All semblance of order was gone. Those who could fled from the field. The others, surrounded by Indians, kept on fighting without hope. At the conclusion of the battle, the Indians had lost only two men, the Americans more than thirty, or about one-third of Perry's command. It was a disastrous defeat; and the whole Northwest—indeed the whole country—was shocked and frightened.

Howard immediately took to the field with about two hundred and fifty soldiers and civilians but found the Nez Percés had retreated to the south bank of the Salmon River. The swirling waters of the river, swollen by the melted mountain snows, formed a barrier he could not cross without boats. While he waited, he received word that Looking Glass, one of the Nez Percés who had earlier gone on the reservation, was preparing to reinforce the fugitives. Although the report proved erroneous, he could not risk having these additional Indians join Joseph's band, so he sent Captain Stephen Whipple to intercept them.

When Whipple reached the reservation, he did not stop long enough to notice that the Indians in Looking Glass's camp were entirely at peace. Instead he charged. Many of the Indians escaped to a nearby woods, where Looking Glass rallied the warriors and led them to join Joseph.

Having made one mistake, Whipple now compounded it. He learned—this time correctly—that Joseph's group had slipped across the river and were now between him and Howard's force. He sent out some ten men to scout the land and prepared for battle, forgetting about Looking Glass, who was now behind him. The scouting party was annihilated by the advancing Nez Percés, who slipped around Whipple and met Looking Glass. All of Whipple's fighting had only strengthened the fleeing Nez Percés.

Then began one of the most extraordinary pursuits in the history of Indian warfare. With reinforcements, Howard again caught up with the Nez Percés, who were now camped on the far bank of the Clearwater River. Opening fire with a howitzer and Gatling guns, Howard attacked. A band of Indians, able to maneuver more easily than the soldiers, crossed the river and attacked Howard's flanks. The fighting continued all day with heavier losses on the Americans' side than on the Indians'; but during the second day, the Nez Percés, who like most Indians were unaccustomed to prolonged battles, realized their hope lay in escape, not in defeating a single contingent of the many soldiers the Americans could send after them.

While some of the warriors occupied the soldiers' attention, the others quickly prepared to move the camp. Having decided they would not be safe in Idaho, they were determined to leave their native country, cross the mountains to the east, and join the Crow Indians in Montana. There, perhaps, the white men would leave them alone. Although they had with them more than five hundred women and children and a large herd of horses, they were able to move along the Lolo Trail more quickly than Howard, who was encumbered with heavy guns and a wagon train.

But the telegraph was on the side of the Americans. At Missoula, Montana,

Captain Charles C. Rawn received word of the Nez Percés' approach. With thirty-five soldiers and two hundred civilian volunteers, he dashed to the eastern end of the Lolo Trail and hastily built a log fort, hoping to hold the Indians long enough to permit Howard to catch up with them. The civilians were not anxious to fight; and when they received assurances the Nez Percés intended to be peaceful, they all went home, while the Indians quietly rode around the now helpless fort and were on their way again.

The Nez Percés kept their word. They made a few purchases at one community, paying for everything they took, but unknown to them, the telegraph had once more spread word of their whereabouts. Colonel John Gibbon, with approximately two hundred men, caught them by surprise at the Big Hole River and charged into their village. Some of the warriors escaped and counterattacked against Gibbon's left flank, killing the officer in command. Once again the soldiers' lack of training told against them. Bewildered by the loss of their leader, they fled toward the center of the camp, which Gibbon now occupied. In the resulting confusion and panic, the Indians captured several thousand rounds of ammunition and were on their way again.

Nelson A. Miles was a rather pompous officer, given to derogating the accomplishments of his peers, but he was nevertheless an able, tenacious military commander. The Nez Percés, after evading several more traps, headed for Canada, where Sitting Bull, the Sioux leader, had found refuge. With approximately six hundred men, Miles raced to cut them off and found them camped in a deep ravine near the Bear Paw Mountains of Montana. Unaware of the soldiers' approach, the Indians were asleep when Miles's men charged. "The tramp of at least six hundred horses over the prairie fairly shook the ground," Miles later recounted, "and although a complete surprise to the Indians in the main, it must have given them a few minutes notice, for as the troops charged against the village, the Indians opened a hot fire upon them." But the soldiers had already encircled the camp, and with the cavalry operating from one side and the mounted infantry from the other, they drove the Indians back into the ravine.

Miles had the choice of trying to enter the village or laying siege to it. A charge, he was certain, would result in high casualties. On the other hand, he was worried that during a prolonged siege, Sitting Bull might come from the north to the Nez Percés' aid. Even if he did, Miles thought he could hold him off until the Nez Percés surrendered. Actually Sitting Bull's band was now too small even if such a strategy had been part of the Indians' mode of warfare.

The fight took place during the first week of January 1878. "The snow and cold," Miles wrote, "caused great suffering to our wounded . . . and while the siege continued, detachments were sent some five miles distant up into the Bear's Paw mountains to get poles with which to make travois and stretchers, knowing that the wounded must soon be transported to the nearest hospital."

The suffering in the Indian camp was worse. After their long trek across the mountains and months of constant flight, the Indians were exhausted and hungry; and looking at the ring of troops that encircled them, they knew that escape was impossible. General Howard arrived just in time to witness their surrender on the morning of January 5, 1878. "As Chief Joseph was about to hand his rifle to me," Miles recalled, "he raised his eyes toward the sun which then stood at about ten o'clock, and said, 'From where the sun now stands, I fight no more against the white man.'"

The road taken by the Nez Percés since Lewis and Clark first penetrated their country had been a long difficult one, and their end as a people free in their own culture had come. But there was still one final drama to be played out. On the way down the river, the officer in charge of the Nez Percés stopped for a few hours at the Mandan agency to pick up supplies. Each of the two tribes was interested in the other. For hundreds of years, as Lewis and Clark learned during their winter in their villages, the Mandans had heard about the mysterious Indians who lived on the other side of the mountains but knew little about them. The same was true of the Nez Percés, who had heard through the Crows about those wiley traders on the Missouri but had never seen them. Thus after centuries, the two Indian cultures came together if only for a short few hours. It was almost like the completion of a circle, the final rending of the veil the mountains had placed between them.

"After leaving the Mandan agency and continuing down the river," Miles wrote, an old Nez Percé "said to the officer in charge, 'Those Mandans back there are bad Indians.' The officer asked him why, and he replied, 'Because they stole two Nez Percé blankets.' Now, in their tremendous march of nearly a thousand miles, together with the severe engagements in which they had taken part, the Nez Percés had lost almost everything. Therefore the officer could not help thinking how much they needed the blankets in the approaching cold weather, and accordingly expressed much sympathy, though of course it was impossible to turn back upstream to recover them. Finally, after giving his strong condemnation to the theft, it occurred to him to ask . . . if the Nez Percés had taken anything from the Mandans. 'O, yes,' he [the old Indian] responded, 'we got away with four buffalo robes.'" One of the old fur traders might have remarked that little had changed—thieving was still a game among them.

The Nez Percés had first been ordered onto the reservation in 1876. They had started their flight in 1877 and, for approximately seven months had eluded the army's efforts to capture them. During this period, they had occupied much of the government's attention, and gained notoriety throughout the Far West, and, during the last stages of their spectacular journey, had been watched with interest by almost all the nation. Although they had occupied the limelight, other events, too, had been turning the Far West from a frontier into the next stage of its development.

The year the peace commissioners were negotiating with Joseph, the people of Colorado were writing the constitution that was a step toward statehood. One of the questions occupying the delegates to the constitutional convention was woman suffrage. Various groups, both in Colorado and across the nation, reminded the delegates that Colorado would receive distinction if it became the first state to permit women to vote. Like most territories, Colorado wanted to avoid all delay, particularly as it hoped to be admitted during the nation's centennial. Woman suffrage, the delegates decided, might cause controversy and slow up Congress's approval, but they did give women the right to vote in school district elections.

On August 1, 1876, Grant announced Colorado's admission, and that fall, Colorado gave his party its three electoral votes, elected Republicans to all statewide offices, and placed a majority of the party in both houses of the state legislature.

Congress was aware that the creation of states did not by itself open up the Far West. What was needed were more people, so once again it passed legislation further expanding the 160 acres originally permitted a settler under the Homestead Act. This was the Desert Land Act. A settler could now obtain an additional 640 acres for $1.25 an acre with three years to pay. Before he could complete his claim, he had to irrigate the land, and the law applied only to certain states and territories, most of them west of the Rockies. In 1878 Congress passed yet another law opening up the public domain. This was the Timber and Stone Act, which provided that 160 acres of land could be purchased in a few specified places at $2.25 an acre, provided it was unsuited for agriculture and the buyer wanted the lumber or stone it contained for his own use. Both these laws, like those passed before them, were subject to much abuse and formed another means by which the unscrupulous gained possession of lands that should have been held for the common good. But the passage of the acts revealed the growing political power of the West as it gained in population and representation in Washington.

The desire for land was not limited to individual speculators. The Southern Pacific, pressing toward the Colorado River under the guidance of the Big Four, wanted the two crossings at Needles and Yuma. To reach the latter, it built its track across a military reservation without first securing permission from the federal government. The Big Four had grown so accustomed to circumventing regulations and bribing legislators they believed themselves above the law. In this instance, their belief was confirmed. Congress quickly granted them the right-of-way they had already taken.

But even Congress had its limits and would not approve the next step the

382

railroad wanted: a charter to cross Arizona and New Mexico and land grants to pay for the work. The charter, along with land grants, had previously gone to the Texas and Pacific Railroad, and Congress was unwilling to duplicate its earlier generosity. So the Southern Pacific secured local charters from Arizona and New Mexico and started building faster than its competitor. In that way, it gained control of one of the southern routes to the West Coast. The other route, farther to the north, was later serviced by the Atchison, Topeka and Santa Fé.

The approach of the railroad brought another change. The governor of Arizona announced that cattle-raising was becoming one of the territory's largest industries. Now that railroads were penetrating the country in every direction, the Far West was preparing to follow the Great Plains as a cattle-raising center.

Three economic forces had played primary roles in opening the West. The fur trade had first carried Americans beyond the Mississippi and Missouri rivers and on to the West Coast; precious ores—and some agriculture—had carried them into the land west of the Rockies; and cattle raising had created the large great ranches that had first caused the settlement of the Great Plains. There mining had played a secondary role, luring people to the eastern slopes of the Colorado Rockies and to the Black Hills. Now cattle was playing a secondary, but important, role beyond the mountains.

The price of silver had been falling steadily from a variety of national and international causes, dropping more than eleven percent on the London market from 1873 to 1878. More than the size of the drop, the steadiness of the decline worried the silver producers, for no relief appeared in sight. When the generally depressed economy made some persons wish to return to a bimetallic standard, the silver producers joined with them in attempting to push such a measure through Congress. The result was the Bland-Allison Act of 1878, which provided for the limited purchase of silver by the Treasury. The act produced neither the adverse repercussions its opponents feared, the economic benefits its proponents had expected, nor an important market for silver. It did, however, create a drain on the Treasury and opened the political divisions that later gave rise to the Populist movement in the days when the frontier had passed.

That time was approaching fast. A part of the country that could talk about currency standards, whose investors were daily watching market fluctuations in the capitals of Europe, whose affairs were being settled in New York and Boston boardrooms and Washington cloakrooms, and which kept an eye on the San Francisco and New York stock exchanges was no longer a frontier. Yet traces of the old life still remained.

In Idaho, the Bannock Indians began to dream of the past and, not yet convinced of the supremacy of the federal government, made a dash to join the Paiutes, who were now in southeastern Oregon. Other discontented members of northwestern tribes, like the Klamaths, joined them, as well as some of the Indians along the Columbia River. Once more General Howard took to the field, this time with considerably better success than when he pursued the Nez Percés.

The Indians fought well, but wherever they turned or dodged, they met detachments of soldiers, who blocked their way. When they reached the Columbia River, they found gunboats stationed along the river to prevent their crossing. The country had changed. The old escape routes were closed, and the ring of armed men seemed to be everywhere. Nothing the Indians did could recapture the past. It was gone, and after about three months of fighting, they surrendered.

The Utes, who had terrorized the Spanish and fought with Carson against the Navajos, rose in a brief and bloody revolt to no avail; and the Navajos themselves, broken in spirit by their exile from their native lands, were crushed forever as a military force. When they were allowed at last to return to their native home, they kept up their old customs, but it was the white traders who found them dyes for their wool and markets for their blankets.

The Apaches, who had fought so long and hard against all white men, were largely on reservations. Many of their leaders were long dead—Cochise and Mangas Colorados among them. Victorio of the Warm Springs Apaches was ready to make peace, but he refused to live away from his home. Others might stay on the reservation at San Carlos; he preferred the risky life of a raiding Indian in what was now a white man's land.

Geronimo, never a leader of the stature of Cochise but always able to find followers, could not resign himself to reservation life. Its constraints, the efforts of Apache warriors to become farmers, the absence of tis-win, the native drink—these were not for him. From time to time he tried the life offered by the reservation and then gave it up in favor of the more dangerous freedom that lay off the reservation.

The miners at Virginia City and most of the other mines west of the Rockies were becoming union members and more interested in a good hourly wages and improved working conditions than they were in striking it rich. Many of them put in a hard day for less than the forty-niners considered a satisfactory reward, but a few men in the Far West still retained the pioneers' independent spirit.

While serving with the army's scouts, Ed Schiefflin had seen what he thought was silver in southern Arizona, and instead of organizing a mining company and selling its shares on the San Francisco Stock Exchange, as the banker Ralston would have done, he went back to look the ground over as soon as he could get out of the army's employ. Those who knew of his plans told him the Apaches would kill him and he would find only his tombstone.

That was the name they gave the town that sprang up around the silver he located, Tombstone, Arizona—another Virginia City, another Montana mining camp, lawless and free and coming late in the youth of the Far West. As the 1870s neared their close, the age of the frontier, in at least a few places, had still a short time to run.

33. ON THE TRAIL A FINAL TIME

Lands bathed in sweeter, rarer, healthier air!
valleys and mountain cliffs!
The fields of Nature long prepared and
fallow—the silent cyclic chemistry;
The slow and steady ages plodding—the
unoccupied surface ripening—
the rich ores forming underneath;
At last the New arriving, assuming, taking
possession,
A swarming and busy race settling and
organizing every where. . . .

—Walt Whitman, 1874

Victorio, leader of the Warm Springs Apaches, had two trusted advisers: his beautiful sister, Lozen, who reportedly had magical powers for locating the presence of an enemy; and a kindly grandfather, Nana, whose tenderness with young children belied his ferocity as a fighter. Refusing to go to the San

Carlos reservation, which he hated, Victorio took refuge at the Mescalero reservation. But the civil authorities swore out a warrant for his arrest on charges of murder. Knowing he stood little chance of a fair trial before a New Mexican jury, Victorio fled, taking with him his two advisers and a band numbering not more than seventy-five warriors and their families.

The months that followed were among the bloodiest in the history of the Southwest. Having determined that the struggle between him and the white men was one to be waged until death, Victorio proved himself a superb leader. Taking advantage of the rough desert country he knew so well, he twisted, dodged, struck the white men, twisted, and dodged again like an evil spirit conjured out of the mountains by some ill-wisher of the white race. No accurate tally of the deaths he caused was ever made, but, taking into account his activities on both sides of the international border, some estimates placed the total at about a hundred and seventy-five.

Both the Mexican and American armies chased him, the troops worn out and bewildered by the constant effort to follow him, to cut him off, to find the secret hiding places in which he momentarily rested. Finally the Mexicans located his temporary camp and crept toward it on a dark night. Their rifle barrels spat years of hatred at the Apaches, and when at last the silence of the desert was restored, Victorio was dead and his band shattered.

Nana took over the leadership. Swiftly he led the remaining warriors north on a devastating raid of vengeance. Like a whirlwind from the mountains, he struck here and there. Then he was gone, taking refuge in the vast and almost impenetrable Sierra Madre of Mexico. The Mexican and American losses had been heavy, but at last Victorio was dead and Nana and Lozen gone.

As the Indians fought and lost one of their last campaigns against their fate, the emigrant trains rumbled westward, loaded with men, women, and children coming to occupy the land and fill its voids. No Pullman cars formed part of the equipment allotted to their use in return for their cut-rate fares. By the time they had pulled into Ogden, Utah, according to Robert Louis Stevenson, who made the trip, the cars "in which we had been cooped for more than ninety hours had begun to stink abominably."

Those enduring the smells and discomforts had been lured west by their own imaginations and by the constant propaganda of the railroads, which were trying to sell their lands and build up their markets. The call these people heard was the call started centuries earlier by Cabeza de Vaca—a vague promise of wealth and better times masking the almost certainty of failure. Talking among themselves, they sounded like Coronado's men around their campfire, full of unfounded optimism and dreams that had no basis. "Hunger, you would have thought," said Stevenson, "came out of the east like the sun, and the evening was made of edible gold."

Those who had come earlier had expected less—a few beavers in their traps, the sight of a newly discovered mountain rising high in the sunlight, a good drunk at the rendezvous once a year, a bit of freedom, and the joy of waking in the morning—alive. To have slept through the night without being discovered by the Blackfeet or Apaches was an accomplishment in itself. They had expected to make a living—what man does not?—but avarice walked the trail with only a few of them.

The discovery of gold had bred the legend of easy wealth—bags of dust or nuggets obtained with little work—of venturing forth a pauper and returning a king. That second wave of emigrants, at least many of them, had come to fill their flattened purses, to find money where the sun dropped behind the ridges. And so had most of the emigrants that crowded later into the railroad's foul-smelling cars. They were to be pitied, not because their hopes were to be frustrated but because their ambitions did not deserve a higher emotion.

The West into which they ventured was not what they had imagined it to be. The new millionaires who acted like nabobs were the conspicuous minority. The obscure majority found conditions much as they were at home.

Even the production at the Big Bonanza, the Cíbola of the Anglo-Saxons, had dropped radically. By 1880, the ore brought to the surface was only a third of what it had been, and the dividends were shrinking. The following year the stockholders received no return; instead they were assessed.

Local government had become expensive with the rising demand for services—and special treatment. Much of the cost fell on individual taxpayers for fear of alienating the big corporations. But even the railroads were unhappy. The representative of one that served Virginia City complained bitterly to the Central Pacific about the high cost of "placing good honest men in the Legislature on whom our Co. could rely."

Others were arguing about the expense of government in terms familiar to more people. The editor of the *Portland Morning Oregonian* in 1880 spoke out against the cost of the school system. "The belief is expressed," he said, "that the machinery of the schools has grown to a too cumbrous and expensive system; that there are too many studies; . . . and those who desire for their children an education beyond the common branches of the old-fashioned common school should pay for it."

Yet the Far West was not submerged in the slough of mining stocks, unemployment in centers like San Francisco, or the high cost of providing the services many of the people had come to expect. The unhappy and underpaid had always before them the dream of staking out their own homestead—that canyon up in the mountains with a clear stream to water a herd of cattle or raise a few crops. All that was required was a little capital, enough for the required improvements and to pay a few living costs. Or there was Tombstone. The Virginia Consolidated might be running down, its owners now millionaires, but its workers about to join the masses of unemployed. But things at Tombstone were humming. The Apaches still wandered through the surrounding land, but too many white men worked at the mines

388

for them to come near the community's board sidewalks or the OK Corral, where visitors left their horses. People made money there. In 1881, the year after Victorio died from his Mexican bullet wounds, the dead of Tombstone were being buried in style, for the Tarbell Undertaking Company bought a hearse with silver trim and gold leaf decoration. It cost eight thousand dollars and had curved glass windows in the front and rear. That was the year the Bird Cage Theater was built. Russian Bill was a regular member of the audience, paying twenty-five dollars a night for his seat. He knew all the bad men and tried to be one of them, but they had little use for amateurs like him. When he finally did commit a crime—he stole a horse—the posse caught him and, unaware that he was not the experienced badman he pretended to be— hanged him. Everyone, including the posse, was sorry afterward.

For those who wanted something less dramatic than Tombstone, there was Bisbee, not far away. The miners were just as tough, but the ore contained copper instead of silver, and the Wells Fargo Company had only to guard the company's payroll, not its product. But the chances for a long-term job were better. Copper was coming out of the Bisbee mines long after Tombstone's greatest days had gone. There were also the big mines in Montana, and a little gold and silver was being discovered elsewhere.

The railroads, which prospered on civilization, not the frontier, remained as anxious as ever to secure each piece of business, each right-of-way. Henry Villard, onetime newspaper reporter and now an eastern financier, believed the owners of a railroad could make money by operating it properly without resorting to stock manipulation and devious construction practices. He had purchased two Oregon transportation companies and merged them. The resulting Oregon Railway and Navigation Company gave him a secure hold on the Northwest, a grip he was determined to maintain. The Northern Pacific Railway, which would come directly into his territory from the east, represented the greatest threat to his monopoly, but he had discounted it for some years. The hard times of 1873 had taken their toll of the company's potential backers, and work on its transcontinental route had stopped.

But now the company was coming to life again, and Villard wanted to buy a majority of its stock. He personally did not have the capital to do this, but if he raised the money publicly and stated his purpose, he was afraid the price of Northern Pacific stock would skyrocket. Therefore he organized his famous "blind trust," giving his investors no inkling of the purpose for which he intended to use their money. In those freewheeling times, with no regulatory commissions to interfere, he could do this; and either his reputation was so good, or the public so willing to gamble, that the $8 million he wanted was soon oversubscribed. Once he controlled the Northern Pacific, he floated a bond issue and began vigorously pushing the railway's construction. It reached the West Coast in 1883, only three years after Victorio's death and two after the opening performance at Tombstone's Bird Cage Theater.

As the Far West became easier and easier to reach, its list of distinguished visitors grew longer. One of the least likely was Oscar Wilde, poet and playwright whose extravagant mannerisms had annoyed even his Oxford classmates. Nothing could have been further apart than this foppish intellectual and the men who had come to San Francisco not long before. But he appeared as a lecturer in 1882 to help the city's people assail the fortress of Europe's culture and advanced thought.

The reception he received was not one of unanimous gratitude. Ambrose Bierce, then writing for a San Francisco publication, was not impressed. "With a knowledge that would equip an idiot to dispute with a cast-iron dog, an eloquence to qualify him for the duties of caller on a hog-ranch, and an imagination adequate to the conception of a tomcat when fired by contemplation of a fiddle-string, this consummate and star-like youth, missing everywhere his heaven-appointed functions and offices, wanders about, posing as a statue of himself, and, like the sun-smitten image of Memmon, emitting meaningless murmurs in the blaze of women's eyes. He makes me tired."

The previous year, the Southern Pacific, pushing its way across Arizona and New Mexico, met the Texas and Pacific just east of El Paso. The southern route, the one favored by the Tennessee postmaster general when he gave out the mail contract to Butterfield, now had its own railroad. Products from the Southwest could be easily carried to larger markets east and west, a miraculous change from the trudging oxen on the Santa Fé trail less than forty years earlier.

The Atchison, Topeka and Santa Fé Railroad had not been idle. Its investors were just as anxious to reach the West Coast as the owners of the Southern Pacific were to reach the East. In 1883 its cars could reach California by going through Needles and then onto the tracks of the Southern Pacific. So it, too, could provide through service and became the third transcontinental railroad. Neither the Southern Pacific nor the Santa Fé was satisfied with the various arrangements they had made, and in subsequent years, they both moved ahead with their own tracks east and west, the Southern Pacific driving on to New Orleans and the Santa Fé building its own facilities in California.

While the United States could construct railroads across the continent and perform other engineering miracles, it had not been able to find a solution to the Indian problem, particularly that of the Chiracahua Apaches. San Carlos was completely unsatisfactory to many of them. They did not like the area, they detested the ill-advised efforts of the government to convert them quickly into farmers, they found the reservation overcrowded, and they knew that the Indian agent in charge, unlike the previous agent, Clum, did not understand them or their ways and was not above cheating them.

J. C. Tiffany was a member of the Dutch Reformed Church like Clum, but his religious affiliation did not prevent him from taking advantage of his government position. A federal grand jury, on the basis of the evidence presented to it, believed Tiffany paid for supplies that were never received, charged for rations for Indians who were not on the reservation, and used both government equipment and Indian labor for his own gain. Since the West was not generally sympathetic to coddling the Indians, the jury's charge was particularly significant.

Some of the Indians accepted these conditions as a way of life and did not rebel against them. Others refused to. When things got too bad they left— there was no way of controlling their movements—and if the soldiers pressed them, they returned, using the reservation as a safe home base whenever they thought they might be tagged by the army. Geronimo, according to one army officer, was in and out of the reservation so often he resembled a jack-in-the-box.

When the Apaches were loose, every man's hand was against them, as they well knew, and they responded in kind. When they wanted horses, they raided a ranch; when they wanted meat, they stole livestock; and when they encountered white men who might interfere with their plans, they killed them. Those white men who lived in cities had nothing to fear. The Apaches carefully stayed away from all large centers of population, adhering to their centuries-old tactic of never starting a fight when they were seriously outnumbered. But the rancher, the solitary prospector, the traveler, all who lived or worked alone or in small groups had to be constantly alert, and many of their days were spent in fear.

In 1882 the army ordered General Crook to return to Arizona—he had been fighting the Sioux on the northern edge of the Great Plains—and settle the Apache question once and for all. As usual, Crook did not move precipitately. His first step was to improve conditions on the reservations and to assure the Indians already there that the government was not, as was rumored, planning to send them to Oklahoma. He also reorganized the Apache police, a group that had become demoralized since Clum's departure.

He next turned his attention to what he considered the crux of the problem, the Apaches' refuge in the Sierra Madre. This chain of mountains, which divides the Mexican states of Sonora and Chihuahua, contains some of the roughest terrain in North America, steep cliffs, deep canyons, rock surfaces that no army could climb, and even today hardly any roads and no settlements in its northern stretches. Few Mexicans ever went there. The country was too fearsome and harbored too many hostile Indians to be attractive even to fleeing criminals. Farther north railroads might roar along the tracks not far from Apache Pass, but those who rode into the Sierra Madre—at the risk of their lives—entered a world where time had been turned back to the days when Lewis and Clark had followed the Lolo Trail. The passing years had had little effect.

As long as the Indians could always take refuge in this strange fortress of theirs, they were almost invincible. They could emerge from the mountains, sweep north on one of their raids, and then dash back across the border and up trails that were known only to them. There they could safely rest until they were ready to raid again, and no army patrols could prevent them from emerging, crossing the border and once more coming north. There were too many miles of desert, too many secret trails through the mountains. Crook decided, therefore, to do what no commander had ever done before: follow them right into the heart of the Sierra Madre.

Before he could launch his campaign, the Indians made another raid north, this time under the leadership of a Warm Springs Apache named Chato. Although disliked by some of the others because of his ambition, Chato was nevertheless a successful fighter. In March 1883, he attacked the camp of some charcoal burners not far from Tombstone. This was the first the Americans knew that another raiding party was in the area. He killed three of the four men, the fourth escaping to spread the news. Then the Apaches attacked another camp and killed one more American. The Indians at San Carlos were in a frenzy, expecting Chato to raid the reservation and forcibly enlist them in his war. The settlers of southern Arizona were also in a panic, for no one knew where Chato's band had gone. Judge H. C. McComas was sure they were farther to the west and was traveling with his wife and six-year-old son not far from Lordsburg, New Mexico, when Chato found him. They killed Mrs. McComas while she was still sitting in the buckboard, sent four bullets into the judge, who crawled about two hundred yards before he died, and kidnapped the McComas' son.

The death of a prominent person like the judge was different from the deaths of obscure charcoal makers. Both Arizona and New Mexico were outraged. The Silver City (New Mexico) *Enterprise* wrote about the two daughters whom the judge had left at home. "Only a few days ago," it said, "this family were together in their home, surrounded by all the comforts and luxuries of life, and were happy in their love for each other. All was sunshine and happiness for these little girls then, but all has changed now, and even the most sympathetic, cannot realize the sorrow that has forever seared the life-spring in the hearts of these little children."

Crook was, of course, blamed for the tragedy. As the army's commander, he was responsible for protecting the lives and property of the people of Arizona and New Mexico, but he had failed. In spite of public pressure, however, he refused to spend his resources on fruitless patrols but continued to concentrate on his invasion of the Sierra Madre.

In one respect, luck favored him. An Indian named Peaches, who had been with Chato, decided to surrender and help the Americans. He reported that the Apaches were now few in number and low on ammunition—replenishing their supplies had been one reason for Chato's raid—and he knew where they usually camped in the Sierra Madre. But Crook also faced a problem with a group that became known as the "Tombstone Toughs." These were civilians from the mining town who thought they could defeat the Apaches even if the army could not. Well equipped with liquor and guns, they marched around southern Arizona to the Mexican border and back almost to San Carlos. Crook had the good sense not to interfere with them, although he took pains to have troops ready in case they should attack the reservation. As he had foreseen, they soon ran out of energy—and whiskey—and returned to Tombstone. Indian fighting took perseverance and skill, not bottles and hot tempers.

A further obstacle to his plans was the nation's international agreement with Mexico. Troops from either country could cross the border only when they were in "hot pursuit" of the Apaches, and even then could not come closer than six miles to any town. Such conditions precluded the campaign Crook intended, and the bureaucrats in Washington, to whom he appealed, failed to help him. Never having fought Apaches themselves, they told him to chase the Indians but abide by the treaty. Crook cut through the diplomatic tangle by conferring personally with the governors of Chihuahua and Sonora. Regardless of what the government at Mexico City might think, they welcomed his help and told him he was free to go where he wished if he could put a stop to the Apaches' raids.

Crook marched over the border on May 1, 1883, at the head of one of the strangest forces in the history of the United States Army—fifty white soldiers and two hundred Apache scouts. Crook had learned that only the most physically fit of the soldiers could keep up with the Apaches or go where they went, and even those picked men sometimes lacked the necessary endurance. So he intended to rely heavily on Apaches. "The two great points of superiority of the native or savage soldier over the representative of civilized discipline," wrote Captain John G. Bourke, who served with Crook, "are his absolute knowledge of the country and his perfect ability to take care of himself at all times and under all circumstances. Though the rays of the sun pour down from the zenith, or the scorching sirocco blow from the south, the Apache scout trudges along as unconcerned as he was when the cold rain or snow of winter chilled his white comrade to the marrow. He finds food, and pretty good food too, where the Caucasian would starve. . . . When his moccasins give out on a long march over the sharp rocks of the mountains or the cutting sands of the plains, a few hours' rest sees him equipped with a new pair—his own handiwork—and so with other portions of his raiment. . . . In battle he is again the antithesis of the Caucasian. The Apache has no false ideas about courage; he would prefer to skulk like the coyote for hours, and then kill his enemy, or capture his herd, rather than, by injudicious exposure, receive a wound, fatal or otherwise. But he is no coward; on the contrary, he is entitled to rank among the bravest."

This army of Indians and white men entered the mysterious Sierra Madre, and later Bourke described the country through which they climbed. "It seems to consist of a series of parallel and very high, knife-edged hills—extremely rocky and bold; the cañons all contained water, either rapidly flowing, or else in tanks of great depth. Dense pine forests covered the ridges near the crests, the lower skirts being matted with scrub-oak. Grass was generally plentiful, but not invariably to be depended upon. Trails ran in every direction, and upon them were picked up all sorts of odds and ends plundered from the Mexicans,—dresses, made and unmade, saddles, bridles, letters, flour, onions, and other stuff."

Following this trail of scattered loot and the directions of Peaches, Crook's strange expedition continued into the Sierra Madre. "The mountains became," Bourke said, "if anything, steeper; the trails, if anything, more perilous. Carcasses of mules, ponies, and cows lined the path along which we toiled, dragging after us worn-out horses."

The trail finally turned into an amphitheater hidden in the mountains. A fresh stream flowed through the middle, and pinnacles of rock formed observation posts for the Apaches, and "their huts," Bourke said, "had been so scattered and concealed in the different brakes that the capture or destruction of the entire band could never have been effected."

At that point the Apache scouts told Crook the white men and the pack train were holding them back. Would he allow them to go on by themselves with a few of the white officers whom they particularly trusted? Crook agreed. There seemed no other way to continue through that wilderness, but his decision showed his trust in his Indians.

Shortly afterward the scouts came to a *rancheria*, and fighting broke out. Many of the warriors were off raiding in the lower lands that flanked the mountains, and the scouts overran the small village. This broke the spirit of the remaining Apaches. Some of them had already been talking about surrendering. Life as fugitives from a superior power had lost its attraction, and the presence of their own people guiding the Americans to their fortress made them feel the future was as dark as the storm clouds that sometimes gathered over the mountains and lashed them with snow and rain.

The Indians did not surrender all at once. That was not the Apache way. Each leader had to discuss the question with his own small band, a system far more democratic than that practiced by most Americans. But one by one they came in to see Crook and agreed to give up.

Getting them out of the mountains and back to the reservation was almost as great a problem as defeating them. Crook did not have enough men to guard them even if it had been possible to do so on those steep trails and in

394

those narrow defiles. So Crook took the courageous course. He accepted the word of each surrendering leader that he would bring his band to San Carlos.

The Indians kept their word. Some of the bands took longer than others, Geronimo's the longest. At the border Crook had a sympathetic officer waiting to receive them and escort them the rest of the way for fear angry settlers might attack them. In fact, a United States marshal did try to arrest Geronimo and carry him off to jail. But the army used a bottle of whiskey to give the officer a good night's sleep, during which they smuggled the Indian leader away. Thus—at least for a time—came an end to the Apache campaign.

Crook, deep in the Sierra Madre surrounded by his Indian allies with an unseen enemy lurking behind the rocks and trees, had reenacted the days of the frontier. He might almost have been a mountain man fighting with the Nez Percés at his side against the Blackfeet during the Battle of Pierre's Hole. But such scenes—such throwbacks to the past—were becoming increasingly rare. Helen Hunt Jackson, the childhood friend of the retiring Emily Dickinson, had deserted Amherst, Massachusetts, and gone on the travels that eventually brought her West and made her aware of the Indian problem. She had already written *A Century of Dishonor* and *Ramona,* both of which helped arouse the public's sympathy for Indians except among those who had seen the mutilated body of a friend or neighbor. She died in 1885, but opinion was already turning, particularly in the East, and a man like Crook was no longer an unquestioned hero. A nation that had no reason to fear Indians had no reason to respect the men who had subdued them.

It was a sign of the times that the Nez Percés, who had once frightened the whole Northwest, were allowed to return from the unfamiliar surroundings of Indian Territory to a reservation in Washington. Even the railroads were being slightly tamed. Having advanced into the West with often ruthless tactics, they, too, were becoming the targets of a higher set of values. Already they had been subjected to several investigations; and in 1885, the Senate appointed the Cullom committee to look at their practices more closely and bring them under better control. They were even having trouble with some of their own workers, as labor unions were spreading into their industry and provoking strikes for better wages and working conditions. The Chinese who had labored laying the track for the Central Pacific would not have understood what this was all about.

In a short time, not only had customs and outlooks changed, but people, too, some of them plunging back into the obscurity from which the young West had raised them. Former Senator Gwin, for example, once a political power in California and a figure in determining the routes across the continent, had never recovered from the disgrace of having chosen the wrong side in the Civil War. He died, a forgotten expatriate, in Paris, also in 1885.

395

What signaled the changing times as much as anything else was a book brought out in 1884 and widely read by those interested in their country. *The Pacific Tourist* was an American Baedeker, designed for readers who wanted to make a pleasure trip through the West. The change was evident in its description of the transcontinental journey. About twenty years before, people going west had followed their ox wagons along the trail, the dust swirling about their heads on a journey better measured in months than days. Now, according to *The Pacific Tourist,* they covered the miles in luxury. "To travelers from the East," it said, "it is a constant delight, and to ladies and families it is accompanied by absolutely no fatigue or discomfort. One lives at home in the Palace Car with as much true enjoyment as in the family drawing room, and with the constant change of scenes afforded from the car window, it is far more enjoyable than the saloon of a fashionable steamer."

At Salt Lake City, where the Mormons had seen their crops nearly destroyed by grasshoppers and wondered if they could survive the winter, the traveler was advised to take hot baths—but not within three hours of mealtime—and then visit the museum. Bozeman, Montana, the early mining camp, was surrounded by several lakes, canyons, and mountains that the tourist might like to see and also offered a convenient tour to the Yellowstone National Park.

At Sacramento, near Sutter's Fort where the Swiss had received the survivors of the Donner party, the visitor was told, "Should you pass through the city in September or October, do not fail to see for yourself the Agricultural Park and the Pavilion." At Monterey, where the Americans had landed to capture California, "the sea bathing is best on the coast north of Point Conception, the beach being especially favorable." Tucson, whose people were once unable to venture into the surrounding country for fear of Indians, now had "a delightful park. Cottonwood trees of only a few years' growth had attained great height under the influence of irrigation, and furnish a shade and cool retreat that everyone must appreciate."

Descriptions like these filled the pages of *The Pacific Tourist,* and a country that looked on itself as a resort for tourists was no longer a frontier. Even Fort Bowie, first established by Carleton and the California Column on their march through Apache Pass, had become almost an anachronism.

"Its position in the Apache Pass," *The Pacific Tourist* said, "made it one of the most important posts in the Territory, for it was long surrounded by fierce and hostile warriors."

Everything was in the past tense. Cochise was not hiding among the rocks, nor the stagecoach racing up the road, prepared for an Indian attack. All was peace and quiet, but . . .

In 1885, Geronimo and a band of warriors with their families wearied once more of life on the reservation. To seek release from the humdrum activity, they had been making and drinking tis-win again and were afraid the government would punish them for their infraction of an important reservation rule—no alcoholic drinks. As the Apaches left, they cut the telegraph wire where it was hidden by the leaves of a tree, tying it together with a leather thong, so no loose ends would show where the break had been made. This gave them an additional lead on the soldiers who once more went in pursuit.

Arizona Territory was wild. Apaches loose again! All that was supposed to be in the past. Lonely ranchers once more started at the night sounds that might merely be a coyote or a browsing horse but also might be an Indian. Crook, weary from long fighting, took to the trail once more.

He and his men now knew the mountains, and the general began an aggressive series of actions, flanking the high peaks with parties of scouts and even crossing over them, a feat that astounded the local Mexicans. With soldiers and scouts on every side, the Apaches realized they could not hold out forever and agreed to talk with Crook.

Wary as always, the place they chose provided them with an easy escape route if the negotiations broke down. Crook accepted this condition, for the alternative was to send hundreds of troops after them in a campaign that could go on for months or longer. After giving them time to state their grievances, he persuaded them to return to the reservation. Once again, he did not attempt to place them under guard, for he did not have enough men to carry out such a move. But this time his luck failed him.

During the night, a seller of mescal entered the Indian camp—some say he was employed by the beef contractors who supplied the army and therefore prospered on warfare. Several Indians became drunk, and as they did, their imaginations began to take over and they pictured a horrible fate awaiting them. The next morning the majority were still willing to go on the reservation, but Geronimo and a small band of warriors had fled.

The news shocked Washington. Many officers and politicians had disapproved of Crook's use of the Apache scouts. Such unorthodox methods were not in keeping with the army's traditions. Surely the scouts had connived with Geronimo. Crook, angry, asked that the authorities either confirm his faith in the scouts or assign him elsewhere. They assigned him elsewhere and replaced him with General Nelson Miles, who had stopped the Nez Percés' flight. Miles was older now and more pompous, and he organized one of the most elaborate Indian campaigns in the history of those wars. Troops roved everywhere, and signal stations on the mountains flashed word by means of mirrors whenever the Apaches were suspected of appearing. But all of this was little avail.

In the end, a few courageous men accomplished what Miles's maneuvers could not. They went to Mexico and persuaded Geronimo to meet a lieutenant whom the Apaches particularly respected. Although not well at the time, the young officer traveled into the mountains and talked to Geronimo in a secret hiding place.

The Apache agreed to give himself up, but his sense of pride and showmanship was such that he would not surrender to a junior officer, only to the commanding general. His demand was in keeping with Miles's own self-importance. Nothing would please the general more than to leave his headquarters and, with no danger to himself and no discomfort, personally take Geronimo into custody. The two men met at Skeleton Canyon in southeastern Arizona, and when they had finished talking, Geronimo realized that further fighting was useless. The frontier was gone, and so were the good, carefree days that had been part of his life.

At Fort Bowie, Miles kept Geronimo a prisoner until the government decided what to do with him. Telegrams flashed back and forth between Washington and Arizona, as the authorities tried to understand the terms on which Geronimo had given himself up—as though he were a foreign nation—and decided what would satisfy both justice and the terrified citizens of Arizona, an impossible combination.

Finally the decision was to march him and his band to the railroad, only a few miles away, and send him east. Overhead the turquoise sky shone clear and unmarked by clouds, and the blue haze was creeping along the foot of the mountains on the other side of the valley. The Chiracahua and Dos Cabezos mountains were empty of Apaches; cattle ranchers were beginning to take them over. The walls of the stagecoach station still stood, but it was falling into disrepair, for travelers now took the railroad. In fact, except for the commotion caused by Geronimo's last outbreak, the chief characteristic of service at the post was boredom. It hung everywhere, and the only place to dispense with it was at the sutler's quarters, a sort of enlisted men's club where many bottles of liquor were sold.

The troops lined up to see the guard march Geronimo and his people to the railroad station. It was a great occasion. In sarcasm, the military band got out its instruments and played "Auld Lang Syne" to the departing Apaches. The notes of the song carried far into the desert air, rising higher and higher against the slopes of the surrounding mountains. But without the soldiers knowing it, the familiar words took on a broader meaning than the band intended. It was not good-bye merely to the last of the Apache warriors who had tried to continue the fight against the white men. It was good-bye to a time and an era, to the Spanish priests in their cowls and the *conquistadores* in their armor coming north in search of Cíbola, to the mountain men crossing the unknown lands, to the settlers in their wagon trains and to the traders making the trip to Santa Fé, to the American soldiers marching to capture the land, to the forty-niners seeking their fortunes, and to all that past that had finally made the lands the Americans' own.

That night as the stars whirled westward, meeting the moist currents

398

pushing to the east, they shone down on the Rockies, the Cascades, the Sierra Nevada, the great Colorado and Columbia Rivers, and as they flickered in the dark, they celebrated the passing of a period in American history—the frontier. What lay ahead was challenging. No one knew what it would be like. But it would be different.

EPILOGUE

The professor lectured us about the Old West. He had read all the books, the journals, the letters home . . . but he didn't know much about cattle, horses, guns, Indians . . . or people. It was like listening to a player piano, which strikes a note for every hole in the roller but doesn't know whether the hole is in the right place.

—Letter from an old-timer, 1896

In the next few years, the Santa Fé Railroad and the Southern Pacific engaged in a rate war that brought fares to a minimum. This encouraged people to flock west in such numbers there were not enough locomotives to pull the needed trains. The Dawes Allotment Act tried to give land to individual Indians, so they could become farmers like white men. It failed of its purpose. The Indians were living in a half-world between their old life and a new one that did not materialize. When the Dawes Act failed, the administrators and

400

politicians—some well meaning, some not—tried other programs. None of them proved successful. Frederic Remington published his pictures of the Apaches, preserving for the future a sense of the campaigns against them. Sheep arrived and cropped some of the better grazing grounds. The white men began shooting at each other instead of at Indians. Rudyard Kipling came West. He had seen the British Empire; now he wanted to see the American. J. P. Morgan attempted to get the railroads to work together instead of trying to outdo each other.

Yosemite, thanks to John Muir, became a national park, and the Sherman Silver Act was passed and slightly helped the miners. Frémont lost his money and lived largely on what Jessie earned. He received a small pension from Congress but died in 1890. The same year the army gave up its post at Fort Bridger, where it had camped the winter of the Mormon War, and Congress passed an act calling for the return of all railroad land grants that had not been earned. The new law did not restore much to the public domain. In this way, bit by bit, the nation went about tidying up the odds and ends left over from the glorious time, or the darkest days, when the sun had looked bright in the west.

Old-timers began to collect their stories. A few historians began to recreate the past time, discussing it with those who still remembered that rapidly vanishing era, then, as the eyewitnesses grew old and died, pored over books and contemporary records. Time gave them a perspective that placed new interpretations on old actions and will eventually make it possible to draw from the West's history the many lessons it has to teach—in the evolution of justice, the role of central government in development, the economics of private versus public financing, the utilization of natural resources, and many other topics of interest and value.

But it was difficult for them to get the sense of it, the feel of cold rain on a stiff slicker, the smell of gunsmoke, the odor of oiled steel, the sound of horses' feet on a stone, the sight of a beaver in a trap, or the uncertain knowledge of whether an approaching Indian was friend or enemy.

These are the things no one understands from reading books, no one can recapture from paper—the inner feelings of the men and the women who, against the most improbable odds, gave us the land we now call our own, who removed the other disputants and placed on us the trust of preserving it for the future—which is the least we can do who shared none of the suffering, none of the worrying, none of the struggling.

ACKNOWLEDGMENTS

The names of individuals and institutions that assisted me with this book would cover a span of many years and compose a list longer than most readers would trouble to peruse. Many of the names would be familiar; many more, unfamiliar; and sadly, some have swung into the saddle for that last, and most dramatic, of rides. The list, however, could not be complete, as some, the possessors of reminiscences and family collections, have specifically requested anonymity.

Since those who helped me the most are already aware of my gratitude, I will limit these acknowledgments to a few who have done special service on this particular volume: the Yale University Library and its staff, Mrs. Joan Rundell and the library of Greens Farms Academy, Mrs. Sylvia Carman, and, as so often, Mrs. C. R. Horton, Jr.

NOTES

The original notes to the sources on which this book is based fill many pages and are too lengthy to reproduce here in their entirety. To have done so would have made this volume both cumbersome and even more expensive without satisfying the needs of any but a small minority of readers. Therefore they have been severely edited.

In doing so, I have been guided by several criteria. Generally speaking I have tried to cite those substantiating sources that are most easily available to the largest number of readers. Thus I have mentioned, when I had them at hand, the later editions of earlier works and the printed texts of original documents even though I myself may have relied on the originals.

Also I have often not mentioned more than one source for a particular statement when a variety of the sources I checked did not substantially differ on any important points. Nor have I cited documents and other primary materials, most of which are relatively difficult for the average reader to obtain, unless they made a material contribution to the text. This has made it possible for me to eliminate many individual cross-references and greatly reduce the length of the notes.

Then, too, I have not included citations to cover events that are generally known. The Louisiana Purchase, as a single example, is sufficiently familiar and well-described to make it unnecessary to provide references to some of the documents that add much in detail, but less in broad outline.

On the other hand, any scholar who wishes to pursue an individual question further may write me in care of the publisher.

1. RUMORS OF TREASURE

In this and the succeeding chapters, I have referred to New Spain as Mexico. For the purpose of this book, the geographical boundaries are approximately the same, and I think many general readers will find the usage less confusing.

Cabeza de Vaca's story is told in his own report. Properly his last name is Nuñez Cabeza de Vaca. As this becomes rather unwieldy, I have followed the custom of other writers and referred to him simply as Cabeza de Vaca. Among the notable efforts to chart the exact route he followed is Hallenbeck's. A detailed account of his journey is contained in my book *Sunlight and Storm*. This also offers more details of Coronado's experience on the Great Plains.

Fray Marcos de Niza's report tells what he thought he saw, and Castañeda wrote a chronicle of Coronado's expedition. The text of this is contained in Winship's volume along with letters from Coronado and other documents relating to that historic journey.

For Ulloa's voyage, I have followed Wagner, who has reprinted the original reports, pp. 15–50.

For Cabrillo's voyage, I have again relied on Wagner. Since Cabrillo's place names did not survive, it is often difficult to locate the spots at which he landed. The problem is further complicated by his errors in latitude, which generally grew worse as he progressed north. Apparently, his tables of the declination of the sun were at fault.

The quotations in this chapter are as follows: Cabeza de Vaca's description of the territory he had seen, pp. 167–76 of his account; Estavanico's attitude, Castañeda in Winship p. 190; Cíbola, p. 203; and also the Hopi villages, 208; Coronado to Mendoza, p. 326; the country near the Grand Canyon, and the description of the canyon's size, p. 209; and Ferrel on Santa Catalina Island, his account, p. 85.

The quotation at the head of the chapter comes from Cabeza de Vaca, p. 149.

2. NEW CONTESTANTS

The courage of the Spanish and Portuguese sailors cannot be overstated. They went into unknown waters either without charts or, at the best, inadequate ones; they had no means of carrying fresh provisions; even their water grew stale. Because they lacked chronometers, they had difficulty ascertaining longitude; thus they were often uncertain of their own position and of the position of their destination. They were also dependent on favorable winds and currents, because their rigging—with its clumsy square sails—made it impossible for them to beat to windward. Thus they could run before the wind but not return against it. Therefore the courses they followed on their voyages resembled loops—one way out, another back. But the question always remained: Was there a way back? For the Spanish voyages mentioned in this chapter, I have relied heavily on Wagner's excellent work. This contains the records of Legaspi's voyage.

For Francis Drake's voyage I have followed Francis Pretty's account in Hakluyt, pp. 145–69. Drake's Bay is now in the Point Reyes National Seashore and is the site of the visitors' center, a rather unfortunate choice, according to many critics, because the building detracts from the marvelous scenery.

The text of the original documents pertaining to the expeditions made by Rodríguez and Espejo at this time are contained in Hammond's volume.

In the record he made of his voyage, Gali said that he had reached the California coast at 37°. This was probably about right. In a French translation, however, it appeared as 57° or just south of the present boundary of Alaska. This created a considerable amount of perplexity.

The text of Unamuno's report is contained in Wagner, pp. 141–51.

For the description of Cavendish's voyage, I have relied on Pretty's account in Hakluyt. Although Cavendish returned to England a wealthy man, he was soon in financial straits again. In 1591 he embarked on another voyage to the Pacific in company with John Davis, who had explored the Canadian coast. The venture was a failure, and Cavendish died at sea.

Castaño de Sosa's records as well as the little that is known about the Leyva-Humana expedition are contained in Hammond's book.

Cermeño's voyage did not receive the attention it deserved from the Spanish authorities. Having failed to discover treasure, a Northwest Passage, or a spectacular harbor, he had not produced those immediate results that the Spanish always desired. But he had greatly enlarged their knowledge of the California coast and had established a rival claim to the one made by Drake. The text of his report of his voyage appears in Wagner, pp. 156–65. Wagner has also traced his course, a difficult task because of the lack of recognizable proper names and the uncertainty of his navigational observations.

The quotations in this chapter are as follows: Drake's reasons for not returning around the Horn, account of Francis Pretty, Hakluyt, pp. 157–58; the natives at Drakes Bay, pp. 158–59; Drake claiming California, p. 161; Gali's description of California, Wagner, p. 135; Cavendish's battle with the Spanish galleon, Pretty in Hakluyt, pp. 284–85; and the news of the defeat of the Armada, pp. 301–2.

The quotation at the head of the chapter is from Francis Pretty's account of Drake's voyage and is in Hakluyt, pp. 161–62. The date is the date they anchored.

3. Hope Will Not Die

The interesting story of Juan de Oñate is told in the two volumes by Hammond and Rey in which they provide not only their own summary of his adventures but also the texts of the pertinent historical documents. Given the Spanish propensity for detailed reports, these are many, although some seem to have been lost. For the sake of brevity, it is not necessary to refer to the specific documents consulted, as they are obvious from the detailed table of contents.

Although Oñate's journey in search of Quivira was important, I have made only passing reference to it, because it covered territory outside the scope of this book, and I have already described it at greater length in my book on the Great Plains.

Hammond has also written a narrative account of Oñate's venture which appeared in the *Publications in History* of the Historical Society of New Mexico.

Vizcaíno's voyage occupies a strange place in history. Largely unproductive in terms of new discoveries or in helping to establish Spain's hold on California, it was nevertheless important, because it resulted in so many of the place names that we know today and because it influenced later Spanish policy in centering settlement on Monterey. An analysis of the voyage and the text of one of the reports is included in Wagner, pp. 168–285.

The principal source for Popé's revolt is Hackett and Shelby's book. In addition to containing a narrative account of the uprising, they have also included the texts of the original documents. Once again, for the sake of brevity, I have not cited the individual documents as they are readily identifiable from the table of contents.

The quotation at the head of the chapter is from William H. Prescott's *The Conquest of Mexico,* vol. 1, pp. 161–62, New York, A. L. Burt Company. No date.

4. Outposts on the Coast

Information about Father Kino may be found in *Father Kino Reports to Headquarters,* Kino's *Historical Memoir,* Watson's collection of some of his letters, and Bolton's *The Padre on Horseback.* Lockwood contains descriptions of the missions.

For concise accounts of the Spaniard's relations with the Pimas and the Indians' subsequent uprising, see Spicer, pp. 118–32 and Faulk, pp. 48–49.

Fray Junípero Serra's life is described in the biography by his devoted disciple Palóu. Obviously Palóu was prejudiced in favor of the man he admired so much and takes his side, particularly in his quarrels with the secular authorities, but he was a conscientious reporter. The Ainsworths' book places the priest's life against a broader background and would be more helpful to those unfamiliar with conditions in Mexico at the time.

The struggles of Fray Junípero with the others in authority in Alta California was a typical Spanish colonial experience and one of the system's great weaknesses. In Fray Junípero's case, the cooperation he received varied in large part with the person currently holding the office of governor, but I have not attempted to detail his ups and downs in a book of this scope.

Anza is often credited with being the founder of San Francisco. Although some of the settlers he brought to Monterey later moved to the bay, the specific choice of a location for the presidio and a mission were made after he departed for Pímeria Alta. This is thoroughly discussed in the book by Bowman and Heizer. They also tell the fascinating tale of the exhumation of his body from the floor of the church in Arisepe, Sonora, and its reburial. This occurred in the second half of the twentieth century and received considerable publicity, particularly on the West Coast.

The basic source for the account of his trip is, of course, his own diary. This is available in the five volumes edited by Bolton and containing Bolton's own narrative introduction. Another account is contained in Font's journal, which provides a cross-check on all that Anza says as well as providing additional information.

For those who would like a shorter account of these two memorable journeys, I would recommend the handsome volume by Pourade, a book that was made possible through the generosity of my old friend, James S. Copley, who, during his lifetime, encouraged many studies of American history.

Supplementing these accounts for this period are the journals of both Juan Crespí and Gaspar de Portolá.

The quotations are as follows: the blacksmith's remarks, Woodes Rogers on the Spanish galleon, pp. 219–21 of his account; Palóu, p. 77; John Adams's comments can be found in George Bancroft's *History of the United States of America*, vol. 5, pp. 320–21, in the edition published at Boston in 1876 by Little, Brown, and Company.

The quotation at the beginning of the chapter is from Palóu's *Life of Junípero Serra*, p. 130.

5. THE AMERICANS COME

In much of the West away from the cities, the historian is often helped by the generally unaltered aspect of the countryside. This does not apply, however, to the rivers. Their strength sapped by irrigation systems, many of them are no longer the roaring torrents of earlier years. This must be borne in mind when considering the importance of the Colorado River crossing.

Cook's voyage and his experiences in North America are recounted in his own journal and in Ledyard's book. The latter was of particular importance, because it later influenced Thomas Jefferson's thinking about the Pacific Coast. The Russian trading post was on Unalaska in the Aleutians, but its impact spread much further. For the Russians' trade was increasingly extensive, and they had discovered the reason for the Pacific Coast's economic importance.

The documents concerning Anza's governorship of New Mexico have been collected in Thomas's book. The tragedy of Anza's life was the brief effect he had on events, but he showed how much could be accomplished by an able administrator and a man of action. The Spanish, however, had reached the point where they needed thousands of such men, not merely a handful, in order to recover from the decline in their power.

Fages kept a diary of his expedition to secure the release of the Yumas' prisoners.

The last days of Fray Junípero Serra and his final frustrations are described by Palóu.

In discussing the Apaches, I have—for the purpose of trying to keep the text more simple—ignored their many subtribes, for these can become quite confusing, and the distinction between them is sometimes relatively meaningless, because at a later date many of these subtribes merged.

Roughly speaking, there were two principal divisions: the Plains Apaches and the Western Apaches who, as their name indicates, lived to the west. These divisions were quite dissimilar, the Plains Apaches being much more like other Plains Indians. The Western Apaches had quite a different way of life, and it was they who gave rise to the famous leaders like Cochise and Geronimo. The reader who is interested will find this subject discussed in considerable detail in my book *Geronimo: A Biography*.

The logs including the logs of Haswell, Hoskin and John Boit, and the remnants of the official log, and many other pertinent documents relating to the voyages of Kendrick and Gray have been collected by Howay on behalf of the Massachusetts Historical Society. Other documents can be found in 25th Congress, 2nd Sess., *Senate Executive Document* no. 470; 29th Congress, 1st Sess., *House Report* no. 456; and 30th Congress, 1st Sess., *House Report* no. 502. Vancouver's voyage is covered in his own account and in the life of him by Godwin. Because of the consequences of Gray's second voyage, he and Kendrick are well remembered, but there may have been other attempts earlier to break the Russians' monopoly.

The Nootka Sound Controversy, as it came to be called, had far-reaching effects. It placed the United States under a serious diplomatic strain, for Great Britain demanded the right to march across American soil in the event of war with Spain, and it gave the British a firm foothold in the Pacific Northwest.

For this latter reason especially, it has an important bearing on the area covered in this book, but I have not had space to treat it in detail.

Alexander Mackenzie kept a journal of his trip to the Pacific, which contains the details of his journey.

The description of Monterey was written by a Frenchman aboard the *Otter*, which was perhaps the first American ship to touch at a California port. It is included in Wagner, "Monterey in 1796."

The descriptions of San Diego and the general condition of the California colonies are from Cleveland and Shaler.

The quotations in this chapter are as follows: Ledyard's comments on trade with the Indians, p. 77 of his book; his description of the Russian village, pp. 98–99; and of the profitable fur trade, p. 70; the quotation involving the three words "and take possession" appears in Boit's log, Howay, p. 398; the description of the Spanish fort, Boit, in Howay, p. 411; Mackenzie's arrival at the Pacific, his journal (the edition edited by Quaife), p. 300; Monterey, Wagner, "Monterey in 1796," p. 176; the fort at San Diego, Cleveland, p. 195; the general condition of the California settlements, Shaler, pp. 76–77; Jefferson on the question of New Orleans, letter of April 18, 1802, to Robert R. Livingston, text in Hofstadter, vol. 1, p. 221; and Senator John Breckenridge's comments on the Louisiana Purchase, speech of Nov. 3, 1803, text in Bartlett, p. 115.

The quotation at the head of the chapter is from Captain James Cook's narrative, vol. 16 in Kerr's edition of 1815, p. 197. The date is the date of writing, not of publication.

6. The Americans Look West

When my book *Sunlight and Storm* appeared, one learned professor complained that I had devoted too much space to Lewis and Clark, apparently overlooking the point I had made that their journal, like Thoreau's *Walden,* is one of the best known but least read classics in America. The story of their adventure is exciting, the character of the two men appealing, and the character of their expedition a signal landmark in the development of the United States. Since the professor also made five distortions or misstatements of fact in his brief comments, his slight abilities as a critic can be ignored, and I will defer to the judgment of the many other readers who thanked me for giving them their first close look at these two heroes.

Their importance should not be underestimated. For their expedition was entirely different from those that had preceded it in North America, a point that is too often overlooked largely because we now take the innovation for granted. I only wish I had more space to give them.

During their long journey, Lewis and Clark carefully kept journals in which they put down everything they did or saw. On their return home, Lewis, who was the more scholarly of the two, intended to edit and combine their journals into one account. His premature death, however, prevented the realization of this plan.

Since Clark felt himself ill-equipped for the task, Nicholas Biddle took it over, working from the original documents and with such help as Clark could give him. The War of 1812 broke out before this was completed, and since his financial talents were sorely needed by his country, he turned the papers over to Paul Allen of Philadelphia. The book appeared in 1814 with Allen's name, rather than Biddle's, on the title page. The later failure of the publisher deprived Clark of any profit.

In 1893, Elliott Coues, who served as a doctor with the army and then as secretary and naturalist of the United States Geological Survey, brought out a new edition. Because of his wide knowledge of the West, he was able to add many explanatory comments. Later the historian, Reuben Gold Thwaites, published the *Original Journals of Lewis and Clark*.

In 1810, before Lewis and Clark's journal appeared, Patrick Gass, who had been a sergeant on the expedition, published his journal, too.

Benjamin S. Barton received the scientific papers of the two captains to edit. Unfortunately he did not finish the assignment, and the papers disappeared. This undoubtedly deprived Lewis and Clark of credit for many scientific discoveries.

The journals are perhaps too long and detailed to appeal to many readers. Bernard DeVoto has edited a shorter version, which retains the spirit of the original and most of the most important incidents. The United States National Park Service has also produced a narrative account of the trip with current descriptions of many of the sites. A brief narrative version of the trip, illustrated with pictures of the country, is contained in Salisbury's book.

The quotations in this chapter are taken from the edition of Lewis and Clark's journals edited by Coues and are as follows: need for meeting Indians after passing the Three Forks, p. 445; the first encounter with a Shoshone, pp. 478–80; the American flag carried in pursuit of the Shoshone, p. 480; the meal after crossing the divide, p. 485; the embraces of the Shoshones, p. 490; and the difficulties after leaving the Shoshones, pp. 579 and 580.

The quotation at the head of the chapter is from Thomas Jefferson's instructions to Lewis, p. xxxi, of Lewis and Clark's journal.

7. BEYOND THE BOUNDARIES

The notes for the preceding chapter contain the principal references for the Lewis and Clark expedition. Again the eastern half of their journey once they left the Rockies is described in more detail in my book *Sunlight and Storm.*

Rezanov's visit to San Francisco is described in his own account and that of Langsdorff, who accompanied him.

Pike's career is well described in Hollon's biography. The firsthand story of his expedition is told in his journals. The role of Wilkinson in this expedition is not clear, and the tracks of the traitor-general are so obscure they cannot be discussed in detail here. Suffice it to say that he was attacking Burr, contemplating the invasion of Mexico, and asking the Spanish authorities for a reward for preventing the invasion of Mexico—all at approximately the same time. Pike was unfortunate to have such a sponsor.

The quotations in this chapter are as follows: Lewis and Clark on their decision to spend the winter on the south shore of the Columbia, pp. 719–20 of their journal; life in camp while waiting for Lewis to return, pp. 724–25; description of December at Fort Clatsop, pp. 738–39; preparations for leaving Fort Clatsop, pp. 901–2; final departure, p. 904; camp near the Nez Percés, p. 1014; sick Indians, p. 1021; the remaining snow as they approached the Bitterroots, p. 1044; heavier snow, pp. 1044–45, and 1045–46; the decision to retreat from the Lolo Trail, p. 1046; their feelings at having to do so, p. 1051; and the trip back over the Lolo Trail, pp. 1056–57.

Pike's description of the Rocky Mountains appears in his journals, vol. 2, p. 345; and his reaction to the request that he go to Santa Fé, pp. 384–85.

The quotation at the beginning of the chapter comes from an appendix to Pike's report and can be found in his journals, vol. 2, p. 94.

8. OUTPOST ON THE PACIFIC

The principal references for Pike's adventures are given in the notes to the preceding chapter.

Washington Irving's *Astoria* remains a classic of American literature as well as an able account of the venture. Irving was a friend of Astor's, who made available to him all the existing papers. This friendship, however, biased Irving in Astor's favor. In addition, some of those who were at Astoria quarreled with him on other points. One was his favorable treatment of Captain Thorn. Terrell's book takes full advantage of modern scholarship and a more dispassionate point of view.

Among the contemporary accounts are two translations of Franchère's book, which specifically criticizes Irving on several points, and the account of Alexander Ross. Hunt's journey is related in his journal as well as in the comments of those who were already at Astoria, and Stuart kept a journal of the trip he made back through South Pass.

Hunt's journey up the Missouri as far as the Arikaras is especially well documented, as a number of people, who returned to St. Louis, kept accounts of both him and Lisa. I have not, however, treated this leg of his journey in any detail in this book.

Astor, of course, was engaged in many other activities besides Astoria. An interesting picture of him appears in Parton's book.

Thompson was one of the finest geographers in the Canadian fur trade but almost unrecognized until the 1880s when Joseph B. Tyrrell, who was working with the Geological Survey of Canada, became intrigued by the accuracy of the existing maps. He learned they were based on some old maps in the Crown Lands Department of the Province of Ontario. Investigation of the origins of these showed Thompson's role and also uncovered many of his original papers. Thompson tells his own story in his journals. James K. Smith's biography gives the story of his life in more succinct terms and, of course, with more background.

The quotations in this chapter are as follows: Pike's two observations on the Spaniards' opinions of Americans are in his journal, pp. 396 and 397; his exchange with the governor at Chihuahua, p. 413; his reaction on returning to the United States, p. 447; the comments on Astor's original scheme and its possible effect, Ross, pp. 4–6; the mouth of the Columbia River, pp. 56–57; entering the mouth of the Columbia, Franchère, pp. 57–58; and Thompson's arrival and his equipment, pp. 82 and 84.

The quotation at the head of the chapter comes from a petition that Astor sent to Congress, requesting permission to import British goods for trade with the Indians. The text appears in Irving, pp. 337–78.

9. Casualty of War

Much of the basic material for the account of the Astoria venture is listed in the notes to the previous chapter. To this should be added Hunt's journal of his trip and also Stuart's.

Considerable differences exist among the various sources relating to the closing days of Astoria. Some say the failure of the *Beaver* to return was caused by its condition and the timidity of its captain; some that Astor had ordered the captain to give preference to the Russians' shipments. Some blame McDougal for failing to resist. Others are more charitable, taking into account his predicament. Alexander Ross says that a group of Boston merchants financed a ship to go to the Pacific and warn American vessels that war had broken out. According to him, Astor refused to contribute to the ship's expense and therefore Astoria received no warning. Irving, who was a friend of Astor's, makes no mention of this point. None of these differences, however, affect the basic outcome.

The quotations in this chapter are as follows: Ross, describing Astor, pp.

284–85; describing the arrival of McKenzie at Astoria, p. 182; on the arrival of Hunt, pp. 182–83; Madison on the state of the nation, Richardson, vol. 1, p. 520; Astor's determination to hold on to Astoria, quoted in Irving, p. 327; Franchère's description of the dealings with McTavish, p. 142; the disillusion of the British naval officers, pp. 150–51.

The quotation at the head of the chapter is from Madison's Fourth Annual Message, Nov. 4, 1812. It appears in Richardson, vol. 1, p. 520.

10. A Time of Change

The War of 1812 had a considerable long-term effect on the United States. For in spite of the nation's many military blunders, it obtained enough success to increase its prestige among the European powers. Pike's role was both militarily and psychologically important. The story of this sad figure, who finally obtained the fame he so much desired only at the cost of his own life, is told in Hollon's book.

Von Kotzebue's account of his visit to San Francisco is interesting for its picture of the breakdown of the Spanish colonial system and for its descriptions of the southward migration of the sea otters and of the Spaniards' roping bears. In later days, when Americans also learned how to use a lasso, western artists—with a degree of artistic freedom—sometimes portrayed cowboys roping wild animals, an extremely dangerous practice. (Bulls and steers can be dangerous, too, but in a different fashion.) Here is an early account of such an activity actually taking place.

When he was not sailing under Bouchard, Corney held a responsible position as a ship's officer with the North-West Company and has left interesting descriptions of its post on the Columbia and other aspects of the fur trade. His life also shows how, in those fluid times, a respectable professional man could be quickly drawn into highly speculative military ventures.

The negotiations over Oregon are somewhat obscured by the lack of detail in some of the British diplomatic records. (Apparently Great Britain did not accord the Oregon question as much importance as some of the other problems then bothering it.) But Merk gives a good summary of the events—with supporting documents—pp. 20–45.

The Long expedition was not directly helpful in the expansion of the United States beyond the Rockies, but it was another important instance of the government assuming the responsibility for exploration and collecting information. The record written by Edwin James is both readable and interesting.

The account of Mexico's independence is, of course, greatly condensed. Iturbide shortly became emperor and was then quickly deposed, leading to decades of bloodshed and uncertain government. A reading of the full story should make Americans glad of their own heritage, but should not give them a feeling of superiority. For the circumstances under which Mexico attempted to achieve an independent government were entirely different from those that prevailed in the United States.

The journey of Hugh Glenn and his party to New Mexico is described in Jacob Fowler's journal. Although I have usually corrected obvious mistakes in quotations to avoid the otherwise necessary *sics,* I have left these as Fowler wrote them, for they have a charm of their own. Thomas James's account is more readable, covers more ground, and gives more detail, for he polished it into the form of a book rather than leaving it merely as a journal. Among the many men he did not like was Hugh Glenn, whom he accused of cheating.

The instructions of the Hudson's Bay Company to George Simpson are included in a letter of February 22, 1822, which is reproduced from Hudson's Bay Company General Letter Book no. 620 in Merk, *Fur Trade and Empire,* pp. 175–76.

George Simpson was not *the* governor of the Hudson's Bay Company, as he is sometimes called. That title was held by the equivalent of the chairman of the board of directors, who was assisted by a deputy governor. The "directors" were members of the committee of the Hudson's Bay Company. Simpson was governor in chief of the Hudson's Bay Company's territories. In modern parlance, he was chief operating officer, North America.

The quotations in this chapter are as follows: Astor's letter concerning the loss of Astoria is quoted in Irving, p. 365; the descriptions of San Francisco in 1816 are in von Kotzebue; the description of Bouchard's attacks on California, Corney, pp. 218 and 210–21; Fowler's two comments on his trip to New Mexico, his journal, pp. 95 and 106-7; and the further description of New Mexico, Thomas James, pp. 173-74.

Monroe's quotation at the head of the chapter can be found in Richardson, vol. 11, p. 117.

11. Growing Ambitions

Even if it had not played such an important role in the early development of the United States, the fur trade would have attracted wide interest because of its romance and adventure. In *Sunlight and Storm* I have dealt in more detail with this business on the Great Plains. For the trade as a whole, including that on the west side of the Rockies, Chittenden's book continues to be a classic, particularly the later edition listed in the bibliography. This includes some corrections that have resulted from the discovery of additional material.

Dale's book contains Ashley's journal of his trip up the Platte, Smith's journal of his trip to California, and other pertinent documents, along with interpretative comments. Morgan's book on Ashley includes additional material of great interest, and his book on Jedediah Smith is also important. James Clyman kept a journal while working for Ashley. Ashley's views of the fur trade were contained in several reports he wrote that will be found in 19th Congress, 1st Sess., *House Executive Documents,* vol. 6, no. 117; 20th Congress, 2nd Sess., *Senate Executive Documents,* vol. 1, no. 67; and 21st Congress, 2nd Sess., *Senate Executive Documents,* vol.1, no. 39. James Beckwourth, the mountain man who later let his fancy embroider some of his stories, is the subject of Wilson's book.

James Ohio Pattie's book, which is one of the classics of the West, tells the experiences of those who trapped out of New Mexico. This part of the fur business produced some remarkable explorations as well as some wonderful stories and helped in the development of a number of frontier heroes like Kit Carson. Because the central route across the mountains later became more important, however, and because the trappers operating out of St. Louis came into more direct confrontation with the British, space has forced me to limit the description of it.

The trade with New Mexico, especially with Santa Fé, also played an interesting and dramatic part in the nation's history. Although it helped to open up the southwest to American merchants, it is largely the story of the trip to and from that distant city. This, in turn, relates more to the Great Plains than to the country west of the Rockies, and I have described it more thoroughly in my book *Sunlight and Storm.* For those who wish more detail about this aspect of American history, the books by Josiah Gregg, Inman, and Vestal are among those recommended.

The quotations in this chapter are as follows: Adams's comments on the Russian ukase, Adams to Middleton, 9/22/23, quoted in Bartlett, p. 170; Monroe's Message to Congress, Richardson, vol. 2, p. 219; Pattie's description of the governor of New Mexico, p. 44; his description of the trapping parties, p. 134.

The quotation at the beginning of the chapter is part of the diary of John Quincy Adams and appears in his memoirs. It is reproduced in Bartlett, p. 187.

12. PAST THE MOUNTAIN BARRIER

Like many active men, Smith did not have much time for keeping journals. (Thus it is that many of the men who have done the most are the least remembered by history.) One of his men, however, Harrison Rogers, kept quite detailed notes that cover much of Smith's travels, although Rogers was unfortunately killed during the Umpquas' attack. His journal and other pertinent information is contained in Dale's book. For the activities of the

British during this period, Merk's edition of George Simpson's journal is important.

For a description of the activities of the trappers working out of New Mexico, the reader may want to refer to Weber's book. As Weber has pointed out, perhaps one reason so little has been known about their activities was their desire to keep them hidden from the Mexican authorities. He describes the misplaced tax law and the tensions between the two groups on pp. 129–33.

The story of Pattie's trip is told in his own account, one of the well-known tales of the trappers. Like many frontiersmen, he had a tendency to exaggerate. Young's story tells about the first part of the journey. In Pattie's original account, he quotes the permit they received from the New Mexican governor and dates it "September 22d, 1829." From the internal evidence and other sources, this was obviously a printer's error, and the date should have been 1827.

Pattie occupies a rather unfortunate place in American western history. Unknown to the general public, he seems to be overly known to western historians and therefore, among the professionals, falls—or nearly falls—into the category of the trite. He is also regarded with considerable suspicion. Some of his dates are in error, and he has also been criticized on other scores. For example, he tells how the California governor tore up the passport issued to his father but then reproduced its text in his book. But this is easily explicable, for on page 234, he explicitly states that he had a duplicate, which he produced later. He has also been questioned concerning his report of the governor's cruelty; and the return of some of the men to California at a later date has been used as evidence against him. On the other hand, there is a considerable difference between being the leader dealing with someone like the governor and merely being a follower who trusts the leader will finally straighten things out. Also the lot of certain persons in the United States at that time was not a particularly happy one, and they were more accustomed to cruelty. (Flogging, for example, was still an accepted punishment in the armed forces.) Other examples of the cruelty of Mexican officials exist that would substantiate Pattie's remarks—for example, the treatment of the Texas Pioneers when, at a later date, they fell into the hands of the governor of New Mexico.

Sylvester Pattie is also sometimes suspected of having intended to go to California in the first place despite a passport that was limited to travel in Chihuahua and Sonora. But if that is the case, he was wasting his time when he went to the mouth of the Colorado. As a woodsman, he knew that beaver did not live on salt water.

Yet there is little question that he had the frontiersman's tendency to exaggerate when relating his adventures to tenderfeet. (Even John James Audubon succumbed to this failing when he described rattlesnakes to a scientific audience in Glasgow.) On the other hand, it hardly seems likely that, as James Ohio Pattie claimed, he vaccinated twenty-two thousand persons in California. The principles of vaccination were, of course, well known. In 1718 Lady Mary Wortley Montagu introduced into England the practice she had learned in Constantinople of vaccinating persons with the pus drawn from a light case. Later Jenner had conducted his experiments, knowledge of which spread quickly. But the doctors I have informally consulted tell me that Pattie's vaccine was undoubtedly dead by the time he reached California. Nevertheless, it would have produced small sores that to an experienced eye might have looked like a real vaccination. It is fortunate that hepatitis was not common in California. Otherwise he might have laid the province low! But in any case Pattie's book makes good reading and much of his information casts light on the life of a trapper and on conditions in California.

Hall Kelley's 1828 memorial to Congress will be found in 20th Congress, 1st Sess., *House Document* no. 139. Many of his other writings as well as a short biographical sketch are contained in Powell's important volume.

An excellent summary of conditions in both the Santa Fé and the fur trade was contained in the Congressional report, 22nd Congress, 1st Sess., *Senate Executive Document* no. 90. This includes statements by people in both businesses.

Bean provides a good account of conditions in California during this period and of the forces that were at play among the various components of the population.

The quotations in this chapter are as follows: Pattie's description of their arrival at the mouth of the Colorado, p. 152; their crossing to Baja California, pp. 133 and 159; his father's funeral, pp. 184–85; the guns, p. 198; his interchange with the governor over the vaccination program, p. 205; the battle at Santa Barbara, p. 225; his desire to return to the United States, p. 231; Kelley on the benefits of a colony in Oregon, Powell, p. 60; Webster on the Union, his works, vol. 3, p. 342; the Santa Fé trade, 22nd Congress, 1st Sess., *Senate Executive Document* no. 90, pp. 33 and 32–33; Webster's remarks on the dismemberment of the Union, his works, vol. 3, p. 342.

Beechey's quotation at the head of the chapter appears in his account of his travels. The date of 1827 is the date he made the observation, not the date on which his account was published.

13. THE TRAILS BECOME BROADER

The settlement—or at least the postponement—of the nullification issue came at a critical time for the outbreak of internecine warfare might well have altered the whole course of America's western movement, postponing it until the United States could no longer be a successful contender.

During this period, the fur business was becoming more routine, since much of the country had been explored—not necessarily in detail—but the traveler knew more and more what in general to expect. Zenas Leonard gives an interesting picture of the trade at this time as well as a firsthand glance at Fitzpatrick, one of the most notable of the mountain men.

Powell's collection of Kelley's writings continues to reveal the glamorous— and popular—view of Oregon that was emerging in the public's mind. John B. Wyeth gives the opposite point of view. Although he was Nathaniel's nephew, his relationship did not prevent his making caustic remarks about the foolishness of men advancing into the wilderness without adequate preparation or knowledge. He was, however, moving against his own times, and his writing probably discouraged few of those who thought of moving West.

Nathaniel Wyeth's two trips west are described in his own journals, and Washington Irving has written an account of Bonneville's venture. Kelley's adventures are related in Powell's book. There must have been more to McLoughlin's obvious dislike of Kelley than the question of the horses or, as some have maintained, that he was interested in keeping settlers out of the area. Kelley seems to have been one of those unfortunate characters who can command neither respect nor affection.

Dana's comments are significant, because he was not a businessman. Therefore he could be expected to be less critical of the Californians than those who were trying to make a living there. Bean, p. 68, has emphasized the slaughter of the mission cattle.

Sources for the missionaries' story are numerous. Lee, Brosnan, and Loewenberg give considerable information. Parker has left his own account, which he published during his lifetime. Whitman received considerable posthumous celebration because of his dramatic death and the controversy over the role he played in saving Oregon for the United States. Among the books that might be consulted by a reader wishing to learn more about this remarkable man are Nard Jones, Mowry, and the excellent two-volume work by Drury. Also valuable is Narcissa Whitman's journal and letter home dated October 26, 1836, a transcript of which was made available to me at the Beinecke Library, Yale University.

Townsend's journal contains an account of his trip and some of the people he encountered.

The quotations in this chapter are as follows: the arrangements with Nathaniel Wyeth, John B. Wyeth, p. 13; the description of Pierre's Hole, Leonard, p. 21; Battle of Pierre's Hole, pp. 22–23; John B. Wyeth's advice to young men, p. 86; Wyeth's determination to return to the Columbia, Irving *Bonneville,* p. 144; Wyeth on the end of his business, a letter included with his journals, p. 101; Kelley's comments on his stay in Oregon come from a book he published in 1852, which Powell has reproduced—the remarks are on p. 143; Dana's comments on the secularization of the missions, pp. 210–11; on the state of California, p. 216; Parker's meeting with the Indians at the rendezvous, quoted in Mowry, p. 53; and Townsend on meeting the Whitman party, pp. 353–55.

The quotation at the head of the chapter is from John B. Wyeth, p. 9.

14. THE MISSIONARIES COME

The story of Texas's struggle for independence is well known and told in most history books dealing with the area. That of California has been less publicized but is recounted in most California histories such as Bean's. Two important points to consider are that Texas was not alone in objecting to the government at Mexico City and that California, in addition to declaring its own independence, was extremely vulnerable to intrusion by Great Britain, the United States, and Russia. This is clearly stated by Alexander Forbes in the quotation that I have used from his book, although he realized that the Russian threat was diminishing.

Those readers wishing to follow more closely the development of Mexico during this period may find useful the books by McHenry and Parkes. McHenry, pp. 109–10, describes in detail the burial of Santa Ana's amputated leg.

The story of Santa Rita del Cobre can be found in my book *Geronimo,* pp. 32–40. Further references to it can be found in Dunn, pp. 314–16, and Ball, pp. 45–47. A description of the Panic of 1837 can be found in Myers, pp. 98–99. Slacum's report is contained in 25th Congress, 2nd Sess., *Senate Executive Document* no. 24. Chittenden's book on the life of de Smet is the primary source for information about that remarkable man. Sutter's activities are described in such works as Zollinger, Schoonover, Dana, Gudde, and in his own diary.

The Texas Pioneers, for all their labors and sufferings, played only a small role in the course of history; but their tale is an interesting one and affected popular opinion, increasing the Americans' dislike of the Mexicans. Since Kendall was a writer by trade, his book gives a vivid picture of what occurred. Loomis's book is also a good account and, of course, gives the story from more than one point of view.

Both Simpson and Wilkes reinforce the impression of Mexican California as a land of corruption and wasted opportunities. For a few, the life there may have had its halcyon qualities, but much of the population led poor existences. Wilkes's report on Oregon and California appears on pp. 518–80 of his book. Some years later, during the Civil War, he became the center of an international controversy, as he was the American commander in the *Trent* affair.

The quotations in this chapter are as follows: the vulnerability of California, Forbes, pp. 92–93; Hugh McCullough's comments on the depression are quoted in Myers, p. 99; Slacum on Oregon, 25th Congress, 2nd Sess., *Senate Executive Document* no. 24, pp. 16–17; de Smet on his first visit to the Indians, Chittenden on de Smet, p. 226; the inexperience of the emigrant party, Bidwell, p. 23; their lack of knowledge of the route, p. 38. Bartleson's reaction to the trip, p. 37; demoralization of the party, pp. 62–63; description of Sutter, p. 75; describing de Smet, pp. 25–26; Kendall on the execution of the two Texans, vol. 1, pp. 320–21 and 323; Simpson on the lack of commerce in California, p. 166; on the Mexican's inefficiency in handling the Indians, p. 196; on the future of California, p. 182; Wilkes on Lee's mission, p. 572; on Whitman's, p. 570; on Fort Vancouver, p. 525; and Kendall on the difficulty of conquering Mexico, vol. 2, p. 425.

The quotation at the head of the chapter is from Parker, p. 13. Although the edition I have used was published in 1844, I have given the date of the earlier edition, 1838, as the remark reflected Parker's views of that time. The trail song is from the autobiographical manuscript of Phinias Cartridge, which was made available to me by his great-grandson.

15. Learning the Land

Hamilton's account gives a good picture of the fur trade, not only in its decline but in its better days as well, for he became acquainted with many old-time trappers. Like many a stranger, he was perhaps a better observer of some of the customs and habits of the mountain men with whom he lived than if he had spent years in the business. His experiences are covered in pp. 6–96 of his book.

The story of the company Hastings accompanied is told in the book that he later published as an emigrant's guide.

Insufficient attention has been given, I believe, to the causes behind the American movement beyond the Missouri. No other country had the same experience. Geographical proximity was certainly a factor, but other circumstances must also have played a role.

Gray, although not entirely reliable, has left a detailed description of the convention to set up a government for Oregon, pp. 336–59, with subsequent events in the following pages.

Frémont was a subject of controversy during his lifetime and has remained so since. Attractive and brilliant, his character was flawed by too much ambition, which led him away from the quiet course of duty. His later performance in California brought about his court-martial and the end of his army career, but he subsequently ran as a candidate for president. Nevins's biography is highly favorable to him. Nevins has also edited his report with slight omissions. For those who want the complete story of his remarkable journey, there is Frémont's original report.

The quotations in this chapter are as follows: Hamilton on Fort Bridger, pp. 64 and 65–66; Hastings on the start of his expedition, pp. 5–6; describing Dr. Whitman, p. 21; on the danger of going from Oregon to California, p. 64; on exchange of views with those coming from Oregon, p. 65; on Sutter's welcome and the desire to persuade others to emigrate, p. 69; Hamilton on Indian insults, p. 31; Gray on the Oregon convention, pp. 340–41; on the statehouse, p. 360; Johnson on the arrival of the emigrants in Oregon, pp. 39–40; on Oregon's government and land claims, pp. 62–63; Frémont on the appearance of the trail to Oregon, p. 128; on his boat and excursions on Great Salt Lake, pp. 152, 153–154, and 155; his discussion of Fort Hall, p. 163; on Mount Hood, p. 182; on Whitman's mission, pp. 182–83; on the emigrants at Fort Vancouver, p. 191; and on the prospects for the return journey, p. 196.

The quotation at the head of the chapter is from Johnson, p. 140.

16. A Time of Expansion

Selections from the correspondence between the United States and Great Britain over the Oregon question are included in 29th Congress, 1st Sess., *Senate Executive Document* no. 1.

For Frémont's expedition, the sources have been listed in the notes for the preceding chapter. Johnson's experiences and opinions are set forth in his book. Johnson's partner and coauthor of the book was William H. Winter. In order to make the text a little less complicated, I have not referred to him along with Johnson every time. For a description of the emigration in 1845, I have drawn on Joel Palmer.

The Senate documents of the period contain much valuable background concerning the controversy with both Mexico and Great Britain, and some of these are specifically listed under the quotations for this chapter.

There is little point annotating the discussion of the origins of the Mexican War. This information is contained in a wide variety of primary and secondary sources. Although it has become customary for Americans to condemn their role in this war, a review of the facts indicates that this self-condemnation may be carried to excessive lengths. Many Mexicans were just as eager to fight as the more bellicose of the Americans and just as sure that they would win. And it must be borne in mind that numerous Americans were obsessed with the specter of another nation's securing sovereignty over the contested territory. Their belief in this specter was real, and they had grounds for thinking as they did. Unfortunately Frémont's aggressive conduct and that of other individual Americans cannot be excused.

The quotations in this chapter are as follows: Packenham's letter to the secretary of state, 29th Congress, 1st Sess., *Senate Executive Document* no. 1, pp. 33–34; Frémont on his decision to go to California, p. 220; his descriptions of crossing the Sierra Nevada, pp. 228, 231, 234, 235, 236, 241, and 245; Calhoun's response to the British ambassador, 29th Congress, 1st Sess., *Senate Executive Document* no. 1., p. 35 and his views on the American claim to Oregon, p. 54; Johnson on the merits of Oregon, p. 70; on Oregon and California, pp. 133–34; Frémont on the international situation, his journal in Nevins, p. 435; Webster on national preparedness, *Works,* vol. 5. pp. 61 and 62; Frémont on the possibility of war, Nevins, p. 435; his reply to Castro, p. 471; excuses for his retreat, p. 472; the secretary of state's statement of Polk's attitude on Oregon, 29th Congress, 1st Sess., *Senate Executive Document* no. 1, p. 62; Polk's message to Congress, Richardson, p. 443.

The quotation at the head of the chapter is from Polk's war message, Richardson, p. 440.

17. MARCHING TO WAR

The state of American preparedness is discussed by Upton, pp. 195–222, along with a discussion of the war in Mexico, although the New Mexico and California campaigns in themselves did not involve enough fighting to influence Upton's study, and therefore he did not include them. The sources for the speeches by Smith and Calhoun are cited in these notes under the listing of quotations.

The negotiations over Oregon, protracted as they were, form a complicated chapter in American history. The sudden settlement of the issue has been ascribed to a number of causes, but it was the mixture, rather than any single one of them, that seems to have produced the results that occurred. For the reader who wishes to follow the story in more detail, Merk's book will be worthwhile.

For Kearny's campaign, I have relied on Cooke's and Emory's accounts. Cooke is especially useful for his description of his reception at Santa Fé. Emory was charged with making a report of the country and the route the army followed, but he also kept a detailed record of the events and went ahead with Kearny while Cooke remained behind to take command of the Mormon Battalion. Emory's report also appears in 30th Congress, 1st Sess., *Senate Executive Document* no. 7.

Thomas Kearny's book contains an account of the march to California and the subsequent events that presents Kearny's side in the controversy that eventually arose.

The quotations in this chapter are as follows: Truman Smith on Polk's policies, speech delivered February 2, 1846, and printed by J. and G. S. Gideon, Washington, p. 19; Calhoun on the possibility of war, speech delivered March 16, 1846, printed by Towers, Washington, pp. 10–11; Polk's message to the Senate, June 10, 1846, Richardson, pp. 449–50; Cooke on his mission to Santa Fé, pp. 27–28, 28, 28–29; on the state of mind of the soldiers,

p. 68; on the prospects of the march to California, p. 71; Emory on Santa Rita del Cobre, pp. 97–98; on the Apaches, both quotations, p. 100; and the Pimas, pp. 134–35.

The quotation at the head of the chapter will be found in Webster's *Works*, vol. 5, p. 156.

18. THE FRUITS OF WAR

The events in California during 1846 and 1847 gave rise to many controversies both then and since. This was natural when so many people, working in an uncoordinated manner, took part in shaping the events and when some of them were more than usually anxious to obtain glory for themselves. Numerous accounts of that period exist, most of them reflecting a particular bias.

Bean contains a summary of the happenings and places them in perspective. Frémont's memoirs, of course, give his point of view. Larkin wrote many letters, some of which are included in Hawgood and Underhill. The navy's story can be found in Neeser and Craven. Lewis's book offers a short selection of some of the documents that reflect an overall picture and would be interesting to a reader who wishes a contemporary source to explore this period further.

Downey and Emory give pictures of the continued march of Kearny's men and the fights in which they were engaged before the reconquest of California. The description of Carson is, to me, particularly engaging. A pipe-smoking horseman is rather unusual; a pipe-smoking rifleman even more so. He had obviously perfected the complicated maneuver involved. The description appears in Downey, p. 215.

The quotations in this chapter are as follows: Emory on the Englishman, pp. 165–66; deaths of the soldiers, p. 170; the night camp, pp. 170–71; the mountain man and the ocean, p. 174; the sailors as infantrymen, p. 179; the battle at the San Gabriel River, p. 186; condition of the soldiers after the battle, p. 186; the final action at Los Angeles, p. 187; and the entrance into Los Angeles, p. 188.

The quotation at the head of the chapter is by Thomas O. Larkin, American consul at Monterey. It was contained in a report that was published in the *Pacific Monthly* in December 1863 and reprinted in Lewis, *California in 1846*, p. 9.

19. VICTORY WITHOUT GLORY

Downey contains a good account of the uprising at Taos. A brief summary appears in Hollon, *The Southwest*, pp. 168–70.

The sensational nature of the Donner party's experience gave rise to many stories of varying degrees of truth. McGlashan checked as many sources as he could and interviewed many of the survivors in an effort to produce a single, authentic account, and his book today remains a principal source for the history of the expedition. In spite of his Victorian sentimentality, to which some readers may object, it is a good, well-written book.

A good deal of material exists on the Whitman massacre. Widespread interest in the tragedy meant that the story of each survivor was carefully sought out. In addition, the testimony offered later at the trial of five Cayuses for the murders added more information. Drury has collated this material and presented an overall account, which will interest those seeking more information.

Gray's book is also of interest, because it is contemporary and therefore exudes a feeling of the times. He was, however, a man of many prejudices. One of his strongest was against the Hudson's Bay Company, a business firm in which he could see little good. His comments, therefore, have to be read with this in mind. He adds to the vividness of his story with quotations from many original documents and accounts.

The quotations in this chapter are as follows: Emory on the end of the war in California, p. 191; lack of food among the Donner party, Georgia Donner, quoted in McGlashan, p. 73; the remains of the Donner party's camp, Edwin Bryant, quoted in McGlashan, p. 183; and the Indians' treatment of medicine men, Wilkes, p. 571.

The quotation at the head of the chapter is from Gray, p. 350.

20. RETREAT AND ADVANCE

Numerous general sources tell about the defeat of Mexico. Often overlooked, however, is the insistence of the Mexicans on fighting, for many of them were confident they could win.

For the continuation of the Whitman story, the reader may wish to refer to the notes for the previous chapter.

Numerous sources, some of which are mentioned in the bibliography, tell the story of the Mormons. Orson Pratt's journal gives an account of the first party of Mormons to reach the Great Salt Lake. Jesse N. Smith, who was considerably younger, tells about the same period from a small boy's point of view and then goes on to describe other aspects of Mormon life, including his trips abroad to raise recruits. Ferris gives the impression of the community early in its history from the point of view of a non-Mormon.

Jesse Smith, p. 13, describes his hunger as a young boy, and pp. 13–14 gives an account of the grasshoppers and the gulls. Larkin's business affairs in 1847 are covered in Underhill, pp. 164–77. A description of Sutter's arrangements over the sawmill appears in Bidwell, pp. 102–3 and 106–9.

The quotations in this chapter are as follows: the Massachusetts legislature on the Mexican War, text in Hofstadter, vol. 1, pp. 343–44; the resolution to set up an armed force in Oregon, Gray, p. 536; the memorial to Congress, pp. 543 and 546; Orson Pratt, on the founding of Great Salt Lake City, p. 80; Polk's message on Oregon, Richardson, vol. 4, pp. 584–85; Bidwell on Marshall's mill and the discovery of gold, pp. 106, 107, 107–8, and 108.

The quotation at the head of the chapter comes from a discourse delivered by Orson Pratt in 1867 and included with his journal, p. 85.

21. STAMPEDE FOR WEALTH

The California gold rush, because of its drama, produced a large quantity of written material in the form of journals and reminiscences. A large number have been consulted in the preparation of this account. A few that have been especially helpful or may be of interest to a reader who wants to pursue the subject further are listed at the end of these notes. Bean, pp. 108–23, gives a good overall summary of what took place. Young's book covers many aspects of mining in detail, not only in California, but elsewhere. He is especially interesting on some of the technical aspects, which he describes in nontechnical language.

Bidwell, p. 109, tells of the surprising lack of excitement that surrounded Marshall's discovery at first. Grimshaw's account gives a good picture of conditions at Sutter's Fort during this early period. He is also responsible for the description of the trial about which he wrote an article that was later reproduced with his full account.

(Place names create something of a problem, because they sometimes changed. For example, as I have noted in the text, Sutter's Fort became more generally known as New Helvetia. Yerba Buena became San Francisco. As these changes would probably only confuse the general reader, I have tried to adopt the name most generally known and use it throughout.)

So many persons made the trip to California and so many of them had a sense that this was a historic occasion of wide interest to those who had remained behind that the number of journals or personal reminiscences is great. All that I can give here are a few that might be of interest to anyone wanting to read a firsthand account of this experience. Kingsley tells about the journey around Cape Horn. Dore provides an example of a man who invested in a ship and cargo for the journey. Cardinell tells about the sufferings of those who went through the American Southwest.

Among the many that are available, two colorful accounts of the California Trail in the north are Stansbury's, which goes only as far as Utah, and Delano's. Steele's experience on a California cattle ranch illustrates what was happening to that business. Neff, pp. 127–46, and Stansbury, p. 134, describe the Mormons' business with the emigrants.

The figures on gold production, the balance of payments, and the

427

government debt come from *Historical Statistics of the United States* published by the United States Department of Commerce. Polk's comments on gold specie and the future of American exports were contained in his fourth annual message. The problem of metallic coin at this period is described in Myers, p. 133. Polk's views on public projects were set forth in his veto message of December 15, 1847.

A clear, but more detailed, description of placer mining in its early stages can be found in Young, pp. 102–24. Delano's description of the change that came over the camp and the murder of the two miners will be found on pp. 349–53. Sprenger's story can be found in Shinn, pp. 191–98. Shinn also contains an interesting study of government in the mining camps. Among other accounts that have provided information for these descriptions and which the reader might wish to consult are Gibson, Osbun, Hannon (editor), Potter, Geiger, Canfield (editor), Manly, Quaife (editor), and Clappe.

The quotations in this chapter are as follows: Bidwell on the discovery of gold, p. 109; Polk on the gold deposits, Richardson, vol. 4, p. 636; Stansbury on the California Trail, p. 22; Delano on the number of emigrants, p. 95; Steele on the sale of cattle, p. 244; the market for emigrants' goods, *The Frontier Guardian,* quoted in Neff, p. 143; Polk's views on public projects, his veto message of December 15, 1847, Richardson, pp. 612–13; Sacramento, Gibson, pp. 43–44, and Delano, p. 251; the miners' earnings and the times when expenses were greater than income, Gibson, pp. 43 and 48; and Delano on the decline of morale in the mining camp, pp. 350–51.

The quotation at the head of the chapter is from Revere, p. 154. The date of his publication was 1872. The date I have used is the date he returned to San Francisco.

22. GOVERNMENT AND JUSTICE

As mentioned in the previous chapter, the story of Sprenger's case is recounted by Shinn, pp. 191–98, Goodwin gives a comprehensive picture of the debates that produced the California constitution.

Bartlett's report contains a detailed account of southern New Mexico and Arizona in the early 1850s as well as some of the adjoining areas in Mexico. It is, of course, the most detailed description prepared by any American up until that time.

The complicated business of Frémont's Mariposa holdings is discussed at some length by Nevins in his biography and by Underhill, pp. 196–97 and 202–15. Sutter gives a picture of his own problems during the gold rush in his *Diary.*

Like most such groups, the San Francisco Committee of Vigilance of 1851 was a semi-secret organization. Many of its members were recognized as such by their fellow citizens, but since they were operating outside the law, they made some effort to conceal their roles. And even in later years, many of them were hesitant in admitting what they had done. They did, however, keep records, and some of them were quite frank in speaking to those interested in California's history. Much of the material thus collected is in the Bancroft Library. For the reader who wants to pursue their story further, two books may be particularly helpful: Bancroft's *Popular Tribunals* and the volume by Williams, who has prepared a careful study of the 1851 committee from the original records. Of particular interest to the reader may be her discussion of the Lewis case and the formation of the committee, pp. 181–85 and 203–6.

The quotations in this chapter are as follows: Webster on the impracticality of slavery in the newly acquired lands, *Works,* vol. 5, p. 382; Clay on behalf of the Union, quoted by Schurz, vol. 2, p. 358; Webster on the Union, *Works,* vol. 5, p. 437; Clay and Webster on the personal effects of the debate, Schurz, vol. 2, p. 365; Cooke's road, Bartlett, vol. 1, p. 294; Mangas Colorados, vol. 1, pp. 300, 301, and 302; public officials, *Evening Picayune,* quoted by Bancroft, *Popular Tribunals,* vol. 1, p. 130; and the San Francisco paper commenting on the crowd's action is the *Herald,* June 5, 1851, quoted by Williams, p. 182.

The quotation at the head of the chapter is from Flint, p. 1223. Although the crowd shouted this in 1856, they might just as well have done so in 1851, for their sentiments were the same.

23. FAILURES OF GOVERNMENT

The gold rush greatly influenced the development of the American clipper ship by increasing the demand for fast vessels. For this effect, see Howard I. Chapelle, *The Search for Speed Under Sail; 1700–1855* (New York, Bonanza Books, 1967), p. 338. The measures introduced by Frémont are listed in Nevins's biography, p. 391. Anderson, p. 115, discusses the initial appropriations for Utah. The federal government's expenditures are given on p. 719, *Historical Statistics.* Hawthorne describes the unfavorable conditions in Oregon, pp. 130ff.

Bergenroth presents a good picture of the lawless conditions in California. Bancroft, *Popular Tribunals,* vol. 1, discusses the Jenkins case in detail as well as other actions of the vigilantes. Williams has brought together the total story of the execution and the coroner's inquest, pp. 208–20, as well as much other information about the movement.

Russell has put together the story of Savage and his dealings with the Indians, pp. 16–24. Coan has gathered the facts dealing with federal Indian policy during the early days of Oregon. Joseph Lane is the subject of

Hendrickson's study on politics and the sectional crisis in Oregon. He describes Lane's dealing with the Indians of southern Oregon, pp. 75–79. Ferris's report on the Mormons is a good example of the misunderstandings that developed between the sect and the outside world.

Meriwether, pp. 137–70, tells of his experiences on becoming governor of New Mexico. Aubry's journal provides a glimpse of the harsh conditions existing in New Mexico and Arizona. Jackson gives us a good picture of the government's road-building program and the question of route.

The quotations in this chapter are as follows: conditions in Oregon before statehood, Hawthorne, pp. 130–31; the defenses of the man on San Francisco Bay and the shift of the criminals to the cities, Bergenroth, pp. 144–45 and 146; Delano on the changing attitudes of the prospectors, p. 373; Ferris on the Mormons, pp. 39 and 290; Aubry discovering gold, p. 360; and the condition of him and his men, pp. 367–68.

The quotation at the head of the chapter is from Whiting's journal, p. 306.

24. Violence and Justice

The story of the vigilantes, whether those of San Francisco or other places in the West, has always proved intriguing. Since those of San Francisco have become so famous, I have treated them in some detail, hoping they will serve as an example of how such movements both developed and operated. The reader who wishes to know more about the committee will enjoy Bancroft's *Popular Tribunals,* but must take into account his strong bias in favor of the vigilantes. A firsthand account is one by Flint, who served as one of the executioners of Cora and Casey.

Those interested in the Mormons' handcarts will find that Hafen has collected much of the original material, including diaries, Mormon press reports, and a commentary that draws the material together.

The quotations are as follows: the editor of the *Herald,* Bancroft, *Popular Tribunals,* vol. 2, p. 78; text of ultimatum, vol. 2, p. 185; the opinion of the Sacramento *Union,* vol. 2, pp. 340–41; the final sentiments of the vigilantes, Flint, p. 1227; the Mormons' offer of financial help to emigrants, the *Millenial Star,* xiv, p. 325 (1852), quoted by Hafen, p. 25; the arrival of the first two companies of handcart emigrants, the *Deseret News,* quoted by Hafen, pp. 77–78.

The quotation at the head of the chapter is from Bergenroth, pp. 148–149.

25. The Stages Roll

Stagecoaches, particularly those following the transcontinental routes, occupy a particularly romantic place in American history; and the stories about them—both fiction and nonfiction—are legion. The reader who wishes to pursue the subject further will find considerable information on the mail routes in Hafen's book. The book by the two Bannings gives a colorful account of Butterfield's operation and is especially useful because the Banning family was in the stagecoach business. They therefore are able to offer some insights that are not generally available elsewhere in the handling of these coaches and their teams.

The notes to the previous chapters dealing with the Mormons and Utah contain references to several sources of information about this remarkable sect and their achievement in turning the wilderness into civilization. In addition, the reader may wish to refer to Hirshson's book for a comprehensive picture of Brigham Young and the organization he fostered. Not all good, but far from all bad, he was an unusual figure. In considering the Mountain Meadows Massacre, the reader should remember the distinctive differences between Indian hostilities in the East and West. In the East, the Indians were often the allies of the competing Europeans. In the American West, they were the common enemy. This is what added to the horror of the massacre. Brooks's book tells the story in considerable detail. Lee's, of course, is sensational. Although he was trying to put himself in a good light, he also did actually witness the event. In his volume on the Utah Expedition, Hafen has done a service in collecting in one place many of the pertinent documents of this extraordinary campaign.

Moody's book gives a good overall picture of the development of transcontinental stage service. The reader should be aware that there were also a number of smaller lines, some of which remained in business, some of which did not, that also played a role in opening the West. Space, however, permits dealing only with the larger ones. Those interested in learning more about the overland mail service will find Hafen's book invaluable. The tale of the Dragoon Station is summarized in Banning, pp. 138–43.

Spencer's book tells the story of Green Russell's search for gold. Moody, pp. 110–24, summarizes Ormsby's report to the *New York Herald*. Banning contains a summary of the report of Dr. J. C. Tucker, which appeared originally in the *Annual Publication* of the Historical Society of Southern California, 1896.

The quotations in this chapter are as follows: Stephen A. Douglas on the Mormons, the *New York Times,* June 23, 1857, quoted by Hirshson, p. 168; Young's remarks to Van Vliet, *New York Tribune,* Oct. 28, 1857, quoted by Hirshson, p. 171; Lee on the Mountain Meadows Massacre, pp. 236–44; Lot Smith and the wagon train raid, originally published in the *Contributor,* Salt Lake City, 1882–83, and reproduced by Hafen, p. 222; comments of Senators Seward and Iverson on the Mormons' resistance, taken from the *Congressional Globe,* 1st Sess. of the 35th Congress and the special session of the Senate, and reproduced by Hafen, pp. 249 and 251–52; and Ormsby on his stagecoach

431

trip, originally in the New York *Herald* and quoted by Moody, pp. 112 and 122.

The quotation at the head of the chapter is typical of frontier humor and appears in a number of places, including Banning, p. 158.

26. ACROSS THE CONTINENT

The references to the duel observed by Dr. Tucker are set forth in the notes to the preceding chapter. A description of the race with the president's message will be found in Moody, pp. 128–32. The debates in Congress over the cost of providing mail service in the West is covered by Hafen, pp. 129–41, and the post office deficits can be computed from the records given in *Historical Statistics of the United States.*

Greeley, of course, speaks for himself in his own reports, which were collected in book form. His discussion of government contracts will be found on pp. 208–9 and 214–17.

The story of the Comstock Lode, being a fascinating part of America's heritage, has been the subject of many books and other studies. For its early days, the reader will find descriptions in Elliott, pp. 61–68, Young, pp. 234–40, and Lyman, pp. 32–52.

As for Greeley's missing the significance of the Nevada discoveries, there were at that time so many reports of gold in various parts of the West that editors had become suspicious. On the other hand, the Colorado discoveries had already received much publicity, and Greeley's investigation of them was to give him a basis for telling his readers whether or not they should join the many others moving to the eastern slopes of the Rockies.

The quotations in this chapter are as follows: Greeley on his leaving Laramie, p. 154; the quality of the mail sent to Salt Lake City, p. 159; on the Mormons, pp. 183–84, 189, and 193; and his description of Nevada p. 234.

The quotation at the head of the chapter is from Buchanan's annual message, delivered in December 1859, Richardson, vol. 5, pp. 552–53.

27. BLESSINGS AND A CURSE

Greeley's observations on California are contained in the last of the reports he submitted on his journey.

As mentioned in the text, the early days of the Comstock Lode are somewhat obscured. There were several assays made, some being higher than others, but all extraordinarily high. For a discussion of this, see Lyman, pp. 363–64.

The Pony Express so captured the imagination of the American people that many books have been written about it. Among those that an interested reader might want to pursue are Driggs, Mattes, Waddell F. Smith, and Bloss. The account by Alexander Majors is interesting, both because he was a participant but also because of his matter-of-fact tone, the expression of a businessman talking about one of his enterprises. Stories of the adventures of individual riders are numerous. The difficulty is distinguishing between those that are true and those that have been embellished. The tale of Pony Bob will be found in Majors, pp. 177–81.

Burton's account of his trip, like Greeley's, is especially important because of his role as a professional, but nonpartisan, observer. We are fortunate that two such writers traveled the central route during the times of the stage-coaches and Pony Express.

Hendrickson gives a picture of the admission of Oregon to statehood. Newsom in his letters, particularly the one dated Feb. 14, 1859, shows the indifference of some people in Oregon to either the gold craze or the wild politics of the time. Newsom saw the future of Oregon in the agricultural use of its rich lands.

The quotations in this chapter are as follows: Greeley on the Yosemite Valley, p. 258; on the redwoods, p. 267; Majors on the stagecoach line, pp. 165 and 166; on the Pony Express, pp. 173–74, on Pony Bob's experiences, p. 179; Burton on Brigham Young, p. 264; on the Mormon faith, p. 457, and on Carson City, p. 552.

The quotation at the head of the chapter is Burton, p. 559. This was the year Lincoln was elected and had been preceded by the bloody struggle for Kansas and other examples of violent politics.

28. THE WAR AND THE WEST

The general references for the story of the Butterfield stage and for the Pony Express will be found in the notes to the previous chapter. The scandal involving Russell has never been fully resolved, and it is not known whether he understood the identity of the bonds when he accepted the first installment of them. He did know later.

The story of the telegraph, not being as dramatic as that of the Pony Express, has received relatively little attention. Dick gives a good picture of its construction, pp. 301–11.

The campaign of the both the Confederacy and the Union is described briefly in Faulk, *Land of Many Frontiers,* pp. 184–99, and Hollon, *The Southwest,* pp. 218–38. Mark Twain's *Roughing It* gives a colorful picture of Nevada as the boom flourished.

The railroad was the subject of many books and government reports. Riegel describes the development of railroads generally in the West; Lewis's book tells about the four extraordinary men who controlled the Central Pacific.

Cremony gives a firsthand account of the advance of the California Column, and Connor, pp. 34–42, tells of the death of Mangas Colorados. He also gives a good description of the mining activities along the Gila River. Browne traveled through Arizona shortly afterward with a journalist's good eye and left behind a description of the problems that the Southwest was having. My own book *Geronimo* deals in some detail with both Cochise's effort to stop the stage and his attack on the California Column.

The quotations in this chapter are as follows: Mark Twain on Carson City, *Roughing It,* vol. 1, pp. 145, 147, and 148; Greeley on the construction of a railroad, p. 324; James Buchanan on the government's role in building a railroad, Third Annual Address, Richardson, vol. 5, p. 573; Browne on conditions in Tucson, p. 134; and Mark Twain on Nevada's prosperity, *Roughing It,* vol. 2, pp. 24–25.

The quotation of Lincoln's at the beginning of the chapter is from his first Annual Message, Dec. 3, 1861, Richardson, vol. 6, p. 58.

29. Civilization Advances

A good discussion of the Homestead Act is contained in Gates, pp. 393–99. His excellent book, prepared for the Public Land Law Review Committee, covers the history of the public domain. Robbins also covers this subject in considerable detail and with additional thoughts. Rohrbough's book will interest those who wish to know more about the earlier history of the public domain and how it was managed. The figures on the land sales's contributions to the federal revenue in the first days of the republic will be found in Dewey, pp. 123–24.

Gates, pp. 335–36, describes the working of the Morrill Act and the rather complicated provision for issuing scrip. The importance of the land grant colleges cannot be underestimated. I spent a weekend with the ambassador from an undeveloped country who told me they were the facet of American education that most interested him. His nation had its quota of graduates from universities like Oxford, Cambridge, and Yale. What they needed were not a select few but large numbers of people who could work building dams, railroads, factories, and perform other such work.

Dimsdale's book tells about Sheriff Plummer from the point of view of one of the vigilantes. Regardless of the reader's attitude toward such activities, the book is exciting with all the elements of real-life melodrama.

Chinese immigration into the United States was negligible until 1854, as *Historical Statistics* shows. That year it leapt upward, only to drop back to considerably lower levels in the following years. This was the result of the Chinese emperor's efforts to restrict the trade.

Bailey gives a good account of the campaign against the Navajos, pp.

149–69, drawing heavily on the official reports of the time to ensure an accurate picture. Elliott, pp. 88–89, tells about the adoption of Nevada's constitution.

The notes to the previous chapter discussing the railroads set forth some material that the reader might want to consult. Ames's book also discusses the financial aspects in considerable detail. Although he is obviously defensive about his family's role, his is one of the few books written by a person with actual investment experience. He therefore provides many sidelights that are not available in other works. Further references to the railroads are included in the notes to the next chapter.

Bowles's book offers a rounded picture of much of the Far West at the close of the Civil War. Dimsdale provides not only the story of Sheriff Plummer but of the social life of the times. His description of the "Hurdy-Gurdy" house appears on pp. 8–11. Warren tells about Mercer's efforts to import women into Oregon, pp. 78–81.

The quotations in this chapter are as follows: The Sacramento *Union* on the start of the Central Pacific Railroad, Jan. 3, 1863, quoted in Kirsch, p. 383; the trade in Chinese, *Harper's Monthly,* vol. 29, no. 169, June 1864, p. 1; Carleton's orders, *The Condition of Indian Tribes,* Washington, D.C., 1867, p. 124, and quoted in Bailey, p. 160; Carson's opinion of the Navajo campaign, Dunn, p. 396; the Humboldt *Register's* opposition to Nevada's statehood, July 23, 1864, quoted in Elliott, p. 88; Bowles on the Comstock Lode and Virginia City, pp. 146, 147, 149, and 154; on Idaho's mines, pp. 313, 314–15; on the effects of hydraulic mining, p. 308; on the Chinese, p. 244; on Oregon, pp. 196–97; Dimsdale on the "Hurdy-Gurdy" house, pp. 8–9 and 10–11; and the quotation from the Seattle *Gazette* on Mercer and the women appears in Warren, p. 79.

The quotation at the head of the chapter is from Dimsdale, p. 8.

30. The Last Spike

The story of the Bozeman Trail and the efforts to keep it open is well told by Johnson. A part of my own book *Sunlight and Storm* is also devoted to it. The fighting took place on the plains, not west of the mountains.

A summary of the Comstock Lode's finances in 1863–65 can be found in Bailey, p. 62. The construction of the Central Pacific Railroad is described in Kraus, who makes good use of contemporary documents. Kraus, pp. 144–57, gives an account of the winter of 1866–67, much of his description being a firsthand account. A series of letters between Hopkins and Stanford, printed in the *California Historical Quarterly,* illustrates the partners' desperate search for funds.

The failure of the partners of the Central Pacific to keep adequate books and the inability of Congress to conduct a thorough investigation into its affairs have left some of its activities rather murky. Some of the more interesting information is contained in the various pamphlets issued by the railroad and by its opponents. One of particular interest was by G. L. Lansing and published by H. S. Crocker and Company on the railroad's relations with the federal government. Another is the attack on the railroad made by Robert S. Graham, "a stockholder and former employee." Roscoe Conkling, the railroad's attorney, prepared a detailed statement to present to the Pacific Railway Commission. This gives a detailed defense of the Central Pacific's activities.

Many quotations from Rusling's report of the West in 1866 appear in Tryon's collection, pp. 755–82, and give a good picture of the more prominent places in that year.

Smith, pp. 241–48, describes the formation of the miners' union and the working conditions in the mines, and so does Elliott. McCoy's classic work describes at firsthand the development of the cattle business, which was to become so much a part of the West.

The homestead figures come from Gates, p. 402. Harpending, pp. 78–112, tells about his own real estate speculations and provides a picture of what it was like to work with Ralston. For a summary of the latter's career, see Bean, pp. 228–32. Harte's difficulties with "The Luck of Roaring Camp" are told by him in a later edition of the story. Muir's observations are well chronicled in his own books.

In his foreword to Dellenbaugh's journal, Goetzmann explains what Powell was doing when he combined his first and second trips in his report.

The quotations in this chapter are as follows: Rusling on Idaho and the Chinese, reproduced in Tryon's collection, p. 756; Portland, p. 758; Los Angeles, pp. 769–70; San Diego, p. 768; Tucson, pp. 781–82; Harte on "The Luck of Roaring Camp," pp. xii, xv, and xvi; and Rae on the railroad and conditions in the West, pp. 78, 79, 184–85, 190.

The quotation starting the chapter comes from Lansing's report on the Central Pacific, p. 44.

31. AFTER THE RAILROAD

The reader who wishes to pursue further the Central Pacific's development after the completion of the transcontinental railroad will find considerable information in the works already cited for previous chapters.

Rae's account of what he saw in the West is especially valuable as it is the account of one unfamiliar with a subject and therefore observant of details that another reporter might take for granted. He lacked, furthermore, the sense of superiority that mars the objectivity of many Europeans exploring the United States.

Ralston's reaction to the possible run on his bank is related in Harpending, pp. 92–95. An interesting example of the freewheeling methods of doing business at that time, its particular significance is its demonstration of the growing commercial interdependence of the West and the East.

The statistics of the increase in homesteads will be found in Gates, p. 418. The figures on the United States population are in *Historical Statistics*. Gates, p. 436, gives the figure for the land offerings in New Mexico, and, p. 378, describes the Hollman Resolution, and p. 456 describes the manner in which speculators were taking advantage of the laws.

In recent years, a few scholars have become convinced that crime was not as rampant in the West as tradition would have it. One factor that has been overlooked by many historians is the effect of the composition of sex and age, which, as any law enforcement officer knows, affects the crime rate. My own studies have indicated that if these factors are taken into account, the crime rate of some of the more notorious western communities may well have been below the crime rate of communities we have never even heard of in this connection. Those who are interested in pursuing the subject are free to write me in care of the publishers. The lack of training of the law enforcement personnel was also a factor that sometimes led to bloodshed. In my book on Sitting Bull I have analyzed the actions of the Indian police who arrested the Sioux leader. Although I tried to be kind to them, their inept performance was directly responsible for Sitting Bull's death. If that had not occurred, the Battle of Wounded Knee might not have followed, and . . .

The events in this chapter dealing with the Apaches are covered in more detail in my book *Geronimo*, pp. 165–94. Schellie gives a good account of the massacre at Camp Grant. Thrapp, whose book makes good reading, dug out the colorful incident of Howard's praying at the meeting with the Aravaipa Apaches. Howard tells his own story in his book.

On the Modoc War, a good description and the texts of some of the current reports will be found in Kirsch, pp. 422–37. The Lava Beds are now a national monument and, like such places operated the National Park Service, well worth visiting. More detailed accounts of the war will be found in Murray, Thompson, and Sproull.

The quotations in this chapter are as follows: Rae on the insularity of California, p. 322; and on the redwood forest, General Land Office *Annual Report,* 1875, and quoted by Gates, p. 418.

The quotation at the head of the chapter is from Bret Harte's poem, "What the Engines Said," *Poems and Two Men of Sandy Bar*, p. 305.

32. THE DYING FRONTIER

The reader interested in pursuing the Modoc War in more detail will find sources of further information listed in the notes to the preceding chapter.

A description of Sue McBeth and her sister Kate, who arrived later among the Nez Percés, will be found in Newell, pp. 96–99. A detailed discussion of the Mint Act in 1873 will be found in Weinstein, pp. 21–50 and in Myers, pp. 192–93 and 202–5. The Timber Culture Act is discussed by Gates, pp. 399–401, and by Hollon in *The Great American Desert,* pp. 142–48.

The discovery of the Big Bonanza is told by Elliott, pp. 133, 135–36 and in a more technical manner by Grant H. Smith, pp. 151–60, and in a more dramatic fashion by Lyman. Wright, who wrote under the name of Dan de Quille, gives a contemporary account. As a local reporter, he was thoroughly versed in mining affairs and observed the scene at firsthand. He often regretted that with his considerable knowledge he could not make more money for himself, but that has often been the fate of the man with the pen or the typewriter.

The death of Cochise is described by Frederick Hughes in articles he wrote for the *Arizona Daily Star,* Jan. 27 and 28, 1886. Wright describes the Virginia City fire, pp. 428–32.

Clum's book gives a full account of the activities of this remarkable Apache agent.

Short accounts of the Nez Percés' flight will be found in Newell, pp. 88–91 and in Josephy's *Patriot Chiefs,* pp. 313–40. A longer account appears in Josephy's book devoted entirely to the subject. Howard gives his version of the campaign in his own writings. Miles, pp. 259–80, describes the flight from his point of view.

A discussion of Colorado's admission to the Union will be found in Ubbelohde, pp. 145–50. The Desert Land Act is discussed in Gates, pp. 638–43, and Hollon, *The Great American Desert,* p. 133; and the Timber and Stone Act, Gates, pp. 550–52, and Hollon, p. 133.

The figures for declining silver prices are computed from the table appearing in Dewey, p. 406. Much confusion occurred during the silver debate, including the establishment of the myth that the antisilver forces had conspired to pass the law of 1873. This fed the emotionalism that surrounded the Populist movement later. For those who wish to study the problem more closely, Weinstein's book goes into it at some length. Myers, pp. 200–2, writes of the Bland-Allison Act in economic terms. Much of the confusion that once prevailed still seems to continue. When my book *Sunlight and Storm* appeared, a professor of western history at a university more noted for its resort surroundings than its scholarship attacked it for not dealing with the silver question and the Populist movement. Apparently he did not know where silver was mostly mined, where the Great Plains were, when the frontier phased out, or when and how the Populist movement began.

The Bannock-Paiute War is well described with a summary and documents in Lonnie J. White.

The quotations in this chapter are as follows: Davis on the conduct of the enlisted men, his report to the adjutant general, reproduced by Kirsch, p. 433; the description of Mackay appears in Wright, pp. 399–400; of Fair, p. 405; the description of Cochise's death is from the account by Frederick Hughes, *Arizona Daily Star,* Jan. 27 and 28, 1886; Wright on the Virginia City fire, pp. 428–29, 430, and 431; the description of the Nez Percés' last battle, Miles, pp. 271 and 273; and his description of the theft of the blankets, p. 280.

The quotation at the head of the chapter is from Miles, p. 339.

33. On the Trail a Final Time

Eve Ball's book gives an interesting and moving account of Victorio. Stevenson's *Across the Plains* is a classic on the railroad trip for those who were not fortunate enough to be able to pay for the best train service. His book *The Wrecker* also contains good descriptions of San Francisco at that time.

The figures for the production and dividends of the Consolidated Virginia can be found in Smith, pp. 260–61. The expense of electing and bribing the Nevada legislature is referred to in a letter quoted by Elliott, p. 160.

The story of Tombstone has been told many times. I remember the community when it had become a ghost town, and the dust blew down its streets and only a few "desert rats" still lived there. Today it is prosperous, restored, and well worth visiting, and the Tombstone Restoration Commission serves as a repository for its history.

I have not, therefore, gone into it in detail, nor have I emphasized the role of the gunman as the West moved from a frontier to a more mature society. The question of justice is, I think, sufficiently handled in the parts of this book dealing with vigilantes. The law enforcement officer was, in many instances, an extension of this same spirit, and his sometimes lonely—and therefore dramatic role—was a natural outcome of the conditions under which he worked. For those who like these stories some of the books that could be recommended are the several by Sonnichsen, including *I'll Die Before I Run,* Breakenridge's *Helldorado,* Haley's *Jeff Milton, A Good Man with a Gun,* and Siringo's *Riata and Spures.* This list, of course, is far from complete.

A summary of the Southern Pacific's advance across the Southwest is in Riegel, pp. 179–84.

The campaigns against the Apaches are handled with much more detail in my book *Geronimo.* Betinez's book is interesting because of its description from the Indian point of view. Faulk's book on the last campaign is excellent, although somewhat marred by his failure to consult the periodicals of the time, which caused him to err describing the one attack led by Geronimo personally on American soil.

The quotations in this chapter are as follows: Stevenson on the emigrant train, *Across the Plains,* pp. 134 and 138; the statement on education, the

439

Portland *Morning Oregonian,* Feb. 21, 1880, quoted by Warren, p. 225; Ambrose Bierce in the San Francisco *Wasp,* 3/31/82, and reprinted in Jackson, p. 345; the McComas's daughters, the Silver City (New Mexico) *Enterprise,* 3/28/83; Bourke on the Apache scouts and the Sierra Madre campaign, *An Apache Campaign,* pp. 46–50, 76 and 79; and *The Pacific Tourist* descriptions, pp. 4, 258, 356, and 360.

The poem of Whitman's at the head of the chapter appeared in *Harper's Monthly Magazine,* Feb. 1874 (vol. 48, no. 285). The issue opened with a highly romantic, well-illustrated poem entitled "Legend of the Cascades." The general tenor of the poem can be illustrated by these few lines picked at random: "The Indian maid, with lover near, Should saunter by thy waters clear, As in the days long flown." The position and treatment of the two poems seemed to symbolize the ambivalent attitude toward the West: a superficially romantic point of view still occupying the first position but being slowly replaced by one that—also romantic—was more in keeping with our times.

EPILOGUE

The quotation at the head of the chapter is taken from a letter included in some family papers that were lent to me by one of the members.

BIBLIOGRAPHY

A bibliography on the subjects covered in this book, if it were to be anywhere nearly complete, would require a sizable volume in itself; even a listing of the magazines, documents, periodicals, manuscripts, books, and other material that I myself have consulted would add numerous pages to this volume without, I believe, appreciably increasing its value to the average reader.

Therefore this is a highly "selected" bibliography, serving to list only those sources specifically mentioned in the notes and a few others that are more or less easily accessible and might be of interest to the general reader.

In doing so, I risk causing distress to those who have translated a single book into a career and take it as a personal offense when their volume's name does not appear. But this risk is no greater than the one I myself run. For while the majority of such persons will keep their grief to themselves, a minority will seek to discredit the offender. The world of books is as full of ambuscades as Apache Pass. But perhaps everyone will remember that this list is not complete, and that many excellent and outstanding works have not been included.

For the same purpose of brevity, in most instances I have not usually made separate entries for coauthors or coeditors, except when they were participants in the action described nor have I listed all the editions of the works that I have consulted.

Adams, Alexander B. *Geronimo: A Biography.* New York: G. P. Putnam's Sons, 1971.

——. *Sunlight and Storm: An Account of the Great American Plains.* New York: G. P. Putnam's Sons, 1977.

Adams, Andy. *The Log of a Cowboy: A Narrative of the Old Trail Days.* Lincoln, Nebraska: University of Nebraska Press, 1964.

Ainsworth, Katherine and Edward M. *In the Shade of the Juniper Tree: A Life of Fray Junípero Serra.* Garden City, New York: Doubleday and Company, 1970.

Aldrich, Lorenzo D. *A Journal of the Overland Route to California.* Ann Arbor, Michigan: University Microfilms, 1966.

Allyn, Joseph Pratt. *The Arizona of Joseph Pratt Allyn: Letters From a Pioneer Judge,* edited by John Nicholson. Tucson, Arizona: The University of Arizona Press, 1974.

Ames, Charles Edgar. *Pioneering the Union Pacific: A Reappraisal of the Builders of the Railroad.* New York: Appleton-Century-Crofts, 1969.

Anderson, Nels. *Desert Saint: The Mormon Frontier in Utah.* Chicago, Illinois: The University of Chicago Press, 1942.

Anza, Juan Bautista De. *Anza's California Expeditions.* 5 vols, edited by Herbert Eugene Bolton. Berkeley, California: The University of California Press, 1930.

See also Pourade, Richard F.

See also Thomas, Alfred Barnaby

Ashley, William. *See* Dale, Harrison Clifford

Aubry, François Xavier (author). *See* Cooke, Philip St. George

Bailey, Lynn R. *The Long Walk: A History of the Navajo Wars.* Pasadena, California: Socio-Technical Books. 1970.

Baldwin, Percy M. *See* Niza, Marcos de

Ball, Eve. *In the Days of Victorio: Recollections of a Warm Springs Apache.* Tucson, Arizona: The University of Arizona Press, 1970.

Bancroft, Hubert Howe. *Popular Tribunals,* 2 vols. San Francisco, California: The History Company, 1887.

Banning, William, with George Hugh Banning. *Six Horses.* New York: The Century Company, 1930.

Barrows, William. *Oregon: The Struggle for Possession.* Boston: Houghton, Mifflin and Company, 1855.

Bartlett, John Russell. *Personal Narrative of Explorations and Incidents in Texas, New Mexico, California, Sonora, and Chihuahua.* New York: D. Appleton and Company, 1856.

Bartlett, Ruhl J., editor. *The Record of American Diplomacy: Documents and Reading in the History of American Foreign Relations.* New York: Alfred A. Knopf, 1954.

Basso, Keith H. *Western Apache Witchcraft.* Tucson, Arizona: The University of Arizona Press, 1969.

Bergenroth, Gustav. "The First Vigilante Committee in California." *Magazine of History*, extra number—no. 151, pp. 143–49. Tarrytown, New York: William Abbatt, 1929.

Bean, Walter. *California: An Interpretative History*. New York: McGraw-Hill Book Company, 1968.

Beechey, Captain Frederick W. *Narrative of a Voyage to the Pacific and Beering's Strait*, 2 vols. London: 1891.

Betzinez, Jason, with Wilbur Surtevant Nye. *I Fought with Geronimo*. Harrisburg, Pennsylvania: The Stackpole Company, 1960.

Bidwell, John. *Echoes of the Past about California*. Chicago: The Lakeside Press, 1928.

Blackwelder, Bernice. *Great Westerner: The Story of Kit Carson*. Caldwell, Idaho: The Caxton Printers, 1962.

Bloss, Roy S. *Pony Express—The Great Gamble*. Berkeley, California: Howell-North, 1959.

Bolton, Herbert Eugene. *The Padre on Horseback: A Sketch of Eusibio Francisco Kino*. San Francisco: The Sonora Press, 1932.

See Anza, Juan Bautista de
See Crespi, Juan
See Font, Fray Pedro
See Kino, Eusebio Francisco

Bourke, John G. *An Apache Campaign in the Sierra Nevada*. New York· Charles Scribner's Sons, 1958.

————. *On the Border with Crook*. Glorieta, New Mexico: The Rio Grande Press, 1969.

Bowles, Samuel. *Our New West: Records of Travel between the Mississippi River and the Pacific Ocean*. Hartford, Connecticut: The Hartford Publishing Company, 1869.

Bowman, J. N. and Robert F. Heizer. *Anza and the Northwest Frontier of New Spain*. Los Angeles, California: Southwest Museum, 1967.

Brackenridge, Henry Marie. *Views of Louisiana, Together with a Journal of a Voyage up the Missouri River in 1811*. Chicago: Quadrangle Books, 1962.

Bradbury, John. *Travels in the Interior of America*. Ann Arbor, Michigan: University Microfilms, 1966.

Breakenridge, William M. *Helldorado*. Boston: Houghton Mifflin Company, 1928.

Brewer, William H. *Up and Down California in 1860–1864*, edited by Francis P. Farquhar. Berkeley, California: The University of California Press, 1966.

Brooks, Juanita. *The Mountain Meadows Massacre*. Stanford University, California: The Stanford University Press, 1950.

Brosnan, Cornelius J. *Jason Lee: Prophet of the New Oregon*. New York: The Macmillan Company, 1932.

Browne, J. Ross. *Adventures of the Apache Country: A Tour Through Arizona and Sonora with Notes of the Silver Region of Nevada.* New York: Promontory Press, 1974.

Buffum, Edward Gould. *Six Months in the Gold Mines.* Ann Arbor, Michigan: University Microfilms, 1966.

Burnett, Peter H. *Recollections and Opinions of an Old Pioneer.* New York: Da Capo Press. Reprinted from the 1880 edition.

Burrus, Ernest J. *See* Kino, Eusebio Francisco

Burton, Richard F. *The City of the Saints and Across the Rocky Mountains to California,* edited and with an introduction by Fawn M. Brodie. New York: Alfred A. Knopf, 1963.

Cabeza de Vaca, Álvar. *The Journey of Álvar Núñez de Vaca.* Translated by Fanny Bandelier. New York: A. S. Barnes & Company, 1905.

Cabrillo, Juan Rodriguez. *See* Wagner, H. R.

Canfield, Chauncey L. *The Diary of a Forty-Niner.* Upper Saddle River, New Jersey: Literature House, 1970.

Cannon, Miles. *Waiilatpu: Its Rise and Fall: 1836–1847: A Story of Pioneer Days in the Pacific Northwest.* Boise, Idaho: Capital News Job Rooms, 1915.

Cardinell, Charles. "Adventures on the Plains: Cardinell's Journal." *California Historical Quarterly,* vol. 1, no. 1 (July 1922), pp. 57–71.

Carson, Kit. *Kit Carson's Autobiography,* edited by Milo Milton Quaife. Lincoln, Nebraska: The University of Nebraska Press, 1967.

Castañeda, Pedro de. *See* Winship, George Parker.

Chittenden, Hiram Martin. *The American Fur Trade of the Far West,* with introduction and notes by Stallo Vinton and sketch of the author by Dr. Edmond S. Meany, 2 vols. New York: The Press of the Pioneers, Inc., 1935.

Chittenden, Hiram Martin and Alfred Talbot Richardson. *Life, Letters and Travels of Father Pierre-Jean De Smet, S. J. 1801–1873,* 4 vols. New York: Francis P. Harper, 1905.

Clappe, Louise Amelia Knapp. *The Letters of Dame Shirley: California in 1851,* introduction and notes by Carl L. Wheat, 2 vols. San Francisco: The Grabhorn Press, 1933.

Clark, Thomas D. *Frontier America: The Story of the Westward Movement.* New York: Charles Scribner's Sons, 1969.

Clark, William. *See* Lewis, Meriwether

Clemens, Samuel. *Roughing It,* 2 vols. New York: P. F. Collier and Son Company, 1913.

Cleveland, Richard J. *Cleveland's Voyages.* New York: Leavitt and Allen, 1857.

Clissold, Stephen. *The Seven Cities of Cíbola.* London: Eyre and Spottiswoode, 1961.

Clum, Woodworth. *Apache Agent: The Story of John P. Clum.* Boston: Houghton Mifflin Company, 1936.

Clyman, James. "Reminiscences and Diaries." *California Historical Quarterly,* vols 4, 5, and 6 (1925–27).

Coan, C. F. "The First Stage of the Federal Indian Policy in the Pacific Northwest." *Oregon Historical Society Quarterly,* vol. 22 (March–December, 1921), pp. 46–86.

Conkling, Roscoe and William D. Shipman. *The Central Pacific Railroad Company in Equitable Account with the United States.* No date. Statement to the California Railroad Commission.

Connor, Daniel Ellis. *Joseph Reddeford Walker and the Arizona Adventure.* Norman, Oklahoma: The University of Oklahoma Press, 1956.

Cook, James. *Journal.* Contained in Robert Kerr's *A General History and Collection of Voyages and Travels,* vols. 15 and 16. Edinburgh, Scotland: William Blackwood, 1815.

Cooke, Philip St. George, *The Conquest of New Mexico and California,* with a foreword by Philip St. George Cooke, III. Albuquerque, New Mexico: Horn and Wallace, 1964.

———. *Exploring Southwestern Trails: 1846–1854.* Journals of Philip St. George Cooke, William Henry Chase Whiting, Francois Xavier Aubry, edited by Ralph P. Bieber in collaboration with Averam B. Bender. Glendale, California: The Arthur H. Clark Company, 1938.

Corney, Peter. *Early Voyages in the North Pacific: 1813–1818,* with introductory material by Glen Cameron Adams. Fairfield, Washington: Ye Galleon Press, 1965.

Craven, Tunis A.M. *A Naval Campaign in the Californias—1846–1849,* a journal edited by John Haskell Kemble. No place. The Book Club of California, 1973.

Cremony, John Carey. *Life Among the Apaches.* Glorieta, New Mexico: Rio Grande Press, 1969.

Crespí, Juan. *Juan Fray Crespí, Missionary Explorer on the Pacific Coast; 1769–1774,* introduction and notes by Herbert Eugene Bolton. Berkeley, California: The University of California Press, 1929.

Dale, Harrison Clifford, editor. *The Ashley-Smith Explorations and the Discovery of a Central Route to the Pacific: 1822–1829.* Original journals. Glendale, California: The Arthur H. Clark Company, 1941.

Dana, Julian. *Sutter of California.* New York: Press of the Pioneers, 1934.

Dana, Richard H., Jr. *Two Years Before the Mast: A Personal Narrative.* Boston: Houghton Mifflin Company, 1911.

Delano, Alonzo. *Life on the Plains and among the Diggins.* Ann Arbor, Michigan: University Microfilms, 1966.

Dellenbaugh, Frederick S. *A Canyon Voyage: The Narrative of the Second Powell Expedition* . . . with a foreword by William H. Goetzmann. New Haven, Connecticut: The Yale University Press, 1962.

de Smet, Pierre-Jean. *See* Chittenden, Hiram Martin

De Voto, Bernard *Across the Wide Missouri,* Boston: Houghton Mifflin Company, 1947.

———. *The Course of Empire.* Boston: Houghton Mifflin Company, 1952.

———. *The Year of Decision: 1846.* Boston: Little Brown and Company, 1943.

See Lewis, Meriwether

Dewey, Davis Rich. *Financial History of the United States.* New York: Longmans, Green, and Company, 1951.

Dick, Everett. *Vanguards of the Frontier: A Social History of the Northern Plains and Rocky Mountains from the Fur Traders to the Sod Busters.* Lincoln, Nebraska: The University of Nebraska Press, 1965.

Dimsdale, Thomas J. *The Vigilantes of Montana.* Ann Arbor, Michigan: University Microfilms, 1966.

Downey, Fairfax. *Indian Wars of the U.S. Army (1776–1865).* Derby, Connecticut: Monarch Books, 1964.

Downey, Joseph T. *The Cruise of the Portsmouth, 1845–1847,* edited by Howard Lamar. New Haven, Connecticut: The Yale University Press, 1958.

Downie, William. *Hunting for Gold,* with a new introduction by Robert Becker. Palo Alto, California: American West Publishing Company, 1971.

Drake, Sir Francis. *The World Encompassed.* Collated with an unpublished manuscript of Francis Fletcher with appendices illustrative of the same voyage and introduction by W. S. W. Vaux. New York: Burt Franklin, no date.

Driggs, Howard R. *The Pony Express Goes Through.* New York: Frederick A. Stokes Company, 1935.

Drury, Clifford M. *Marcus and Narcissa Whitman and the Opening of Old Oregon,* 2 vols. Glendale, California: The Arthur H. Clark Company, 1973.

Dunn, J. P., Jr. *Massacres of the Mountains.* New York: Archer House. No date. (Originally published in 1886.)

Edwards, Frank S. *A Campaign in New Mexico.* Ann Arbor, Michigan: University Microfilms, 1966.

Elliott, Russell R. *History of Nevada.* Lincoln, Nebraska: The University of Nebraska Press, 1973.

Emory, W. H. *Lieutenant Emory Reports,* introduction and notes by Ross Calvin. Albuquerque, New Mexico; The University of New Mexico Press, 1951.

Fages, Pedro. "Diary of Pedro Fages: The Colorado River Campaign: 1781–1782," edited by Herbert Ingram Priestley. *Publications of the Academy of Pacific Coast History,* vol. 3, no. 1 (May 1913).

Faulk, Odie B. *The Geronimo Campaign.* New York: Oxford University Press, 1969.

————. *Land of Many Frontiers: A History of the American Southwest*. New York: Oxford University Press, 1968.

Ferrel, Bartolomé. *See* Wagner, H. R.

Ferris, Benjamin G. *Utah and the Mormons*. New York: Harper and Brothers, 1854.

Ferris, Robert G. *Lewis and Clark: Historic Places Associated with Their Transcontinental Exploration (1804–06)* Washington, D.C.: National Park Service, 1975.

Fletcher, Francis. *See* Drake, Sir Francis

Flint, Edward P. "My Recollections of Vigilante Days." *Sunset: The Pacific Monthly,* vol. 32, no. 6 (June 1914).

Font, Pedro. *Diary: The Anza Expedition of 1775–1776,* edited by Frederick J. Teggart. *Publications of the Academy of Pacific Coast History,* vol. 3, no. 1 (March 1913).

————. *Font's Complete Diary: A Chronicle of the Founding of San Francisco,* translated and edited by Herbert Eugene Bolton. Berkeley, California: The University of California Press, 1933.

Forbes, Alexander. *California: A History of Upper and Lower California,* with an introduction by Herbert Ingram Priestley. San Francisco: John Henry Nash, 1937.

Fowler, Jacob. *The Journal of Jacob Fowler,* edited by Elliott Coues. New York: Francis P. Harper, 1898.

Franchère, Gabriel. *A Voyage to the Northwest Coast of America*. Chicago: R. R. Donnelley and Sons, 1954.

————. *Adventure in Astoria: 1810-1814,* translated and edited by Hoyt C. Franchère. Norman, Oklahoma: The University of Oklahoma Press, 1967.

Frémont, John Charles. *Memoirs of My Life with a sketch of the life of Senator Benton by Jessie Benton Frémont*. Chicago: Belford, Clarke and Company, 1887.

————. *Report of the Exploring Expedition to the Rocky Mountains*. Ann Arbor, Michigan: University Microfilms, 1966.

Gallegos, Hernán. *See* Hammond, George P.

Gass, Patrick. *A Journal of the Voyages and Travels of a Corps of Discovery . . . during the Years 1804, 1805, and 1806*. Philadelphia: no publisher, 1810.

Gates, Paul W. *History of Public Land Law,* with a chapter by Robert W. Swenson. Washington, D.C.: U.S. Government Printing Office, 1968.

Geiger, Vincent and Wakeman Bryarly. *Trail to California: The Overland Journal of Vincent Geiger and Wakeman Bryarly,* edited with an introduction by David Morris Potter. New Haven, Connecticut: The Yale University Press, 1945.

Godwin, George. *Vancouver: A Life: 1757–1798*. London, England: Philip Alan, 1930.

447

Goetzmann, William H. *See* Dellenbaugh, Frederick S.

Goodman, Cardinal. *The Establishment of State Government in California: 1846–1850.* New York: The Macmillan Company, 1914.

Graham, Robert S. *Central Pacific Railroad: Facts Concerning Its Past and Present Management.* By a stockholder and former employee. San Francisco, 1889.

Gray, William H. *A History of Oregon: 1792–1840.* Portland, Oregon: Harris and Holman, 1870.

Greeley, Horace. *An Overland Journey from New York to San Francisco in the Summer of 1859,* edited, and with notes and introduction by Charles T. Duncan. New York: Alfred A. Knopf, 1964.

Gregg, Josiah. *Commerce of the Prairies,* edited by Max L. Moorhead. Norman, Oklahoma: The University of Oklahoma Press, 1954.

––––––. *Diary and Letters.* Norman, Oklahoma: The University of Oklahoma Press, 1941.

Grimshaw, William Robinson, *Grimshaw's Narrative,* edited with preface and notes by J. R. K. Kantor. Sacramento, California: Sacramento Book Collectors Club, 1964.

Hackett, Charles Wilson. *Revolt of the Pueblo Indians of New Mexico and Otermín's Attempted Reconquest: 1680–1682,* 2 vols, introduction and annotations by Charles Wilson Hackett; translations of original documents by Charmion Clair Shelby. Albuquerque, New Mexico: The University of New Mexico Press, 1942.

Hafen, Leroy R. and Ann W. Hafen. *Handcarts to Zion, the Story of a Unique Western Migration: 1856–1860.* Glendale, California: The Arthur H. Clark Company, 1960.

Hafen, Leroy R. *The Overland Mail: 1849–1869.* Cleveland, Ohio. The Arthur H. Clark Company. 1926.

––––––, editor. *The Utah Expedition: 1857–1858. A documentary Account of the United States Military Movement under Colonel Albert Sidney Johnston and the Resistance by Brigham Young and the Mormon Nauvoo Legion,* edited with introduction and notes by LeRoy R. Hafen and Ann W. Hafen. Glendale, California: The Arthur H. Clark Company, 1958.

Hakluyt, Richard. *Voyages of Elizabethan Seamen to America,* selected and edited, with historical notices by E. J. Payne. London: Thos. de la Rue and Company, 1880.

Haley, J. Evetts. *Jeff Milton: A Good Man with a Gun.* Norman, Oklahoma: The University of Oklahoma Press, 1949.

Hallenbeck, Cleve. *Álvar Núñez Cabeza de Vaca: The Journey and Route of the First Europeans to Cross the Continent of North America: 1534–1536.* Glendale, California. Arthur H. Clark Company, 1939.

Hamilton, W. T. *My Sixty Years on the Plains.* Norman, Oklahoma: The University of Oklahoma Press, 1960.

Hammond, George P. "Don Juan Oñante and the Founding of New Mexico." *Publications in History,* vol. 2 (October 1927). Historical Society of New Mexico.

Hammond, George P. and Agapito Rey. *Don Juan de Oñate, Colonizer of Mexico: 1595–1628,* 2 Vols. Albuquerque, New Mexico: The University of New Mexico Press, 1953.

———. *The Rediscovery of New Mexico: 1580–1594: The Explorations of Chamuscao, Espejo, Castano de Sosa, Morlete, and Leyva de Bonilla and Humana.* Albuquerque, New Mexico: The University of New Mexico Press, 1966.

Hannon, Jessie Gould. *The Boston-Newtown Company Venture: From Massachusetts to California in 1849.* Lincoln, Nebraska: The University of Nebraska Press, 1969.

Harpending, Asbury. *The Great Diamond Hoax and Other Stirring Incidents in the Life of Asbury Harpending,* edited by James H. Wilkins with a foreword by Glen Dawson. Norman, Oklahoma: The University of Oklahoma Press, 1958.

Harte, Bret. *The Luck of Roaring Camp and Other Stories.* Boston: Houghton Mifflin Company, 1906.

———. *Poems and Two Men of Sandy Bar.* Boston: Houghton Mifflin Company, 1912.

Hastings, Lansford W. *The Emigrants' Guide to Oregon and California.* New York: De Capo Press, 1969.

Hawgood, John A. *America's Western Frontiers.* New York: Alfred A. Knopf, 1967.

Hawthorne, Julian *The Story of Oregon,* 2 vols. New York: American Historical Publishing Company, 1892.

Hendrickson, James E. *Joe Lane of Oregon: Machine Politics and the Sectional Crisis, 1849–1861.* New Haven, Connecticut: Yale University Press, 1967.

Henry, Alexander and David Thompson. *The Manuscript Journals of Alexander Henry and David Thompson,* edited by Elliott Coues, 3 vols. New York: Francis P. Harper, 1897.

Hirshson, Stanley P. *The Lion of the Lord: A Biography of Brigham Young.* New York: Alfred A. Knopf, 1969.

Hofstadter, Richard, editor. *Great Issues in American History: A Documentary Record,* 2 vols. New York: Vintage Books, 1959.

Hogg, Garry. *Union Pacific: The Building of the First Transcontinental Railroad.* London: Hutchinson of London, 1967.

Hollon, W. Eugene. *The Great American Desert, Then and Now.* New York: Oxford University Press, 1966.

———. *The Lost Pathfinder: Zebulon Montgomery Pike.* Norman, Oklahoma: The University of Oklahoma Press, 1949.

————. *The Southwest: Old and New.* New York: Alfred A. Knopf, 1967.

Horgan, Paul. *Great River: The Rio Grande in North American History,* 2 vols. New York: Rinehart and Company, 1954.

Howard, Harold P. *Sacajawea.* Norman, Oklahoma: The University of Oklahoma Press, 1971.

Howard, Oliver Otis. *Autobiography,* 2 vols. New York: Baker and Taylor Company, 1907.

————. *Famous Indian Chiefs I Have Known.* New York: The Century Company, 1908.

Howay, Frederic W., editor. *Voyages of the "Columbia" to the Northwest Coast: 1787–1790.* Boston: The Massachusetts Historical Society, 1941.

Hungerford, Edward. *Wells Fargo: Advancing the American Frontier.* New York: Random House, 1949.

Hunt, Wilson Price. *See* Stuart, Robert

Inman, Henry. *The Old Santa Fé Trail: The Story of a Great Highway.* Minneapolis, Minnesota: Ross and Haines, 1966.

Irving, Washington. *Bonneville.* New York: Thomas Y. Crowell and Company, no date.

————. *Astoria or Anecdotes of an Enterprise Beyond the Rocky Mountains.* New York: John W. Lovell Company, no date.

Jackson, Joseph Henry, editor. *The Western Gate: A San Francisco Reader.* New York: Farrar, Straus and Young, 1952.

Jackson, W. Turrentine. *Wagon Roads West: A Study of Federal Road Surveys and Construction in the Trans-Mississippi West, 1846–1869,* with a foreword by William H. Goetzmann. New Haven, Connecticut: The Yale University Press, 1952.

James, Erwin. *Account of an Expedition from Pittsburgh to the Rocky Mountains.* Ann Arbor, Michigan: University Microfilms, 1966.

James, Thomas. *Three Years Among the Indians and Mexicans,* edited, with an introduction by Milo Milton Quaife. New York: The Citadel Press, 1966.

Johnson, Dorothy M. *The Bloody Bozeman.* New York: McGraw-Hill Book Company, 1971.

Johnson, Overton and William H. Winter. *Route Across the Rocky Mountains.* Ann Arbor, Michigan: University Microfilms, 1966.

Jones, Nard. *The Great Command: The Story of Marcus and Narcissa Whitman and the Oregon Country Pioneers.* Boston: Little, Brown and Company, 1959.

Josephy, Alvin M., Jr. *The Indian Heritage of America.* New York: Alfred A. Knopf, 1968.

————. *The Nez Percé Indians and the Opening of the Northwest.* New Haven, Connecticut: The Yale University Press, 1965.

————. *The Patriot Chiefs.* New York: Viking Press, 1961.

Kearny, Thomas. *Generai Philip Kearny, Including the Conquest of the West,* with a preface by Frank Monaghan. New York: G. P. Putnam's Sons, 1937.

Kelley, Hall J. *See* Powell, Fred Wilbur

Kendall, George W. *Across the Great Southwestern Prairies,* 2 vols. Ann Arbor, Michigan: University Microfilms, 1966.

Kingsley, Nelson. *Diary of Nelson Kingsley: A California Argonaut of 1849,* edited by Frederick J. Teggart. *Publications of the Academy of Pacific Coast History.* vol. 3, no. 3 (December 1914).

Kino, Eusebio Francisco. *Correspondence of Eusebio F. Kino, S. J. from New Spain with Rome,* English translation with notes by Ernest J. Burrus. Rome, Italy: Institutem Historicum Societatis Jesu, 1954.

————. *Kino's Historical Memoir of Pimeria Alta,* 2 vols, translated, edited and annotated by Herbert Eugene Bolton. Cleveland, Oho: The Arthur H. Clark Company, 1919.

Kirsch, William and William S. Murphy. *West of the West: Witnesses to the California Experience, 1542–1906.* New York: E. P. Dutton and Company, 1967.

Kotzebue, Otto von. *Voyage of Discovery in the South Sea and to Behring's Straits in Search of a North-East Passage: Undertaken in the Years 1815, 16, 17, and 18.* London: Printed for Sir Richard Phillips and Company, 1821.

Kraus, George. *High Road to Promontory: Building the Central* [now the Southern Pacific] *Across the High Sierra.* Palo Alto, California: American West Publishing Company, 1969.

Langsdorff, George Heinrich von. *Langsdorff's Narrative of the Rezanov Voyage,* translated by Thomas C. Russell. San Francisco: The Private Press of T. C. Russell, 1927.

Lansing, G. L. *Relations Between the Central Pacific Railroad Company and the United States Government.* San Francisco: H. S. Crocker and Company, 1889.

Larkin, Thomas Oliver. *First and Last Consul,* A selection of letters edited by John A. Hawgood. San Marino, California: The Huntington Library. 1962.

Ledyard, John. *A Journal of Captain Cook's Last Voyage.* Chicago: Quadrangle Books, 1963.

Lee, John D. *Mormonism Unveiled, Including the Remarkable Life and Confessions of the Late Mormon Bishop, John D. Lee.* St. Louis, Missouri: Vandawalker and Company, 1892.

Leonard, Zenas. *Narrative of the Adventures of Zenas Leonard.* Ann Arbor, Michigan: University Microfilms, 1966.

Lewis, Meriwether and William Clark. *History of the Expedition of Lewis and Clark,* edited by Elliott Coues, 4 vols. New York: Francis P. Harper, 1893.

————. *The Journals of Lewis and Clark,* edited by Bernard De Voto. Boston: Houghton Mifflin Company, 1953.

————. *The Original Journals of Lewis and Clark,* edited by Reuben Gold Thwaites. New York: Dodd, Mead and Company, 1904–5.

Lewis, Oscar. *The Big Four: The Story of Huntington, Stanford, Hopkins and Crocker, and the Building of the Central Pacific.* New York: Alfred A. Knopf, 1966.

————. *California in 1846, Described in Letters from Thomas O. Larkin and Others.* San Francisco: The Grabhorn Press, 1934.

Lockwood, Frank C. *Story of the Spanish Missions of the Middle Southwest.* Santa Ana, California: The Fine Arts Press, 1934.

Loewenberg, Robert J. *Equality on the Oregon Frontier: Jason Lee and the Methodist Mission: 1834–1843.* Seattle, Washington: The University of Washington Press, 1976.

Loomis, Noel M. *The Texan-Santa Fé Pioneers.* Norman, Oklahoma: University of Oklahoma Press, 1958.

Lyman, George D. *Saga of the Comstock Lode: Boom Days in Virginia City.* New York: G. Scribners, 1934.

McCaleb, Walter F. *The Conquest of the West.* New York: Prentice-Hall, 1947.

McCoy, Joseph G. *Historic Sketches of the Cattle Trade of the West and Southwest.* Ann Arbor, Michigan: University Microfilms, 1966.

McGlashan, Charles Fayette. *History of the Donner Party.* Ann Arbor, Michigan: University Microfilms, 1966.

McHenry, J. Patrick. *A Short History of Mexico.* Garden City, New York: Doubleday and Company, 1962.

Mackenzie, Alexander. *Alexander Mackenzie's Voyage to the Pacific Ocean in 1793,* historical introduction and footnotes by Milo Milton Quaife. New York: The Citadel Press, 1967.

————. *The Journals and Letters of Sir Alexander Mackenzie,* edited by W. Kaye Lamb. Cambridge, England: Hakluyt Society, 1970.

Majors, Alexander. *Seventy Years on the Frontier: Alexander Majors' Memoirs of a Lifetime on the Border,* with a preface by "Buffalo Bill" (General W. F. Cody). Denver, Colorado: The Western Miner and Financier Publishers, 1893.

Manly, William Lewis. *Death Valley in '49,* with a foreword by John Stephen McGroarty. New York: Wallace Hebberd, 1929.

Marcy, Randolph B. *Thirty Years of Army Life on the Border,* with an introduction by Edward S. Wallace. Philadelphia: J. B. Lippincott Company, 1963.

Mattes, Merrill and Paul Henderson. "The Pony Express: Across Nebraska from St. Joseph to Fort Laramie." *Nebraska History,* vol. 41, no. 2 (June 1960).

Meriwether, David. *My Life in the Mountains and on the Plains: The Newly Discovered Autobiography,* edited and with an introduction by Robert A. Griffen. Norman, Oklahoma: The University of Oklahoma Press, 1965.

Merk, Frederick. *The Oregon Question: Essays in Anglo-American Diplomacy and Politics.* Cambridge, Massachusetts: The Belknap Press of Harvard University, 1967.

Miles, Nelson A. *Personal Recollections,* introduction by Robert M. Utley. New York: Da Capo Press, 1969.

Moody, Ralph. *Stagecoach West.* New York: Thomas Y. Crowell Company, 1967.

Morgan, Dale L. *Jedediah Smith and the Opening of the West.* Indianapolis, Indiana: Bobbs-Merrill, 1953.

————, editor. *The West of William Ashley.* Denver, Colorado: The Old West Publishing Company, 1964.

Mowry, William A. *Marcus Whitman and the Early Days of Oregon.* New York: Silver, Burdett and Company, 1901.

Mulder, William and A. Russell Mortensen, editors. *Among the Mormons: Historic Accounts by Contemporary Observers.* New York: Alfred A. Knopf, 1967.

Mullane, William H. *Apache Raids.* Privately published, 1968.

Murphy, William S. *See* Kirsch, William

Murray, Keith A. *The Modocs and their War.* Norman, Oklahoma: The University of Oklahoma Press, 1959.

Myers, Margaret G. *A Financial History of the United States.* New York: Columbia University Press, 1970.

Neeser, Robert Wilden. *The Navy's Part in the Acquisition of California, 1846–1848,* reprinted from the *United States Naval Institute Proceedings,* vol. 34, no. 1, whole no. 125.

Neff, Andrew Love. *History of Utah: 1847 to 1869,* edited and annotated by Leland Hargrave Creer. Salt Lake City, Utah: The Deseret News Press, 1940.

Nevins, Allan. *Frémont: Pathfinder of the West.* New York: Longman's, Green and Company, 1955.

Newell, Helen M. *Idaho's Place in the Sun.* Boise, Idaho: Syms-York, 1975.

Newmark, Harris. *Sixty Years in Southern California,* edited by Maurice H. and Marco R. Newmark. Los Angeles, California: Zeitlin & Ver Brugge, 1970.

Newsom, David. *The Western Observer: 1805–1882.* Portland, Oregon: Oregon Historical Society, 1972.

Niza, Marcos De. "Discovery of the Seven Cities of Cíbola," translated and edited by Percy M. Baldwin. *Publications in History,* vol. 1 (Nov. 1926). Historical Society of New Mexico.

Palmer, Joel. *Journal of Travels over the Rocky Mountains.* Ann Arbor, Michigan: University Microfilms, 1966.

Palóu, Francisco. *The Founding of the First California Missions,* including letters of Serra Palóu and Galvez; translated and arranged by Douglas S. Watson, assisted by Thomas W. Temple II. San Francisco: Nueva California Press, 1934.

———. *Palóu's Life of Fray Junípero Serra,* translated and annotated by Maynard J. Geiger. Washington, D.C.: Academy of American Franciscan History, 1955.

Paré, Madeline Ferrin. *Arizona Pageant: A Short History of the 48th State,* with the collaboration of Bert M. Fireman. Phoenix, Arizona: Arizona Historical Foundation, 1965.

Parker, Samuel. *Journal of an Exploring Trip.* Ithaca, New York: Andrus, Woodruff and Gauntlett, 1844.

Parkes, Henry Bamford. *A History of Mexico.* Boston: Houghton Mifflin Company, 1950.

Parton, James. *Life of John Jacob Astor.* New York: The American News Company, 1865.

Pattie, James Ohio. *The Personal Narrative of James O. Pattie of Kentucky.* Ann Arbor, Michigan: University Microfilms, 1966.

Pike, Zebulon Montgomery. *The Journals of Zebulon Montgomery Pike With Letters and Related Documents,* edited and annotated by Donald Jackson, 2 vols. Norman, Oklahoma: University of Oklahoma Press, 1966.

Potter, David M. *See* Geiger, Vincent.

Portolá, Gasper de. "Account of the Sacred Expedition," vol. 1. *Publications.* Academy of Pacific Coast History, 1910.

Pourade, Richard F. *Anza Conquers the Desert: The Anza Expeditions from Mexico to California and the Founding of San Francisco: 1774–1776,* with extensive quotations from the journals of Anza and others. San Diego, California: Copley Books, 1971.

Powell, Fred Wilbur, editor. *Hall J. Kelley on Oregon.* Princeton, New Jersey: Princeton University Press, 1932.

Pratt, Orson. *Exodus of Modern Israel Diary,* compiled by N. B. Lundwall. Salt Lake City, Utah: N. B. Lundwall, no date.

Quaife, Milo Milton, editor. *Pictures of Gold Rush California.* New York: The Citadel Press, 1967.

Rae, William Frazier. *Westward by Rail: The New Route to the East.* New York: Promontory Press, 1974.

Revere, Joseph W. *Keel and Saddle: A Retrospect of Forty Years of Military and Naval Service.* Boston: James R. Osgood and Company, 1872.

Rey, Agapito. *See* Hammond, George P.

Rezanov, Mikolai Petrovich. *The Rezanov Voyage to Nueva in 1806,* translated and revised by Thomas C. Russell. San Francisco, California: The Private Press of T. C. Russell, 1926.

Richardson, James D., editor. *A Compilation of the Messages and Papers of the Presidents: 1789–1897,* 10 vols. Washington, D.C.: Published by Authority of Congress, 1899.

Riegel, Robert Edgar. *The Story of the Western Railroads.* Lincoln, Nebraska: The University of Nebraska Press, 1964.

Riesenberg, Felix, Jr. *The Golden Road: The Story of California's Mission Trail,* edited by A. B. Guthrie, Jr., New York: McGraw-Hill Book Company, 1962.

Robbins, Roy M. *Our Landed Heritage: The Public Domain: 1776–1936.* Lincoln, Nebraska: The University of Nebraska Press, 1962.

Rogers, Woodes. *A Cruising Voyage Round the World,* with an introduction by G. E. Manwaring. London: Cassell and Company, 1928.

Rohrbough, Malcolm. *The Land Office Business: The Settlement and Administration of the American Public Lands, 1789–1837.* New York: Oxford University Press, 1968.

Rollins, Phillip Ashton. *See* Stuart, Robert

Ross, Alexander. *Adventurers of the First Settlers on the Columbia River.* Ann Arbor, Michigan: University Microfilms, 1966.

Russell, Carl P. *Firearms, Traps, & Tools of the Mountain Men.* New York: Alfred A. Knopf, 1967.

———. *Guns on the Early Frontier.* New York: Bonanza, 1957.

———. *One Hundred Years in Yosemite: The Story of a Great Park and Its Friends,* Yosemite National Park: Yosemite Natural History Association, 1968.

Salisbury, Albert, and Jane Salisbury. *Two Captains West: An Historical Tour of the Lewis and Clark Trail.* New York: Bramhall House, 1950.

Schellie, Don. *Vast Domain of Blood: The Story of the Camp Grant Massacre.* Los Angeles, California: Westernlore Press, 1968.

Schurz, Carl. *Life of Henry Clay,* 2 vols. Boston: Houghton, Mifflin and Company, 1887.

Scrugham, James G., editor. *Nevada: A Narrative of the Conquest of a Frontier Land,* 3 vols. Chicago: The American Historical Society, 1935.

Settle, Raymond W. and Mary Lund Settle. *Saddles and Spurs: The Pony Express Saga.* New York: Bonanza Books, 1955.

Shaler, William. *Journal of a Voyage Between China and the North-Western Coast of America,* introduction by Lindley Bynum. Claremont, California: Saunders Studio Press, 1935.

Shaw, Reuben Cole. *Across the Plains in '49,* edited, with an introduction by Milo Milton Quaife. New York: The Citadel Press, 1966.

Shinn, Charles Howard. *The Story of the Mine as Illustrated by the Great Comstock Lode of Nevada.* New York: D. Appleton and Company, 1896.

Simpson, George. *Fur Trade and Empire: George Simpson's Journal,* edited with a new introduction by Frederick Merk. Cambridge, Massachusetts: Harvard University Press, 1968.

———. *An Overland Journey Round the World During the Year 1841 and 1842.* Philadelphia: Lea and Blanchard, 1847.

Siringo, Charles A. *Riata and Spurs*. Boston: Houghton Mifflin Company, 1927.

Smith, Grant H. *The History of the Comstock Lode: 1850–1920*. Reno, Nevada: The Nevada School of Mines, 1943.

Smith, James K. *David Thompson: Fur Trader, Explorer, Geographer*. Toronto: Oxford University Press, 1971.

Smith, Jesse N. *Journal: 1834–1906*. Edited by Oliver R. Smith. Provo, Utah: Jesse N. Smith Family Association, 1970.

Smith, Waddell F. editor. *The Story of the Pony Express*. San Rafael, California: Pony Express History and Art Gallery, 1960.

Sonnichsen, C. L. *I'll Die Before I'll Run: The Story of the Great Feuds of Texas*. New York: The Devin-Adair Co., 1961.

Spencer, Elma Dill Russell. *Green Russell and Gold*. Austin, Texas: University of Texas, 1966.

Spicer, Edward H. *Cycles of Conquest: The Impact of Spain, Mexico, and the United States on the Southwest, 1533–1960*. Tucson, Arizona: The University of Arizona Press, 1967.

Sproull, Harry V. *The Modoc Indian War: 1872–1873*. Lava Beds National Monument, California: Lava Beds Natural History Association, 1969.

Stansbury, Howard. *An Expedition to the Valley of the Great Salt Lake*. Ann Arbor, Michigan: University Microfilms, 1966.

Steele, John. *In Camp and Cabin: Mining Life in California During 1850 and Later*. Chicago: R. R. Donnelley and Sons, 1928.

Steffens, Lincoln. *The Autobiography of Lincoln Steffens*. New York: Harcourt, Brace and Company, 1931.

Stevenson, Robert Louis. *Across the Plains*. New York: Charles Scribner's Sons, 1918.

Stuart, Robert. *The Discovery of the Oregon Trail: Robert Stuart's Narratives*, includes an account of the *Tonquin*'s voyage and Wilson Price Hunt's Diary. Edited by Phillip Ashton Rollins. New York: Charles Scribner's Sons, 1935.

Sutter, John August. *The Diary of John Sutter*, with an introduction by Douglas S. Warren. San Francisco: The Grabhorn Press, 1952.

Terrell, John Upton. *Furs by Astor*. New York: William Morrow and Company, 1963.

———. *Journey Into Darkness: Cabeza de Vaca's Expedition Across North America, 1528–36*. London: Jarrolds Publishers, 1964.

Thomas, Alfred Barnaby, editor and translator. *Forgotten Frontiers: A Study of the Spanish Indian Policy of Don Juan Bautista de Anza, Governor of New Mexico, 1777–1787, from the Original Documents in the Archives of Spain, Mexico and New Mexico*. Norman, Oklahoma: The University of Oklahoma Press, 1932.

Thompson, David. *See* Henry, Alexander

Thompson, Erwin N. *Modoc War: Its Military History & Topography,* with a preface by Keith A. Murray. Sacramento, California: Argus Books, 1971.

Thrapp, Dan L. *The Conquest of Apacheria.* Norman, Oklahoma: The University of Oklahoma Press, 1967.

Townsend, John Kirk. *Narratives of a Journey Across the Rocky Mountains to the Columbia River.* Fairfield, Washington: Ye Galleon Press, 1970.

Tryon, Warren S., compiler and editor. *A Mirror for Americans: Life and Manners in the United States, 1790–1870, as recorded by American Travelers.* Chicago: The University of Chicago Press, 1952.

Twain, Mark. *Roughing It,* 2 vols. New York: P. F. Collier and Son Company, 1913.

Ubbelohde, Carl. *A Colorado History.* Boulder, Colorado: Pruett Press, 1965.

Underhill, Reuben L. *From Cowhides to Golden Fleece: A Narrative of California, 1832–1858, Based Upon Unpublished Correspondence of Thomas Oliver Larkin.* Stanford University, California: Stanford University Press, 1946.

U. S. Department of Commerce. *Historical Statistics of the United States: Colonial Times to 1957.* Washington, D.C.: U. S. Government Printing Office, 1960.

U. S. National Park Service. *Lewis and Clark: Historic Places Associated with their Transcontinental Expedition (1804–1806).* Prepared by Roy E. Appleman. Washington, D.C.: U. S. Government Printing Office, 1975.

U. S. Political Documents. This is a bound collection at Yale University Library.

Upton, Emory. *The Military Policy of the United States.* Washington, D.C.: Government Printing Office, 1907.

Vancouver, George. *New Albion.* Typescript copy of those parts of the second volume of the first edition of George Vancouver's Voyage. Made under the supervision of Charles B. Tarrill. Includes notes of George Davidson. 1913. This is at Yale University Library.

Vaux, W. S. W. *See* Drake, Sir Francis

Vestal, Stanley. *The Old Santa Fe Trail.* Boston: Houghton Mifflin Company, 1939.

Vorpahl, Ben Merchant. *My Dear Wister: The Frederic Remington-Owen Wister Letters,* introduction by Wallace Stegner. Palo Alto, California: American West Publishing Company, 1973.

Wagner, Henry R. "The Discovery of California." Includes the report of Bartolomé Ferrel. *California Historical Society Quarterly,* vol. 1, no. 1 (July 1922), pp. 36–56.

———. "Monterey in 1796." *California Historical Society Quarterly,* vol. 1, no. 1 (July 1922), p. 174.

————. *Spanish Voyages to the Northwest Coast of America in the Sixteenth Century*. San Francisco: California Historical Society, 1929.

Warren, Sidney. *Farthest Frontier: The Pacific Northwest*. New York: The Macmillan Company, 1949.

Watkins, T. H. *Gold and Silver in the West*. Palo Alto, California: American West Publishing Company, 1971.

Weber, David J. *The Taos Trappers: The Fur Trade in the Far Southwest, 1540–1846*. Norman, Oklahoma: University of Oklahoma Press, 1970.

Webster, Daniel. *The Works of Daniel Webster*, 6 vols. Boston: Little, Brown and Company, 1872.

Weinstein, Allen. *Prelude to Populism: Origins of the Silver Issue, 1867–1878*. New Haven, Connecticut: Yale University Press, 1970.

White, G. Edward. *The Eastern Establishment and the Western Experience: The West of Frederic Remington, Theodore Roosevelt, and Owen Wister*. New Haven, Connecticut: The Yale University Press, 1968.

White, Lonnie J. *Hostiles and Horse Soldiers*, with a foreword by Merrill J. Mattes. Boulder, Colorado: Pruett Publishing Company, 1972.

Whiting, William Henry Chase, *See* Cooke, Philip St. George.

Whitman, S. E. *The Troopers: An Informal History of the Plains Cavalry, 1865–1890*. New York: Hastings House Publishers, 1962.

Wilkes, Charles. *Voyage Around the World*. New York: George P. Putnam, 1851.

Williams, Mary Floyd. *History of the San Francisco Committee of Vigilance of 1851*. New York: Da Capo Press, 1969.

Wilson, Elinor, *Jim Beckwourth: Black Mountain Man and War Chief of the Crows*. Norman, Oklahoma: The University of Oklahoma Press, 1972.

Winship, George Parker. *The Coronado Expedition: 1540–1542*. This volume also contains the Spanish texts and translations of Casteñeda's account and the *Relación Postrera de Sivola* and translations of letters from Mendoza to the king and Coronado to Mendoza and the king, the *Translado de las Nuevas, the Relación del Suceso*, the narrative of Jaramillo, the report of Alvarado, and testimony concerning those who went on the expedition. Chicago: The Rio Grande Press, 1964.

Winter, William H. *See* Johnson, Overton

Wright, William (Dan De Quille). *The Big Bonanza*, introduction by Oscar Lewis. New York: Alfred A. Knopf, 1947.

Wyeth, John B. *Oregon*. Ann Arbor, Michigan: University Microfilms, 1966.

Wyeth, Nathaniel J. *The Journals of Captain Nathaniel J. Wyeth with the Wyeth Monograph on the Pacific Northwest Indians Appended*. Fairfield, Washington: Ye Galleon Press, 1969.

Young, Brigham. *Letters of Brigham Young to His Sons;* edited and introduced by Dean C. Jessee, with a foreword by J. H. Adamson. Salt Lake City, Utah: Deseret Book Company, 1974.

Young, Otis E., Jr. *Western Mining,* with the technical assistance of Robert Lenon. Norman, Oklahoma: The University of Oklahoma Press, 1970.

Zollinger, James Peter. *Sutter: The Man and His Empire.* New York: Oxford University Press, 1939.

INDEX

Specific battles, Indian tribes, forts, railroads, and treaties are listed under the general heading to which they belong.

461

Bidwell, John, 20, 168–169, 193, 231
Bierce, Ambrose, 390
Big Bend National Park, Texas, 191
"Big Bonanza," name given to the final discovery at the Comstock Lode, which see.
"Big Four," term used for the partners in the Central Pacific and Southern Pacific Railroads, which see.
Big Hole River, 380
Big Williams River, 55
Bighorn Mountains and River, 105, 111, 113, 133
Birch, James E., 285
Bird Cage Theater, 389
Bisbee, Arizona, 389
Bismark, North Dakota, 372
Bitterroot Mountains and River, 90, 97–98, 169
Black, Andrew, 139
Bland-Allison Act, see silver, government policy toward.
Bodega Bay, California, 116, 124
Bonilla, Francisco Leyva de, 16
Bonneville, Benjamin, 20, 153
Bosque Redondo, New Mexico, 24, 334, 335
Bouchard, Hypolite, 19, 123
Bourke, John G., 393–394
Bowles, Samuel, 24, 338–340
Bozeman, Montana, 396
Bozeman Trail, 344
Brannan, Samuel 227, 234, 256, 260
Bridger, James, 158, 226
Bridger, Mary Ann, 221
Buchanan, James, 23, 284–285, 288, 289, 294, 323
buffalo, 39, 51
Burton, Richard, 313–314
Butterfield, John, 23, 286, 290–291, 292–298, 317–318

Cabeza de Vaca, Álvar Nuñez, 15, 28, 33–34
Cabrillo, Juan Rodríguez, 15, 40–41
Cache la Poudre Canyon, 132, 180
Calhoun, John C., 189–190, 198
California: 22, 190–191; American conquest of, 175, 205–212, 214–215; condition under Mexican rule, 138, 162, 170–171; condition under Spanish rule, 122–123; economic change under American rule, 230; effect of gold on, 234–236, 241, 244–245, 251–252; effect of railroads on, 358–359; Greeley on, 306–307; independence, 20, 161–162; land routes to, 61, 71; Solís's revolt, 143; statehood, 249–250; strategic importance (see also Philippines, trade with), 43–44

California Column (see also Carleton, James H.), 23
California, Gulf of, 35, 55
California Trail: This term was used to designate the last part of the route west after it had separated from the Oregon Trail. It was also sometimes used to designate the entire route to California. For information on, see specific explorers and emigrants.
camp, see Forts.
Canada, 164–165
Canby, Edward R. S., 324–325, 332, 368
Cañon, Colorado, 101
Canyon de Chelly, Arizona, 335
Captain Jack, 25, 368–371
Cárdenas, García López, 38
Carleton, James H., 325–326, 333–335
Carson, Kit, 24, 145, 158, 180, 193, 202–203, 208, 211–212, 334–335
Carson City, Nevada, 303, 305, 314, 321
Carson River, 312
Carson Valley, Nevada, 311
Cascade Mountains, 27, 29, 91, 186
Casey, James P., 271, 272–274
Castro, José, 193–195
Catalina Mission, Baja California, 141
Catholics (see also individual missionaries and missions), 56, 156, 166–167, 175–176, 220, 223
cattle ranching and hides, 134–135, 241, 348, 383
Cavendish, Thomas, 16, 46–47
Cedar City, Utah, 290
Cenozoic Era, 28, 29
Century of Dishonor, A, 25, 395
Cermeño, Sebastian Rodríguez, 16, 47–50
Chama River, 51
Chamuscado, Francisco Sánchez, 15
Charbonneau, Jean Baptiste ("Pomp"), 88
Chato, 392
Chief Joseph, 25, 371, 377–381
Chihuahua, Mexico, 104, 164
Chinese immigrants, 333, 340, 344, 345, 347, 353, 359, 362–363
Chinese fur trade, see fur trade, Chinese.
Chiracahua Mountains, 317, 398
cholera, 165
Cíbola, 35–36, 37, 38
Civil War in the West, 23, 318–319, 324–328, 338
Clark, William, see Lewis and Clark Expedition.
Clay, Henry, 250
Clearwater River, 91, 160, 379
Clemens, Samuel, 320–321, 328, 350
climate, 27–28

465

469